*Irish Film Censorship*

For Emer, with love

# IRISH FILM CENSORSHIP

## *A Cultural Journey from Silent Cinema to Internet Pornography*

KEVIN ROCKETT

Co-editor: Emer Rockett

FOUR COURTS PRESS

Set in 10.5 on 12.5 point Ehrhardt for
FOUR COURTS PRESS LTD
7 Malpas Street, Dublin 8, Ireland
e-mail: info@four-courts-press.ie
http://www.four-courts-press.ie
*and in North America*
FOUR COURTS PRESS
c/o ISBS, 920 N.E. 58th Avenue, Suite 300, Portland, OR 97213.

A catalogue record for this title
is available from the British Library.

ISBN 1–85182–844–3 hbk
1–85182–845–1 pbk

Printed in Great Britain
by MPG Books, Bodmin, Cornwall.

# Contents

# Illustrations

*Plates between pages 192 and 193*

*Plates between pages 288 and 289*

### CARTOONS AND NEWSPAPER PUBLICITY

### TABLES

# Acknowledgments

As the introduction notes, most of the research for this study was undertaken at the National Archives of Ireland and at the premises of the Official Film Censor. Special thanks are due to both institutions. Likewise, I gratefully acknowledge Dublin City Council's archive where much of the research for chapter 2 was undertaken, and the Military Archives where chapter 8 was substantially researched.

Since I moved to Trinity College Dublin in 2000, I have been the beneficiary of its positive research support culture, not least by being made a Fellow of the university in 2004, but also through its Start-Up Fund for new academic staff which helped to facilitate this and other research work, and the Arts and Social Sciences Benefactions Fund which provided a grant for the purchase of the book's film stills. On a more personal level, I would like to express appreciation of my colleagues at the School of Drama in terms of their support and their intellectual companionship. I am also grateful to Seamus O'Connor who made available his PhD research materials on Irish film censorship prior to the public release of the film censors' records, and more particularly to Ruth Lysaght and Eugene Finn who undertook additional research at the National Archives of Ireland and elsewhere for this study. Thanks to copyright owners for the use of film images quotations; the British Film Institute for supplying copies of most of the film stills; the National Library of Ireland for illustrations 3–6; Luke Gibbons for the *Dublin Opinion* cartoons; Mary Macken for the photograph of her husband, Christopher Macken; and Sheamus Smith and John Kelleher for the photographs of the other film censors. At Four Courts Press, special thanks to Michael Adams and Martin Fanning for responding so positively to the project.

Gratitude inadequately describes the debt I owe to my wife Emer for the extensive intellectual contributions she has made to this book beyond her editorial assistance. Her knowledge of cinema from its beginnings to postmodernism, as well as cultural and theoretical debates surrounding visual practice, film and the internet, among many others, have helped to shape the framework of this study. Finally, I would like to thank her and our two young sons, Matthew and Stephen, for their support, love, and enduring all that is necessarily involved in such a large project.

# Preliminary notes

All films are American unless stated or otherwise indicated by the context in which the film is mentioned. All films in the main texts are referenced, while those in the notes are selectively referenced.

Upper case is used for Official Film Censor and the shortened Film Censor and Censor when referring to the particular individual acting as single Censor; this also applies to deputy (or assistant) Film Censor, or a collective of Official Film Censors. Lower case is used for film censors to refer to all censors other than the Official Film Censor, but including the Official Film Censor if coupled with the Censorship of Films Appeal Board censors or any member thereof.

In 1998, all except current 'active' records were transferred from the offices of the Official Film Censor to the National Archives of Ireland. In total, over 100 volumes of film censors' material are now held there. These consist principally of:

1. *Registers of Films Censored Books*. Written in pen and ink, these are six large-format ledgers which list in alphabetical order the decisions made by Official Film Censors on each film submitted by the distributor from 1929. It records whether a film has received a 'pass' (indicating approval without cuts), a 'reserve' (that is, with a cut or cuts), or a 'reject' (banning) decision. Additionally, the distributor's (or renter's) name is included, as is the length of the film (in feet, usually), the censorship fee and whether an appeal was lodged. Covering the years 1929–1964, these are held at the NAI 98/26/1 to 98/26/6.

2. *Record of Films Censored Books*. These ledgers list the films submitted for censorship. The first two volumes (98/27/1 and 98/27/2) cover the period from January to September 1928; thereafter up to June 1981 is registered in volumes 98/27/3 to 98/27/48. There are 44,700 films in all are recorded therein.

3. *Censor's Decision Reserved Books*. These duplicate books, which begin in January 1928 (98/28/1) continue to January 1979 (98/28/43) and record 12,900 reserved decisions. They had a detachable top copy which was sent to the distributor with a 'memo of exceptions' giving details of the cuts required to be made to the film before it could be awarded a certificate for public exhibition.

4. *Reject Books*. These large-format ledgers are the only documents which date

from the beginning of national film censorship. The five volumes at the National Archives begin in February 1924 (98/29/1) and continue to December 1972 (98/29/5). They record the Censor's decision when a film has been banned. In the early decades of censorship, the Official Film Censor often gave an explanation for his adjudication and, in turn, provided this report to the Appeal Board if an appeal was lodged. A film is also recorded as a reject when a distributor refuses the cuts demanded by the Censor. In order for the film to proceed to the Appeal Board, a Reject is recorded. Combined with the Reserve books, these volumes proved during the research for this study the most valuable in illuminating the policies of Official Film Censors. (Except for Reject books, records prior to 1928 seem to have been lost.)

5. *Appeal Board Journals.* These ledgers record the decisions of the Censorship of Films Appeal Board, and often include the Official Film Censor's reasons for rejecting a film. Following the viewing of the film, the chairman noted the decision, and the those in attendance are usually recorded. On rare occasions (and not until the 1960s/1970s) a division within the Appeal Board members is recorded. The first ledger dates from 1946, though the Board's decisions prior to that date are recorded as part of the Film Censor's reports.

6. Volumes held at the National Archives also include the amounts paid by distributors in film censorship fees while the censors' notebooks (or jottings during screenings) for certain periods are also there.

7. *Official Film Censor's Annual Report.* The Film Censor prepares an annual report to the Minister for Justice in which he provides a statistical summary of the operation of the office during the previous calendar year. In addition, a one to two-page commentary is included by way of a confidential report to the minister. Unlike the statistical summary which has been freely available, the confidential reports have not been released to the media or libraries (exempting the first printed report for 2003), extracts from these are published here for the first time. They continue to be held at the Official Film Censor's offices. The reports for the years 1926, 1928 and 1947 are missing, while those for 1925 and 1944 are incomplete.

# Introduction

They can't censor the gleam in my eye.

Charles Laughton, *1935*.

'Impetuous. Homeric.' When Official Film Censor Richard Hayes viewed in June 1952 John Ford's *The Quiet Man*, which for many, notwithstanding its Hollywood origins, is the quintessential Irish film, he ordered that this (apparently) knowing but ironic observation on the broken condition of Sean Thornton's (John Wayne) huge bed the morning after his marriage to Mary Kate Danaher (Maureen O'Hara) by Michaeleen Oge Flynn (Barry Fitzgerald) should be deleted. He took this decision even though the audience know that it is the result of Sean's anger and frustration at her refusal to sleep with him following his failure to secure her dowry from her brother Will (Victor McLaglen), and not their love-making. Indeed, that night he had slept alone in his sleeping bag in the adjoining room and it was some time before the marriage was consummated. Hayes had already determined that an earlier scene in which another reference to the bed, and more specifically, the intimate activities within it should be cut. 'Ah, a man'd have to be a sprinter to catch his wife in a bed like that,' sleeven Feeney (Jack MacGowran) says as he interrupts Mary Kate's private observation of the bed's delivery, though the first part of his comment was allowed: 'Is that a bed or a parade ground?', a question of sufficient ambiguity to warrant reflection from a viewer.[1]

Such treatment of comic and mild references to sexual relations, even between married people, serves as a warning that the narrative which follows is an often dispiriting account of how many key cinematic representations were systematically suppressed in Ireland during cinema's most productive periods. As will become clear, Irish film censors from the 1920s to the 1970s took an extreme, at times an absolutist, if necessarily perversely logical, view of how sexuality, private fantasy and desire should or, more pertinently, should not be represented. Despite the levels of censorship, cinema, whether in terms of the films themselves with their engulfing aesthetic, the sumptuous darkened spaces of private-public interface in which they were screened, or the spin-off industrial products and media interest in the lives of the stars, carried a powerful charge and *frisson* largely unavailable in or through other popular media. Consequently, this study also concerns audience resistance to the censors' attempt at total repression, as much as it is an account of institutional film censorship. In a country which since

the mid-1960s, but, most particularly and intensively since the 1990s and the growing wealth of the modern Irish economy, has experienced a sea change in attitudes
towards traditional notions of morality and authority, most obviously with regard to
institutional religion and the inter-relationship of citizen and state, the extent of control over the cinema images that adults were permitted to consume from the 1920s to
the 1970s is hard to imagine, let alone justify. In the mapping of this material, the close
relationship and the collusion, which operated between the Catholic church, politicians, and the civil service will be explored.

Notwithstanding the relative scarcity of serious research into Irish film censorship, an episode of the successful satirical 1990s television series, *Father Ted*, set on
fictitious Craggy Island off the west coast of Ireland, offers a comic account of such
church intervention and how that intervention is no longer possible in modern Ireland.
The narrative, trading on the traditional notion of European art cinema as risqué[2] features an attempt by the local bishop to have a French film, *The Passion of Saint Tibulus*,
withdrawn from the local cinema because the Pope regards it as blasphemous.
Reluctantly, Fr Ted (Dermot Morgan) and his dim-witted side-kick Fr Dougal (Ardal
O'Hanlon) go to the cinema to voice their protest, but end up staying to see the film.
Bewildered, they wake up the next morning in their almost adjoining single beds and
try to make sense of the film.

> Fr Ted: What was that all about?
> Fr Dougal: You're asking the wrong person there, Ted. I couldn't make head
> nor tail of it.
> Fr Ted: I know for a fact that St Tibulus wore more clothes than that. He was
> from Norway or somewhere. He'd have frozen to death.
> Fr Dougal: You know why St Tibulus tried to take the banana off the other
> lad?
> Fr Ted: That wasn't a banana, Dougal.

After further pressure from the bishop, the two priests hold a public protest outside
the cinema, but their presence and sensationalist review only helps to make the film a
commercial success, such that even their colleague, the foul-mouthed and otherwise
disheveled dipsomaniac Fr Jack (Frank Kelly), goes to see it in his first visit to the
cinema since a Sharon Stone season! Acknowledging that 'nobody takes a blind bit of
notice' of their efforts, the two priests abandon the protest. Outraged, the bishop threatens to transfer them to remote missionary locations. Meanwhile, Fr Jack has discovered a video in the bishop's bag. It transpires to be an amateur video, which recalling
the real-life events around Bishop Eamon Casey and his fathering a son, features the
bishop frolicking on a Californian beach with his lover and their young son. Their new
insight into the bishop's private life ensures that they will remain on Craggy Island.
While it would seem that Ireland had certainly radically transformed by the 1990s with
these and other satirical representations of previously untouchable, even taboo, subjects, being generally available on television and elsewhere, nevertheless, though *Father
Ted* was originated by Irish writers and actors working for British television, it was

two years before RTÉ had the courage to show it. Less than two decades earlier the episode (indeed the whole series) would have been banned, if made at all.

In the current 'liberal' era in which Irish society is pledged to transparency and openness of information it is worth recalling that the history and cultural implications of Irish film censorship is something that the Department of Justice, which administers censorship, would have rather remained unexplored, this is arguably the case at least until the late 1990s when the key issues raised by a debate on film censorship *appear* to be in the past, or have been replaced by an unfolding story of political and economic corruption and bureaucratic mismanagement. As recent as 1986 the then Minister for Justice, Alan Dukes TD, no doubt on the advice of his civil servants, wrote to inform me that access to the Official Film Censor's office records was being denied on the basis that the relationship between the Film Censor and film distributors who submit films for certification was akin to a confidential commercial contract. Since the files 'contain details of private commercial arrangements between the censor and various film distributors it would be regarded as a breach of confidence to release this information.'[3] This ruling applied even to the titles submitted in the 1920s and 1930s. Mr Dukes' successors, including now-disgraced politician Ray Burke (1990),[4] took a similar approach, while the publication of prohibited video titles from 1994 failed to budge the secrecy surrounding the Film Censor's office. (Of course, for essential practical reasons the Censorship of Publications Board publish lists of prohibited titles in a practice that goes back to its inception.) Later, justification for the refusal to release film records to the National Archives of Ireland (NAI) – their proper location under the Archives Act, 1986 – was that these were 'active files' needed for the day-to-day running of the Censor's office.

The impetus of the Freedom of Information Act, 1997, which facilitates access to decisions made *after* April 1998, led the Official Film Censor Sheamus Smith in response to a further request from me seeking the deposit of film censorship records, including those prior to this date, at the National Archives[5] to finally do so, and, it is there that much of the research for the present study was undertaken. At the Archives, I am grateful to Tom Quinlan in particular for the speed with which he catalogued and made available the 100 plus volumes of the film censors' records. Subsequent thanks is due to Film Censors Sheamus Smith and his successor John Kelleher who permitted me to examine more recent 'active' records still held at their Harcourt Terrace premises. As a result, for the first time, a detailed insight into the operation of film censorship in Ireland contextualized through a discussion of over 1,000 representative films and reference to almost as many again, based upon an examination of about 18,000 of the more than 50,000 censors' decisions made under the Censorship of Films Act, 1923, is possible. Prior to this, information had to be filtered through a number of sources, including film distributors and newspaper reports, not all of which could be deemed reliable or objective. Heretofore, the history and effects of censorship have largely been confined to literary texts with the exemplary work remaining Michael Adams' *Censorship: the Irish Experience* (1967). Unfortunately, the impact of censorship on cinema has been rarely and then only partly treated: for example, in Donal Ó Drisceoil's *Censorship in Ireland, 1939–1945* film censorship is the focus of one chapter, and

because of the book's publication in 1996, necessarily only contains limited information on how the censors treated films, though, ironically, the Irish Military Archive,
where some of the research for chapter 8 was undertaken, has long been open to film
researchers. That a special 1980 issue of the now-defunct Arts Council magazine, *Film
Directions*, edited by David Collins, which includes my own first article on the issue
– 'Film Censorship and the State' – continues to be cited is evidence in itself of the lack
of scholarly material on Irish film censorship.[6]

While the literary is placed centre-stage in Irish cultural production, often to the
detriment of film (as well as other arts), not least in the direction cinema has often
been pushed, increasingly since the mid-1970s and most particularly the 1990s, Irish
cinema has emerged as a new vibrant and sometimes challenging medium of expression, even if that voice more often than not in the 'Celtic Tiger' era seemed to be focused
on the international, especially American market. In acknowledgment of the cultural
importance and currency of film, Ireland's relationship to the screen in terms of indigenous and foreign cinema, as well as film representations of Ireland, the Irish and their
history has been already substantially written through such books as Kevin Rockett,
Luke Gibbons and John Hill's *Cinema and Ireland* (1987), Martin McLoone's *Irish
Film: The Emergence of a Contemporary Cinema* (2000), Lance Pettit's *Screening
Ireland* (2000), Emer Rockett and Kevin Rockett's *Neil Jordan: Exploring Boundaries*
(2003), Ruth Barton's *Irish National Cinema* (2004), Harvey O'Brien's history of Irish
documentary *The Real Ireland* (2004), and catalogued in Kevin Rockett's *The Irish
Filmography* (1996), such that a significant absence in Irish films studies until this publication has been censorship. The focus of this particular work, however, is primarily
limited to the treatment of *all* films by the Irish state of which, since 1923, about 2,500
theatrical films have been banned and between 10,000 and 11,000 cut. These are discussed through a representative rather than exhaustively complete selection of films
with particular emphasis on the most popular and commercially and/or critically successful examples. In that way, it is not a comparative study. Nevertheless, no apology
is made for this focus on the specific, as otherwise, given the sheer volume of material, it would have become either diluted or too unwieldy. In the first instance, it was
necessary to produce in a single volume the entire cultural history of film and related
censorships (most especially of video censorship fully introduced in 1994 and which
has resulted in the banning of over 3,000, largely pornographic, titles), not just to mark
cinema's coming-of-age in Ireland, but to trace the changing cultural, social and political climate, for as Cheryl Herr notes in her study of James Joyce, the anatomy of censorship is the anatomy of culture.[7] Similar histories produced elsewhere including those
by, in Britain, James Robertson (1985 and 1989) and Anthony Aldgate (1995), and in
the USA, Gregory Black (1994 and 1998), also seem to adopt this same methodology,
though some, such as Annette Kuhn (1988) and Lea Jacobs (1991) have focused on
specific moments or themes, in this case analyses informed by feminist film theory,
while Doherty (1999) has narrowed the focus to the early 1930s.

Given this situation and my own frustrated attempts to gain access to the primary
material, the question as to why the Film Censor's office refused in the past to provide

information to interested journalists and other writers and academics since the 1960s must be posed. At one level, it may be answered by the ingrained secrecy and paranoia of a government department which has fought internal subversion since the early 1920s, or the fact that the Department of Justice represents one of the last major bastions which believes it is the institution, rather than the citizen, which should take priority within Irish society. At another level, it was, as has often been acknowledged by those involved in the censorship process, the fear of ridicule. Indeed, the sorry tale of this book not only traces how a particular form of the most conservative Christian ethos held a grip for fifty years on a popular entertainment, and the extent to which this *policy* incorporated the most innocuous of films, even those aimed primarily at children, including *The Lady and the Tramp* (Hamilton Luske, Clyde Geronimi, Wilfred Jackson, 1955), where the line of reassurance to an expectant father, 'Old Doc Jones has never lost a father yet,'[8] was deemed offensive, but it also suggests that the state's paternalistic treatment of its subjects was little different to that of the colonizer.

Censorship is necessarily a blunt instrument, so blunt that one can forget that there are precise structures and ideological certainties in place not just so it may be established, but administered. While this study is designed to shed light on this most secretive of government activities and highlight and contextualize the extent of the process, it no less offers a salutary warning to future legislators and interested parties that the language of censorship must be precise and not vague, all encompassing, subjective or otherwise ambiguous and impressionistic, as has been and largely continues to be the case. Likewise, it points to the conclusion that education, not restriction, is the best defence against problematic or potentially dangerous representations.

Perhaps the most fundamental question to censorship is, under what dispensation can a society deny access to its *adult* population *any* words and images, particularly if these representations are not recordings of actual criminal activity? Also it is necessary to examine the relationship of reality to representation and the viewer's imagination or perception and the law. There is, after all, no definite way to (fully) control private fantasy even if that fantasy is located in the morally, ideologically or legally odious realm, and where such would be deemed by the state to be desirable or appropriate. Nevertheless, the question may already have become redundant with the open access of the internet. However, we should remember that the supposedly 'democratic' nature of this medium is little more than a myth and the internet is in the process of being more fully incorporated into the global capitalist economy as well as becoming the object of increased surveillance, as discussed in chapter 7. Additionally, one must be cognizant of the evidence that there is widespread ignoring by parents and guardians of the age classifications imposed on films and videos/DVDs by the censors. It is not, in general, film exhibitors or video renters who allow underage access to films, but relatives and friends, either directly or indirectly through negligence. That said, there is anecdotal evidence to suggest that exhibitors have illegally and frequently screened imported films without the Irish censor's certification at least up until the 1970s.

Lastly, it must be remembered that there is no one version of a film. During the research process for this book considerable use was made of pre-recorded videos, and the taping for personal use of television transmitted versions of films submitted to Irish censors. Though seemingly complete, if not always in their correct (widescreen) format, in a great many instances either the television station, or, as often, the video distribution company had in fact, without advertising or in any way acknowledging their intervention, cut the film in order either to achieve, ironically, the kind of rating into which Irish film censors sought to straitjacket commercial cinema from the 1920s to the 1960s, namely the general certificate, or universal rating, or so as to achieve a more convenient or marketable length. Two such examples illustrate this. The Irish film censor cut one line from Alfred Hitchcock's comedy *Mr and Mrs Smith* (1941).[9] This occurs when estranged husband Robert Montgomery is told by an acquaintance that when he eventually returns to his wife, played by Carole Lombard, that 'That isn't all she'll like.' However, not only is this line, suggestive of sexual activity following a reconciliation, cut in the 4 Front video version but so, too, were other scenes, thus reducing the film's original running time by about four minutes. More pertinently, perhaps, is the treatment of *Tom Jones* (1963, GB). This adult film was approved with 21 cuts in 1964 to make it conform to the General Certificate category,[10] but the 1994 4 Front version (which carries a [British] PG [Parental Guidance] rating, indicating that it can be seen by children but only with parental permission), is almost *thirty minutes* shorter than the original film release (99 minutes on video; 129 minutes in the original cinema release version). For the film's 1989 reissue, director Tony Richardson cut seven minutes, and it is probable (though the information is not included) that is the version (running to 123 minutes) that was released on DVD in Ireland in 2004 and rated PG, making it fit for viewing generally, but in the case of children under 12, under parental guidance. (Clearly, the Trades Description Act has yet to be extended to video/DVD releases!) If by different processes and to the service of different ideologies – moral and commercial – the accessible, though butchered, films still remain at some level cultural vehicles of desire and imagination, and remind us that the experience at the cinema in Ireland was, if unique, no less valid than elsewhere.

" Give that ould devil a prod, Jim, or we'll be late for the Betty Grable film."

1 Little illustrates better the contrast that existed between the lives of Irish cinemagoers and the often sumptuous, materialist and secular world of the cinema, both onscreen and within the cinema itself, than this cartoon, taken from *Dublin Opinion*

# CHAPTER I

# *A clash of popular cultures*

One of the greatest dangers of ... films is not the Anglicisation of Ireland,
but the Los Angelesation of Ireland.
James Montgomery, *Official Film Censor, 1923–1940*[1]

Cinema's arrival in Ireland at the end of the nineteenth century was broadly contemporaneous with the establishment of a number of organizations whose most
explicit goal was the encouragement and development of a distinctively Irish identity whether through the unsuccessful attempt to restore the Irish language as the
vernacular; the cultivation of Gaelic sports, music and dancing; or, the reimagining
of the Irish as 'the wise and simple man' who goes 'To a grey place on a hill / In grey
Connemara clothes / At dawn to cast his flies,' but who sadly transpires to be 'A man
who does not exist, / A man who is but a dream.'[2] While great efforts were made to
achieve this, still greater energy was expended in trying to restrict imported, most
especially English commercial entertainments and popular publications which were
deemed anathema to the Irish cultural nationalist project. Clearly, when these nationalist protectionist campaigns were, as moreover was the case, underpinned by the
moral certainties of the institutional Catholic church, the hostility against the invading cultures increased substantially.

In Ireland, as elsewhere in Europe, in the late nineteenth century, engaging in
'healthy' outdoor and morally uplifting recreations, no doubt as a corrective to the
growth in industrialization and capitalism, was encouraged by a great many cultural
idealists. While the histories of the various organizations involved in the promotion of
these activities, most particularly the Gaelic League and the Gaelic Athletic Association,
has been extensively documented and discussed, less attention has been paid to the
physical display and (though the word would not be used in such puritanical quarters)
the 'beauty' of the body in this culture. If Gaelic sports were promoted as an active
leisure and communal activity and as a means of asserting a distinctive Irish identity
(amateur, not professional like English soccer), they no less acted as political 'training
grounds' for those promoting Irish national self-determination, something seen at its
most public in the substitution of hurling sticks for guns in military drilling during the
preparations for the 1916 Rising. Furthermore, these sporting activities allowed for a
form of physical contact that contrasted, on one level, with the psychic interiority of

the commercial entertainment experience, and on another, with the repressed cultural terrain of Irish catholicism and the denial of the (sexual) body.

One such organization, the radical feminist and nationalist group Inghinidhe na hÉireann (Daughters of Ireland), declared in its constitution upon formation in 1900, that while it aimed 'to encourage the study of Gaelic, of Irish literature, History, Music and art,' it also sought 'to discourage the reading and circulation of low English literature, the singing of English songs, the attending of vulgar English entertainments at the theatres and music hall, and to combat in every way English influence, which is doing so much injury to the artistic taste and refinement of the Irish people.'[3] Such a contrast of the 'Gaelic as high art' against 'low' popular English culture necessarily suggests the inroads which had been made by the 'alien' culture into the Irish psyche and the uphill battle to reappropriate the Irish imagination for itself. It also contains a distinct whiff of middle-class snobbishness and dismissal of 'low' culture, which was indicative of the organization's social bias, including of its chief promoter, Maud Gonne. Often in broad alliance with the Catholic church (though, importantly, radical secular voices from this period too often are neglected in Irish historiography and cultural studies), which sought to suppress all deviations from the Catholic sanctioned nuclear family (including the reporting of divorce cases in the popular British press), it was almost inevitable that they, and the cultural nationalist project more generally, would be viewed as excessively puritanical and joyless. Additionally, reflecting the bourgeois fear of the body and its *representations*, it would also be opposed to those popular (and 'commercial') entertainments that traded on the display of the body or otherwise engaged in suggestive or risqué language or behaviour. In a predominantly rural society where reticence (or at least privacy) as regards the body was the norm, these often brash displays of women's bodies, such as in the can-can music hall dance craze of the 1890s, were, at the very least to the moral guardians and cultural leaders, challenging. Needless to say that cinema which, beyond its initial fascination with the depiction of 'innocuous' reality, at its most fundamental centers on the (voluminous and sensuous) physical – if not always in its most charged or erotic form – was an already marked medium. Conceivably, it was this aspect of the medium that informed the emerging Irish state's policy of control, suppression and censorship. Rather than adapt and use the medium for their own ends, as was the case, for example, in the Soviet Union during its revolutionary period where the cinema was placed center-stage and gave rise to an artistically rich avant-garde tradition, Ireland simply tried to contain its threat.

Of no less concern was the space in which these different activities were enjoyed. While Gaelic sports take place outside, 'under the sky,' in a healthy, if often physically brutal, environment, by contrast, commercial entertainment unfolds in a hothouse atmosphere, usually at night, or in any case from which (God's) daylight is excluded and under the most 'artificial' conditions, the implications of which will be discussed below. Importantly, the communal environment of the *seanchaí*'s storytelling around the cottage hearth, promoted by cultural nationalists, is of a radically different order to that of commercial entertainments, not least because in the latter instance, the audience is considerably larger. More pertinent is the cinema audience's interrelation with the pleasurable object, characterized, on one level, by capitalism and, on another, but related level, by *private* voyeurism.⁴ As Irish novelist Elizabeth Bowen, writing in 1938, describing her experience of the cinema, notes that it offers

> *The delights of intimacy without the onus*, high points of possession without the strain ... And apart from this – how seldom in real life (or so-called real life) does acquaintanceship, much less intimacy, with dazzling, exceptional beings come one's way ... Rapture lets me suppose that for *me alone* they display the range of their temperaments, their hesitations, their serious depths. They live for my eye. Yes, and I not only perceive them but am them; their hopes and fears are my own: their triumphs exalt me. (Emphasis added.)⁵

Furthermore, the cinema and indeed the (vaudeville) theatre audience carries within itself a potentially dangerous *frisson* as for the most part it consists of strangers who as such are subject to the (pleasurable) dangers, real and imagined, that chance encounters often produce. Indeed, this extra-textual interaction between audience members is invoked in James Joyce's *Ulysses*, through the memories of Molly and Leopold Bloom. Bloom's recollection of the theatrical experience of his youth is defined by an insistent sensuousness and physicality, and the aroma of women's scent: 'the mingling odours of the ladies' cloakroom and lavatory, the throng penned tight on the old Royal stairs (for they love crushes, instinct of the herd, and the dark sexsmelling theatre unbridles vice).' While it is this super-presence of the body, both on and off the stage, which Molly objects to and leads her to declare that it will be 'the last time I'll go there to be squashed like that for any Trilby or her barebum,' she nonetheless enjoys, or, as Bloom would reason, even courts through 'her crocus dress ... lowcut, belongings on show,' the sexual interest of other audience members. In this regard, she refers to a 'gentleman of fashion staring down at me with his glasses.' In contrast, Bloom jealously remembers a 'chap in dresscircle staring down into her with his operaglass for all he was worth.'⁶

A rare description in Irish literature of the subversive and transgressive pleasures and dangers of cinema which serves to starkly highlight the hidden desires of the audience, something about which the censors were only too acutely aware, appears in Liam O'Flaherty's 1926 novel *Mr Gilhooley*. The eponymously named retired civil engineer, who is 'in full possession of all his faculties and of all his lusts,'⁷ drunkenly wanders down Dublin's Grafton Street with his mind a miasma of confused thoughts. He approaches the Grafton Street Picture House and enters the darkened cinema where a (silent) film is showing. 'On the screen were Americans dancing in a cabaret, while behind a curtain, on the screen, of course, a dark man was whispering to a half-naked girl.'

> A faint perfume reached Mr Gilhooley ... This perfume was a curious feminine scent, which was familiar to him, for he was a habitué of the cinema for

certain reasons; and that curious feminine scent is peculiar to the cinema. So many well-dressed women sitting in silence in the half-darkness. There was an air of mystery about it. An air of romance and of *remoteness from actual life*. With the mind drugged by the spectacle on the screen, *the body hidden from observation by the darkness, yet in contact with others, eavesdropping on the absurd display of emotion exhibited on the screen, passions were aroused which in the cold air outside would bring a flush to the cheek* ... A feeling of extraordinary passion pervaded his body. *His movements were no longer under control of his brain.* He could not see, and had he tried to speak at that moment his lips could have uttered no sound. Moisture filled his eyes. He was intoxicated with passion. To the degree that he had been miserable a minute ago, suddenly he had now become deliriously happy, plunged suddenly into that intoxication of the *voluptuary by the environment, which suggested strange things to his imagination*, and by the prospect of a subtle amusement to which he was addicted. (Emphasis added.)[8]

Sitting beside a middle aged woman he begins

> to take part in this peculiar form of debauchery ... His self-centred passion merely toyed with the subtlest form of lust, which does not depend on the object desired, but on the suggestions brought to bear on the object. He touched her knee again and it seemed there was a slight response ...[9]

Gilhooley's hand moves upwards and suddenly the previously compliant woman jumps up and leaves the cinema noisily. In fear, Gilhooley imagines that the woman will return with an attendant and point him out as the audience join her in a chorus of 'Pervert. Away with him. Lynch him,' and he would be publicly ruined and disgraced. No such reaction occurs and his fear is replaced by shame: 'He was in the throes of the mania of guilt which follows in the wake of a perversion,'[10] and he ends up feeling sorry for himself.

Of course, that he fears retribution, is not so much superego induced as reflecting the presence of the law and local authorities within the cinema space, who acting as the censors of the physical environment, sought, as much as possible, to contain such extra-textual attractions through the regulation by their 'Inspector of Places of Public Resort'. For example, prostitutes and alcohol were banned, while, as discussed in chapter 2, they were also engaged in a struggle over the degree of lighting within the cinema.[11] After all, it was the Public Health Committee of Dublin Corporation which appointed the first Irish film censors in 1916. (The only known recorded account of an alleged sexual assault in the cinema was in 1932 when a man was charged and found not guilty with feeling another man in the Camden de Luxe, Dublin.)[12]

In addition to the dynamics of audience (and the medium), was the venue's location within the city, which consequently lends a fundamentally different experience and meaning than that of the countryside. If, as Raymond Williams[13] remarks at the opening of *The Country and the City*, that 'country' and 'city' are 'very powerful' words, in the Irish context, treated as binary opposites, their ideological resonance is even more pronounced than elsewhere. While the 'country' has been represented within mainstream nationalist historiography, as well as much of nineteenth- and early twentieth-century literature, and the visual arts as the site of authentic Irishness, the city within this tradition has, for the most part, been unfavourably contrasted against it, even though James Joyce did bring a modernist discourse to bear on the city as a means of unpacking the dichotomy and turning the focus not just on his native Dublin, but on the broader cultural inheritance. In doing this, he employed the techniques of a new modernist fiction as well as drawing on a philosophical and methodological framework provided by cinema to explore space and time, most especially the latter.[14]

Of course, overarching both modernist and traditionalist approaches to the Irish city is a particular type of engagement with popular culture and the description of everyday life. In her study of James Joyce's writings and their relationship to popular culture including the press, plays, pantomimes, and the music hall, in particular, Cheryl Herr[15] analyzes the social class, national, and economic bases of popular culture in Ireland in the late nineteenth and early twentieth centuries. What becomes clear is the prominence of the British presence in commercial theatres and music halls and that despite the constraints of censorship, at least with regard to 'suggestive' or risqué songs, imposed as much by Dublin's theatre owners seeking a 'respectable' middle-class clientele as by Dublin Castle, English music hall type and related entertainments were the main commercial fare of all classes in Dublin. (Although the exact social composition of the audience remains a matter of some conjecture – we know that while certain Dublin film exhibition venues in the early period, such as the Ancient Concert Rooms and the Rotunda, or later the Grafton, were favoured by the middle classes, the city's dominant cinema audience was working-class, or, at least, clerical grades and other aspiring lower middle-class men and women.) Furthermore, Dublin was the most important 'provincial' centre for such 'cultural' exports, even though Dublin audiences were likely to interpret or read these, at least in part, oppositionally. For example, such acts, which offered to their (British) largely urban proletariat target audience critiques of the upper classes and authority figures, would in Dublin, if not necessarily in Belfast, be read as also critiquing English colonialism in Ireland. Irish culture, on the other hand, as it entered an expansive phase during the same period was built around amateur sports, Irish language classes, and amateur drama. Simultanously, the 'Literary Revival' would dominate the high art cultural agenda. Consequently, as commercial entertainment, viewed by many as being soiled by its commodification in the market, was predominantly English, the contrast between Irish and English culture in Ireland was usually clear-cut, though Dublin venues such as Dan Lowrey's Star of Erin Theatre of Varieties, where the first moving pictures were shown in Ireland in April 1896, regularly featured Irish acts.

As popular fiction, and, from the 1860s onwards, the popular press, included writings on socially divisive topics such as divorce, an alliance between nationalists and Catholics against imported popular media emerged. More broadly, the development in the nineteenth century of popular 'panoramic writing' (to use Walter Benjamin's term) with its accounts of 'the tiniest corners' of everyday urban life together with illustrative lithographs (subsequently, the basis of the cheaper everyday press), brought to the masses a new philosophical vision. Through these written and visual micro-narratives 'a sense of the density of everyday experience, of its lived complexity,'[16] was conveyed which inevitably challenged the dominant ideology and the meta-narratives of religion, capitalism and the (re)formation of Irish culture and identity. As a significant section of the cinema audience was drawn from the readers of such popular publications, it was not long before the cinema too became the target for similar criticisms. However, the threat and liberation posed by film and the cinemagoing experience far outstripped the print-based media.

Cultural-nationalist ideology was to a large extent formed by elevating a putative rural pastoral harmony above the perceived degradation of the city. Although Irish modernists such as John Eglinton, writing in 1899, could celebrate technology and modern communications – 'The epics of the present age are the steam-engine and the dynamo, its lyrics the kinematograph, phonograph etc.'[17] – and Joyce could establish formally, if not actually, Dublin as a 'modern-ist' city, the dominant strain within Irish cultural nationalism displayed an overt hostility to modernity and urbanization. Douglas Hyde, founder in 1893 of the Gaelic League, an organization dedicated to the replacement of the English language by Irish as the vernacular, and who in 1938 became President of Ireland, 'dreaded', as historian Joe Lee put it, 'the threat of a modernised Gaelic Ireland as intensely as the prospect of a modernised anglicised Ireland.'[18] Or, as one of the leading figures of the Literary Revival, Lady Gregory, complained, her imagination 'is always the worse for every sight of Dublin.'[19]

This prejudice against (an urban) modernity, and its corollary, the celebration of the pastoral, was not a product of rural dwellers but of urban, specifically Dublin-based, intellectuals, writers and artists operating within the context of the colonial experience. While the urban was associated with centers of capitalist concentration and colonial administration, the struggle for the land, literally and figuratively, was fought for a different economic and cultural order, both of which could be termed self-sufficient and protectionist. Choosing the country was a rejection of the trappings of the colonial Other as well as an attempt to enter a romantic arcadia with man pitted not against man but against nature. Conjoined to this escape into an imagined pre-Conquest Ireland was the fostering of the Irish language which became linked with potential Irish economic fortunes. The influential D.P. Moran, editor of the *Leader*, the main Irish-Irelander journal during the first half of the twentieth century, put it this way:

> An English-speaking Ireland, with English thoughts and ideas, can never do anything but drift; but an Irish speaking Ireland, looking at Irish interests from an Irish point of view, can become prosperous and content.[20]

Such complacency, and materialistically unfounded optimism, about the economic well-being of Irish citizens was to prove disastrous in the decades following independence. Indeed, some Irish language enthusiasts such as Hyde regarded language as 'not merely *expressing* thought but as *creating* it.'[21] From language *alone*, cultural and other values would arise 'organically from the Gaelic past, in place of the derivative, vulgar, meretricious modes of feeling produced by an "imposed" English materialist culture.'[22] It is unsurprising therefore to discover that cinema, a technologically-based urban medium produced for the urban classes, should be regarded with suspicion by those who sought to create a mythical Gaelic past.

There are two main issues concerning the cinematic representations of urban experience in the Irish context. One is how the Irish themselves were represented both by foreigners and by themselves; and the other, which forms the central theme of this book, is how representations of urban America with its overt secularism and consumerism, and to a lesser extent urban Britain, were received in Ireland. When representatives of the pioneering Lumière Brothers visited Ireland in 1896 and 1897 to screen films and to make some of the first moving picture images of Ireland, a new way of seeing the Irish countryside and the city was initiated. A selection of Irish film footage was included in the Lumières' catalogue – 25 items, mostly 50-second segments, featuring the two cities (Belfast and Dublin) which were visited, and the train journeys from Belfast to Dublin, and Dublin to the port town of Kingstown (now Dún Laoghaire). The scenes of city streets and shots from trains were similar to those filmed throughout the world by the Lumières' cameramen, and likewise are marked by a structured absence of rural life. Even though some of the images in the train journey films are of the countryside, in these, the countryside becomes abstracted and reduced to lines of speed such that it has a dreamlike, even eerie quality. It is as if the countryside is ethereal, separated by the train from that which is being filmed and from the medium which is filming it. These early moving picture images of the countryside, compared with the bustling, busy, communal, even aggressive sense of the city which is conveyed (such as the Dublin film of the Fire Brigade, a popular choice for both cameramen and audiences in all cities), are in stark contrast with the emptiness of the countryside.

It has been argued that the experience of the countryside in Ireland (and, presumably, elsewhere) at the time of famine, has a 'shock' of modernity akin to that experienced by urban dwellers. In an article, 'Montage, Modernism and the City,' Luke Gibbons[23] asks: 'In a culture traumatized by a profound sense of catastrophe, such as Ireland experienced as late as the Great Famine, is there really any need to await the importation of modernism to blast open the continuum of history?' Whatever the relevance of this as a philosophical enquiry into the collective imagination, culturally or representationally one only has to look at the first Lumière films shot in Ireland to realize that there *is* a fundamentally different experience of modern life being recorded. It is the difference between the 'hyper-stimulus'[24] of the city – which, in Irish cities, ironically, was formed in part by the agricultural 'invasion' of the city as pigs and cows were exported through Dublin Port – and the emptiness of the countryside. The sensory assault of everyday life, the defining element of modernity, can be seen even in these fixed-camera shots, such as the view of O'Connell Street shot in September 1897, the oldest surviving moving picture of the capital.

With the absence of critical and dynamic urban representations in both the official culture and in cinematic representations of their own urban centers, Irish people
were left with a comprehensive set of representations of urban life produced by
Hollywood. But, as is explored in chapters 2 to 6, they did not see Hollywood as predominantly viewed either by Americans or by British cinemagoers. Instead, they saw
a radically contrasting world and lifestyle which necessarily challenged traditional Irish
notions of morality and order and highlighted their own material lack, both personally and as a nation. Furthermore, this cinema offered a new, more complex and
ambiguous perspective on Ireland's relationship to America and the Irish migrant, not
least in films which were directed by or featured Irish-born or Irish-Americans.
Exemplary in this regard is the first fiction film made in Ireland, *The Lad from Old
Ireland* (1910), in which the ambitious agricultural worker goes to New York, leaving behind his sweetheart, becomes prosperous and is elected to political office, but
forgets his pining lover. In the meantime, he has been seduced not just by wealth and
privilege, but he is clearly attracted to a 'loose' New York beauty, that is, until he gets
a reminder to return home, which he does, and arrives in the nick of time to save his
sweetheart from eviction.[25] Most of those who left were seduced by one aspect or
another of America and, indeed, one of the themes of Catholic bishops' Lenten pastorals during the 1920s and 1930s was that the cinema was showing a way of life
which, when compared to the poor pay and conditions being experienced in Ireland,
was likely to encourage emigration, as, no doubt, it did, at least on a psychic level. As
the Bishop of Ardagh and Clonmacnosie Dr MacNamee, put it in 1937, in regard to
'the emigration of girls to Great Britain':

> they are lured, perhaps, by the fascinations of the garish distractions of the
> city, and by the hectic life of the great world as displayed before their won-
> dering eyes in the glamorous unrealities of the films ... For it is not the least
> of the sins of the cinema to breed a discontent that is anything but divine in
> the prosaic placidity of rural life.[26]

Writing in 1944 when 22 million cinema tickets were being sold in Ireland annually,
B.G. MacCarthy, a Lecturer in Education at University College Cork, also focused on
the rural marginalized, or, at least, on the most economically and socially-disadvan-
taged of the rural population:

> It is interesting to consider the average farm labourer walking five or six miles
> ... to go to the pictures, and then that long way home again in our Irish rain.
> What has he seen that has the slightest relation to life as he knows it? He has
> seen nightclub queens covered by a few spangles, Chicago gangsters talking
> a peculiar argot, society playboys babbling airily of Reno divorce. He has seen
> crooning cowboys, coal-black mammies, typists clad in Schiaperelli models
> living in luxurious flats, and millionaires living in Babylonian palaces, he going
> home to fall into his bed in a loft, to rise the next morning and feed the pigs.
> What does he make of it all?[27]

Of course, we will never know, because such voices from the Irish countryside are not recorded, certainly as regards the effect of the cinema on their imaginary life. Like others, though, the cinema transported them, however fleetingly, out of the general drudgery and loneliness of their lives. For that alone, the cinema can be regarded as a positive social and cultural force.

Not least of that which singled out the cinema as an alternative space to official Irish culture, for all classes, and allowed Irish audiences, as much as their American counterparts, to experience 'difference,' was very often the architecture and decor of the buildings themselves, the prestigious ones in particular. Their combined modernist/Art Deco designs, and their contrasting though similarly *unIrish romantic* 'atmospheric' interiors, provided a relief against the dearth of a dynamic modernist impulse elsewhere in Ireland where, in terms of architecture, neo-classical and Victorian styles predominated. The buildings themselves, such as Dublin's Savoy (opened 1929), the Theatre Royal and nearby Regal (1934–1935), and the Adelphi (1938), like those in Belfast were in the International Style, though those in Dublin resonated more with Art Deco ornamentation. Provincial Ireland was no different, with most towns and cities having at least one such example; indeed it was often the only major modern building in the region. As architectural historian Sean Rothery notes,[28] 'by the early 1930s the cinema in Ireland was to become possibly the main outlet for designs in a modern idiom.' He adds[29] that when the Ritz, Athlone opened in 1939, with its white walls, large areas of glass, flat roofs and porthole windows, 'it must have seemed an exotic, exciting and even bizarre newcomer to this old market town.'

The cinema itself was *relatively* unsupervised and warm, and in this respect at least, first-run Irish cinemas were similar to those elsewhere. If many cinemas offered a sumptuous environment – central heating, plush carpets, sensuous decor and seating – which contrasted with the cold, poorly-lit, wooden floored, or at best linoleum covered floors, of working-class homes, or the equally spartan living conditions of many in the agricultural sector, others coded this in fantastic ways. The interior of Dublin's Savoy, for example, was designed in a Venetian style, and included paintings of the Doge's Palace and a proscenium arch in the shape of a Venetian bridge. The dark blue ceiling was lit such that it resembled the night sky. The Theatre Royal also had 'a simulated outdoor decorative scheme with spot lighting imitating a starry sky' while 'balustrading and oriels completed the illusion of an exotic outdoor southern piazza.' The Savoy, Cork (1931–1932), Rothery writes,[30] was 'the most elaborate and outrageous atmospheric interior in Ireland and probably hard to equal in Britain.' The Venetian theme included a painting of the Grand Canal and other Italianate frescoes on the walls. The proscenium arch was, like its Dublin namesake, in the shape of a Venetian bridge, this time with a 'Romeo and Juliet' balcony. The *Architectural Review* at the time described it as 'Ireland's most beautiful Theatre.'

Writing in the *Irish Cinema Handbook* in 1943, a promoter of International modernism, architect Alan Hope, who snobbishly dismissed these 'romantic' cinema interiors as being founded on the 'insistent belief that cinema is an escape from the reality of the world to the warmth and comfort of a modern Arabian night,'[31] missed so much of what was and is cinema's attraction. Writing five years earlier, the conservative theatre and film critic, Gabriel Fallon, later a deputy Film Censor, was more attuned to these extra-textual experiences and warned against these 'Temples of the New Entertainment' with their darkened interiors and plush-covered armchairs. Cinema was 'an escape from reality, a drug. And for the nationalist, the economist, the sociologist, the moralist … it remains … a menace.'

> Consider a visit to the cinema. The foot sinks comfortably into the carpeted floor as the usherette guides you carefully to your place. Your body relaxes in the ease of the well-sprung, generously padded seat of plush … The whole place is restful, soothing, somnolent … Worries vanish. Then you lift your eyes (or rather your eyes are lifted) through the semi-darkness to the brightness of the illuminated screen. Your attention is caught and held, carried along. *The experience is pleasurable, attractive, fascinating, penetrative. With your body off duty, it may be that your mind is off duty too.* (Emphasis added.)

Fallon, who regarded the influence of the cinema as 'tending towards moral, artistic and intellectual degradation,' described how cinemagoing affected what he called the 'unsophisticated'. He continued: 'Observe our young men, and more particularly, our young women, cinemagoers all. Notice the Clark Gable moustaches, the coiffures à la Garbo. Remember the Valentino side locks …'[32] Indeed, this mimicking of the stars as an attempt to move beyond the stifling emptiness and repression of (1930s) Ireland, is explored in a Seán Ó Faoláin story, adapted for cinema by Thaddeus O'Sullivan as *The Woman Who Married Clark Gable* (1985). Incidentally, for O'Sullivan, the atmosphere evoked equally recaptures the importance of the weekly visit to the cinema that he enjoyed when he was growing up in the otherwise bleak 1950s. For most cinemagoers, sophisticated or not, this flight of fantasy, or the vicarious enjoyment in the free flow of desire was precisely what they wanted, as Elizabeth Bowen's 'confession' on her reasons for going to the cinema attests:

> I go to be distracted (or 'taken out of myself'); I go when I don't want to think and need stimulus; I go to see pretty people; I go when I want to see life ginned up; charged with unlikely energy; I go to laugh; I go to be harrowed; I go when a day has been a mess of detail that I am glad to see even the most arbitrary, the most preposterous, pattern emerge; I go because I like bright light, abrupt shadow, speed; I go to see America, France, Russia; I go because I like wisecracks and slick behaviour; I go because the screen is an oblong opening into the world of fantasy for me; I go because I like story, with its suspense; I go because I like sitting in a packed crowd in the dark, among hundreds riveted on the same thing; I go to have my most general feelings played upon.[33]

A more recent local study of women and cinemagoing in Waterford led Helen Byrne to observe that while talking with one of her interviewees she got a real sense of the importance she and other working class women associated with their visits to the cinema. It was their time, where in the dark of the cinema, beyond prying eyes, they could let their thoughts flow with the narrative and forget the responsibilities of family and endless domestic chores. They could look without being looked at. In the cinema, they could take pleasures in seeing strong and beautiful women and handsome men, they could become enveloped in love stories, take pleasure in seeing women who answered back, had confidence, glamour, smoked in public and wore trousers with no mind to current predominant Irish conventions.[34]

What follows is the story of how the state, and other institutions, most notably the Catholic church, and mostly men, who, fuelled by repressive ideologies, or the hysterical need to control and direct the hearts and minds of others, tried to stop cinemagoers experiencing at times, liberating, subversive and transgressive pleasures, even if these pleasures in another context, as has been well argued, could be seen to be vehicles of reinforcing the (American) status quo and monolithic culture, such as in the negative (or regressive) positioning of women and other marginal or minority groups. It is also a narrative of the failure of this project. While censorship attempts to repress that which threatens bourgeois hegemony, it is powerless against, and may well stimulate, negotiated or entirely oppositional readings or discourses. Put another way, meaning, as we know, can never be fully determined because of the subjective nature of reception and the *relative* freedom by which an audience can understand or interpret images or narratives. One of the consequences of this is the gap that often exists between public and official reception of fiction film content, such as is exemplified in a review of the first programme screened at Ireland's first full-time cinema, the Volta, at 45 Mary Street, Dublin which was opened and very temporarily managed by James Joyce in December 1909. Included in the programme, and arguably the catalyst for Joyce opening the cinema was the Italian film, *Beatrice Cenci* (Mario Caserini, 1909). Based on a real historical event and popularized by Percy Byssey Shelly in his play *The Cenci* (1819), it tells of a daughter who kills her father after he sexually assaults her. The *Freeman's Journal* commented that it was 'hardly as exhilarating a subject as one would desire on the eve of the festive season [Christmas 1909],' yet the film 'was very much appreciated and applauded.'[35]

If as will become clear, the 'anti-cinema' campaigns were characterized by a middle- and upper-class bourgeois desire to contain, as much as possible, expressions of the physical both on and off the screen – given that polite society requires the body to be denied and transformed into a silent, odourless, senseless object without desire – nevertheless, the traces of sensuality and desire, stubbornly remain, if often in a truncated and at times almost unrecognizable form. The fictional Bloom and Gilhooley, in common with their fellow *real* audience members, know that the dangers and the pleasures afforded by cinema are not merely located in the film itself, but float in a non-rational ether around the film object. Indeed, this blurring of private and public on the one hand, and imagination and reality on the other, a defining feature of the cinema experience, is intensified in the even more immersive world of cyberspace, where our censorship journey ends, at least with regard to what could be defined as moral censorship. The history of overt 'political' censorship of film and television presented in chapter 8 concludes the narrative.

### INDUSTRIAL REVIVAL!
A NEW BRITISH CINEMA IN O'CONNELL STREET, DUBLIN.

" TO-NIGHT WE MAN THE BEARNA BAOGHAIL."

**2** The context of the phrase, taken from the National Anthem, 'A Soldier's Song', is the soldiers' manning of the 'gap of danger' in order to win Ireland's freedom from 'the Saxon foe'. Here, the Irish-Irelander journal *The Leader* (21 December 1929:493) mocks the President of the Executive Council William T. Cosgrave's (right) attendance at the opening in November 1929 of Dublin's 3,000-seat Savoy cinema, by Associated British Cinemas, whose managing-director John Maxwell is seen thrid from left. The cinema's opening film, a musical, *On with the Show* (Alan Crosland, 1929), had 'many glimpses of semi-nudity' cut by Film Censor James Montgomery

CHAPTER 2

# Setting the agenda

From the point of view of morals it might be profitable to draw a parallel
between the use of the Cinema and the use of Whiskey. Both are used as a
stimulus, or to produce a change in one's mental state ... Either may be good in
suitable quantities for suitable people, but, being strong stimulants, must be
administered in dilution to the young or unstable.
Max Drennan, *Professor of English, University College Galway, 1917.*[1]

## ORIGINS OF FILM CENSORSHIP IN IRELAND

The first major controversy concerning the cinema in Ireland focused on the 1910
filmed contest between the ex-world heavyweight champion, James J. Jeffries, and the
reigning champion, Jack Johnson, 'a person of color.'[2] The boxing genre, together
with the travel and passion play genres, were among early cinema's most popular
entertainments.[3] Though exhibition (projected or in 'peep' shows)[4] of boxing films
– celebrating movement and the body at a time when there was a growing awareness
among the urban populace of fitness and physicality[5] – was popular as early as 1894,
it was only with the screening of the James J. Corbett and Bob Fitzsimons fight of 17
March 1897, that the fight film became established internationally. The choice of St
Patrick's Day was no accident as 'Gentleman Jim' Corbett and his predecessor as
heavy-weight champion, John L. Sullivan, were Irish-American sporting heroes.
(Corbett took the title from Sullivan in 1892.) *The Corbett–Fitzsimons Fight*
(Veriscope, 1897), 'one of the first full-length performances devoted exclusively to
motion pictures'[6] was specially staged for filming[7] and ran for about 100 minutes
when premièred in New York City on 22 May 1897. The film was shown in Ireland,
as were the *Fitzsimons–Jeffries* (American Vitagraph Company, 1899) and
*Sharkey–Jeffries* (Biograph, 1899) fights.[8] The latter, a 25-round contest which went
all the way, ended with Jeffries defeating Sharkey who was known as *The Irish Sailor.*
Indeed, that these two films were shown as a double bill, along with *The Great Passion
Play*, from Christmas Eve 1900 onwards at Limerick's Athenaeum gives some indication that the controversies about fight and passion play films which emerged a
decade later were not a feature of early cinema even in a city such as Limerick with

31

its strong Catholic activist constituency. Many fight films were also restaged for film, though without the actual boxers, predominantly by Siegmund Lubin during 1899–1900. Though these 'fakes' were initially resisted by the audience who expected the real thing, they soon became an established part of variety entertainment and, as Musser observes, became 'the poor man's way to see the fight.'[9] It seems that after this period (1897–1900) screened prizefights waned in popularity. However, in Ireland at least, there was a resurgence of interest with a number of boxing films screened from the end of the decade through to 1914.

One of the most interesting cultural dimensions to the screening of boxing films was women's attendance. In general, women were excluded from the homosocial world of boxing and wrestling, but writers on American cinema, including Charles Musser and Miriam Hansen,[10] have noted how such films drew not only a cross-section of social classes, but women to the screenings. On the one hand, contemporary American accounts suggest that the exhibition space offered a more controlled and less visceral environment than the boxing arena as the 'absence of noise, blood, and the sounds of distress' made the film more palatable to women's sensibilities. (The film was, after all, a 'reproduction', not the real thing.) On the other hand, it was suspected that many attended 'with the expectation of being shocked and horrified.'[11] Whatever the reason, more pertinent is that it allowed (Irish middle-class) women access to, and to assert themselves in, what had been hitherto an exclusively male sphere.[12] Equally, it opened up the notion of women's desire: 'Suddenly they had access to the forbidden and could peruse the semi-naked, perfectly trained bodies of the male contestants.'[13]

Although there is no evidence as to the extent of (middle-class) women's attendance at such films, it would seem that it parallels the American experience. From an *Irish Times* review of films screened at the Empire Palace Theatre (formerly Dan Lowery's Star of Erin Music Hall; now the Olympia Theatre, Dame Street, Dublin) on 15 November 1897 which describes the audience as fashionable – 'Such as one is accustomed to see in a first-class playhouse, and included a large number of ladies'[14] – women's presence is clear. This is supported by advertisements for the Rotunda, Dublin's most important film exhibition venue during the 1900s, in which references were regularly made to the availability of carriages following afternoon screenings (when, of course, working-class people and middle-class men would be working). Indeed, the advertisements for the Johnson-Jeffries fight declared that while it was 'Never before Equalled in Old Dublin's Annals,' it was 'Patronised and Applauded by Clergy, Ladies and the Very Elite of Society.'[15] Considering this pattern and the marketing of the *Johnson–Jeffries Fight* it is safe to assume that middle-class women were expected to patronize the film. This view is reinforced by the fact that the *Johnson–Jeffries Fight* was planned to open at the (respectable) Rotunda just prior to Horse Show Week which was (and is) one of the major annual social events for middle- and upper-class, urban and rural men and women. Secondly, the ticket prices ranging from one to five shillings were comparable to those of variety theatres, and were probably the most expensive cinema tickets to be issued in Ireland.[16]

That the Irish audience had witnessed a number of fight films prior to the Jeffries–Johnson 1910 bout in Reno, Nevada, which had passed without debate, suggests that it was not boxing per se that drew the ire of the authorities during the subsequent controversy, but race, and specifically, Johnson's victory. Another view must be that the authorities saw an opportunity to try indirectly to introduce censorship as two previous Johnson victories, including when he won the heavyweight championship, were shown in Ireland. Regarded by some as the greatest heavyweight boxer of all time, in the first decade of his career, Johnson was forced to fight only other African-Americans such as Sam Langford and Sam McVey because of racism in the USA, but, eventually, he tracked down the reigning heavyweight champion, Canadian Tommy Burns, who had been avoiding him, to Australia where he comprehensively defeated him on Boxing Day, 1908, the film of which was shown in Ireland.[17] Back in the USA, Johnson defeated the world middleweight champion, Stanley Ketchell, in October 1909, the film of which was also seen in Ireland only a few months before the Johnson–Jeffries contest.[18] Both of these films seem to have been shown in Dublin without protest from the archbishop or anyone else. After Ketchell's defeat, there were calls for a 'Great White Hope' to defeat Johnson. In the absence of any credible white challenger, James J. Jeffries, who retired as champion in 1904 after a successful career, was prevailed upon to fight Johnson. By now 44 years old, Jeffries faced Johnson on 4 July 1910. Johnson won the contest and went on to hold the title until defeated in Havana, Cuba in 1915. A flamboyant character, the reaction to Johnson was not just generated by his colour, but by his perceived arrogance, such as taunting white opponents in the ring, living an extravagant life-style, and having white girlfriends.[19] Nevertheless, it was usually unacceptable in early cinematic representation to have an African-American or other ethnic groups including the Irish and Jews, beat a 'respectable' (that is, middle-class WASP) white man other than in a comic context.[20] This volatile issue of race and the underlying white suprematism, would be most explicitly brought into focus through the screening of *The Birth of a Nation*, D.W. Griffith's 1915 historical epic featuring the American Civil War and its aftermath in the South.[21]

When J.T. Jameson, who had been running highly successful film seasons at the Rotunda for almost a decade, acquired the Irish film rights to the Jeffries–Johnson contest, the film already had a problematic history, and had failed to be given a European screening. In America, the fight had generated an intense reaction from whites, which, no doubt, was reinforced by the match being fought on American Independence Day. Fear of race riots arose in some parts of the USA, and the subtext of commentaries in Britain indicated similar fears if the film was shown there. Consequently, London County Council (LCC), in what was in effect Britain's first film censorship decision, took the lead and told exhibitors on 12 July 1910 that it was 'undesirable' to screen the film,[22] a decision also taken in Germany. Despite this, or perhaps because of it, Jameson paid a 'substantial price'[23] for the Irish rights, and advertised it as the 'first public exhibition outside America.' Though the film was to prove successful – its popularity attested to by its two-week long run and its six shows daily, including one at 10.30 a.m. to facilitate visitors to the Horse Show – on 20 August, the day of its planned opening, it appeared that the film might not be shown at all.

The catalyst for the Irish agitation against the film was the Lord Mayor, Michael Doyle, who sought the support of Archbishop Walsh and Sir John Ross of Bladensburg, the Chief Commissioner of Dublin Metropolitan Police, in having the film banned. Doyle later claimed that he had received strong objections to the film from American visitors to Dublin as well as from a number of prominent Irish people.[24] In his sympathetic reply to Doyle, Walsh acknowledged the LCC's 'strong opinion' against the film, and pointed to the (malign) influence of the context within which a film is viewed:

> The Horse Show ... has its drawbacks, and, amongst them, one of a very demoralising kind. Things being as they are, the cinematograph display will be attended by *crowded audiences*. (Emphasis added.)[25]

He resignedly concluded that all they could do was to 'register a protest against it.'[26] With such a lukewarm response from Dublin's most influential arbiter on moral issues, Doyle tried to use an administrative mechanism, the Cinematograph Act, 1909, to further his plan. He approached Dublin Corporation's Inspector of Places of Public Resort, Walter Butler, an employee of the Corporation since 1882, who had been looking after cinema exhibition for a number of years prior to his appointment in April 1910 as the official charged with administering the provisions of the Act. Under the terms of the Cinematograph Act, from 1 January 1910 all buildings in which films were due to be screened had to be licensed by the local authority. The Act was passed following fatalities in a number of European countries when buildings in which the inflammable nitrate film then in use caught fire. While the Act was ostensibly designed to ensure that cinema buildings were safe, some MPs, most notably T.M. Healy of the Irish Parliamentary Party, suspected that the Bill's real purpose was film censorship.[27] Indeed, Home Secretary Herbert Gladstone 'was not averse to seeing local authorities use safety powers for control over the arts when these were transmitted to the discontented masses.'[28] Therefore, while Butler had no authority as yet to regulate a film's content, he used his powers, which included deciding on the location of projection rooms, storage of films, and assessing the position and numbers of seats,[29] at least in relation to the Jeffries–Johnson fight to try and prevent it (because of its content) from being screened. Indeed Butler, with Doyle no doubt in the background, and Jameson, were engaged in a protracted tussle over the Rotunda's licence for more than six weeks before the fight film was due to be screened, with Butler introducing ever more ludicrous complaints about the building's suitability for film screenings.

The first obstacle to the granting of the licence for the Rotunda was the failure of Butler's office to inform Jameson that a fee had to be paid in advance of inspection. When this was paid on 5 August Butler agreed to examine the premises but 'condemned the electrical fittings as unsuitable and dangerous.' However, at Jameson's insistence Corporation officials examined them and 'pronounced them to be absolutely perfect, [with] the calibre of the cable more than [meeting] the requirements of safety.' When Butler ordered the removal of the projection box, claiming that it obstructed an exit, Jameson borrowed the Theatre Royal's, which had already been passed by Butler, and when one approved by the London County Council arrived that was installed in its stead. Following these further changes Jameson invited the police to inspect the building and Inspector McCabe declared himself satisfied with it. McCabe then met Butler, who was planning legal action against Jameson, and enquired as to whether he would now stop the legal proceedings. Butler made another visit to the Rotunda and found a new 'fault'. He demanded the curious and potentially dangerous condition that an air shaft be installed from the projection box to the outside, a feature which would only help fan the flames if there was a projection box fire, and consequently not allowed by other local authorities. Jameson made the alteration, but this time Butler complained about the length of the air shaft. As a result, by the time of the scheduled first screening of the *Johnson–Jeffries Fight* the licence had still not been issued.[30]

Following the Lord Mayor's letter to Sir John Ross, Superintendent Byrne and Inspector McCabe were dispatched to report whether the screening was in breach of the 1909 Act. When they arrived at the Rotunda for the film's first showing Jameson informed them that as the film was on safety stock, it was not subject to the 1909 Act which only governed combustible nitrate film, and consequently he was not breaking the law. (Only non-inflammable film was allowed for export by the USA.) He then invited the police to attempt to set fire to the film stock, which they failed to do, and assured them that he had applied for a licence only as a matter of form and that 'nothing obscene, brutal or objectionable'[31] was in any of the pictures shown.

Though this opinion of the non-objectionable nature of the film was supported in a long review by the *Irish Times*[32] in which the writer remarked that there was neither a 'taint of brutality' in the film nor a 'display of racial animosity,' even if the white crowd left the fight somewhat 'disappointed [and] dejected,' Archbishop Walsh was not convinced. While the *Times* could point to the film's relatively neutral presentation of the fight that had allowed it to be screened widely in the USA, where in New York and Brooklyn alone it had been shown in eleven cinemas, Walsh focused on the 'brutalising' nature of boxing. Though such films were viewed in the USA as promoting 'criminality by feeding the bestial in man,'[33] perhaps it was the imprint of conservative Victorian morality and the lack of expression of the physical which restrained Walsh from making explicit the question as to the 'propriety of exhibiting semi-nude human figures to a promiscuous assembly' or to women,[34] although he did worry about viewing the film in a large crowd. Unlike his counterparts in the USA, Walsh failed to draw parallels between the boxers' selling of 'their bodies for merchandise as surely as the harlots of the street,'[35] which indicates a general suppression of the erotic within the Irish context, something that is made obvious in the next chapter.

Perhaps prompted by the experience of the *Jeffries–Johnson Fight*, Dublin Corporation's Public Health Committee (PHC) which was responsible for overseeing the implementation of the provisions of the 1909 Act, enquired of the Corporation's Law Agent, Ignatius J. Rice, as to the extent of their power under the Act. He advised that they could 'use their discretion as to the imposing of conditions'[36] in a licence given to a cinema or other such buildings used for film exhibition. This was a mild interpretation of the law since following the precedents being set in England it was clear, even by 1910, that the Cinematograph Act could be interpreted beyond its sole provisions dealing with public safety. Indeed, by the end of the Act's first year in operation, the courts ruled that local authorities were not confined to imposing safety conditions on cinemas, a decision which the Home Office had almost certainly anticipated.[37] This allowed councils in England to restrict cinema opening hours; to forbid unaccompanied children from attending the cinema after 9.00 p.m.; to close cinemas on Sundays; and, most controversially, to censor a film's content.[38] Rice's liberal, but reformist position may be explained by his view of cinema as 'an innocent and healthy form of recreation,' which could do 'the poorer classes ... no harm'.[39] That this was accepted by the members of the PHC owes to the various business interests of the committee. This is most clearly illustrated in the prosecution in late 1911 of two Dublin cinemas, the Volta, Mary Street, and the Electric, Talbot Street, both owned by the then Lord Mayor, J.J. Farrell (1911–1912), and a member of the PHC. By having live musical accompaniment with films screened on Sundays the cinemas had contravened the separate six day music licence required by venues which played live music. However, as 'silent' films were almost never screened without some audio accompaniment – music, lecture, or other sound effects – a cinema, in effect, could not operate without a music licence, and strictly speaking, it had to close on Sundays. Despite this, and while later requiring cinemas to close during Sunday evening religious services, Dublin Corporation from the beginning issued seven day cinema licences. Music (and dancing) licences were issued annually by the Recorder at Green Street Courthouse, Thomas Lopdell-O'Shaughnessy KC, a Sabbatarian, who during the following few years took a more strict line with regard to the cinema, especially Sunday opening, than Rice did. Indeed, when Rice was asked to assist in the case against Farrell, he asked the PHC to consider that cinemas 'do a great deal of good by offering a counter attraction to other less desirable forms of amusement,' a comment which echoes the American reform movement's campaign for the cinema as an alternative to the saloon.[40] Unsurprisingly, the PHC, including Farrell, seem to have agreed with the Law Agent and did not display any enthusiasm for restrictions to be attached to the licence. Resistance to the imposition of conditions relating to the content of films was no doubt led by Farrell and other business interests on Dublin Corporation.

The PHC together with Butler, the Inspector of Places of Public Resort who enforced the committee's decisions, was pivotal in regulating businesses in Dublin. Responsible not just for overseeing such public health regulations as sanitation and ventilation, as well as approving bye-laws relating to safety in a new building, it could also condemn or demand alterations to an existing one. However, by the 1900s Dublin Corporation's elected members were mainly Catholic small businessmen, especially from the grocery and publican trades (even J.J. Farrell's original premises at 44/45 Talbot Street – the Electric Theatre, which was a tobacconist/stationers and footwear warehouse prior to its conversion – was perhaps no bigger than those of many of his fellow councillors), and often as already noted their other interests lay in an uneasy relationship to their responsibilities as councillors. Since some of them were also tenement landlords, they, like their retail business colleagues, had a vested interest in ensuring control over the manner in which health and building bye-law regulations were enforced. Many of the numerous notices to improve or demolish dwellings issued to landlords were not acted on. Indeed, an alderman of the Corporation and a member of the PHC was the owner of a tenement house which collapsed in 1902 killing one person and injuring many others,[41] while in 1913 a housing enquiry revealed that 16 of a total of 79 Dublin Corporation members owned 89 tenements and second-class houses. In this context, Corporation members proved adept at defending their own economic interests while displacing responsibility for many of the city's social problems on to the British Parliament or Dublin Castle's Local Government Board, often through the device of rhetorical nationalist flourishes. Unlike in most other European cities, there was little interest in regenerating (or even representing) the city.[42] As Mary Daly dryly observes, 'Public Health in Dublin Corporation does not appear to have aroused widespread commitment, either from officials or from politicians.'[43] She goes on to make a more telling ideological point:

> The lack of political commitment on the Dublin housing question is in marked contrast to the attention given to the social and economic problems of rural life. This reflects the relative political weakness of Irish cities; their stagnation during the nineteenth century, and an undefined feeling that urban Ireland was somehow alien to the true Irish identity. Dublin housing lacked the powerful sympathies of the Roman Catholic clergy, in marked contrast to the land question ... Unlike rural landlords, tenement owners tended to be nationalist sympathisers.[44]

Thus, Dublin Corporation promoted nationalist and Catholic aspirations in a period of imminent Home Rule rather than engaging with the city's social problems. Cinema, though, was to present a more complex challenge to this approach since it raised the difficulty for some councillors and their friends that their self-interest intersected with the dominant Catholic moral and nationalist cultural attitudes of an increasingly confident Catholic-nationalist majority. When changes were eventually forced upon the PHC, J.J. Farrell, who had been the committee's vice-chairman in 1912 and chairman the following year, was ideally placed to negotiate the best arrangement for Dublin exhibitors.

The PHC finally introduced non-safety related conditions for cinema licences in 1913 when it was presented with a comprehensive set of conditions by Lopdell-O'Shaughnessy, who had been the Recorder since 1905. Although his powers over the cinema did not extend beyond issuing music licences, in February 1913 he positioned himself so as to influence the Corporation into adopting new cinema licence conditions. On 21 February the Recorder refused to issue a music licence to the promoters of a new 194-seat cinema, the Picture House at 30 Henry Street (formerly the World's Fair), until 'proper conditions' appeared in the licence, adding that he would not grant 'an open licence'.[45] No doubt this was motivated by the controversy which had been building up for a number of weeks about the imminent release of Sidney Olcott's life of Christ, *From the Manger to the Cross* (1912). Though this was the first major dramatization, the filmed passion play was already a popular genre with about forty films based on a biblical theme having been produced.[46] These films were usually accompanied by a 'reverent' lecture, and also, in some instances, moving pictures, lantern slides, and religious music. Irish exhibition of religious films goes back to at least October 1898 when *The Passion Play at Oberammergau*, a film in twelve shots, was shown in the Rotunda's Concert Room.[47] However, what is interesting in the Irish context is that even though occasional Irish religious items were included in cinema programmes – for example *The Pilgrimage of Croagh Patrick* was shown in Rathmines Town Hall, Dublin, in August 1905[48] – the number of religious themed films appears to have been relatively low. (Such films were rarely mentioned in newspaper advertisements.) That said, prior to Christmas 1902 the North American Animated Picture Company's *The Vatican Series* (director, Ralph Pringle), which included footage of Pope Leo XIII, was screened in Dublin's select Antient Concert Rooms, Great Brunswick Street (more recently known as the Academy Cinema, Pearse Street). It was at this venue where Olcott's film was also planned to be shown.

A private screening of *From the Manger to the Cross* was held on 29 January 1913 and similar to its initial London (3 October 1912) and New York (12 October 1912) screenings a broad spectrum of clergy were invited. Those who attended were generally in favour of the film, while those who boycotted it, such as the *Irish Catholic*,[49] and a number of prominent Protestant clergy and lay people, began a campaign to have it banned. If the film raised the issue as to the suitability of religious films for commercial exhibition,[50] in Dublin (and, by extension the whole of Ireland), it also served to sharpen sectarian divisions, with Protestants in general opposed to any film featuring a materialization of Christ. This prohibition and distrust of the image had been central to the Reformation, which at one level was fought over the issue of representation. Catholics, with their sumptuous churches and idols, took an altogether more relaxed view of such representations, and, more broadly, the issue of how the Sabbath should be observed or celebrated. The denial of pleasure on the Sabbath, a feature of Protestantism, was only half-heartedly complied with by Catholics who, for example, allowed Sunday opening of cinemas under the jurisdiction of the Catholic majority in Dublin Corporation, while the Protestant-controlled boroughs of Rathmines and Rathgar, and of Kingstown banned Sunday openings.

*From the Manger to the Cross* posed a very particular challenge to Protestants as not only was it filmed in Palestine and Egypt at the actual locations mentioned in the Bible, but it was made in a time of transition from early cinema's 'primitivism' towards the classical style of narrative continuity cinema, something which gave the film a more powerful impact than previous filmed passion plays. Earlier films were usually shot in a tableau style with theatrical painted flats as the background, 'more like the illustrations in a Sunday School book';[51] they were, in effect, filmed plays. While sharing aspects of the tableau form with the earlier films, *From the Manger to the Cross*, nevertheless, used close-up and medium shots, as a result of which 'the people and the surroundings had a tangible solidity that may have contributed to that feeling of sacrilege.'[52] Perhaps the strength of the response against the film was also in part attributable to Olcott's 'imaginative direction' which, according to Kinnard and Davis, gave it 'an emotional charge'.[53] Of the daily newspapers, it was the Protestant/unionist *Irish Times* that was most agitated following the film's private screening. In what would be the first of three editorials on the subject, it reasoned that 'the permanent result of the constant exhibition of such "reproductions" before the casual frequenters of the "picture palaces" must be the cheapening of religion,'[54] and concluded that the film was 'not wanted' in Ireland. In this context, a committee, which appears only to have included Protestants, was formed to try to stop the film's commercial release. On 24 February, less than a week before the film was due to open in Dublin, an application was made to the Recorder to have the licence of the Antient Concert Rooms suspended for two months, or else revoked altogether, on the grounds that *From the Manger to the Cross* was an unsuitable film. In its three column summary of the one day court hearing, the *Dublin Evening Mail* commented on the 'storm of indignation [which] had been aroused by the proposal to exhibit the film.' Even though clergymen, including the President of Blackrock College, Fr N.J. Brennan, and Fr John Gwynn SJ, who had seen the film and reported that its 'exhibition would do immense good' as the Catholic church sought to 'make sacred things part of the daily lives of people,'[55] opponents of the film were appalled at the religious theme being exploited for commercial ends; as an *Irish Catholic* editorial put it, the film was 'Trading on God,' making 'Lucre from Christ'.[56] Much of the discussion in the court case centred on the film's use of professional actors in contrast to the amateur 'actors' participating in the passion play at Oberammergau, who had refused to perform for the screen.

The Recorder had no power to prohibit the screening since he had found no violation of the music licence. Towards the end of his judgment, however, he declared that he 'would not hesitate to express his opinion on the case and the evidence.' The representations in *From the Manger to the Cross*, he was reported to have remarked, were

> indefensible, and nothing less than a traffic for money in the most sacred of sacred subjects. It was ... the exploitation of the mystery of the Incarnation and Atonement by a syndicate for personal gain ... [H]ow odious this was to those for whom Calvary was alike the refuge and the hope.[57]

His comments were echoed by religious campaigners seventy-five years later when, in 1988, Martin Scorsese's *The Last Temptation of Christ* was released. As with *From the Manger to the Cross*, the Irish response to *The Last Temptation of Christ* mirrored what had occurred internationally, but unlike *The Last Temptation of Christ*, *From the Manger to the Cross* was a commercial success, as well as acting as a rallying point for those opposed to religious films. The wheel came full circle in 2004 with the release by born-again Catholic Mel Gibson of *The Passion of the Christ*, his controversial version of Christ's last twelve hours, one of the most commercially successful films ever, not just in Ireland, but worldwide.

Following the failure to get the injunction against *From the Manger to the Cross*, the *Irish Times* urged its readers to boycott the film because it deemed it to have exploited 'the sufferings of Christ for commercial purposes.'[58] However, the protest committee went further, and in a veiled threat warned that the exhibition 'may lead to something in the nature of a riot.' This announcement was condemned by the *Times*: 'no Dublin Protestant will want to interfere with [the] right' to view the film, no more than the vigilance associations had the right to prohibit the circulation of certain publications through intimidation.[59] A 'public indignation meeting' was held at the Mansion House on 28 February to register further opposition to the film. Chaired by the Revd R. Walsh, who represented the Church of Ireland Archbishop of Dublin, Dr Peacocke, among the speakers were the Revd Thomas C. Hammond of the Episcopalian Church of Ireland, one of the applicants for the court injunction against the film; the Revd J. Denham Osborne DD, a Presbyterian and one of the signatories of the circular discouraging attendance at the private screening of the film; the Revd William Bracken, a Methodist; and Pastor Hugh D. Brown, a Baptist. During the meeting it was stated that the scene of the Crucifixion was cut from the film as a result of pressure from protesters, and John Leech KC, who acted for the plaintiffs in court, called for 'strict censorship over cinema films' and restrictions on films which were contrary 'to public morals, decency and religious instincts'.[60] Judging from its third editorial on the controversy following this meeting, the *Irish Times* clearly did not share the implied demand in Leech's speech for state censorship. In what was probably the first reasoned, even liberal, Irish view of state film censorship, it declared that such censorship 'may readily become State tyranny' and again defended the right of people to see the film. It added that it did not want to see cinema 'submitted to the same sort of illogical, and blundering supervision from which the drama now suffers,' but suggested that it must be made amenable to two forms of censorship. Film producers 'must guarantee decency and absence of vulgarity,' and audiences and local authorities, especially Dublin Corporation, should exercise the right of veto.[61] It also regretted the absence of Catholic speakers at the meeting.[62] This sectarian aspect of the campaign, which can also be detected in the court proceedings against the film, illustrates perhaps two complementary aspects of Irish society at this time. Catholic exclusiveness was not just confined to the formal institutions of the church but to the daily activities and campaigns of lay people.[63] To have Protestants involved in a campaign in which Catholics were also participating had to be on Catholic terms, as was demonstrated by censorship agitation later in the decade and in the 1920s. On the other hand, Protestant groups, such as those participating in the *From the Manger to the Cross* controversy, helped set the agenda for campaigns which were later successfully carried through in their own inimitable way by Irish Catholics.

Ironically, when *From the Manger to the Cross* finally opened on 3 March, it was in a bigger venue than the Antient Concert Rooms. The PHC inspected the Concert Rooms on 26 February, two days after the court case, and demanded alterations to it, as well as forbidding the use of the gallery. As a result, the applicants for the cinema licence abandoned the decision to exhibit films there.[64] However, one of the promoters of the screening of *From the Manger to the Cross* had recently remodelled the 1,200-seat Phoenix Picture Palace at Ellis Quay and it was decided to open the film there. Though extra police were on duty at the cinema for the screening, they were not needed, and the manager of the cinema, Cathal MacGarvey, described the criticism of the film as 'unnatural'.[65] He introduced the film with a 'gracefully-worded' speech which alluded to high art by noting that the film was based on the religious paintings of the French artist Tissot.[66] He then placed the film within a religious context by asking the audience to remain silent throughout the film, not to smoke, and that, as in churches, men and boys should remove their hats. According to the *Freeman's Journal*,[67] these demands were 'obeyed absolutely,' and organ music of 'a devotional character' was played during the film. In this enthusiastic report of the film, the newspaper remarked on the impossibility of the film, at least in its first three sections, causing offence to anyone 'unless it be a person who is opposed to religious art of every description.' Though the writer suggested that the scourging at the Pillar and the mocking of the Jews should be omitted, he reported that the Crucifixion scene had been shortened since the time it had been shown to the invited audience. The 'only objection a Catholic could take' was that the Protestant Bible was the source of the film's intertitles, a complaint also made in the *Irish Catholic*.[68] Nevertheless, the *Journal* concluded, 'a Catholic at least' could find nothing to complain about beyond these qualifications.[69] This sharply contrasted with the Protestant/unionist *Dublin Evening Mail*, which declared, albeit in a neutral report, that the film 'ought never to have been produced' and regretted its Dublin screening.[70]

Despite their objections to the film, it did not restrain the *Mail* and other newspapers from carrying advertisements for it. The most elaborate of these in the *Mail* was published when the film's distributors turned the religious divisions provoked by the film to their own advantage. On 15 March a full front page advertisement carried the endorsement of prominent Catholic and Protestant clergy, both Irish and English, including Fr Brennan of Blackrock College, Fr William J. Doherty of the Catholic Pro-Cathedral, the Revd T.H. Seale of Trinity College's Philosophical Society, and the Provost of Trinity College itself. It rather cheekily highlighted the Pope's support for the film, though this was of dubious origin and led to further agitation in the columns of the *Irish Catholic*.[71]

*From the Manger to the Cross* proved to be a huge commercial success, probably helped by the controversy and its attendant publicity. Demand was such that the three daily shows were supplemented by a 12 o'clock matinee. The 'enormous and very general demand'[72] continued during Holy Week and until 6 April, except when the cinema was closed at Easter. The cinemagoing public chose to ignore those 'leaders' agitating against attending the film as they had done during the screening of the Jeffries–Johnson fight in 1910. Despite the apparent defeat of the anti-film, pro-censorship campaigners, the debate surrounding *From the Manger to the Cross* helped to set in train a series of events which eventually led to formal film censorship being introduced in Dublin. Following the failure to cajole cinemagoers into boycotting such films, lay and religious activists, encouraged by the Recorder, pressured Dublin Corporation into introducing new film censorship conditions in the cinema licence. On the day it visited the Antient Concert Rooms and refused it a licence, the PHC also agreed to a meeting with the Recorder, whose idea it seems to have been, to co-ordinate the issuing of licences to cinemas. To that end the PHC appointed a sub-committee to meet him. It is clear from the meeting's outcome that the Recorder had more in mind than the mere co-ordination of licences.

Obviously well versed in the precedents being set by both the British local authorities and the courts, the Recorder recommended that all Dublin licences should contain conditions as were then required in large provincial towns in England. These included the class of film to be shown; the non-admittance of disorderly persons; direct power to revoke licences; and Sunday opening to be confined to between 1.30 p.m. and 7.00 p.m., and 8.00 p.m. and 10.30 p.m., the latter condition an acknowledgment by the Recorder that Sunday opening could not be stopped completely in Dublin City. It was also proposed that licences should be granted from 31 October each year to coincide with the issuing of music and dancing licences. However, he stated that the granting of licences was optional and, for example, could be refused on the grounds that there were enough cinemas in a particular district. He also requested that prior to the renewal of a licence an annual report be furnished to the PHC by its inspectors and by the police on the manner in which the cinema had been run during the previous twelve months. Finally, the Recorder considered the issue of censoring film content. He reported the recent appointment of a Censor in London, a reference to the establishment of the British Board of Film Censors (BBFC), an industry body, which introduced from 1 January 1913 self-regulation of film content as a means of trying to head off state-regulation of film.[73] In its first year, the BBFC refused to certify twenty films, though this was its highest number outside of the war years until 1931.[74] The PHC sub-committee agreed with the Recorder and ordered that one of the conditions of the licence should be that only films bearing the mark of the Censor should be allowed to be exhibited in Dublin 'so as to ensure that nothing of an objectionable nature would be shown.'[75] Similarly, they approved all the Recorder's other suggestions with the exception of Sunday evening closing.

The PHC were 'strongly of the opinion' that more disturbance would be caused to religious worship by the arrival at the church shortly after 7 o'clock and the departure prior to 8 o'clock on Sunday evenings than would be the case if cinemas were open between these hours.[76] Of course, the religious objection to Sunday evening opening was on the grounds that those attending the cinema between 7 and 8 o'clock should be in church and, in this regard, the PHC's apparent concern over disrupting church services disguises the fact that Sunday was by far the best day of the week for the box office. As a result, any restriction on Sunday cinema attendance was fiercely resisted. This was demonstrated quite conclusively later in the decade when, following criticism by the Recorder of the uninhibited opening of cinemas in Rathmines on Sundays, an alliance of Protestant churches successfully campaigned to have the cinemas in the autonomous Dublin Urban District of Rathmines and Rathgar closed completely on Sundays from 1917 to 1920. This action displayed not just the Protestant Sabbatarian position, but also the disdaining middle-class attitude to the cinema.[77]

When the text of the cinema licence was placed before Dublin Corporation in October 1913 there were two other specific clauses: 'No known prostitutes or thieves'

could be admitted, or allowed to remain on the premises; and more generally in a pre-
emption of the all-inclusive and ill-defined terms in the Censorship of Films Act, 1923,
'nothing shall be presented which is licentious or indecent or likely to produce riot,
tumult or breach of the peace.'[78] In 1913 further pressure was mounted on the PHC
when the Dublin Juvenile Advisory Committee of the Board of Trade sought to restrict
the attendance of children at cinemas. They proposed the inclusion of a clause banning children of school-going age from cinemas during 9.00 a.m. to 3.00 p.m. and
after 9.00 p.m. unless accompanied by an adult. The PHC unanimously approved the
clause and recommended to the full council of the Corporation that the age limit for
unaccompanied children attending cinemas after 9.00 p.m. be set at 12 years, two years
older than that sought by the Juvenile Committee.[79] On the surface these restrictions
may appear a hardship to exhibitors but in reality they were not. While the first proposal was obviously aimed at truancy, the second was unlikely to affect cinema audiences in that few children under-12 were likely to be out alone after 9.00 p.m. Indeed,
such a restriction may have had the beneficial effect of encouraging more adult patron-
age at a time when exhibitors were searching for 'respectable' adult audiences. No
doubt this was in the mind of the PHC's Chairman J.J. Farrell, when he deemed that
conciliation and compromise were the most effective means of protecting the nascent
film business from undue interference.

Following a letter to Dublin Corporation from the Representative Managers of
the London County Council Elementary Schools on the 'use and abuse of the cinematograph,' which was considered at its meeting of 6 October 1913, the PHC was
charged with preparing a report on the topic for the council. This was submitted
three months later by the PHC chairman.[80] Farrell pointed out that a United Kingdom
Board of Film Censors (the BBFC) had recently been appointed, and that one of the
conditions of the Corporation's licence since October 1913 was that all films exhibited to the public had to bear the mark of a censor. It was intended that from I March
1914 all films released were to carry the mark of this censor, though the report omitted to state that the BBFC's decisions were not binding on the film trade. Since the
Corporation's licence did not specify that only a Dublin censor's certificate was
required, but any other 'whose judgement is accepted by the Corporation,' in practice the BBFC certificates came to be accepted, at least for awhile, as suggested indirectly by Farrell. At this early stage the BBFC had only two prohibitions – nudity,
and the materialization of Christ[81] – the latter, ironically, which would almost certainly have caused *From the Manger to the Cross* to have been banned had the BBFC
been operating when the film was released.[82] However, it was a number of years
before the BBFC gained sufficient authority to impose its will on a less than compliant film business. Even then its decisions could be overturned by local authorities.
Nevertheless, Farrell and other exhibitors must have been satisfied that a reasonable
compromise had been achieved. This relatively mild form of censorship would be
challenged by the Vigilance Committees.

### THE IRISH VIGILANCE ASSOCIATION AND
### DUBLIN CORPORATION FILM CENSORSHIP

The predominatly Protestant group opposed to *From the Manger to the Cross* did not pursue a more general film censorship policy.[83] That task was taken up by the well-established and powerful Catholic vigilance committees which were initially formed to counter imported 'evil literature'. If the Catholic Truth Society, formed in 1899, attempted to do this through their own uplifting Catholic publications, the vigilance associations engaged in more direct action against the press and other print media.[84] This was later extended to other forms of popular culture, including the cinema, which was gaining an ever more secure foothold in Ireland, and as the circulation and consumption of cinema was less diffuse than the print media, it provided opponents with an easily identifiable target.

The campaign against 'evil literature' originated in Limerick in early autumn 1911 and by the end of that year it had developed a national profile under the leadership of the Dublin Vigilance Committee. Vigilance committees were established throughout the country, usually with overt clerical involvement and in association with established Catholic bodies, such as the Catholic Young Men's Association in Dublin. Simultaneously, there was a growth in mass movements of the Sacred Heart devotions and of the Temperance Pioneers, which helped to put the activities of the vigilance committees into the mainstream of Catholic action. The vigilance movement expanded so rapidly that on 1 July 1912 a meeting held at Dublin's Mansion House had an over-flow of 20,000 people. Presided over by the Lord Mayor, it was attended by the Lord Lieutenant, Lord Aberdeen, a Catholic, whose public endorsement was central to the movement's growth to 100 local vigilance committees.[85] He had been President of the National Vigilance Committee in England for fifteen years, and was currently the President of the International Bureaux for the Repression of White Slave Traffic. At the meeting, messages of support were read from the Pope; the head of the Irish Catholic church, Cardinal Logue; and Archbishop Walsh of Dublin, who had been the most ardent critic among the hierarchy of the popular press since his appointment to the Dublin Archdiocese in 1885.[86]

The committees, later incorporated into a national organization – the Irish Vigilance Association – sought restrictions on the availability of British newspapers and magazines in Ireland, as well as 'suggestive' postcards. It lobbied or coerced sellers of British 'popular' Sunday newspapers in particular to show their compliance with the association by displaying a vigilance card. Those who refused were targeted for boycotting by the committees. Since editions of the imported newspapers were ordered by resident British garrisons such as Limerick and Clonmel, the campaign developed a nationalist dimension. Nevertheless, it was estimated that 40,000 copies of English Sunday newspapers were sold in Dublin alone,[87] which indicates that such publications also had an Irish (working-class) readership. Though support for the campaign was readily forthcoming from the *Irish Catholic*, the fact that it was promoted by D.P. Moran's Irish-Irelander publication, the *Leader*, indicates a co-mingling of moral and political, or Catholic and nationalist issues. As Louis Cullen observes in his account of the vigilance committees, 'the nationalist element was as strong as the religious.'[88] This is further illustrated by the *Leader* setting out, six months prior to the 'evil literature' campaign getting fully underway, terms of reference which were to feature in the nationalist/Catholic hybrid that was central to the vigilance committees motivating doctrine.[89] Similarly, almost from the beginning, in October 1911, both the Irish Branch of the Ancient Order of Hibernians,[90] then undergoing a huge expansion following the lifting of the clerical ban on the organization as a 'secret society' in 1904, and the Council of Sinn Féin, supported the 'evil literature' campaign. The weekly *Sinn Féin* declared at the time that

> We are glad that a movement is afoot to stem the poisoned flood that is pouring into the country, and its promoters will need all and deserve all the support they can get ... [It is] a crusade against immoral literature.

Some of the reports of English divorce cases, the paper complained, were 'a disgrace to the Editor and management who permitted them to be published, and a reflection on the decency of the community which could tolerate them.'[91]

In 1913 the Gaelic League announced its support for the vigilance committees' campaign 'in the most unmistakable language.'[92] This broadening of its support base allowed it to declare its identification 'with the national life of Ireland, and with the inspiring ideal of reviving the traditions of the Island of Saints and Scholars.'[93] Such a statement indicates all too clearly that the vigilance committees, ultimately under clerical control,[94] viewed their task as extending beyond the narrow focus of the campaigns in which they were engaged. As this increasingly powerful and determined alliance of religious and cultural groups began to push Dublin Corporation towards introducing more formal film censorship procedures, resistance was to prove much more difficult than in the past.

While the *Irish Catholic* lent its support to the campaign against *From the Manger to the Cross*, and published weekly reports on the anti-publications campaign of the vigilance committees, it was not until 1915 that the Dublin Vigilance Committee (DVC) finally instituted a campaign for further film censorship. The *Irish Catholic* had already signalled the need for such a campaign when in March 1913 it prominently published a letter from Catholic activist F.P. Carey which concluded, now that '"immoral literature" was vanquished, so, too, will the immoral picture be abolished, particularly as regards the cinema houses of this Catholic capital of Catholic Ireland.'[95] Later in 1913, during the course of the introduction of the first comprehensive set of conditions to the Corporation's cinema licence, the circular from the Representative Managers of London County Council Elementary Schools on the 'use and abuse of the cinematograph' was considered by the Council. When referred to the PHC it appeared that it would lead to further film censorship restrictions. In March 1914, five months later, the report prepared by J.J. Farrell was considered by the full council. This intimated that the concerns expressed by the Elementary Schools Managers were answered by the conditions introduced in the cinema licence adopted in October 1913. This did not satisfy some members of the Corporation who tabled a motion that the PHC's report not be accepted and that the Elementary Schools' Managers' circular be referred to the Committee of the Whole House. Among those voting in favour of the motion, which was carried by 28 votes to 20, were five future Dublin Corporation censors: Councillor Patrick Lennon, Alderman William O'Connor, Andrew (later Sir Andrew) Beattie, Michael Brohoon, and Dr Myles Keogh (a TD in the 1920s and 1930s).[96] At its meeting the following month a letter incorporating a formal resolution on the cinema from the Confraternities Central Council (CCC) – the body which had provided the impetus to the vigilance committees and their 'evil literature' campaign since 1911 – was also considered. The CCC protested against the films being shown in Dublin cinemas; called upon Dublin Corporation to institute 'a proper Civil Censor Board'; and asked that all cinemas be closed on Sundays.[97] On the suggestion of the Lord Mayor the proposal was referred to the Committee of the Whole House, where it languished with the Elementary Schools Managers' circular for more than a year. In May 1915, a year later, the Committee of the Whole House reported to the full council that no further communications should ensue with either organization.[98]

The Dublin Vigilance Committee was initially reluctant to include the cinema and other commercial entertainments among its activities, but in the absence of any other organization, the DVC wrote to Dublin Corporation during the run up to their 1915 annual demonstration in Dublin requesting a meeting on the subject of objectionable films. The resolution in support of this was moved by Councillor William T. Cosgrave (later President of the Irish Free State) at the meeting of 9 August,[99] and it was agreed that the DVC deputation would be received at the council's next meeting.[1] The *Irish Catholic* welcomed the new initiative and lauded the broadening of the campaign against the popular press to take account of theatres, music halls and cinemas, 'which are becoming such a source of danger to public morals.'[2]

The DVC's President, Thomas J. Deering, a solicitor, circulated a letter to the members of the Catholic hierarchy seeking public support for this new campaign. On 11 September, the *Irish Catholic* carried a detailed account of the demonstration under the title 'Fighting a Plague' and printed messages of support from the Catholic bishops which had been read at a rally held at the Mansion House. One of these was from Bishop Gaughan of Meath who wrote that 'these picture houses are now in every small town, and are sure to degenerate and do incalculable harm if not strictly supervised.' His prescription that 'strict supervision in Dublin [would] do much to save us in country towns,'[3] highlights the pivotal position accorded to Dublin Corporation and the recognition that provincial local authorities were without sufficient resources to adequately assess films released in their districts. While some local authorities outside Dublin did censor films, most seem to have accepted the approval or otherwise of Dublin Corporation.

In his address to the Mansion House meeting, Fr Paul OFSC called for 'an organised effort' to deal with cinemas and music halls as he echoed the meeting's tone

> Pestilent literature is bad enough. It is a poison which secretly but effectively corrupts the heart and undermines the virtues of home and country; but its dreadful havoc is outdistanced by the pernicious effects of the filthy picture screen.

This was of further concern as he believed that the great majority of the cinema's audience were 'young [and] innocent' children.[4] The motion on extending the vigilance committees' brief to include theatres, music halls and cinemas was proposed at the meeting by Richard Jones JP, who had been the chairman of the Richmond Asylum Board for seventeen years. It was addressed by Michael Comyn KC who declared that the vigilance committees' objective was 'to preserve the ancient purity and characteristics of [the Irish] race.'[5] The resolution was carried without dissent, and a special sub-committee of the DVC was set up to supervise the new campaign.

The following day a DVC delegation led by Deering and including Fr Paul[6] met Dublin Corporation to record their concern about the screening of objectionable films in certain unspecified cinemas. During the discussion with the council, Fr Paul felt that the councillors 'were thoroughly in sympathy' with their objectives.[7] The councillors expressed their support for the DVC, and according to the *Dublin Evening Mail*,[8] the Lord Mayor James M. Gallagher, promised that 'any machinery of the Corporation would be set in motion at once'[9] to aid the campaign. Even J.J. Farrell, who felt impelled to state that 'none of the picture houses with which he was connected exhibited objectionable matter,' offered full support and called for the naming of disreputable cinemas.[10] This appears not to have been done. Though he suggested that exhibitors had lost money 'by refusing to show sensational or suggestive pictures,' he was of the opinion that

> in the long run ... clean houses always paid. The majority of managers in Dublin would not only be with the aims of the Committee, but would subscribe to any fund organised for the purpose of purifying places of entertainment in the city.[11]

A week later the next major public event of the anti-cinema campaign took place. Ironically, action by an exhibitor helped fuel the DVC's campaign. *A Modern Magdalen* (Will S. Davis, 1915), an adaptation of C. Haddon Chambers' 1902 play, was booked at the Bohemian Picture Palace, Phibsborough, for three days from 13 September. One of those who attended the opening night screening was William Larkin of Sherrard Street, Dublin, who had on two previous occasions publicly objected to films screened at the Bohemian,[12] and its sister cinema, the Sandford, Ranelagh. The controversy over the latter arose when, in July 1915, *Neptune's Daughter* (1914) was shown. Directed by Irish-born, but Hollywood-based, Herbert Brenon, and starring the scantily-clad swimming star Annette Kellerman in her first film role, it had been denounced on the Sunday prior to its screening by a local priest. Though this may have prompted Larkin's objection, it had the opposite effect to that intended as 'scores could not obtain admission' due to the demand for tickets.[13] It is probable that this particular incident encouraged the DVC to publicly announce the extension of its campaign two months later.

Larkin returned to the Bohemian on the second night of the run of *A Modern Magdalen* with some supporters, including two DVC activists, Peter Tierney and Richard Jones, both of whom gave evidence at Larkin's subsequent trial. During the screening of the film Larkin and others hissed their disapproval of it. Eventually, he began screaming that a board of censors was necessary in Dublin. His loud shouts frightened some members of the audience and a degree of panic ensued with, apparently, women in particular rushing to the front of the cinema. Larkin then went outside where he made a speech from the steps of the cinema, blocking the exit in the process. The police were called by the Bohemian's manager, Ernest Matheson, and Larkin was taken into custody. He was charged with causing a disturbance resulting in a stampede among the audience, and obstructing the entrance by making a speech outside the cinema. At a court hearing the next day, attended by members of the DVC and clergy, he was granted bail. His prosecution was pursued on complaint from the Bohemian's owner, Frederick Arthur Sparling, who explained that as owner of both the Bohemian and the Sandford he was seeking to stop Larkin's interruptions at his cinemas.[14] The trial proper began in the Northern District Court on 11 October. The defence claimed that in the 'Mad Cap Scene' of the film, Katinka, 'the modern Magdalen,' dances topless on the table. Others, corresponding to contemporary accounts of the film's content, stated that this was not so, and that her shoulders were merely showing. It was not the first, nor the last, occasion when a would-be censor saw more (or less) in a film than other members of the audience. Giving evidence in support of Larkin, Peter Tierney claimed that the film 'ridiculed religion,' and was 'an insult to Christianity'. The modern Magdalen, he complained, 'did not show any sorrow,'[15] even though the film sees Katinka reconciled with her labourer boyfriend after she saves his life when she goes to work as an army nurse having left her wealthy lover.[16] A large number of prosecution witnesses corroborated the evidence against Larkin and declared that they had not found anything objectionable in the film. This view was reiterated by Mr Swifte, the presiding magistrate, after he suspended the trial for a week in order to view the film. Having seen the film, Swifte announced that there was nothing improper or indecent in it, and he found Larkin guilty as charged, fined him 5s., and ordered him to pay 15s. costs.[17] Despite the conviction, the trial had provided an early opportunity to bring the DVC's anti-cinema campaign to public attention, and it may have proved a phyrric victory for Sparling and other exhibitors.

In the meantime, the DVC's sub-committee on music halls, theatres and cinemas was formed on 1 October 1915. Its immediate concern was to apply pressure to alter the 'suggestive' hoardings outside places of entertainment and elsewhere in the city. The sub-committee's membership is not known, but one can assume that it included at least some of those who attended a meeting with the Public Health Committee a month later. This 13-man[18] delegation was led by Deering and included Fr Paul and solicitor Mr F.J. Little. These three presented the DVC's case for Dublin Corporation film censorship to the meeting, which was presided over by Alderman J.J. Kelly and attended by the Lord

Mayor. In his report[19] of the meeting to the full council, the chairman of the PHC, Joseph Isaacs, stated that the PHC had agreed to postpone granting the twenty-six cinema licences for 1915 until the Vigilance Committee had been communicated with. They had supplied the DVC with a list of the places in respect of which applications for renewal of the licence had been made. The Law Agent's advice was obtained as to whether the Corporation had the power to withdraw or revoke a licence if an exhibitor was convicted of screening an 'immoral picture'. It was a condition of the licence, the Law Agent, Ignatius J. Rice, reminded the PHC, that 'no licentious or indecent pictures' were to be shown. The Vigilance Committee also formally requested the right to submit their views when the renewal of licences was under consideration. They had already received permission from the Recorder to be represented when music licences were under consideration, and the PHC also agreed to this request. The Vigilance Committee informed the PHC that as a result of 'repeated complaints as to the class of entertainment,' they had 'exercised supervision over the Cinema Theatres for some time past.' They had found no 'serious' complaint, with the exception of one unnamed cinema. In an undoubted reference to *A Modern Magdalen*, and trying to turn that legal setback to their advantage, the delegation asked that cinema managers give an undertaking in future that such films should not be exhibited in Dublin.

The delegation submitted alternatives to a number of the clauses in the Corporation's cinema licence, including a request for Sunday closure from 6.30 p.m. to 9.00 p.m. This was partly accepted by the PHC when it recommended the closure of cinemas from 6.30 p.m. to 8.30 p.m. The Vigilance Committee also pressed for a requirement that cinemas should never be totally dark[20] and that they should be closed on Christmas Day and the Wednesday, Thursday and Friday preceding Easter Sunday. Both of these amendments were accepted. Additionally, it sought to extend the Corporation's condition that 'nothing shall be represented which is licentious or indecent, or likely to produce riot, tumult, or breach of the peace,' to include the phrase 'licentious or indecent *tendency*'.[21] Though this very general amendment was not accepted, a provision was made that written notification prohibiting a film could be given to a licensee or a cinema manager by the Corporation's agent who exercised his delegated powers under the Cinematograph Act. At this stage it seemed that film censorship would operate similar to that for theatres. A prohibition order could be served on an exhibitor after the film was in distribution and, thus, no structure for prior censorship would be used, except that operated by the still unacknowledged British Board of Film Censors, which satisfied the formal censorship requirements of the licence. The delegation also requested that if the Corporation had the power, a censor should be appointed, and if no such power existed, a committee composed of the Corporation and citizens, or entirely of citizens, should be empowered to supervise and investigate complaints. However, the PHC ignored this suggestion in its report to the council which refined its earlier condition on the appointment of a censor.

In proposing the appointment of a censor for the City of Dublin the PHC recommended that 'other public censor' replace the more restrictive alternative – 'other public censor whose judgement is accepted by the Corporation'[22] – that was already in use.

This important amendment, which would potentially allow any national or international censor to be accepted by an exhibitor, irrespective of the Corporation's wishes, was not immediately noticed by the DVC. This was due in part to the fact that the report was not formally approved by the PHC until August 1916, nine months after the meeting with the DVC, while it was not considered by the full council until two months later. Nevertheless, the PHC seems to have been in agreement with the general thrust of the Vigilance Committee's recommendations. In their meeting of December 1915, one month after their negotiations with the PHC, the DVC geared itself up for a lobbying campaign of Dublin Corporation councillors to ensure the approval by the whole council of their amendments. An intimidatory tone can be detected in their approach to the councillors, as reported in the *Irish Catholic*. Members of the Corporation 'will be interviewed by deputations from the Committee in order to urge ... the importance of adopting the [PHC's] recommendations.' It was during this meeting that the Irish Vigilance Association (IVA) was established, with the DVC renamed as the IVA (Dublin Branch).[23]

As already noted, the PHC, much to the irritation of the IVA, did not treat the issue with any urgency. At the IVA's annual general meeting in January 1916 it was reported that visits to cinemas were to be recorded for future use and no doubt to maintain pressure on the Corporation.[24] Three months later, the IVA's honorary secretaries, Laurence O'Dea and James J. Hayes, wrote to the Corporation urging the appointment of film censors.[25] When during its 7 June meeting the Corporation was asked, in a motion proposed on behalf of the IVA by Councillor Devlin and seconded by Patrick Lennon, what had been done about this, it responded by referring it to the PHC.[26] By this stage the PHC was receiving a further opinion from the Law Agent as to its censorship powers. He advised that the Corporation was empowered to prohibit the screening of any particular film, a view informed by the recent British court action against the controversial film adaptation of a novel by Victoria Cross, *Five Nights* (Bert Haldane, 1915, GB), which concerns a love affair between an artist and his cousin. It had been banned by many local authorities in Britain, and the Law Agent's analysis was endorsed by the PHC at its meeting on 7 June when an order was made formally appointing Walter Butler and Councillor Patrick Lennon as censors. In cases where there was 'any doubt' they were advised to consult with the Catholic and Protestant archbishops of Dublin.[27] The decision to appoint censors was communicated to the IVA in a letter two days later on 9 June and published in the *Irish Catholic* along with a letter from the IVA dated 20 June expressing exasperation at the length it had taken to do so and saying that it would not have happened without their considerable pressure.[28] Though the IVA were consulted by the PHC before the appointment of Butler and Lennon,[29] the organization was far from happy when the conditions governing censorship in the licences to be issued in October were made known two months later.

The revised licence conditions approved by the PHC at its meeting on 15 August and sent to the full Council for endorsement, included the clause that the PHC or its appointees could accept 'any other public censor' rather than be bound by the ones the PHC had delegated its powers to under the Cinematograph Act. Dublin Corporation were not due to consider the revised conditions until 2 October and thus the IVA had ample time to mobilize against what it deemed an even less satisfactory proposal than already existed. A letter was sent by the IVA to the councillors of 'the Metropolis of a Christian and Catholic nation' asking for an alternative to the provision 'any other public censor'. They declared that this clause could be interpreted as applying to any part of the world, which may not even be Christian. The Corporation could, the IVA declared, 'apply a Home Rule principle without reference to any outside body or authority whatever.'[30]

The following week the IVA's Fr Fottrell SJ forwarded to the *Irish Catholic* a letter from Archbishop Walsh to him. In the letter he supported the 'memorial' being sent by the IVA to the PHC for the alteration of the licence: 'I cannot conceive any ground on which it can be objected to, or its prayer refused.'[31] With such heavyweight pressure being applied the councillors were certain to give in. On 2 October a Vigilance Association delegation consisting of Thomas Deering and the Revd Canon Dunne PP, VG, met the council to press for the change.[32] At the adjourned council meeting a week later the PHC Chairman Joseph Isaacs, tabled the PHC's recommendations. Councillor Moran then moved an amendment that the words 'or any other public censor' be deleted from the motion. He proposed the alternative wording promoted by the IVA: 'or any Censor duly appointed in Ireland, pursuant to the Cinematograph Act 1909.' Of the 79 members of Dublin Corporation, 47 voted on the amendment, only 4 of whom were against it: Councillors Isaacs and John Ryan TC, and Aldermen William McCarthy and William T. Dinnage.[33] Displaying an attitude which undoubtedly reflected the intimidatory nature of the campaign, an anonymous letter in the *Irish Catholic* declared that these four should be 'vigorously opposed' at the next election unless an explanation of their 'extraordinary vote' was forthcoming. Since, unusually, the letter was printed on the front page of the newspaper it obviously reflected the newspaper's editorial policy.[34]

The comprehensive success of the campaign was a powerful declaration that the Catholic church would intervene effectively where it determined that its interests lay. In this regard these and other campaigns ensured that any new Irish nation-state, whether Home Rule within the Empire or, from 1918, an independent state more loosely linked to Britain, would be challenged to enforce strict moral regulations on the Irish people. But, while the IVA, as a vanguard organization of the Catholic church, succeeded in its primary objective of introducing Dublin Corporation film censorship, it could not control the inefficiency and ramshackle amateurism with which these regulations were often administered.

## DUBLIN CORPORATION FILM CENSORSHIP, 1916–1923

The task of administering the new censorship regulations had been assigned by the Public Health Committee to Walter Butler and Councillor Lennon in June 1916, months before their formal appointment as film censors by Dublin Corporation on 9 October 1916. In addition to amending the cinema licence to the satisfaction of the IVA, the council also gave a specific directive to its new censors. It ordered that Butler, as the Officer of the Corporation authorized to administer the Cinematograph Act,

> report to the Public Health Committee the exhibition of any film which, *even though passed by the Board of British Censors* is, in his opinion, licentious, or indecent, and in any such instance the Public Health Committee if they think fit, direct a prosecution, and take the matter into consideration in any application for the renewal of the licence. (Emphasis added.)[35]

Six months before Butler's appointment as a censor, he reported that 'the managers of the numerous cinema houses in Dublin had been found most willing to comply with any changes suggested by the members of the Vigilance Committee or by [himself] by way of cutting out parts of pictures to which exception would be taken.'[36] Thus, a degree of control was already being exercised even before his formal appointment as film censor. By the end of the year, though, only 5 films had been viewed: 4 were passed and 1 was forbidden to be exhibited.[37]

It soon became evident that even with Lennon's assistance Butler could not carry out the hugely increased workload of viewing all the films released in Dublin while continuing to inspect the physical condition of cinemas, theatres and other places of public resort. As a result, following suggestions from the Dublin Vigilance Committee, the Dublin Watch Committee, and the Juvenile Advisory Committee of the Board of Trade, in early 1917 the PHC appointed Mrs E.M. Smith and Mrs A. O'Brien as Honorary Lady Inspectors of Theatres and Places of Public Resort. Similar to already established practice in the USA,[38] these middle-class women 'reformers' were instructed not only to examine film content but to act as moral surveillance officers within the cinema space. They were to call attention 'to any indecency which they may observe'; to report on whether children and young girls were 'accompanied by proper persons'; and 'to draw attention to any film likely to morbidly affect young persons.' They were also required to attend to the implementation of the Corporation's safety guidelines.[39] (That 'Lady' censors were appointed without controversy is further indication that middle-class women were regular cinemagoers in Ireland.)

It is perhaps no coincidence that the first issue of Ireland's first film publication *Irish Limelight* should appear in January 1917 just as the film trade was feeling under increased pressure from all sides. In an article in the magazine's second issue entitled 'First Take the Mote out of Thine Own Eyes' it did not mince its words over the decision to appoint 'Lady Inspectors'. Unfavourably contrasting the middle-class censors with the predominantly working-class cinema audience, the writer, echoing the Corporation's Law Agent, Ignatius J. Rice five years earlier, enquired whether the PHC had

> nothing more important and urgent to do than lend its aid and support to the cranks whose sole ambition is to curtail and, if possible, suppress altogether

the forms of amusement which alone help to brighten and cheer the comparatively monotonous existence of the majority of the masses.[40]

Despite the strength of the industry's voice the religious and political consensus favoured film censorship. Indeed, in an article, 'The Cinema and Its Dangers', in the *Irish Monthly* the following month, Max Drennan, Professor of English at University College Galway, called for 'rigorous control and inspection' of all cinema shows by a local inspector, 'perferably an educated woman'.[41]

In the IVA's 1916 annual report the organization's president, Thomas Deering, berated the Corporation for the 'unnecessary and unaccountable' delay in establishing film censorship while ignoring the recent appointment of Irishman T.P. O'Connor as president of the British Board of Film Censors.[42] Deering urged 'citizens' to send reports of objectionable films to the censors at City Hall.[43] Such a film was likely to be the uncensored one, and with this in mind *Irish Limelight* reported in its March 1917 issue that the leaders of the film trade were 'making great efforts to organise the industry with a view of doing away with the uncensored film.'[44] To this end and to help counter the activities of the Dublin film censors, *Irish Limelight* called on exhibitors to 'fortify' their position against the 'narrow-mindedness of these professional moralists' by establishing a trade association. The magazine was seeking an exclusively Irish 'defensive alliance'[45] of exhibitors even though an Irish branch of the Cinematograph Exhibitors' Association of Great Britain and Ireland already existed with prominent exhibitor David Frame[46] as president, and John Carley as secretary. Later in 1917 the Dublin and South West of Ireland Exhibitors' Association was formed with Frame as President. In 1920 this organization was renamed the Theatre and Cinema Association of Ireland, TCA(I), with Frame continuing as president. It was the largest such body in the country with thirty-eight members. A smaller organization existed in the south of the country and there was another exhibitors' organization based in Belfast. As the *Irish Times* reported in 1921, the association, originally formed for 'protective purposes to avert trade disputes,' was succeeding 'admirably' as it was working amicably 'with the various trade unions'.[47]

While disputes over wages and working conditions with trade unions were an ongoing aspect of all businesses, one of the primary concerns of exhibitors during the 1910s was to secure an efficient and relatively restrained censorship. In addition to T.P. O'Connor's appointment to the BBFC, another development during 1916–1917 helped to secure the acceptance of the existing censorship regimes of the BBFC and the local authorities. The National Council of Public Morals had instituted an enquiry into the physical, social, moral and educational influence of the cinema, with 'special reference' to young people. The Cinema Commission established by the council published its report in October 1917. To the relief of the film trade it was generally favourable to the status quo and 'did much to dampen the general criticism of the cinema.'[48] The only Irish submission quoted in the report came from the Dublin Metropolitan Police who stated that the film situation in Dublin was satisfactory:

No films of an indecent nature have been exhibited in the city, although in one or two instances private persons have taken exception to films which might perhaps be regarded as suggestive, but which did not justify police action.

While there had been some instances of juvenile offenders alleging that their crime had been motivated by seeking the admission price to the cinema, it was observed that children 'who steal for this purpose would equally steal to gratify any other keen desire, and it can scarcely be said that the cinema can be held responsible for such crimes.'

Indeed, in light of subsequent debates on the cinema in Ireland, and more generally on the effects of the media on children, together with the duties of the Lady Inspectors as moral guardians to the young, what is surprising is how limited the discourse was surrounding the baneful effects of cinemagoing on young people, most especially with regard to imitative behaviour. On the whole, the Chief Commissioner concluded, 'having regard to the working of the Dublin picture houses, ... the cinema is a source of much innocent amusement.'[49] Such a benign view was not held by either Cardinal Logue of Armagh or Archbishop Walsh of Dublin. In a letter to the IVA in February 1917, Cardinal Logue advised them to turn their attention to cinema which was 'spreading through the country, like wildfire' with a 'very pernicious effect upon the young.'[50] In his Lenten Pastoral for 1917 Archbishop Walsh also roundly condemned cinema, a factor which aided the IVA in their resistance to the exhibitors' attempt to liberalize the opening hours of cinemas on Sunday evenings.[51]

In early 1917 the PHC was 'informed' that 'certain' cinemas opened on Sunday during the hours prohibited by the licences. As a result, a circular was ordered to be sent to the proprietors calling attention to the matter, and pointing out that the conditions of the licence must be observed.[52] In late March 1917 J.J. Farrell let it be known that he intended to put down a motion to Dublin Corporation at its meeting on 2 April seeking a change in the cinema licence which would allow cinemas to open at 8.00 p.m. instead of 8.30 p.m. on Sunday evenings. This was immediately denounced by the IVA and Archbishop Walsh,[53] while the Confraternities Central Council[54] and the IVA wrote to the Corporation demanding that Farrell's proposal not be passed. The IVA asked that a delegation be allowed address the Council prior to the meeting of 2 April 1917. Monsignor Dunne PP, VG and Fr Powell of the IVA outlined the organization's objections to the suggested change.[55] Farrell, no doubt well aware of the intensity of clerical opposition, did not put his motion to the meeting. It is possible that he may have been merely testing the strength of the response such an amendment would provoke. It was not the only victory of the IVA in 1917.

Following the IVA's success with the appointment of Lady Inspectors, it sought to increase lay involvement in film censorship. On 13 August 1917 William (Liam) R. McGuirk, the IVA's secretary, wrote to the PHC urging the appointment by the Committee of two nominees of the IVA as censors. He stated that the IVA's president had met with Walter Butler and Councillor Lennon to discuss film censorship. Though the IVA had to 'admit with pleasure that the Censors have done everything possible

... and undoubtedly there has been a considerable improvement in consequence of their exertions,'[56] there were still many uncensored films 'exhibited without the Censors' knowledge, ... with the result [that] some of them [were] not free from objectionable features.' Since it was 'quite impossible' for two censors, who had other duties to perform, to carry out 'adequately' the censoring of films, they recommended, with Butler's support, the appointment of Eugene McGough and Aeneas J. Murray as additional censors. Both men, who were of independent means and 'of education and standing in the City,' would devote their spare time to carry out the work, 'without fee or reward, solely in the interests of the citizens.' The PHC 'carefully considered' the request, Chairman Lorcan G. Sherlock reported, and recommended to the council that the two men be appointed censors from 1 November 1917 to 31 October 1918, the period for which the licences were issued.[57] At its meeting of 8 October the council approved the appointments. Despite the increase in film censorship activity some exhibitors continued to ignore the Corporation's censorship conditions. In summer 1917 the film *Evidence* (Edwin August, 1915) was screened in which 'some of the episodes ... were considered of a licentious nature by one of the Censors.' The film was shown before being censored and 'a warning was sent to the proprietor that in the event of a similar occurrence [the PHC] would be obliged to refuse a renewal of the licence.' A notice to that effect was sent to all the cinemas drawing attention to the licence conditions in that regard.[58] Such a direct threat to exhibitors' livelihoods was sufficient to bring them into line and no similar episode is recorded in the reports of the PHC.

No matter how compliant exhibitors were, or restrictive censorship was, there was always a campaigner who, because of hostility to popular culture in general, or more usually, a conservative attitude to sexual morality, would seek even further restrictions on the cinema. In early 1918 one of the *Evening Herald*'s regular columnists, the anonymous 'Jacques', explicitly challenging the Irish censors – 'What are our censors doing?' – initiated a campaign against 'smut' in music halls and cinemas by highlighting representations of women. Following visits to twenty cinemas, he reported seeing pictures

> depicting bedroom scenes suggestive and objectionable; women running around partly dressed pursued by men ditto; 'funny' men getting entangled with women obviously of loose morals (this picture was disguised in comical (!) camouflage, but smut oozed from it). I saw pictures dealing with sacred matters of marriage and child-birth (these pictures are simply lozenged smut coated with sentiment to make them attractive); I saw pictures making light of marriage and treating trivially or otherwise with sexual questions.[59]

Three weeks later, after a large and favourable correspondence had been generated by the campaign, Jacques interviewed the film censor who was most sympathetic to his point-of-view, Vigilance Association appointee Eugene McGough. McGough acknowledged that film censorship remained haphazard, and while the censors attended trade shows and made 'surprise visits' to cinemas, some of which were 'simply shocking,' not all films were viewed. He intimated that he had 'often discovered foul, filthy incidents pourtrayed [*sic*] on the screen,' and suggested that 'such pictures dealing with sexual matters should be prohibited by law and the houses showing them should be heavily penalised.' Elsewhere in the interview he declared that 'the strong arm of the law' may be necessary to deal with some of the 'revolting' films coming from the USA and England. Noting that cinema managers ignored, or delayed implementing, requests for cuts in films, he supported the call for state censorship of films.[60] These comments proved too much for one of the lady inspectors and another censor. They are recorded in the reports of the PHC as stating that they were 'at variance with that recorded in the interview.'[61] The controversy did not endear McGough to the PHC, who despite his declared 'independent' means on appointment as a censor, applied for, but was refused, a grant for out-of-pocket expenses incurred in carrying out his censorship duties.[62]

It is perhaps surprising that McGough's provocative statements against exhibitors were not responded to by *Irish Limelight*. Instead it sought to show up the inefficiency of the censorship system. In its February 1918 issue, published at the time of the Jacques/McGough campaign, it reported that *Camille* (J. Gordon Edwards, 1917) had to be shown three times to the censors before it was passed uncut, which was hardly surprising given that the film features the exotic and transgressive Theda Bera as a mistress at the French court. This 'wibbly-wobbly' policy was the result of three of the four censors holding honorary and unpaid positions, complained the magazine. *Irish Limelight* also reported that when a film was shown at a trade show with more than one censor present different points of view on the film would be expressed by the censors.[63] Three months later *Irish Limelight* reported that forty films were on the 'black list' compiled by Dublin Corporation.[64] Friction between the distributors and censors continued during 1918, as the censors extended their control over film releases.

One of the censors reported to the PHC that he had seen copies of correspondence from the head of a film company advising them not to send certain films to Dublin 'as the censors and Exhibitors were strict.'[65] This was no doubt a sensible precaution by the distributors, who quickly adopted this self-censorship policy as a means of saving time and resources by not bringing to Dublin from London films they knew had little chance of being passed by the Vigilance Association's censors. Of more serious concern was Gaumont Film Company's complaint that one of the censors, whom Gaumont declined to name, 'passed comments' on the films being shown during trade shows.[66] It is not recorded in the PHC's Reports whether the intimidation of distributors and exhibitors which is implied in the censor's actions was reprimanded by the Committee. Though no further complaints of this nature feature in the reports, the fact that Gaumont formally complained to the PHC indicates an uneasiness in the film trade at the operation of Dublin's film censorship. No doubt further strains were put on that relationship when the Vigilance Association successfully canvassed the PHC to introduce a requirement that a certificate of censorship be exhibited on cinema screens prior to the screening of a film from 10 February 1919.[67] Nevertheless, the exhibitors at least proved generally compliant with the Corporation's censorship as was evidenced by a deputation from the Dublin and South of Ireland Kinematograph Association which met the PHC in 1919. The exhibitors were seeking remedies to the difficulties they were experiencing with the pre-censorship of short comedies and last minute substitute films. While 'big films' could be censored before being shown to the public this was proving difficult with the shorter and substitute films which often arrived just before they were due to be screened. The exhibitors assured the PHC that they 'were anxious to comply with the Corporation's requirements' and undertook to arrange with the renters that the censors would have 'timely notice of films not already censored.'[68]

Two years later, in 1921, the *Irish Times* could report that 'the duty of censoring [films] seems to be carried out satisfactorily in Dublin,' and the trade shows, where the censors were 'given full scope to exercise their authority,' served the useful function of enabling films to be censored. Commenting that most cinema managers (of which, according to the newspaper, in 1921 there were twenty-seven in Dublin City and immediate suburbs) actually 'welcome[d] the presence of the censors, as it relieves them of much responsibility, and safeguards them against subsequent criticism,' it went on to observe that 'there is whole-hearted co-operation in preserving a moral tone in accordance with Dublin's fair name.'[69]

If these comments suggest that the censors were operating a restrictive censorship regime, the total numbers of films banned and cut, even accounting for self-censorship on the part of film distributors (the extent of which is as yet uncertain), demonstrate that perhaps the periodic complaints by the more extreme censors and their allies about its ineffectiveness were justified. Indeed, as Dublin Corporation's film censorship evolved, an increasing number of films were released uncut and fewer films were banned.

Table 1: Dublin Corporation film censorship[70]

| | Viewed | Passed | Passed with cuts | Banned |
|------|--------|--------|------------------|--------|
| 1917 | 185 | 132 | 28 | 25 |
| 1918 | 454 | 412 | 24 | 18 |
| 1919 | 600 | 539 | 39 | 17 |
| 1921 | 873 | 845 | 12 | 16 |

*Note*: The figures for 1920 are not available.

By 1921 exhibitors had come to accept Dublin Corporation's inefficient if reasonably benign film censorship. While Dublin set the pace for film censorship, at least in Catholic parts of Ireland, local authorities outside the capital could exercise further film censorship, but, according to the IVA, no more than six had done so.[71] While the IVA would remain disaffected until a stricter censorship regime was introduced, the *Irish Times* reported that exhibitors and pro-censorship campaigners alike seemed reasonably satisfied with the arrangements.[72] As a result, the changes which independence brought were all the more traumatic, especially for exhibitors and distributors.

TOWARDS NATIONAL FILM CENSORSHIP

In a lecture entitled 'Practical Patriotism' delivered in 1917, one of the founders of the
Dublin Vigilance Committee, Fr MacInerney OP of St Saviour's, Dublin, warned that
if the film censorship measures recently introduced by Dublin Corporation did not
'prove effective,' then 'a stricter censorship on more systematic lines' could be
demanded. He reiterated the clarion call of the Catholic-nationalist majority, that they
were fighting for 'the grand old cause of Faith and Fatherland,' and argued that
'Christian morality and national welfare go hand-in-hand, and that whatever is injurious to morality is also injurious to the best interests of the nation.'[73]

As if to acknowledge Fr MacInerney's view that morality and nationality, the clerical and the secular, were conjoined in the fight for censorship, Dublin Corporation's
councillors became increasingly active in the process of film censorship itself. Upon
the resignation of Walter Butler as Chief Film Censor in early 1919, Patrick T. Daly,
the PHC's chairman who had replaced Councillor Lennon as a censor in 1918,[74] was
joined by three other councillor-censors: Peter O'Reilly, Michael J. Kelly and William
McCarthy, making a total of six censors, including the IVA's Eugene McGough and
Aeneas Murray. These six censors were re-appointed for 1920/21,[75] but in early 1921
there began an exponential expansion in the number of councillor-censors and the
appointment of more outsiders to the position. All members of the PHC became censors from January 1921, including its chairwoman, Mrs Jenny Wyse-Power, a long-
time campaigner for Irish social and political rights. They were joined by five members of the IVA, which besides McGough and Murray were Mrs J. Fogarty, Mrs
McKean and Miss S. Russell-Stritch.[76]

It is unclear what precipitated the change in policy but one of the effects was that
at a conference of the Honorary Film Censors on 5 July 1921 it was decided that no
cuts would be allowed to censored films: films would now only be approved or banned.
Under this new regime, greater emphasis was to be placed on the pre-censorship of
films, and exhibitors were to be warned about the 'objectionable practice' of altering
film titles without notifying the Censor's Office.[77] The net effect of these changes was
that a larger number of films were viewed by the censors. Whereas 600 films were
viewed by them in 1919, by 1921 the number had increased to 845, though the number
of films banned actually dropped by one.[78]

It was in this context that the PHC hosted a broad-based conference on Film
Censorship in late 1921 to review the operation of local authority film censorship.
Held on 13 and 30 December, it concluded that 'it was not considered possible to delin-
eate any special qualifications as being essential [for censors] other than broad-mind-
edness, common sense, and moral sensibility.' If the first two were not always to the
forefront in the actions of the Corporation's Vigilance Association censors, the more
ideologically-determined last qualification allowed for, and indeed validated, clerical
involvement. The conference confirmed that the Catholic church-influenced approach
of the activists was being adopted by the promoters of the event and agreed that besides
the IVA's nominees, the Priests' Social Guild, a Catholic Action group, should supply

six additional censors.[79] At the regular council meeting of the Corporation a few days later, on 2 January 1922, Mr M.J. Moore proposed a motion requesting that the two archbishops of Dublin be asked to nominate film censors. Despite seconding the motion, Jenny Wyse-Power said that there was no need for the Catholic archbishop to nominate censors as the Priests' Social Guild would be involved in censorship, but she proposed that the Church of Ireland Archbishop of Dublin, Dr Gregg, be asked to nominate six.[80] It was also agreed at the conference to establish a Court of Appeal comprising three censors who had not previously seen the film under appeal. Perhaps the conference's most momentous resolution was that for reasons of practical application it was not going to issue two types of certificates, 'one for adults and one for children'. Films were to be censored 'with a view to their being seen by all.'[81] It was a prescient decision in view of how Irish Free State film censorship would be administered within three years.

A delegation of film distributors and exhibitors 'expressed the willingness of the Cinema Trade to assist in the matter of Censorship as far as possible.'[82] They were obviously unwilling to publicly criticize film censorship, especially considering that on the second day of the conference censorship activists were concerned with detecting films which were 'cut' by renters and exhibitors prior to their submission to the censors.[83] The censors were keen to retain local control over film censorship as on those occasions when the issue of a national film censorship arose it was deferred until the PHC 'had explored the problem fully, and were in a position to put definite suggestions before the National Government.'[84] Nevertheless, the matter was given a degree of topicality when a communication from the Clerk of Castlebar Urban District Council was considered at the conference. He complained that some of the films being shown in Castlebar were 'improper', but the local exhibitors used against him the fact that they had been approved by Dublin Corporation. While disclaiming responsibility for the action of exhibitors outside their jurisdiction, the councillors pointed out that a particular film may not have been submitted to the Corporation's censors before travelling to provincial Ireland, and even if it had been, there was no guarantee that it would be the version of the film shown in Dublin. (Indeed, as noted in the Introduction, the [often deliberate] confusion between different versions at times allowed for Irish audiences to see material that would not have been deemed appropriate in the Irish context. Clearly, on second and subsequent film runs it was unlikely that exhibitors would have always been able to access the approved Irish version, something that seems might have been the case in many second-run cinemas as late as the 1970s, even though by then it was a clear breach of the law to screen non-state censored films in commercial cinemas.) The conference recognized the dilemma facing urban and rural councils outside Dublin whose resources were too limited to censor films locally. As a result, the Clerk suggested the need to approach Dáil Éireann with a view to appointing an Irish Board of Film Censors.[85] Indeed, the pre-independence Dáil Éireann had passed a motion in 1920 favouring national film censorship.[86] A week after the censorship conference the *Irish Times*, which only three months earlier had reported its satisfaction with the status quo, doubting whether

'even one exhibitor could be found to advocate a state censor,'[87] now voiced its support for national film censorship. It remarked that the issue of censorship 'is one
which sooner or later must be dealt with on a national basis.'[88] Such a radical change
in attitude it would seem was caused by the PHC's 'drastic order'[89] only to pass films
without cuts.

The IVA wasted no time after the approval of the Anglo-Irish Treaty by Dáil Éireann to press for national film censorship. On 28 February 1922 a deputation from the
IVA waited on members of the Dáil in order to present their views on censorship.
However, as the *Irish Times* regrettably reported, no such meeting took place. Despite
the 'general unanimity ... that any scheme which may be adopted should operate for
Ireland as a whole, so that the present absurd anomalies would be abolished,' it added
that neither Dáil Éireann nor the Provisional Government were likely to give the matter
immediate attention given the increasing political instability (which led to civil war a
few months later).[90] During the same week a delegation from the Irish Cinema
Exhibitors Association met the PHC to discuss the resolve to confine censors' certificates to those films passed uncut for general audiences. Though it agreed to suspend
the ruling, no other decision was taken. In the *Irish Times* report[91] on this encounter,
it recommended a study of T.P. O'Connor's 43 Rules on Film Censorship and quoted
O'Connor as favouring cuts to films when necessary. Two weeks later, another *Irish
Times* article stated that 'the case for reform [was] urgent' and noted that the inefficiency with which the unwieldy and often unco-ordinated group of PHC censors administered censorship caused difficulties for censors and exhibitors alike. This was illustrated by the example of how some films recently passed by Dublin Corporation were
objected to, or rejected by some other local bodies, and the absurd case where up to
half the censors viewed a film on three different occasions before finally, and without
unanimity, approving it. Also noted was that despite the controversy over 'improper
films' the percentage of rejections 'is surprisingly small, especially when it is remembered that no "cuts" are now permitted.' From 1 January to 9 March 1922 the PHC
censors had viewed 211 films, of which all but 13 were passed, with a decision on 9
of these being reserved for further consideration. Finally it reported that the PHC was
in communication with the Provisional Government on the matter and 'the importance
of the subject' was 'fully appreciated' by the government.[92] Shortly afterwards, the
newspaper called for the establishment of a National Board of Censors.[93] Indeed the
Corporation itself recognized the inadequacies of its own system. On 1 May 1922 a
motion proposed by Alderman McDonagh TD and seconded by Jenny Wyse-Power
that 'Dáil Éireann be asked to appoint a Board of Film Censors for all Ireland' was
passed unanimously.[94]

In this context what emerged from the December 1921 conference was the promotion of policies which gave the initiative to those advocating national film censorship and the realization by councillors that local authority censorship was inef-
fective. Arguably, the convening of the conference at the same time as the Anglo-Irish
Treaty was being debated by the Dáil is perhaps evidence enough that the campaigners were laying the groundwork for mass media legislation in the new state.

The proposal approved by the PHC, that only general certificates be issued (that is no film classification), was in practice how state film censorship mostly operated in Ireland during its first forty years. It is no surprise, therefore, to learn that the PHC's chairwoman during the turbulent 1920–1922 period, Jenny Wyse-Power, became one of Ireland's first national film censors in 1924. Thus, in parallel with Dublin Corporation film censorship was the formulation of what might constitute national film censorship.

Pressure on the Corporation was increased later in 1922 when the secretary of the Priests' Social Guild and administrator of Dublin's Pro-Cathedral, Fr John Flanagan, sent a letter jointly signed by him and Liam R. McGuirk, secretary of the IVA, to the Lord Mayor asking that the council meet the committees of the two organizations. The 'matter of urgent public importance' which the committees wanted to place before the council was the 'defects in the system by which cinema films are censored in Dublin.'[95] The deputation raised with the council whether films were being shown uncensored in Dublin and whether any of the censors had an interest in films. After some discussion, the matter was postponed for a fortnight when it was proposed to consider a motion from Councillor Daly, the PHC's chairman during 1922–1923 and the Corporation's longest serving councillor-censor. At the council meeting of 27 November, he pursued these allegations when he sponsored a motion calling for a sworn enquiry to be established by the Local Government Board to see: (a) had any of the censors been negligent in their duty, and (b) whether the allegations that some censors were financially interested in the film business or in the cinemas where such films were shown were true. This was again deferred until written charges were received from the IVA.[96] However, when these were received and considered by the Municipal Council on 29 January 1923, Daly's motion was dropped.[97] Whether the allegations were substantiated, or were imprecise and consisted of hearsay, is unclear from the outcome of the council meeting. Nevertheless, the episode had, from the pro-censorship campaigners' point-of-view, at least two beneficial effects: an inter-denominational group had been formed to pressurize the council on the matter, and the allegations served to further discredit the council's own film censorship regime.

Another of the censors, Councillor George A. Lyons, the PHC's chairman during 1923–1924, moved a motion at the next council meeting on 19 February 1923 which stated that since the Corporation 'has been forced to accept responsibility for a system in which we have no confidence' all warrants issued to the film censors should be revoked and the Corporation's officials should 'take all necessary steps to abolish all film censoring' on behalf of the council. The motion also stated that 'the system of censoring films cannot be perfected until such time as the Government can see its way to establish a national system of film censoring.' Though postponed,[98] and on 5 March ruled out of order, this and other pressure during the previous year had the desired effect on the government. At the same time as Lyons' motion was being placed before Dublin Corporation, the Minister for Home Affairs, Kevin O'Higgins, met an inter-denominational delegation which pressed for a system of national film censorship. Within less than three months, on 3 May 1923, O'Higgins published the Censorship of Films Bill. Not only was it one of the first Bills to come before the Free State Parliament but it was independent Ireland's first piece of media censorship legislation. It was also to provide an early illustration of how closely church and state would operate in the new country.

3 Under the Censorship of Films (Amendment) Act, 1925, all film publicity material had to be passed by the Censor. On occasion, an advertisement was 'amended' even after it was published, which was perhaps the reason why in 1967 Raquel Welch suddenly disappeared from the *Evening Herald* (27 October) the day after being included in the advertisement.

CHAPTER 3

# Free expression in a free state?

I take the Ten Commandments as my Code.
James Montgomery, *Official Film Censor, 1923–1940.*[1]

## CENSORSHIP OF FILMS ACT, 1923: THE POLITICAL CONSENSUS

As part of its campaign to get the new Irish Free State parliament to pass national film censorship legislation, the Irish Vigilance Association said that local authority censorship was being carried out 'by make-shift arrangements,' and admitted that the censors 'were unequal to the large amount of work to be done.' Acknowledging that few pictures of 'an openly bad character' were being exhibited, nonetheless, they suggested that the censors felt obliged to pass films 'of which their better judgement disapproves,' lest their decision to ban would be challenged in the courts, a situation which 'might prove disastrous' to the vigilance movement. Broadening the debate as it linked its moral concerns with issues of Irish national identity, the IVA argued that the 'tastes' of some judges were not 'harmonise[d] with the Traditional Irish moral sense.' Indeed, the association went on to declare that 'the majority' of the films shown in Dublin 'would be better not shown to our people.' While they were 'not manifestly immoral or bad,' given that such films had been already forbidden, they were 'un-Irish' and 'unhealthy'. This would remain the case as long as the supply of films to the Irish market was 'English and Foreign'. A further issue raised by the organization was the relationship of Dublin to the rest of the country. Films which were passed in Dublin were 'found to offend outside Dublin.' There should be one censorship for the whole country, the IVA argued, as well as 'one moral standard' and 'whatever offends an intelligent Irish Provincial Audience should offend a Dublin Audience.' If that was not the case, then Dubliners 'must level up'. In this regard, the IVA hinted, a single censor might not reflect the values of provincial Ireland.[2]

Before the Irish Free State government published a Bill to provide for national film censorship, the Minister for Local Government, Ernest Blythe, sent a circular to the local authorities seeking their views on the administration of film censorship. According to a speech made in the Dáil by the Minister for Home Affairs, Kevin O'Higgins, 'There was a general, a unanimous feeling amongst [them] that there should be a uniform censor-

ship for the country.'[3] This view was strongly reinforced by an inter-denominational delegation from bodies 'interested in the moral welfare of the people'[4] who met O'Higgins
on 28 February 1923 and made the already well-established case for national film censorship. The 'thoroughly representative' delegation, as O'Higgins described them,[5] consisted of Fathers Lawrence and Flanagan of the Priests' Social Guild; Fr Tomkin SJ,
Milltown Park; Thomas J. Deering and Liam McGuirk of the IVA; the Church of Ireland's
the Revd T.W.E. Drury; the Revd Dr Denham Osborne of the Social Reform Committee
of the Presbyterian Church, who was one of the signatories of the circular promoting
the boycott of *From the Manger to the Cross* in 1913 as discussed in chapter 2; and
Walter Butler.[6] Blythe, speaking in the Senate, highlighted the ineffectiveness of local
authority censorship in Ireland which was 'not very well done. It is not merely that it is
not uniform, but that as it is done on a voluntary basis, it often happens that the films
are not censored at all.'[7] The introduction of national film censorship would mean that
local authorities would lose their power to impose conditions 'as to the character or
nature of the pictures to be exhibited' in premises to which a cinema licence referred.[8]

When O'Higgins introduced the Censorship of Films Bill, 1923 in the Dáil, he justified bringing it in 'even in times like the present' (the Civil War was continuing),
because there was a 'considerable and growing demand for the measure.' He described
the Bill as a 'non-contentious measure,'[9] and predicted that it would proceed rapidly.
Published on 3 May, it had passed all stages in both the Dáil and the Senate by 21 June,
a clear reflection of the consensus on the issue in the new Irish parliament. The Act[10]
provides for the appointment by the Minister for Justice (the new term for the Minister
for Home Affairs) of an Official Film Censor and a 9-person unpaid Censorship of
Films Appeal Board. The duration of tenure for the Official Censor is determined by
the minister, while the members of the Appeal Board are appointed for renewable five-
year terms. The Act declares that from the introduction of national film censorship no
moving picture can be exhibited in public unless the Official Censor has certified that
'the whole of such film is fit for exhibition in public.' A certificate is not to be issued
if the Censor is 'of the opinion that such picture or part thereof is unfit for general
exhibition in public by reason of its being indecent, obscene or blasphemous or because
the exhibition thereof in public would lead to inculcate principles contrary to public
morality or would be otherwise subversive of public morality.' Certificates can carry
conditions which limit either the place of exhibition or the class of persons, such as an
age group, to whom a particular film can be shown. In addition to the Censor's powers
to issue limited certificates or ban films, he or she can authorize the deletion of part
of a film deemed objectionable and the part is to be surrendered to the Censor, 'who
shall retain it in his possession.' All decisions adversely affecting a film – banning, cutting and issuing of a limited certificate – can be re-examined by the Appeal Board.
However, the right of appeal is reserved for the film's distributor; no member of the
public or an interested organization, such as, for example, the IVA or the Knights of
St Columbanus, can officially seek to alter the Censor's decision. The decision of the
Appeal Board is final, but when the members of the Board present are equally divided,
the Official Censor's original decision is confirmed.

The debate on the Bill in both the Dáil and Senate provided an early opportunity for members of the Oireachtas to record their views not just on cinema and censorship, but more indirectly on the relationship of Irish culture to foreign popular culture. The most enthusiastic endorsement of the Bill came from Cumann na nGaedheal TD William Magennis, who was also Professor of Metaphysics at University College Dublin, and who claimed to be a regular cinemagoer. During the debate, Magennis declared that the minister and the drafters of the Bill deserve 'the highest credit for providing the [Irish Free State] with an agency like this, which helps to realize our Gaelic traditions.' He added:

> Purity of mind and sanity of outlook upon life were long ago regarded as characteristic of our people. The loose views and the vile lowering of values that belong to other races and other peoples were being forced upon our people through the popularity of the cinematograph. … [The Bill] is helping all the objects of the Gaelic League, because it is exactly like gardening. You have to attend to the pests and plagues that beset your growing vegetation as well as to cultivate the ground.[11]

Such a statement was characteristic of many extreme anti-cinema campaigners worldwide, but in this instance it found a ready echo in the most senior government circles. His views were sympathetically received by O'Higgins, who remarked that Magennis 'provided grounds for serious consideration … as Film Censor.[12] Though he does not seem to have offered his services as Censor, he accepted the position as the first chairman of the Appeal Board. In the 1920s Magennis also became involved in the campaign which led to the Censorship of Publications Act, 1929, and from 1933 until his death in 1946 he was a member of the Censorship of Publications Board and its chairman for the last four years of his tenure.

It was Magennis' contention that the 'rising generation require[d] to be protected from an environment that [was] certainly not conducive to good morals.'[13] For him, the cinema was such an environment in that it offered a 'veiled presentation of vice' where 'the pernicious things [were] not always obviously so.'[14] This, coupled with the lack of primary education of the majority of the cinema audiences, made them unable

> to discriminate judiciously between what … is attractive and admirable as a piece of photography [and what at the same time] is seductive and prejudicial to a proper life and to a proper outlook upon life. Our people have not been trained in these things.[15]

Elaborating, he arrived at what is central to cinema – the power of the image – and indirectly acknowledged the ultimate futility of film censorship. What constituted the danger for Magennis was that such 'vice' films had a 'seductiveness of artistic treatment.'[16] Indeed, Walter Benjamin, though coming from the opposite side of the European political spectrum, maintained this view and remarked on the camera's ability to turn even abject poverty into an aesthetic object 'by handling it in a modish, technically perfect way.'[17] In effect, Magennis was forced to concede that the censors could suppress plot elements which infringed Catholic morality, but they were helpless against the seductiveness of the image itself (with meanings hidden from official culture), irrespective of its content. He favoured a Board of Censors rather than one Official Censor and proposed that a cinema licence be withdrawn after two films were deemed to be objectionable. Indeed, he went so far as to declare that the only reason he did not propose that a person who was fined repeatedly for offences under the Act 'should be deprived of citizenship altogether' was that he would be thought a 'fanatic'.[18] Although this extraordinary suggestion was not even discussed by the Dáil, it serves to illustrate the unbalanced way in which some Catholics, who were also cultural nationalists, viewed the imported mass media.

One of the few criticisms of the Bill came from Thomas Johnson, leader of the Labour Party, who, like Magennis, was concerned with the appointment of a single Censor, though for diametrically opposite reasons. Questioning if an individual Censor, or a Board, could give 'anything like satisfaction to the present generation or, just as important, to the next generation,'[19] he asked whether

> you could choose one man, or even a small board of appeal, who will not be extravagantly puritanical, or, on the other hand, careless, and whose conceptions of morality and social order are too narrow and perhaps old-fashioned. It is rather a risky undertaking.[20]

Notwithstanding this (mild) opposition to the Bill, he pointed out that nearly all the films objected to had already been censored by a 'distinguished Irishman' (T.P. O'Connor, the president of the British Board of Film Censors).

Johnson chose not to challenge the sections of the Bill dealing with private morality, knowing probably that he had little chance of altering these provisions even if he so wished, but succeeded in substituting the term 'public morality' for 'social order' as a basis for restricting films. He argued that the words 'social order' could restrict educative or propagandist films:

> If this or any such scheme had been in operation, say, in 1914 or 1915, 'social order' would have meant one thing. Today it would mean another. 'Social order' to some minds has a very narrow meaning, and pictures designed to subvert social order may simply mean pictures with a message which do[es] not seem to fit in with the particular Censor's view of certain property relations.[21]

O'Higgins assured Johnson that there would be 'no war on new ideas, but rather on old and unsavoury' ones.[22] However, history was to prove him wrong. Nevertheless, he accepted Johnson's amendment that 'contrary to public morality,' a phrase from the Constitution, be substituted for 'social order'.[23] If this amendment was designed

to allow for the exhibition of oppositional political films in Ireland then it was a failure. As the second Film Censor, Richard Hayes, stated in a 1947 interview: 'Anything
advocating Communism or presenting it in an unduly favourable light gets the knife.'[24]
By then, the first Film Censor, James Montgomery (1870–1943) had made wide use
of the Act's 'subversive of public morality' provision to ban or cut films which bore
little relationship to the concerns over public morality expressed during the 1923 debate.

After passing all stages in the Dáil by 28 May the Bill went to the Senate where
it had an even speedier passage than in the Lower House. When introducing the Bill
to the Senate, Ernest Blythe gave an unexpectedly restrictive account as to how he
viewed the Official Censor's task. Contrary to the majority view, he indicated his support for individual choice, a reflection perhaps of his Protestant background and not
of his otherwise conservative Irish cultural outlook. He said he did not believe there
were too many improper films, and added that he had never seen such a film. He
acknowledged that occasionally films were shown which ought not to have been
screened, and which were 'calculated to have a bad effect from a moral or other point-
of-view on those who would see them.' Declaring he did not take 'too puritanical [a]
view,'[25] he anticipated that through the Bill it would be possible to have film censorship administered

> in a broadminded way, and that it will not be a finicky, restricted, or puri-
> tanical censorship, but one in which due care will be taken of public morals,
> and that there will not be any attempt to carry the thing too far, or deal with
> it in what would be called a grandmotherly way.[26]

Such an approach was not favoured by the Catholic censors who came to dominate
its proceedings.

Other contributors to the relatively short debate in the Senate echoed the extrem-
ism, such as that of Magennis which had been voiced in the Dáil. Senator James
McKean, for example, regarded the cinema as 'a sort of propaganda for materialism.'
Everything in the cinema appeals 'to the senses and [does] not … appeal at all to …
judgement.' Films, he asserted, were '"penny dreadfuls" … in a realistic form,' and
young people needed to be protected from 'that class of thing'. Consequently, he proposed an amendment, which was defeated, that all persons under-16 be forbidden from
entering cinemas unless they were with a school group supervised by their teachers.[27]
This view had also been expressed in the Dáil where Gavin Duffy complimented as
'simply splendid' a Bavarian law which forbade under-18s from the cinema.[28] In proposing his amendment, McKean blamed the anti-Treaty IRA activities during the previous year on the cinema, which put 'realistic productions … before the youth of the
country.' Acting on what they viewed, he claimed that the Irregulars 'put into practice
what they saw on [*sic*] the films.'[29] In his contribution to the debate, Senator W.B.
Yeats, who, ironically was to become, albeit for a brief period, a member of the first
Appeal Board, displayed a barely disguised contempt both for views such as McKean's,
and for the cinema itself: 'We see only the evil effect, *greatly exaggerated in the papers*,

of these rather inferior forms of art ... I think you can leave the arts, superior or inferior, to the general conscience of mankind.' (Emphasis added.)[30]

While Yeats took a characteristically lofty view of the Bill, only Senator Peter de
Loughry recorded his outright opposition to the proposed legislation, and argued in
favour of the appointment of those engaged in the film business to the Appeal Board.[31]
However, the only amendment made to the Bill by the Senate was the debarring of
anyone engaged in film exhibition or production from the Board. An amendment put
forward by Senator William Barrington would have greatly increased the Censor's
powers to restrict political films. He proposed that after the new formulation on 'public
morality' the phrase 'or otherwise undesirable in the public interest' should be added.
This amendment was firmly rejected by Blythe who stated: 'I think it would be better
not to have the Bill at all than to have a Bill that would put such powers into the hands
of the Censor.'[32] In practice, Blythe's surprisingly liberal and flexible interpretation of
the Act was disregarded. The criteria for censoring films were so subjective that the
politicians, in effect, allowed considerable leeway to the censors in the administration
of the Act, which they regularly interpreted in 'a grandmotherly way'.

After the 1923 Act became law, the Minister for Justice was surprised that he was
still receiving complaints from around the country 'protesting vehemently against the
nature of the films that were being exhibited.' On inquiry, he discovered that the cause
of this was the films' publicity matter. Though the films themselves were being rigor-
ously cut, the original posters which often showed passionate scenes and carried risqué
taglines, conveyed the impression that the deleted parts were still in the film. These
posters 'did considerable harm.'[33] As a result, the minister introduced the Censorship
of Films (Amendment) Act, 1925, which gave the Film Censor power to vet all a film's
promotional material using the restrictive criteria set down in the 1923 Act: pictorial
posters, cards, handbills, or other representational advertisements, as well as film trailers, had to be submitted to the Censor for approval. During 1929–1940 inclusive,
7,596 such pictorial advertisements were rejected by the Censor using this new power.[34]

Characteristically, William Magennis, by now chairman of the Appeal Board, made
the most lengthy contributions to the Amendment Bill debate. As the person most experienced in censorship, his views carried considerable weight. He complained that while
the tenor of a film could be altered by the Censor's cuts, the newspaper advertisements
provided access to the non-censored film and enabled the reader to go to the cinema
and, in effect, experience some of the original film's subversive pleasures.[35] All of his
comments were directed towards 'safeguarding the young from the deleterious and
dangerous influences we know are there.' However, he accepted the powerful attraction of the cinema for such young people.

> No one can exaggerate ... the extent and depth of influence on the growing
> generation that is being exercised by the cinema. It is the popular high school.
> It is the university of the people, and most of what they are going to learn
> about life and conduct they will learn by the visible, actual examples shown
> to them on the screen.[36]

Later in the debate he drew attention to the importance of colour in attracting the audience, and its lurid quality and visceral impact:

> The colouring makes an enormous difference to some of these posters, especially where semi-nude figures are in question, and what is harmless enough and might be passed by anyone not too prudish, could not be permitted and could not be tolerated in colour for promiscuous and general exhibition on the posters in a town.

Revealing once more the social class basis of his critique of cinema, he went on:

> Inside a picture gallery, where these things are for the entertainment of people of culture, or where they are for the higher education of those aspiring to culture, these things are absolutely right, and I would contend defensible, but as a stimulus to pruriency, as sensational items and as things intended to appeal to the lower instincts, they should not be tolerated to deface the hoardings of our towns or villages.[37]

Despite lengthy considerations of film censorship in both houses of the Oireachtas, there has been inadequate public discussion on the administration of the 1923 Act. The censors, all political appointees, in collusion with the Department of Justice, have surrounded their tasks with secrecy. This has had the effect of inhibiting debate about film censorship. Unlike the campaigns that were later mounted against the more restrictive aspects of censorship of publications, it was not until the late 1950s that the first sustained questioning of film censorship began to appear in the national press. Had there been a clearer anticipation at the time about how the legislation would be interpreted, there might have been less than the complete endorsement of the new Act by the national press.

The *Freeman's Journal* welcomed the Bill as 'an honest and well considered attempt ... to deal with a delicate and difficult problem,' though the editorial presciently observed that 'everything will depend on the capability of the men who are appointed.' The writer added that 'a great deal will hang on the sympathy, insight, and sense of balance of the individual censor.'[38] The *Irish Independent* regarded the Bill as 'a step in the right direction,'[39] while the *Irish Times* described it as 'shrewd and sensible'. The latter observed that 'some speakers in the Dáil ... seemed to think that indecency would be the Censor's chief problem,' but, anticipating Magennis' concern with the image itself, suggested that 'it will be his simplest problem':

> We have seen in Dublin ... dozens of films which, while not 'indecent' tended to produce, by their longdrawn out ineptness, vulgarity and triviality, a cumulative effect that was positively poisonous. This kind of stuff will furnish the censor's real problem, and we shall judge him by his handling of it.[40]

The *Irish Times* was indeed right since the general tone of films which might produce an adverse cumulative effect on cinemagoers became a constant refrain among campaigners who sought more stringent film censorship. The subject also regularly surfaces in the film censors' reports.

For the *Irish Catholic* the Censorship of Films Act was merely the first step in the legislative campaign against imported popular newspapers and magazines, music halls and theatres.

> We are unfeignedly glad that the [Irish] Free State Government has ... taken a first step towards the defence of public morals ... We trust that the action now taken ... is but the initial item in a programme of reform which shall aim at the suppression of all indecent performances in theatres and music halls, and in the exclusion from Ireland of the evil books and newspapers which are now being dumped in such large quantities upon our shores![41]

The test for the *Irish Catholic*, as well as for other groups campaigning for film censorship, would be in the selection of those who would interpret and administer the Censorship of Films Act. These groups would not be disappointed.

## IRELAND'S FILM CENSORS

During the course of the Dáil debate on the Censorship of Films Bill Professor Magennis expounded at some length on the effect exposure to cinema would have on the censors. He asserted that the ordinary person did not have the defences or *immunity* which was required for viewing films. Only medical doctors, who had built up this immunity through their work in combating diseases and visiting the most deprived working-class slums, would be capable of dealing with the pestilence of cinema. For Magennis, cinema appears to have been little more than a latter-day plague, and, while his advice was not strictly followed, it is true that doctors (medical and psychiatric) have featured prominently among Ireland's Official Film Censors, all of whom have been men.[42]

It is convenient to divide the nine men who have occupied the office of Official Film Censor into three distinct categories. The first category covers the period 1923–1956. It includes the first two Censors – James Montgomery and Dr Richard Hayes – who held the office between them for more than thirty years (1923–1954), and the third Censor, Dr Martin Brennan (1954–1956). Their formative roots were in the struggle for Irish independence, and while they did not have any background in cinema, they pursued literary and academic interests outside their chosen professions: a gas company employee in the case of Montgomery, and medical practitioners in the cases of both Hayes and Brennan. Similarly, the two Censors who followed – Liam O'Hora (1956–1964), and another doctor, Christopher Macken (1964–1972), a War of Independence veteran – had no background in film, but unfortunately they lacked the relative sophistication of their predecessors. As a result, they found themselves increasingly out-of-step with Irish social and cultural mores during a turbulent decade, the 1960s. The third group can be traced from Dermot Breen's appointment in 1972 to the present. Having been Director of the Cork Film Festival since its foundation in 1956, he was the first appointee with direct involvement in the cinema. His successors, Frank Hall (1978–1986), Sheamus Smith (1986–2003), and John Kelleher (2003–) continued this tradition. Hall had been a television personality and satirist, Smith a managing director of the National Film Studios of Ireland during 1975–1982, while Kelleher had worked in RTÉ for many years, and had established a successful film and television production company.

Only with the appointments of James Montgomery and John Kelleher was the post publicly advertised. In a memorandum from the Department of Justice to the Department of the Taoiseach in 1948 on the occasion of Richard Hayes' retirement at the age of 70, it was stated that shortly before Montgomery retired, a decision was made that the post of Film Censor was not a Civil Service Commission appointment.[43] The memo records:

> So many people would regard themselves as fit for the post that it would be impossible to restrict competition to a reasonable field, and that the final selection might easily be made on proper qualification which would prove to be of little value in practice.

Furthermore, 'the position is a dignified one, of an assured social standing, and it would not be possible to limit competition by prescribing any professional or special qualifications.' At that time the salary was £1,115 per annum and the post was a temporary one. It was a position where only one month's notice on either side was required but, the memo thundered, 'it may be terminated without notice and without cause assigned in the event of misconduct.' What 'misconduct' which might arise, would, presumably, concern either the Censor's personal life, or if the Official Censor deviated from the prescribed terms of reference set down by the Department of Justice. As these 'guidelines' have never been published (indeed may never have been written down), and Film Censors were forbidden at least until the 1960s to give interviews concerning their office,[44] it has been difficult in the past to gauge precisely their performance as Censors and to assess the role of the Department of Justice in that process. With the newly available details on the fate of the films submitted for certification it is now possible to reconstruct the decision-making process of the film censors. However, the lack of detailed information on the operation and policy of the Appeal Board remains a hindrance in examining its actions, as unlike the first Film Censor in particular, generally no rationale for the decision is given. The Board merely records an affirmation or otherwise of the Film Censor's decision. The points of difference between the two branches of censorship were largely limited to cuts or the class of a certificate to be issued, while on rare occasions a film was banned by the Board after only having been cut by the censor.

Just as the Censors fit into particular categories, so too do the various Appeal Boards. The first period covers 1924 to 1964, while the second extends from 1965 onwards. The first Board was appointed on 29 February 1924, almost four months after Montgomery took up the post of Film Censor on 1 November 1923. Joining the chairman, Professor William Magennis, were two clergymen, the Revd T.W.E. Drury and the Pro-Cathedral's Fr L. Sheehan CC. Their appointments established the tradition, which still continues, of having one Protestant and one Catholic cleric on the Board. While Drury stayed on the Board for thirty years, Sheehan resigned within two years and was replaced by the formidable Canon (later Monsignor) Michael Cronin. An international authority on Thomist philosophy, Cronin was the author of the two-volume *The Science of Ethics* published in 1909, the same year that he became the first Professor of Ethics and Politics at University College Dublin. In 1930 he was appointed Vicar-General of the Dublin Archdiocese, a position re-confirmed in 1941 by the new Archbishop of Dublin, Dr John Charles McQuaid. A strict traditionalist interpreter of Catholic theology, Cronin wrote the widely distributed book aimed at Catholic lay people, *Primer of the Principles of Social Science* (1927), which displays a strong antipathy towards many elements of the modern world, including socialism and the emancipation of women.[45] It is probable that such experienced theologians would have carried most influence, not just with regard to religious films, discussed below, but when there was a perceived deviance from traditional Christian values such as with regard to divorce or illegitimacy in films. This was confirmed by Magennis' successor as chairman, Labour Senator John T. O'Farrell, who, during the 1930 debate on the amending of the Censorship of Films Act to allow for the censoring of sound films, pointed out that at least in relation to religious films, 'the Board … largely defers to clerical opinion on the Board.'[46] O'Farrell also remarked that 'the number of pictures rejected *in toto* by the Film Censor but passed by the Board is absolutely negligible.'[47]

Montgomery, writing in 1936 to Monsignor Curran of the Irish College, Rome, told his correspondent that the Board was in tune with his thinking:

> The [Appeal] Board as at present constituted, includes representatives of the learned and professional classes. There are two clergymen (one Catholic, the other – Church of Ireland), a University Professor, a Dramatist, an Architect, a member of the Senate, and a Medical Doctor. There are also two ladies, of whom one is an M.A., and both are Gaelic scholars.[48]

In practice, though never officially acknowledged, there was close co-ordination between the Official Censor and the Appeal Board. On occasion, the chairperson or another member of the Board would view a film with the Censor prior to a ruling being given to the distributor. While this is not strictly speaking outside the terms of the Act, it must call into question the supposed-independence of the Board. In one instance recorded by Montgomery early in his career as Censor, he had ensured the support of the chairman before banning a film 'in order to silence any suggestion of personal bias which might be made by the renter.' He had taken this course of action as the particular distributor recently had had other films banned and he feared that the renter would receive a sympathetic hearing from the Board as a result. Needless to say, the chairman supported the Film Censor.[49] One area of disagreement between the Board and Montgomery recorded in the 1920s concerned representations of national difference in war films. In his report for 1927, Montgomery stated that some of the films banned by him were subsequently passed by the Appeal Board, either with or without cuts, because the Board would not accept his formula which equated 'inflaming racial hatred' with the Act's clause, 'subversive of public morality.'[50]

In the 1920s the Appeal Board also included among its members writers and Senators, W.B. Yeats and Oliver St John Gogarty; previous Dublin Corporation censors, Senator Jenny Wyse-Power and Dr Myles Keogh TD; and Ernest H. Alton, a classical scholar who was Professor of Latin at Trinity College and one of the College's three independent TDs. The appointment of members of the Oireacthas to the Board ended in the 1930s. While nobody who is gainfully involved in film production or exhibition can be appointed to the Board, it has also been the case that no informed members of film cultural bodies, such as the Irish Film Society, have ever been made members of the Board, though the Film Society's Liam O'Leary did deputize for the Film Censor during holiday periods in the 1940s.[51] The pattern, where it exists, shows that those who expressed antipathy towards the urban, modern values of commercial cinema in the 1920s or 1930s were most likely to be nominated to the Board. This is evident in the appointment in 1933 of the rural dramatist T.C. Murray, a schoolmaster from West Cork. As a writer whose themes were 'the frustration of the loveless marriage, the tragedy of exile, the slavery of the hired farm hand, the problem of the spoiled priest and the bleak years of the old,'[52] it is not to be expected that he would show much sympathy towards, or understanding of, for example, the gangster films of the early 1930s. Another appointment in the 1930s was that of Mrs M.J. McKean, a Dublin Corporation film censor in 1922 and wife of the aforementioned Senator James McKean. Though the post-war years saw less nationally-known people acting as Board members, the pattern, established by the 1930s, of deviating little from the norms set down by the Official Censor continued largely unaltered until the complete revamping of the Appeal Board in 1965.

THE FAMILY AS THE UNIT OF THE STATE

The question as to the type of censorship policy which the Film Censor and the Appeal Board pursued is answered succinctly by James Montgomery in a letter to Monsignor Curran in 1936. The 'Catholic interests are well guarded,' he reported, because the Appeal Board 'consists of seven Catholics, and two Protestants – who are in full accord with our attitude to divorce and "the family as the unit of the State".'[53] Such a comment makes transparent what was at the core of his and the Board's policy: all decisions were being made in the first instance on the basis of whether or not films conformed to, or challenged, the monogamous nuclear and Christian family. Within a few months of taking office Montgomery was dealing with a hostile film trade that regarded such a film censorship regime as being too harsh. As the Minister for Justice, Kevin

O'Higgins, speaking in the Dáil in March 1924, noted, the film trade 'did not give much assistance when the arrangements for censorship were first being made.'[54] Indeed the distributors engaged in a boycott of censorship which began in February 1924, but the action had collapsed by the following June.[55] The chairman of the Appeal Board, William Magennis, anticipating the distributors' threat of the withdrawal of films from Ireland, told a delegation of distributors from London that the Irish Free State 'would rather have no films than the ones forbidden.'[56] The distributors accepted defeat and recognized that they had no option but to work within the already very strict policy being pursued by Montgomery and the Board. This change subsequently led to two pre-censorship effects: the major distributors, based in London and operating through regional offices in Dublin, withheld certain films from the Censor knowing they were likely to be banned, or cut others prior to submission. Apart from the prosecution on 6 September 1927 of an exhibitor at Carna, Co. Galway, for screening a film without displaying the Censor's certificate,[57] as was required by the Act, there is no other known prosecution of an exhibitor in such circumstances. After initial resistance to the Act, distributors and exhibitors alike fell into line. However, in early 1925 Montgomery expressed irritation at being presented with *Tarnish* (George Fitzmaurice, 1924), a film which features an unfaithful husband. In his report after banning the film, he commented that 'it is without exception the most vulgar film I've seen. One would fancy – after fourteen months' experience – that the film trade would have learned that such filth won't be tolerated in Saorstát Éireann.'[58]

One of the difficulties in assessing the extent of Irish film censorship is establishing the number of films, already in distribution in Britain, that were deliberately withheld from the Irish Censor. An even more problematic task is in confirming the particular version of a film submitted. In the first case it is possible to look at the absolute number of films submitted to the Irish Censor compared to the number released in Britain. At certain times there is as much as a 10 per cent differential between the two countries. With regard to the second case, the Irish Censor recorded the footage of the films submitted (this was essential to arrive at the cost of censorship as the distributor paid a fee based on the amount of footage submitted) and where known these are compared with the British release footage figures. It appears from the frequency with which Montgomery refers to it, that pre-submission cutting by distributors was particularly prevalent in the early 1930s, especially in 1933. This is not a surprising revelation as American cinema of this period was pushing the boundaries of what was acceptable on the screen in the years prior to the formal adoption of the Hays Code and the establishment in 1934 of the Legion of Decency. This helps to explain why Montgomery banned more films in 1931 and 1932 than in any other years he was in office. Cutting of films prior to their submission posed particular difficulties for him, not least of which was his annoyance at being cheated of seeing the whole film. When assessing Dorothy Arzner's *Christopher Strong* (1933), he reported that

> since this film was heavily cut before presentation to me, it will be necessary – in the event of this not being the showing copy – to notify me of the import

of another copy – or to give me a written guarantee that the imported copy is exactly similar to the one I have seen. Some step must be taken to ensure that the parts not shown to me might, inadvertently or otherwise, be inserted in second copies imported.

He added that 'the Revenue [Commission] reports all imports to me, but eternal vigilance is a hardship.'[59] From time to time, distributors did try to resist Montgomery's mutilation of their films, but they rarely got the benefit of the doubt, even when films were returned a second or third time for re-showing to the Censor.[60]

Montgomery was, in general, as inflexible in his decisions as he was witty and sharp in the manner he discussed the films. Noting in his first annual report that nearly 20 per cent of the films submitted for certification were objectionable, Montgomery went on, 'these undesirable parts dealt principally with indecent dancing [and the] customs of the "divorcing classes" in England and America. The general tone of the films is akin to the immorality of the Restoration drama, without its wit.'[61] Montgomery had viewed 1,307 films between November 1923 and October 1924. He had passed without cuts 1,037 films (79.3 per cent), passed with cuts 166 films (12.7 per cent), and had banned 100 films (7.7 per cent). The Appeal Board made only 4 alterations to Montgomery's rulings: it passed one film without cuts and a further 3 films with cuts.[62] The figures for 1923–1924 tell only part of the story. In 1925, 1,205 'Drama' films were submitted, of which 115 were banned (9.5 per cent), and 172 were cut (14.3 per cent). In the 'Interest' category, 552 films were submitted and none were banned or cut, while in the 'Educational' category (which was not subject to censorship fees), none were banned or cut, but 6 were rejected as not coming within the rubric of 'educational.'[63] During his full tenure in office, 1923–1940, Montgomery banned a total of 1,905 films. In 124 (6.5 per cent) of these cases, the Film Censor's decision to ban a film was reversed by the Appeal Board, while another 220 films banned by the Censor (11.5 per cent) were passed with cuts, making a net total of 1,561 films banned during the period.[64] (This figure may be compared with the 1,841 books banned by the Censorship of Publications Board during its first sixteen years in operation, 1930–1945.)[65] Overall, the Censor's decision was upheld by the Appeal Board in 410 (54 per cent) of the 754 appeals ruled on during 1923–1940.[66] This dramatically contrasted with the modest number of films banned by Dublin Corporation's film censors. Unsurprisingly, as we will see from evidence of the individual decisions, Montgomery's principal target was drama, especially feature films. In his report to the Minister for 1927 he wrote of his regret in not being able to discern any 'general improvement in the moral tone of the films' and complained about 'the importance given to "Sex Appeal" by some producers' which lead to many rejections. He elaborated that

> Many fine stories are spoiled and distorted both morally and artistically by the intrusion of scenes of sexual passion, and one is forced to conclude that *incidents of little dramatic value*, such as Cabaret orgies, semi-nude dancers,

bathing pools for vulgar 'new rich' revels, and bedroom and dressing room scenes, are introduced to pander to morbid and unhealthy tastes. There is a growing tendency to exhibit the erotic intimacies of lovers: such episodes *give the onlooker the uncomfortable feeling of an intruder*. One would not willingly witness these intimacies in real life, and even on the stage there is an amount of reticence in dealing with them, but it seems reserved for the 'Peeping Tom' mentality that has evidently intruded into certain cinema studios. (Emphasis added.)[67]

It is clear from this commentary that Montgomery was hostile to anything which deviated from traditional Catholic teaching on the family and society. It is somewhat ironic though that what he chose to highlight as impairments to a moral cinema – spectacle and voyeurism – are actually the essence of Hollywood, even if it is narrative that is most often discussed. His reports were liberally sprinkled with a litany of complaints: films were morbid, unhealthy, unsavoury, pornographic, vulgar, filthy, lustful, macabre, objectionable, offensive. All of this 'debauchery' gave 'moral nausea' to any 'normal person'. However, Montgomery's *normal* person was of a limited type as he illustrated in an unfavourable social class contrast between theatre and cinema audiences. In the draft of his 1931 report to the minister he explained:

> I am not trying to say that the morality of the stage is superior to the 'talkies,' but it must be remembered that the stage attracts a sophisticated adult audience and that the following of the development of a play calls for the exercise of thought. We have thus the anomaly of a sophisticated and limited audience for comparatively reticent productions, and a most highly sophisticated entertainment offered indiscriminately by the Cinema to the unsophisticated masses.[68]

In this passage Montgomery hints at the possibility of both literary and film texts not being fully determined or having fixed meanings, and accordingly recognizes the need for the audience to 'complete' that which is signified or to produce meaning. But for him the 'sophisticated' middle-class theatre audience can be trusted to interpret a play or a film according to the dominant ideology given to them through education, while the 'unsophisticated' cinema audience cannot. Therefore, not only is every film potentially subversive at the level of the image, as Magennis noted, but the narrative can invite an oppositional reading, or alternatively, it is open to being too literally interpreted and can indicate a course of imitative action. When Montgomery banned *The River Pirate* (William K. Howard, 1928), a decision upheld by the Appeal Board, he was explicit with regard to the latter point:

> Just think of its effect on young people; sympathy is excited for a robber and a murderer, and the officers of the law are shown in an unsympathetic light. There is an escape from prison, condoned by a warder, shown with instruc-

tive detail. I have constantly in my mind when dealing with underworld films, the memory of the crowd of children from the neighbouring slums attending the Picture House in Pearse [Street, Dublin].[69]

Likewise, after banning *Carmen* (Jean Murat, 1927), although it was passed with cuts by the Appeal Board, Montgomery commented that 'one must dismiss memories of opera, [the] novel and drama, and remember that this is a work for the screen with a dangerous appeal to the unsophisticated by its flattery of the passions.'[70] In ordering cuts to George Cukor's *Camille* (1937), an adaptation of Alexandre Dumas' *La Dame aux Camélias* featuring Greta Garbo, he observed that 'it may be advanced that [Verdi's opera *La Traviata*] is [of] the same theme, however the censorship is dealing *only with morality* irrespective of art.' (Emphasis added.)[71] Montgomery was, of course, applying these elitist norms to the cinema in a paternalistic manner not dissimilar to previous campaigners against popular publications and the music hall. Taking a strict moral and civil law approach, he ruled that cinema needed to be cleansed of embarrassing and 'illegal' subject matter. As divorce was illegal in the state (and constitutionally prohibited in 1937), then cinematic representations of such 'illegal' activities should be forbidden. Triangular relationships, illegitimacy, birth control, abortion, homosexuality, and prostitution were some of the other themes which infringed these laws and, consequently, were banned and cut from films.

As a result, *My Husband's Wives* (Maurice Elvey, 1924) was banned because it featured an extra-marital affair and was deemed to be 'subversive of public morality'. The film concerns Vale Harvey (Shirley Mason) who invites an old school friend, Marie Wynn (Evelyn Brent), to her home unaware that she was once married to her husband, William (Bryant Washburn). To Vale's discomfort, Marie tries to resume her relationship with William and an upset Vale dreams of an affair between her husband and an Italian actress (Paulette Duval). William, on discovering Marie's designs, asks her to leave, thereby allowing the Harveys to be reconciled. Commenting in his characteristically subjective manner, Montgomery equated such relationships with those of primates: 'In this picture the monkey house morality begotten of such a social condition is apparent.'[72] *True as Steel* (Rupert Hughes, 1924) was banned for somewhat similar reasons. On a trip to New York, married businessman Frank Parry (Huntley Gordon) becomes infatuated with married Eva Boutelle (Aileen Pringle), manageress of a cotton mills. Though their affair develops, Eva refuses to divorce her husband, despite the fact that Frank is willing to divorce his wife so that they can marry. When Frank returns home, his wife (Cleo Madison) forgives him. For Montgomery, this film had 'all the defects of the class of picture which made ... Censorship a necessity. It reeks with sex, conjugal infidelity and of course – divorce.'[73] After ordering cuts to *Secrets* (Frank Borzage, 1923), which includes a scene of marital infidelity, he wrote that 'the moral is apparently – satisfy your passions with other women and you will be justified if you love your wife and she loves you.'[74] Montgomery was not fooled by the Hollywood formula of the wife forgiving her wayward husband in the last scene or having an 'illicit' relationship regularized. As he put it when ordering cuts to *Beggar's Holiday*

(Sam Newfield, 1934), which features a criminal who eventually goes straight for the love of a woman: 'There is the usual sop to censorship in the last reel.'[75] While the status quo is re-established at the end of the Hollywood film, a condition of classical narrative resolution, Montgomery sought to deny audiences the pleasure of identifying with transgressive activities before such closures were effected. However, it is in the gaps opened up by classical cinema, especially in the second act, which have been most productively explored, particularly by feminist film theorists seeking a progressive or subversive reading of Hollywood.[76] He could not, as already noted, suppress the pleasure inherent in the image itself.

In 1939 an exasperated Montgomery lectured a renter after he had submitted *Women in the Wind* (John Farrow, 1939):

> It is a waste of money to import divorce films. Divorce or the remarriage of divorced people during the lifetime of the discarded partner, is bigamy. It is now in the constitution of this country. All [material] relating to the possibilities of the marriage of the hero and heroine in this film must come out – *even if it spoils the story*. So, if the renter wishes, he may make these cuts – and let me see how they work. (Emphasis added.)[77]

The renter, somewhat unusually, requested that the film be banned, and the Appeal Board duly obliged.[78] One rare exception to Montgomery's rule on divorce was the Academy Award winning musical biography hit of showman Florenz Ziegfeld, played by William Powell in *The Great Ziegfeld* (Robert Z. Leonard, 1936), which was passed with cuts of 'semi-nude wrigglers' and the 'allusions to Sex Appeal.' Montgomery explained his decision in allowing the representation of Ziegfeld's divorce from Anna Held (Louise Rainer) and subsequent marriage to Billie Burke (Myrna Loy) with recourse to historical fact: 'The divorce and remarriage, being *actual history*, justify my passing them.' (Emphasis added.) He also reported that he 'couldn't ban, for instance, Napoleon's Royal Divorce for the same reason.'[79]

Notwithstanding the Catholic church's promotion of large families, representations of any 'embarrassing' matters dealing with personal morality or the human body were as forbidden on the cinema screen as they were repressed elsewhere in Irish society. Cinematic exploration of such topics was judged and conditioned by Montgomery's reference to the Victorian notion of *reticence*. When he ordered cuts to *Gentlemen Are Born* (Alfred E. Green, 1934), he wrote that 'celebration of conception is not usual in Ireland. We are a gabby nation, but we have our limits of reticence.'[80] Such a comment gives credence to the popular myth of Ireland as a literate rather than a visual people, and suppresses the, at times, sexually explicit depictions in Irish art, such as the predominantly medieval sheela-na-gig carvings of splay-legged women displaying exaggerated genitalia – even if these were used by the church to represent lust and the temptation of man by woman.[81] *The Marriage Cheat* (John Griffith Wray, 1924) was only passed subject to the cutting of 'the entire episode of the childbirth' as he deemed it 'unfit for an audience in which children might be present.'[82] When ordering the cutting of a childbirth scene in *The World Changes* (Mervyn LeRoy, 1933), he remarked that 'this office will soon be like a branch of the Rotunda [Maternity Hospital]. The next Censor will require a certificate in midwifery.'[83] This theme was again returned to when he ordered extensive cuts to Michael Curtiz's *Four Wives* (1939) which 'bulges with babies, and is better fitted for the Rotunda than for this office.' He complained that 'it will dispel the cabbage myth from the child mind' and contrasted Irish and American male attitudes to conception:

> American men seem to ballyhoo the baby from its conception to its almost public delivery. It is perhaps, the right thing to do (certainly better than birth control) but, there is to an Irishman an indecent lack of reticence in the whole proceeding. Think it out: the hospital scenes must at least be dealt with drastically. You'd almost want a midwife to cut it.

He noted when passing the trailer that it was 'unfit for exhibition to a juvenile or adolescent audience' because it 'tells too much' and 'would embarrass young unmarried women' as it was 'far too intimate'.[84] While Montgomery suppressed any hint of childbirth in the case of married women whose 'dignity' he sought to protect, he was unrestrained in his condemnation of unmarried mothers. Any sympathy he may have had for such women was confined to those whose 'transgression' was accompanied by remorse. Such was not the case in *Reveille* (George Pearson, 1924, GB) a film he banned in 1924, the central figure of which 'is an unmarried mother who expresses more pride than regret for her lapse.'[85]

In this context, it is to be expected that any references to birth control or abortion were cut, or films with such themes banned. Cecil B. DeMille's jungle adventure *Four Frightened People* (1934) was passed only after the 'birth control stuff' was removed. Indeed, Montgomery noted that he 'could easily reject this [film] for the "comic" relief of the sexy lady urging birth control in the jungle.'[86] References to birth control were cut from the drama *South Riding* (Victor Saville, 1937, GB),[87] and from *To Mary – with Love* (John Cromwell, 1936), a romantic comedy, the genre in which British or American cinema could most easily raise the topic in the 1930s.[88] Michael Curtiz's *Alias the Doctor* (1932) was only passed after he made cuts which were 'intended to get rid of the fact that Stephan [(Norman Foster)] procured [an] abortion,' and that he had engaged in an 'illicit intimacy'. In keeping with his general instructions following the cutting of a film, the published synopsis had to be amended in order to suppress any hint of the abortion. Montgomery also worried about the attitude of the medical profession to 'the main situation,' how Stephan's brother Karl (Richard Barthelmess), who is studying medicine takes responsibility for the abortion, is imprisoned, and later becomes successful while masquerading as his dead brother: 'Is it moral?' wondered Montgomery.[89] *Ann Vickers* (John Cromwell, 1933) was cut for similar reasons, and in order to detach the film from its literary origins – Sinclair Lewis' notorious novel *Ann Vickers*, banned by the Censorship of Publications Board – he ordered the title to be changed to *Ann's Romance*.[90]

*Gone with the Wind* (Victor Fleming, 1939) included a number of these prohibitions, but because it was perhaps the most prestigious American film of the sound era, Montgomery spent a considerable amount of time, and was unusually conciliatory, in dealing with it. Not only did he view the film at least twice, negotiate with Neville, MGM's local manager, but entertained the American Minister David Gray on two occasions and who sought to have the Censor's proposed cuts modified. Montgomery demanded thirteen cuts when he viewed the film in May 1940; he met Neville five days later, and in August Gray went to the Censor's office seeking modification of the cuts, and he returned less than three weeks later for the reshow. None of this was in the public domain; indeed, Montgomery commented after seeing Neville on 28 May to discuss the trailer, that 'everything hush hush. A marathon of endurance.' They met again on 3 June.

The cuts Montgomery demanded are familiar ones from his years in office. These include the scene of Scarlett O'Hara (Vivien Leigh) with her black maid as she is being dressed and she re-arranges her bosom with a look of sexual allure to make herself more attractive to men at the barbecue. The subsequent 'stripping her at a glance' comment at the event was also cut. In addition, the scenes concerning Melanie (Olivia de Havilland) giving birth in Atlanta were cut from the time practical preparations are being made through to the mother's screams at birth, and the appearance of the baby. Later scenes concerning procreation, including Scarlett and Rhett's (Clark Gable) honeymoon conception of Bonnie, were also prohibited. Even more problematic were the events surrounding Scarlett's second pregnancy. In his jealousy, Rhett believes she still pines for Ashley and when the pair are seen in a compromising hold, Rhett forces her to attend a party alone at Ashley's house. When a humiliated Scarlett returns from the party in her red dress that Rhett had forced her to wear, she finds him drunk. Dispirited, but still in love with her, Rhett follows Scarlett to the stairs where he grabs her, and the explicit moment – the passionate kiss between the pair – before he carries her upstairs is a clearly coded prelude to their love-making. MGM agreed to the deletion of the kiss at the foot of the stairs so as not to make it so obvious as to why she was being carried upstairs. Indeed, Montgomery demanded cut the three shots of kisses of the couple the first time they accept each other; these were too 'passionate and prolonged'. In fact, he was concerned about cutting the later kiss as 'the tyranny of continuity would almost demand the act of conception to be screened.' Forlornly, he asked, 'Why not let imagination a chance?' The couple, however, separate the next morning and it is only when Rhett returns from Europe with Bonnie it is revealed that she is pregnant. Most disturbing for Montgomery was Scarlett's reaction to Rhett's indifference when she tells him that she is pregnant. Following his hurtful comment – 'Who's the father?' – and realizing the impossibility of a reconciliation, she throws herself downstairs and kills the unborn baby. Before the single brief reconciliation that had led to this ill-fated pregnancy she had told him, in an allusion to the availability of birth control, that she would not have any more children to which Rhett implies that he could divorce her for that. Like the other scenes which present Scarlett as a sexually-independent woman, this scene was cut. Other scenes 'edited' were the attempted rape of Scarlett in the woods, which was re-created by Montgomery as an attempted robbery as he cut the shot of the close-up of the leering white man seen from Scarlett's point-of-view, a familiar rape-coded shot.[91]

Another taboo subject was homosexuality. Alert to the double-meaning of the term, he ordered the 'homosexual joke,' 'the boys with love below the Dixie line,' to be cut from the Al Jolson vehicle *The Singing Kid* (William Keighley, 1936).[92] Prostitutes, with or without a 'heart of gold,' or even when showing remorse for their 'sinful ways,' were invariably cut. While Josef von Sternberg's *Dishonored* (1931), a spy drama set in Vienna and featuring an army widow (Marlene Dietrich) who has turned to prostitution and later becomes a spy, was initially banned, it was subsequently cut for resubmission by the distributor, and eventually passed with cuts. Montgomery's cuts included the infamous seduction scene with the line, 'Shall I go on with my undressing?' Montgomery wondered: 'Is patriotism an excuse for prostitution?' (As there is no reference to prostitution in the Censor's report it is safe to assume that the distributor had removed the offending scenes.) The certificate was issued 'subject to the synopsis of the story being amended to agree with [the] version of [the] film as passed.'[93]

Yet another sensitive subject, and one which violated both civil and religious law, was suicide. Among the films banned by Montgomery in his first year in office featuring representations of suicide or attempted suicide were the society melodrama *Ladies Must Live* (George Loane Tucker, 1921) which also featured divorce; the romantic melodrama, *Java Head* (George Melford, 1923) in which Manchu Princess Taou Yuen takes an overdose of opium and dies, leaving her husband – who only married her so that she would not be put to death – free to marry his true sweetheart; yet another melodrama, this time domestic, *A Woman's Woman* (Charles Giblyn, 1922), in which an unappreciated mother discovers independence and success as a business woman, but which (in)directly leads to her husband – who has taken up with a young widow – divorcing her, her daughter who is refused marriage attempting suicide, while her son is killed avenging his sister: subsequently, she gives up her business and starts a new life for all her remaining family; and *Let Not Man Put Asunder* (J. Stuart Blackton, 1924) in which two couples marry and then divorce, but later, one couple reunites while the woman of the other dies and her grief-stricken ex-husband commits suicide. Montgomery claimed to be concerned at the possibility of copycat suicide attempts. When he ordered cuts to *Little Friend* (Berthold Viertel, 1934, GB), he noted that 'suicide by gas is becoming quite common owing to its ease, and I have been repeatedly recommended by the late Coroner and by the police to delete it from all films.' He went on: 'Its appeal to a morbid and precocious child in this instance is dangerous.'[94] Similarly, the successful sombre romance-melodrama western, *The Virginian* (Victor Fleming, 1929), based on Owen Wister's 1902 novel which offered a definite version of the cowboy as a heroic nature's gentleman and featuring Gary Cooper as the eponymous nameless man-of-action cowboy, was only passed after cutting by the Censor:

I don't want the gruesome scene of the men with the noose around their necks.
Cut every shot of this no matter how much sentimentality you sacrifice ...
Children are imitative and I don't want to be held accountable for the hanging of some child in the Saorstát when playing cowboys. I won't pass the
episode of the child with the rope around its neck.[95]

It was not just films dealing with the family in the broadest sense – divorce, re-marriage, and extra-marital affairs – or the sexualized body, which were viewed with suspicion and curtailed, but any representations of the Catholic church.

## THE CENSORS DEFEND THE CATHOLIC CHURCH

Montgomery would not tolerate any criticism of the Catholic church as an institution,
allow 'irreverent' films based on the Old or New Testaments, or have church sacraments screened, the latter decision made on the dictate of the archbishop of Dublin.[96]
The treatment of the gangster film *Angels with Dirty Faces* (Michael Curtiz, 1938)
shows how sensitive the censors were to representations of the Catholic church. It was
passed only after Fr Connolly's (Pat O'Brien) 'lie' was cut. At the end of the film gangster 'Rocky' Sullivan (James Cagney) replaces his bravado with a display of mock cow-
ardice as he is being led to the electric chair. Afterwards, Fr Connolly visits the juvenile delinquents known as the Dead End Kids and 'lies' when he tells them Rocky died
'yellow': 'It's true boys, every word of it. He died like they said.' Montgomery, quoting Catholic doctrine, maintained that 'no motive however good can excuse a lie,' and
so 'the priest's lie must come out.'[97] With such moral certainties applied to the *fictional
representation* of a priest's cinematic lie (made, it must be emphasized, in the interests
of 'good', so as to demystify Rocky in the eyes of his young followers), there was little
chance for any cinematic criticism of the Catholic church as an institution or of its
belief systems being allowed on Irish cinema screens. Indeed, he banned *The Garden
of Allah* (Rex Ingram, 1927) because it concerned a priest who broke his religious
vows and as a result, it was not 'a desirable subject for exhibition in Ireland,'[98] a comment which reveals the Censor's casual disregard for the Act's terms of reference.

*In a Monastery Garden* was banned because, according to Montgomery, it 'would
give offence to Catholics everywhere.'[99] After banning *The Man in the Iron Mask* he
wrote that it was

an historical distortion unfit for exhibition from an educational standpoint.
The casuistical Richelieu, the murderous Mazarin and the Sultanic Louis are
not edifying patterns from the moral angle and the anti-Catholic aspect is
offensive.[1]

Later he banned films depicting the life of Christ or cut those which included the
monstrance or the sacraments. In his 1925 report on *I.N.R.I.* (Robert Wiene, 1923,

Germany) about a sentenced revolutionary murderer who converts and repents after
a prison chaplain tells him the narrative of the life of Christ, Montgomergy wrote that
'I have made a rigid rule to reject films in which Christ is materialised,' a policy, of
course, in operation in Britain since the establishment of the BBFC in 1913. He went
on to say that

> in this picture I consider that the meeting with Mary Magdalene is shown
> with a lack of reticence, and the excessive details showing crucified torture,
> excite horror rather than reverence. I think that the attitude of the Ober-amer-
> gau players – who refused to act for the films – was quite right.[2]

Somewhat ironically his sentiments recall the commentaries on much of medieval eccle-
siastical sculpture which celebrates the sensuous, and, at times, gruesome world of
bodily pleasures and tortures.[3] However, Montgomery attributed his difficulties with
this graphic art of display to its vulgar and democratic origins, and to his own refined
sensibility and appreciation of fine art. He mistakenly, though characteristically, believed
that high culture was marked by reticence.

Another reason why he banned *I.N.R.I.* – a decision upheld by the Appeal Board,
even when a re-edited version of the film was submitted – and similar themed films,
was due to a concern over the viewing context. His comments echo the debate surrounding *From the Manger to the Cross*, discussed in chapter 2:

> One must consider the environment in which the picture is to be shown, and
> decide if it is proper to exhibit it as part of the entertainment offered in a
> Cinema Theatre. I have no power to impose restrictions or conditions which
> might ensure its reverent reception by the ordinary picture house audience.[4]

In 1928 Montgomery cited this report when he banned Cecil B. DeMille's epic life of
Christ, *The King of Kings* (1927), but on this occasion the Appeal Board passed the
film with cuts. Montgomery had written, somewhat dramatically given the film's content (it even begins with the redemption of Mary Magdalene), of his regret 'that in this
instance the approach to "the Greatest Story in the World" should be through a bed in
a brothel, with an attempt to suggest a Hollywood sex triangle.'[5] Ironically, Catholic
theologian and Professor of Dramatics at St Louis University, Fr Daniel Lord SJ, who
later played a pivotal role in American film censorship, was Catholic adviser to the film.

One of the first films that Montgomery ordered to be cut because it featured the
Catholic mass was Erich von Stroheim's *The Wedding March* (1928). Commenting on
a scene set in a Catholic church, he wrote:

> In the church scenes there are incidents that are anything but reverent. The con-
> versation regarding the heiress is probably essential, but the sacred ceremonies
> that are in progress at the same time display the cynical disregard of Hollywood
> for the sincere feelings of Catholics. The Elevation, and the bells for it, must

come out, and the conversation must be curtailed to the essential minimum. During the procession the full view of the Monstrance must come out.[6]

In the 1930s he ordered the Monstrance and the Benediction to be removed from feature films, including *Call of the Flesh* (Charles Barbin, 1930),[7] as well as from newsreels. He told *Movietonenews* that the blessing of the pilgrims in Lourdes, as well as the Monstrance, had to be cut.[8] In his report in 1938 on a film about the Holy Ghost Fathers, Montgomery wrote that 'His Grace the Archbishop [of Dublin] will not allow the Canon of the Mass, or the Monstrance in procession or Benediction, to be shown in Dublin cinemas. Delete the Benediction.'[9] The Benediction was also ordered cut from a film of the Eucharistic Congress in 1935: 'By order of the Archbishop this must never be shown in a picture house.'[10] By 1937 this prohibition was extended to a newsreel of the Pope, who was ordered cut from an edition of *Movietonenews*.[11] Shortly afterwards, a religious film, *The Call to Orders* (submitted by the film's producer, Fr Horgan) was viewed by Montgomery with Monsignor Cronin, who seems to have acted as an adviser to the Censor on such films, and later the Censor ruled that the film was 'unsuitable for public exhibition.'[12] Even the Shirley Temple film *The Little Colonel* (David Butler, 1935) was not immune: 'A joke about a sacrament will not be tolerated in this country … there must be no allusion to baptism.'[13]

Considering Montgomery's hostile attitude to limited certificates, it is strange to discover that some of the few offers he made of such a certificate was in connection with films about religious life. Besides confining *The Call to Orders* to limited audiences,[14] he was also emphatic in his refusal to certify *Cloistered* (1937), a story about the cloistered French Good Shepherd Order, for general exhibition, and even remarked that the trailer was 'sheer commercial sensationalism and [in] bad taste.' He continued:

> I cannot understand how such scenes of cloistered life have been released for exhibition. What is the purpose? It is fine photography, but some Catholics and high ecclesiastics to whom I showed the film, were pained and indignant. If the Renter insists I'll issue a limited certificate for exhibition in such places as the Father Matthew Hall under the auspices of the 'Fathers'. All scenes showing the Canon of the Mass, and the Holy Communion must be deleted.

He was so determined to ensure that the film would not be distributed in Ireland that he even offered the renter a refund of the censorship fee if the film was withdrawn. Nevertheless, the film was issued with a certificate after Monsignor Cronin saw it.[15] Beyond the more formal areas of objection on grounds of civil or religious law, Montgomery applied his litmus test of 'reticence' (or lack of it) to assess whether a film conformed to his views on the limits of the public display of the female body. In this respect he regularly objected to representations of what he called 'semi-nude' women.

THE CENSOR'S DESIRE: 'SEMI-NUDITY,' 'BALLETS' AND 'NIGHTCLUB LIFE'

Montgomery devised a unique lexicon in his censorship reports. Of primary concern to him was the state of undress of the female characters. 'Semi-nude' encompassed any exposed area of the female anatomy below the neck, including women in dance costumes or underwear, taking off stockings or other clothes, and bathing. Usually linked with 'semi-nudity,' especially in nightclubs or cabarets, was dancing, which in his parlance was oddly called 'ballet'. Alert to the erotic and sensuous resonances of representations of women and men in various states of undress, Montgomery observed, perhaps with classical art in mind, that 'absolute nudity might be less offensive than this semi-nudity which in my opinion is pornographic.'[16] If we understand pornography as revealing too much, and eroticism as being impregnated with desire, it is clear that semi-nudity falls into the latter category (though nudity does not necessarily belong to pornography). It would seem that Montgomery's *desire* is to fix, or empty the image of a *frisson* or temptation, so that he is not overwhelmed by it and thereby can occupy a position of control in relation to the image. This notion of distance and control has been identified as a key characteristic of western representational art from the Renaissance until the late-nineteenth century, and indeed of classical Hollywood cinema. However, what makes cinema so much more powerful, or subversive to the dominant drive to control, is that it refuses or problematizes the (single) point-of-view inscribed in painting (or the novel) through the extra dimension of movement.[17] The moving image can never be fully contained or arrested. Furthermore, as Benjamin puts it, a film 'can be analyzed much more precisely and from more points-of-view than those presented on paintings or on the stage.'[18]

The contradictions in Montgomery's approach to representations of female nudity[19] may be seen in his treatment of scenes of rape or attempted rape, which, in general, he cut. In Alfred Hitchcock's *Blackmail* (1929, GB) a key sequence of deception and attempted rape was cut. Ironically, given the esteem in which Montgomery held high art, the 'deviant' is an artist. Blinded, perhaps, by the desire aroused in Montgomery by the woman changing her clothes to pose as the artist's model, he described the attempted rape and the woman's subsequent killing of her attacker as 'the sex struggle,' although it is obvious that all sexual advances made are unwelcome and resisted. He ordered that 'the unstripping [sic] and dressing and the passionate kiss prior to and including the sex struggle' be curtailed. He merely noted that 'this film is restricted to adult audiences in Great Britain, and that such restriction is not enforced in Saorstát Éireann.' Later, he rejected the film and it was passed by the Appeal Board.[20]

The films which received closest scrutiny were those set in theatres, music halls, cabarets and nightclubs, or drew on the erotic possibilities of the Old Testament stories, so well exploited by Cecil B. De Mille. Chorus lines, or scenes set in the dressing rooms of the performers, were a constant cause of complaint. From *New York Nights* (Lewis Milestone, 1929) the 'views of chorus girls coming down ladder steps,' 'orgiastic' scenes, and a drunken woman,[21] were cut, while 'chorus girls in ... indecent costumes' were deleted[22] from *The Singing Kid*. Ordering a series of cuts from *After*

*Midnight* (Monta Bell, 1927), which 'barely escapes rejection', of garters, dancing and a drunken woman, Montgomery expressed his annoyance at such films thus: 'It is almost impossible to "clean" scenes of night life and the underworld.'[23] A close-up of the legs of girls dancing was cut from the musical review *Paramount on Parade* (Dorothy Arzner, 1930): 'In the opening trick shot there is a display of bare legs only. The ballet in this reel is far too nude. The hips are exposed, and the trunks are barely (barely is the right word) covered.' Montgomery warned sternly, 'better not have to submit it twice, so cut drastically. I want it out.'[24] Similarly, the musical *Gold Diggers of 1933* (Mervyn LeRoy, 1933) – 'a euphemism for a certain type of woman of very easy virtue' – was closely scrutinized, and had about seven minutes cut from it,[25] and the Mae West/Cary Grant comedy *I'm No Angel* (Wesley Ruggles, 1933) was banned, even though renter Paramount cut 1,480 feet (about seventeen and a half minutes) from the film before submitting it,[26] while the film which made West an international star, *She Done Him Wrong* (Lowell Sherman, 1933), banned in Australia, Finland and Austria, was not even submitted to the Irish Censor.

'Ballet,' whether in a chorus line or a biblical epic, was allowed only if he considered the characters suitably dressed or he did not regard it as erotic. In 1926, in his report on *The Queen of Sheba* (J. Gordon Edwards, 1921), he wrote that

> this Biblical Ballet is evidently designed to display the figure of the Queen of Sheba [(Betty Blythe)], which it does to the greatest possible extent. There are few scenes in which she is not semi-nude. Is it desirable to allow this Hollywood 'triangle' [Sheba, Solomon and his wife, Amrath] to be shown as a picture of the story told in the Old Testament?[27]

Montgomery expressed outrage at the number of films in the early sound era which had more 'suggestive' dancing as their focus. *Flirtation Walk* (Frank Borzage, 1934) was passed with cuts after appeal only when the Hula was cut: 'The hip-wagging Hula is frankly and designedly a sex dance,' and is 'poison for adolescents'.[28] The British film *Everything Is Rhythm* (Alfred Goulding, 1936) allowed him to contrast the American and British cinemas' treatments of dancing in the mid-1930s.

> Of one thing I am certain and that is that I never will pass the indecent 'costume' of brassiere and trunk, the hula, and the rumba. This was my attitude when America spewed this dirt, now that America has dropped it, and England is emphasising it, my attitude is unaltered.[29]

After ordering the cutting of a taxi dancer in *Asleep in the Fleet*, an MGM short, in 1933, Montgomery used the occasion to place such films in the context of the contemporary controversy in Ireland surrounding the alleged indecency taking place in Irish dance halls and their environs. Indicating his support for restrictions of such venues, he remarked that 'there is a justified outcry against dance halls in Ireland and [*Asleep in the Fleet*] shows all that is said against them.'[30] The campaign led to the passing of the Dance Halls Act, 1935 which regulated through licence the operation of dance halls. In ordering cuts to *Father O'Flynn* (Wilfred Noy, 1935, GB), a film whose exteriors were shot in Ireland, he suggested that though it 'might be called "Stage Irish," ... the girl dancing on the village green shows more leg than ever I've seen on any village green in Ireland, *better amputate them.*' (Emphasis added.)[31] Films set in the late-nineteenth century, such as *Sunrise* (F.W. Murnau, 1927),[32] *Dreyfus* (F.W. Kraemer, 1931, GB),[33] and *Way out West* (James W. Horne, 1937),[34] all of which featured the can-can, were also cut, though he regretting having to approach *Sunrise*, which was cut in six places (especially semi-nudity and kisses in the first two reels), 'through the spectacles of the [1923] Act which is concerned with morality rather than with art.' Montgomery told the distributor when cutting *The Woman Between* (Victor Schertzinger, 1931) that 'I require the complete deletion of *each* and *every* shot of the can-can dancers. When the panic exit is shown, some of the Can-Can girls are in it with their skirts up in front.'[35] Two epics of the late 1930s were not immune from the can-can embargo: *In Old Chicago* (Henry King, 1938) which features an Irish family against the backdrop of the burning of Chicago,[36] and the already discussed *Gone with the Wind*,[37] one of the last films which he censored.

The prohibition against 'semi-nude' women extended to non-fiction films, and came into play when, in the 1930s, beauty contests became a popular entertainment. *Pathé Pictorial* was told in 1936 to delete shots of girls 'indecently "clad" in brassieres and trunks.' Though Montgomery was all too aware that such costumes were part of the shows in Dublin theatres and cine-variety houses such as the Royal, he was adamant that he would 'not accept the Royal as a criterion of decency,' and argued that if he were to pass such films it would be the end of his efforts to keep these costumes off the screen.[38] Ironically, what could be seen live on the stage was forbidden on the screen, indicating that Montgomery regarded screen representations as being more influential than reality. Indeed, he elaborated on the scale and power of the image when he contrasted the effect of figures in the swimming baths with their projected and magnified images on the screen.[39] It may also be remarked that his decision on the banning of *actual* beauty contests lies uneasily against his passing, in the same year, of *The Great Ziegfeld* which featured an *actual* divorce and highlights the distinction he obviously made between representations of historical fact and of present-day reality. In summary, it seems that he disapproved of representations of the present if they did not accord with his vision of Ireland, and instead favoured a somewhat nostalgic recreation of the past and held to a traditional notion of Irish women. This is evident in his response to a 1933 Paramount short, *Beauty Contest*, which featured Irish girls:

> I will not be responsible for the showing of Irish girls in single-piece bathing costumes on the screen. I consider that it is pandering to exhibitionism, and absolutely at variance with our women's reputation for the *old-fashioned virtue of modesty.* One girl (Scottish) is shown in a brassiere and on no account will she pass. If the first scene showing semi-nude boys and girls all together is deleted, and the close-ups of the girls' figures showing full lengths

in single piece costumes are cut out I'll pass the film, if not, better appeal. (Emphasis added.)[40]

Despite Montgomery's confidence in his ability to adjudicate on films and of institutional support in that task, he felt somewhat disabled through his inadequate viewing facilities. Without the advantage of seeing the image magnified, he believed that he missed unseen details which would effect the viewer's reception and interpretation of the film.[41] Pre-empting another if more famous 'censor' – Disney's 1940 version of Carlo Collodi's talking cricket (*Pinocchio*, Ben Sharpsteen and Hamilton Luske) who puts on his spectacles in order to better enjoy the suggestive can-can dancing marionettes – he told the renter of *Paramount on Parade* in 1930 that

> on a larger screen and with stronger light than I have at my disposal the concluding part of this reel may give many glimpses of semi-nudity which I cannot define. [You are] advised to cut if so. I'm having mirror arcs installed. They will be in action for the re-show.[42]

Even if he did not share Benjamin's celebration of popular culture,[43] Montgomery indirectly anticipates his thesis that the cinema belongs to the world of science whereas art belongs to magic and ritual, and that cinema is to vision what Freud is to the unconscious. As is clear in the comment above, Montgomery cast himself as a scientist who wishes to penetrate the film's meaning, and diagnose and 'amputate' its malignancy, but is without a sufficiently powerful microscope to do so. He regularly complained about the size of the screen onto which the films he viewed were projected and worried that the magnified image on the cinema screen would have an overwhelming effect on the audience.

### THE IRISH CINEMA AUDIENCE

One of the myths of Irish film exhibition has been that the Irish are the greatest cinemagoers in the world. While there is evidence to suggest that Irish cinemagoing in the 1990s was at a slightly higher per capita rate than the European Union's average, such was not the case in the 1930s. The first comprehensive statistical analysis of Irish cinemagoing was carried out by Thekla Beere in 1934–35 and published in 1936. Beere demonstrated that while Dublin accounted for about 60 per cent of Irish cinemas' box office, the per capita Irish rate of cinemagoing at 6 visits per annum, or 11 million admissions in 1934, was less than one-third Britain's rate of 22 visits to the cinema per annum. Even Dublin's rate of 23 visits per annum compares unfavourably with British cities, such as, for example, Liverpool's 35 visits per annum. Beere commented on the most public manifestation of Irish cinemagoing, the famous Dublin cinema queue. She observed that these queues were most likely to be for the cheapest priced seats as the most expensive ones were outside the financial reach of most working-class cinemagoers, who – confirming Montgomery's prejudice – formed the bulk of the audience: 'There may often be a queue outside and many empty seats inside.'[44] This view is borne out by the fact that the wage of the average Dublin working-class family was only about two-thirds that of their British counterpart. Nevertheless, as I have suggested elsewhere,[45] the importance attached to cinemagoing as *the event of the week* indicates that despite the severity of film censorship, the experience of going to the cinema was central to the lives of a great many people, especially children, young adults and court-ing couples, in urban areas.

One of the major obstacles in attempting to draw some general conclusions about cinemagoing is the nostalgic manner in which childhood and young-adulthood is remembered by most people. Nevertheless, we need to appreciate two points: firstly that there was direct intervention at the level of the plot by the film censors, as out-lined above, and, secondly, as recognized by Montgomery when cutting such films, that there remained the overwhelming emotional impact or viscerality of the cinematic image itself *irrespective of its content*. Though Montgomery tried to 're-edit' Hollywood narrative cinema to fit an ideal notion of Irish society, even his sanitized version of the films still sharply contrasted with the Ireland of the 1920s and 1930s. There existed on the cinema screen a world of excitement and glamour, of difference, which was absent elsewhere in Irish life for most cinemagoers. There was also the display of con-sumer delights which were unobtainable in Ireland for large numbers of people until many decades later and which were only directly experienced through emigrants' let-ters and their home visits. It is not surprising, therefore, that bishops and others should blame the cinema for anything from emigration to the spread of materialism in Ireland.[46] Rather than confront the challenge of popular culture, Montgomery adopted, what has been called in another context, 'the imperial strategy of infantilizing the native culture.'[47] Montgomery literally applied this colonial inheritance to the cinema by treat-ing all cinemagoers as children. This is despite the fact, as he himself acknowledged, that the 'girls' and 'boys' were sexualized young adults who did more in the cinema than watch films. In his report on *Four Wives*, he makes reference to 'the unmarried young girl sitting and holding hands with her … boyfriend in the *darkest part of the cinema.*' That he suggested they would 'blush' or be 'embarrassed'[48] at the on-screen activity of childbirth revealed his awareness, if then suppressed, of their knowingness: blushing can only take place in the presence of (disavowed) knowledge. Indeed, William Magennis was even more explicit in what he thought happened in the cinema. During the 1923 Censorship of Films Bill debate, he had no doubt as to who constituted the audience for such films. Giving a sketch outline of what he regarded as a typical film about the elopement of a young couple, he reported that 90 per cent 'of the audience looking on at that are lovers.'[49] While the censors knew that sexually-active (even if in a most limited way) young people were attending the cinema, they continued to treat them as children.

As noted above, during Montgomery's almost seventeen years in office, he banned 1,905 films, or 1,561 after appeal, a figure which can be compared with the 177 films banned by the British Board of Film Censors during 1924–1940.[50] With the exception of the Irish War of Independence feature film *Irish Destiny* (George Dewhurst, 1926, Ireland), banned for political reasons in Britain, I have not been able to identify any other film of this period banned by the BBFC which was even submitted to the Irish censor. Indeed, I would doubt if any such films were offered for Irish distribution. Montgomery and his successors during the first forty years of film censorship certified almost all films for general audiences. That is to say, all films were certified or banned on the basis that even the youngest child could see them. The BBFC, by contrast, had an 'A', or adult rating from 1913, and introduced a 'H' for horror films in 1933 and an 'X' for films confined to over-16s in 1951. The Irish policy inevitably threw up contradictions and anomalies. In passing *Odette* (Luia Murat, 1927) with cuts, he wrote:

> It is obvious that a film which in England can be shown to adults only requires some attention in Ireland where children and young persons are admitted to all cinema theatres without restriction. It is not very clearly shown, but it certainly may be inferred that Odette is living in adultery with the gambler. I don't want to emasculate the story, but I fancy that if it were suggested that she is merely a decoy and not the mistress of the gambler that the story would be just as effective. It is hardly conceivable that she could love such a brute. The kissing on the breast etc. in the first reel might be cooled somewhat.[51]

Montgomery's remark that the relationship between Odette and the 'brute' is 'hardly conceivable,' and the film would be improved by its deletion, perhaps reveals his own desire to be overwhelmed and immersed in a world of fantasy: something he is fearful that the 'unsophisticated' working-class audience also want. Surprisingly as a viewer, it would seem that he does not want to occupy a critical distance to the on-screen events, at least in this instance.

In the 1930s, as in later decades, this policy came under strain with the developing horror genre. During 1933–1941, a total of 32 films received the 'H' rating from the BBFC. Montgomery treated these films on the basis of their suitability so as to be given general certificates. Severe cuts were ordered by Montgomery to *King Kong* (Merian C. Cooper, Ernest B. Schoedsack, 1933), which in Britain had less than a minute cut.[52] He advised that the film 'is not a "horror" to the sophisticated but it is too much for children [and that] the Renter must prune the film to enable [him] to issue a General Certificate.' Among the scenes cut were the screaming during the first encounter with Kong; the Brontosaurus mauling the man on the tree; shots of men being eaten and crushed; and, of course, the scene where Kong puts his hand in through the bedroom window and takes away the sleeping, though subsequently, screaming woman (Fay Wray).[53] When passing with cuts *The Hunchback of Notre Dame* (William Dieterle, 1939), Montgomery recorded: 'This is a horror,' and rather pathetically, and inaccurately, given his power to issue limited certificates under the Act, claimed, 'it's a pity that I can't prevent children's admission.'[54] Perhaps we see here the hidden hand of the Department of Justice forbidding him from doing so, an issue discussed in chapter 5.

Montgomery took the view that to certify a film 'fit for exhibition to Adults only would excite morbid and unhealthy curiosity, and tend to tempt the excluded categories to evade the law.' As such he believed it was not 'judicious' to do so and made an effort 'to pass only such films as are considered fit for family entertainment.'[55] Indeed, less than three months before his retirement as Film Censor in October 1940, he recalled that an 'A' certificate had never been granted by his office. This comment was made in the course of his report detailing a visit to him by the American Ambassador to Ireland, David Gray, who was seeking modifications to the cuts, outlined above, that Montgomery had demanded to *Gone with the Wind*. Gray seems to have been no more successful in his mission than the legions of distributors and exhibitors who preceded him.[56] While Montgomery may or may not have independently originated this 'General Certificate' policy, it was to remain the dominant approach of Irish film censors until the mid-1960s.

### THE CENSOR'S TREATMENT OF IRISH SUBJECTS

During this period, Ireland had almost no indigenous film industry,[57] a fact lamented by Montgomery.[58] Consequently, representations of the Irish were largely produced by foreigners, primarily British and American filmmakers. In addition to the difficulties Montgomery had with the cinematic image and mainstream narrative, these foreign- produced representations were received with hostility by him on at least two levels – those that employed stage-Irishness, and those that represented Irish history and politics. As he himself noted, the Censorship of Films Act did not give him 'power to reject insults to Ireland,'[59] therefore, in order for him to contain such images, he interpreted his brief very broadly, and at times, it can be argued, knowingly overreached his statutory powers. He banned or cut films which he deemed to be libelous, impudent, mischievous, ridiculing or contemptuous of the Irish (terms not in the Act).

The stage-Irish films that he focused on were mostly of two types, Jewish-Irish stories set in New York which had the further charge of being offensive to religious sensibilities, and Irish emigration narratives. After viewing *The Shamrock and the Rose* (Jack Nelson, 1927), which he banned, Montgomery commented negatively on the representations of the rabbi and the priest and asserted that 'we in Ireland should stop – at least in our own land – the exhibition of offensive "stage-Irish" pictures' just as 'we are banning films which hold up other nations to contempt and ridicule.'[60] Likewise, the adaptation of the hugely popular play about an Irish-American and Jewish couple, *Abie's Irish Rose* (Victor Fleming, 1929), he found not just to be a 'stage Irish-Jewish travesty of marriage,' but was 'likely to offend religious and racial susceptibilities.' He rejected it as being 'subversive to public morality,' and was supported in his decision by the Appeal Board.[61] The comedy of two Irish feuding mothers, and their children who have secretly married, set in New York, *The Callahans and the Murphys* (George Hill, 1927), which had already caused controversy among Irish groups in the USA,[62] was banned by the deputy Censor, James Holloway, a person who is more associated with the theatre than the cinema. He believed that it was 'calculated to hold the Irish people up to ridicule and contempt,' a decision once again upheld by the Appeal Board.[63] Citing the same reasons, and using identical language – the 'ridicule and contempt' of the Irish – Montgomery banned *Finnegan's Ball* (James P. Hogan, 1927), in which Irish emigrants temporarily cross the class divide in the USA, and added that he considered it 'an impertinence' for it to have even been presented for certification.[64] The emigration story *Irish Hearts* (Byron Haskin, 1927) received the same treatment from him, and later from the Appeal Board. This film opens in Ireland and has its heroine, Sheila (May McEvoy), leaving her worthless boyfriend, Emmett (Warner Richmond), to migrate with her father to America. Emmett turns up in America, but on the day they are due to marry, he jilts her for a flapper. Meanwhile, Sheila has befriended a wholesome American, Rory (Jason Robards), and they decide to get married. Though his reasons for banning the film are not known,[65] perhaps it was the exposure of the fallibility of the Irish male that proved too much for him. This is supported by his changing the title of *Kept Husbands* (Lloyd Bacon, 1931) to *Rich Wives*.[66] It would seem Hayes felt similarly in that he replaced *Are Husbands Necessary?* (Norman Taurog, 1942) with *Mr and Mrs Cugat*.[67]

Montgomery paid even closer attention to British films about the Irish than he did to their American counterparts. 'No Catholic girl,' he recorded, 'would treat marriage as Lily treats it [in *The Lily of Killarney* (George Ridgwell, 1929, GB), an adaptation of Dion Boucicault's *The Colleen Bawn*] by urging her husband to commit bigamy.' He also complained that the priest in the film 'is shown pocketing – with a meaning leer – money for the "poor box" and condoning robbery for a share of the booty. He is also shown as semi-illiterate in some of the stage-Irish' intertitles. A series of cuts were ordered to what had been described by *Bioscope*[68] as a 'modernised version' of the play to ensure that Lily was not seen offering to return her wedding ring.[69] When commenting on the sound version of the play, *Lily of Killarney* (Maurice Elvey, 1934, GB), once more he regretted 'not having power to stop Stage Irish' films, but proceeded to order a series of cuts designed to 'render the film less offensive.'[70]

Though he praised the key indigenous feature film about the War of Independence, *The Dawn* (Tom Cooper, 1936), in his annual report to the Minister for Justice,[71] he closely scrutinized films dealing with Ireland's struggle with Britain, especially adaptations of Irish 'realist' writers. For example, the two very different versions of Liam O'Flaherty's novel *The Informer* – Arthur Robison in 1929 and John Ford in 1935 – were banned by him, though Ford's film was subsequently passed with cuts by the Appeal Board. Commenting on Robison's adaptation, Montgomery said that it was a

> sordid show of Chicago gun men, armed police and prostitutes ... shown at gunplay and soliciting in the standard slum of movieland. It is offered as a realistic picture of the underworld of Dublin. It is a pity that the citizens cannot take an action against the producers for a libel on our city. I refuse to grant a certificate for the exhibition of this impudent and mischievous distortion.[72]

He was no less withering about Ford's film:

> One thing can be said with truth of the Black and Tan war, and that is that the prostitute and brothel had nothing to do with it. In this sordid but clever production, one is led to think differently. [It is] a sordid brutal travesty of the Black and Tan period. The prostitute and brothel tone which is given to the struggle is offensive and untrue. The production is very clever and artistic but it is unfit for Exhibition in this country. The issue of a cut by this censorship might be taken as … the approval of a gross libel.[73]

Some Irish-American Catholics associated with the Legion of Decency took a similar view, and when it was condemned by the Legion in Chicago in particular it led to a national controversy.[74] Montgomery passed Alfred Hitchcock's 1930 version of Sean O'Casey's Civil War play *Juno and the Paycock*, which had been the subject of controversy when first performed at the Abbey Theatre in 1924, most especially concerning how unmarried Mary Boyle becomes pregnant. (The American title of the film was *The Shame of Mary Boyle*.) This aspect of the film was probably 'cleaned-up' by Montgomery, but the film itself was too much for some citizens. When it was screened in Limerick, local Catholic activists seized and destroyed the film.[75] Ironically, Montgomery had passed uncut another controversial film, *Smiling Irish Eyes* (William A. Seiter, 1929), which was withdrawn from distribution when the Savoy Cinema, Dublin was attacked by cultural activists because of the film's 'stage-Irish' characteristics.[76] This type of direct action against such films was later condoned by Montgomery, if only ambiguously so, when he wrote in relation to the 'vulgar libel' of the Irish, *Outside of Paradise* (John H. Auer, 1937), a musical comedy mainly set in an Irish castle which also had 'risky' and 'suggestive' bedroom scenes, that 'if I were a member of an audience where an exhibitor had [the] temerity to show it, I know what I'd do.'[77]

## SOUND CINEMA AND NARRATIVE CONTINUITY

As early as his first report to the Minister for Justice in November 1924,[78] Montgomery displayed awareness of the imminence of sound cinema. Drawing attention to an article in *Kine Weekly* on spoken prologues to pictures, he proposed that in such cases 'jurisdiction … should lie with the Police or with some Dramatic Censor,' and seemed to advocate that the law as applied to the theatre be used for sound cinema. This is surprising, not least because censorship of the theatre is governed by the police who can take a prosecution against a production only *after* a play has been performed. By the time of his 1927 report, though not having a sound cinema apparatus on his premises, he had already been viewing films with synchronized sound in the Phonofilms' format, courtesy of Grand Central Picture House, O'Connell Street. When the proprietor withdrew from him this facility, he viewed them without sound, but with a copy of the scenario. Later, he ruled that all sound films must be submitted with scripts.

Montgomery alerted the department to 'great developments' in the area of sound films
and suggested that 'it may be necessary in the near future to frame regulations to meet
the new conditions.'[79] By 1929 the issue had become more urgent as he still did not
have either the technical apparatus or, it would seem, the statutory power to censor
the increasing number of sound films.

Between March and December 1929 Montgomery viewed, without hearing the
sound or reading the explanatory intertitles, a total of 158 sound features and 172
short sound films. He complained that he was unable to deduce the plot and was
obliged to stamp the certificate with the legend, 'Plot and sound not censored.'[80] As
Jenny Wyse-Power, a member of the Appeal Board, told the Senate in May 1930, without the benefit of sound there is uncertainty as to the female characters' roles: 'you do
not know what the woman's position is ... She may be the wife or she may be the mistress.'[81] One form of dealing with this situation, a later report revealed, was through
the establishment of local bodies 'all over the country' that 'visit[ed] the cinemas and
[took] the law into their own hands ... preventing some exhibitors from screening certain films.'[82] A synchronous sound apparatus was eventually installed in the censors'
viewing room in June 1930. By then, the Oireachtas had passed the Censorship of
Films (Amendment) Act, 1930 empowering the censors to censor sound films as they
would silent films.

The 1930 debate offered another opportunity for members of the Oireachtas especially Fianna Fáil TDs and Senators who, of course, were not members of the Dáil
during the previous two debates, to record their views after almost seven years of
national film censorship. One of the contributors to the debate was Fianna Fáil's Francis
Fahy TD. Admitting that he rarely went to the cinema, he registered concern at 'the
general tone or the moral' of films, which, he was told by friends, was 'demoralising'.
According to him, films were 'supporting certain types of immorality' even if 'there
might not be a single scene or sentence to which you could take objection.' He called
for the general tone of a film to be censored, as it 'might upset the whole teaching
received in the schools, nationally and morally.'[83] Professor Alton TD, a member of
the Appeal Board, responded by saying that 'the general tone' of a film was always
taken into consideration by the Board.[84] In calling for a more strict interpretation of
the Act, Thomas Derrig TD, who became Fianna Fáil's first Minister for Education in
1932 and served in that post until 1948, declared that there 'should be a definite ruling
with regard to modern society dramas, shooting scenes, night club life and bedroom
scenes.' He demanded that children be excluded from all films 'which are simply a
mass of corruption from beginning to end.'[85] He also suggested that TDs be given the
opportunity to attend the Censor's screenings and pass comments on the films, a proposal ignored by the Minister for Justice.[86] During the Senate debate Chairman of the
Appeal Board J.T. O'Farrell, articulated some of the dilemmas which he thought the
Board faced.

It is hard to say what type of mentality one should take as a standard. It is
said you may pass certain [types of films] for cities which you cannot pass for

a simple country population, but against that is the argument: are you to take the simplest mentality of the whole country as a standard upon which you should base your judgement in all cases?[87]

Montgomery, supported by the Appeal Board, clearly took the 'simplest mentality ... as a standard' and set his face against both adult/children and urban/rural distinctions in film certification.

In his report for 1931, Montgomery complained that the difficulties of censorship had 'increased considerably' with the advent of sound cinema, but it was not so much in the way articulated by members of the Oireachtas. In the past he had been able to delete 'objectionable scenes and subtitles, or to amend subtitles ... without spoiling continuity.' It was 'comparably easy to preserve the main theme; as the objectionable parts were very often over-statements (a common fault of entertainments designed for the inattentive), or spicy additions, which had little or no bearing on the story.' Indeed, as was the case with *Odette*, he had proudly regarded his sanitizing of the film as improving it. This approach was no longer possible to the same degree: 'Dialogue and incident are now so interwoven that a film which might be salved by deletions under the old conditions, must be rejected.' To justify the extent of his bannings in 1930 and 1931, Montgomery continued in his characteristic paternalistic style that 'total rejection in many cases is fairer to the Cinema public, than the passing of a mutilated story; besides, cuts are so obvious that they defeat the object of censorship, by exciting morbid curiosity regarding the parts eliminated.' He correctly realized that censorship or any form of repression only works if that which is repressed is completely eradicated and does not draw attention to itself. He pointed to the further difficulty with Sound on Disc films as it was technically impossible to erase the sound from the disc. Montgomery restated that 'the principal reasons for cuts and rejections were stories enlisting sympathy for divorce and bigamy, cynical episodes of marital infidelity, semi-nudity, indecent costumes, suggestive songs and dances, and intimate bedroom scenes.' He also made reference to the fact that 'the growing tendency to portray brutality and degradation' had even provoked a warning to film producers from the British Board of Film Censors, about whose activities he was well informed.[88]

In a repeat of the concerns he expressed in 1930 about the effect cutting was having on narrative continuity, Montgomery reported to the minister the following year, when he banned 208 films, the 'complete displacement' of silent by sound films. Characteristically, he transferred blame for his extensive culling on to film producers and the cinema audience:

> The 'talkie' goes far beyond the limits of reticence imposed by common decency or even the very free stage plays of to-day... I am not trying to say that the morality of the stage is superior to the 'talkies,' but it must be remembered that the stage attracts a sophisticated adult audience and that the following of the development of a play calls for the exercise of thought.

To reach this 'unsophisticated' audience, a cinema of narrative integration was developed, which according to Montgomery's misreading of it, blinded as he was by social elitism, is not within the tradition of nineteenth-century literary realism, but is entirely new:

> In order to bring its stories within the grasp of the meanest and inattentive intelligence a convention called 'continuity' has evolved. It is the effort of the machine to provide for its votaries a substitute for the thought which is essential to the stage play. When imagination will create a mental bridge between dramatic episodes on the stage – the cinema leaves no hiatus, it projects a literal continuity of realistic events – an emphasis [on] the obvious.[89]

By now Montgomery was becoming concerned about audience awareness of the censors' actions. 'It is not my business to sub-edit a film in order to preserve continuity,' he argued. 'I feel that my duty ends when I indicate the parts of a film which are forbidden by the Act. I try in most cases to "save" the story, but many complaints are justly made by the public of irritating and apparent cuts.' He then tried to blame the renters for the problem, who 'with the exercise of care and judgement could secure coherency.' If the renter 'feels that the ordered deletions will spoil the film, he should refuse to show it.' He repeated that 'the public has become so accustomed to literal continuity, that any effort to break away from it is resented.' Interestingly, he added that 'efforts of advanced Directors to produce films which call for intelligent attention, lead people to blame the Censor for "cuts" which were never in the film.'[90] But then all cinema, to varying degrees, functions by oscillating between an opening up and closure or denial of desire. It is from these gaps, the spaces of uncompleted desire, that the audience derives pleasure, and not just from the fullness or clarity of knowledge they may have of the plot. While suture theory may argue that classical cinema through its continuity editing works to contain or stitch the spectator into the film's world, it remains the case that the multiple possibilities imagined by spectators of each scene cannot be shown. This is because the director (within mainstream classical cinema) is forced to operate according to a linear logic and is required to make a single choice: only one ending is screened. Consequently, no censor can ever succeed in repressing the viewer's desire.

In observing that silent cinema might possibly have become an 'independent art,' Montgomery noted that a number of 'difficult' stories had been '"cleaned" effectively'. Since sound cinema was 'a parasite' of the theatre, film producers 'gave us "back stage" ad nauseam.' Seeing the often very erotic early musicals which were to give Montgomery and his successors such difficulty, he reported that 'we are surfeited with reproductions of sexy stage plays filmed from a footlight angle, but with an added realism foreign to the stage.' He also condemned 'realistic' gangster dramas, early sound cinema's most successful genre, as well as the frequent 'intimate scenes of eroticism, and gruesome details of crime' in films.[91] For example, he cut further the already-cut version of *The Public Enemy* (William A. Wellman, 1931).[92] Lamenting the fact in his report

1 *The Woman who Married Clark Gable* (Thaddeus O'Sullivan, 1985, Ireland)
Set in 1930s Dublin, this short film suggests the importance of the cinema (even if in, as we now know, a crudely truncated form) as a means to escape repressive reality. Validating the censors' anxiety around imitative behaviour, George (Bob Hoskins) 'becomes' Clark Gable for his wife Mary (Brenda Fricker).

2 Façade of the Volta Cinema, 45 Mary Street, Dublin.
The first dedicated cinema in Ireland, it was opened on 20 December 1909 and managed briefly by writer James Joyce before he returned to his home in Trieste. It acted as a catalyst for the rapid expansion of film exhibition and distribution in Ireland during the 1910s, and it continued as a cinema until the late 1940s.

3 The sumptuous interior of the Savoy Cinema, O'Connell Street, Dublin, designed by architect Mitchell of London, opened in 1929. The safety curtain featured a painting of the Doge's palace in Venice, the proscenium arch echoed a Venetian bridge, the dark blue ceiling which was lit indirectly suggested a night sky, while the balconies and windows were of a florid Venetian design.

4 'The most elaborate and outrageous atmospheric interior in Ireland' was that of the Savoy Cinema, St Patrick's Street, Cork, designed by Moore and Crabtree (1931–32). Like the Savoy, Dublin it had a Venetian theme. The safety curtain featured a painting of the Grand Canal, Italianate frescoes adorned the walls, the proscenium arch was rendered as a Venetian bridge, 'with a "Romeo and Juliet" balcony,' while 'Mannerist brackets, sugar-stick columns and balustrading' made it 'a true palace of fantasy and dreams.' (Sean Rothery, 1991:193.)

5  The Ritz Cinema, Athlone, Co. Westmeath, designed by Michael Scott (1938–39). While many of the
cinema exteriors were relatively restrained, with the notable exceptions of the flamboyant Art Deco-styled
Savoy, Cork, or the Carlton, Theatre Royal and Regal in Dublin, the Ritz, incorporating many of the features
of modern Dutch architecture – 'with its white walls, large areas of glass, flat roofs and porthole windows' –
must have appeared 'an exotic, exciting and even bizarre newcomer to [the] old market town.' (Sean Rothery,
1991:192.)

6  The Green Cinema, St Stephen's Green, Dublin, designed by Jones and Kelly (1934–35). Like many Irish
cinemas, the exterior, four storeys high with horizontal steel windows, was unremarkable, but the interior
which remained intact until the 1970s was 'pure and polished Art Deco … with a splendid curved false ceiling, housing concealed lighting.' (Sean Rothery, 1991:190.)

**7** James Montgomery, Official Film Censor, 1923–1940
Ireland's first and longest serving Film Censor who, guided by theological certainty, set a strict moral blue-print that remained largely in place until the mid-1960s. Unlike many of those who followed, he knew, perhaps too well, the seductive and dangerous power of the cinematic image.

8 Dr Richard Hayes, Official Film Censor, 1940–1954
Though he appreciated the usefulness of limited certification (something resolutely rejected at Governmental level), he conscientiously continued the policy of assessing cinema according to traditional Christian moral law and the dominant ideology of the sanctity of the (Irish) family.

9 Dr Martin Brennan, Official Film Censor, 1954–1956
Despite the cultural changes that had occurred, if not in Ireland, certainly in cinematic representations and the emergence of a youth culture, Brennan, the shortest-serving Censor, was perhaps more strict than his predecessors, and seemed particularly concerned with the family and the role of women.

10 Liam O'Hora, Official Film Censor, 1956–1964
Though faced with an increasing number of adult films, he was constrained by his employers, the Department of Justice, from issuing limited certificates. Consequently, he remained within the increasingly anachronistic mould of his predecessors.

11 Dr Christopher Macken, Official Film Censor, 1964–1972
At a time of increased thematic boldness, he sought to hold back the wave of liberalism in the cinema, and with a reforming Appeal Board appointed shortly after he became Censor, a major chasm emerged between the two branches of censorship. Macken is seen here in his role as a Fianna Fáil Councillor and Dublin's Deputy Lord Mayor in the early 1960s.

12 Judge Conor Maguire, Chairman of the Censorship of Films Appeal Board (1965–1973) and Dermot Breen, Official Film Censor (1972–1978)
As chairman of the Appeal Board, Maguire carried through the new policy of issuing limited certificates, a practice consolidated by Breen, who was the first appointee with a background in the cinema.

**13** Frank Hall, Official Film Censor, 1978–1986

Another transitional figure, who, despite shades of liberalism, remained bound by a conservative attitude particularly evident with regard to representations of the church and 'problematic' areas of sexuality including birth control, abortion, and homosexuality.

**14** Sheamus Smith, Official Film Censor, 1986–2003

Notwithstanding the loosening up of censorship visible from Breen onwards, Smith was the first liberal Film Censor. He tried to avoid the cutting of films, and reinterpreted his role as that of classifier. Although he banned relatively few films, some of these decisions were controversial.

15  John Kelleher, Official Film Censor, 2003–
Building on the liberal agenda of his predecessor, he is continuing to move away more fully from notions around censorship as state protectionism to those of transparency and of servicing the public by way of providing a consumer guide to the films certified. By now, morality, or at least a (strict) Catholic nationalist interpretation of it, has been replaced by consumerism, a fitting reflection of the new Ireland, which contrasts with the immediate post-colonial period.

16  Official Opening by the Minister for Justice Maire Geoghegan-Quinn TD on 12 May 1994 of the extension to the Film Censor's building, Harcourt Terrace, Dublin, providing additional space for the video censors (above). Photographed left to right: John Keith, Ger Connolly, Violet Ennis, Tony Stapleton, Audrey Conlon, the Minister, Official Film Censor Sheamus Smith, Olga Bennett and Tras Honan.

17 *The Lily of Killarney* (George Ridgwell, 1929, GB)
Father Tom (Wilfred E. Shine) visits Eily O'Connor (Pamela Parr) where she is entertaining her 'husband'
Hardress Cregan (Cecil Landeau). Though passed with cuts by Montgomery, he complained that its tone 'is
anything but commendable to the Irish people.' He resented the stage Irishisms, the treatment by 'a Catholic
girl' of marriage, and the priest, a 'semi-illiterate', who is 'shown pocketing, with a meaning leer, money for
the "poor box" and condoning robbery.'

18 *Abie's Irish Rose* was rejected by Montgomery in 1929 'as subversive to public morality'.
Defying their parents, Jewish Abie Levy (Charles Rogers, centre) marries Irish Catholic Rosemary Murphy
(Nancy Carroll) in an Episcopal church. On Mr Levy's demand, they have a Jewish wedding, after which
Rosemary's father (J. Farrell MacDonald, left) arrives with a Catholic priest (Nick Cogley) for a third cere-
mony. Montgomery wrote in his report that this 'stage Irish-Jewish travesty of marriage is likely to offend reli-
gious and racial susceptibilities.'

19  *The Callahans and the Murphys* (George Hill, 1927, USA)
Controversial 'stage-Irish' comedy focusing on two feuding New York Irish mothers, one of whom, Mrs Murphy (Polly Moran) looks after her wayward boy Dan (Lawrence Gray). According to deputy Censor Joseph Holloway, who viewed it in 1927, the film was 'calculated to hold the Irish people up to ridicule and contempt'; as a result he banned it, a decision upheld after appeal.

20  *The Quiet Man* (John Ford, 1952, USA), was passed with cuts by Richard Hayes, 1952.
Bright and early, Michaeleen Oge (Barry Fitzgerald) arrives with his IRA friends (Charles B. Fitzsimons, Sean MacClory) bringing Mary Kate's (Maureen O'Hara) dowry (including most prominently a cradle) that her brother Will initially withheld. They explain that though Will agreed to this after the couple left, they did not like to disturb their 'Homeric' wedding night. The irony is that they have yet to sleep together.

**21** *Mambo* (Robert Rossen, 1954, Italy/USA)
It was not the Communist sympathies of the director that caused this unusual romance about a saleswoman who becomes a famous dancer difficulties with the Irish Censor, but the on-screen transgressive images, including that of a 'semi-nude' woman dancer, based around ritualized desire and a 'kiss'. Of, course, for Martin Brennan, the subversive nature of the dance was no doubt heightened by race.

**22** *Singin' in the Rain* (Gene Kelly, Stanley Donen, 1952, USA)
The eroticized spectacle, or the nearest simulation of actual sex, was perhaps nowhere more apparent than in the musical. From this most accomplished and self-reflexive musical, Richard Hayes, in an almost futile attempt to sanitize the film, demanded cut the shot of Clarisse's (Cyd Charisse) extended leg and of 'her raising her foot higher'. He also requested that the subsequent dance of Clarisse and Don (Gene Kelly) be 'tone[d] down'.

**23** *Incendiary Blonde* (George Marshall, 1945, USA)
If Irish censors could regard the dangerous and immoral if seductive images of dancers and others as alien to the Irish experience, this was certainly problematized in Marshall's film which is about the life of Jazz Age 'rather indecent' nightclub singer and Broadway star, real-life Irish-American Texas Guinan (Betty Hutton). She and her 'semi-nude' chorus girls were cut by Richard Hayes (1945).

**24** *Young Cassidy* (Jack Cardiff, John Ford, 1964, GB)
In this adaptation of Seán O'Casey's autobiography, Rod Taylor as Johnny Cassidy rescues Daisy Battles (Julie Christie) from a street mob and takes her home where she appears before him in a negligee. Film Censor Macken ordered the trimming of 'these shots to avoid the obvious conclusion.'

**25** *Summer of '42* (Robert Mulligan, 1971, USA)
This nostalgic coming-of-age narrative, 'told with much humour, some pathos and a profusion of schoolboy profanity', was deemed to be 'generally impermissible' and banned by the deputy Censor. When her boyfriend is killed during World War Two, lonely Jennifer O'Neill feels pity for virginal adolescent Hermie (Gary Grimes) and seduces him.

**26** *I Want a Divorce* (Ralph Murphy, 1940, USA)
Despite the film's title, the recently-married couple, Joan Blondell and Dick Powell, do not really want to separate in this light comedy. Before he issued a certificate for the film in 1941, Richard Hayes demanded that the title be changed to the moralizing *The Tragedy of Divorce*. Such a practice of re-titling was not unusual, but more generally was accompanied by cuts to the film.

**27** *Animal Crackers* (Victor Heerman, 1930, USA)
Chico (left) and Harpo (right) slug it out as Groucho and Margaret Dumont look on. The Marx Brothers with their punning, slapstick physicality and their lechery, clearly challenged Montgomery in 1931, who, struggling to 'define' the 'so many gags and so much objectionable business,' passed the film with cuts. It was, subsequently, banned by the Appeal Board when the renter appealed the cuts.

for 1931 that he had to give 'a definite reason' for refusing a certificate, he noted that 'vulgarity as an element of comedy is growing.' He found it very difficult 'to define where it insinuates itself into indecency, obscenity, or immorality,' the general criteria in the Act under which he was operating, though the word 'immorality' does not appear in the statute.[93]

Despite his uncertainty, it did not stop him from banning after initially suggesting fourteen cuts, in July 1931, the Marx Brothers' *Animal Crackers* (Victor Heerman, 1930), a rejection upheld after appeal: 'There are so many gags and so much objectionable business that I find it difficult to define them.'[94] Two years later the Marx Brothers' *Horse Feathers* (Norman McLeod, 1932) was cut in thirteen places.[95] The problematic scenes featured kissing, 'mauling,' Groucho's puns and *double entendres*, and what one writer has called Harpo's 'silent lechery'.[96] In both cases his reports focus exclusively on the films' comic if perverse content, but there is no broader discussion of comedy or the culture of laughter and its radicalizing function: 'Laughter demolishes fear and piety ... thus clear[s] the ground for an absolutely free investigation.'[97] Similarly, no mention was made of the films' non-linear structure or their *gramatica jocosa*, wherein lay – though Montgomery was unable to articulate this – what was perhaps most offensive to him, a subversion of logic and order. However, to have acknowledged this would have inadvertently forced him to reconsider his dismissive and class-based attitude to Hollywood's classical realism which operates according to the rules of cause and effect. It is the films' form as much as their comic narrative or imagery that places them within the American carnivalesque tradition, of which one of the functions is to challenge the symbolic order.[98] Put another way, carnival seeks to subvert good manners and rationality, blur borders and dismantle categories: it celebrates in-betweenness, confusion and anarchy.[99] In summary, it can be argued that Montgomery was frustrated when it came to any film which challenged the status quo, and when it came to the Marx Brothers' two pronged attack, his wit left him and he humourlessly tried to impose a 'moral order' on the anarchic and subversive events.

## THE 'CLEAN SCREEN' CAMPAIGN AND IRELAND

From the early 1920s in the USA, campaigns were initiated to force the American film industry to change the content of the films it produced. According to the campaigners, cinema should be uplifting; assert the traditional values of society; and help to reinforce its institutions. Films should steer clear of social, moral or political issues unless they asserted the status quo. The sharp end of this struggle was with regard to the adaptations of modern literature, especially the work of writers such as John Dos Passos; William Faulkner; Eugene O'Neill; Sinclair Lewis, as discussed above; F. Scott Fitzgerald, whose *The Great Gatsby* (Herbert Brenon, 1926) was banned in Ireland where it was described by the Film Censor as 'a very disagreeable story of the dirty menagerie called Society in movieland';[1] and Ernest Hemingway, whose *A Farewell to Arms* was the subject of a major controversy when made into a film[2] and was banned in Ireland in 1932. Their view of America generally undercut the pastoral, rural, anti-urban ideology of the reformers (and the Irish censor), but it was precisely these modern writers who were favoured by urban cinemagoers. Foremost among the reformers' concerns was the notion that these cinematic adaptations of the modernist novel were far more corrupting than the reader's silent mental imagery.[3]

After a series of scandals involving the private lives of Hollywood personalities, the industry itself established in 1922 a trade body, the Motion Picture Producers and Distributors of America (MPPDA) as a means of combating demands for federal film censorship and to resist organized pressure from both Protestant and Catholic quarters. This organization was headed by Will Hays, formerly Postmaster-General in a Republican Administration, who was given wide powers by the industry, and used them to insert, for example, clauses in actors' contracts governing their private lives. He also set about censoring films prior to and after production. The first attempt at formalizing censorship rules were the 11 'Don'ts' and 26 'Be Carefuls' introduced in 1927. The 'Don'ts' were: 1. Pointed profanity; 2. Nudity; 3. Illegal drug traffic; 4. Any inference of sex perversion; 5. White slavery (that is, prostitution); 6. Miscegenation; 7. Venereal diseases; 8. Childbirth scenes; 9. Children's sex organs; 10. Ridicule of clergy; and 11. Wilful offence to any nation, race or creed. The 'Be Carefuls' list included deliberate seduction of girls; men and women in bed together; the institution of marriage; rape or attempted rape; religious ceremonies; surgical operations; the national flag, and sedition.[4] It is clear from this list that prior to films reaching the Irish Film Censor extensive restrictions were imposed on film content, even if the Don'ts and Be Carefuls were treated cursorily by many producers as they were not binding on the industry. Following pressure from film trade publisher Martin Quigley, an Irish-American Catholic, with advice from Fr Daniel Lord, editor of *The Queen's Work* – a publication promoting Catholic ethics and morality among young people – and who made a name for himself in 1915 with an attack on George Bernard Shaw in *Catholic World*,[5] a self-censorship code was drawn up and adopted by Hays. Hays saw this measure as a way of incorporating the industry's critics into the production process. Popularly referred to as the Hays Code, the Motion Picture Production Code, though formally adopted by the film industry in 1930, remained voluntary and advisory.

The principles which underpinned the Code were that both Catholic and Protestant reformers

> wanted entertainment films to emphasize that the church, the government, and the family were the cornerstones of an orderly society; that success and happiness resulted from respecting and working within this system. Entertainment films ... should reinforce religious teachings that deviant behavior, whether criminal or sexual, cost violators the love and comforts of home, the intimacy of family, the solace of religion, and the protection of law. Films should be twentieth-century morality plays that illustrated proper behavior to the masses.[6]

Fr Lord, the Code's chief drafter, argued that as Hollywood films were entertainment in the first instance, they carried a special moral responsibility required of no other entertainment or communications medium:

> Their universal popularity, cutting across social, political, and economic classes and penetrating local communities, from the most sophisticated to the most remote, meant that filmmakers could not be permitted the same freedom of expression allowed producers of legitimate theatre, authors of books, or even editors of newspapers.[7]

It was conservative middle-class morality re-packaged. The Code, one historian of the Catholic church has noted, was 'hopelessly out of sympathy with the creative artistic mind of the twentieth century.'[8] Nevertheless, the Code's promoters were determined to get their way and issued detailed instructions to Hollywood as to what should, and more pertinently, should not, be in films. Audience sympathy for a wrong-doer, adulterer, criminal, or otherwise was to be squeezed from cinema. In the middle of America's worst-ever economic Depression, filmmakers were also being told not to depict unemployment, poverty, or starvation, as these subjects were deemed 'immoral' within the terms of the Code. Such a policy was a two-edged sword. On the one hand, the repression of socially-challenging films would help social stability, but, on the other hand, it indirectly encouraged a cinema of excess and glamour, epitomized by MGM in the 1930s. It must be remembered, though, that unlike in Ireland, much of American culture of this period, especially its cinema, promoted the ideology of consumerism as the contemporary form of capitalism, a policy which was deemed 'immoral' by church leaders as well as by censors in Ireland. In Ireland, too, it was the 'realism' of aspects of both American and European cinema which attracted most favourable comment.[9] The non-violent struggle of people against social exclusion (searching for jobs, housing, poverty in general) would have been welcomed in Ireland, even if deemed 'subversive' in America. In other areas, Irish censors would have been in agreement with their American counterparts, such as in the suppression of representations of contentious issues – birth control, abortion, premarital sex, divorce, or racism in America, including the lynching of African-Americans in the South – all of which were deemed propagandist by the Code's formulators.

'The Twelve Commandments'[10] as the Code's twelve sections were popularly referred to were: 1. *Crimes against the Law*: 'The technique of murder must be presented in a way that will not inspire imitation'; 'methods of crime should not be explicitly presented'; 'illegal drug traffic must never be presented'; nor should 'the use of liquor in American life, when not required by the plot or for proper characterization.' 2. *Sex*: 'The sanctity of the institution of marriage and the home shall be upheld. Pictures shall not infer that low forms of sex relationship are the accepted or common thing'; adultery 'must not be explicitly treated, or justified, or represented attractively'; 'scenes of passion ... should not be introduced when not essential to the plot'; 'excessive and lustful kissing, lustful embraces, suggestive postures and gestures, are not to

be shown'; and 'in general passion should be so treated that these scenes do not stimulate the lower and baser element'; seduction or rape 'should never be more than suggested ... and never by explicit method'; 'sex perversion or any inference to it,' white-
slavery, miscegenation, sex hygiene (that is, birth control, abortion) and scenes of actual
child birth 'are never to be presented'; and 'children's sex organs are never to be
exposed.' 3. *Vulgarity*: 'The treatment of low, disgusting, unpleasant, though not necessarily evil, subjects should be subject always to the dictates of good taste and a regard
for the sensibilities of the audience.' 4. *Obscenity*: 'Obscenity in word, gesture, reference, song, joke, or by suggestion ... is forbidden.' 5. *Profanity*: 'Pointed profanity
(this includes the words, God, Lord, Jesus, Christ – unless used reverently – Hell, S.O.B.,
damn, Gawd) ... is forbidden.' 6. *Costume*: Complete nudity 'is never permitted';
'undressing scenes should be avoided'; 'indecent or undue exposure is forbidden'; and
'dancing costumes intended to permit undue exposure or indecent movements in the
dance are forbidden.' 7. *Dances*: 'Dances suggesting or representing sexual actions or
indecent passion are forbidden'; and those which 'emphasize indecent movements are
to be regarded as obscene.' 8. *Religion*: 'No film or episode may throw ridicule on any
religious faith'; 'ministers of religion ... should not be used as comic characters or as
villains'; and 'ceremonies of any definite religion should be carefully and respectfully
handled.' 9. *Locations*: 'The treatment of bedrooms must be governed by good taste
and delicacy.' 10. *National Feelings*: 'The use of the Flag shall be consistently respect-
ful'; while 'the history, institutions, prominent people and citizenry of other nations
shall be represented fairly.' 11. *Titles*: 'Salacious, indecent, or obscene titles shall not
be used.' 12. *Repellent Subjects*: 'The following subjects must be treated within the
careful limits of good taste: actual hangings or electrocutions as legal punishments for
crime; third degree methods; brutality and possible gruesomeness; branding of people
or animals; apparent cruelty to children or animals; the sale of women, or a woman
selling her virtue; [and] surgical operations.'

The twelve sections were preceded by three general principles. Firstly, 'no picture
shall be produced which will lower the moral standards of those who see it. Hence the
sympathy of the audience should never be thrown to the side of crime, wrongdoing,
evil or sin.' Secondly, 'correct standards of life, subject only to the requirements of
drama and entertainment, shall be presented.' Thirdly, 'law, natural or human, shall
not be ridiculed, nor shall sympathy be created for its violation.'[11] While the Code was
accepted by the industry (and was one which even Montgomery approved of), with
the advent of the Depression in 1929–1930, and the introduction of sound cinema,
with its huge commitments of capital, American film producers pushed the boundaries
of what was permissible. With their profits of the 1920s turned to crippling losses in
the early 1930s (box office revenue dropped from $730 million in 1930 to $527 million in 1932), the studios often disregarded the Code and produced more risqué films,
most especially those starring Mae West. Also in the front line of controversy were the
crime genre films such as *Little Caesar* (Mervyn LeRoy, 1930), passed uncut by
Montgomery, *The Public Enemy*, and *Scarface* (Howard Hawks, 1932). Frustrated at
the failure of Hollywood to observe the Code, in 1933 the Catholic church set in motion

a campaign which was to culminate the following year in the establishment of the Legion of Decency, an organization designed to give popular backing to the Hays Office. 'The moral force of the Catholic Church,' Hays records in his memoirs, 'gave the *coup de grace* to Code-breakers.'[12] It was not moral power with which Hollywood was concerned, but the threatened economic boycott by the Legion's 11 million members who had pledged only to attend cinemas showing films with a new Production Code Administration (PCA) seal of approval. As those cinemas which accepted the new PCA policy accounted for more than 80 per cent of American cinema's box office, any large budget film had to conform to the Code or it would be excluded from the most lucrative cinemas and consequently suffer a loss.

Scripts and the finished films would now be adjudicated by a more powerful PCA run by Joseph I. Breen, an Irish-American friend of publisher Martin Quigley, Fr Lord, and many Catholic bishops, including Bishop Cantwell of Los Angeles, one of the prime movers behind the Legion of Decency. Breen, a journalist by profession, was rabidly anti-Communist and anti-Semitic, while also being a deeply religious person. He wasted no time in imposing his will on the American film industry, but it was not until 1935 that the full extent of the changes became apparent. As part of the new arrangements with Hollywood, it was agreed that the version of a film exported was the one approved of by the Legion.[13] Even so, lay and religious Catholic activists in Ireland complained about the limitations of the American campaigns as they sought further restrictions on those films approved of by the Legion of Decency and the PCA. For example, both the National Film Institute of Ireland, a Catholic body formed in 1943 which had the Papal Encyclical on the cinema, *Vigilanti Cura* (1936), as its frame of reference, and the Knights of St Columbanus, issued ratings for films already certified for commercial release in Ireland.[14]

During the hiatus in American film censorship in the early 1930s, Montgomery continued to focus in his annual reports on, as he put it in early 1933, 'the tendency of producers to cater for a sophisticated adult, rather than a general audience.' While the previous year had shown 'a marked advance in all branches of production, ... unfortunately the entertainment value in most films was in inverse ratio to their moral and ethical content: There is a steady decline, presaging an eventual contempt for Christian Standards.' He observed that the 'most charming scenes are invariably made the vehicles for insidious and subtle innuendoes.' However, he was pleased to report a drop in the number of gangster films, and those made, he observed, were divided between 'the morbid and sensational' and 'maudlin sentimentality, or to the triumph of the law.'[15] This comment anticipates the reorientation of the gangster genre from its archetypal anti-heroes of the early 1930s, such as the characters played by Edward G. Robinson and James Cagney, towards the promotion of the forces of law and order, especially the FBI, as the heroes in such films as *G-Men* (William Keighley, 1935), a film approved of by no less a person than the head of the FBI, J. Edgar Hoover, who was even consulted on the film's casting.[16] Montgomery regarded such films as 'a variant within the dangerous "Gangster" category. It has all the old sensational gun-man methods, but the halo is shifted from the "tough-guy" to the "cute-cop".'[17] Montgomery records his first encounter with the 'thriller' in 1932. This film type 'deals with the macabre, the bizarre, and the horrible. As a rule it is not sexy, but agonising scenes of cruelty and sadism are surely subversive of public morality.' Meanwhile vulgarity in comedy continued to give him trouble: 'it is a matter of definition, which makes it difficult to deal with.'[18]

In 1933 Montgomery was reporting an increase in the cutting of films – necessitating reviewing of the films – and the number of appeals. He regarded this as a reflection of the 'ever growing difficulties of censorship, owing to Hollywood's harping on sex, crime, and sly pornography.' Again, he regretted that while Hollywood was becoming more sophisticated, films suitable for 'family entertainment' were becoming fewer: 'There is a deliberate attempt to inspire erotic sensations in the adolescent, by means of "close-up" kisses, furtive sex excitements, and immodest situations slurred over by sensationality, and sensuous music.' While gangster and horror subjects were decreasing, there was an increase in stories inviting 'sympathy for the condonation of murder, of perjury to save a lover, and for taking the law in one's own hands.' These themes, he complained, 'are presented so plausibly, that it is difficult to convince some people that they are subversive of public morality, and that their poison is insidious and cumulative.'[19] The year was a watershed as the Catholic church's campaign was soon to prove successful with the Production Code finally being imposed on the American film industry. Since American cinema generally accounted for between 80 and 90 per cent of all the films released in Ireland, the long line from film script in Hollywood to the Irish Censor's offices in Dublin, contracted. Hollywood was about to make Montgomery's job much easier.

Despite the changes in Hollywood, Montgomery's report for 1934 remains gloomy, but perhaps this was to be expected as the changes in the PCA did not really take effect until the 1935 releases:

> Notwithstanding the 'Clean Screen' campaign, the number of films fit for family entertainment are [sic] not increasing. Since the advent of 'sound' the majority of pictures have evolved into absolute 'adult' fare. The problem of providing pictures fit for children seems ... to be insoluble.

As a means of encouraging children's film programmes, Montgomery established a record of films suitable for children.[20] This is somewhat ironic given his decision only to certify films suitable for this category. Indeed, in November 1934 he wrote in his report on *Men in White* (Richard Boleslavsky, 1934), a medical drama featuring an abortion which was almost certainly cut prior to submission, that 'the futility of this job sickens me. Clean screen. Moryagh!'[21] Nevertheless, the following year Montgomery could enthusiastically report that his 'pessimistic remarks about unsuitable films' made in 1934 did not apply to the 1935 releases. This change, which he correctly attributed to the 'Clean Screen' campaign, was evident in the significant drop in the banning of films – from 208 in 1931 to 58 in 1935, while in 1936, he would only ban 20 – and there were fewer appeals and re-shows. He also outlined what he believed to be an important shift in the content of films:

> The so called 'cleanliness' consists in the toning down of the erotic note ...
> One aspect of the reform is the substitution of sadism for salacity, particu-
> larly in the morbid and macabre pictures known as 'Horrors'.

According to Montgomery, horror films, 'with their unpleasing naiveté, [were] apt to
excite an amused contempt in the normal adult,' and were 'unquestionably unfit for
exhibition to children or to nervous or sensitive adults.' Though he went on to note
that such films did not offend against the Censorship of Films Act, he warned that 'if
their import continues or increases, some action may become necessary.'[22] He also reiterated his dislike of 'G-Men' films. In a letter to W. Cresswell Reilly, Chief Censor of
the Commonwealth Film Censorship in Australia, with whom he was in regular correspondence, he expressed disappointment in the 'Clean Screen' drive not having
reached English film studios.[23]

Britain was, in a way, a refining intermediary between Hollywood and the Irish
censors. It had its own industry, which supplied about 10 per cent of the films released
in Ireland; a censorship system; as well as being the distribution centre which decided
on the films (and in what version) to be sent for Irish certification. Similar to the Hays
Office, the British Board of Film Censors published criteria governing its decision-
making process. The original version of these was the 43 Rules of 1917 set down by
T.P. O'Connor. In its 1926 annual report, the BBFC set out 73 grounds in seven sections – religious, political, military, social, questions of sex, crime, and cruelty – under
which films would be cut prior to certification or banned. In the religious category, the
prohibition on the materialization of Christ was restated, while among the warnings
given were scenes with 'irreverent quotations of religious texts'; 'travesty and mockery of religious services'; 'Holy vessels amidst incongruous surroundings'; and 'comic
treatment of incidents connected with death,' or 'realism in death bed scenes.' While
many of the points in the political, military, and social categories were designed to
ensure that national institutions, such as the monarchy and the army, were represented
largely uncritically, other clauses in these categories ensured that 'Bolshevist propaganda' was not promoted, or there were no 'equivocal situations between white girls
and men of other races'; in other words, the American prohibition on miscegenation
was reinforced. Drunken people (especially women), mental institutions, workhouses,
and hospitals were to be treated with caution. Discretion was advised in relation to
'orgy scenes'; 'girls' clothes [being] pulled off, leaving them in scanty undergarments';
'men leering at exposure of women's undergarments'; abortion; 'criminal assault on
girls'; 'scenes in and connected with houses of ill-repute' (that is, brothels); and 'marital infidelity and collusive divorce.'

The 15 items in the section entitled 'Questions of Sex' were: 'The use of the phrase
"sex appeal" in subtitles; themes indicative of habitual immorality; women in alluring
or provocative attitudes; procuration; degrading exhibitions of animal passion; passionate and unrestrained embraces; incidents intended to show clearly that an outrage
[that is, a sexual assault] has been perpetrated; lecherous old men; white slave traffic;
innuendoes with a direct indecent tendency; indecorous bathroom scenes; extenuation

of a woman sacrificing her honour for money on the plea of some laudable object; female vamps; indecent wall decorations; [and] men and women in bed together.' Likewise, the section on crime which incorporated prison, executions, drug-trafficking, and suicide, was not dissimilar to its American counterpart. The final section on cruelty covered both children and animals and included a clause pertaining to girls and women fighting. Brutal fights and realistic scenes of torture were also discouraged.[24]

Despite the existence of the Hays Code and the BBFC's rules, Montgomery found himself in open confrontation with American and British distributors since his appointment. Though his attitude to American cinema began to mollify in the mid-1930s, he remained unhappy about British cinema, which saw a certain resurgence in the 1930s on the back of the quota requirements of the British Cinematograph Act, 1929. For example, in April 1937 he recorded in his report on *The Frog* (Jack Raymond, 1937, GB) that America had cut out semi-nudity, but England had not. The film had scenes with cabaret dancers over which he was in 'complete conflict' with the distributor, though Montgomery's rejection was overturned by the Appeal Board:

> The censor holds that the British notion of cabaret dancers' dress, that is brassiere, and trunks, with black stockings and garters leaving part of the leg exposed, is indecent. The renter contends that it is not, and says he will always appeal against the deletions of such shots ... This shows that British studios still rely on pornographic spice.[25]

Nevertheless, during his last five years in office, Montgomery continued to report positively to the Minister for Justice on the 'continuance of the "Clean Screen" Crusade' in the USA.[26] However, he also recorded his disquiet at horror films during 1935 and 1936, and pointed to evidence of 'eroticism [having] been replaced by an undoubted note of cruelty,'[27] and, ever-alert, detected in 1938 'a tendency ... to return to the old "Happy Ending" secured by divorce.'[28] Nevertheless, the same year he praised 'a few really excellent films' that had been made in England. In 1939, his last full year as Film Censor, Montgomery could report that the 'influence of the "Clean Screen" movement still prevails.' There were only 13 appeals on moral grounds compared to 23 in 1938.[29]

By the end of his term, therefore, Montgomery was satisfied on a number of fronts: he had comprehensively imposed his will on Irish film exhibition, while gaining the support of the Appeal Board, and the confidence of Ministers for Justice and civil servants. In fact, he regarded his last decade in office as a 'sinecure' after seven years of 'chaos'.[30] He had also evolved the office into one of social prestige, which is clearly reflected in the booklet printed to commemorate his retirement as Film Censor at the age of 70. President Douglas Hyde led the tribute of more than 250 people from all walks of life, as well as film companies, including those with whom he had been in closest combat. Among those contributing to Montgomery's retirement fund of almost £650 were exhibitors and distributors, including British Lion, MGM, Paramount, Pathé, RKO Radio, 20th Century-Fox, and United Artists.[31] It was hardly affection which led to this display of largesse; it was more like good politics.

## JAMES MONTGOMERY'S LEGACY

T.C. Murray, a close friend and member of the Appeal Board, described James Montgomery as 'a deeply reflective and profoundly religious man,' in an obituary in the *Irish Press* in 1943.[32] The *Irish Times* paid its respects to him in a front page article by suggesting that the non-controversial nature of his decisions be regarded as 'a tribute to the soundness of his judgement and to his tact and courtesy in dealing with people.' The article quoted Montgomery's own summary of his task – 'I act as a moral sieve' – and, more humorously, cited his remark that on the whole, he found the films 'more silly than sinful'. It also recorded one of the recurring themes of his term in office: 'One of the greatest dangers of our films is not the Anglicisation of Ireland but the Los Angelesation of Ireland.'[33]

This notion was central to a wide-ranging article he had contributed in 1941 to *Studies* entitled 'The Menace of Hollywood,' in which he displayed a shrill, conservative Catholicism (the Censorship of Films Act, he explained, was 'a sort of sin-filter'). He stated that while the newly-formed Irish Free State was still in danger of Anglicization, it was combating that particular influence through schools, colleges and universities as it sought 'to foster a national culture.' Hollywood films, however, were undermining this national project:

> Every evening boys and girls, from our educational institutions, crowded the Picture Houses in the cities, while in every little town – and in some remote villages – people flocked from shop and farm to the cheapest of all amusements – absorbing ideas of life, which, with few exceptions, were vulgar and sensational. Could any people for long preserve a distinct national character in [the] face of such a bombardment?[34]

For the new Irish state engaged as it was in a narrow cultural nationalist project surely this alone was a compelling argument in favour of indigenous film production. Yet the link between what the censors saw and the need for an indigenous film industry was not made by policy-makers. When a proposal came before the government in 1937 seeking support for the Abbey Theatre to work with the American theatrical group Shuberts in order to adapt Abbey plays for the screen, President Éamon de Valera, echoing American censorship campaigns to control film content at the pre-production stage, conveyed concern as to the particular plays that would be selected.[35] In something of a reprise of his 1937 statement, de Valera approved in 1946 a nominee of Archbishop McQuaid, Fr Cormac OFM, to sit on a board which would oversee production if a proposed Irish film studio was to go ahead.[36]

The *Studies* article also expressed Montgomery's reductive attitude towards the cinema. For him, the Hollywood film producer, whose object is 'mass entertainment,' must appeal

> to the dullest intellects and the smallest minds, and there is no surer sign in the world of a small mind than inattention. Therefore inattention in an audi-

ence makes for stereotyped forms of entertainment – direct, emphatic, vehement. Hence the continuous sensationalism.[37]

He blamed the coming of sound for heightened realism and contrasted Hollywood
with French and German cinemas, which, for him, had demonstrated that 'literal realism' was not essential to a successful cinema.[38] Citing Emil Jannings' performance in
*The Last Laugh* (F.W. Murnau, 1924, Germany) – though not in *The Blue Angel* (*Der
blaue Engel*, Josef von Sternberg, 1930, Germany) which he banned for its 'lustful
degeneracy'[39] – and Charlie Chaplin in *The Gold Rush* (Charlie Chaplin, 1925), he
observed that 'if only speech had been delayed a while, an admirable "silent" convention would have arrived.'[40] Conflating narrative development with moral concerns,
the article complimented the activities of the Legion of Decency. In a pointed racist
comment he declared that prior to the formation of the Legion some of the films representing 'womanhood' were

> so far below the standard of oriental morality that they lowered all decent
> conceptions of manly honour and womanly virtue. Triangle plays are the
> revolts of passion against a high ideal. They take the pleasure calculus as a
> criterion and challenge the whole Christian trend of marriage.

Censorship, Montgomery concluded, is 'as necessary as supervision is to insure pure
food and drugs.'[41]

It may seem that these attitudes were somehow an aberration, that film in Ireland
was singled out for special treatment. Yet, if we recall J.H. Whyte's summary of the
dominant ideological views of the period, we should not be too surprised as to how
vigorously cinema was controlled:

> The years 1923–37 reveal, so far as religious values are concerned, a remark-
> able consensus in Irish society. There was overwhelming agreement that tra-
> ditional Catholic values should be maintained, if necessary by legislation.
> There is no evidence that pressure was needed to bring this about: it appears
> to have been spontaneous. The two major parties, bitterly though they dif-
> fered on constitutional or economic issues, were at one on this. Mr Cosgrave
> refused to legalise divorce; Mr de Valera made it unconstitutional. Mr
> Cosgrave's government regulated films and books; Mr de Valera regulated
> dance halls. Mr Cosgrave's government forbade propaganda for the use of
> contraceptives; Mr de Valera's banned their sale or import. In all this they had
> the support of the third party in Irish politics, the Labour party. The Catholic
> populace gave no hint of protest. The Protestant minority acquiesced. The
> only real opposition came from a coterie of literary men whose impact on
> public opinion was slight.[42]

Such limited opposition did not extend to film censorship. Indeed, if a comment by
Oliver St John Gogarty during the debate on the Censorship of Films (Amendment)

Bill, 1930 is to be taken as representative of the literary establishment, there was little hope of support from that quarter for an easing of film censorship. During the course of a lengthy contribution to the debate, he 'strongly support[ed]' the minister 'in his desire to censor talkies.' He added that if the minister 'had the courage of what is the conviction of many people who dealt with censorship, he ought to abolish [sound films] utterly out of the country.' He complained that 'we allow this cosmopolitan form of attacking the emotional nature of the country to go unchecked.' For Gogarty, cinema consisted of 'the three appeals only tolerable to the mass of humanity, that is sex, blood and murder.' That, he continued, 'is the reiterated and unchanged theme of every cinema picture.'[43] Despite the one-sided nature of the Irish experience, internationally, negative attitudes to the cinema in many cases were no less severe than they were in Ireland. The Irish experience was in fact commented on favourably worldwide shortly after the introduction of the 1923 Act. It received positive comment in Italian, Australian and New Zealand newspapers, with proposals in some American cities to adopt similar measures there.[44] How then, given the extent of their power and the consensual acceptance of the restrictions on Anglo-American cinema, did the Irish censors view their achievements during the 1920s and 1930s? Surprisingly, perhaps, they regarded it in an embattled and defeatist manner.

Writing in 1944 of his experience of Irish film censorship and cinema generally, William Magennis propounded that cinema, 'in its portentous range of influence,' had become 'a sinister rival of the Universal [Roman Catholic] Church.' Its 'ideology is a degraded paganism,' he asserted. Magennis' rhetorical flourishes display not so much the success of Irish film censorship in stemming the secularist and materialist tide of Anglo-American social and cultural influences through the cinema, but despair at the impossibility of achieving the Catholic and nationalist ideological purity which he, Montgomery and other censors were seeking to realize. Despite the suppression of any films dealing sympathetically with non-traditional sexuality or urban mores, for most cinemagoers the pleasure of going to the cinema and enjoying even truncated films continued to override the strictures about the cinema's alleged pernicious influence which emanated from lay and religious anti-cinema campaigners. Montgomery, unlike Magennis' more crude Catholic nationalism, sought to appeal to a high art constituency, but his conclusions were no less pessimistic and anti-democratic, and in that, they shared with the dominant strand of the Frankfurt School epitomized in the work of Adorno, Horkheimer and Marcuse concerning the baneful effects of mass culture:

> Most arts appeal to the mature; the art of the Cinema appeals to every class – mature, immature, developed, undeveloped, law-abiding, criminal. Music has its grades for different classes; so have literature and the drama. The art of the cinema – combining, as it does, the two fundamental appeals of looking at a picture and listening to a story – at once reaches every class of society. By reason of the mobility of a film, the ease of picture distribution, and the possibility of duplicating pictures in large quantities, this art reaches places unpenetrated by other forms of art. Because of these two facts, it is difficult

to produce films for a certain class of people. The cinema theatres are built for the masses – the cultured and the rude, the young and the mature. Films, unlike books and music, can with difficulty be confined to certain selected groups.[45]

If Montgomery and Magennis could write at the end of their long censorship careers in such gloomy tones, there was little chance that the tide of challenging films in the post-War period could be held back indefinitely. Nevertheless, Montgomery's successor as Official Film Censor, Richard Hayes, continued the policies of his predecessor. While the 'Clean Screen' movement was to be swept aside in the USA and Europe in the 1950s, it was to be more than another two decades before films made for adults were released without mutilation in Ireland.

**PASSED FOR UNIVERSAL EXHIBITION.**

4 Though the likeness is not that of James Montgomery, unquestionably *Dublin Opinion*'s target was the Film Censor who confined all his decisions to general certificates, and was prolific in his cutting of films, even if his interventions often meant a radical reworking of the film's narrative.

# CHAPTER 4

# *Orthodoxy maintained*

There is a simple moral code, and there are principles on which civilisation and family life are based. Any ignoring of these or any defiance of them in a picture bans it straightaway as far as I am concerned.

Richard Hayes, *Film Censor 1940–1954*.[1]

## RESISTANCE TO CHANGE

If James Montgomery's background was an unusual one for a Film Censor, his successor, Richard Hayes, was equally remote from film culture. A medical doctor, Hayes (c.1882–1958) had played a prominent role in the Irish independence struggle. He had been imprisoned twice, the first time, after the 1916 Rising for his part in the Ashbourne, Co. Meath, engagement, and again in 1920, by which time he was the Sinn Féin MP for East Limerick and a member of the Volunteer Executive. Subsequently, he supported the Treaty and remained a member of the Dáil until 1926. In 1934, he was appointed as the government nominee to the Abbey Theatre Board by President de Valera, with whom he grew up in Bruree, Co. Limerick, a position he retained until his death. According to one historian of the Abbey Theatre, during his service, he was 'the most devoutly Catholic member of the Board.'[2] Simultaneously, he pursued a distinguished career as a writer contributing to a wide range of publications, including the *Irish Statesman*, *Dublin Magazine*, *Studies* and the *Irish Monthly*, and in 1951, he was awarded the Legion of Honour by the French government for his academic work on Irish migration to France. However, more interesting to this project is the 1918 Public Health Circular No. 1, for the Sinn Féin Public Health Department.[3] Co-authored with Kathleen Lynn it contained dire warnings about the spread of syphilis by soldiers after World War One. Given the association in Ireland between disease and foreign popular culture, it is worth quoting the ideologically-loaded assessment of the threat posed by syphilis echoing as it does the metaphors of contamination which were used by Catholics and nationalists alike to describe how the cinema wrought havoc on the putative purity of rural Ireland in particular:

> This infection will extend its ravages even to the rural districts. Official returns prove ... that [syphilis] is almost unknown in Ireland outside the British mil-

itary centres ... [However,] among a people like ours, whose blood has no immunity against it, the history of the disease elsewhere shows it will spread rapidly and extensively ... The Irish people themselves must see to it that *their* Small Nationality will not have her living children and yet unborn children stricken with a blighted curse ... We owe it to the race that we will not be guilty of a hideous national sin ... Hideous deformities of the body, more hideous deformities of the mind, moral perversities, lowered vitalities, the suffering and sense of shame made keener [for those who inherit the disease] by their guiltlessness – such is part of the disastrous legacy that no inconsiderable portion of the next generation will receive from ours unless effective measures are adopted to deal with this threatening evil.

The writers concluded that 'the problem is more of a social than a purely medical one.' They recommended that there should be compulsory detention of infected soldiers until they were cleared of the disease. On 1 November 1940, Hayes at 58 years of age, became the first government appointee as Film Censor, a position he retained until 1954 (two years beyond the retirement age of 70).

Slotting seamlessly into Montgomery's moral position, his first report to the Minister for Justice echoed his predecessor's complaints: 'I regret to note a tendency to revert to the pre-clean screen type of film. There are quite a number of lascivious dance scenes that call for drastic censorship.' 4 However, given the tone, and that subsequently Hayes refrained from making any such generalized statements, Montgomery may have contributed to this report. In fact, Montgomery acted as an adviser and deputy Censor to Hayes until at least November 1942, four months before his death. Indeed Hayes' refusal throughout his career as Censor to offer substantial comment or analysis only allows evaluation to be made on the basis of the decision itself. Little access is given to the censorship process.

At a cultural level, the Second World War triggered, or at least coincided with a paradigmatic shift. Defined schematically, the new culture was more aggressively consumerist and promoted in its various forms, the culture of desire. If the 'New Look' of fashion through its characteristic ultra-feminine curves seemed to epitomize the new cultural norm, no less so did music and films, which increasingly began to represent more sexually- and erotically-explicit roles for women and men, and later sexualized youths. While American post-war film, the dominant cinema in Ireland, was characterized by an uncertainty of direction in that it offered, at one level, the politically informed 'New Movie' of directors such as Elia Kazan, at another, the big budget spectacle which celebrated technology (3D, widescreen, CinemaScope, etc.), and yet another, the youth films which challenged traditional values and promoted the immature hero epitomized by James Dean. Nevertheless, each of these forms were bound together in an attempt to still the decline of the audience which was migrating geographically to the suburbs, and culturally to television. If in their various approaches they never fully succeeded, they did move filmmaking out of a pre-war classicism and, in terms of content, as was the case with much literature and theatre of the period which was often the source for the more challenging films, into an adult world which freely explored sex and sexuality. It was (to Hayes' discomfort) during this period that adult films became an established part of European and American cinemas. In many western countries, such films, made as they were with an adult audience in mind, were categorized according to the age of the viewer. In 1951, Britain changed its classification system to accommodate the new trends. Whereas the 'A' certificate in use since 1913 had allowed under-16s to attend a film accompanied by a parent or guardian, and the 'H' certificate regulated horror films, the new 'X' certificate banned under-16s from attending such films. 'X' certificates were designed to restrict 'sordid films dealing with unpleasant subjects,' but were also intended to allow films 'which, while not being suitable for children, [were] good adult entertainment and [were] films which [would] appeal to an intelligent public.'5

As noted in the previous chapter, Montgomery, during his seventeen years as Irish Film Censor, had only issued general certificates, which were equivalent to the BBFC's 'U', or universal certificate. Limited certificates, he explained in his retirement, 'might arouse the curiosity of adolescents – at a dangerous age – and tempt them to gain admission to a Picture House under false pretences – thus fostering a contempt for the law.'6

His justification was based on an awareness that censorship which is made explicit (in this case through classification) actually accentuates rather than erases that which has been deemed morally or otherwise offensive. For Montgomery, of course, it was sexuality rather than legality that was of most concern. Despite the practice of refusing limited certificates it was only in 1945, for the first time, it was given official articulation. The Minister for Justice, Gerald Boland, told the Dáil that it was the view of the Official Censor and the Appeal Board that such certificates would serve only to 'arouse unhealthy curiosity'. Consequently, he reported, the censors 'thought it better to endeavour to ensure that no film is passed if it contains anything which would be seriously injurious to young minds.'7

However, during the previous few years, Hayes had recorded his regret at not being able to issue adult certificates, especially for horror films. On one occasion in 1943 he extracted a promise from an exhibitor that under-15s would not be admitted to *Dr Renault's Secret* (Harry Lachman, 1942),8 a film in which a scientist, reversing Darwinism, turns a human into an apeman. This arrangement clearly proved unsatisfactory, as six months later in his report on *The Return of the Vampire* (Lew Landers, 1943), he complained that 'guarantees from renters about excluding children from these [horror films] are useless and [are] not observed.'9 Again in 1944 he reiterated his concern stating that he would have passed *House of Frankenstein* (Erle C. Kenton, 1944) despite its 'unhealthy atmosphere of terror and horror,' with an over-16s limit, but, in a blatant denial of the powers available to the police under the 1923 Act, he argued that there was 'no machinery for enforcing' such a restriction.10 The following month Hayes also refused a certificate to the 'fantastic' and 'distinctly irreverent' *Between Two Worlds* (Edward A. Blatt, 1944) which dealt 'rather frivolously (and skittishly) with the question of life after death,' and was open to misinterpretation by young people. As was the case with *House of Frankenstein*, he displaced his part in banning the film on to 'prevailing circumstances' or the inadequate state policy of the failure to make arrangements to show the film 'exclusively to adults.'[11] Nevertheless, both films were subsequently passed with general certificates by the Appeal Board. Perhaps as a result of the Appeal Board's more lenient policy, he passed with cuts the horror film *The White Gorilla* (Harry Fraser, 1946) in 1946,[12] but aware that the BBFC certified it as an 'Adults Only' film, he advised that Irish exhibitors 'should surely exercise some discretion regarding the admission of children.' Given Hayes' desire to use, if sparingly, restricted certification and the provisions for doing so under the 1923 Act (albeit publicly denied), it was, as became evident almost fifteen years later, and which is discussed in the next chapter, undoubtedly the Censor's masters in the Department of Justice who closed down this option. Indeed, the minister's view of limited certificates as dangerous and 'arousing unhealthy curiosity' remained unchanged throughout Hayes' career. Speaking in December 1953, at the end of Hayes' tenure, only the slightest modification of the 1945 position could be registered, whereas in 1945 Boland had declared that they had 'never' been issued, in 1953 he reported that they were 'seldom' issued.[13] Thus, while Hayes' references to the limitations of general certificates indicated a greater flexibility and openness than his predecessor to limited certificates – a policy shift he would have welcomed with regard to European cinema – his mentors clearly refused to sanction any substantial change to the general certificates' policy.

Notwithstanding the minister's 1945 Dáil speech, Hayes, writing in 1947 about Marcel Carné's *homage* to the theatre, *Les Enfants du Paradis* (*Children of Paradise*, 1945, France), again articulated his desire for a more sophisticated classification, noting that though he 'would have little hesitation in granting it a certificate for adult audiences,' he could not recommend it for '*universal* exhibition'.[14] In this swansong of French Poetic Realism, actress Nathalie (Maria Cassarès) loves mime artist Baptiste (Jean-Louis Barrault), who loves the enigmatic and unknowable Garance (Arletty), who in turn has many lovers including a murderer, Lacenaire (Marcel Herrand), an actor, Frédérick Lemaître (Pierre Brasseur), and wealthy Count de Montray (Louis Salou), with whom she lives unmarried. Garance goes away for six years with the Count, but on her return to Paris, she and Baptiste express their love for each other. However, by this time, he has already married Nathalie with whom he has a child. Unsurprisingly, whatever the merits of this 'outstanding' film, it was for Hayes automatically debarred from general exhibition because Garance was 'a lady without moral sense and with many lovers,' and not even the film's 'delicate' and subtle treatment could save it. The film went to the Appeal Board, which passed it with five cuts, including the final scene in which Baptiste's attempt to follow the departing Garance was deleted, thus suppressing for Irish audiences their continuing love for each other, and maintaining the illusion that he and Nathalie would remain married. The relative generosity and understanding expressed by Hayes and the Appeal Board towards *Les Enfants du Paradis* was not, in general, extended to American cinema (another indication of the social class bias of censorship).

Writing about *Kiss Tomorrow Goodbye* (Gordon Douglas, 1950), its low art origins allowed Hayes to dismiss it as 'a brutal gangster film without a redeeming feature,' and comment that even if there were an adult certificate 'the picture [would still be] unfit for presentation.'[15] Such an attitude prevailed when discussing other challenging realist dramas of the post-war years and, it seems, with the notable exception of *The Snake Pit* (Anatole Litvak, 1948), Hayes had largely abandoned any attempt to introduce limited certificates by the late-1940s. He continued to observe that certain films were 'unsuitable for general presentation,' and, as a result, he banned them, such as in the case of William Wyler's tale of 'marital infidelity' with Jennifer Jones and Laurence Olivier, *Carrie* (1952), 'a picture in which it is impossible to do sufficient cutting to make it unobjectionable.'[16]

This effective, if crude, solution was revised for the pioneering film about mental illness, *The Snake Pit*, which, notwithstanding Hayes' appraisal of it as 'a very fine film,' was in its original version banned by both him and the Appeal Board. The film centres on Virginia (Olivia de Havilland, who won an Oscar for her performance), who marries Robert (Mark Stevens), but, incapable of coping with married life, is hospitalized where she receives the horrific electro-shock treatment. However, under the care of the sympathetic Freudian analyst, Dr Kick (Leo Genn), who traces her illness to childhood trauma, she recovers and is reconciled with her husband.

In his report, Hayes noted that while 'from beginning to end there is nothing said or shown infringing on the moral law or in any way liable to deprave or corrupt,' but, 'in this country where there is only [one] Cert, the picture may not be a fitting one for *general* presentation.' Acknowledging that he may have 'viewed it too severely from a strict medical standpoint,' he refused a certificate 'with some reluctance and misgiving'.[17] The Appeal Board were of a similar view and 'very regretfully' banned the film.[18] No doubt this response encouraged the distributor to submit a 'revised' version (the distributor's cuts are not listed in the reports), and in September 1949, six months after originally viewing it, Hayes passed the 'revised' film with fourteen additional cuts, mainly of dialogue. Among the cuts demanded was of a scene in which Virginia is put in a strait-jacket after being terrorized by a sadistic nurse, who, in a familiar trope of this subgenre of asylum-horror which includes the German expressionist *The Cabinet of Dr Caligari* (Robert Wiene, 1919), is later incarcerated as a mental patient. More interestingly, Hayes also attached two conditions to the certificate.

The managing-director of distributors 20th Century-Fox, as well as exhibitors, were obliged to sign an 'agreement form' then in use in England accepting that the film was to be treated 'as an *Adult* film, i.e., children under 18 are not to be admitted to its presentation.' A notice to this effect was to be exhibited 'prominently' in the foyer of every theatre where the film was showing. Additionally, exhibition of the film was to be restricted to cities and towns of over 5,000 persons.[19] This somewhat unique geographical condition arguably makes explicit censorship as cultural infantilization, revealing the attempt to insulate rural Ireland from the modern world, or, more broadly, exposes the fragility with which such areas were viewed. Generally speaking, the main threat posed by the modern world, at least from the censors' viewpoint in the 1940s and 1950s, came from representations of the break-up of the nuclear family and expressions of physical pleasure between the sexes. More sinisterly, Hayes' concern that the scenes in the mental hospital were too 'realistic' from an Irish perspective may also reveal his own awareness of the appalling conditions in Irish mental hospitals at this time, something which the society at large did not wish to confront. The caring treatment of Dr Kick is sharply contrasted by the scenes in the overcrowded state-run asylum with its often cruel regime. Such a geographical quarantine was applied on at least one other occasion when, in 1962, the originally banned French film *Le Defroqué* (*The Renegade Priest*, Léo Joannon, 1953), featuring an 'unfrocked priest,' was restricted by Film Censor Liam O'Hora to over-18s in the towns of Dublin, Cork and Limerick.[20]

### THE OLD RELIABLES

As already shown, Hayes did try, albeit half-heartedly, to modernize the Irish film censorship regime, though his complaints to distributors about general certificates as expressed in his reports were not followed up by action. Indeed, in an interview which Hayes gave to *The Bell* – a non-sectarian and liberal literary publication, edited by Seán Ó Faoláin, which was a leading critic of the Censorship of Publications Act – nine months after his appointment as Film Censor, he declared a strong preference for European 'art' cinema and French films in particular.[21] He recalled how he had recently viewed an unnamed French film and with considerable regret felt obliged to ban it because of its themes: 'It was filled with adultery and abortions and God knows what. But what acting, what wonderful restraint! It gave me a real pang to have to reject it. I don't think I've ever seen such beautiful photography, such exquisite acting.' Reiterating his disdain for 'vulgar' American cinema, he added that he found himself 'wondering if, after all, it wouldn't be less harmful to Irish morals than Hollywood.'[22] However, most Irish film releases were American and Hayes could not continue Montgomery's absolutist policy. Not only was the film industry changing worldwide in the post-war years, but Irish society was slowly beginning to awaken from its protectionist slumber.

Nevertheless, Hayes applied the 'family first and last' policy to European cinema as much as to its American and British counterparts. In 1943 Dublin's Astor Cinema, the picture house which most frequently showed European or specialist films at this time, advertised Marcel Pagnol's *La Femme du Boulanger* (*The Baker's Wife*, 1938, France) as an over-18s film even though such a condition was not attached to the certificate and seems to have been one of Hayes' 'informal' limited certificates. The (Catholic) *Standard* reported the cinema's manager as saying that it was the Censor who had imposed an adults only restriction, but Hayes pointed out that the film had received a normal 'suitable for public exhibition' certificate, although he added, that the exhibitor had been advised to 'show discretion as regards the audience.' In any case, the *Standard* could observe that the film as screened was no longer *The Baker's Wife*, but 'only the Baker'. All that remained of 'the wife's unsavoury intrigue' was enough 'to justify the powerful interpretation by Raimu of the husband who has overwhelming proof yet refuses to accept the fact that his wife has been unfaithful.' It was 'not a very savoury theme,' and some of the French dialogue and English sub-titles were still deemed objectionable.²³ Besides cutting the scenes of the wife's sexual desire and adultery, Hayes also cut shots of a priest being carried on a teacher's back, and a sermon by the priest.²⁴ While the wife's adultery in the film was reduced by Hayes to the husband's point-of-view, it does serve to highlight the type of pressure on the Censor which became increasingly common during the post-war period. However, his relative sympathy for French cinema (he was, after all, a Francophile) did not extend to other European, never mind American or British, cinemas.

As themes such as adultery or sexual promiscuity more frequently became the subject-matter of European, American and British cinemas, the distance grew between what Irish audiences were allowed to see and what was available elsewhere. In *The Bell* interview, Hayes said, in comments which could easily be attributed to Montgomery, that he did not maintain 'crime and sordid themes should be banned in the Cinema no more than they should be in the theatre,' but, he declared, 'evil must not be presented in the guise of good, and when presented must not tend to be debasing or subversive.' Like his predecessor, who had sought unsuccessfully to contain the power of the image, he said that it was not usually dialogue but visuals which were most regularly cut. Top of his agenda in this regard was 'lascivious dances' of which he believed there was an 'appalling spate' in most of the big American musicals. 'Vulgarity' is what he found in them.²⁵ While Montgomery described Dorothy Arzner's musical *Dance, Girl, Dance* (1940) – a film that was later claimed as a 'progressive' text by feminist film critics²⁶ – as harking 'back to the monkey house morality of 1931' and banned it,²⁷ when re-submitted to Hayes a few months later he too rejected it, a ban upheld after appeal. Likewise, 'lascivious' dances were cut from Busby Berkeley's *Strike up the Band* (1940),²⁸ while the can-can, the rhumba, the boogie-woogie, and the jitterbug were also cut from films. Even the documentary *Fishing in Hawaii* had two shots of a hula dance trimmed.²⁹ 'Semi-nude girls' also continued to be cut from musicals, including in the popular *Road* movies series, starring Bob Hope and Bing Crosby, at least four of which were trimmed.³⁰ Irish-American musical stories were not free from the Censor's scissors with cuts to *Sweet Rosie O'Grady* (Irving Cummings, 1943),³¹ *Shine On Harvest Moon* (David Butler, 1944),³² and *Incendiary Blonde* (George Marshall, 1945),³³ while one of the most erotic scenes in the innovative musical *Singin' in the Rain* (Gene Kelly, Stanley Donen, 1952) was mutilated. In this film, Clarisse (Cyd Charisse) is introduced through the camera following her extended stockinged leg as she raises her foot, a shot which was cut, but which, 'narratively', attracts Don (Gene Kelly). Their subsequent dance, especially when she drops to the floor, was also cut. Overall, the consequence of the excisions was to damage the balance of the whole number.³⁴

The 'unpleasantness' of many films, Hayes told *The Bell*, could be traced back to 'frivolity'. The treatment of divorce, he maintained, illustrated this, implying that it was not a fit subject for humorous entertainment. Bearing in mind Irish people's attitude to divorce, he said that 'one has … to be very careful not to allow any light or frivolous treatment of marriage to appear on the screen.'³⁵ As a result, Hayes reported that in July 1941, shortly before his interview, he had ordered the title of the social comedy *I Want a Divorce* (Ralph Murphy, 1940) to be retitled *The Tragedy of Divorce*.[36] He also changed the titles of other comedies: *Honeymoon For Three* (Lloyd Bacon, 1941) became *Easy to Love*,[37] *Married Bachelor* (Edward Buzzell, 1941) became *A Bachelor Looks at Marriage*,[38] *The Night Before the Divorce* (Robert Siodmak, 1941) was shorten to *The Night Before*,[39] and *Misbehaving Husbands* became *Henry Goes Haywire*.[40]

Despite these changes, he told the interviewer, he had been criticized 'in several quarters' for permitting films dealing with divorce although they were pictures in which the subject was treated seriously. In his defence of limited references to divorce, Hayes declared that since such pictures illustrated a life so far removed from that in Ireland they were 'on an almost entirely different plane.' Such apparent liberalism was, of course, tempered by Hayes' manicheanism and provincialism.

> I say it emphatically – that each film in which divorce is a feature ought to be judged by one standard alone: Is it an incentive to Divorce or does it condone it – ennoble it in any way? If it does either of these things, then it is not a film for the Irish public.[41]

The impression Hayes gives in *The Bell* interview is of a person seeking to be more open and liberal as regards previously forbidden topics, but this public face is not evident in the generality of his decisions, such as with his attitude to limited certificates.

In his initial report after rejecting *Accent on Love* (Ray McCarey, 1941) in October 1941 he commented that divorce is presented 'as a desirable refuge from marital troubles' and that 'the marriage bond is treated lightly.' Consequently, he held that 'its attitude to divorce offends the civil and moral law of this State.' A month later, the film was cut and passed, no doubt with all references to divorce deleted from the film.[42] After banning *Skylark* (Mark Sandrich, 1941) the same month, a ban upheld by the Appeal Board, he said that its 'light treatment of marriage' and 'the usual divorce denouement' made the film 'unfit for general exhibition'. He added that the 'apparent reconciliation' of the couple at the end 'does not lessen the unfitness of its presentation.'[43] Ten years later, Hayes was still maintaining as strict a policy when he viewed *Surrender* (Allan Dwan, 1950), a film which contains a range of 'unsavory' themes, including divorce and marital infidelity, 'with scarcely a redeeming feature.' He patronizingly added that only the 'most morbid' could complain about not seeing it.[44] While Montgomery occasionally allowed representations of divorce and re-marriage by 'real' historical characters, his sole concession to the issue as noted in the previous chapter, Hayes was more strict. According to him *The President's Lady* (Henry Levin, 1953), about American President Andrew Jackson who 'lives with another man's wife as her husband after a divorce,' was putting 'glamour' on their life together and 'the entire film [was] a justification of divorce.'[45] *Bad Lord Byron* (David McDonald, 1948, GB) concerned the 'notorious amours' of the infamous writer, and therefore he could not justify its release with a general certificate.[46] Like his predecessor, Hayes usually reserved the greatest opprobrium for representations of extra-marital affairs, or adultery as he preferred to call it.

William Wellman's *Roxie Hart* (1942), a comedy burlesque set in the Roaring '20s, was for Hayes 'an unsavoury picture' with its themes of 'murder, marital infidelity, disputed paternity, and finally a woman leaving her husband for another man.' He considered the film 'unpresentable to an *ordinary* audience.' (Emphasis added.)[47] John Huston's *In This Our Life* (1942) was another 'sordid picture of marital infidelities, suicide, etc.' with 'an unhealthy atmosphere ... in which all moral considerations are discarded.'[48] Elia Kazan's *The Sea of Grass* (1947), which he cut in nine places, was 'objectionable ... by reason of the marital infidelity of the "heroine", who bears a child to her lover.' The story 'is so constructed that sympathy is often aroused for her, while as well a certain glamour is put on her infidelity.'[49] Even Julien Duvivier's adaptation of Tolstoy's novel of adultery, *Anna Karenina* (1947, GB), was banned by Hayes because as presented on the screen it was 'a story of marital infidelity, adultery and suicide.' The decision was reversed by the Appeal Board, probably because of the film's literary origins rather than out of any approval of its theme.[50]

Hayes' position as regards illegitimacy, a feature of *The Sea of Grass*, was, like divorce, 'entirely a matter of presentation and approach to the subject.' If it was 'frivolous', this didacticist declared, 'out it goes.'[51] Comedies with illegitimacy storylines, such as *One Wild Oat* (Charles Saunders, 1951, GB), which 'deals with the embarrassment of a married man when confronted with the mother of a supposed illegitimate child of his,'[52] and *Honeymoon Deferred* (Mario Camerini, 1951, GB), 'eminently an Adult film,'[53] were also banned by Hayes. Others were severely cut, such as *That Night with You* (William A. Seiter, 1945), in which there was dialogue of a 'dubious and indelicate' kind regarding the paternity of the central character,' and to which he ordered fifteen cuts.[54] A story of an unwed mother who brings up her son as her 'nephew', *To Each His Own* (Mitchell Leisen, 1946), was banned, a decision supported by the Appeal Board. Hayes wrote that the illegitimate child was 'the offspring of a one day's amour between her and a flying officer.'

> The theme is worked out in such a way that *a certain sympathy is aroused right through for the mother, while a glamour is created around illegitimacy.* Though the film may be unobjectionable for adults, it is quite unsuitable for young people. (Emphasis added.)[55]

Hayes regarded the introduction of an illegitimate child towards the end of *The Corn is Green* (Irving Rapper, 1945) as 'something of an afterthought,' and as a result it was passed with fourteen cuts designed to eliminate 'what is at times the outspoken dialogue regarding the child.'[56] In 1947 Hayes banned *Her Sister's Secret* (Edgar G. Ulmer, 1946), but in an indication of the slightly more flexible approach being adopted in the post-war years by the Appeal Board, even though its composition had changed little since Montgomery's time as Censor, the ban was reversed by them,[57] something they also did with *One Wild Oat.*[58] This is surprising as *Her Sister's Secret* follows the path familiar from *To Each His Own* with a young woman getting pregnant following a brief affair with a soldier. The child is then passed off as her sister's, and 'the ruse turns out fairly successfully,' but 'such a subject is quite unsuitable for presentation.' Similarly, *Blossoms in the Dust* (Mervyn LeRoy, 1941) had cut from it the two lines: 'There are no illegitimate children. There are only illegitimate parents.' This denial by Hayes corresponds with contemporary secular and religious official attitudes, and reflects the intolerance of an era in Irish society in which any deviation from dominant patriarchal and Catholic norms was harshly treated, and when women were blamed or deemed totally responsible for illegitimate births while the role of men in such relationships was elided. It was not until the 1990s that the full horror of the Irish 'homes' where unmarried women and their children were incarcerated was exposed by personal testimonies, social historians, and television documentaries.

The related subjects of birth control and abortion continued to be totally suppressed. In *Blossoms in the Dust* there is perhaps a hint of abortion when it is stated that 'he's trying to say that motherhood in a case like your wife's is extremely dangerous,' a scene cut by Hayes.[59] From *The Doctor and the Girl* (Curtis Bernhardt, 1949) Hayes demanded that the 'preliminaries to and details of' what he euphemistically called 'an illegal operation' be cut.[60] Two years later in 1951 three other films were submitted for certificates dealing with abortion, two of which were banned, the other severely cut. *Street Corner* (Albert Kelley, 1949), which was banned, a decision upheld after appeal, was 'an indelicate film dealing with views on sex education and a young unmarried woman who finds herself about to have a child, and who goes to an abortionist.'[61] *Beyond the Forest* (King Vidor, 1949), 'an unsavoury film' featuring 'adultery, murder and abortion,' was also banned,[62] while *Detective Story* (William Wyler, 1951) was only granted a certificate after being initially banned by both Hayes and the Appeal Board. Following its re-submission to the Censor in a 'revised version' the film was approved with cuts, but no certificate was issued as the cuts demanded were so extreme that the distributor must have decided not to release it. Hayes even acknowledged this when he commented that 'the elimination of this unsavoury feature would leave the picture meaningless and without interest.' When the revised version of the film was submitted three months later in January 1952, Hayes observed that it still had 'the same objectionable features'. In the film, crusading police detective Jim McCloud (Kirk Douglas) becomes estranged from his wife Mary (Eleanor Parker) when he discovers that the abortionist whom he is pursuing had performed an abortion on his wife before she met him, and she had kept it secret from him. As a result of the operation she has been unable to have children. The cuts were designed to ensure that this central narrative element, as well as the contemporaneous death of a girl following an abortion, were suppressed.[63]

Hayes also maintained his predecessor's policy of suppressing anything to do with pregnancy, childbirth, or sexual assault, such that the words 'I'm pregnant' were deleted from Michael Curtiz's *I'll See You in My Dreams* (1952),[64] while 'Maternity' on hospital doors, as well as references to birth and to triplets were removed from *That's the Spirit* (Charles Lamont, 1945).[65] However, five years later, Hayes did allow comments about having a baby in *Mrs Mike* (Louis King, 1949), but in an echo of Montgomery's treatment of a similar event in *Gone·with the Wind*, the scene in which Kathy (Evelyn Keyes) has labour pains was cut.[66] The rape-revenge story *The Accused* (aka *Strange Deception*, William Dieterle, 1948) had its central narrative element, the attempted rape of a female academic by a student, cut by Hayes.[67] More drastically, he banned Ida Lupino's 'unsavoury film' *Outrage* (1950) because it dealt with 'a criminal assault on a girl and its psychological effects' on her, Hayes' oblique reference to rape and the trauma associated with it. He added that it was 'not a [suitable] subject for a film'[68] though this film and Lupino as director, producer and actress was later explored by feminist critics searching for a rare female voice in Hollywood in the 1940s and 1950s.[69] As a result of Hayes' actions, cinematic representations of women remained straight-jacketed within an idealized form of official ideology: happily-married, free of sexual desire, and producing children mysteriously, while men were not seen as sexual aggressors even in films dealing with sexual assault or rape.

Like Montgomery, one of the difficulties with Hayes' 'cleansing' approach to cinema was that the whole narrative logic of a film could be erased or radically transformed by him. For example, of the five cuts demanded in the adaptation of an Oscar Wilde story, *The Picture of Dorian Gray* (Albert Lewin, 1945), most were of Wilde's suggestive aphorisms, such as 'There's only one way to get rid of a temptation and that's to yield to it'; 'Faithfulness is merely laziness'; and 'I believe she loves you so much you have no need to marry her,' a comment which concerns the developing relationship between Dorian (Hurd Hatfield) and Sibyl Vane (Angela Lansbury), a young vaudevillian singer. While she is at Dorian's house, he decides to emulate his mentor's (George Sanders) behaviour and test her innocence. When he asks her not to leave him alone – 'don't go home' – she turns away from him and goes to the door. Dorian resumes playing the piano, but she returns to the drawing-room, with the clear implication that she has decided to spend the night with him. The Censor, however, cut out the phrase 'don't go home,' allowing only the sentence about not leaving him alone, thus assigning quite a different, and apparently 'pure', meaning to her actions.[70] Whatever about the transgressive nature of Hollywood sexuality, and the (minor) degree of latitude accorded to it in Ireland, when the censors were confronted with representations of non-mainstream, or even 'pagan', religious practices Catholic orthodoxy was enforced.

### RICHARD HAYES AND RELIGION

When James Montgomery viewed John Ford's well-regarded Depression-era *The Grapes of Wrath* (1939) a few months before his retirement, he cut five scenes. While three of these were brief, but still 'indelicate,' references to Rosie Shannon Joad's pregnancy, two others did not conform to his theological views. On his return home from four years in prison, Rosie's brother, Tom (Henry Fonda), meets Casey (John Carradine), an ex-preacher, who has lost the 'Call' and the 'Spirit'. Casey says, in dialogue which the Censor regarded as reflecting 'the lust of revivalism,' that at his prayer meetings he used to give the girls 'glory' until they 'about passed out and then I'd go to comfort them and always end up by loving them.' Casey continues in this vein, announcing that the Holy Spirit was 'Love,' and declaring that 'there ain't no sin ... and there ain't no virtue,' asserting that what was important was 'what people does.' His rejection of the traditional God is reinforced when he concludes that his 'heart was not into saying Grace,' even when people set out food for him. Tom laughs at his method of seducing girls and tells him he should get a wife. The linking through Casey of sex and religion within a 'pagan' framework is given credence at the end of the film when Tom tries to articulate his own philosophy which is 'pantheistic' according to Montgomery, and consequently cut. Speaking to his mother, perhaps for the last time, before he leaves the migrant labour camp, and after seeing the trials and tribulations experienced by his own family, he says that he agrees with Casey that 'a fellow ain't got a soul of his own. [He is] just a little piece of a big soul – The one big soul that belongs to everyone.' Linking this pantheistic view, that God is everything and everything is God, to social and economic justice for the poor, a radical Catholic theological position which became popular from the 1960s onwards with the advent of 'liberation theology,' he goes on to say that 'wherever there is a fight so hungry people can eat,' or 'a cop beating up a guy, I'll be there.'[71]

Hayes went a step further than Montgomery when he ordered cut entirely from Disney's classic animation film *Fantasia* (Ben Sharpsteen, 1940) the scientific talk which introduces the section depicting Igor Stravinsky's *The Rite of Spring*.[72] Instead of representing the composer's series of tribal dances – which had been controversial since its première performance in 1913, as, in Stravinsky's words, it sought 'to express primitive life' – Disney and his team decided, as the narrator puts it, to visualize it as a form of 'pageant, as the story of the growth of life on earth.' (The original ballet had featured a virgin sacrifice to prehistoric Russian gods.) It is 'a coldly accurate reproduction of what science thinks went on during the few first billion years of this planet's existence.' So, 'now imagine yourselves,' the narrator tells the viewer, 'out in space billions and billions of years ago looking down on this lonely tormented little planet spinning through an empty sea of nothingness.' Hayes declared that this speech gave 'an entirely materialistic view of the origin of life' and cut it. (Although Disney's own 1990s booklet on the film does regard this section as the 'most disturbing,' albeit the 'most modern'.[73]) The earth's origins are depicted as a molten mass and the episode continues to the extinction of the dinosaurs, with primitive dance music on the soundtrack. Somewhat similarly, Hayes demanded cut the Darwinian-view of the origin of species as expressed in the documentary *Monkey Land up the Barito* [or *Bainto*] *River*. In this film the words, 'our ancestors' and 'our forefathers' in reference to monkeys, were deleted.[74] Indeed, as late as 1958, Howard Hawks' *Monkey Business* (1952), had references to 'Darwin theory' removed,[75] while *Murder by Contract* (Irving Lerner, 1958) had the line 'the human female is descended from the monkey' cut.[76] This fundamentalist and anti-materialist view of creation inevitably ensured that any depictions of Christianity, especially Catholicism, its rituals and institutions, including the sacraments, were approached with extreme caution and sensitivity.

William A. Wellman's *The Ox-Bow Incident* (1943), for example, had a scene cut in which a Mexican is seen kneeling and making Confession,[77] while a priest reciting a Psalm was the only cut ordered to *Joan of Paris* (Robert Stevenson, 1942).[78] Vincente Minnelli's musical fantasy *Yolanda and the Thief* (1945), in which a con-artist (Fred Astaire) tries to convince a wealthy convent-educated girl (Lucille Bremer) that he is her guardian angel, was cut, including shots of a statue of an angel in a procession.[79] He banned the Michael Powell/Emeric Pressburger film set among a community of nuns in the Himalayas, *Black Narcissus* (1946, GB), because they are 'all under the spell of the sinister Oriental environment' before they 'go to pieces'. It has 'a sex atmosphere right through' it, Hayes recorded, and many would regard it as 'a travesty of convent life.' He was concerned that it would be 'misunderstood' in Ireland because they would associate it with 'the old caricatures' of convent life, a comment which, if deemed an accurate reflection of popular contemporary thinking, suggests that the fantasy projected on to the sexual dynamics in convents (either between nuns themselves or between nuns and local priests) was a widespread one. Hayes was particularly concerned with the representation of the convent's Superior, Sister Clodagh (Deborah Kerr), an Irish-born character, whom, he said, was 'more reminiscent of a Hollywood Star than of the head of a religious Order.'[80]

Whatever the justification, even the Irish box office hit, and reverential film, *The Song of Bernadette* (Henry King, 1943), about the 'apparition' seen by Bernadette Soubirous (Jennifer Jones) at Lourdes was cut in six places. Hayes ordered cut a key scene in which the sceptical dean of Lourdes (Vincent Price) enquires of Bernadette as to whether she understands what 'I am the Immaculate Conception' means after the 'Lady' in the Grotto offered this as explanation as to whom she was. The dean explains the Catholic dogma of the Immaculate Conception: how Mary 'was preserved from all stain of Original Sin even from the first instance of her presence in her mother's womb,' as she was later due to bear Jesus Christ, the Son of God. Bernadette declares that she does not understand it. The dean reflects, and states, 'Why should you,' but the continuation of his sentence was cut, '*great scholars have wracked their brains about it for centuries.*' This cut suggests Hayes regarded the (historically accurate) comment that (secular) scholars, or merely human beings, interpreting the actions of God was contrary to Catholic theology. Frustrated at his inability to use theology with Bernadette, the dean reverts to tautology (is a person an 'event' or not?) to prove her wrong:

> Perhaps you can grasp this one thing. If the Most Blessed Virgin were to speak, she could not say of herself: 'I am the Immaculate Conception.' All she could say would be: I am the fruit of the Immaculate Conception. *Birth and conception are events, but a person is not an event. You can't say I am conception, I am birth.* Consequently, your lady is guilty of an inexcusable blunder. You must admit that. (Emphasis indicates where the Censor cut the speech.)

The innocent Bernadette replies that 'the next time I see her, I will tell her, your reverence.' The exasperated dean then uses his authority to try to bring her under his power,

'As your confessor, I beseech you, renounce this falsehood,' as he seeks to get her to admit that it was family members who suggested the phrase so that she 'might become important in men's eyes.' Hayes, though, ordered cut the preface 'As your confessor' with its implied criticism of the institutional Catholic church. The dean gives up after failing to shake Bernadette's belief in the apparition. Shortly afterwards, when a Professor of Psychiatry tries to commit Bernadette to a mental hospital, the dean comes to her defence and thwarts the plans by the local imperial prosecutor (Peter Cushing) to end public support for her. Later, the dean tries again unsuccessfully to get her to retract the phrase 'I am the Immaculate Conception.'

Two other cuts concern the hostile and sceptical nun in charge of Bernadette's training in the convent, Sister Marie-Therese (Gladys Cooper), who expresses her resentment that in spite of her own (masochistic) suffering through work and prayer, she cannot believe Bernadette's story of the apparition, and asks for proof because she is overcome by the 'monsters of doubt and hate'. The serene and subservient Bernadette reveals a cancerous tumour on her own knee and later a doctor diagnoses that she has the painful condition of tuberculosis of the bone of which she has been suffering quietly. Contrite, Sister Marie-Therese hurries to the chapel where, before the altar, she confesses to not believing Bernadette and being 'filled with hate and envy'. In both scenes, Hayes demanded cut the word *hate*, suggesting that nuns, or indeed the clergy more generally, in the cinema were not allowed such negative and sinful emotions.[81]

Just as early cinema had used magic and spectacle to attract audiences to the cinema, the 1950s saw a return to a celebration of technology with the biblical epic serving as one means of helping stem the decline in cinema audiences. *Quo Vadis?* (Mervyn Le Roy, 1951) concerns the pagan and decadent lifestyle of Rome under Nero (Peter Ustinov), who is ultimately overthrown by the Christians led by Peter and Paul. Many of these films, whether Old Testament or corrupt Rome, were a means of exposing the female anatomy and bypassing Hollywood censorship. While one cinematically unusual and ideologically repulsive shot of a young woman slave passionately (and fetishistically) kissing the statue of her master was cut from *Quo Vadis?* by Hayes, two main areas were severely curtailed. Unsurprisingly, the scenes of 'decadence,' sometimes only dancing, before Nero were censored, as was the repeated observation that a young Christian woman, Lygia (Deborah Kerr), was 'too narrow in the hips' for Nero. Scenes depicting 'brutality,' including where the giant, Ursus (Buddy Baer), kills a bull in the public arena by breaking its neck in order to protect Lygia who is tied to a pole, were also cut. Towards the end of the film, Hayes cut Nero's strangling of his mistress Poppaea (Patricia Laffan), who had encouraged him to oppress the Christians, and, shortly afterwards, Acte's killing of Nero with a dagger after he proves too cowardly to do it himself as the mob attacks the palace, making a total of fifteen cuts to the film. Despite the Censor's concern at the brutality of some of the later scenes, the graphic representations of lions attacking the Christians in the arena, as well as a number of them being burned at the stake, martyrdom style, were not cut as they could be justified within masochistic if heroic Christian ideology. In both these instances, their joyful singing at the time of death, which unsettles Nero, perhaps allowed for this Christian myth to be seen even by Irish children.[82] However, these later scenes may have been cut by the distributor. Such a practice of cutting films prior to submission is clear from the treatment of Alfred Hitchcock's *I Confess* (1953), which concerns a priest, Fr Michael Logan (Montgomery Clift), who is wrongly accused of murder.[83]

In *I Confess*, Fr Logan hears a confession from a murderer and finds himself accused of the crime. In the meantime, a girlfriend from his youth and before his ordination, and now married, Ruth (Anne Baxter), seeks his help against a blackmailer. Prior to the film being submitted to Hayes, the film's distributor, Warner Bros, cut 423 feet (about five minutes) from the film, clearly demonstrating the company's sensitivity to how Catholic themes would be regarded in Ireland. Despite these cuts, Hayes banned the film, describing it as 'not a suitable one for general presentation,' though the Appeal Board later passed it.[84] The cuts by Warners represent one of the few recorded insights we have into how distributors censored films prior to submission to the Irish Censor. In this instance they were designed to suppress Ruth's relationship with Michael prior to her marrying Pierre (Roger Dann), and despite her continuing love for Michael, of which Pierre is aware. When Michael re-enters their lives after he is suspected of murder, Ruth tells Pierre that she was never, nor even pretended to be, in love with him. While this was retained by the Censor, her comment to her husband, 'You can leave me,' was cut, thus ensuring that any reference to their possible separation or divorce was denied.

Also trimmed were flashback scenes in which Ruth and Michael, years before he becomes a priest, dance and kiss prior to his leaving for the war. On his return two years later, to escape rain, he spends a night in a shelter with Ruth, who, unbeknown to him, is married. This leads to her being blackmailed by an unscrupulous lawyer, Vilette (Ovila Legare), who is in fact murdered during a robbery by Otto, an employee at the priest's residence. When Michael is silenced by Otto's admission of guilt to him in the confessional, Ruth feels obliged to reveal to the police a meeting she had with Michael in order to discuss the continuing blackmailing of her on the night Vilette was killed. Ruth arranges a further meeting with Michael to warn him that he is about to be arrested for Vilette's murder. During this meeting she expresses her continuing love for him, a scene which was completely cut by Warner Bros. Unsurprisingly, in her interview with the police her expression of love for Michael at the time of her marriage was also removed. The comment by a juror, 'I believe what the prosecutor said [that] there must have been many more times' when the lovers met, was also cut by Warners, as was a scene following his acquittal when he walks through the hostile crowd outside which displays a lack of respect for him: 'Take off that collar – Preach a sermon, Logan.' It is only at this point that the guilt felt by Otto's wife at Michael's treatment leads to the truth being revealed.

The Appeal Board overturned Hayes' ban, accepted Warners' cuts, but added one of their own. Though Warners had cut part of the scene between Ruth and Michael on the night before he left for the war, the Appeal Board demanded that the complete scene be removed. The view taken by the Board seems to be have been that this soft-focused adolescent love scene, in which the couple dance and kiss, was not an appro-

priate one for a future priest. In Catholic Ireland, priests were not to have any emotional attachments or sexual desire even before joining the priesthood. Like the Virgin
Mary, they were to be represented as 'immaculate'. Just as Montgomery sought to represent American cinema of the 1920s and 1930s, Hayes attempted to re-make the
cinema of the 1940s and 1950s according to a particular, repressive Catholic ideology.
This is especially true of his treatment of *film noir*, the most interesting new cinema
'genre' of the period.

### 'FILM NOIR' AND 'HARD-BOILED' THRILLERS

*Film noir* encompasses a range of films which have certain recurring thematic and
stylistic features. *Noir* films are most often set at night, are characterized by a dark
and brooding style, and usually feature cynical and conniving characters who are
enveloped in a world of crime and amorality which is pervaded by a sense of sexual
transgression. One key narrative feature of *noir* which separates this group of films
from most of the Hollywood product, and which feminist film critics have long noted,
is that the women characters are often the controlling agents in the films, even if, in
the end, such women are killed, imprisoned, or re-inserted within the domestic sphere
for their 'transgression' of patriarchal norms.[85] On the other hand, male heroes in
*noir* and 'hard boiled', or tough guy, films are often characterized by masochistic
impulses, whether being manipulated by 'dangerous' women or being repeatedly beaten
up as they search for 'meaning' or a solution to unexplained events which have been
visited upon them.[86] On the surface, one would expect such films to be anathema to
Irish film censors and many were, but perhaps what is most surprising is that while
the most obviously transgressive films were banned or cut, those featuring the bru-
talization of the male hero were often allowed. Perhaps, *noir's* masochistic male characters found a ready echo in the dominance of woman, especially the nurturing mother,
of official Irish ideology.

    Of the 96 censors' examinations of *noir* and hard-boiled films (90 by the Censor,
6 by the Appeal Board), 49 were passed uncut by the Censor, including films such as
*The Maltese Falcon* (John Huston, 1941), *Dead Reckoning* (John Cromwell, 1947),
*Lady in the Lake* (Robert Montgomery, 1947), *The Naked City* (Jules Dassin, 1948),
*The Night has a Thousand Eyes* (John Farrow, 1948), *The Asphalt Jungle* (John Huston,
1950), *On Dangerous Ground* (Nicholas Ray, 1952), *Panic in the Streets* (Elia Kazan,
1950), *Where the Sidewalk Ends* (Otto Preminger, 1950) and *The Woman in the Window*
(Fritz Lang, 1944).[87] Forty-one films were passed with cuts (usually with less than three),
such as in *Force of Evil* (Abraham Polonsky, 1948)[88] (one cut), *In a Lonely Place*
(Nicholas Ray, 1950)[89] (three cuts), *The Killers* (aka *A Man Alone*, Robert Siodmak,
1946)[90] (one cut), *The Blue Dahlia* (George Marshall, 1945)[91] (one cut), *Pickup on
South Street* (Samuel Fuller, 1953)[92] (one cut), *Ruthless* (Edgar G. Ulmer, 1948)[93] (one
cut), *Side Street* (Anthony Mann, 1950)[94] (one cut), *They Live by Night* (Nicholas Ray,
1949)[95] (one cut), and *The Big Heat* (Fritz Lang, 1953)[96] (two cuts). More extensive

cutting was visited on *The Lady from Shanghai* (Orson Welles, 1948)[97] (twelve cuts), *The Bribe* (Robert Z. Leonard, 1949)[98] (nine cuts), *The Dark Corner* (Henry Hathaway, 1946)[99] (five cuts), *Gun Crazy* (aka *Deadly is the Female*, Joseph H. Lewis, 1950)[1] (five cuts), and *The Fallen Sparrow* (Richard Wallace, 1943)[2] with a record, at least within this genre, of thirty-eight cuts. A total of 13 rejected films went to the Appeal Board, of which 6 were passed, including *Double Indemnity* (Billy Wilder, 1944)[3] and *The Glass Key* (Stuart Heisler, 1942),[4] while of the 7 rejects upheld by the Board, the most prominent are *High Sierra* (Raoul Walsh, 1941),[5] *Kiss Tomorrow Goodbye* (Gordon Douglas, 1950),[6] *Mildred Pierce* (Michael Curtiz, 1945),[7] and *The Postman Always Rings Twice* (Tay Garnett, 1946).[8] In the one film on which it was asked to adjudicate on cuts, *Farewell My Lovely* (aka *Murder My Sweet*, Edward Dmytryk, 1944),[9] of which Hayes had ordered eleven, it overturned Hayes' decision. One further feature of these films is that in the main they were submitted to the Film Censor in the version released in Britain. Nevertheless, in some instances this policy was not observed: *Pickup on South Street*, was released in Britain at 6,863 feet in Britain,[10] but submitted at 7,230 feet to the Irish Censor; *Kiss of Death* (Henry Hathaway, 1947) was released in Britain at 8,857 feet and submitted at 9,157 feet;[11] and *On Dangerous Ground* was released in Britain at 7,243 feet, but submitted at 7,373 feet. In all, 7 such instances (allowing for a twenty-five feet margin of error between the two countries) have been identified among the 114 films examined, while 11 films were submitted to the Irish Censor in shorter versions than the British release film. This pattern, though, was not, as indicated, unique to *noir*, but can be detected across most decades and all genres.

Hayes' comments after banning Howard Hawks' *The Big Sleep* (1946) summarize his view of *noir*. It was 'a thoroughly immoral' and 'unsavoury' film where '*the entire atmosphere* is sordid, and there are many suggestive situations, and not a little double-meaning dialogue.' (Emphasis added.)[12] These sentiments were echoed in his report on Michael Curtiz's 1945 *Mildred Pierce*, in which a housewife, Mildred (Joan Crawford), leaves her husband, becomes economically independent, sees her daughter kill her spiv boyfriend and being jailed, before she returns to her estranged husband and the domestic sphere. It was 'a sordid, unsavoury picture' where 'the sanctity of marriage is treated as a joke and moral considerations of any kind are ignored.' There were, he continued, 'seductive situations, dubious dialogue, murder and an accommodating husband.'[13] Hayes' (deliberate?) misreading of the film (the husband is far from 'accommodating') is further evidence of the juxtaposition of the idealization of women and of misogyny which permeate the censors' reports.

When first submitted, Michael Curtiz's *Casablanca* (1942) was banned under the Emergency Powers Order (EPO) – discussed in chapter 8 – as it was deemed to infringe Irish neutrality during the war. On re-view in June 1945 after the EPO had been lifted, Hayes passed the film with cuts. These were designed to suppress Rick's (Humphrey Bogart) and Ilsa's (Ingrid Bergman) love affair in Paris. Although she believed herself to be a widow, the Censor seems to have approached the film as her still being married, and so her relationship with Rick was deemed contrary to an Irish Catholic perspective.[14] This is illustrated in a key scene set in Rick's office when she comes to see

him and tries to convince him to hand over the letters of transit which would allow
her and her husband, Victor Laslo (Paul Henreid), to escape from the country. Rick
refuses even at gunpoint and tells her that she would be doing him a favour if she shot
him. At that point, Ilsa breaks down, embraces him, and says, in a section cut by the
Censor, 'The day you left Paris. If you knew what I went through. If you knew how
much I loved you, how much I still love you.' They kiss. In the following sequence,
which was passed, Ilsa explains that she had been married prior to her meeting him,
but had been told that Victor had been killed trying to escape from a German concentration camp, but she found out on the day she was due to leave Paris with Rick
that he was still alive and needed her. Now, she tells Rick, she will never have the
strength to leave him again, and that Victor can continue with his work without her.
While this explanation was allowed by the Censor, the dialogue, and embraces, which
follow it were cut:

> Rick: All except one. He won't have you.
> Ilsa: I don't fight it [our love] anymore. I ran away from you once, I can't do
>      it again. I don't know what's right any longer. You have to think for both
>      of us. For all of us.
> Rick: All right, I will. Here's looking at you kid.
> Ilsa: I wish I didn't love you so much.

The second major cut was in the film's denouement at the airport. Until then Rick has
not revealed how he will use the two letters of transit, but perhaps it will be for himself and Ilsa. He surprises the French Chief of Police, Louis (Claude Rains), by firstly
telling him to fill one out in Laslo's name, thus, it would appear, removing him from
the scene, but he then gives up Ilsa and tells him to put her name on the second. Ilsa
protests, 'No, Richard, no, I, I', as she is torn by her conflicting emotions about staying with him or leaving with Laslo. Hayes demanded cuts from this moment right
through Rick's less-than-convincing explanation, that she could end up in a concentration camp, and her painful responses to him:

> Ilsa: You're saying that only to make me go.
> Rick: I'm saying it because it's true. Inside us, we both know you belong with
>      Victor. You're part of his work, the thing that keeps him going. If that 'plane
>      leaves the ground and you're not with him you'll regret it. Maybe not today,
>      maybe not tomorrow, but soon and for the rest of your life.
> Ilsa: But what about us?
> Rick: We'll always have Paris. We didn't have it, we lost it until you came to
>      Casablanca. We got it back last night.
> Ilsa: When I said I would never leave you.
> Rick: And you never will. I've got a job to do, too. Where I'm going you can't
>      follow. What I've got to do you can't be any part of.

With this cutting, Hayes succeeded in diluting, if not entirely eliminating, the most important narrative element, the intense relationship between Rick and Ilsa while they were in Paris. As a result, his final words to her were more likely to be interpreted by Irish audiences as referring to the debilitating effects of the war rather than to their affair: 'Ilsa, I'm no good at being noble, but it doesn't take much to see that the problems of three little people don't amount to a hill of beans in this crazy world. Someday you'll understand that. Now, now. Here's looking at you kid.' Even in 1974 following a query from RTÉ which intended showing the film, the Film Censor told the television station that the only cut which had not been restored to the film since the 1940s was the crucial scene in Rick's office beginning 'The day you left Paris ...' which reveals Ilsa's continuing love for Rick.[15]

Similar treatment befell *The File on Thelma Jordan* (Robert Siodmak, 1949), in which a married man with children, Cleve Marshall (Wendell Corey), is ensnared in a murder cover-up by, in typical *noir* fashion, a woman. Cleve, an assistant district attorney, first meets Thelma Jordan (Barbara Stanwyck) when she reports a fictitious prowler at her aunt's home where she lives and from whom she plans to steal jewels. Thelma traps the district attorney in a romantic tryst as a means of ensuring protection after the robbery, which she carries out in collusion with her low-life husband, Tony Laredo (Richard Rober). The robbery goes wrong, and she accidentally shoots dead her aunt, for which she is arrested. However, Cleve, an unhappy man, becomes infatuated with her and subsequently takes charge of the murder case, but deliberately loses it, which results in her acquittal. Desperate to see her, he goes to her home, but by now she has developed feelings for him, and racked by contradictory emotions, causes a car accident which kills Tony and fatally injures herself. At the hospital, Cleve holds her hand before she dies. As he leaves the hospital with his friend, Chief Investigator Miles Scott (Paul Kelly), whom Thelma had originally intended to entrap and to whom she has just confessed, Cleve realises that his career is over.

The Censor cut the film in a simple way, deleting all the intimate scenes involving Thelma, a total of ten kisses and embraces, mostly with Cleve, but also, surprisingly, with her husband. He also cut the erroneously described 'fondling' of Thelma's hands by Cleve in the hospital and his key line (to Miles) explaining his motivation for throwing the case, 'I loved her.' It might appear that such cuts were designed to suppress Cleve's transgression, but his marriage and legal career is ended by his involvement with Thelma. Before he walks away alone, he tells Miles he will 'go somewhere, try to start again,' and get in touch with his wife Pamela (Joan Tetzel), 'later'. There is no secure, happy ending in a *noir* film, and even the Censor cannot save the family from being represented in all its darkness and contradictions.[16]

Perhaps, blind to the radically different sexuality of *noir*, Hayes also misread, according to a traditional male Catholic ideology, Billy Wilder's *Sunset Boulevard* (1950) which he banned. He dismissed the film as being centred around 'the infatuation of a wealthy middle-aged ex-film star,' Norma Desmond (Gloria Swanson), for a young man, Joe Gillis (William Holden), whom she 'loads' with 'favours' before 'finally seducing him' and becoming 'his mistress'. However, far from being a mistress, Norma, for much of the narrative, retains her power over Joe, who is more akin to a gigolo. She finally succumbs to insanity and shoots him dead, ironically when he decides to become a man and, by rejecting her, his passivity, by taking a younger lover (Nancy Olson). The Appeal Board disagreed with Hayes and passed the film with one cut.[17] It took a similarly lenient view of Charles Vidor's *Gilda* (1946) after Hayes had submitted a wholly negative report on the film. This is 'a sinister unpleasant film,' he wrote, with 'sex, passion right through but without moral considerations.' There were 'numerous sensual scenes and several murders'. After considering cuts to it, he decided that these would have to be 'so drastic, that it would leave the picture meaningless.' The Board approved the issuing of a certificate for the picture subject to the cutting of Rita Hayworth singing two songs, including her sexy, exhibitionist rendition of 'Put the Blame on Mame.'[18] The superficial reading of the scene by the censors failed to appreciate the subversive nature of the song and its performance in which the visual and the aural textures undercut its voyeurism. Such a literal reading of the 'performance' also fails to take into account the destabilizing of the narrative through (dance) movement.[19]

While Hayes' objection to physical brutality in the cinema was not confined to *noir* films, it certainly featured as a regular issue. *Noir* and the hard boiled/crime films were the offspring of the quintessentially urban genre of the 1930s, the gangster film, which had troubled his predecessor. The controversial *Scarface* (1932), for example, was never allowed an Irish release, despite being submitted for a certificate in the 1930s, 1940s (under the title *Gang War*), and, again, in the 1950s. Hayes considered it a 'particularly brutal picture, dangerous for presentation to young people,' and, like other commentators, expressed concern at the 'strong suggestion of incestuous passion'[20] between the anti-hero and his sister (something not as clearly inscribed in the film as is often claimed, nor, indeed, is it unique to 1930s films).

Such cuts of brutality which Hayes ordered to *noir* films included the 'brutal scene' where 'Moose' attacks Marlowe (Dick Powell) in Amthor's (Otto Kruger) apartment in *Farewell My Lovely*,[21] and the 'rather brutal gun scene' between Joe, Ficco and Baner in *Force of Evil*.[22] Fight scenes, whether in the ring or on the street, were deleted or 'toned down', such as in *The Set-Up* (Robert Wise, 1949), where boxer Stoker (Robert Ryan) is beaten by a gang. Hayes' successor, Martin Brennan, continued to ban or cut *noir* films, such as Robert Aldrich's *Kiss Me Deadly* (1955), which was extensively cut. Many of the cuts concerned private investigator Mike Hammer's (Ralph Meeker) relationship with his secretary and lover, Velda, including a night-time visit to her, in which it is clear that besides her affair with him, she uses her sexuality to gather information from suspects. The Censor cut this scene which features lines such as Velda's, 'One thing led to another.' In the film's final scene, Gabrielle, the *femme fatale*, kills her scientist lover, who has been seeking the 'great what's it,' after he tells her he intends to leave without her. Before he is killed, he patronizingly thanks her 'for all the creature comforts' she has given him, a line cut by the Censor. Gabrielle's final line is a classic female *noir* comment. 'Kiss me,' she says to Hammer as she points the gun at him, 'the liar's kiss that says something else.'[23] In *noir* films, the assertive heroine may be killed, but in the process the hero has suffered both mentally and physically. If a married man enters the criminal world, then the consequences can also be destructive, though Irish audiences were denied such a view of married life in the 1940s and 1950s.

*Scarlet Street* (Fritz Lang, 1945), in which Christopher Cross (Edward G. Robinson) is brought into the orbit of seductress Kitty (Joan Bennett) and her criminal boyfriend Johnny (Dan Duryea), was banned by Hayes in 1946, but like many other films of this era, it was not re-submitted for a certificate until the 1960s, when it was passed with cuts. Even then, bedroom scenes in the apartment rented by Kitty and Johnny were cut. Censor Liam O'Hora at that time demanded more than two minutes cut from one long 'morning-after-the-night-before' scene which implies that Kitty and Johnny have slept together, though Kitty appears from the living-room in her nightdress to greet the hung-over Johnny.[24] One of the most daring and popular *noir* films was Tay Garnett's adaptation of James A. Cain's controversial novel *The Postman Always Rings Twice* (1946). 'It was the usual triangle,' but, Hayes added, 'without a relieving feature' and he denied it a certificate, 'even for adult audiences.' It was a 'base, sordid picture into which moral considerations of any kind do not even faintly enter,' a view endorsed by the Appeal Board as it upheld the Censor's decision.

Like *Scarlet Street*, it was not until 1962 that *Postman* was re-submitted to the Censor when it was passed with cuts. O'Hora appreciated the still-powerful impact of the on-screen relationship between Cora (Lana Turner) and Frank (John Garfield), about which he had to be 'particularly careful,' and doubted whether he should pass it at all. O'Hora's cuts included the first key scene in which Cora acknowledges her attraction for Frank, and after a feeble 'Please don't,' kisses him. The cuts sought to suppress the passionate intensity of the adulterous relationship which leads to their murder of her husband, the elderly and tedious Nick (Cecil Kellaway). Despite the cuts, the 1962 Irish version of the film maintained the sexual dynamism between the two with its innate eroticism repeatedly expressed in the looks exchanged between them from their first meeting onwards. In this scene at the diner, which was left intact by the Censor, Cora's body is seen from Frank's point-of-view, and, as the camera then focuses on her eyes, it is clear that she is as interested in him as he is in her. Still worried after cutting the film, O'Hora advised the distributor that he 'may have to delete entirely the Cora-Frank episodes' which follow their first kiss, but this suggestion to change entirely the content of the film does not appear to have been pursued. These scenes are crucial to the central plot element, the killing of Nick, and in which their motivation – their love for each other, or at least their intense passion – is explored. In one scene, Cora explains that she has been the object of desire of 'all the guys' since she was 14. When she was down-and-out she accepted Nick even though she told him when they got married that she didn't love him. After Nick's murder, Frank and Cora stay at the diner, but she is furious at his co-operation with the district attorney. It is all the more ironic, therefore, that O'Hora cut her attorney Keats' line, that people were talking about 'an unmarried man and woman living under the same roof.' It was in the nature of O'Hora's moral blindness that he subtly misreads the film and fails to record Keats as saying that people were talking about the unmarried couple 'living *together*'. Indeed, after Cora and Frank get married, and when she renews her love for him on her return from her mother's funeral, she tells him she is pregnant. This scene, in which a remorseful Cora believes she is 'giving one back' to the world after Nick's death, was not cut by the Censor. As in Hollywood, Cora's guilt at her transgression is strengthened at the end by the Censor, who also allowed her death to be seen, and Frank's belief that 'wherever they'll be' after his execution, they will be together, a comment which could be interpreted as suggesting happiness in the afterlife, thus, perhaps, overturning the film's retributive ending.[25]

While *film noir* presented a direct challenge to the censors due to its representations of sexual transgression and physical brutality, it might be thought that the repressed circular narrative which ultimately reinforces the status quo in *Brief Encounter* (David Lean, 1945, GB) would have been acceptable to Hayes. Though contemporaneous with *noir*, *Brief Encounter* is, of course, a very British film, by the end of which the wife (Celia Johnson) goes back to her husband, while her putative lover (Trevor Howard), with whom she has only symbolically consummated the 'affair,' leaves for Africa. Because the film concerns 'the entanglement' of a man with a married woman, who 'lies to her husband regarding her intrigue,' and contains 'numerous seductive and indelicate situations,' the film was banned, a decision upheld by the Appeal Board. Other objectionable features were that 'the pair part with regret and without remorse,' that she then contemplates suicide, all of which leave the audience with 'a certain sympathy' for their 'amorous relationship,' and though Hayes does not spell it out, that is because Johnson's husband, to whom she returns, appears such a bore.[26] The film was re-submitted for a certificate in early 1962 in a slightly longer version than in 1946, indicating prior cutting by the distributor at that time, and was passed uncut.[27] Liam O'Hora, at least, understood the difference between the sterile middle-class English sexuality between Johnson and Howard, on the one hand, and the erotic charge between Americans Turner and Garfield, on the other. No better contrast can be made either in the 1940s or in the early 1960s as to why American cinema was pre-eminent over its British counterpart.

## TENNESSE WILLIAMS AND THE CENSORS

The plays of Tennessee Williams, often explorations of sexuality, infidelity and moral depravity, were the *bête noirs* of American theatre and, during the 1950s in particular, also of the cinema, notwithstanding their considerable sanitization in that medium. In total, between 1950 and 1970 fifteen of his plays were adapted for the screen. The second of these adaptations, *A Streetcar Named Desire* (Elia Kazan, 1951), led to a recognition that, as one American film censor put it, 'censoring … is not [about] morality but taste.'[28] However, references to homosexuality remained taboo and only after a titanic struggle against the film industry's Irish-American Catholic censor, Joseph I. Breen, was the fundamental narrative element – the rape of Blanche du Bois (Vivien Leigh) by her brother-in-law Stanley (Marlon Brando) – allowed to remain in the film, albeit in an implied manner. Despite the play's transformation, *Streetcar*, nominated for nine Academy Awards and winner of four, was a critical success and encouraged the American film industry to become more confident and aggressive in making films with more challenging themes. This was given further impetus when, in 1952, the legal basis of film censorship was considerably modified following the American Supreme Court decision on 'The Miracle,' the second episode in Roberto Rossellini's two part Italian film, *L'Amore* (aka *Woman/Ways of Love*, 1948).

In 'The Miracle' a young peasant woman, seduced by a stranger whom she imagines to be St Joseph, becomes pregnant and believes that the child is the product of a miraculous conception. The film was banned in New York on the grounds that it was 'sacrilegious'. However, according to the Supreme Court, sacrilegious was too vague and indefinite to be a standard for censorship. Such a 'broad and all-inclusive' term, the court argued, sets the censor 'adrift upon a boundless sea amid a myriad of conflicting currents of religious views, with no charts but those provided by the most vocal and powerful orthodoxies.'[29] More importantly, by acknowledging the constitutional right of film to free speech without legal interference, the court reversed the position on film censorship in force since 1915 whereby movies were seen exclusively as a business, and thus not entitled to exercise such rights, but were susceptible to laws governing commerce. While this ground-breaking judgment was successfully cited in defence of other films in the following years, unfortunately, in the Irish context there was only one dominant orthodoxy and *L'Amore*, which does not seem to have been submitted to the Film Censor, was certain to fall foul of the subjective, but all-embracing, blasphemy provision of the 1923 Act.[30]

No less central to the encouragement of more liberal and transgressive cinematic representations was Otto Preminger's 1953 romantic comedy *The Moon is Blue*, adapted from the Broadway hit by F. Hugh Herbert. The film, with sparkling dialogue, which concerns a 'professional virgin', Patty O'Neill (Maggie McNamara), and her relationship with two men (William Holden, David Niven) was refused the Legion of Decency's seal of approval and condemned by the organization. Nevertheless, the film's production company, United Artists, resigned from the Production Code Administration and released the film without the Legion's seal. When the financial return on the film was ten times greater than its production costs, it was clear to the American film industry that the Legion could be defied successfully. Notwithstanding its breakthrough in America, the film ran into censorship difficulties with the British Board of Film Censors, which cut it from 8,962 to 8,550 feet (or just under five minutes),[31] but despite a number of viewings by Irish censors during 1954 to 1956, no certificate was issued. Although Censor Martin Brennan admitted that 'the dubious situations [were] delicately handled,' he argued that the film's dialogue was 'very direct ... very suggestive,' and much of it 'capable of double meanings,' noting that it would be 'impossible to cut the film without interfering with the plot.' When two years later Brennan viewed such a version cut by a 'few hundred feet' by the distributor, he maintained the ban because there were still 'suggestive' scenes and dialogue which the renter refused to cut further, a decision upheld by the Appeal Board.[32] The adaptation of Tennesse Williams' play, *Baby Doll*, directed by Elia Kazan (1956) – a story about the marriage of a child-bride and a middle-aged man which includes an adulterous affair – and other films in a similar mould, led to a revision of the Production Code with less restrictions on films dealing with sex and religion. (This did not impact in Ireland for more than another decade.)

Besides *The Moon is Blue*, no less than eight adaptations of Williams' writings were refused certificates at least initially by Irish censors: *The Rose Tattoo* (Daniel Mann, 1955);[33] *Baby Doll*;[34] *Suddenly, Last Summer* (Joseph L. Mankiewicz, 1959);[35] an adaptation of *Orpheus Descending*, *The Fugitive Kind* (Sidney Lumet, 1959);[36] *Summer and Smoke* (Peter Glenville, 1961);[37] *The Roman Spring of Mrs Stone* (Jose Quintero, 1961);[38] *Sweet Bird of Youth* (Richard Brooks, 1962);[39] and *This Property is Condemned* (Sydney Pollack, 1966);[40] while *Period of Adjustment* (George Roy Hill, 1962), a comedy about marriage difficulties, which had to be toned 'down drastically,' was passed with eight cuts.[41] Nevertheless, the somewhat tame adaptations of two of Williams' key plays, *A Streetcar Named Desire* and *Cat on a Hot Tin Roof* (Richard Brooks, 1958), were both released in Ireland, albeit, in versions which radically altered and recast the films' characterizations and meanings.

In *Streetcar*, Blanche, a school-teacher, arrives in New Orleans from the small town of Laurel to stay with her pregnant sister Stella (Kim Hunter) and Stella's husband Stanley, a factory worker, whom Blanche regards as crude and common. Over a period of five months her neurotic and uppity behaviour grates on Stanley, who is suspicious of her propriety and her reasons for staying in their apartment, and begins to enquire into her past. He discovers not only that she was involved with a number of men, but was dismissed from teaching following an affair with a 17-year-old student, and sub-sequently, after being ordered to leave her hotel because of her male visitors, she came to New Orleans. Meanwhile, romance blossoms between Blanche and a friend of Stanley's, Mitch (Karl Malden), and the couple hope to marry. However, when Stanley reveals to him Blanche's sordid life, he, unlike Stella who refuses to believe it, brutally rejects her. On the night Stella goes to hospital, Stanley arrives home drunk, and begins to intimidate the increasingly delusional Blanche. Eventually, he forces himself on her. On her return from hospital Stella is disturbed by Blanche's accusatory raving about Stanley, but Eunice, Stella's friend and a neighbour, urges her to believe in Stanley's innocence. By now, Blanche's mental heath has deteriorated further, and a doctor, whom she thinks is a suitor, escorts her from the house to hospital. After she leaves, Stella pushes Stanley away, swearing that he'll never touch her again (but such a resolution has already been undermined in the opening scene by their mutual sexual attraction for each other).

Hayes made a total of twenty-seven cuts to the film: twenty following the initial viewing and a further seven after a subsequent screening.[42] The effect of these was the removal of Blanche's sexually promiscuous past, her rape by Stanley, and an unex-plained break-up of Mitch and Blanche. What is left is a slightly volatile household into which a neurotic woman arrives, gets on her brother-in-law's nerves, and, after a series of rows with a suitor and her brother-in-law, is taken away to a mental institu-tion. It is hard, in Hayes' version, to decipher the type of woman Blanche is. Certainly,

Stanley's physicality and brutality have been toned down; Mitch's two-faced and ulti-mately pathetic character is confusing, while Stella is converted into an anguished sister and content wife without sexual urges or the ability to stand up for her sister. Indeed, the first cut Hayes made, the passionate reconciliation of Stella and Stanley following an argument, in which she embraces her contrite husband and runs her hands sensu-ously over his back, is central to the depiction of the 'animalistic' attraction and helps to contexualize what is, in effect, an inter-class relationship.

The first scene cut which indicates Blanche's unstable personality is when a young newspaper collector arrives at the apartment. She tries to seduce him, but the scene was cut from where she says, 'Cherry, Cherry, make my mouth water,' and asks to kiss him, 'Just once, softly and sweetly on your mouth.' At that they kiss and the boy leaves, looking back askance. In other scenes also, the nature of her transgressive desire was suppressed, as were the unpleasant and conniving aspects of Mitch's character. Following Mitch and Blanche's romantic involvement, she acknowledges her enjoy-ment of his kiss on a previous occasion, but in a section cut by the Censor, she goes on to say that 'it was the other little familiarity that I felt obliged to discourage. I didn't resent it! Not a bit in the world! In fact I was somewhat flattered that you desired me!' Just as this denies Mitch's attempt to sexually exploit Blanche, the next part of her speech was retained to suggest that she is a moral woman: 'But, honey, you know as well as I do that a single girl, a girl alone in the world, has got to keep a firm hold on her emotions or she'll be lost!' Again, the Censor intervened and cut Mitch's response: 'Lost?' and Blanche's next line: 'I guess you are used to the type of girl that likes to be lost,' a line which implies that Mitch may be less than 'pure'.

Stanley's comment to Stella about Blanche that 'she's no lily,' was cut by Hayes as part of his attempt to sanitize her past. Stanley goes on to report the gossip from a supply-man at the factory that Blanche was living a promiscuous life in Laurel. However, the lines thereafter were cut: 'and everybody else in the town of Laurel knows all about her. She is as famous as if she was the President of the United States, only she is not respected by any party!' Similarly treated by Hayes were Stanley's reports of how Blanche lived in a cheap hotel which turned a blind-eye to her behaviour before even-tually evicting her, and how she lost her job following her involvement with the 17-year-old boy. After Stanley informs Mitch about Blanche's past, and Mitch decides to end their relationship, Stella is upset, but Stanley, in another line cut by the Censor, tells her that Blanche's 'future is mapped out for her,' implying continued unmarried promiscuity, or worse. He extensively cut the dinner scene during which Blanche tries to assert herself, justifies her past and makes an attempt to rebuild her relationship with the hostile Mitch. Hayes first of all removed Mitch's interrogation of her, 'Didn't you stay in a hotel called the Flamingo?' and Blanche's response, 'Flamingo? No! Tarantula was the name of it! I stayed at a hotel called the Tarantula Arms.' 'Tarantula,' Mitch enquires. 'Yes,' says Blanche, 'a big spider. That's where I brought my victims.' But, after re-viewing the film, he cut the rest of the paragraph, which actually provides some explanation for her behaviour. According to this, it was 'panic' which drove her from one man to another after the death of her (homosexual) husband. Blanche goes on to say that three men in Laurel with whom she was involved, 'have tied an old tin can to the tail of the kite.' After the second viewing, he also cut Blanche asking Mitch what he wants, his grabbing and kissing of her, after which she asks him to marry her. It is at this point that he looks at her in disgust and declares (in another line which was cut): 'You're not clean enough to bring in the house with my mother.'

The other major narrative element in the film deleted by the Censor was of Stanley's intimidation and (implied) rape of Blanche, with, for example, Stanley's suggestive comments to Blanche, that they are alone, and that his silk pyjamas into which he changes are the ones he wore on his wedding-night, cut. Consistent with the earlier cuts which go someway to cleanse Blanche's character and history (many of) Stanley's vicious comments including his invitation to her – 'Let's have a little rough-house' – which act as a prelude to his physical assault of her that begins when she tries to walk by him, were cut. The Irish Censor unsurprisingly removed the rest of the scene in which Stanley rapes her.

Having altered Blanche, re-oriented Mitch's motivation, and eliminated Stanley's verbal and physical assaults on Blanche, it only remained for the tidying up of the final scene in which Stella becomes aware through Blanche's disturbed conversation that Stanley raped her. Stella tells Eunice, in a section of the scene cut by the Censor, that 'I couldn't believe her story and go on living with Stanley. I couldn't.' Though Eunice is firm, 'Don't you never believe it. You got to keep on going, baby,' later Stella warns Stanley never to touch her again. Meanwhile, Stanley tells his card-playing friends, including Mitch, in a further cut line: 'I never once touched her.' However, the Censor decided that in his version of *Streetcar* Stella and Stanley could continue to live happily ever after, now that Blanche has been removed to a mental hospital. Such radical reworking of *Streetcar* was not even mentioned in the Irish reviews of the film. The *Irish Times*, for example, unfavourably contrasted the film with *Cry, the Beloved Country* (Zoltan Korda, 1951, GB), which was released the same week, and concentrated on the quality of the actors' performances.[43]

While American censors had successfully suppressed the references to homosexuality in *Streetcar*, by the time *Cat on a Hot Tin Roof* was made, both American and British cinemas were beginning to include homosexual characters and themes, exemplary were such films as *Suddenly, Last Summer*, *Serious Charge* (Terence Young, 1959, GB), *Oscar Wilde* (Gregory Ratoff, 1960, GB), *The Trials of Oscar Wilde* (Ken Hughes, 1960, GB), *Devil's Advocate* (1961), *Victim* (Basil Dearden, 1961, GB). *Advise and Consent* (Otto Preminger, 1962), *The Children's Hour* (William Wyler, 1962), and *The Pleasure Girls* (Gerry O'Hara, 1963, GB). Most of these, unlike *Cat* ..., which Liam O'Hora described as 'the roughest picture' he had passed to date and added that he was 'taking a chance in letting it through,'[44] were, at least initially, banned or not even submitted to the Censor. While Williams' play had turned on the suspicion that Brick had been sexually involved with his friend Skipper, and that Brick's wife, Maggie, had set out to seduce Skipper in order to prevent the relationship, under censorship pressure the film disregarded the possible homosexual affair of Brick and Skipper and focused on Brick's belief, despite her protestations to the contrary, of her affair with

Skipper when Brick was suffering from a sports injury. Skipper, following a bad performance in an important game, committed suicide. Central to the film is how the possible affair continues to affect Brick and Maggie's marriage.

The film is mainly set in the mansion of the 28,000 acre ranch owned by Big Daddy (Burl Ives) and his family, which includes sons Brick (Paul Newman) and Cooper (Jack Carson), their respective wives, Maggie (Elizabeth Taylor) and May (Madeleine Sherwood) and her and Cooper's children. The occasion for the gathering is Big Daddy's return from hospital after a check-up, and though he has a terminal illness, the family collude in the lie that he is in good health. While Cooper and May connive to inherit the estate and their children also display less than wholesome traits, Brick, an alcoholic, constantly feuds with Maggie, the 'cat' of the film's title. All reference to Maggie as cat were cut, including lines such as, 'I feel all the time like a cat on a hot tin roof' (Maggie); 'We'd smell alike. Like a couple of cats in the heat' (Brick to Maggie); 'Maggie, the cat' (Brick); and, shockingly, but untrue, 'Sired by Brick out of Maggie the cat' (Maggie to May and her family). After a second viewing, O'Hora ordered cut a further reference in the dialogue to 'Cat on a hot tin roof,' but, clearly he felt constrained in not being able to alter the film's title, as one of his predecessors might have done.

O'Hora made the same number of cuts to *Cat on a Hot Tin Roof*, as Hayes had to *Streetcar*, twenty-seven, and claimed that 'despite the extensive cutting … continuity has been preserved.' The crisis between Maggie and Brick, the centre of the film, was somewhat modified by O'Hora. The underlying tension between them, and with his parents, was largely cut such as when one of Brick's irritating nieces says, 'You're jealous just because you can't have babies,' and Maggie tells Brick she went to a gynecologist who told her she could have children, but Brick replies to this attempt at reconciliation by stating viciously that he cannot stand her. Likewise, arguments between the couple with lines such as, 'Would you like to live alone?' and 'Take a lover' were cut.

In their bedroom, Maggie tells Brick that she lied to his family about her pregnancy, but by now Brick realizes he loves her. They embrace, and Brick takes a pillow as they do so and throws it on the bed. From the film's final image, a point-of-view shot from the pillows towards the couple in the background, it is clear they will make love and she will conceive, thus ensuring a happy ending. However, no doubt troubled by the sex, O'Hora issued a blunt final instruction to the distributor: 'Cut out the shots of pillow at the finale.' But perhaps the coupling only partly accounts for his decision to leave unresolved the happiness of the couple. This view can perhaps be reinforced if we look back to an earlier scene which the Censor ordered cut. Big Daddy says to Brick: 'They say Maggie sleeps on the bed and you sleep on the sofa. Is that true or not?' While this line was cut, the next line was left in: 'If you don't like Maggie, get rid of her.' Clearly, O'Hora was of the same viewpoint, even if the latter implied divorce, a normally forbidden theme, but in this case just punishment for Maggie's (possible) adultery.[45] O'Hora's cleaned-up version, about eight minutes shorter than the British one, which had received an over-16s 'X' certificate, was given an over-18s certificate, though this seems to have been another informal arrangement as there is no official record of this decision. Even so, the *Irish Times* commented that, 'rather surprisingly,' the film did not share the same fate as other Williams' films, but complained that

> the censor's scissors from time to time cause little breaks in the action and dialogue, and, since these usually occur when some aspect of the plot is about to be clarified, seeing the picture as it is shown to us is inclined to be something of an imaginative exercise.

The writer went on to question why the film had received an over-18s rating since 'it is almost a highly moral picture, about a young wife with highly normal desires.'[46] Despite such complaints which were to recur with increased frequency from the mid-1950s onwards, Irish film censorship still tried to hold back the tide of adult films.

## MARTIN BRENNAN: THE SHORTEST-SERVING CENSOR

Throughout his tenure in office, Richard Hayes maintained a religious rigidity with regard to marital relations, the litmus test of Irish film censorship for thirty years. Indeed, less than a month before his retirement, he removed from the eight Oscar-winner *From Here to Eternity* (Fred Zinnemann, 1953) all kissing and embracing between Warden (Burt Lancaster) and the Commanding Officer's wife Karen (Deborah Kerr), including the iconic scene when they make love on the beach as the water washes over them. Also cut were Karen's subsequent verbal attacks on her husband for his extra-marital affairs and her seeking a divorce to marry another man.[47] Hayes' successor, Martin Brennan, remained bound to this repressive tradition, but also tentatively responded to the changes in mainstream cinema. A prominent figure in the War of Independence, he had worked as an assistant to Professor Delargy in collecting West of Ireland folklore; had undertaken research in philology and Irish dialect with Professor Ó Máille of University College Galway;[48] had been the poll-topping Fianna Fáil TD for Sligo from 1938 to 1948; and in between these careers had practiced as a medical doctor. With such a background, similar to his two predecessors, there could be little confidence that he would react positively or progressively to the increasingly challenging cinema of the 1950s, especially the films which explored youth culture, sexuality and adult relationships.

Brennan, appointed Official Film Censor in January 1956, but died in office two and a half years later, banned his first film, *Cage of Girls* (*La Cage aux Filles*, Maurice Cloche, 1949, France), within a few days of taking up the post. It is the story of Micheline (Danièle Delorme), a young girl whose home is dominated by her brutal stepfather; her involvement with a married fairground employee after running away with him; her time in reform school; her involvement with criminals; and further imprisonment until a new life beckons with a childhood sweetheart.[49] No commentary was attached to the decision, a situation which became a feature of Brennan's tenure in office, though three months later, when he banned Luis Buñuel's surreal study of juvenile delinquency in Mexican slums, *Los Olvidados* (submitted under its English-language title, *The Young and the Damned*, 1950, Mexico), he went beyond his remit, in subjectively judging the film as having 'no merit'.[50]

Brennan, together with Mr E.C. Powell, a Principal Officer in the Department of Justice, who often deputized for him,[51] stuck by many of Hayes' and Montgomery's policies, including those relating to religion. He forbade Catholic sacraments to be shown, a continuation of the Thomist belief in the devaluation of the Divine by the image, or indeed media devaluation which marks the post-modern,[52] and remained sensitive to the position of the Catholic church. For example, he banned the adapted stage farce *See How they Run* (Leslie Arliss, 1955, GB) because the bishop was shown in 'a very unfavourable light,' nevertheless, the Appeal Board passed the film with cuts.[53] During this time, Powell banned the powerful and frightening film about a psychopathic preacher (Robert Mitchum), *The Night of the Hunter* (Charles Laughton, 1955), because it was 'brutal, sadistic and immoral,' a decision upheld by the Appeal Board.[54]

The adulterous affair between Sarah (Deborah Kerr) and Maurice (Van Johnson) was enough to ensure that the adaptation of Graham Greene's novel *The End of the Affair* (Edward Dmytryk, 1954, GB) would be banned.[55] However, it was the mystico-religious content which gave Brennan most trouble. Adopting the patronizing style so familiar from the Montgomery years, Brennan conceded that while it 'might be suitable for exhibition to a very select and discerning audience, ... there are too many theological implications which are far above the normal cinemagoer's ability to grasp' to make it fit for public exhibition. The film's moral dilemma begins when Sarah believes that Maurice has been killed by a bomb and prays to God that if He returns Maurice to life she will end their affair. It was this, Sarah's meditation on death, her dialogue with God despite her being a non-believer, which Brennan found problematic and to be beyond the conceptual grasp of 'ordinary' cinemagoers. When she seeks solace in a Catholic church, a priest tells her that if she doesn't believe in God, she can break the vow, but, unconvinced, she responds that if there is a God and He placed the thought in her head, she hates and resents Him for doing so. Her non-belief is soon converted to belief, followed by the flow of happiness at her realization. Returning home, she finds Maurice there with her husband, Henry (Peter Cushing), and comes to regard this as a divine test. Despite her resolution to end the affair, she reconciles herself both to the affair and to her new-found belief in God. However, she promises to stay with Henry when he declares that he cannot live without her. Already ill, Sarah tries to avoid Maurice by going out on a wet night but she becomes more sick and dies. After her death, Maurice post-humously receives a letter from Sarah saying that she is in love with him and believes in God. Maurice concludes that he, too, believes, but needs time to assimilate it.

A few months later, in July 1955 the influential International Catholic Cinema Office (OCIC) held its annual conference in Dublin. It was hosted by the National Film Institute of Ireland and was opened by the Institute's patron, the Archbishop of Dublin, John Charles McQuaid. As in previous years, the OCIC selected a film of the year. The winner was Elia Kazan's *On the Waterfront* (1954), which had won eight Oscars, including Best Picture of 1954. Suggested by real events of criminal infiltration of the trade union movement at the New Jersey docks in the late 1940s, this gritty and violent story ultimately resolves itself as an upbeat morality tale in which, through the intervention of a priest, Fr Barry (Karl Malden), and romantic love, corruption is challenged and defeated. The OCIC cited the 'sublime significance' of the film's message 'in the social, human, moral and spiritual spheres.' The citation went on to declare that 'this film shows the profound action of the Church in the person of a priest, who in the midst of shamefully exploited dockers, courageously undertakes to secure the triumph of social justice.'⁵⁶

The film centres on the actions of Terry Malloy (Marlon Brando), a former boxer, now a docker and a disgruntled member of Johnny Friendly's (Lee J. Cobb) gang, who finally does the decent thing and testifies against them. From the beginning he is more a tool to be exploited than an actor, and unwittingly lures Joey, the brother of Edie (Eva Marie Saint) to whom he is attracted, to his death at the hands of the gang. Though his association with Edie, a 'pure' school-teacher, suggests that Terry possesses tenderness and morality, he is nevertheless irritated by Fr Barry's attempt to organize the dockers to take back control of their union. Terry asks Edie early on as to Fr Barry's 'racket', and when she points out simply that 'he's a priest,' Terry responds, in a line cut by Brennan, 'oh, are you kiddin, so what, that makes no difference.' Yet later, he confesses his role in the gang to Fr Barry on discovering that his brother, Charley (Rod Steiger), one of the racketeer leaders, has been killed after he refuses to kill Terry for co-operating with the Waterfront Crime Commission. Following his brother's death, Terry goes to the gang's bar with a gun intending to kill Friendly. Fr Barry finds him there and disarms him. Afterwards, Fr Barry tells the barman, 'give me a beer,' and then says, 'make it two,' as he orders one for Terry. Brennan cut these lines as he did not want the priest to be ordering drink. He also cut the phrase 'go to hell' which is uttered twice by Terry to Fr Malloy when he enters the bar, but these cuts were later cancelled. Following Terry's public testimony against the gang, they brutally beat him in a scene ordered 'drastically cut' by Brennan. Bloodied but undaunted, Terry leads the dockers back to work having broken the power of the gang.⁵⁷ When the film was released to generally favourable reviews, the editor of the *Sunday Independent* inserted a special statement on the film page explaining why it would not be reviewed by that newspaper. Objecting to the 'horrible and brutal' violence from which 'any sensitive person must recoil,' it claimed that 'the insidious penetration of this type of film can do untold harm, especially to young people,' and went on to recommend that parents 'advise' their off-spring not to see the film. 'For ourselves,' the editor concluded, 'we refuse to review it.'⁵⁸

Following the established patterns, Brennan suppressed references to the sexual and maternal body, removing, for example, all shots of a woman in labour from *David* (Paul Dickson, 1951, GB);⁵⁹ comments on birth and babies, including the line, 'You don't even know why a woman gives birth in nine months instead of twelve,' from *Not as a Stranger* (Stanley Kramer, 1955);⁶⁰ and two references to pregnancy in *A Kid for Two Farthings* (Carol Reed, 1955).⁶¹ However, he showed a bit more flexibility when such elements were in a comedy, such as when confronted with the inimitable British juvenile and scatological humour of *Doctor in the House* (Ralph Thomas, 1954), the first in the successful series. Just as his predecessors would have, he demanded cut a nurse's reference to bed pans; a woman's comment to a medical student, Simon Sparrow (Dirk Bogarde), that her husband had slept through childbirth since their third child; and Sir Lancelot's (James Robinson Justice) chiding of another medical student who is told after an incorrect diagnosis that he will not stay in practice long if he sends everyone under 60 to the ante-natal clinic. Nevertheless, a scene with medical students treating babies, and Simon's articulation of his fear that he hopes mothers don't start producing babies during the following eight hours (when he's on duty), were passed. A lecture with comments including 'hormones control emotions,' and that humans are just a collection of cells and nerve impulses, which, despite its humorist context, would have been deemed too materialistic a decade earlier, was also passed. Similarly, other previously forbidden lines, such as the advice by a foreigner, Stella, to Simon as he is nervously preparing to go on a date, 'When you make love to her, do not be too English, be a bit more aggressive,' was allowed, though a medical student's lascivious comment to a nurse, 'You succulent starched uniform with a soft centre,' was cut.[62]

Any instance of semi-nudity (usually featuring the woman's midriff and legs even if occasioned by the wearing of bathing costumes)[63] and the attendant dance numbers within musicals remained one of the Censor's prime targets. Films as various as the Danny Kaye vehicle *Knock on Wood* (Norman Panama, Melvin Frank, 1954),[64] *Kiss Me Kate* (George Sidney, 1953),[65] *The Human Jungle* (Joseph M. Newman, 1954),[66] *There's No Business Like Show Business* (Walter Lang, 1954),[67] *Mambo* (Robert Rossen, 1954, Italy/USA),[68] *Underwater!* (John Sturges, 1955),[69] and *Ain't Misbehavin'* (Edward Buzzell, 1954)[70] were just some of those cut. Indeed, Brennan's humourless approach to the job led him to cut the line from *Ain't Misbehavin'*, 'I didn't know you with your clothes on.' Brennan was also unimpressed with kissing. The question, 'Does he ever want to go beyond kissing?' in *Picnic* (Joshua Logan, 1955) he deemed too bold for Irish audiences.[71] Likewise, a kiss with a native islander in the Burt Lancaster China Seas adventure *His Majesty O'Keefe* (Byron Haskin, 1953, GB) was ordered curtailed,[72] as were kisses in, among many others, *Knock on Wood, Three Coins in the Fountain* (Jean Negulesco, 1954),[73] and *Killer's Kiss* (Stanley Kubrick, 1955).[74] For narrative reasons (suppression of an on-going relationship), the kiss between Mark and Margot at the beginning of Alfred Hitchcock's *Dial M for Murder* (1954) was cut,[75] thus undermining a key motivation in the film. Indeed, the forced kiss and propositioning (that they should meet in New York) of widow Cary Scott (Jane Wyman) by the minor character Howard in the subversive and incisive melodrama, *All That Heaven Allows* (Douglas Sirk, 1955), accounted for three of that film's five cuts. The other cuts concerned Kay reporting to her mother Cary the hurtful accusation that Cary's affair with the considerably young and socially inferior Kirby (Rock Hudson) had begun while her husband was still alive. The final cut was of Cary's doctor who, breaking ranks with the bourgeois community, encourages the widow to grab love and become reconciled with Kirby, reminding her that until now she was 'ready for a love affair, but not for love.'[76] Despite Sirk's reputation as a maker of fine women's pictures much of his work, including *Summer Storm* (1944) (with twenty-eight cuts)[77] and *Scandal in Paris* (aka *Thieves' Holiday*, 1946), (with seventeen cuts),[78] had already been severely dealt with by Hayes, before his successor was asked prior to cutting *All That Heaven Allows* to adjudicate on *There's Always Tomorrow* (Douglas Sirk, 1956). Though he banned the film, the decision was reversed after appeal, notwithstanding the fact that the film concerns the renewal of a relationship between married Fred MacMurray and ex-girlfriend Barbara Stanwyck.[79]

Alfred Hitchcock's *Rear Window* (1954) brought a number of these elements – semi-nudity, dancing, kissing, sexual expression – together. Of the ten cuts, four were of Miss Torso, such as when she is bending with her back to the camera and when she removes her bra. Other scenes which were 'drastically curtailed' were the kisses, even if crucial to narrative development, between L.B. Jeffries (James Stewart) and Lisa Freemont (Grace Kelly). While apparently he allowed the scene in which Lisa reveals she has brought her nightgown with the intention of spending the night at Jeffries' apartment, (although these shots may have been cut prior to submission), he ordered cut Jeffries' line, 'Sure, like staying here all night uninvited.' The only other dialogue cut was when Stella (Thelma Ritter), his nurse, offers the opinion that 'When General Motors has to go to the bathroom ten times a day, the whole country is ready to let go.' Her persistent suggestion that economic (or the socio-political) health of a society is intertwined with the body and personal health, which was later explored by anthropologist Mary Douglas[80] was formed when prior to the Wall Street Crash she was attending to a General Motors executive who was suffering from a kidney ailment. Finally of note was the cutting of the attempted sexual assault by a young man on Miss Lonelyhearts in her apartment.[81] Such sexual assaults were totally forbidden. Indeed, the central plot element, the rape of a young woman, in *No Peace among the Olives* (Giuseppe de Santis, 1950, Italy), was cited by Brennan's assistant E.C. Powell as the reason for banning the film,[82] while a few days later Brennan rejected *Cell 2455 Death Row* (Fred F. Sears, 1955) on 'grounds of brutality' as it concerns a 'convicted rapist's criminal career' in which the 'emphasis is laid on his sordid exploits and brutal attacks on couples parked in deserted spots.'[83]

However, all of these themes remained as minor elements in the censorship process as Brennan maintained his focus on the primary issue, representations of the family and the role of the woman. His reading of *The Last Time I Saw Paris* (Richard Brooks, 1954) illustrates a certain misogyny, or at best, double standard in relation to women. After the Liberation in Paris vivacious Helen (Elizabeth Taylor) marries American soldier Charles Wills (Van Johnson) but the marriage quickly deteriorates as he fails to gain success as a novelist. He becomes an alcoholic and, with Helen increasingly absenting herself with friends and suitors, he begins an affair with many-times-married Lorraine. Brennan summarized this mélange as the 'husband *appear*[ing] to be unfaithful' and the wife being 'unfaithful'. (Emphasis added.) In fact, Helen rejects the one person with whom she might have had an affair, failed tennis star turned gigolo, Paul

(Roger Moore), who proposes to keep her 'on the side' allowing her to remain married. This 'particularly objectionable scene' is erroneously described by Brennan as Helen 'offer[ing] to divorce her husband,' which she does not do. On abandoning Paul, she fails to gain entry to the family home because of her husband's drunken state, and, in the rain, goes to her sister's house, catches cold, and eventually dies of pneumonia. The 'pleasant if sad ending' sees Helen dead and the reformed alcoholic widower regaining his young daughter from Helen's sister.[84]

Any transgression of married life, especially by the wife, remained forbidden, even if, by comparison to previous censorship practice, somewhat loosened. In the crime film *The Big Combo* (Joseph H. Lewis, 1955) the search is on for Alicia (Helen Walker), the apparently-dead wife of gangster Brown, who is said to be living in Sicily with another gangster. When she re-appears, the film was partly amended by Brennan so as to ensure that there was no reference to her marriage, but enough remained for an audience to deduce that Brown is living with Susan, his girlfriend of four years, and that he is unfaithful to his wife.[85] *The Deep Blue Sea* (Anatole Litvak, 1955, GB), an adaptation of a Terence Rattigan play concerning marital infidelity, was banned by Brennan, a decision upheld after appeal, but the Censor's reasoning concerning divorce differs from that of his predecessors. While the central female character is divorced before she leaves her first husband, this 'does not justify their reconciliation afterwards, without a second divorce and subsequent marriage,' a situation which was 'contrary to common law in any country,'[86] a (convoluted) argument, it would seem, for divorce as a means of maintaining narrative symmetry, or just another excuse to ban a film.

Brennan also banned the 'fine film' *The Rains of Ranchipur* (Jean Negulesco, 1955) because it 'unfortunately' treated marriage 'far too lightly,' but the Appeal Board took a contrary view. While it cut out the more obviously (physically) transgressive aspects of the relationship between married Edwina (Lana Turner) and her Indian lover, Dr Softi (Richard Burton), the fact that the double transgression – miscegenation and a triangular affair – was allowed indicates the Board's increasing divergence from the Censor's more rigid decisions,[87] but perhaps the Board were appeased by the fact that despite their expressions of continuing love the status quo is restored when, following an earthquake, Softi chooses to serve his community rather than leave with Edwina who then departs with her husband. Similarly, while Brennan banned the breakthrough film about drug addiction, *The Man with the Golden Arm* (Otto Preminger, 1955), the Board was (more liberally or more literally) only concerned with shots of 'semi-nude ladies' in the background of a nightclub scene. While there is an eighty feet (less than one minute) difference between the film's length as seen by the Censor and the Board, it still hardly accounts for the ideological differences between the two branches of censorship, with Brennan arguing that the film's 'realistic depiction of the mental and physical torments of a drug addict, the prison scenes and the heavy losses at poker' made the film unsuitable for general exhibition,[88] even though it was a 'fine' film and one that 'may deter would-be drug addicts.' The Board also reversed his ban on *The Constant Husband* (Sidney Gilliat, 1955, GB), a comedy with Rex Harrison who on recovering from amnesia realizes he is wed to more than one woman.[89] However, more often than not, the Board upheld Brennan's decision to ban a film. Examples include *The Seven Year Itch* (Billy Wilder, 1955),[90] *The Sleeping Tiger* (Joseph Losey, 1954, GB),[91] *French Cancan* (Jean Renoir, 1955, France),[92] *The Scarlet Hour* (Michael Curtiz, 1955)[93] and *Autumn Leaves* (Robert Aldrich, 1956).[94]

Despite the mild 'loosening' up of film censorship in the mid-1950s, noted above, it remains the case that Brennan banned proportionately more films than his predecessor. While Hayes passed uncut an annual average of 60 per cent and banned 4.4 per cent of the total number of feature films submitted during the period 1945–1953, Brennan in 1954 passed uncut only an annual average of 51 per cent and banned almost 8 per cent. (The remaining films were those passed with cuts.) Therefore, in all categories, Brennan was stricter than Hayes, and as is indicated during his second year in office, his decisions were proceeding in an even more restrictive direction. In 1955, for example, he passed uncut only 40 per cent of the films viewed and banned another 10 per cent, whereas two years earlier, in 1953, Hayes passed uncut 61 per cent of the films viewed and banned only 4.7 per cent. Had Brennan not died in 1956 it is probable that Ireland was destined for an extended period of severe film censorship that was already shown to be out of touch with international trends. The treatment of youth-oriented films helped to sharpen the tentative debate evolving around Irish film censorship.

### 1950S YOUTH CULTURE AND IRISH FILM CENSORSHIP

Following the belated post-war recognition that the universal family audience had begun to fragment in the wake of new leisure activities, notably television, and demographic changes such as the expansion of suburban living, a new youth audience was courted. Among the innovations championed were youth-oriented films set against a realist background of the home, the school or the streets. The first such film was the controversial *City across the River* (Maxwell Shaw, 1949),[95] about Brooklyn youths who become involved in murder. Though it had been shot in a semi-documentary style to heighten the realist effect, a technique influenced by the pioneering city film *The Naked City*, it was only with the release of *The Blackboard Jungle* (Richard Brooks, 1955), set in a vocational high school in an unnamed city and concerning 'juvenile delinquency,' a topic of increasing social concern in the 1950s in both the USA and Britain, that the realist aesthetic became central. *Blackboard Jungle* also signaled the coming-of-age of the teenage cinema audience, and the emergence of the 'teenpic' as a marketing strategy, which developed over the following five years. Central to this development was the 'exploitation film', a maligned category of film which favoured the bizarre, and whose increasingly daring and explicit subject matter was deemed 'timely and sensational'.[96] Like other commentators, *Variety* was critical of teenpics, declaring in 1956 that many within the industry considered such films 'undesirable'.[97] Even so, it was clearly a response to the 'rise of the privileged American teenager'[98] during the second half of the 1950s. However, while the teenager could be treated as a definable and marketable group in America, such was not the case in Ireland due to the relative economic misery until the 1960s, and then not to the same extent. Indeed, it could be argued that it was not until the economic boom of the 1990s that the Irish teenager (as we will see in chapter 7) became more completely a target of consumer exploitation as well as of benign bureaucratic and institutional attention. While Irish teenagers of the 1950s could feel empathy through cinema and music with their American and British counterparts, they lacked the employment income (or pocket money) to engage in their consumer choices of clothes or cars. Usually they had to wait until adulthood and well-paid employment (and then only in the 1960s) to enjoy 'luxuries' routinely available to Americans a decade earlier.

While *Rebel without a Cause* (Nicholas Ray, 1955), with its angst-ridden and rebellious middle-class youth, 'the first American teenager,' played by James Dean, could be passed uncut by E.C. Powell in April 1956,[99] in part, no doubt, because the violence is internalized, *Blackboard Jungle* could not be viewed so benignly. As Thomas Doherty observes, throughout the film 'there is a real sense that the terms of the social contract between young and old have changed. On film at least, the relationship had never been so frightening, ambivalent, or antagonistic.'[1] It had caused an outcry when released in the USA in March 1955, while in a number of European countries it became a *cause célèbre*. At the 1955 Venice Film Festival, for example, it was withdrawn following pressure from the American ambassador.[2] In Britain, after four viewings of the film during March–August 1955, the BBFC divided on whether to ban or cut the film, and invited the film's distributor, MGM, to submit a cut version for consideration. The approved version, with twenty cuts and with an over-16s 'X' certificate, reduced the film's footage from 9,051 to 8,482 feet, over six minutes of screen time.[3] The Irish censor[4] viewed the film in May 1956, ordered five cuts, trimming an additional minute from the BBFC version, released nine months earlier. Though he followed the British example by insisting that it could only be seen by over-16s, one of the rare limited certificates of the 1950s, Powell's cuts were not concerned with the film's violence, but the traditional obsession with sex and the body with particular focus on that which might ordinarily affect heterosexual 'normal' adults. Though he passed the sexual assault by a student on teacher Lois (Margaret Hayes), which is beyond cultural acceptance, but which also allows for the heroic male to save the woman, he twice cut dialogue between married couple Rick (Glenn Ford) and Anne Dadier (Anne Francis). On the first occasion, during a celebratory dinner on the occasion of Rick's appointment as a teacher, Anne, who has already lost a baby, articulates her worries about her pregnancy, and asks Rick, 'You don't mind my being this way,' to which he reassuringly replies, 'How could I mind?' However, the rest of the sentence was cut: '*I'm responsible aren't I.*' The second cut occurs when Rick returns home to Anne having rescued Lois, and she reveals in a playful manner her anxiety about Lois as a rival: 'You didn't think I was very sexy, did you.' Rick: 'I thought you were irresistible.' Anne: 'Prove it.' While no sexual contact occurs between them, the *mise en scène* – Anne lying on the bed – makes it clear enough what the final sentence means. Such sanitizing was even more necessary in potentially adulterous instances. Towards the end of the film,

Brennan cut Lois' speech in which she makes explicit her desire for Rick. Lois: 'With me, maybe. Don't you. Don't you.' Rick: 'Ah, I guess not.' Lois: 'You'd like to, alright, but you're married, you're married and I'm bored. You're afraid and I'm choosy. You can't be choosy or you live alone.' Rick: 'You keep thinking that way you're going to end up in a mess of trouble.' In so doing, Brennan maintains Lois' purity by disallowing her transformation from prey to predator. In another scene, Rick's comment that 'even a prostitute makes more than' a teacher was removed. The one vicious physical assault in the film, when the student gang attack Rick and fellow teacher Josh in an alley, was also curtailed. Nevertheless, the *Sunday Independent's* film reviewer, Noel F. Moran, warned despite the official limitation pertaining to the film, 'keep the children away from it.'[5]

Many of the rebellious youth films were centred around the male worlds of motorcycles and automobiles, and their various coming-of-age rituals. Exemplary is *The Wild One* (Laslo Benedek, 1954), which had caused considerable controversy in the USA, mainly due to the lack of retribution meted out to the film's social outcasts, a motor-cycle gang. Brennan, in a decision upheld by the Appeal Board, banned it, describing it (with the exception of one unidentified scene) as a film without merit, about 'thirty or forty irresponsible, law flouting, sadistic motor cycle riders who terrorise a town for a day and a night.'[6] It was also banned by the BBFC eight months later, a ban which remained in force until 1967, though some local authorities, including Belfast, passed it for exhibition using their powers under the Cinematograph Act, 1909. Columbia, the film's distributor, taking on board the BBFC's proposal that another ending might be less problematic, issued another version. However, the BBFC reaffirmed its ban,[7] while, interestingly, the Irish Censor passed it with five cuts, mostly of fights and other violence, but when it opened in February 1956 the *Irish Times* was quick to point out the 'trite "crime does not pay" ending grafted on' to pass censorship.[8] This highly unusual difference between the Irish and British treatment of the film may be explained, in part, by the absence of motorcycle gangs in Ireland and, thus, the British censors' concern with imitative behaviour was clearly not an issue. However, the re-submitted version of *The Wild One* was 724 feet (or over eight minutes) less than the one assessed originally. A clone of this film, *Motorcycle Gang* (Edward L. Cahn, 1957), was treated leniently with Liam O'Hora ordering just one cut to it,[9] although Roger Corman's motorcycle gang movie, *The Wild Angels* (1966), was banned a decade later.[10] Indeed, Hayes' reason for banning *Cosh Boy* (Lewis Gilbert, 1952, GB), which showed 'the activities of a group of adolescent gangsters who stop at nothing, not even murder, to raise money,' was precisely his fear of imitative behaviour. For him, the film was 'dangerous' to show as 'some of the methods ['the young thugs'] adopt are vividly shown.' Also, one of the youths is seen seducing the sister of another which results in her becoming pregnant. Five years later, the film was submitted to O'Hora, but by then an *apparent* degree of liberalization was in evidence as he passed the film with just two cuts, one of which was of the line 'Take off your coat. Make yourself comfortable,' prior to an extended kissing session which needed to be toned down. A further cut was of the aggressive line, 'Ah, get stuffed you.' However, 218 feet (two and a half minutes) had been cut from the film prior to its re-submission.[11]

The 1940s had seen occasional crime films featuring teenagers or young adults, such as the *noir* films *They Live by Night* with one cut (a kiss),[12] and *Gun Crazy*,[13] an altogether more controversial film with five cuts. These cuts mainly concerned the sexual relationship between the central characters, Bart and Laurie, rather than their psychopathology (and gun-obsessions). The cuts included the comment by freak-show proprietor Packie describing the pair's mutual gazing at each other as being 'like a couple of wild animals,' and the scenes between the now married couple in which their sexual relationship is made explicit. The first of these is when they are on the run from the police, Bonnie and Clyde-style, and Laurie says to Bart that, 'The next time you wake up, Bart, look over at me lying there beside you. I'm yours, and I'm real,' to which he replies, 'Yes, but you're the only thing that is, Laurie. The rest is a nightmare.' The second occurs near the end of the film when they articulate their desire for one other: Laurie: 'Know what I've been waiting for all my life?' Bart: 'Tell me.' Laurie: 'Tonight.' Bart: 'Do you want to hear something?' Laurie: 'What?' Bart: 'So have I.' Laurie: 'Darling, let's go home.'

These films did not dwell very much on the environmental factors underlying anti-social behaviour, even if in a popular Freudian way childhood trauma is seen as the root of Bart's pathology. However, by the mid-1950s, 'environment' as explanation for juvenile crime and delinquency had very much come centre-stage. Don Siegel's *Crime in the Streets* (1956), for example, aligns itself with a sociological explanation for the activities of adolescents in New York tenements. The film features gang warfare and frequent violence, as well as a near-the-surface homosexual theme, with a social worker attempting to wean the central character Frank away from violence. Frank's behaviour, it is suggested, originated with the physical brutality meted out to him by his now-absent father. In the end, he is apparently rehabilitated, but with the adolescent violence, at best, just contained. For Liam O'Hora, the film, which received an 'X' certificate in Britain, was 'too much [preoccupied] with sex and violence' marked by 'a sort of moral and social degeneracy,' and was without 'purpose'. In short, he considered the film as having 'no value whatever as a tract for the times.' Whatever about the efficacy of this comment in an Irish context, his real concern was revealed later when he noted that the film was 'primarily intended for adolescents' or, rather 'adolescents would certainly display great interest in the picture.' The Appeal Board agreed with him and the ban was upheld.[14]

Some of the solutions to the (cinematic) juvenile delinquency problem must have seemed a bit bewildering (and secular) to a 1950s Irish audience. While the resolution of 1930s and, more particularly, 1940s American problem-youth films was through a moral authority figure such as streetwise priest Fr Barry in *Angels with Dirty Faces* (1938), or the priests played by Bing Crosby in *Going My Way* (Leo McCarey, 1944) and *The Bells of St Mary's* (Leo McCarey, 1945), by the 1950s such a mediating figurehead had been replaced by a person of science, such as the psychologist/psychiatrist and the liberal, well-meaning social worker. In short, by one who sought solutions through the (emotional and physical) 'environment'. This shift, while indicative of the changes – the loosening grip of parental authority and the move away from religion – occurring in American and British society, was largely irrelevant in a country such as Ireland where these professionals did not come centre stage until the 1980s, and, as elsewhere, their ascent was facilitated by the decline of religion within the society.

By the end of the 1950s, though, another shift occurred, with the benign environmental explanation giving way to an altogether more dangerous screen character, the sociopath, or what Thomas Doherty calls the 'reptilian young psycho'.[15] An early example is *Compulsion* (Richard Fleischer, 1959), which concerns 1920s rampaging thrill-seeking killers, based on real characters, whose exploits were advertised with the provocative tag-line: 'You know why we did it? Because we damn well like doing it.' Considering this attitude has parallels to that of *Natural Born Killers* (Oliver Stone, 1994) (discussed in chapter 6), it is surprising that O'Hora ordered just one cut, that of a model.[16] More important are the other 'psycho' movies which followed, most especially Michael Powell's *Peeping Tom* (1960, GB) and Alfred Hitchcock's *Psycho* (1960) discussed in chapter 5. Indeed, this move from unexplained action to analyst to social worker to the psychopath who 'deep down inside him [is] no good' is at once popularly recognized and traced in the ridiculing song, 'Gee, Officer Krupke' of *West Side Story*. In their mock court, the Jets claim leniency, first on account of their 'bringing up-ke' and being psychologically disturbed, and then because society has played a terrible trick on them, leaving them sociologically sick, 'Juvenile delinquency is purely a social disease.' However, the truth, it is finally suspected, may be that they are simply bad.[17]

## ROCK 'N' ROLL AND ELVIS' PELVIC GYRATIONS

If *Blackboard Jungle* brought juvenile delinquency to mass cinema audiences, *Rock around the Clock* (Fred F. Sears, 1956) established rock 'n' roll as the defining cultural expression of 'rebellious' youth of the 1950s and 1960s. Already uniquely experienced in making films for specific audiences, pioneering teenpic producer Sam Katzman announced in 1952 that 'we got a new generation, but they got the same old glands.'[18] With this in mind, he produced *Rock around the Clock* which became the first film to successfully target teenagers to the exclusion of adults, thus setting in train a plethora of teen-oriented music films. Upon its release, *Rock around the Clock* generated enormous excitement with teenagers dancing (and rioting) in cinema aisles. Unsurprisingly, 'moral panic' campaigns and calls for the film's banning followed in the wake of such a show of youthful exuberance. In Ireland, the film received a general certificate without cuts from deputy Censor E.C. Powell[19] and the film caused quite a stir even in provincial centres. In Sligo, where it was screened in November 1956, extra gardaí were drafted in anticipation of the 'mass hysteria' which had been aroused wherever it was shown. They were not disappointed.

The atmosphere was electric ... but in the foyer as the starting time neared, and with hundreds still outside fearful that they wouldn't get in, the mood soon changed to desperation as the word spread that the cinema was full. A tremendous crush developed ... Things got so out of control that ... a Garda had to draw his baton to prevent injury to a crowd jammed in the cinema's entrance.

Those unable to gain admission moved to the street outside and held an hour-long impromptu rock 'n' roll session 'under the anxious eyes of the law.' Meanwhile, inside the cinema 'ushers roamed the aisles and did their best to maintain order as the infectious rhythm sent the audience into a frenzy.' Despite the anxiety of the authorities 'no serious incidents occurred' during the film's seven showings, including a special midnight screening. However, a member of Sligo Corporation, Councillor J. Dolan, dismissive of both the reality of a teenage subculture and its aesthetic or other merits, denounced the local 'hep-cats' as 'hysterical nit-wits in drain-pipe trousers *copying* what they had seen across channel.' (Emphasis added.)[20] Notwithstanding the patronizing view of the teenagers engaging in imitative behaviour, the film clearly proved that there was a market for rock 'n' roll films in Ireland and that Irish teenagers regarded themselves as part of the international trend even though their financial circumstances was dire, their society repressive, the 'official' culture alienating, and their future bleak with emigration often seen as the only solution.

In early 1957 four such films were submitted to the Irish Censor: *Rock, Pretty Baby* (Richard Bartlett, 1956) in which a high-school rock-band tries to win a musical competition, was passed with five cuts, mostly of teenagers 'necking';[21] *Don't Knock the Rock* (Fred F. Sears, 1956), from *Rock around the Clock*'s producer/director team, which was passed with two cuts of female dancers;[22] *The Girl Can't Help It* (Frank Tashlin, 1956), which featured Little Richard, Gene Vincent, and Eddie Cochran, was passed with five cuts;[23] and Elvis Presley's debut feature, *Love Me Tender* (Robert D. Webb, 1956),[24] which was passed. What almost all these films based themselves around, including the later British ones such as the Cliff Richard's film *Expresso Bongo* (Val Guest, 1959, GB), was the intergenerational conflict triggered by rock 'n' roll. As in many teen films, there was a merging of genres, the musical with the crime film in the case of *Bongo*.

In *Expresso Bongo*, which was passed with cuts by Liam O'Hora, Bongo (Cliff Richard), an aspiring teenage rock 'n' roll singer, is managed by hustler Johnny (Laurence Harvey), whose girlfriend Maisie (Sylvia Syms) is a Soho stripper, though all scenes of the Soho strip-show were cut with the exception of a section of the show being recorded for a BBC television documentary. Also cut were scenes showing unmarried Johnny and Maisie living together in a small flat with a very visually-present double-bed, and her line to him, 'Well there's not much point in putting on my things at the theatre if I have to take them all off again here.' Sensitive to Cliff's youth following, the Censor cut all references to religion, even though they were mild and certainly could not be construed as blasphemous, though Johnny, cynical as ever, sees in the use of religion by the sincere Bongo a means of promoting the singer's career. When older singer Dixie enters Bongo's life, among the scenes cut was one in which she seduces him, including a scene in which she massages his bare body with oil.[25]

By a curious coincidence, two of the key teenpics of the 1950s, *I Was a Teenage Werewolf* (Gene Fowler Jnr, 1957),[26] which was passed uncut, and *Jailhouse Rock* (Richard Thorpe, 1957), were released the same week in Dublin. The *Irish Times'* Cinema Correspondent commented that 'a lower form of entertainment' than *I Was a Teenage Werewolf* 'would seem hard to imagine,' but 'the usually-discriminating' Adelphi Cinema achieves it 'by giving us the ineffable Elvis Presley' in *Jailhouse Rock*.[27] *I Was a Teenage Werewolf* combined two features of the teenpic, a teenage problem story that evolves into a horror film as the 'problem' youth becomes metamorphosed into a werewolf under the regressive hypnosis therapy of a psychiatrist. With a brilliant marketing campaign behind it, the film became a US coast-to-coast sensation. Unlike many of the other and often condescending teen pictures, it explores the terrain of teen culture independent of parental sanction or endorsement and concentrated on how teenagers viewed themselves as a subculture. The problem, ultimately, for the 'werewolf' is that he is unable to fit into his own peer group.

To draw the parallel with *Jailhouse Rock*, as the writer did, betrayed the hostility which these teen-oriented films generated. Indeed, there is no better illustration of the changing cultural experience of young Irish people in the late 1950s than the different generational responses to Presley both as musician and film star. In 1956 he had his first number one hit, 'Heartbreak Hotel,' and *Love Me Tender*, which – like many other rock films, capitalized on the popular success of *Rock around the Clock* – was released in America. The film premièred in Ireland in early 1957, and despite the *Sunday Independent*'s film reviewer, Noel Moran, ridiculing of Elvis' 'crude physical gyrations,'[28] Elvis enjoyed immense popularity in the country as the *Sunday Independent*'s annual popularity poll showed later that year when he toppled the (Catholic and more restrained) Bing Crosby from his twenty-five year reign as Ireland's most popular screen star. The poll, Moran observed, 'fell far short of what we expected as a reflection of national taste.'[29] The following year *Jailhouse Rock* was passed with a cut to reel 2 where a 'rather too unclad' dancing girl 'more or less fills the screen.'[30] Despite the critical opprobrium of the *Times* and others, *Jailhouse Rock*, unlike many of the other teen rock pictures, respects and positively acknowledges both its lead performer and its teenage audience. Even though Elvis' many later films would not represent in such a sympathetic way rock 'n' roll and its subculture, nevertheless, he remained a potent force even in the truncated films seen in Irish cinemas. O'Hora, and more particularly the Appeal Board, were all too aware of that as they tried to contain his impact on young people. As Thomas Doherty says more generally of the teenpics, while their plot lines were often 'dopey', this misses the point of the films, as they were 'a ritual occasion for self-celebration.' They were 'occasions for public demonstrations of teenage presence, identity, and solidarity.' No matter how paternalistic a film was towards rock 'n' roll, or how accomodationist its plot, such films legitimized teenage subcultures and often celebrated the 'rebellious exhilaration' of the music.[31] Of course, as the 'genre' became popular, crude exploitation was not far behind. *Teenage Rebel* (Edmund Goulding, 1956), for example, was based on a play (*A Room Full of Roses*) concerned with the effect divorce has on children, and accordingly three cuts were ordered by the Irish Censor.[32] The film did not deal with teen subculture, notwithstanding its marketing campaign which suggested it did.

Towards the end of 1958, O'Hora viewed one of Elvis' most incisive films, *King Creole* (Michael Curtiz, 1958), and ordered eight cuts. 'This picture is a tough one for me,' he commented, 'particularly so because it features the controversial Presley who has such an appeal for *uneducated* adolescents.' (Emphasis added.) Among the cuts was the scene in the School Principal's office near the beginning where Danny (Presley) is told he will not be allowed to graduate, a cut which eliminates details of his family circumstances. Danny explains that he has worked hard before and after school to earn money because his father, a trained pharmacist, is unable to get work. It is a scene which tries to give a rational basis for Danny's rebelliousness. Another major cut was when Danny meets Nellie (Dolores Hart) for their first date and he tricks her into going to a hotel with the object of having sex with her. When Nellie realizes at the hotel room door what Danny's intentions are, she embarrasses him by declaring that she thought him a 'nice boy', implying one with middle-class mores like herself. He weakly responds that he thought she knew 'the score', but he abandons his subterfuge. When this scene is referred to later, it, too, was cut to ensure that the audience is unaware of Danny's attempt to seduce Nellie.

The Censor's intervention also suppressed the exploitative relationship between Fields (Walter Matthau) and Ronnie (Carolyn Jones). When Fields is drawing Danny into his net, he demonstrates his power over Ronnie by demanding she walk over to them and lift her skirt. Fields says, 'Show the kid your legs ... And there's nothing wrong with the rest of it.' Later, Fields sends one of his men to take Danny to his apartment where Ronnie has been ordered to 'do anything' for him while Fields sleeps in an adjoining room. Danny refuses the offer but agrees to stay to make it appear he has been with her. During this sequence, Ronnie explains the power which Fields holds over her and she gives a graphic account of her oppression. During this exchange, Fields appears and a fight between him and Danny ensues, which ends with Ronnie and Danny escaping. The effect of the Censor's cuts was to neutralize the relationship between power, money and sex in keeping Ronnie in the exploitative relationship. Two songs were also removed from the film. One is a 'banana' song by performer Mimi, and the other is probably (the report does not specifically identify the song) Presley's rendition of 'King Creole', which was cut no doubt because of the singer's 'pelvic gyrations'. The renter appealed the cuts and in his report to the Board in October 1958, O'Hora revealed how much 'trouble' he had had, 'particularly from Headmistresses of girls' schools,' regarding Elvis' 'most suggestive abdominal dancing'. He said that he had viewed the film twice, but added that 'Presley's abdominal gyrations are much more restrained than in previous pictures,' and his presence had not given him the trouble he had anticipated. However, the Appeal Board, as was their right even when considering appeals against cuts, banned the film.[33]

*King Creole* was Elvis' last film before he went into the army for a two-year stint and, thereafter, his films lose the intensity of *Jailhouse* and *Creole* and become increasingly conservative and cautious. However, O'Hora was clearly nervous when he viewed *G.I. Blues* (Norman Taurog, 1960), an Elvis vehicle made with the full co-operation of the American military in Germany while he was in the army. 'I have to be particularly careful,' he wrote, because 'this picture will be seen mostly by teenagers in *this* country.' The main area of concern for O'Hora was not Elvis' 'pelvic gyrations,' but the sexual activities of the soldiers since one of the story-lines concerns an unmarried mother. The Censor provided a 'Montgomery' solution to the problem when he told the distributor that he had preserved continuity in the film and the only 'slight deviation' from the story was that he had 'married' soldier Rick and German girlfriend Marla. In fact, what he effected through a series of cuts was to ensure that the unmarried pair are reconciled after she avoids him because of their baby and her awareness of a previous relationship he had in America. Thus, lines such as Rick's, 'We're gonna be married,' and Tulsa's (Elvis) response, 'You want me to be best man?' were cut. No, replies, Rick, 'We need a babysitter,' for the time they are away being married. Later, Rick says that he 'already had a licence to marry' Marla when he finally locates her, but with this line cut, a further reference to 'licence' could be interpreted by an Irish viewer as a motorcar or other licence. Another cut on this topic was between Tulsa and his girlfriend, Lily, when he tells her he is babysitting for a buddy 'who just ran away to get married.' As a result, this already sanitized US Army propaganda film ensures that the theme of pre-marital sex was suppressed. When Rick and Marla return and are with the baby once more an Irish audience would have assumed that they went off on a short, but mysterious holiday. Further cuts included a scene where another GI, Cooky, and his girlfriend Tina are kissing on a couch. Despite the fact that Tina has her feet on the ground at all times, O'Hora ordered a cut because Cooky *appears* to be 'on top' of her. Another sub-plot concerns a bet among the soldiers that Chad will spend a night with the 'icy' Lily, a dancer, whose pelvic gyrations, incidentally, in her nightclub act are far more suggestive than Elvis'. A deletion was ordered to the nature of the bet, he had to stay 'till dawn', and later when it is revealed to Lily that Tulsa would 'spend the night with you, alone.' By then the pair have fallen in love and Tulsa has abandoned the bet, thus ensuring his pure intentions and moral integrity, a far cry from the pre-army Elvis.[34] Nine months later, *King Creole* was resubmitted to the Censor, no doubt because the distributor was trying to cash in on the continuing commercial success of Elvis as a recording and screen star.

On the surface, it would appear that this time O'Hora was more liberal, ordering just two cuts. However, the version submitted at 9,268 feet was 1,113 feet (thirteen minutes) less than the one submitted three years earlier. Indeed, the only cuts left to be made in 1961 were of the line, 'It's gotten so that I look longer at a dancer with clothes on than one without,' and the scene in which Fields offers Ronnie to Danny.[35] Two weeks later, O'Hora viewed *Wild in the Country* (Philip Dunne, 1961), in which hillbilly Elvis is involved with three women. Commenting that he was 'being more than lenient' in passing the film, he noted that it had 'quite a few problems,' but it is clear that his real anxiety was that 'the presence of Elvis Presley [would] ensure its being seen by ninety-five per cent of our teenagers and adolescents.' He ordered sixteen, mostly dialogue, cuts.[36] Six months later he reiterated this fear when he viewed Elvis' *Blue Hawaii* (Norman Taurog, 1961), noting that 'because of the age-group of the potential viewers, I have to be particularly careful.' However, he ordered just four cuts, two of which were restored by the Appeal Board. The first of the cuts overturned was a rather innocent scene in which Chad's (Elvis) girlfriend Maile (Joan Blackman), loses her bikini top while swimming and has a blouse brought to her in the water by a dog, while the first of three cuts concerning 17-year-old tourist Ellie (Jenny Maxwell) was also restored. During her first attempt to seduce Chad, Ellie surprises him with a kiss and when this fails to arouse him, she takes off the dress she is wearing over her swimsuit, thus inviting him to view her body. While the Board cancelled these two cuts, it supported the Censor in two others. One of these shows Ellie going to Chad's hotel room and, having once more failed to entice him to seduce her, lies back on the bed and says suggestively, 'I am in bed.' Another part of the scene cut was when Ellie says defiantly to Chad that 'I don't wear britches,' implying, of course, no underwear, but Chad, who calls her 'Miss oversexed' and 'Miss No Britches Bardot,' clearly has no intention of encouraging her. In his report to the Appeal Board on *Blue Hawaii*, O'Hora voiced his concern that 'ninety-nine per cent of the viewers of this picture will not be more than nineteen years of age.' Presley had been one of 'the bogeys' of his office for the previous five years and he went on to list the various 'representations and even delegations' – from the Catholic Women's Secondary Schools Federation, Church of Ireland, Presbyterian Church, and other religious and educational bodies – who had approached him because of 'the suggestiveness of every single picture in which Presley figured.' While *Blue Hawaii* was 'by no means his worst ... I thought that I should make the few cuts I did because of the age-group of the potential viewers.'[37]

By the end of the 1960s Elvis had made more than thirty increasingly sanitized, and censorially uncontroversial films. Nevertheless, the Censor's alertness to the erotic power of Elvis for girls and young women, and the physically liberating aspects of rock 'n' roll and rhythm 'n' blues in general, serves to highlight that emerging from beneath the apparently rigid and conservative Irish social scene was an assertive youth consciousness. This had been demonstrated by the response to *Rock around the Clock* in 1956 and was to be repeated ever more publicly during the following decade and beyond. If Irish culture could not provide the expressive release for the post-war generation, then imported mass culture, music and the cinema in particular, could do so, even if the latter was circulated in a truncated and highly-diluted form. Having said that, though, we need to be reminded that there was a mainstream conservative streak to 1950s teenage film and music, and the person most associated with that movement was singer and actor Pat Boone. The 'Clean Teen' films at the end of the decade which were at least as popular as Elvis' movies, such as Boone's *Bernardine* and *April Love*, both directed by Henry Levin in 1957, and *Mardi Gras* (Edmund Goulding, 1958), feature the clean-living and sexless teenager. So sanitized were these films that Boone refused, on religious grounds, even to kiss a girl on-screen. Yet, even these films, which

Thomas Doherty has described as existing in a 'never-never land' with 'well-behaved middle class youngsters with few blemishes,'[38] were often seen as too risqué for Irish teenagers. For example, O'Hora ordered ten cuts to the musical *Where the Boys Are* (Henry Levin, 1960),[39] in which four college girls spend a vacation near a military base in search of men, while the more innocuous *Gidget* (Paul Wendkos, 1959), featuring teen-idol Sandra Dee, was actually banned, a ban upheld after appeal. O'Hora regarded it as 'too much preoccupied with sex – adolescent sex – for my liking.'[40] However, given the undeniable conservatism of these 'Clean Teen' pictures, and even Elvis' post-army films, it is perhaps only nostalgists who remember a continuing radical or even critical presence in teen films after their initial flurry in the mid-1950s. It was not until the counter-culture of the late 1960s/early 1970s that another (albeit brief) flurry of 'authentic' youth-oriented commercial films were seen.

## CHAPTER 5

# From protectionism to 'liberalism'

I'm a virgin, Isak. That's why I talk so daringly.
Sara in Ingmar Bergman's *Wild Strawberries* (1957), cut by
Censor Liam O'Hora.[1]

PETER BERRY AND FILM CENSORSHIP

If cinematic representation (of the 'excesses') of human nature and sexuality (and what such images and narratives might provoke) always concerned the censor, this became, as already noted, more pronounced in the late 1950s as a result of the growing boldness of cinema, but also because of the changing nature of Irish society as can be seen in the response to *Rock around the Clock*. Following the death of Martin Brennan in office on 25 June 1956, the Official Irish Censor who was appointed to deal with these transformations was an unlikely one. In August 1956 Liam O'Hora became the first of the post-independence generation to be appointed to the position. Much of his early career had been spent in Palestine where he had joined the police force in 1938 and worked in various other capacities including as an arabic interpreter to the Australian Army, as well as in the Colonial Civil Service and in public relations. When he returned to Ireland, he became manager of the Gaiety Theatre in 1948, and while there, studied law, before being called to the Bar in 1954. Given such a background, it is possible that family connections may have aided his elevation to the role of Censor. His brother was Fr Cormac of Mount Argus, who had become involved in the Bernard Shaw/Gabriel Pascal film studio project in 1946/7 on the recommendation of Archbishop McQuaid,[2] while his cousin was Dr William Philbin, bishop of Down and Connor. Having such relatives, one could not imagine him responding sympathetically to the increasingly transgressive, youth-oriented, more sexually explicit and realist British and American cinemas of the late 1950s and early 1960s, and the pressure from exhibitors who saw Irish box office revenue decline from 1956 onwards.[3]

Unsurprisingly then, in January 1957, in his first annual report to the Minister of Justice, O'Hora expressed the difficulties he envisaged in the context of the recent liberalization of American film censorship:

Henceforth the problem of film censorship will be somewhat aggravated because of a certain lowering of standards by the Motion Picture Code Administration in Hollywood. Producers will be dealing with topics that hitherto have been completely taboo or at least portrayed in a most subdued manner. Homosexuality will have its place in the new films as well as other forms of sexual perversion and excess.[4]

The following year O'Hora wrote that he was right in his forecast, especially with regard to films 'preoccupied with the subject of sex.'

Some of the pictures were genuinely pornographic in part and the new Hollywood attempt at holding the mirror up to nature is almost entirely lacking in the finesse and balance that the Frenchman René Clair or the Italian Vittorio de Sica can impart to the most sordid of screen portrayals.[5]

Given the fact that de Sica's films, including *Indiscretion of an American Wife* (*Stazione Termini*, 1953, Italy/USA), which had been banned by Brennan when the distributor refused to accept eight cuts, a ban upheld after appeal,[6] and that only five months earlier O'Hora himself had cut *Umberto D* (1952, Italy) in seven places,[7] such that the distributor chose not to pursue a certificate, his defence of European cinema was more than a little hollow. Later, O'Hora would also cut in four places de Sica's *Two Women* (*La Ciociara*, 1960, Italy/France),[8] which further made such a reference seem not just to be a gratuitous inaccuracy, but, which once again serves to place (hypocritically) European cinema within a high art tradition apart from the vile and vulgar industrial product of America (and even Britain).

Nevertheless, O'Hora practically responded to new British and American cinema by issuing three limited certificates during 1957 for films with 'peculiarly adult themes'. One of these was for *The Seventh Sin* (Ronald Neame, 1957), a remake of a 1934 adaptation of a Somerset Maughan story, 'The Painted Veil', set in Hong Kong and China, in which an adulterous woman, played by Eleanor Parker, redeems herself during an epidemic. Despite the limited certificate, he also ordered cuts, and even though 'the adulterous episodes' were difficult 'to circumvent' – 'Nothing is left to the imagination ... as Carol and Paul are revealed, *in flagrante delicto*' – he reported that he had successfully cut the film while preserving 'logical continuity'.[9] However, O'Hora's 1957 annual report pointed out that 'the Department of Justice does not approve of my issuing limited certificates.' Though thanking him for his 'guidance,' O'Hora was also being indirectly critical of Peter Berry, the powerful senior civil servant at the Department of Justice, who was responsible for overseeing film censorship at this time. While nothing is on public record from the 1950s about Berry's attitude to cinema, a decade later as Secretary of the Department of Justice, he opposed the liberalization of publications censorship in 1967 when the Minister for Justice, Brian Lenihan, introduced the 'twelve year rule' which automatically unbanned all books after twelve years.[10] It is also probable that Berry was unhappy when Lenihan liberalized film censorship in 1965, discussed below.

The question of limited certificates 'is rather a sore point with me,' O'Hora wrote, 'as I am constantly being rebuked – by the press, the public, and occasionally the renters

– for not using my powers more frequently.' He also noted that 'even the Appeal Board' had at times pointed out to him that he was so empowered to issue such limited certificates under the Act. Indeed, he went so far as to declare that he was 'rather amazed that so many people seem to have read the 1923 Act.' Although O'Hora initially acceded to the 'wishes' of the department by not issuing limited certificates in 1958,[11] in the three months following the submission of that year's report, perhaps in defiance of Berry, he issued three. The first of these was on 18 February 1959 for *Cat on a Hot Tin Roof* (already discussed in chapter 4), while less than three weeks later on 6 March 1959 he passed with cuts *I Want to Live!* (Robert Wise, 1958), which, were it not intended for exhibition to adults, 'might have [been] rejected ... entirely.'[12] The film centers around real-life prostitute Barbara Graham (Susan Hayward) who was executed for murder. Despite the (perhaps unofficial) agreement with the renter to confine it to an adult audience, O'Hora ordered five cuts designed, in part, to suppress the references to prostitution, and almost certainly to drugs, though he seems to have missed the significance of the (marijuana) 'cigarette' being passed in the opening sequence. He deleted lines such as 'I'll rub oil all over your body so's you won't get too bad a burn' spoken by one of the film's seedy males as he tries to get Barbara to go away with him for the weekend, as well as removing an 'obscene gesture' by Barbara. The effect of these was that the film's length was reduced by five minutes on the British release version of 120 minutes, while the film carried an 'adults only' certificate specified by renter United Artists in the leasing contract for the film.[13] The following month, *Sister Letizia*, which deals with cloistered life, was also given an over-18s limited certificate.[14] Berry intervened again, but O'Hora made no reference to this in his annual report for 1959 sent to the Minister in February 1960.[15] However, in May 1961, in a supplementary report sent to a civil servant, Mr Toal, which dealt exclusively with the issue of limited certification, he wrote that after issuing three such certificates in 1959, 'Berry advised ... as to the definite departmental view on the granting of limited certificates.' Accordingly, he 'absolutely refused to issue any ... since ... [their] conversation.' He added that his attitude to certification was accepted by the renters 'and nowadays even the most persistent among them rarely raises the matter at all.'[16] Consequently, during O'Hora's last five years in office I have been able to identify only one limited certificate issued by him. This was for *Le Defroqué*, with its unique geographical audience quarantine, which is discussed in the previous chapter.

Unfortunately, the Appeal Board also treaded cautiously with regard to limited certificates, but, as it was independent of Peter Berry, potentially it could have opened up film censorship. That said, the conservative nature and long-serving composition of the Board (for example, J.T. O'Farrell, had held the post of chairman since 1929 and was not replaced until 1965) militated against radical change and, thus, during 1954 to 1964, it issued only eleven limited certificates. It was not until the revamping of the Board in 1965 that full use was made of the 1923 Act's limited certificate provisions. The very first limited certificate issued by the Board was in October 1954 for the French film, *Father Unknown* (*Né de Pere Inconnu*, Maurice Cloche, 1950), ten months after the Minister for Justice, Gerald Boland, told the Dáil that such limited certificates had 'seldom' been granted. For Brennan, as *Father Unknown* 'rather glorifies illegitimacy,' it was 'unsuitable for general exhibition' and as he was 'not prepared to give a limited certificate,' he banned the film. On appeal, the Board ordered just one cut – a sub-title which referred to the 'dreadful words ... adultery and bastard' – before issuing an over-18s certificate.[17] The following year, the Board issued two such certificates, one for *Prisoner of War* (Andrew Marton, 1954)[18], set in a prison camp in communist Korea, and the other for the science fiction film *The Quatermass Experiment* (aka *The Creeping Unknown*, Val Guest, 1955, GB). Both of these had been banned by Brennan, the latter only after the renter refused to make the nine cuts which had been requested. These concerned the monster, its 'pulsating' tendrils and his victims (screams, mutilated faces and arms), though, as ever, there was an objectionable intimate scene, in this case the opening of the film in which a young couple cavort in a haystack.[19] The Board only issued one other limited certificate during the rest of the decade. That was for the biographical film about New York's Irish-American Mayor Jimmy Walker, *Beau James* (Melville Shavelson, 1957), which O'Hora had banned because of the 'adulterous relationship' between Walker and singer Betty Compton. Like other censors who ignored the provisions set by the 1923 Act, or were afraid to defy his departmental mentors, he added that he would have been willing to issue a certificate 'if it could be insured that [it] would be viewed by adults only, since its subject matter is treated in a reasonable manner.' On appeal, the film subsequently received an over-18s certificate with just one cut.[20] Two and a half years later, the Board issued its next limited certificate, this time an over-16s one for *House on Haunted Hill* (William Castle, 1958), which O'Hora had regarded as an 'amalgam of horror and sex' that 'might be alright for adults,' but not for adolescents or children.[21] Two weeks later, they awarded an over-18s certificate without cuts to *Summer of the Seventeenth Doll* (aka *Season of Passion*, Leslie Norman, 1959, USA/Australia), which again had been banned by O'Hora even though he thought it 'could be shown to adults.'[22] Maintaining its commitment to granting such certificates, the Board approved with one cut and an over-18s certificate, the marry-and-murder comic film, *Bluebeard's Ten Honeymoons* (W. Lee Wilder, 1960, GB), which O'Hora had banned,[23] and later in the year issued an over-18s certificate for the milestone controversial 'horror' *Peeping Tom* (Michael Powell, 1960, GB).

O'Hora was unimpressed with the Board's decisions, especially after he had been brought under departmental control by Berry in 1959. In his report to the Minister for 1960, written in January 1961, O'Hora complained that the Board had reversed four of his (1960) rejections: *Summer of the Seventeenth Doll*; the British horror film, *Behemoth, The Sea Monster* (Douglas Hickox, 1958);[24] the film of slum life and drug addiction, *Let No Man Write My Epitaph* (Philip Leacock, 1960);[25] and the influential lesbian film, *Mädchen in Uniform* (submitted as *Girls in Uniform*, Leontine Sagan, 1931, Germany).[26] He reported on having raised the change in Board policy with Berry, noting that it placed him 'in a rather invidious position'. While the Appeal Board was confined to the same legal and statutory terms of reference as himself, it frequently issued limited certificates, and

it will not surprise me if it grants even more in the future because of the prevailing trend towards the making of entirely adult pictures and the incessant
and increasing pressure of every kind from the renters. The practice of the
Appeal Board in granting limited certificates leaves me open to a constant
demand for the granting of the same facilities.

Nevertheless, he accurately observed that the Appeal Board 'generally upholds my decisions quite consistently.' Indeed, he was keen to emphasize his empathy with the Board
the following year in his first report to the new Minister for Justice, Charles Haughey,
drawing attention to the fact that it had adjudicated on only seventeen films, of which it
reversed only one of his decisions, and partially reversed two others: 'The incumbent of
this office,' he recorded, 'has never before received such vindication from the Appeal
Board.' He added that 'the Board's attitude is further proof of the trend of films today.'
Yet only four months later he regarded the Appeal Board as negating his efforts as it
appeared 'to continue, and even to extend' the granting of limited certificates, particularly
in relation to horror pictures.[27] A month later in June 1961, the Board viewed the Hammer
horror film, *The Curse of the Werewolf* (aka *The Wolfman*, Terence Fisher, 1961, GB),
which had been banned by O'Hora, and gave it an over-16s certificate with four cuts.[28]

Additionally, in his report for 1962 to the Minister for Justice, O'Hora complained
that the Board had passed without limited certificates *Adam and Eve* (*Adan y Eva*, Alberto
Gout, 1956, Mexico), adapted from *Genesis*, and *Nights of Rasputin* (*L'Ultimo Zar*, aka
*The Night They Killed Rasputin*, Pierre Chenal, 1960, Italy/France). He had banned both
films, the first because of nudity,[29] and the second because of its unsuitablity for children.[30] Given that exhibitors outside Dublin refused to handle *Adam and Eve*, while those
taking *Nights of Rasputin* imposed a voluntary restriction on persons under-18 years-of-
age being admitted, O'Hora felt justified in his comment that this seemed 'to indicate a
most definite and indeed deliberate lowering of the standards [by the Appeal Board] than
[had] hitherto prevailed.' He went on to write that 'scores of pictures rejected in the past
are relatively mild compared with the two ... mentioned. So the news has gone abroad
that the Appeal Board will not be so finicky in the future.'[31] O'Hora's bitterness at the
Board may be explained by their relative independence of action, as, unlike himself, they
were not under the thumb of the Department of Justice. For the first time since 1923,
there emerged a minor chasm between the Film Censor and the Board.

Some renewal of the co-ordination policy of the past between the Board, Censor,
and Department of Justice officials must have occurred as O'Hora does not record any
further complaints against the Board during his last fifteen months in office. Indeed, the
Board only resumed issuing limited certificates following the appointment in April 1964
of O'Hora's successor, Dr Christopher Macken. The Board issued two before its term
of office expired later that year. In July 1964, the downbeat comedy *Only Two Can Play*
(Sidney Gilliat, 1962, GB) based on Kingsley Amis' novel and starring Peter Sellers, which
was previously banned by O'Hora, was passed with cuts and its viewing restricted to
over-18s,[32] while two months later the film adaptation of William Golding's novel *Lord
of the Flies* (Peter Brook, 1963, GB), banned by Macken, was approved without cuts

with an over-16s certificate.[33] The Board also reversed Macken's banning of *The Masque of the Red Death* (Roger Corman, 1964, GB);[34] *Black Torment* (Robert Hartford-Davis, 1964, GB), an eighteenth-century ghost story;[35] and the short, *Position of Trust* (GB), despite having 'illicit sex and blackmail'.[36] It is perhaps interesting to note that architect Sam Stephenson, who had been appointed to the Board in April 1964 by Charles Haughey, was party to the some of these decisions, and that he was the only one to be re-appointed to the new Board though not initially. The consequences of the bolting down of the hatches during 1962–64 was that the campaign for changing the general certificate policy grew in intensity. Unsurprisingly, perhaps the treatment of horror films was to the fore of the public controversy.

HORROR FILMS

Since the 1920s it was horror more than any other genre which had exposed the contradictions and restrictions of the general certificate policy and defined the censors' approach to limited certificates. Certainly, the censors saw to it that sexually explicit films, or those which infringed the 'family only' policy were cut or banned, but horror films – largely Dracula, Frankenstein, and werewolf films of the 1920s to the 1940s, and the more sexually explicit ones of the 1950s and 1960s – most frequently led to calls for the issuing of limited certificates and caused the greatest unease among censors and public commentators alike. Before considering the censors' response, a brief summary of horror is necessary.

Horror is primarily concerned with what Julia Kristeva terms the 'abject', a place where meaning collapses or where boundaries are crossed.[37] Broadly speaking, horror's function is to question (self-) identity and certainty and show the continuum of man with the rest of the universe (the cosmoglogical), the psyche or interior (the psychological), animal (the biological) and machine (the technological), and to expose the fragility of life, civilization, and its values, even if the text is tamed by a neat closure or ultimately is made to serve a conservative rather than radical or progressive agenda. Exemplary is horror's interest in the world of the undead, that is, those who have passed to another state – death – yet still remain in the material and/or human world, such as the vampires of Bram Stoker's *Dracula* (1897). While vampires rise from the dead at night, the protagonist of Mary Shelly's *Frankenstein: A Modern Prometheus* (1818) seeks to create life from death by reviving a corpse, 'the most sickening of wastes'.[38] Another popular trope, though most closely associated with German Expressionist cinema, is that of the döppelganger, or the dual personality. This is often scientifically induced as in Robert Louis Stevenson's *Dr Jekyll and Mr Hyde* (1886). Here the struggle is between good and evil, or the values and behaviour of a 'surplus repressed'[39] society and a liberated amoral animal nature. Elsewhere, the boundary between human and animal is more explicit as in werewolf narratives, while Oscar Wilde's *The Picture of Dorian Gary* (1891) becomes the classic tale of those who try to defy old age and death, and thus retain perpetual youth but at an enormous price. Wilde's story blurs image and reality as the eponymous character becomes his beautiful and youthful portrait while the painting itself ages. Its aptness as a metaphor for the cinematic image is one that has been well rehearsed. In short, horror affects the sense of self by challenging or transgressing boundaries – psychological, spiritual, physical, social, national, etc. – whether intimately (in terms of the body) or more broadly, as in the case of Armageddon-type scenarios.

While these literary originating stories – Dracula, Frankenstein, Dr Jekyll and Mr Hyde – as well as many tales by Edgar Allan Poe and those that featured the exotic world of mummies and voodoo formed the blueprint of cinematic horror, their ability to produce a sense of (fearful) possibility was greatly enhanced by the inherent qualities of cinema. If these most obviously included movement and scale, and later, sound and colour, no less important, and from a censor's perspective, perhaps, most potent, was the cinema audience. Horror's isolated (if transgressive) reader was replaced by a mass audience with an all together more unstable and powerful dynamic, and which James Montgomery and other censors feared, was largely uneducated. Arguably, regardless of its form or content, horror articulates, at least to some degree, the anxieties or fissures in society at a particular moment and, as such, can be used to read or understand a culture. However, until relatively recently, this 'low' and popular form has received little of the cultural or academic analysis accorded to other genres within cinema such as the gangster, western, thriller, and even musical.[40] Yet, unlike those constructing the critical canon, the censors have always been alert to the dynamics and meaning of horror, even if they often could not contain its excesses, except through banning.

An early example of horror, banned by Montgomery, was Tod Browning's *The Unknown* (1927). It tells of a strangler (played by Lon Chaney) wanted for murder who disguises his identity (and two-thumb hand) by blackmailing a doctor into amputating his arms, and then, under the stage name of Alonzo the Armless Wonder, performing a knife-throwing act using his feet. He is killed when he jealously attempts to injure strong man Malabar (Norman Kerry), who is in love with Estrellita (Joan Crawford), and whom she has come to love, despite having spurned both Alonzo and Malabar out of a neurotic dislike of all men because of how she has been treated in the past. For film critic Phil Hardy *The Unknown* is 'one of the truly great silent movies,' and is unusual 'in the depth and darkness of its undertones of sexual phobia.'[41] But, it was this, of course, which Montgomery wanted to suppress. He regarded this 'chamber of horrors' as 'unfit for general exhibition.' Apart from its 'cruelty,' he complained that 'the heroine is almost semi-nude in the opening scenes,' while the last reel is 'unhealthy sensationalism'. He concluded with a warning endorsed by the Appeal Board which upheld his banning order: 'Think of its effects on youngsters or even on nervous adults.'[42]

In the early 1930s there was a huge expansion in the number of horror pictures produced within the American film industry. While Tod Browning's *Dracula* (1931) and James Whale's *Frankenstein* (1931) were to the forefront of this development, a great many other horror films were released, many without any interference from the Irish censors, though we do not always know the version of the film submitted. For example, the 1930 sound version with additional sequences directed by Ernst Laemmle and dialogue by Frank McCormack of Rupert Julian's 1925 *Phantom of the Opera* was passed uncut,[43] as was another Universal film, *The Cat Creeps* (Rupert Julian, 1930),[44] and the somewhat pedestrian British adaptation of Arthur Conan Doyle's detective novel which pits Sherlock Holmes, the epitome of rationality against the supernatural, *The Hound of the Baskervilles* (V. Gareth Gaundry, 1931).[45] However, the censors were becoming alert to the evolving horror genre as their treatment of *Dracula* and *Frankenstein* shows. With *Dracula*, which was passed uncut in Britain, though the submitted version seems to have had seven minutes cut,[46] the Irish renter was simply ordered to 'delete some of the horrors' (from what would have been this shortened version) and a certificate was granted in June 1931.[47] *Frankenstein*, viewed eight months later, was treated much more harshly. While the version submitted was probably the British one which had been issued with an 'A' or adult certificate and from which a total of seven minutes had been removed (including the monster fatally impaling the hunchback),[48] Montgomery, in his typical response to horror films, recorded that he could not grant the film a general certificate whereby audiences 'containing children or nervous people' might see it. Indeed, he argued that it was unsuitable 'even [for] an adult audience' because 'it panders to the morbid and unhealthy minded,' while its 'cruelty and brutality would have a demoralising effect on many.' Arguably, it was the film's insistence on the innate innocence of the monster which proved too much for Montgomery. It is after all a most moral, if also sentimental and viscerally engaging film, which places the inevitability of the monster's ultimate savage behaviour on society and its prejudices and fears, and more specifically on the scientist's sin of transgressing the human condition and playing God. The Appeal Board took a more lenient view and passed it.[49] This was also the case with the 'very heavily cut' *Dr Jekyll and Mr Hyde* (Rouben Mamoulian, 1931)[50] which had been banned by Montgomery as 'the lengthy remnant' was still unfit for general exhibition.[51] Similarly, the Board passed *The Mummy* (Karl Freund, 1932), which though passed in Britain, had been rejected by deputy Censor Joseph Holloway because of 'semi-nudity' towards the end of the film.[52] (Unfortunately, all the Censors' reports to the Board pertaining to films viewed by the Board prior to 1946, and more importantly, the Board's Minute Books recording details of cuts, are missing from the records.)

In March 1932, *Murders in the Rue Morgue* (Robert Florey, 1932), a film influenced by the germinal Expressionist film *The Cabinet of Dr Caligari*, was submitted. Again, though the version submitted to the Irish Censor was most likely that which had been cut and passed with an 'A' certificate by the BBFC,[53] the Irish Censor ordered *only* three cuts before issuing it with a general certificate. Besides the injunction to shorten the fight scene on the bridge and to delete close-ups of a dagger, the main cut was of the torture and death of a girl (Arlene Francis) picked up by the mad doctor/fairground hypnotist Dr Mirakle's (Bela Lugosi) servant. Taken to the laboratory where Mirakle is experimenting on man/ape blood mixing, he extracts blood from her and she dies screaming on the rack.[54] The following year, *Doctor X* (Michael Curtiz, 1931), a film concerning a murderous scientist (Preston Foster) being investigated by a reporter (Lee Tracy), was submitted. Yet again, the Irish Censor probably viewed the British version from which six minutes had been cut prior to submission to the BBFC and trimmed a further 205 feet. Montgomery told the renter that he could only issue a general certificate and ordered him to 'cut to that standard.' Among the scenes to be edited was one in which the renter was to reduce considerably 'the tension of horror' while the struggle between the murderer and the reporter was to be 'cut to the limit.'[55] As already discussed, it was Montgomery's aim to strip cinema of its lure, whether, in this instance, as narrative appeal (suspense), or as hypnotic (often erotic) image.

In response to the public controversy following the increasing number of horror films, in 1933 the BBFC introduced a new category of certification. To the 'U' (universal, or in Irish terms, general certificate) and 'A' (adult) was added 'H' for horror. While the first film to be certified 'H' was *The Ghoul* (T. Hayes Hunter, 1933, GB) had just two shots cut by the Irish Censor, one of 'the Ghoul' cutting a symbol on his breast, and another of a close-up,[56] the next 'H' viewed by the Irish Censors, *The Invisible Man* (James Whale, 1933) was passed uncut,[57] as was *The Vampire Bat* (Frank Strayer, 1933),[58] and *The House of Doom* (aka *The Black Cat, The Vanishing Body*, Edgar E. Ulmer, 1933).[59] Indeed, a feature of Irish censorship in the 1930s, especially after the introduction of the restrictions on the American film industry following the establishment of the Production Code Administration in 1934, is how few horror films were banned or cut. Among other horror films passed uncut were *The Bride of Franskenstein* (James Whale, 1935),[60] *The Mark of the Vampire* (Tod Browning, 1935),[61] *The Hands of Orlac* (aka *Mad Love*, Karl Freund, 1935),[62] *The Raven* (Louis Friedlander, 1935),[63] *The Werewolf of London* (Stuart Walker, 1935),[64] all of which received 'H' certificates from the BBFC, *Dracula's Daughter* (Lambert Hillyer, 1936)[65] and *Revolt of the Zombies* (Victor Halperin, 1936).[66] Nevertheless, if the Code was largely responsible for producing films palatable for an Irish audience, it could be argued that horror, if it was not graphically rendered or imbued with an erotic or sexual sense, was not, given Ireland's post-colonial and troubled history, an anathema to the Irish psyche. Indeed, crossed boundaries and the refusal of clarity have often characterized the Irish experience, while the practice of waking the dead, together with pagan and gothic traditions, have tamed death and the non-rational. Nevertheless, a more obvious reason beyond the fact that the versions submitted had been censored already, is that a number of key horror films of the 1930s were not submitted, or submitted much later, to the Irish Censor. One such film is *Freaks* (aka *Forbidden Love, Nature's Mistress, The Monster Show*, Tod Browning, 1932), the best known of the films released in the 1920s and 1930s which featured human oddities and which the BBFC banned and only passed in 1963 with an 'X' certificate, while, as discussed in chapter 7, when it finally came before the Irish censors in 1999 it was banned.[67] The story focuses on a number of such performers who though shown with compassion, assert their mutual support for one another by a vengeful attack on a 'normal' woman by turning her into a hideous and chicken bodied creature after she conspires to kill her dwarf husband. In keeping with the new medicalized view of abnormalities, some copies of the film were prefaced with a statement that such freaks were being eliminated by science. Difference was clearly been coded as abnormal disease or condition and stripped of its magical and exotic aura, perhaps a factor in the film's relative lack of success at the box office. Other films not submitted were the anomalous early grind-house exploitationer, *Maniac* (Dwain Esper, 1934), with poor cast and production values and featuring nudity and grotesque scenes that look forward to 1980s body horror, and the classic adaptation of H.G.Wells' *The Island of Dr Moreau*, *Island of Lost Souls* (Erle C. Kenton, 1932), which in Britain, presumably not because of the film's raw climatic revolt of the beast-men, but the scenes of vivisection, had been banned on three occasions by the BBFC, before it being eventually approved in 1958.[68] In Ireland it was submitted six months later, whereupon it was banned.[69]

As already referred to in the discussion of the 1930s, Montgomery refused to issue limited certificates and so films such as *King Kong* and *The Hunchback of Notre Dame* had to be cut to ensure their suitability for children. When he was unable to prune the film, banning became a necessity as was the case with *The Dark Eyes of London* (aka *The Human Monster*, Walter Summers, 1939), a British 'H' film, in which a mute giant (Bela Lugosi) is manipulated by the proprietor of a home for the blind into drowning insured people.[70] Although his successor, Richard Hayes, did not, at least until near the end of his tenure, have to face anything like the same number of horror films, his report on *The Return of the Vampire* (1943) reveals a similarity to Montgomery in his concern about the power of the image. He noted that 'macabre stories are relatively harmless to read … It is a very different matter when presented realistically on the screen.' Notwithstanding his decision to ban the film because of its 'strong appeal to the morbid and prurient, young and old'[71] (as well as ignoring the notion of realism being applied to a vampire film), distributors may have regarded Hayes as being more lenient than his predecessor. Hayes' more relaxed approach can be seen in his treatment of *White Zombie* (Victor Halperin, 1932), the first zombie movie which also had been viewed by Montgomery.

'One of the underground classics of horror,'[72] *White Zombie* concerns Madeline (Madge Bellamy) and her fiancé Neil (John Harron) who are due to be married in Haiti at the home of Beaumont (Robert Frazer). However, their host desires Madeline and in order to bring her under his control, enlists the help of sugar mill owner and zombie master 'Murder' Legendre (Bela Lugosi) who also desires her. During his rescue of Madeline from Beaumont's prison-like gothic castle, Neil kills the two men and Madeline is released from the spell. When Montgomery viewed the film in 1932 he decreed that it was 'unfit for General Exhibition' and banned it because 'the pagan superstition of the Zombie or soul-less is a negation of Christian doctrine.' The Irish renter, though, was given a 'chance to amend' the film and the re-submitted version was passed.[73] Interestingly, when Hayes viewed the original film nine years later, he found no objection either to the theme or the scenes with the 'soulless' zombies. Indeed, he didn't bring to bear any deep philosophical concerns or symbolic understanding, but confined his intervention to the graphic. He ordered just two changes to the film: one as Madeline is changing for her wedding in her underwear with her midriff visible, while the other concerned the 'gruesome' death of Beaumont's servant Silver (Brandon Hurst), who is taken by the zombies and thrown into a swirling pool of water.[74] Otherwise, the film's themes of the supernatural and of three different men desiring Madeline, as well as, for children, the undoubtedly frightening episodes in the graveyard, especially as the zombies recover Madeline's coffin from the crypt after she has 'died', were apparently allowed uncut. While the erotic or exploitative possibilities of a zombieized woman was not fully explored in this film (though many of the symbolic exchanges, such as the red rose being proffered by Beaumont to Madeline, or her scarf wrapped in a large candle by 'Murder', carry explicit erotic messages), the film, like *I Walked with a Zombie* (Jacques Tourneur, 1943), viewed two years later, contained the ability to transgress the 'family' policy.

In line with much horror of the time, *I Walked with a Zombie* situates horror at one remove from America and the familiar. Here a Canadian nurse, Betsy (Frances Dee), travels to the West Indies to look after Jessica (Christine Gordon), the zombieized wife of sugar mill owner Paul Holland (Tom Conway). Though the film contains potentially frightening undertones of voodoo and possession, Hayes' concern focused on the more mundane adulterous relationship between Jessica and Paul's half-brother Wesley (James Ellison). In a scene referred to by Hayes as 'The British Grenadier Song' he made his only cut. As Betsy and Wesley are having a drink at a cafe, a street singer sings in a censored verse of the sterility of Jessica's relationship with her husband and her subsequent affair with Wesley: 'The Holland man he kept in a tower / A wife as pretty as a big white flower / She saw the brother and she stole his heart / And that's how the badness and the trouble start.'[75] Another verse, which appears not to have been cut, reveals that Jessica and Wesley wanted to leave the island, but Paul refused to let them go. Later, Paul's mother tells how she had access to voodoo and caused Jessica to become a zombie. By then, Betsy and Paul, her employer, have fallen in love, but she does not transgress, except symbolically, his marriage vows, and works, unsuccessfully, to restore Jessica to well-being. It is Wesley who, in the end, takes Jessica to the sea where they both drown. This scene of 'murder' and 'suicide' also seems to have been allowed, perhaps because it facilitates the two 'innocent' parties, Betsy and Paul, who are now free to fully acknowledge their love, and gets rid of the already spiritually dead Jessica and the immoral Wesley.

In films such as *I Walked with a Zombie*, and other horror films produced by Val Lewton,[76] one could argue that 'normality' is questioned. As Jancovich observes, 'the modern world is seen as one of repression and control, in which alienated characters become lost in a paranoiac landscape where fantasies and realities become indistinguisable.'[77] Commenting on Tourneur in the context of a later film, *Night of the Demon* (aka *Curse of the Demon*, Jacques Tourneur, 1957, GB), to which Liam O'Hora made one major cut concerning 'spiritualism,'[78] Phil Hardy observed that Tourneur's

> extraordinary placing and handling of the camera imbue seemingly ordinary surroundings with a brooding sense of menace. The trees, objects of simply unlit areas darkly obtruding in the foreground suggest the presence of implacable forces waiting to pounce on vulnerable, isolated figures ... an object lesson in atmospheric horror.[79]

It was films with features such as these which led to Hayes' timid complaints about the limits of the general certificate system during 1943–1944 in particular (outlined in chapter 4). And while he tried to contain the more explicitly horrific visual conventions of this wide-ranging genre, the non-specific, often all-pervasive, brooding sense of menace and eroticism like *film noir's* sense of (transgressive) sensuality, could not be suppressed.

The most frequent cinematic representation of the 'undead' is found in the Dracula cycle. Hayes cut *Son of Dracula* (Robert Siodmak, 1943) in just one place, the 'distorted faces of the Count and Frank' towards the end of the film.[80] However, though a relatively mild film, as Hardy points out, the 'morbidly erotic side' of the vampire/young woman relationship is explicit in the Count's (Lon Chaney) wooing of a Southern belle (Louise Albritton) who 'ecstatically embraces' vampirism in order to share immortality with him.[81] *House of Dracula* (Erle C. Kenton, 1945), with its trio of monsters – Dracula, Frankenstein and the Wolfman – had greater difficulty with the Censor, again not because of eroticism, which is quite minimal, but because of its possible blasphemy, a theme to which all censors were very alert even though the Christian symbol of the cross is seen in a positive and powerful light. Hayes ordered seven cuts, especially of those scenes in which Dracula tries to entice the doctor's assistant Melissa into discarding her crucifix. Cut were his lines: 'Forsake the cross so you can join me' in the other world and 'Cast away the cross so that you may join me there.' Other cuts included the attempted suicide by the man/werewolf and the murderous behaviour of the mad doctor/scientist as he is in the process of becoming a vampire when he strangles villager Siegfried, and then kills his hunchbacked woman assistant while he is reviving Frankenstein.[82] Another film featuring a wolfman who, in this instance, ends up being burned alive as a result of a providential bolt of lightning, was *The Mad Monster* (Sam Newfield, 1942), made in the wake of the successful *The Wolfman* (George Warner, 1941), which was submitted to the Irish Censor belatedly in 1952 following its unbanning in Britain that year when it received an X' certificate, as well as a disclaimer on blood transfusions. Unsurprisingly, it was banned by Hayes because of the general certificate policy.[83] A similar situation arose with *Jungle Jim in the Forbidden Land* (Lew Landers, 1952), one of a series of films starring Tarzan actor Johnny Weissmuller. According to Hayes, the film, aimed mainly at young people, while not strictly speaking a horror, would have received an 'H' rating in Britain had it been submitted because it consisted of 'almost continuous scenes of brutality and cruelty.' When a cleaned-up version was submitted, Hayes remain unsatisfied, but the renter successfully appealed to the Board and Hayes' decision was reversed.[84]

An image central to vampire films is the lifting of the coffin lid prior to the vampire's rising from his/her day's rest. Despite a recurrence of a version of this within the Irish tradition of the corpse apparently rising, not from the sealed earth-bound coffin, but from a table during the wake, albeit treated in a comic manner such as in Dion Boucicault's *The Shaughraun* (1874) – a trope extensively used in early cinema[85] – viewed from a position of official Catholic and repressed culture, this image was deemed transgressive. Thus, in *Dead Men Walk* (Sam Newfield, 1943), not submitted to the Irish Censor until 1950, which features a man killing his evil twin who returns to 'life' as a vampire to seek revenge, the scene in which 'Old Kate' takes off the coffin's lid and the subsequent scenes of the hunchback (Dwight Frye) trundling along with the coffin prior to the vampire (George Zucco) rising up were cut.[86] To the 'morbid and fantastic film' *Before I Hang* (Nick Grinde, 1940), in which a scientist (Boris Karloff) working on a rejuvenation serum turns killer when he uses the blood of a murderer, Hayes cut four murders, as well as scenes of strangling and 'neck-fracturing'.[87] For the Censor, scenes of strangulation were always problematic, such as those in *The Mummy's Curse* (Leslie Goodwins, 1944),[88] but notwithstanding Hayes' status as a medical doctor, that the 'scientific experiments' ended in tragedy was important in so far as it fed into the dominant fear of (scientific) progress and served as a warning against playing or usurping God.

Jekyll and Hyde, or variations on the dual nature of man, or the border between man and beast, has been one of the staples of cinematic horror. One version submitted to the Irish Censor was Victor Fleming's 1941 *Dr Jekyll and Mr Hyde*.[89] Given Ireland's official attitude to sexuality, it is interesting that Hayes didn't read the symbolic and transgressive meaning of the protagonist's (Spencer Tracy) bodily transformation, which he allowed uncut. Nevertheless, he did understand the sexual charge in the relationship between Jekyll, most particularly as Hyde, and the lower-class Ivy (Ingrid Bergman). Jekyll meets Ivy when he and his friend Lanyon (Ian Hunter) rescue her from a violent suitor. Taking her home, Jekyll is drawn to her sensuality which contrasts with his upper-class fiancée Beatrice (Lana Turner). In the first of five cuts to this sequence, Ivy takes off her blouse, which is followed with her telling an aroused Jekyll that she thought she was being picked up by a couple of 'toffs'. A third cut involves Jekyll leading her on with the line, 'Your eyes are pools of desire,' and her taking off her stockings. These preliminaries result in them kissing, a scene observed by Lanyon. A final 'doubtful scene' occurs when Ivy tells Jekyll that 'I ain't no, ain't no …,' but the word prostitute is not delivered, and Jekyll replies, 'I know you are not.' Cut, too, was the following scene of Jekyll and Lanyon discussing the night's events in a cab on the way home during which Jekyll's fascination with Ivy is clear. The by now truncated scenes of Jekyll's cross-class fascination had stripped the film of its double duality: good man/bad man (Jekyll/Hyde); virginal woman/sexual woman (Beatrice/Ivy). In fact, to ensure that Jekyll remains faithful to Beatrice, and in keeping with repressing non-Catholic sanctioned relationships, Hayes largely deleted the bad animalistic Hyde and his 'adulterous' behaviour, including his invitation to Ivy to join him in 'debauchery'. He cut the montage sequence which includes 'Ivy lying seminude,' as Hyde asserts for the first time his personality, while the final three cuts concern Hyde's visits to Ivy's lodgings where their unholy couplings, it is hinted, occur.[90] However, Hayes' intervention – twelve cuts in all – devalue the impact of Dr Jekyll's ultimate destruction and, indeed, throw into confusion the nature of the debate between the doctor and the bishop (C. Aubrey Smith) at the dinner party early in the film. During the exchange, Jekyll outlines his theory of good and evil being in continuous conflict in the soul and his research as attempting to tip the balance in favour of good.

Yet for the bishop, Jekyll's project, which has failed to find favour within the medical establishment, amounts to tampering with God's work. Thus isolated from his religious and professional peers, Jekyll discovers his animalistic 'evil' self in his visceral dealings with Ivy, and as it becomes more dominant, he is killed as a result.

Towards the end of his term in office, Hayes got a glimpse of the gruesome and 'ordinary' direction horror was taking when he viewed *House of Wax* (André de Toth, 1953), photographed in 3-D. In it, a mad sculptor/academic, Professor Jarrett (Vincent Price), murders people in order to transform them into 'realistic' mannequins for his wax museum. Hayes cut a number of scenes, including one in which Jarrett steals a woman's dead body from a roomful of shrouded corpses, specifically ordering cut a shot which reveals the woman's head. Also deleted was a mannequin which has its head guillotined at the museum, featured close-ups of heroine Sue's head and shoulders as she is about to be immersed (naked) in a vat of wax and turned into a mannequin, as well as the close-up of a needle which is about to be administered to her by Jarrett. (After she is rescued, her thanks to a police officer for loaning her his coat, a reference to her prior nakedness, was allowed.) Hayes' report on the film concluded rather weakly with a 'suggestion' to the renter that children should not be admitted to the film.[91]

Hayes' successor, Martin Brennan, seems largely to have been untroubled by horror, with *The Mad Magician* (John Brahm, 1954) – an attempt to reprise Vincent Price's role in *House of Wax*, but in this instance as a murderous magician – one of the few such films he cut.[92] However, he banned *Gorilla at Large* (Harmon Jones, 1954) because 'the appearance of the huge gorilla should be much too terrifying for any *normal* audience.' (Emphasis added.)[93] During his tenure, the related science fiction genre came to the fore, with Brennan adjudicating on the 'brutal, sadistic' *Quatermass Experiment*. When the renter refused to make the nine cuts which were required for a general certificate, the Board issued one of its rare over-18s certificates without requesting any cuts.[94] Interestingly, the film's producers Hammer, when realizing they had an innovative film on their hands, chose to emphasize its 'X' quality by renaming it *The Quatermass Xperiment*. Such a strategy was in keeping with a general trend towards the sensational which was designed to encourage a jaded audience back into the cinema following the social and economic changes that occurred in the 1950s.[95] The attempt by Irish distributors to attach a degree of notoriety to such films became more prevalent later in the decade when trailers for films with reference to a film's 'X' certificate were ordered cut on numerous occasions by Liam O'Hora. While these were probably the British cinema trailers, distributors were not shy at pretending that the Irish version of the film was more risqué or horrific than it actually was.

In the interregnum between Brennan's sudden death in June 1956 and Liam O'Hora's appointment six weeks later, civil servant and deputy Censor, E.C. Powell, viewed the influential science fiction film, *Invasion of the Body Snatchers* (Don Siegel, 1956). Rather than being concerned with the zombie-izing of the population of a small American town by the pods from outer space, a narrative element which has often been read as a reference to communism (though arguably equally applicable to capitalism, globalization, or the blandness of modern culture), Powell kept his focus on the infringement of traditional values, ordering cut a scene, early in the film, in which a brief reference is made to divorce in Reno. Becky (Dana Wynter) meets old flame Miles (Kevin McCarthy), who has also divorced recently. He comments that though they are 'life brothers,' the difference between them is that while he is paying 'dues' (alimony) she is collecting it. A later scene featuring the two was also cut. After fearing she was about to be zombieized, or replaced by an emotionless alien duplicate, Miles brings Becky to his house. As she is boiling eggs for breakfast, Miles says to her in an exchange about their previous spouses cut by Powell: 'Did you do this for your husband?' Becky responds: 'Did your wife do this for you?' Miles replies: 'Oh, yes, she liked to cook.'[96] All of the impending doom, and the overwhelming of the community by the alien pods, was left intact. As long as Irish audiences believed that marriage was indissoluble, then aliens or no aliens, life went on.

Powell also initiated O'Hora into the job, for which he was 'deeply indebted'. As he reported to the Minister for Justice, James Everett TD, in early 1957, it was Powell 'who acted as my mentor' for the 'first weeks'.[97] O'Hora bore the brunt of the radical transformation of the horror genre as he was confronted by a range of films which would almost automatically have received an 'X' certificate in Britain. Despite his stated desire to issue more limited certificates, O'Hora declared that some films should not be seen even by adults. One example is *The Black Sleep* (Reginald Le Borg, 1956) in which the formula of creation turning on creator is played out through a Victorian brain surgeon who, experimenting on humans so as to achieve the means to restore his comatosed wife, produces freaks who turn on him. After viewing it in early 1957, he described it as 'not just ordinarily horrific,' but 'it is even clinically so.' He went on to say that while it was 'utterly unsuitable for children or adolescents,' it was also 'not the kind of picture that might be considered for a limited certificate.'[98] By 1959, though, O'Hora was coming under sustained pressure concerning his approach to horror films. He told the Board following his rejection of *The Horrors of the Black Museum* (Arthur Crabtree, 1959, GB), in which a writer induces his assistant to commit ghoulish murders which he then writes about for his sensation-seeking public, that he had received 'countless protests' during the previous few months. Some of these had come from 'thinking people of every walk of life' and he had had letters from parents which had convinced him that he had been 'too lenient' in granting certificates for horror. While the Board upheld his decision to ban the film, when it was re-submitted in 1961, he approved it with four cuts, and the title was changed to *The Black Museum* (an indication, perhaps, of the evolution of horror, especially as transformed by *Psycho* and *Peeping Tom*, the importance of which is discussed below).[99] The sequel to *Black Museum*, *Circus of Horrors* (Sidney Hayers, 1959, GB), was banned in 1960.[1] Two months earlier, O'Hora had banned the British film, *Behemoth, the Sea Monster*, and in his report to the Board on that film he said that there was a 'strong campaign' in Ireland against horror films for children, but, as noted, the Board ignored his advice and reversed the decision.[2]

Like America's Universal before them, Britain's Hammer Films was central in the revitalizing of the horror genre, especially through their ace director Terence Fisher, and later Roger Corman who offered a further spin to gothic horror with his nine adaptations of the stories of Edgar Allan Poe. *The Curse of Frankenstein* (Terence Fisher, 1957) was the 'breakthrough' film of the genre in the postwar era,[3] in part because of its innovative use of colour – the first British horror to be so shot – but also because it shifted the focus away from the creature, as was the case with the Universal films of the 1930s and 1940s, to the creator, in this instance Baron Frankenstein. When released in London in May 1957 with just one major cut, a shot of Frankenstein (Vincent Price) dropping the bird-pecked highwayman's head into a vat of acid,[4] it was, like *The Quatermass Experiment*, a box office sensation, notwithstanding or perhaps because of the opprobrium poured on it by newspaper reviewers such as the *Observer's* C.A. Lejeune who described it as 'among the half-dozen most repulsive films I have encountered.'[5] While such critics denigrated British horror and science fiction films in favour of 'quality' British 'realist' cinema, the Irish Censor's agenda was more narrowly focused. When O'Hora viewed the film in June 1957, he declared that he had come to the conclusion that it was 'too powerful a combination of horror and sex' to allow for its exhibition in Ireland and duly banned it. In his report to the Appeal Board, he asserted that he was not influenced 'in the slightest' by the controversy that it had caused in Britain, but re-stated his difficulty with the 'too powerful' coupling of horror and sex. The Board agreed and upheld his decision. Fifteen months later, a cut version was passed by O'Hora with a further five cuts, most of which concerned the accumulation by Frankenstein of body parts for the 'creature' – clearly too materialistic an approach to life. Thus, the Censor demanded a more extensive cut than in Britain to the scene (already cut by the distributor) of the dead highwayman. Prior to his head being immersed in acid, cut in Ireland as in Britain, O'Hora cut from the point commencing with dialogue concerning how the birds had eaten out his eyes which suggests the viciousness and brutality of the natural world. Other 'horror' shots deleted were the close-up of the stolen dead pianist's hands and the episode in which Frankenstein buys the eyes. Additionally, the destruction of the creature at the end of the film, when he is first set alight by Frankenstein, and then, falls through a skylight into the vat of acid, was also edited. True to form the Censor found 'sex' in the sub-plot of the relationship between Frankenstein and the maid Justine (Valerie Gaunt). Though only one line, 'In a different way, of course,' was actually cut, this was a reference by Frankenstein to how Justine was 'servicing' him by comparison to his fiancée Elizabeth (Hazel Court). Another explicit scene between Frankenstein and Justine was almost certainly cut by the distributor since no reference is made to it in the report, and the 1958 version is either 86 or 353 feet less (the reports are contradictory) than that submitted the previous year. This concerns Justine telling him that she is going to have a child, and his retort, 'Why choose me as a father?' It is also possible that lines delivered by Frankenstein in relation to the creature, 'I've created a being,' and 'I'll give you life again,' may have been cut as they could have been interpreted as blasphemous. (If elsewhere, as noted in relation to *Before I Hang*, such tampering with life was allowed as a cautionary warning, the important distinction is that *human* life afresh is not created.) With some relief, the *Irish Times* observed, the Censor had successfully 'scissored out … some of the more lurid visual obscenities.'[6]

By the time the cut version of *Curse of Frankenstein* was passed, O'Hora had already approved with five cuts its sequel, *The Revenge of Frankenstein* (Terence Fisher, 1958, GB). While he had described it as 'so much hocus-pocus,' he also considered that many of its scenes 'would horrify the squeamish.' These included shots of a severed hand, red meat being fed to a monkey and its eating it, and details of a surgical operation.[7] Reinforcing the view that the 'blasphemous' lines in *Curse* were removed, he ordered cut from the trailer, 'I am the first man to create another human being.'[8]

Discussing the difference between the narratives of Frankenstein and Dracula, Phil Hardy observed that though each deals 'with the same terms' they do so 'from opposite sides of an imaginary fence.'

> While Dracula is the disquieting survival of a feudal social order into the era of 19th-century business and scientific rationalism, Frankenstein presents the horrors of that rationalism, deploring its tendency to interfere with the old-established religiously fixed order of things.

He goes on to note that Fisher in his later horror films gave the characters different inflections, such that his Dracula films explore the return of the feudal, anti-rational repressed, while in the Frankenstein films, 'sexual deviance is a by-product of excessive rationality.'[9] It is no surprise, therefore, that Hammer and Fisher should turn to the Dracula legend as their next major project after *Frankenstein*. Nevertheless, perhaps because *Curse of Frankenstein* had, at least initially, failed to get a certificate, and no doubt, in part, because it had been condemned elsewhere for 'the way it conveyed the erotic aspects of the vampire's relationship with his female victims,'[10] Hammer's *Dracula* (aka *Horror of Dracula*, Terence Fisher, 1958, GB), was less challenging and was passed uncut by the Irish Censor,[11] while the less effective *The Brides of Dracula* (Terence Fisher, 1960, GB) when viewed by O'Hora in 1960 was passed with just one cut, that of a section of a fight in which vampire killer Van Helsing (Peter Cushing) is being choked by vampire Baron Meinster (David Peel) prior to his biting of him.[12] Though O'Hora recognized that he was assessing yet another film which elsewhere children were not permitted to see, this time Hammer's *Kiss of the Vampire* (aka *Kiss of Evil*, Don Sharp, 1962, GB),[13] nevertheless, he let it through with just two cuts, one of which was of the attack by bats on the vampire's white-robed disciples at the end of the film.[14] However, the film's central theme, the duality of puritan repression and vampire orgies, may already have been deleted or toned down by the renter.

Fisher also regenerated the Jekyll and Hyde story in *Two Faces of Dr Jekyll* (aka *House of Fright*, 1960, GB). In this film, he continues his exploration of 'the ambiguous attractions of "evil",' which, once again, is equated 'with indulgence of sexual desire unfettered by moral codes.'[15] As a result, it is unsurprising that O'Hora described it as 'an amalgam of sex and brutality' before banning it. The ban was upheld after appeal,[16] and reaffirmed in 1962 even with 2,542 feet cut prior to submission.[17] (There was no appeal on that occasion.) In assessing the dual personality film *The Curse of the Werewolf*, which was the first film to emphasis the werewolf's anti-Christian aspect which had elsewhere been established[18] – the film for example uses the symbols of Christianity (the bell-ringing at the beginning and end of the film, Christmas Day), as part of the ironic counterpoint, or 'mocking parallels,' of the werewolf and Jesus[19] – O'Hora, as might be predicted, focused his attention not just on the film's horrific aspect which he deemed to be 'too horrific to be fit for children,' but on the 'near blasphemy' which would 'cause grave offence to all practising Christians.' Problematic was the coincidence of the birth of the future werewolf with the celebration of the Nativity and the 'extraordinary pseudo-theological justification by a Catholic priest for the existence of werewolves,' which was 'too absurd for words'. Though O'Hora banned the film, the Board passed it with four undetermined cuts and an over-16s certificate.[20]

As part of its project following its acquisition of Universal's horror catalogue, Hammer re-launched one monster after another. *The Mummy* (Terence Fisher, 1959, GB) was one of these and, as in earlier versions of the sub-genre, scenes of choking, and in this instance, a 'tongue being removed with forceps,' were cut.[21] The Dorian Gray story got its outing in *The Man Who Could Cheat Death* (Terence Fisher, 1959, GB), but despite O'Hora's complaints that it 'should be seen by adults only,' he gave it a general certificate with eight cuts.[22] With such blatant contradictions evident in the administration of Irish film censorship, some liberal commentators became uneasy at the trend of horror releases. Contrasting, in 1961, the different treatment of Britain's 'New Wave' cinema with horror, the *Irish Times'* Fergus Linehan attacked the 'archaic censorship laws' which allowed the showing of horror films to children while forbidding adults to see 'a tasteful treatment of the tragedy of Oscar Wilde,' a reference to the recent banning of *two* very contrasting 1960 British feature films dealing with Wilde and his homosexuality, the black and white *Oscar Wilde*, which looks to the 1950s, and the stylish *The Trials of Oscar Wilde*. He went on to say that the censorship policy had deprived Irish audiences of several of the best examples of British cinema.[23] It was another four years before the policy was changed and, consequently, in the meantime, a great many horror films were released with general certificates (moreover in a cut version) which elsewhere were receiving over-16s or over-18s certificates.

Roger Corman's horror films are obvious examples. They were receiving 'X' certificates in Britain, but as mostly edited versions, general ones in Ireland.[24] While his witty, if gruesome, *A Bucket of Blood* (1959) was banned by O'Hora,[25] the majority of his films were approved. These include *The Pit and the Pendulum* (1961), the second of his Poe adaptations which got through with three cuts (these were mainly references to adultery and debauchery);[26] *Premature Burial* (1961), the third in the Poe series, which in 1962 received a general certificate, without cuts it would appear;[27] the fourth Poe film, *Tales of Terror* (1961), was released with only shots of a decomposing face removed;[28] the seventh in the series, *The Haunted Palace* (1963), although banned by deputy Censor Gabriel Fallon, was passed uncut by the Board with a limited certificate;[29] while the eight and ninth Poe films, *The Masque of the Red Death*,[30] with its devil-worshipping central character (Vincent Price), and *The Tomb of Ligeia* (1964, GB),[31] respectively, were released when the Appeal Board reversed the newly-appointed Censor Christopher Macken's decision to ban them. The first of Corman's Poe adaptations, *House of Usher* (aka *Fall of the House of Usher*, 1960),[32] despite its incestuous theme, and the fifth and sixth in the series, *The Raven*[33] and *The Terror*,[34] both 1963, were passed uncut. If this list illustrates the inconsistencies in Irish censorship it also clearly points to the growing distance, as noted in the previous section, between the Board and the strict regime of O'Hora and later Macken.

A discussion of horror would, of course, be incomplete without treating the two milestone films, *Psycho* and *Peeping Tom*. Together they are often cited as the beginning of modern horror in that horror is no longer located in the exotic or different but is normalized and brought into the family. In both films the highly disturbed young man at the center of the story embarks on a misogynistic killing spree: Mother-fixated Norman Bates (Anthony Perkins) in *Psycho*, and Mark (Carl Boehm) who suffers from the lingering effects of a father-induced childhood trauma in *Peeping Tom*. By the time O'Hora viewed both these films (*Peeping Tom* in May and *Psycho* in August 1960), they already carried the weight of opprobrium of American and British reviewers. His response was to ban them, commenting not just on their unsuitability for a general audience but even for an adult one. He reported that *Peeping Tom*, 'an amalgam of sex, sadism and horror,' had never 'been shown to children anywhere [and] I do not feel that children should see it here either.'[35] Similarly, he found *Psycho* to be 'horrific in the most sadistic manner.' While 'the straightforward sex scenes [undoubtedly, a reference to the film's opening scene] might be coped with ... deviational ones [were] impossible to handle.'[36]

Although the distributor of *Psycho* did not initially appeal the banning, *Peeping Tom*'s renter did and was successful. The Board only cut one scene which ran for about four minutes in reel 2 and imposed an over-18s certificate. However, the Board's apparent 'liberal' attitude is somewhat tempered by a newspaper report which stated that twelve minutes were cut from the film,[37] presumably, the British release version which had also been the version O'Hora had seen, a view confirmed by a note in the records which refers to a 're-edited version' being viewed by the Board.

Nevertheless, the offensive scene – Mark, a motion picture cameraman moonlighting as a photographer of female models for the soft-porn stills market – indicates a continuing fear of the image and (low) culture industry in that it is the 'dirty' photograph rather than the reality – prostitutes and the voyeuristic and sadistic killings – which are repressed. Despite being cut and released with a limited certificate, the *Irish Times'* cinema correspondent described it as a 'nauseating piece' of filmmaking when it was released in October 1960. The writer went on to say that it 'disgusted me as much as anything I can remember seeing. It is hands down the nastiest piece of work of the year, and of most other years as well.' The reporter asked rhetorically, 'Why have we a censorship at all if it is not to protect [us from] such films as *Peeping Tom?*'[38]

To be fair, this response echoed the British reaction. Indeed, the British censor, John Trevelyan had wanted Mark to be portrayed as suffering from a pathology (revolted by physical sex) rather than as 'a sexual sadist' who was aroused by the killings, but despite the pressure, director Michael Powell had made only minor changes.[39]

A re-edited version of *Psycho*, and forty-seven feet shorter than the film viewed in 1960, was re-submitted for a certificate in 1961, eight months after it had been banned. In a note to the distributor, O'Hora, in revising his doubt on the film's appropriateness for adults, conceded that it was 'strictly for adults,' but that it had to be altered to 'make it suitable for exhibition to children.'[40] On this occasion, it was passed with seven cuts, all of which serve to sanitize or repress the visceral experience of the characters. The first of these is in the film's opening scene in which Sam (John Gavin) and Marion (Janet Leigh) are in a hotel room getting dressed after having made love. Though this scene was largely left intact, there was an important dialogue cut: Marion's reminder to Sam, 'And you have to put your shoes on.' While women regularly kick off their shoes to be more comfortable, men (it would seem) take them off for a purpose, and it is likely to signal the removal of their trousers. The Censor undoubtedly read the comment as making explicit the fact that Sam had been naked. The main cuts, of course, concern Norman's voyeuristic and murderous activities. Two of the three shots were cuts of Norman (and the audience) spying on Marion through the key-hole prior to his/the mother's killing her. Her undressing was cut, but after she puts on the dressing gown she was allowed to be seen, as was Norman's final look at her. The shower scene was also subject to O'Hora's gaze. While the early part of the scene was allowed, including the menacing transvestite arrival of Norman, and the stabbing, it is only when *blood* appears that he intervened. It should be recalled that the viewer does not actually see the knife stabbing Marion's flesh; the blood is only seen when it is being washed away by the shower water. Thus, Marion is allowed to 'sink slowly' down the wall of the shower, but then the precise directive emerges: 'No gobbets of blood, etc. Cut shots of blood flowing in bath water. Flowing water OK when blood ceases.' Later, Norman comes down from the house to clean up the mess in the cabin, but, as he leaves, he twice says 'blood' to his 'mother'. Because we *hear*, and do not *see*, the blood, these words are allowed. Thus, the Censor decreed, 'Cut shot of Norman's hands saturated with blood and subsequent washing. Cut shots of blood in bath etc.' The effect, then, is not to erase the murder and show it in all its messiness and physicality, but to make it safe, and palatable. Ironically, he makes unnecessary Norman's compulsive and, from a psychological point-of-view, futile, ablutions. Similarly, when private detective Arbogast (Martin Balsam) arrives at the motel and is killed by Norman while he is snooping around the house, O'Hora ordered the distributor to 'drastically curtail the repeated stabbing. One stab is surely enough.' Yet if one stab can be viewed as non-gratuitous, it also suggests a more rational act than the frenzied killing by a *mad* man. Arguably, such cutting, while it robs the visceral grotesque and vicarious pleasure from the audience, also makes the murders more obscene. But then, references to the basis of Norman's pathology, his oedipal jealousy at his mother's relationship with a married lover, and his subsequent killing of them both, was also curtailed. When the Sheriff's wife tells Sam and Marion's sister, Lila (Vera Miles), that 'Norman found them dead together *in bed*,' the last two words of the sentence were cut. However, in the film's final scene after Norman has been apprehended, the psychiatrist reports that Norman murdered his mother and her lover – in an Irish moral context 'lover' could be most easily interpreted in its more innocent rather than active meaning. He describes his mother as 'clinging, demanding' and the introduction of the man seemed to him as if he was being abandoned by her for the lover. Indeed, also trimmed were shots of Norman's mother's skeleton when it is on the floor. Another cut included Arbogast's questioning of Norman as to whether he spent the night with Marion. Here the Censor was more alert to the ordinariness, if crudity, of the query and the audience's desire, rather than Norman's (perverted) sexuality.

If *Psycho* and *Peeping Tom* then can be seen as transformative, not least in the movement in *Psycho* from the 'haunted house tradition' to the modern clinical rational terror through the shower murder, another sub-genre of this new horror was the demonic child. Though both films discussed feature the dysfunctional adult child, their evil stems not so much from them but their parents. So, despite their shift away from traditional narratives, the innocence of childhood is never challenged. Prior to the 1960s, it was extremely rare for children to be represented as anything other than the sometimes mischievous off-spring who could annoy but never repel their parents and other adults, or as the victims of either the capitalist system or parental disputes, especially marriage breakdown. In short, they were rarely the agents of negative action, except, perhaps, in such coy representations as those featuring Shirley Temple or her imitators.[41]

However, films such as *Village of the Damned* (Wolf Rilla, 1960, GB) and its sequel, *Children of the Damned* (aka *Horror!*, Anton Leader, 1964, GB), delight in the evil or manipulative child while exposing the alien nature of childhood. In both films, women give birth to alien super-human children. In an Irish context, these two films also throw up one of the contradictions inherent in the literal approach adopted by the Irish Censor. While references to pregnancy were cut, he failed to appreciate that the women of child-bearing age in the remote English village had been impregnated miraculously in a form of a mass 'immaculate conception'. This implantation by aliens, or as is revealed in the sequel, humans from one million years in the future, occurs when all the inhabitants of Midwich are knocked out for a number of hours. Four of the five cuts to *Village* were to references of the impregnation, including that of Milly (Pamela Buck), a spinster, who visits Dr Willers (Laurence Naismith) and in distress tells him, 'I've never, it's impossible.' The other cuts included the local vicar (Bernard Archard) saying that one of those pregnant 'is only 17'. While the sentence, 'no way of accounting for their condition,' was allowed by O'Hora, an exchange concerning the rapid growth, including the use of X-rays, of the 'perfectly formed' foetuses was deemed too 'clinical'. The only other cut was of a 'suicide' provoked by the increasingly murderous emotionless child-aliens.[42] *Children of the Damned*, which focuses on six 'alien' children from different continents who, fearing human curiosity in them, go on a killing spree, was also cut to disguise the alien impregnation of women. While the word 'womb' was removed, a longer cut concerned the paternity of the chief alien child, Paul (Clive Powell), whose mother is visited by a psychologist and a geneticist investigating the child-genius phenomenon. Deciding that the neurotic mother cannot be the source of Paul's brilliant intelligence, they enquire about his father. These lines, left narratively ambiguous at this point, imply that she is an unmarried mother, which, indeed, she is. But, like those in the earlier film, she did not have intercourse before impregnation.⁴³ By cutting the references to pregnancy, the issue of the mysterious conception is left for the audience to deduce from the remaining evidence. If such cuts imply a reticence or a strict morality and go some way to distort the film's narrative, ironically they served to erase what, from an official cultural view, would have been regarded as blasphemous – miraculous conception.

While both these films suggest a coupling of evil and the child, ultimately it is displaced on to that which is unnatural or non-human. *The Innocents* (Jack Clayton, 1961, GB), an adaptation of Henry James' *The Turning of the Screw* (1898),⁴⁴ sets up a narrative that is too human, too natural, albeit one that has regard to the supernatural. The story concerns how two children, Miles (Martin Stephens) and Flora (Pamela Franklin), are affected by the deaths of the intensely passionate Quint (Peter Wyngarde) and his lover Miss Jessel (Clythie Jessop) and their corruption which is suspected and feared by their repressed and spinsterly governess Miss Giddens (Deborah Kerr), who, having learnt about the amoral lovers and seeing them in an (hallucinatory?) vision, becomes sensitive to the children's sinister behaviour, most especially Miles'. In order to keep the film within the conventions established by Irish film censorship, O'Hora cut the film in eight places.

While clearly the cuts serve to sanitize the children, arguably, they also function, as is the case with much Irish film censorship before its liberalization in the mid-1960s, to deny fascination or voyeurism. That O'Hora cut a scene in which the governess persists in asking about the lovers after he had allowed the housekeeper's comment describing how Quint and Miss Jessel, often watched by the children, used rooms lit 'by daylight as if they were dark woods,' which not so subtly implies sexual activity, suggests his desire to 'save' Miss Giddens. It is the talking, the imagination and probing which becomes the target, not the reality. Conceivably then, his first cut of the film can be seen in a more complex light. In it, Mrs Gross laughs at the governess, 'Oh Miss, are you afraid [Miles]'ll corrupt you.' If this is read straight – the boy is bad – a reading validated by his expulsion from school, it carries too the housekeeper's alertness to Miss Giddens' prudish behaviour and suggests that she might be projecting on to the boy her own sexual fantasies. But then O'Hora is careful to delete Miles' line to Miss Giddens which he records thus, 'A damned dirty-minded bitch.' Indeed, such an insult might be seen as a valid description of Miss Giddens and therefore be problematic as it would force the audience to work through the relationship between perception and reality. The cut is also noteworthy as these are not the words spoken by Miles whose actual comment is 'A dammed hussy. A damned dirty-minded hag.'⁴⁵ Such an error presumably arose as a result of O'Hora following a script rather than listening to the dialogue – here, as elsewhere, the Censor favoured the (literal) literary, over the film. However, the most obvious effect of the cut is to protect the interlinking of childhood and innocence by denying Miles access to such profanities. As such it mirrors an earlier cut that involves Flora using obscene language. Deleted is Mrs Gross' comment, 'In all my years, and I have known a foul tongue or two in my time, never have I heard such obscenities ... to have heard such filth from a child's mouth.'

In line with traditional policies on metaphysics and religion, O'Hora intervened on the issue of possible and actual possession and so further diluted Miss Giddens' and, indeed, Mrs Gross' lurid fantasies. Though he left intact the line that Miss Jessel was 'hungry for him,' a bold statement of female animal desire which on another occasion might well have been erased, the follow-through lines were cut: 'For his arms, for his lips, but she can only reach him; they can only reach each other by entering the souls of the children and possessing them.' According to Mrs Gross, they have already done this, that the 'children are possessed,' that 'they live and know and share this hell.'

The evil child trope was, of course, evident in the 1960s. Exemplary is the more realistic, though nonetheless as difficult to the cult of the innocent child, *Lord of the Flies*, which, as mentioned, was passed after appeal with Macken regarding the conversion of 'the quiet and gentle temperaments' of the group of schoolboys 'into an exhibition of cruelty and savagery,' as 'inciting' in its horror scenes and unsuitable for public exhibition.[46]

## ART CINEMA AND IRISH CENSORS

Another set of films, at the opposite spectrum to horror, that pushed the boundaries of Irish film censorship in this era was the broad category of 'art' cinema. Theoretically, these films should have been endorsed by the Irish censors as they would seem to fulfill the censors' desire for a cinema of ideas akin to that of the theatre and literature. Indeed, the term *cinéma d'art* was coined in France in 1908 as a means of attracting the middle-classes to the cinema with adaptations of bourgeois novels and plays, a development copied by other countries, including the USA. In Ireland, Richard Hayes had revealed, early in his censoring career, his preference for Continental European, especially French films. And, of course, the Irish Film Society (IFS) had been catering for this minority audience since 1936, as Irish exhibitors were slow to show non-Anglo-American films. With the support of Fianna Fáil's Minister for Finance, Sean MacEntee, the IFS's film programmes were made exempt from import duty from 1939 onwards and, as a result, the Society greatly expanded its activities during the following decades.[47]

While the first *films d'art* were conventional adaptations of bourgeois writing, the term developed to one which described a type of European cinema which tended to be low or medium budget productions that were experimental in their techniques and narrative, and could be seen in contrast to classical (often high budget) Hollywood's dynamic linearity governed by the logic of causality and economy. Instead of Hollywood's hero, who is psychologically rounded only to the extent that is demanded by the attempt at verisimilitude and the narrative, in European or Art cinema, there is greater emphasis on characterization (even if we never know or under-

stand, let alone empathize, with the character), ambiguous situations, elliptical dialogue, and often a refusal of narrative closure.[48] In short, such a cinema often refuses
the simplicity of mainstream classical cinema where every problem or obstacle can be
overcome, and as a result, can often create a reflective, if somewhat uncomfortable
or alienating space for the viewer which may challenge the political, social, or other
status quo and dominant ideology. Perhaps unsurprisingly then, much of European
cinema has not been popular with audiences seeking, certainly on the formal level, a
less challenging cinema or one that is bound up with visceral and emotional experiences. Censors, on the other hand, have often responded to that cinema with bewil-
derment. Ironically, while Irish censors have tended to ignore the obviating circumstances or context that led the various Hollywood characters to 'sin' and
misdemeanour, when faced with these 'immoral' acts without their naturalizing backdrop they remained dissatisfied, but more than that, confused. This is perhaps best
expressed by Liam O'Hora, who, exasperated after viewing Michelangelo Antonioni's
modernist and somewhat alienating and slow *L'avventura* (1960, Italy) in which the
sterility of modern man and his disconnectedness is explored, wrote – in a preemp-
tion of *Father Ted*'s Fr Dougal cited in the preface – that he found the film 'very difficult to make head or tail' of. Nevertheless, he focused on the fact that it had 'more
than its share of erotic episodes,' and, accordingly, ordered eight cuts, including all
the love-making scenes.[49] Antonioni's second film of the trilogy begun by *L'avventura*,
*La Notte* (aka *The Night*, 1960, Italy/France), and similarly starring the sensuous
Monica Vitti, fared no better, with scenes involving 'the nymphomaniac' near the
beginning of the film totally cut. The final scene in which the husband and wife 'are
obviously having sexual intercourse' was deemed 'too prolonged'.[50]

Historically, art films have been more explicitly erotic than commercial films and
during the heyday of American film censorship (1934 to the mid-1960s), such films
were often regarded as sex films, while, with the advent of French poetic realism in
the 1930s and Italian neo-realism the following decade, it became bound to realism.
The notion of the *politique des auteurs* in the 1950s refocused the concept towards a
more self-consciously artistic and intellectual cinema in which the industrial became
subservient to the cultural with the director regarded as the film's (sole) author. The
French New Wave later in the decade and in the 1960s consolidated the idea of an
auteurist cinema. As a result of these developments, and with the elevation of a select
band of film directors to canonical status, those whose work were deemed to be more
consistently creative and personally expressive than others, allowed for the concept of
art cinema to encompass non-European directors (Ford, Huston, Welles, Kurosawa,
Ray, et al.), a position, as we will see below, which informed film critic Ciaran Carty's
newspaper campaign in the late 1960s/early 1970s when he sought to have the work
of such auteurist filmmakers made exempt from Irish film censorship by giving their
films automatic certification (without cuts).

The increasing number of non-English language films released in Europe in the
post-war years, especially those from Italy and France, was acknowledged by Hayes
when he began recording the nationality of films submitted to him in 1951. It is no

accident, perhaps, that Hayes should have chosen 1951 as the starting date, as this was when Britain introduced the 'X' certificate which greatly aided the distribution of European films there.[51] In 1951 in Britain non-American films accounted for 8.8 per cent of the films registered for distribution.[52] By contrast, in Ireland the figure, excluding British films, was only 2.5 per cent (13 of 520 films over 2,000 feet), while the annual average submitted during 1951–1959 was only 7 per cent. In Britain, films over 3,000 feet, well outside the half-hour tourist and other documentaries which were included in the Irish figures, were an average of nearly 16 per cent per annum, and accounted for nearly one-quarter of all films distributed in this category in 1959. The total numbers of these films for the period 1951–1959 were 324 non-Anglo-American films over 2,000 feet *submitted* to the Irish Censor, while 743 films over 3,000 feet were *distributed* in Britain. Besides reflecting the conservative policies of Irish exhibitors and distributors, the figures help to illustrate Ireland's isolation from cinemas other than those of the USA and Britain and reinforces the view of Ireland's primary dependency on the Anglo-American product.

Table 2: Nationality of films over 2,000 feet submitted in all categories to the Official Censor, 1951–1964

| | 1951 | 1952 | 1953 | 1954 | 1955 | 1956 | 1957 |
|---|---|---|---|---|---|---|---|
| American | 454 | 391 | 403 | 320 | 351 | 336 | 362 |
| British | 53 | 61 | 82 | 137 | 100 | 90 | 96 |
| French | 3 | 10 | 7 | 13 | 7 | 26 | 26 |
| Italian | 3 | 4 | 10 | 16 | 6 | 13 | 12 |
| German | – | 1 | 1 | 1 | 2 | 3 | 8 |
| Irish | – | 2 | 1 | – | 1 | – | 2 |
| Other | 7 | 4 | 4 | 6 | 3 | 17 | 5 |
| TOTAL | 520 | 473 | 508 | 493 | 470 | 485 | 511 |

| | 1958 | 1959 | 1960 | 1961 | 1962 | 1963 | 1964 |
|---|---|---|---|---|---|---|---|
| American | 350 | 292 | 237 | 231 | 203 | 193 | 206 |
| British | 122 | 292 | 147 | 129 | 105 | 103 | 85 |
| French | 26 | 16 | 19 | 16 | 14 | 19 | 11 |
| Italian | 11 | 10 | 26 | 19 | 21 | 27 | 18 |
| German | 6 | 12 | 12 | 7 | 6 | 6 | 3 |
| Irish | 3 | 3 | 4 | 2 | 3 | 2 | 3 |
| Other | 7 | 6 | 27 | 16 | 23 | 17 | 17 |
| TOTAL | 525 | 446 | 472 | 420 | 375 | 367 | 343 |

*Source*: Official Film Censor's Annual Reports

Notwithstanding the infrequency and the new-found status of non-English language films being submitted to the Irish Censor, those that were viewed were treated with the same narrow restrictions imposed on their American counterparts, as evidenced in the discussion of *La Femme du Boulanger* in the previous chapter. This is further demonstrated in the treatment of Italian films, of which 196 were submitted during the years 1951 to 1964. For example, two key neo-realist films – the somewhat melo-dramatic *Bitter Rice* (*Riso Amaro*, Giuseppe de Santis, 1948) which despite being per-vaded by a sense of overt eroticism through Silvana (Silvana Mangano) and her hot pants, offers a neo-realist vision in terms of the primacy of the landscape and its doc-umentary realist aesthetic, and *Paisà* (aka *Paisan*, Roberto Rossellini, 1946) which in its six distinct episodes explores the interrelationship between the liberating Americans and the Italians – were cut. In *Bitter Rice*, whose title Hayes changed to *The Harvesters*, there were ten cuts, including Silvana's suggestive dance at the film's begin-ning and the showing of her leg while sitting on a bed,[53] while in *Paisà* the third episode concerning the loss of innocence in post-Liberation Rome, was cut in the spot where the two original lovers, Fred and Francesca, lie on her bed and where she is undress-ing.[54] This destabalizes the narrative as the contrast between Fred's memory of Francesca from six months before, and her work now as a prostitute, is so acute that he fails to recognize her as the young vivacious woman he met on the day the American Army entered Rome. It was not the only Rossellini film to be censored. Scenes of tor-ture towards the end of *Rome, Open City* (*Roma, Città Aperta*, Roberto Rossellini, 1945, Italy),[55] were cut as was the beating of Karin by Antonio in *Stromboli* (Roberto Rossellini, 1949, Italy), a critical and commercial failure at the time of its release, in part, as a result of the 'immoral' and scandalous behaviour of Ingrid Bergman leav-ing her husband to live with Rossellini, whom she married in 1950.[56] His 'Envy' episode in *The Seven Deadly Sins* (Eduardo de Filippo, Jean Dreville, Yves Allegret, Roberto Rossellini, Carlo Rim, Claude Autant Lara, Georges Lacombe, 1952, France/Italy) in which a woman is jealous of her husband's pet cat, was one of the 'sins' cited by Hayes when he banned the film. Although it was later re-submitted with cuts by the renter, and cut further by the Censor, the Board banned the film after the renter appealed the cuts.[57] Rossellini's most critically successful film featuring Bergman, the mediative *The Lonely Woman* (aka *Viaggio en Italia*, *Strangers*, Italy, 1953), which was hailed as a masterpiece by the critics of *Cahiers du Cinéma*, was cut in two places, one which was of Venuses and a nude on bull statuary. Also cut was a scene in which Alex (George Sanders) is with a prostitute.[58]

The foremost Italian director of the post-war period, Federico Fellini, who stretched the concept of neo-realism to incorporate a more magical and spiritual meaning of truth such that fantasy and reality merge, not only had his films, all marked by a rich sumptuous quality, cut, but many of them were banned, at least initially. *La Strada* (*The Road*, 1954, Italy) was rejected by Martin Brennan, primarily on account of Zampanò's (Anthony Quinn) (unmarried) relationship with the girl (played as a simple trusting Chaplinesque figure by Giulietta Masina), his treatment of her generally, and his affair with the widow, a decision upheld by the Appeal Board, though not before it divided evenly on the decision, and then on re-viewing it, banned it. Even so, the version submitted was 7,097 feet, already 2,308 feet less than its British counterpart.[59] Re-submitted in 1961, it was passed by O'Hora with four cuts designed to ensure that no physical relationship existed between Zampanò and the girl. Thus the scenes where they become sexually intimate, and later refer to each other as husband and wife, were cut, as were references to his previous mistress, Rosa. Such a pattern of cuts is familiar from the censors' treatment of American cinema where physical or carnal relationships were forbidden between unmarried people, or indeed marriage may have been seen to be undermined.[60] Two of Fellini's most popular films were also banned. The 'contentious [and immoral] picture' *La Dolce Vita* (aka *The Sweet Life*, 1960, Italy/France) which offered an uncomplicated and spectacular insight into the decadent world of Rome society inhabited by the central character played by Marcello Mastroianni (and no doubt autobiographical for Fellini) who detests its shallowness yet remains trapped by its allure, was 'too full of sex' for O'Hora, and, on appeal, the Board,[61] while Macken banned the Oscar winning *8-1/2* (*Otto e Mezzo*, 1963, Italy), another autobiographical-based film, but one which foregrounds, in a sometimes complex way, artistic creation and the production of a film. The decision was not appealed initially, but two years later, the film was passed by the Board with four cuts.[62] Macken also banned Fellini's first colour film, the surrealist and visually sumptuous fantasy *Juliet of the Spirits* (*Giulietta degli Spiriti*, 1965, Italy),[63] about a woman's fear that her husband is cheating on her, while his deputy Gabriel Fallon banned *Satyricon* (1969, Italy).[64] *Fellini's Roma* (1972, Italy) which many regarded as a partial return to his earlier work, was also banned, but the renter appealed against the cuts and it was passed uncut with an over-18s certificate four months later. However, the Board seems to have made an informal arrangement with the distributor that it would be shown only at Dublin's International cinema, which specialized in art house product at this time, and 'then [be] withdraw[n] from circulation.'[65]

Other Italian directors whose work was 're-edited' included Vittorio de Sica, as noted above, whose *Umberto D* seen as 'a celebration of neorealism and a lament for its death'[66] was censored in six places, including references to pregnancy and a scene of a couple leaving a brothel (or in O'Hora's parlance, 'a house of assignation').[67] Nevertheless, no certificate was issued, thus suggesting that the renter did not want to distribute a mutilated version of the film. More than a decade later in 1964, Luchino Visconti's 'rather adult picture' about the Rigorismento, *The Leopard* (*Il Gattopardo*, 1963, USA/Italy), was viewed by Macken who deleted references to sexual activity, including where the Prince (Burt Lancaster) speaks disparagingly to his Jesuit confessor about his wife, 'I am a vigorous man. How can I find satisfaction with a woman who makes the sign of the cross in bed after each embrace. And, often can only say, "Jesu Marie." Seven children I have. Seven. And do you know something, Father? I have never seen her navel.' Interestingly, at least in terms of gender bias which is repeated throughout the history of Irish film censorship, is that the rest of his justification is allowed: 'She's the real sinner.' Other cuts concerned Angelica (Claudia Cardinale) and her relationship with the Prince's nephew, Tancredi (Alain Delon), who tells her a story at dinner in which he describes a break-in to a convent while he was fighting with Garibaldi's troops. Frightened, the nuns huddled at the chapel's altar, expecting to be raped or otherwise assaulted, 'martyrs,' Tancredi calls them, 'yelping like bitches in heat,' but one of the men laughs at them and says they will return if these elderly nuns can supply them with novices. Other scenes cut also involved Angelica, whose description of her bed (no doubt regarded as doubly offensive), by the Prince's shooting companion is removed: 'Her bed sheets must smell like the perfume of paradise,' while an exchange between her and Tancredi, who refers to a remote room in the palace as one where his ancestors indulged in 'infractions of the rules' when 'they were bored with love,' was also deleted.[68]

French cinema, which followed America and Britain in terms of quantity of films submitted, fared no better than its Italian counterpart. However, it must be remembered that not all European films were art films, and, indeed, this often careless equation of the two has, at times, disguised the fact that the vast majority of films produced in Europe are comedies, costume and police dramas, or other popular genre films (often imitations of Hollywood) which are usually not seen outside their national territory because of their culturally specific nature. One such example viewed by Hayes was the 'typical French [*sic*] farce' *Bambino* (*Taxi di Notte*, Carmine Gallone, 1950, Italy), which he banned because of its 'suggestive and double meaning' dialogue concerning the paternity of a baby discovered by a Roman taxi driver in his car. 'However suitable and unobjectionable it may be for France [*sic*] with its different ... attitude[s]' it was not deemed suitable for Ireland.[69] Similarly, a French film viewed by O'Hora, *Honour Among Thieves* (*Touchez pas au grisbi*, Jacques Becker, 1954), an influential *policier*, was cut in seven places,[70] which reinforces the view that the censors approached these European genre films in a manner not dissimilar to American cinema.

France was well known for its provocative sexuality on the screen from an early stage, though, as ever, such representations were curtailed in Ireland. When the classic humanist anti-war film, Jean Renoir's *La Grande Illusion* (aka *Grand Illusion*,1937, France) which explores the interrelationship of the prisoners particularly with regard to the operation of the class-system beyond national identity, was viewed by O'Hora more than twenty years after it was made, he remained focused on the scene in the prisoner-of-war camp where a French officer (Jean Gabin) talks about how women's fashions have changed on the outside, 'They've cut their hair short, too,' he says, which elicits the response from another inmate, 'It must be like sleeping with a boy,' a line cut by the censor. Indeed, this articulation of homosexuality is one that is hinted at elsewhere in the film. Shortly afterwards, reference is made to 'sleeping around' but the script supplied to O'Hora reported the term as 'unfaithful', and he ordered the subtitle to be so changed.[71] Martin Brennan had banned already the (hetero)sexual but 'indecent, suggestive and immoral' *French Cancan*, Jean Renoir's tribute to the French music hall.[72] Clearly, the can-can and its licentious undertones were still too strong for 1950s Ireland.

More pertinently and painfully for that decade in Ireland were films such as *The Light across the Street* (*La Lumière d'en Face*, Georges Lacombe, 1955, France), which probes 'the problems of sexual frustration' that confront a young married couple. With the husband impotent, the film focuses on the wife's 'temptations and longings and her husband's frustrations and jealousies.' Having received an 'X' in Britain, it was rejected by O'Hora because he found it unsuitable for general certification, but the ban was reversed by the Board.[73] Because of widespread sexual ignorance during this period and later, the attempt by the new Irish television station to sensitively educate Irish people on topics such as male impotence led, in 1962, shortly after it began broadcasting, to the first major censorship controversy regarding the new Irish medium, as is discussed in chapter 7.

It was the provocative sexuality of, first, actress Martine Carol, and then Brigitte Bardot, which helped to give French cinema its scandalous reputation. In a series of erotic-comedies, which were popular with both women and men, Carol brought a sexual daring to the cinema. Exemplary is the adaptation of Zola's novel, *Nana* (Christian-Jaque, 1955, France). Condemned for 'pandering to the fantasies of Fourth Republic men,'[74] it was banned by O'Hora in 1958,[75] a decision not appealed. This representation of the 'liberated' and sexually alluring woman transcended the stodgy conservatism of the French 'cinema of quality' of the early 1950s, which would shortly be sidelined by the formal and thematic innovations of the French New Wave. By then, it was neither the intellectual cinema of Jean-Luc Godard or the humanism of François Truffaut which had come to epitomize French cinema, but Bardot had already emerged as Europe's premier sex icon. Her status was established in 1956 with the release of *Et Dieu créa la Femme* (*And God Created Woman*, Roger Vadim, 1956, France). Although it was not submitted to the Irish Censor, elsewhere, especially in the USA, it transformed the image of French cinema from its art house ghetto into being regarded as part of mainstream cinema. Alert to this development, O'Hora commented after viewing *Heaven Fell That Night* (*Les Bijoutiers du Clair de Lune* aka *The Night Heaven Fell*, Roger Vadim, 1958, France/Italy), that 'in its theme and ... treatment' the film was 'unsuitable' for Ireland, because, apart from the story of a girl on the run with a killer, 'Miss Bardot so successfully wears nearly nothing that some of her appearances in the picture would have to be excised no matter what the other circumstances might be.' The ban was upheld by the Board.[76] Arguably, the unconscious description 'successfully' goes some way to suggest the Censor's personal desire.

By this time – 1958 – the French 'New Wave', at least in its first non-explicitly political form of the late 1950s to early 1960s, which may be loosely defined as a reaction against an earlier literary based French cinema and bourgeois sensibility, was established with the release of *Le Beau Serge* (Claude Chabrol, 1958) and François Truffaut's *The 400 Blows* (*Les 400 Coups*, 1959) Ironically these two films recalled the poetic realist work of Vigo and Renoir rather than, in terms of technique, ushering in a new era. For the most part, these and other films, including Jean Luc-Godard's *A Bout de Souffle* (aka *Breathless*, 1959), employed the codes and techniques of counter-cinema, such as for example fast non-linear editing, as well as celebrating the low forms of Hollywood and popular culture while focusing on contemporary and relevant issues affecting young adults, including issues around sexuality, desire and identity. Despite its cultural importance, O'Hora granted *The 400 Blows*, which was an autobiographical story of a troubled childhood, little leniency. Cut were the subtitle: 'The boss is sleeping with the new typist,' which young Doinel's (Jean-Pierre Leaud) father says at dinner one evening at home, and 'rough – too rough' was the lengthy exchange with the psychologist at the reform school when she asks whether he has slept with anyone, to which he replies that he had tried to engage a prostitute, but when he arrived at her place, she was out.[77] Other Truffaut films ran into trouble with the Irish censors, including his evocative ménage à trois *Jules and Jim* (*Jules et Jim*, 1962), which had established him as a director of considerable stature, was banned in 1966, four years after it was made, a decision upheld by the more 'liberal' post-1965 Appeal Board.[78]

More disturbing is the treatment of Agnès Varda, perhaps the foremost French woman director whose *Cleo – Between 5 and 7* (*Cléo de Cinq à Sept*, aka *Cleo – From 5 to 7*, 1962) established her as a filmmaker of international renown and whose earlier *La Pointe Courte* (1954) has often been suggested as the beginnings of the French New Wave. Focusing on a confident female protagonist pop singer, the Irish Censor chose not to see the positive liberation of the woman, but honed in on comments concerning nudity and sleeping arrangements, such as a man saying: 'I've had enough of leaving at 2.00 a.m. … It's all night, or nothing,' and the reply: 'Nothing, then.' Other cuts included Cleo's friend Dorothy seen in the nude and Dorothy's question to Cleo: 'Don't you talk to him [José] in bed?' The long section of Cleo with the soldier she meets casually and with whom she has an extended conversation, including a discussion of nudity, was cut in three places: Cleo to soldier: 'To me nudity suggests guilty secrets. Night-time, illness.' Soldier: 'How can you say that?' Cleo: 'It's how I feel,' and shortly afterwards on the bus the soldier says: 'We need nakedness, as we need summer.' Cleo: 'What do you mean?' Soldier: 'Things are simple when you're naked. Love, birth, the water, the sun, the beach.' Later, also while they are on the bus, the soldier describes having seen a baby in an incubator: 'It's moving, seeing someone naked, even a stripper.' Cleo: 'You must be moved often.' Soldier: 'No; nudity isn't that frequent.'[79]

Louis Malle's *The Lovers* (*Les Amants*, 1959), a film which helped to consolidate international interest in French New Wave cinema, was assessed by O'Hora, who was concerned, through a series of cuts, to delete what he called 'the capers upstairs after they all retire,' and other sexual activity, including the love-making in the boat, the only part of which was allowed was when the boat stops and they climb ashore.[80] Perhaps such interference explains why so many New Wave films were not submitted to the Irish Censors, but a more pertinent point may be that Irish exhibitors were (and are) overly conservative in their screening practices and were too wedded to Anglo-American cinema to release a broad range of world cinema. Nevertheless, those small Irish film distribution companies, Egan Film Service, Hibernian and Elliman Films, which sought to introduce European films to Ireland (since they did not have access, in general, to American studio productions), must have been discouraged by the censors' treatment of these alternatives to American cinema.

Besides the dominant Italian and French cinema (almost 60 per cent of all non-English language films submitted during 1951–64), and to a lesser extent German cinema (which accounted for another 10 per cent), little interest was shown in cinemas outside western Europe, with some small exceptions including that of Poland, Japan and Sweden, or, more particularly, the auteurist cinema of Ingmar Bergman. In 1960, the popular and influential Polish film, *Ashes and Diamonds* (*Popiól y Diament*, Andrzej Wajda, 1958) – the richest and most baroque of his trilogy (begining with *A Generation*, 1954, and including *Kanal*, 1956) exploring the psychology of the war and post-war years – was submitted to O'Hora. Like other films of the post-Stalin era of filmmaking in which previously unexamined subjects were filmed, it is characterized by romantic pessimism (of which the lead character, anti-hero as well as anti-communist, Maciek, is a prime example), and preoccupied with the legacy of the Second World War as well as 'with the subjection of the individual to the forces of history.'[81] O'Hora cut the film in seven places, the first of which was a reference to being a communist, but he at least acknowledged that he could only 'request' the renter to cut it, as unlike his predecessors who routinely cut 'political' allegiances or commentaries with which they disagreed, the Censor knew that the 1923 Act did not explicitly exclude such references. The other cuts were predictable ones mainly dealing with the relationship between Maciek (Zbigniew Cybulski) and barmaid Krystyna (Ewa Krzyzanowska). One such cut concerned Maciek's invitation to her, 'Room 17. First Floor. 10.30,' but, despite the cut, the look between them indicates the nature of the conversation, even though the line, 'You won't regret it,' at this stage is meaningless and ambiguous. In his hotel room, scenes between the pair were cut, including a lengthy bed scene and after love-making when they talk about themselves. Also removed from this scene was a friend of Maciek listening outside the bedroom door. Towards the end of the film, Maciek articulates to Krystyna that he has discovered what love is as they wander through a ruined chapel with a cross in the foreground and he talks about how in the past he sought to survive, but is now less certain. Shots of a man hanging were ordered cut from this scene, even though the religious resonance of this execution of an informer could not reasonably be deemed 'blasphemous'. Perhaps, the Censor was concerned with the horror of it.[82] Four years later, Macken viewed Roman Polanski's universally acclaimed feature debut, *Knife in the Water* (1962, Poland), which is an intense and subtle psychological drama of a married couple who take a young man aboard their yacht. He ordered three excisions. One was of the still forbidden word 'bastard,' another concerned a nude woman in a boat, while the third was a 'prolonged sensuous kiss'.[83] Polanski's later, equally disquieting and troubling, films were treated even more harshly: *Repulsion* (1965, GB), his first English-language film, was banned by a deputy Censor, Mr J. Shiel, a decision upheld by the Appeal Board.[84] while *Cul-de-Sac* (1966, GB), was banned by Macken, but, after appeal, it was given an over-18s certificate with seven cuts, especially of Teresa in the nude and being whipped, and Albert being buried.[85]

*Rashomon* (aka *In the Woods*, Akira Kurosawa, 1951) was the breakthrough film in the west for Japanese cinema, having been awarded best foreign film at the 1951 Venice Film Festival and released in Britain in 1952. However, it was another five years before it was submitted to the Irish Censor, although the version (7,648 feet) was unusually longer (178 feet) than the one released in Britain.[86] Set during a bandit's trial as the events surrounding the rape of a noblewoman and the killing of her husband are recounted, this formally radical film with multiple points-of-view questions the nature of memory and reality, but these merits were ignored by O'Hora who banned it because he (crudely) found it to be 'sordid and immoral'. The decision was appealed and it was approved provided the 'embrace' of the woman by the bandit was 'substantially shortened' and that all references to 'seduction' were eliminated.[87] The rather delicate word 'embrace' is used to hide the film's sexual assault, or as happens elsewhere in the censors' reports, it can refer to consensual sexual relations.

Richard Hayes' decision in 1951 to begin to record the nationality of films submitted to him was no doubt in recognition of the changes in post-war cinema. These can be seen in the renewal of the film festival at Venice and the establishment of one at Cannes, both in 1946, which brought to the fore new national cinemas. For example, the critical endorsement given to *Rashomon* in 1951 was the first major European recognition of film from outside the Occident. As the decade progressed, this non-western cinema was brought to wider attention. A Japanese film, Teinosuke Kinugusa's *Gate of Hell* (1953), won the best film at the 1954 Cannes Film Festival, while Satyajit Ray's *Aparajito* (*The Unvanquished*) of India took best film at Venice in 1957. Also, of course, European cinema, especially Italian and French, began to reach new (foreign) audiences outside those countries. Only twice at Cannes and not once at Venice did an American film win the best film award during the years 1951–60. Such changes in film production and distribution began to percolate through to Ireland during the decade, if not at the rate seen in Britain. As O'Hora stated in his report for 1956, two first-run cinemas in Dublin were 'devoted entirely' to the exhibition of Continental films 'and it certainly makes our work here no easier because many of these films, whatever their artistic and creative merits, grossly transgress the moral standards that prevail here.'[88] Unfortunately, that was the limited manner by which cinema was judged. There was no room for considering film within any other context than that of an abstract and detached morality which de facto was not actually always practiced in Ireland. Pre-eminently in this period, the films of Ingmar Bergman provided the most complex challenge to the censors.

Arguably, Bergman, at least of the 1950s and 1960s, is the quintessential European art film director. Often viewed as having a dark and brooding cinematic sensibility, and utilizing symbolic imagery, central to his work is an almost forensic interrogation of the modernist (divided) self, sexuality, relationships, and personal beliefs, especially those focused on metaphysical explorations of God and death.[89] The first of Bergman's films to be viewed by an Irish censor was *Wild Strawberries* (*Smultronstället*, 1957, Sweden). The film painfully dissects an old academic's spiritual death and alienation over the course of a physical journey, a device found in other Bergman films. As he drives to be honoured for a lifetime of academic achievement, Isak (Victor Sjöström) is told by his young hiker companion, Sara (Bibi Andersson), in a line cut by the Censor because it contains the forbidden word 'virgin': 'I'm a virgin Isak, that's why I talk so daringly.' (If one accepts her logic, it may say much about Irish society and the 'purity' of the censors that such a line was cut. Such a supposition is given support by the recent scandals surrounding the Catholic church's checkered past and the extent of the reality of sexual abuse that is now known to have existed, particularly in state-supported institutions.) During the journey, they pick up a couple following a car crash which seems to have been precipitated by the wife, Berit, trying to hit her husband, Sten. The conversation turns to what O'Hora regarded as 'rather peculiar references to being a Catholic,' and he ordered it cut. 'Do forgive me, please,' Berit says, 'As we said when we were kids I was going to hit my husband but the road curved. God punishes some sins at once. Eh, Sten? You're a Catholic.' Later in the car, Sten says to Isak's daughter-in-law, Marianne: 'You don't seem hysterical. Little Berit is. Do you know what that means to me?' Marianne replies: 'You're a Catholic,' and Sten adds: 'That's how I survive. My wife and I ridicule each other. She's hysterical, I'm Catholic. We depend on each other, you understand. It's pure egoism we haven't killed each other.' If confusion was O'Hora's reason for deleting this section, a more honest or brighter (Irish Catholic) censor would have objected to equating Catholicism with neurosis, in this case hysterical masochism. The third cut concerned a flashback memory from 1917 when Isak watches as his wife is seduced by a man who aggressively pulls her down as she initially resists, then sits on top of her, and after love-making when she is fixing her dress. She talks about her husband's insensitivity, that 'he doesn't give a damn about anything.' The cut to this scene ordered by O'Hora was when the man 'actually gets astride' the woman, thus allowing, it would seem, the adulterous affair and the husband's perverted (or masochistic) voyeurism, but not the sex act.[90] Again, the Censor's contradiction remains to cut before we see 'the action,' but after it has been initiated, thus allowing the audience to fill in, imagine more or less, and regard it as either violence or sex or both.

Perhaps following the commercial success of this film, other Bergman films were submitted. While *Wild Strawberries* was submitted three years after it was made, *Summer Interlude* (*Sommarlek*, aka *Illicit Interlude, Summerplay*, 1951, Sweden), which O'Hora viewed two months later, had to wait nine years for an Irish release. The film concerns the memories of a prima ballerina (Maj-Britt Nilsson) who recalls a summer she spent with a lover who died tragically. Though O'Hora described it as a 'sophisticated Bergman picture,' he deemed it unsuitable for general exhibition and banned it, a decision upheld after appeal. When re-submitted in 1964, it was passed with two cuts by Macken. These included a scene of the couple in bed together, and he also deleted the line, 'I would like to spit in His face,' probably because he regarded it as blasphemous.[91] By the time O'Hora viewed Bergman's medieval drama of rape and revenge, *The Virgin Spring* (1960, Sweden), the film had already won the Academy Award for Best Foreign Film (1960). The only cut to the film was of the rape sequence, which was ordered to be 'drastically' curtailed. In this scene a teenage girl is travelling through a forest to deliver candles for mass when she meets three goat herders, all brothers, two young men and a boy. After encouraging her to share her food with them, which she does willingly, the men rape and then kill her. Her father, a devout religious man, extacts his revenge when he kills all three of them after they seek shelter at his house. Unusually, words and references

which would have been automatically cut from a mainstream commercial film seem to
have been allowed. These included the phrase 'bastards beget bastards' and, in a further
reference to pregnancy, a girl is told that she is acting like an animal, 'a wildcat.'[92] Such
limited 'leniency' may owe less to the film's status as an art film or its Academy award,
which, in a sense commercialized it, and more to the relative randomness of what is after
all a subjective and uneven censorship process.

The elegant ironic romantic comedy, *Smiles of a Summer Night* (*Sommarnattens
Leende*, 1955, Sweden) which had brought Bergman to international fame, was also
submitted in 1964. Revealing that he viewed Bergman's, and by extension other art
films, differently to mainstream commercial cinema, O'Hora remarked that 'if this film
were for general distribution,' he 'would reject it out of hand.' This rather detached
but witty piece, on which the Broadway musical *A Little Night Music* (1973) is based,
is set in the late nineteenth century and centers on Fredrick, his wife Anne, their son
Henrik, their maid Petra, Fredrik's ex-mistress, Desirée, her current lover, Count Carl-
Magnus, a soldier, and his wife, the Countess. Ironically, in spite of the complexity
(and adulterous nature) of many of the relationships, O'Hora's primary objective seems
to have been to disguise the fact that married Anne was still a virgin and that unmarried Petra was not, with lines such as 'first time' and 'she's untouched,' as well as the
two women discussing it, cut.[93]

Despite these excisions designed to 'protect' Anne and/or the sanctity of marriage,
a great many other lines of dialogue remained which would have been cut from a mainstream commercial British or American film, but, perhaps, because the film was submitted on 16mm, thus denying it a mainstream commercial cinema release, O'Hora
knew it would be largely confined to 'art' cinema audiences. Numbered among these
are Anne's comment to the promiscuous Petra that, 'Nearly everything that's fun is a
sin,' and her reply, 'Then I'll shout hurrah for sin,' and a series of references to Fredrik
and Desirée, including Fredrik wrongly calling his wife, Desirée, and it would appear,
Desirée's needling of Fredrik, 'It amazes me that you can experience touches of emotion above the navel'; 'I was a playmate to brag about, but were you going to marry
me?'; and, 'Besides, you had other women. Can you deny that?' Also allowed was dialogue concerning the disputed paternity of Desirée's son, when her lover of six months,
Count Carl-Magnus, a soldier on nine hours' leave (five of which he will spend with
his wife), arrives at her apartment while she is entertaining Fredrik. Passed too were
other normally forbidden encounters, including Henrik as a disillusioned theology student being encouraged by Petra to feel her breasts.

*Through a Glass Darkly* (*Sasom i en Spegel*, 1961, Sweden), is the first in
Bergman's bleak sparse 'chamber music' trilogy in which the (non)existence of God is
explored, as is man's isolation and alienation. It also touched on the most sensitive of
cinematic representations with an explicit incest scene. While Macken had objected to
references, early in the film, by a young wife to her husband concerning the role of a
healthy wife for the production of children, he was most concerned with the scene in
the hulk of a ship 'where incest appears obvious.' Later, when the boy tells his father
what has happened with his sister, a reference to incest, Macken again intervened.[94]

Despite the liberalization of film censorship which became manifest from 1965 onwards, and the sometimes more sympathetic treatment of art cinema, Bergman's films continued to suffer. *Persona* (1966, Sweden), in which he moved away from the metaphysical in favour of human psychology and interaction, was initially banned by Macken, but then passed by the Appeal Board with three cuts and an over-18s certificate.[95] *The Rite* (*Riten, The Ritual*, 1969, Sweden), which was his first film made both for theatrical release and television, was not unexpectantly – given the film's anti-censorship point-of-view – also banned, but cut after appeal and given an over-18s certificate,[96] a process similar to what happened to his only English language film *The Touch* (*Beröringen*, 1971, Sweden/USA).[97] No matter how many European art films challenged the censors, they seemed to do so only in a minor way when compared to the raw realism of British 'New Wave' cinema of the late 1950s/early 1960s. Interestingly, though, the censors' treatment of such films helped to jolt some film reviewers into demanding changes to the grading system.

## THE PUBLIC STRUGGLE FOR LIMITED CERTIFICATES

Ironically, given that the situations explored within British 'New Wave' and social problem cinema of the 1956–1963 period little affected Irish society, these films were to the forefront of the public debate which emerged in Ireland concerning children and adult audiences. More than any other body of work, this distinctive group of films was used by film reviewers to expose the contradictions exacerbated, if not caused by, a lack of grading. Besides the standard preoccupations with various social problems such as juvenile delinquency, prostitution, homosexuality, race, inter-class relationships, extra-marital affairs, contraception and abortion, the films were marked by a more explicit exploration of sex and nudity, no doubt fuelled by European cinema, while the more downmarket British sexual comedies often enjoyed risqué dialogue of a particular type of male adolescent humour, a 'genre' which runs from the *Doctor* and *Carry On* series beginning in 1954 and 1958, respectively, to the *Confessions* series of the 1970s.[98]

It is perhaps strange to record that the only evidence of restrictions on *Violent Playground* (Basil Dearden, 1958), a British film dealing with juvenile delinquency in which a junior liaison officer in the Liverpool slums falls in love with the sister of an arsonist, does not concern its theme, but the name of one of its characters. In the film, the aptly named Mary de Valera Murphy was renamed by the Censor as Mary Murphy. The then-Taoiseach, it seems, was to have a monopoly on the name, a private arrangement O'Hora recorded having made with the distributor.[99] However, this mild rebuke belies the treatment of such films by the Irish censors because many of the key British films of the period were banned, with distributors in many cases not bothering to go to the Appeal Board, or, alternatively, re-submitting butchered versions of the film. Some of the headline films of the British 'New Wave' were repeatedly banned by Irish censors. *Room at the Top* (Jack Clayton, 1958), for example, was rejected in 1959,[1] a decision upheld almost two years later by the Appeal Board, by which time the Censor recorded that he had seen three different versions of it, the last being 936 feet (or around eleven minutes) less than the original. Notwithstanding that 'much of the adulterous overtones, the erotic love-making and all the crude dialogue have been removed,' O'Hora told the Board in February 1961 that he 'could not pass the film for general exhibition.'[2] Re-submitted in June 1964 in its complete form, the new Censor rejected it, a decision reversed by the new Board. To complicate the film's fate, the distributor decided to add some scenes deleted before the Board saw the film, so it adjudicated on it once more, this time passing it with three cuts.[3] (The film was eventually released in 1967.) *Saturday Night and Sunday Morning* (Karel Reisz, 1960, GB) was 'far too realistic both in theme and treatment' for exhibition in Ireland and, consequently, suffered a similar fate. Banned in 1960, a decision upheld on appeal,[4] it was finally released in 1972 when it was issued with an over-18s certificate by the Board. Indeed, *Look Back in Anger* (Tony Richardson, 1958, GB), the film whose title reflected the era of Britain's 'Angry [and masochistic] Young Men,' was also banned initially.[5] Though the decision was not appealed, the film was re-submitted in 1962 when it was passed with four cuts despite the Censor complaining that it was 'a very adult picture'.[6] Other films denied included those dealing with juvenile delinquency and the problems of young people, such as *Cosh Boy*, noted in the previous chapter, and the sexually provocative *Beat Girl* (aka *Wild for Kicks*, Edmond T. Greville, 1962, GB).[7]

As also noted in the previous chapter, films with homosexual themes were routinely banned or cut, as it would be another two or even three decades before advocates of gay rights would get a sympathetic or supportive mainstream public hearing, but even in the present barely disguised hostility towards homosexuals emanates from the institutional Catholic church and its more zealous activists. British films with such themes cut or banned by Irish censors include *Serious Charge*,[8] which was banned with the decision upheld after appeal, and when re-submitted in 1962, it was banned again; *Oscar Wilde*;[9] *The Trials of Oscar Wilde*;[10] *Victim*;[11] *A Taste of Honey* (Tony Richardson, 1961);[12] and *The Leather Boys* (Sidney J. Furie, 1963), in which, according to O'Hora, 'the only heterosexual person in sight is the hero himself.'[13]

Likewise treated were British films which featured abortion, such as *The Kitchen* (James Hill, 1961)[14] and *The L-Shaped Room* (Bryan Forbes, 1962).[15] Of course, American films with abortion narratives were also suppressed, such as in *Blue Jeans* (Philip Dunne, 1959);[16] *The Interns* (David Swift, 1962);[17] and *Love with the Proper Stranger* (Robert Mulligan, 1964),[18] while films that had prostitution as a prominent element were invariably banned. These include *The Flesh Is Weak* (Don Chaffey, 1957, GB);[19] *Passport to Shame* (Alvin Rakoff, 1959, GB), in which a taxi driver tries to rescue his girlfriend from prostitution;[20] *The World of Suzie Wong* (Richard Quine, 1960, GB), which is set in a brothel and features a Chinese prostitute;[21] *The World Ten Times Over* (aka *Pussycat Alley*, Wolf Rilla, 1963, GB);[22] and 'the perverse theme' in the London sex comedy featuring Harry H. Corbett and Diane Cliento, *Rattle of a Simple Man* (Muriel Box, 1964, GB).[23] Like their American counterparts such as the influential gangster movie, *Underworld USA* (Samuel Fuller, 1960), which was cut in six places,[24] British films featuring the criminal underworld were routinely denied an

Irish release by the Censor. While *The Small World of Sammy Lee* (Ken Hughes, 1962) was banned because it is set against a background of London's striptease clubs,[25] *The Criminal* (aka *The Concrete Jungle*, Joseph Losey, 1960, GB) was banned as much for its 'blatantly disrespectful conduct of Mass,' and the nude pin-ups juxtaposed with the statues of the Blessed Virgin in a prison cell, as for its broader critique of the underworld and prison conditions.[26]

With such widespread banning and cutting of films in the early 1960s, it was inevitable, especially within the context of the process in train of modernizing and internationalizing of the Irish economy (if not of the culture and society), that resistance to the general certificate policy would emerge. In his report for 1960 O'Hora detailed the 'stresses and strains' he felt he was under: from the correspondence columns of the *Irish Times*; the British press, particularly the Beaverbrook newspapers; and cinema trade periodicals 'everywhere'. They 'all attempt to decry our work in a manner more polemical than objective or factual.' He went on to state that 'the amazing thing is that the Appeal Board is never attacked.' He argued that the main reason is that his 'decriers are able to single me out as an individual and they know I have no powers of reply.' He explained that the reason for the pressure was that 'productions were now longer and more expensive and that rejection now means more to the producer than in the past.' But, he continued, 'I doubt if anyone could be sensibly *more liberal* than I am and with many pictures my limits of tolerance are utterly strained to save them from rejection.' (Emphasis added.)[27]

In his last report to the minister, O'Hora singled out the *Sunday Independent* for special mention. He declared that they had 'specifically accused me of deliberately failing in my duty' because of not having granted limited certificates. 'That this newspaper should be the *enfant terrible* of advanced picture viewing is somewhat surprising as until very recently it refused even to review current films which did not meet with its approval on moral grounds.'[28] O'Hora's comments in relation to the *Sunday Independent*, and though not named, its film reviewer Des Hickey, came at the time when Hickey and his colleague, Fergus Linehan at the *Irish Times*, had raised the temperature considerably as regards the issuing of limited certificates. It came at the end of a decade of periodic campaigning by the newspapers for limited certificates. However, the campaign had begun not for the wider availability of 'advanced picture viewing' for adults, but for more conservative moral ends designed to protect children from adult narratives, the other side of the 1960s' liberal argument in favour of an adult cinema. Whatever their ideological differences, conservative and liberal commentators alike shared the view that limited certificates should be introduced.

Unlike his predecessors, then, O'Hora was faced by a new generation of writers on the cinema who became increasingly hostile to the perceived anomalies of Irish film censorship. These film reviewers, notably those at the *Sunday Independent* and the *Irish Times* during the late 1950s and early 1960s, sought to change the almost-complete prohibition on grading of films, while also objecting to the widespread cutting of films released. In this, the first sustained critique within the national press, they began to question the censors' authority and the administration of censorship. In the

1950s, these challenges often centered not just on the absence of limited certificates, but on the protection of children from adult drama and horror films, even when these had already been severely cut by the Censor. The *Sunday Independent's* Noel Moran was one of the earliest and most frequent critics of the self-imposed dilemma being faced by the Film Censor, such as in the case of *Rashomon* which the film reviewer described as being 'strictly for adults with strong stomachs,' despite, as noted above, its being released in a truncated version.[29] Perhaps in recognition of the cultural transformation of European exhibition, as early as 1956 Moran was highlighting the need for change, and in his review of *La Donna del Fiume* (*The Woman of the River*, Mario Soldati, 1954, Italy/France) he complained about the absence of adult and universal certificates. His defence of the film's screening, but only for an adult audience, provoked a strong response from his readers.[30] The following year in the course of a review of *The Secret of Sister Angela* (*Le Secret de Soeur Angele*, Léo Joannon, 1956, France/Italy), a film about a young novice who is attracted to an escaping criminal, but on their departure he returns to prison, she to the convent. Moran described it as 'a provocative theme for an adult audience.'[31]

While the censors may have reluctantly begun to accept that such activities as adultery and prostitution actually existed, other topics such as rape remained taboo. The central plot element in Otto Preminger's *Anatomy of a Murder* (1959) was the criminal trial of a man accused of raping a woman. In the courtroom scene words such as sperm, contraception and penetration were used as part of the film's graphic examination of the alleged rape. These terms were, of course, acceptable as part of a 'real' trial and Preminger successfully defended the film when a prosecution was attempted in the American courts against it on grounds of obscenity. However, in Ireland, not only was rape excluded from public discourse, but there was a refusal even to acknowledge that it might exist in Catholic Ireland. (It was to take another decade or more before public debate on such subjects developed and when it did emerge more completely in the 1980s, it overwhelmed the media, and all public discourse seemed for a short time stuck on the opening up of the female (sexual) body and means of reproduction.) As a result, *Anatomy of a Murder* was released in a version which must have bewildered Irish audiences. All references to rape were cut from the trial scene which makes up a large part of the film.[32] In Britain the film had received an 'X' certificate from the BBFC with just one minute trimmed, whereas in Ireland about fifteen minutes were removed.[33] The *Irish Times'* anonymous cinema correspondent exasperatedly commented that 'the censor has dissected *Anatomy of a Murder* to an extent that makes it practically incomprehensible.'[34] This led an incensed letter writer to complain to the *Irish Times*.[35] In reply, the cinema correspondent observed that 'the wonder ... is, not that so many films are cut or refused certificates, but that so many are allowed entry and that so much is left untouched that could do with excision.' Indeed, as he observed, many films were screened which wouldn't have had a 'ghost of a chance' fifteen years earlier. However, that said, the cuts are frequently 'futile and childish. To remove all reference to the crime of rape, as was done [in *Anatomy of a Murder*] ... is to try and pretend that such crimes do not exist, an attitude which strikes one on consideration as showing a considerable contempt for the moral strength of our people.' Instead of working through notions of paternalism and the contradictions within Irish culture, he concluded that such 'infuriating' cuts largely represent an attempt by the censors to remain within the Act's terms of reference while avoiding 'extremes of puritanical narrow-mindedness.' To ameliorate the problem he called for the grading of films according to the British model.[36]

A few years later in 1963, another film with rape as a central theme, the interracial drama *To Kill a Mockingbird* (Robert Mulligan, 1962), suffered the same fate as *Anatomy of a Murder*. This germinal film, now on the American school curriculum, which makes a plea for (racial) tolerance, represents the points-of-view of two children and their friend, and their relationship with their father Atticus (Gregory Peck), a lawyer who defends a black man wrongly accused of rape in the early 1930s. O'Hora approached the film as he would any other concerning rape, but, in this case, felt obliged to offer the observation that it 'is a very adult film as the Renter appreciates. I want to tone down the rape overtones; *nothing will be really missed*, I think, by any adult of *any maturity* whatever.' (Emphasis added.)[37] Apart from the acknowledgment that censorship may not be complete and the operation of the viewer's active reading whereby meaning extends beyond what is actually shown, in this instance the argument is somewhat disingenuous and is surely open to critique. At the core of white neurosis and prejudice against black people is the threat of miscegenation which moreover is manifest in the notion of a black sexuality out of control: the rapist. (It should come as little surprise that such a myth is central to one of the founding films of classical cinema, D.W. Griffith's 1915 white supremacist *The Birth of a Nation*.) As a result, one of the four cuts demanded by O'Hora was the response by the racist Ewell when he sees his daughter Mayella hold a black man, Tom Robinson. Ewell forces her to accuse Tom of raping and beating her, whereas in fact it is he who beats his daughter for consorting with Tom. In the subsequent court case where Atticus defends Tom, references to rape were cut at three points. That O'Hora allowed through uncut the all-white, all male jury finding Tom guilty of rape, his attempt at escape in which he is shot dead, and Ewell's attempt to kill Atticus' children and his own suicide, suggest inconsistencies in the Censor's decisions. Race and rape, it would seem, were regarded as more 'dangerous' than violence and suicide, even though the former were non-issues within official culture.

It is perhaps indicative of the type of society in Ireland at the time that the controversy surrounding the Boulting Brothers' *I'm All Right, Jack* (1959, GB) did not concern its contentious representations of workers and trades unions, but its opening and closing scenes set in a nudist camp. But then, as noted elsewhere, often it was such lesser 'side-show' or incidental 'attractions' of the (sexualized) body or immoral and flawed behaviour that was elevated beyond the meaning and context of the film's overt content. Though British cinema of this period is rightly remembered as exploring more challenging themes such as race, class and homosexuality, in its 'realist' films, there also developed in the 1950s a revisiting of the 'saucy' British tradition which had its predecessors in the 'naughty' seaside postcard and the risqué music hall joke. However, those nudist camp sequences of *I'm All Right, Jack* do not function as mere titillation – there are no bare female breasts, for example (this would be exploited within a decade in both mainstream British and American cinema) – but offer images of anti-industrial, pastoral bliss which contrasts with the film's otherwise recriminatory comedy about employer/employee relationships. When O'Hora cut these sequences, which totalled about two minutes,[38] the Boulting Brothers in a letter to the *Irish Times* attacked the Irish Film Censor's 'fuddy-duddy attitudes'. The Boultings declared that they would 'have no truck' with the Censor's decision. They added that there was 'nothing lewd or licentious in either the banned scenes, or the film.' The Boultings hoped their decision not to release a cut version of the film would 'focus attention on the glaring need for reform' of Irish film censorship.[39]

Almost immediately a lively correspondence appeared in the *Irish Times* with satirist and lay Catholic activist John D. Sheridan writing in defence of the Censor,[40] with others following.[41] Brian Cleeve, an ex-film reviewer and later a novelist and broadcaster, sought to define a middle ground of rational debate,[42] but this quickly dissolved with John Manning's attack on Sheridan's 'condemnation before examination'.[43] In turn, Sheridan sought to satirize Cleeve's reasoned reply[44] and an 'ex-nudist' wrote to declare that the climates of Northern Europe were unsuited to nudist camps![45] Neil Renton[46] had written to make the case for grading, and, indeed, a week later at the Fianna Fáil Ard Fheis, Seán Lemass, elected Taoiseach five months earlier, addressed such a motion from the Cork branch of the party. In opposing it, Lemass, in his only known comment on film censorship, made an explicit association between censorship and food regulations. In so doing he displayed a surprising conservatism which belies his image as a modernizer: 'We regard these [film and book censorship] regulations as being exactly in the same category as other regulations which prevent the sale of putrid meat or contaminated milk.'[47] The motion favouring grading of films was lost.

When *I'm All Right, Jack* was submitted to the Appeal Board by the film's distributor, British Lion, the Censor's decision was upheld.[48] Private negotiations followed between British Lion and the Boultings, with the filmmakers 'bow[ing] to finance' because Irish distribution of the film was worth £10,000,[49] and the film was awarded a general certificate on 1 November 1960, almost fourteen months after the Censor first saw it. The film itself was reviewed approvingly when it was released in December 1960 with the *Irish Times* headline reporting 'Still All Right, Jack.'[50] However, Noel Moran's successor as film reviewer in the *Sunday Independent*, Ken Shaw, reported that the film had a new opening sequence 'which seems to have no bearing on the story proper.'[51] The controversy over *I'm All Right, Jack* indicated that there was at least the beginnings of a public debate about Irish film censorship, even if the nature of that debate was tentative. Yet, among reviewers, and especially among the censors themselves, the balance continued to favour strict censorship and, in the main, the issuing of general certificates.

The early 1960s marked some small changes in the censorship code. Films previously banned were now being re-submitted, perhaps because of minor encouragement from the Appeal Board, but more likely as a result of pressure on exhibitors seeking a

**28** *The Wedding March* (Erich von Stroheim, 1928, USA)
Cripple Mitzi (Fay Wray, above) prays for forgiveness for her sexual transgression with the aristocratic Prince
Nicki (Erich von Stroheim), who, though also in love with her, accepts the arranged marriage to the wealthy
magnet's daughter played by Zasu Pitts. 'In the church scenes there are incidents that are anything but reverent ... The sacred ceremonies that are in progress ... display the cynical disregard of Hollywood for the sincere
feelings of Catholics.' (Banned by James Montgomery, 1929.)

**29** *From the Manger to the Cross* (Sidney Olcott, 1912, USA)
This early life of Christ, shot in Egypt and Palestine, and mostly using biblical quotations as its intertitles, proved, despite its reverence and artistic merit, to be most controversial in Ireland. In this scene, Mary (Gene Gauntier) and Joseph (Montague Sidney) look at 'their' son, Jesus.

**30** *The King of Kings* was banned by Montgomery in 1928, but passed with cuts after appeal.
Jesus, the Christ (H.B. Warner) presides over the Last Supper with his disciples. 'I have a rigid rule to reject films in which the figure of Christ is materialised ... I am bound by this rule. I regret that in this instance the approach to "the Greatest Story in the World" should be through a bed in a brothel, with an attempt to suggest a Hollywood sex triangle.'

**31** *Monty Python's Life of Brian* (aka *Life of Brian*, Terry Jones, 1979, GB)
Singing 'Always Look on the Bright Side of Life', Brian (Graham Chapman) finds himself amongst the thieves on Calvary after being mistaken throughout his life for Jesus. This zany parody by the British ensemble was deemed blasphemous and banned by Frank Hall in 1979, a decision confirmed by the Appeal Board. It was finally certified for over-18s in 1987 by Sheamus Smith.

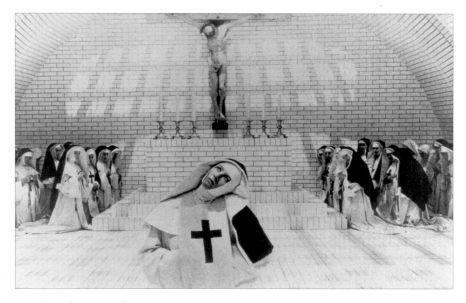

**32** *The Devils* (Ken Russell, 1970, GB)
Arguably, at the extreme end of Russell's work, which is as lavish as it is controversial, this adaptation of Aldous Huxley's *The Devils of Loudun*, is set in a seventeenth-century convent and deals with possession. The sexual reverie of nuns (including Vanessa Redgrave, above) was sufficient to ensure Christopher Macken's banning of the film (1970).

**33** *The Garden of Allah* (Rex Ingram, 1927, USA)
Father Adrien (Ivan Petrovitch) joins a Trappist monastery but leaves when the lure of women becomes irresistible. He meets and marries devout Domini (Alice Terry), but returns to the monastery to do penance when she becomes pregnant. Montgomery banned it in 1928 because 'a priest who has broken his vows is not a desirable subject for exhibition in Ireland.' Subsequently, it was passed with cuts after appeal.

**34** *Angels with Dirty Faces* (Michael Curtiz, 1938, USA)
Priest Jerry Connolly (Pat O'Brien) tries to demystify gangster Rocky Sullivan (James Cagney) in the eyes of the Dead End Kids and to that end lies about his death. Driven by an absolutist morality, and a desire to suppress all images that might negatively impact on the Catholic church or its servants, Montgomery declared that 'No motive however good can excuse a lie,' so 'cut the lie.'

35 *The Song of Bernadette* (Henry King, 1943, USA)
In this box office hit, the Dean of Lourdes (Vincent Price) tries to get Bernadette (Jennifer Jones) to retract he claim ot have witnessed an apparition of the Blessed Virgin. It was one of six cuts by Richard Hayes in 1944 primarily designed to eliminate even implied criticism of the Catholic church. (A more traditional cut, earlier in the film, was of the children with clothes drawn up as they cross the stream.)

36 *Lamb* (Colin Gregg, 1985, GB)
Idealist Christian Brother – Brother Sebastian / Michael Lamb (Liam Neeson) – with the troubled and epileptic Owen Kane (Hugh O'Conor) reach the end of their journey before Lamb drowns Owen rather than return him to the reformatory. Lamb proves unable to commit suicide. Though the climate had changed such that a negative representation of the religious could be allowed, and the film passed uncut, some thought this unwise.

**37** *The Curse of Frankenstein* (Terence Fisher, 1957, GB)
Baron Frankenstein (Peter Cushing) shows a sculptor's hands for his creature to his sceptical collaborator Paul Krempe (Robert Urquhart), an altogether 'too powerful a combination of horror and sex to allow for its exhibition' in Ireland. Of course, all Frankenstein films were problematic in their relationship to creation and the creator's usurping of God. (Liam O'Hora, 1957.)

**38** *The Innocents* (Jack Clayton, 1961, GB/USA)
Cut in eight places by Liam O'Hora (1962) in order to contain the references to possession, the obscenities and the screams. Demonic Miles (Martin Stephens, bottom) and his sister Flora (Pamela Franklin) are affected by the deaths of the intensely passionate Quint (Peter Wyngarde, above) and his lover Miss Jessel (Clythie Jessop).

**39** *The Masque of the Red Death* (Roger Corman, 1964, GB)

In this seventh in Corman's Edgar Allan Poe series, Juliana (Hazel Court) experiences the terror of being betrothed to the Devil, an increasingly popular trope within horror, from *Rosemary's Baby* onwards. According to Christopher Macken, who banned it in 1964, 'the blasphemy throughout ... and the scenes of horror make this film unacceptable for general exhibition.' Nevertheless, the ban was reversed after appeal.

**40** *White Zombie* (Victor Hugo Halperin, 1932, USA)

Under the spell of zombie-master 'Murder' Legendre (Bela Lugosi, center), Madeline (Madge Bellamy) is sent to kill her husband Neil (John Harron), but her love for Neil overcomes the spell, while Madeline's betrayer (Robert Frazer, right), is poisoned by Legendre. Cut by Montgomery, he stated that 'this horror is unfit for General Exhibition – the pagan superstition of the Zombie or soul-less is a negation of Christian doctrine.' (1932)

**41** *The Wild Bunch* (Sam Peckinpah, 1969, USA)
Mapache (Emilio Fernandez) slits the throat of gang member Angel (Jaime Sanchez), one of the many cuts made by the Appeal Board. The film had been initially banned by deputy Censor Gabriel Fallon 'on the grounds of its sadistic violence' with many of the western's sequences regarded as 'orgies of brutality', while others were 'objectionable from a sexual point of view.' (1970)

**42** *Peeping Tom* (Michael Powell, 1960, GB)
Blind Mrs Stephens (Maxine Audley) is another potential female victim of serial killer cameraman Mark (Carl Boehm), but is saved because of her (emotional) strength and insight, and his love for her daughter Helen (Anna Massey). 'This picture is an amalgam of sex, sadism and horror, and has not been shown to children anywhere in the world. I do not feel that children should see it here.' (Liam O'Hora, 1960.)

**43** *The Man with the Golden Arm* (Otto Preminger, 1955, USA)
In this controversial and powerful film, Hollywood's first foray into drug addition, which defied the Production Code's taboo of on-screen depictions of drug abuse, Frankie (Frank Sinatra) shoots up. Unsurprisingly, it was banned by Martin Brennan, but it was passed in 1956 by the Appeal Board with cuts including shots of 'semi-nude ladies'.

**44** *The Snake Pit* (Anatole Litvak, 1948, USA)
In a mental asylum, disturbed Virginia (Olivia de Havilland) sits on the forbidden carpet. 'I fear that in this country where there is only [one certificate] the picture may not be a fitting one for *general* presentation. It is possible that I have viewed it too severely from a strict medical standpoint ... Its presentation [is to] be limited to cities and towns of over five thousand in population.' (Richard Hayes, 1949.)

**45** *A Streetcar Named Desire* (Elia Kazan, 1951, USA)
The films of Tennessee Williams, as would be expected, caused great difficulties for the Irish Censor. While his wife is in hospital having their child, Stanley (Marlon Brando) intimidates his sister-in-law Blanche du Bois (Vivien Leigh) before he rapes her. Twenty-seven cuts were demanded by Richard Hayes (1952), but these could not contain the animalistic charisma that Brando exudes.

**46** *Rashomon* (aka *In the Woods*, Akira Kurosawa, 1951, Japan)
During the trial of Tajomaru the bandit (Toshiro Mifune, above), one of the flashbacks shows him kissing (or raping?) the murdered nobleman's wife Masago (Machiko Kyo). Liam O'Hora regarded the award-winning film which introduced post-war Japanese cinema to the west as 'sordid and immoral'. On appeal, the ban was changed to cuts with the embrace (above) 'substantially shortened' and all references to 'seduction' cut.

**47** *A Clockwork Orange* (Stanley Kubrick, 1971, GB)
One of the gangs 'perform' a rape in a theatre. The film (an adaptation of Anthony Burgess' novel), is relentless in its grim delight of a young thug motivated by Beethoven, violence and sex, and offers a pessimistic judgment of idealist notions around social containment of violence. Banned by Breen (1973), and later withdrawn from British and Irish distribution by the director, it was passed by Smith in 2000.

**48** *Of Human Bondage* (Henry Hathaway, Ken Hughes, 1964, GB)
The destructive but loving relationship between Philip (Laurence Harvey) and Mildred (Kim Novak) erupts in violence. This third, and perhaps least successful, adaptation of Somerset Maugham's novel, though made in Ireland at Ardmore Studios, was banned by Christopher Macken who deemed it 'unsavoury' and 'subversive of public morality.' (Passed by the Appeal Board with nineteen cuts, 1965.)

**49** *Blackmail* (Alfred Hitchcock, 1929, GB)
While being sexually assaulted, Alice White (Anny Ondra) kills her attacker. 'Curtail to a decided minimum the unstripping [*sic*] and dressing and the passionate kissing prior to and including the sex struggle ... Remember that this film is restricted to adult audiences in Britain, and that such restriction is not enforced in Saorstát Éireann.' (James Montgomery, 1929.)

50  *Anatomy of a Murder* (Otto Preminger, 1959, USA)
Defence attorney  Paul Biegler (James Stewart) displays the rape victim's underwear as the rapist's daughter
(played by Kathryn Grant) tells how she found it. 'This is a most controversial picture for me to pass, pruned
though it has been ... The utterly clinical dialogue is my main objection to this picture.' (Passed with fifty-
three cuts, which were designed to eliminate all references to the rape, Liam O'Hora, 1959.)

51  *I Can't ... I Can't* (aka *Wedding Night*, Piers Haggard, 1969, Ireland)
Fearful of pregnancy because of her mother's death as a result of a miscarriage, and bound by the Catholic
church's prohibition on 'artificial' contraception, a newly-married woman (Tessa Wyatt) recoils from her
husband (Denis Waterman) and later attempts suicide. It was cut by the distributor before submission, and
then by the Censor (1972), despite being made in Ireland.

**52**  *Gold Diggers of 1933* (Mervyn LeRoy, 1933, USA)
Three performers in the stage show. 'Gold digger is a euphemism for a certain type of woman of very easy virtue. So, the title won't pass. In reels one and two there is so much semi nudity, indecency and double meaning gags that I don't see how to deal with them … The extreme end of the reel [8] is disgusting … the drunken love-making is disgusting … The story is really one of the seduction of men by a type of woman.' (Banned by James Montgomery, 1933; passed with cuts after appeal).

**53**  *Working Girls* (Lizzie Borden, 1986, USA)
This film treats prostitution as an 'ordinary' and viable alternative to traditional employment. Here two middle-class working girls and their madam – Louise Smith, Amanda Goodwin and Ella McElduff – chat between clients. The film, which has a quasi-documentary style, resolutely refuses voyeurism, titillation, and stereotypes, and foregrounds the banality of the work, was banned in 1987 by deputy Censor Jerome Hegarty.

**54** *Docks of New York* (Josef von Sternberg, 1928, USA)
Sadie (Betty Compson) and Lou (Olga Baclanova) ply their trade in a bar on New York's docks. 'The story of sailors and dockside prostitutes. A very cleverly produced film … but highly tainted fare for general consumption, being spiced with lust, suicide and murder. There is a disgusting travesty of marriage.' (Banned by James Montgomery, 1929; ban upheld on appeal.)

55 *Scarface* (aka *Gang War*, Howard Hawks, 1932, USA)
Gangster Tony Camonte (Paul Muni) and his sister (Karen Morley) hold out against the police. 'This is undoubtedly anti-gangster propaganda, and law is triumphant, but ... such films pander to sensationalism.' Re-confirming Montgomery's 1932 ban, Hayes in 1941 wrote that 'there is ... a strong suggestion of incestuous passion between its central figure and his sister.' (Ban renewed in 1953.)

56 *Natural Born Killers* (Oliver Stone, 1994, USA)
Juliette Lewis and Woody Harrelson who play the murderous honeymoon couple pose for the camera. This highly self-conscious film which is a satire on media violence and the public fascination with it, was banned by Smith in 1994 because of fears of imitative behaviour. It was subsequently released on video in 2001, but not before it had caused considerable controversy with theatrical screenings under club conditions refused.

product suitable for the changing production and exhibition environment, with less 'family' films being produced in the context of a declining and fragmented audience. Thus, *The Wicked Lady* (Leslie Arliss, 1945, GB), 'a film of lust, adultery and murders' according to Hayes in 1946 when he banned it,[52] a decision confirmed in 1947 when he viewed a 'revised' version of the film which had 522 feet cut under the title *Wicked Lady Skelton*[53] was resubmitted in 1960 to O'Hora. Nevertheless, he agreed with Hayes (and the Appeal Board, which on both occasions had upheld the decision),[54] but it was passed with six cuts by the Board,[55] and eventually released in January 1961.[56] Another 1940s film to have been treated similarly was King Vidor's steamy melodramatic western *Duel in the Sun* (1946) which features a half-Indian transgressive woman (Jennifer Jones) and her relationship with two brothers. (At the time it was often referred to as 'Lust in the Dust'.) During a long censorship process in 1947–1948, it ended up with thirty-three cuts, and then seems to have been banned.[57] Re-submitted in 1961, it was passed with three cuts, including the rape scene, or in O'Hora's description, 'seduction scene,' which had to be 'drastically curtail[ed]'.[58]

Despite these chinks of light, the policy of general certification dogged Irish cinema, forcing distributors to cut films prior to submission, an approach which invariably failed to satisfy the Censor. For example, the British film *A Kind of Loving* (John Schlesinger, 1962), which concerns the consequences for a young couple who get married because of the woman's pre-martial pregnancy, and had been passed uncut with an 'X' certificate by the BBFC, but in Ireland, even though it had been cut prior to submission, nine further cuts were demanded to conform to the general certificate standard.[59] At the time, Fergus Linehan observed that

> The minor renaissance which has taken place across the water … has largely passed us by here due to … the anomalies of a censorship system which makes no distinction between a ten and a thirty-year old. Thus, we have had no chance to see *Room at the Top*, *Look Back in Anger*, *Saturday Night and Sunday Morning*, and *A Taste of Honey* to name but a distinguished handful.

As for *A Kind of Loving* the Censor had left it 'annoyingly in flitters'.[60]

The banned and cuts list is long for British Cinema of this period, but the core point of Linehan's complaint concerned the access by children to films which had been produced with an adult audience in mind but which might prove disturbing even in their cut form for children. Likewise, other film reviewers sporadically drew attention to the anomalies within the system and highlighted the inefficiency of a grading system that relied on the discretion of cinemas' screening policies, as in the case of *This Sporting Life* (Lindsay Anderson, 1963, GB) and *Look Back in Anger*, released the same week in Dublin, where local cinema managements imposed an age limit on admittance.[61] While *Sporting Life* had been passed in a version cut by 2,754 feet prior to submission, the *Irish Times*' reviewer sarcastically observed that *Look Back in Anger* 'reaches us after four years, the censor having, apparently, made up his mind that we can now be permitted to know that men sometimes live with women who aren't their wives,'[62] even though the relationship between Richard Harris and Rachel Roberts seems to have been largely deleted from *Sporting Life*.[63]

The *Sunday Independent's* Des Hickey eventually led the effective newspaper campaign in favour of limited certificates. His frequently expressed argument was simple – when films become 'outspoken' a system of graded certificates is 'sorely' needed.[64] *Return to Peyton Place* (Jose Ferrer, 1961), the prequel of which, *Peyton Place* (Mark Robson, 1957) had been banned,[65] typified the problems with the then-current process. In 1962 the film was finally released, but with a general certificate, having been butchered by ten minutes with, it seemed, any dialogue 'of moral consequence' excised.[66] Notwithstanding Hickey's misinformed accolade to the Censor on the release of *Term of Trial* (Peter Glenville, 1962, GB), which he believed was cut only briefly in two places and given an over-18s certificate thus allowing a 'rare occasion to see a provocative piece of cinema in its original form,'[67] – in fact, the film had been cut in eight places and there is no reference to an over-18s certificate in the Censor's report of six weeks earlier[68] – his campaign remained focused. However, it was his comments on the treatment of the sentimental comedy *The Courtship of Eddie's Father* (Vincente Minnelli, 1962) which exposed the ridiculousness of Irish film censorship and kick-started a public debate. In his Sunday column, Hickey published a line which had been cut from the film, but its relative mildness – 'I don't want to marry one of those ladies in the cartoons with skinny eyes and big bosoms' – only caused, as he recalled later, readers to laugh, and 'the structure of our censorship [to begin] to crack.'[69] Though John D. Sheridan wrote in support of the Censor's decision to remove the line, he only succeeded in 'hastening the victory of the enemy with his astonishing tactics.'[70] He helped to fuel the debate on film censorship and ensured, as many such censorship controversies have proved, that the opposite result to that intended by the complainant was achieved.

Nevertheless, a more liberal film censorship regime was not aided by the appointment on 7 April 1964 of 63-year-old Dr Christopher Macken as Film Censor, in succession to Liam O'Hora, who died suddenly on 22 March. An elected Fianna Fáil member of Dublin Corporation for ten years, he had run unsuccessfully for the party in the 1954 and 1957 general elections. It was his running mate on those occasions, Charles J. Haughey, the Minister of Justice in 1964, who appointed him Film Censor even though he 'knew nothing about film.' But like earlier censors he believed that his medical career and his experience in psychiatry (he had taken a graduate course in psychiatry and had worked for five years at St Brendan's Hospital, Grangegorman, an institution for the insane) lent him a 'better understanding of human nature.'[71] (This is something which seems to have continued in more recent media censorship debates with the foregrounding of psychologist/psychiatrist based experts.) Given his background, it is not surprising that like his predecessor Dr Richard Hayes, he expressed a preference for didactic and realist films, ones 'which teach a lesson ... that point to what could happen and what happened.'[72] Such was hardly propitious to commercial and indeed 'art' cinema, and so it proved to be. Before Macken could fully impose his restrictive will on film releases, pressure began to mount on the minister for new directives to be given to the censors. Despite Haughey's commitment to law reform in his three years at Justice[73] unfortunately it did not extend to film censorship. Even when in July 1962 the cinema owners called for the grading of films,[74] Haughey refused to act and rejected their argument that this would help stem the decline in audiences. He told the Dáil that the downturn in audiences was happening worldwide and could not be blamed on the Irish film censorship system. Anyway, if it were the case, that could not justify the lowering of standards.[75] During 1963 and 1964 he continued to reject any change in the censorship arrangements.[76] Fortunately, in October 1964 Haughey was moved to Agriculture and his replacement at Justice, Brian Lenihan, was more open than any other previous Minister for Justice to the mounting criticism against film censorship policy.

Initially, this seemed not to be the case when during the Fianna Fáil Ard Fheis in November 1964 Lenihan made a distinction between theatre and film censorship. He declared that the 'experience in other countries clearly indicates that notices [for a restricted film] tend to attract people who would not ordinarily attend such a film.' Perhaps the mind-set of Peter Berry, the Department's Secretary, its most senior civil servant, was behind this comment, but this differentiation between high and low culture was a recurring trope in censorship debates, and which provoked Hickey into making a sarcastic attack on Lenihan's speech. He observed, undoubtedly correctly, that 'the theatre in Ireland has a respectability which the cinema lacks.'[77] Shortly afterwards, when Macken's decision to ban *Of Human Bondage* (Ken Hughes, 1964) was revealed,[78] quite uniquely, as Hickey pointed out, MGM's chief in Ireland and the film's local distributor Jack Lyons complained to Lenihan about the decision even though hithertofore there had been a 'policy of outside film companies not [interfering] with the operations of our Film Censor.' Hickey also noted the hypocrisy of banning the film after three million dollars had been spent in Ireland on its making.[79]

For the first time renters and exhibitors were willing to go on the record to point out what was happening to their product. British Lion's Sam Parker reported that Alexander Singer's *Psyche '59* (1964, GB), Alvin Rakoff's *The Comedy Man* (1964, GB) and Michael Winner's *The System* (1964, GB) had been banned, and Fred Zinnemann's *Behold a Pale Horse* (1964) and Carl Foreman's *The Victors* (1963, GB) had been cut, while Stanley Kubrick's *Dr Strangelove: Or, How I Learned to Stop Worrying and Love the Bomb* (1963) remained unreleased because Kubrick had refused to accept the cuts demanded by both deputy Censor Mr J. Shiel and the Appeal Board. In all other countries it had been shown uncensored.[80]

*Dr Strangelove* had been cut in three places by Shiel in April 1964. The cuts were: the whole scene in which Miss Scott (Tracy Reed) is seen in a bikini as she answers the phone and is later joined by her lover, General Turgidson (George C. Scott); the exchange between General Jack D. Ripper (Sterling Hayden) and Captain Mandrake (Peter Sellers) in which the general talks about love-making, his concern about 'fatigue' and 'loss of essence,' and how women sense his power; and the scene which follows Major 'King' Kong (Slim Pickens) riding the nuclear bomb to explosion, when the wheel-chair bound scientist Dr Strangelove (Peter Sellers) expounds his theory as to how people could survive for 100 years in mineshafts following a nuclear explosion.

He proposes that the human race could be bred by living underground with a ratio of ten 'sexually stimulating' women to one man. Shiel cut all references to such imaginary promiscuity, a decision which left (for an Irish audience) a mysterious reference to mineshafts when Ripper tries to convince the President (Peter Sellers, again) to endorse the plan, that is, just before the film's final moments of total nuclear destruction. Unusually, Sam Parker, the local manager of the film's distributor, British Lion, wrote to J.T. O'Farrell, the chairman, shortly before the Appeal Board viewed the film. He said that he had pointed out to Shiel when the film was being censored that 'it was a most serious subject on which sex, or discussions of sex had no possible bearing on either the theme or the ultimate end.'[81] Parker's disingenuous plea was in vain because a few days later the Board upheld the cuts.[82] The inevitable outcome of such censorship, at least in commercial terms, was summed up by Colman Conroy, head of Odeon's operations in Ireland, who pointed to the 'acute' shortage of product: 'The number of films being rejected is affecting our circuit throughout the country.' Des O'Keefe, general manager, Adelphi-Carlton cinemas, endorsed this view. The united front now seen by the distributors and exhibitors could, according to Hickey, 'mean the end of a sorry regime of film censorship.'[83]

The following week Lenihan called in the exhibitors' body, the Cinema and Theatre Association of Ireland, to discuss the issue. He agreed to view a number of films on their recommendation so as to assess the difficulties they were experiencing. While revealing this development in the most prominent front page story in the *Sunday Independent* 'FILM CENSORSHIP: A SENSATIONAL TURN', Hickey reported that the films to be viewed would include the banned and cut films *The Victors*,[84] *Marnie* (Alfred Hitchcock, 1964),[85] *Becket* (Peter Glenville, 1964, GB),[86] the adaptation of Edna O'Brien's banned novel *The Lonely Girl* (1962), *Girl with Green Eyes* (Desmond Davies, 1964, GB),[87] and *For Those Who Think Young* (Leslie Mortinson, 1964),[88] which had been given a 'U' certificate in Britain.[89] Exhibitors and distributors knew there was one weapon in the Minister's armoury which could effect speedy change in censorship policy: the imminent appointment of a new Censorship of Films Appeal Board. It was to be the beginning of a new era for Irish film censorship.[90]

5 *Shake Hands with the Devil* (Michael Anderson, 1959). The politically unacceptable tag line (*Evening Press*, 22 May 1959) was removed from the following day's newspaper.

# CHAPTER 6

# *The Film Censors and the new 'liberalism'*

> I think that a film is a director's work and he is
> the only one really entitled to cut it.
> Sheamus Smith, *Official Film Censor, 1986–2003.*

## THE APPEAL BOARD AND LIMITED CERTIFICATES, 1965–1972

A dominant view of the 1960s in Ireland is that it represents the period from when (post)modernity and liberalism began to displace notions of (patriarchal and institutional) tradition. In real terms, it saw insular Catholic Ireland open out to international influences – largely through the media and cultural production – which brought in their wake secular and liberating forces, something, of course, which the cinema in Ireland, albeit in a truncated manner, had been doing for decades. These changes included greater individual control over human reproduction, which led to increased sexual activity; the involvement of more women in the workforce; and more broadly the raising of the status of women from their singular preoccupation in the home as defined in the 1937 Constitution, such as through the lifting in 1973 of the marriage ban on women working in the civil service. If accumulatively these altered the social fabric and impacted on the nature of the family and home, not least in its affecting fatherhood and men's status as provider, and indeed, continue to do so, increasingly since the 1990s and particularly with the decline of the 'Celtic Tiger' economy in the early 2000s the view of this cultural shift as progressive has been challenged and problematized. As one might expect, critics of this post-1960s secular liberalism have come most consistently, if not exclusively, from the right in a debate which has foregrounded issues relating to childcare; the breakdown of the traditional nuclear family such that there is a significant proportion of people in Ireland living in alternative arrangements including co-habitation and single parent homes, which are often not protected by any legal framework should difficulties arise; sexual (ir)responsibility and the growing reality of teenage sexual activity which has led to an increase in STDs and teenage and/or unwanted pregnancy; crime rates, and in particular the relatively new phenomenon of random street violence by young males, and the social disturbances and other (violent) instances caused by late night drinking; and increasing house prices which seem to preclude single and even many double income families, most especially in Dublin and other urban centres, from owing their own home. However, the changes have been less dramatic or instant than as has often been imagined, but slowly emerged out of and overwhelmed the dominant repressive ideological sensibility. This is evident in film censorship which has been shown to parallel the experience in other areas of Irish life. The 'revolutionary' breakthrough in this sector was to allow a provision – limited certification – in a 42-year-old statute to be fully activated, but it was more than another two decades before this 'liberal' policy was consolidated.

In December 1964, shortly before the appointment of a new Censorship of Films Appeal Board, the Minister for Justice, Brian Lenihan, told the Dáil of his sympathy with regard to limited certification and revealed that he had listened to film trade representatives, 'who expressed strong disagreement with the standards of censorship,' and as a result, he decided to view the particular films which they had identified for him.[1] Lenihan also informed the Dáil that he intended to 'reconstitute' the Board when it came up for renewal.[2] Indeed, some of the members of the outgoing Board had been in charge of appeals for an exceedingly long time. The chairman, 78-year-old John T. O'Farrell, had served continuously in that position for thirty-five years, prior to which he had been a board member since 1924, while other members had been appointed in 1941, 1942, 1946, 1953, 1958 and 1959. Only architect Sam Stephenson, later responsible for the controversial civic offices on Wood Quay and the Central Bank building, Dublin, who had been appointed in April 1964 by Charles Haughey following the death of one of the censors, was re-appointed, and then only after a vacancy became available in late 1965.

In January 1965, 43-year-old Judge Conor Maguire was appointed chairman of the new Appeal Board. Two of the members were the traditional clerical appointments. These were the Revd John Desmond Murray, ordained in 1939 and Church of Ireland incumbent at Dalkey since 1955, who replaced the Revd W.W. Rooke who had served on the Board since 1953, and Fr Michael J. Browne DCL, who had worked under John Charles McQuaid at Archbishop's House during the 1940s and early 1950s before being appointed to Harold's Cross Parish, Dublin, who took over from Canon Thomas O'Donnell, a Board member since 1941, when he had replaced Monsignor Cronin. Continuity with the previous Board was also seen in the appointment of William Coyne MD, indicating a continuing preference for doctors as censors, and in the selection of Irish Transport and General Workers Union (ITGWU) official, John F. Carroll PC, who took over from fellow trade unionist, Thomas O'Reilly, who had served since 1953. Both of these appointments were in recognition of the ITGWU as the trade union which organized film exhibition and distribution workers. In 1973 Carroll replaced Judge Maguire as chairman,[3] a position he retained until 1997. For the first time, the 1965 Board included a third clergyman, a Jesuit, Fr John C. Kelly, but after only nine months he moved to Italy, leaving an opening which Stephenson then filled. Of all the clerics of the various boards only Fr Kelly's views are publicly known, as he gave an interview in the November 1965 issue of the Catholic monthly, *Assisi*. Though he had taken the position with 'some hesitancy', as Des Hickey reported, during his short tenure he 'helped to bring a touch of sanity to film censorship in Ireland.'[4] The other members of the Board were John (Jack) A. O'Connor, District Justice Alfred A. Rochford, and Mrs Helena Ruttledge.

The new Appeal Board quickly transformed Irish film censorship, though Macken resisted the new dispensation. He reverted to the all-embracing undefined phrase from the 1923 Act in his (short) reports to the Appeal Board. The films he rejected (42 in 1965, his first full year in office) were almost universally deemed to be 'subversive of public morality,' a phrase he applied indiscriminately to the very different 'macabre production' of *The Tomb of Ligeia* and unremarkable if at times playful comedy, Ingmar Bergman's *The Devil's Eye* (*Djäävlens Öga*, 1960, Sweden),[5] both banned in early 1965. The range of subjects rejected by him varied from the 'bigamy' of *The Remarkable Mr Pennypacker* (Henry Levin, 1958);[6] 'the continuous unhealthy treatment of sex' in *Sex and the Single Girl* (Richard Quine, 1964);[7] 'striptease joints, prostitution, narcotics and nudity' in *The Troublemaker* (Theodore Flicker, 1964);[8] the 'brutality' of *The Hill* (Sidney Lumet, 1965, GB);[9] rape and prostitution in *Sylvia* (Gordon Douglas, 1964);[10] the 'trial honeymoon' of *I'll Take Sweden* (Frederick de Cordova, 1965);[11] and the 'degrading depths' of the London beatnik scene in *The Party's Over* (Guy Hamilton, 1965, GB).[12] Other films banned by him in 1966 included Max Ophuls' *La Ronde* (1950, France) a narrative of interconnected love affairs which displays the director's sumptuous baroque visual style and his reputation as a consummate stylist who understood the importance of *mise en scène*;[13] Richard Lester's fast paced bouncy comic tribute to the swinging sixties *The Knack* (aka *The Knack … and How to Get It*, 1965, GB)[14] made around the time of his two films featuring the Beatles: *A Hard Day's Night* (1964) and *Help!* (1965); Vittorio de Sica's upbeat hit comedy *Marriage Italian Style* (*Matrimonio all'italiana*, 1964, Italy) staring Sophie Loren and Marcello Mastroianni;[15] Clive Donner's farce *What's New, Pussycat?* (1965, USA/France) written by Woody Allen and starring Peter Sellers;[16] Roman Polanski's surrealist disquieting *Repulsion*[17] dealing with mental breakdown which won the Silver Bear at the 1965 Berlin Film Festival; Luis Buñuel's grim iconoclastic *Nazarín* (1958, Mexico)[18] about an earnest priest whose aim is to bring Jesus' message; and John Schlesinger's *Darling* (1965, GB)[19] which, reflecting the superficiality, amorality and ennui of the sixties, had much in common with more elitist modernist filmmakers such as Antonioni, and which was described by Bosley Crowther of the *New York Times* as 'the tale of a London photographer's model who goes from bed to worse.'[20]

Clearly, Macken did not discriminate between mainstream commercial films and those belonging to the European art cinema tradition. For him, content not context was paramount. However, in a western society that was increasingly becoming secular and materialistic and in which the grand narrative of religion and morality was being challenged, it is less than surprising that the films being submitted reflected this. If Ireland historically had been out of sync with the rest of Europe and North America, by virtue of the media, particularly television, increased travel, the shift towards an internationalized economic policy, and Ireland's joining of the European Economic Community in 1973, that was no longer the case. Nevertheless, Macken's decision to ban representations that were contradictory to official Ireland even if they found a reality in everyday society and within the public imagination, was a logical one within the confines of his ideological remit. While censorship is necessarily limiting and paternalistic, as well as regressive, when its mechanisms or reality become apparent and the level of repression is recognized, it is no longer sustainable in its current form as Lenihan understood. Before him, others too appreciated this fact, not least among them James Montgomery who had some anxiety concerning the *technical* issues surrounding the introduction of sound cinema in the early 1930s and the difficulties it would present to his job, and, as discussed in chapter 8, Thomas Coyne, Controller of Censorship, who feared that if cutting was too extensive and hence apparent, it would open up the whole process of censorship to ridicule. If television and media were highlighting the problem of censorship in the 1960s, it was only an earlier and weaker manifestation of what would happen with video in the 1980s and the internet in the 1990s. The solution favoured then, as now, was what Lenihan had indicated to the Dáil in 1964, limited certificates and classification. Whatever about the crudity of such certification, or the potential fostering of prurient fascination, as Montgomery feared, when a film was released only theatrically (prior to video, that is), at least it could be satisfactorily monitored. It was with this mandate of social compromise that the new Appeal Board introduced four limited certificates: under-12s accompanied by an adult, over-16s, over-18s, and occasional over-21s (issued only on four occasions).

While the view has persisted that bannings ceased altogether with the new Board and films were being approved uncut, albeit with limited certificates, this is not the case. Of the 42 films banned by Macken in 1965, the Board only passed 3 uncut, although it is likely that at least one of these had been cut prior to submission.[21] Twenty-four of them were approved for over-18s; 2 for over-16s, and one with an under-12s with adult certificate, while the significantly large remainder of 13 (or over 30 per cent) had the reject decision affirmed. The latter category included a number of films whose subject matter continued to be suppressed for Irish audiences, such as the sexually-provocative teen film, *Beat Girl*;[22] Billy Wilder's lewd farce, *Kiss Me, Stupid* (1964);[23] the sixties compilation film of female film stars, including scenes many of which had been cut from films or had contributed to their banning in previous decades, *The Love Goddesses* (Saul J. Turel, Graeme Ferguson, 1965);[24] one of Italian horror specialist Mario Bava's many films which caused censorship difficulties, *Black Sabbath* (*I Tre Volte della Paura*, 1963, Italy);[25] the exploration of the instablility of a sexually-repressed young Frenchwoman (Catherine Deneuve) in *Repulsion*; and by contrast, Swinging Sixties London featuring sexually uninhibited Julie Christie in *Darling*; the hit comedy about a man's sexual conquests and his friend's attempts to emulate them in *The Knack*; and *La Ronde*.

When it came to films cut by Macken but awarded a general certificate, the Board was not as liberal as it is retrospectively imagined, though, in comparison with what went before, it was perceived as being 'revolutionary'. One of the main features of the censors' interventions in films in the latter part of the 1960s and afterwards was to try to contain the increasingly explicit sexual activities taking place in intimate bedroom settings. Thus, when the 1963 film *Torpedo Bay* (Charles Frend, Italy/France) was viewed by Macken in January 1965, his instruction to the renter was to delete the bedroom scene where a woman doctor and the commander are in bed together.[26] The biographical picture about playwright Sean O'Casey, *Young Cassidy* (Jack Cardiff, John Ford, 1964, GB), viewed later in the month, had to be cut 'to avoid the obvious conclusion' that Johnny Cassidy (Rod Taylor) and Daisy Battles (Julie Christie) were making love. In this scene, which takes place after Cassidy rescues Daisy from a riot, she tells him she has an 'uncle' who looks after her and follows this up with suggestive comments about mending his trousers, before appearing in front of him in a negligée, whereupon he takes her to bed. The other scene cut was also of a woman, Bessie Ballynoy (Pauline Delany), who tries to seduce the reluctant Johnny before the Black and Tans interrupt their activities, but not before she makes derogatory comments about her 'pathetic' husband.[27]

Three months later, Macken edited the hugely popular Greek drama *Zorba the Greek* (Michael Cacoyannis, 1964, GB) in twelve places, many of these cuts concerned Zorba's (Anthony Quinn) earthy comments on sexuality and belief, such as when he says that 'if a woman sleeps alone it puts a shame on all men' and 'if a woman calls a man to her bed and he will not go ...' While these lines were cut to ensure the explicitness of his comments was suppressed, the intervening lines were allowed: 'God has a very big heart, but there is one sin he will not forgive. I know, because a very wise old Turk told me,' which seems to suggest that God's word is being invoked in a general sense, however the context is provided by the Turk's cut line about the 'sin' of a woman not going to a bed when called there. It is a neat piece of editing à la Montgomery, who similarly was always on the lookout to turn such sexual explicitness to a religious/moral end. Another instance of this policy is when Zorba gives advice to Basil (Alan Bates), son of a Greek migrant to England, who dithers over his interest in the widow. Zorba tells him, 'If God went your way there would be no Christmas. He did not go to church. He went to Mary, and Christ was born. He went that way. Mary is the widow.' Other scenes cut include Zorba with a young prostitute, Lola, whom he meets in a bar in Athens, and the reminiscence of the dying prostitute (Lila Kedrova) as she recalls her activities during World War Two with the soldiers of various armies, including the line, 'So they undress me.' Zorba, too, recalls the war and bitterly recounts what he did for his country, including 'raped women,' words removed by the Censor. Also cut were the love-making scenes between Basil and the widow, including when she takes off her clothes and the morning after when he is in bed with her. As a result of the widow's 'transgression,' the villagers attack her, but before killing her they molest her. A scene of clothes tearing and breast-pulling was cut, yet, contradictorily, the more violent killing of her with a knife was allowed.[28] But then violence and death are less problematic in the Irish context to the (sexualized) body. Even as late as 1989 in Margo Harkin's *Hush-a-Bye-Baby*, the central teenage Goretti vainly hopes that she is suffering from cancer rather than being pregnant.

In other films, too, scenes of seduction continued to be trimmed, including the dialogue in *Love Has Many Faces* (Alexander Singer, 1964),[29] in which a teenager explains the consequences of her seduction, 'I was only 17. Too young to get married

...' while *Seduction of Julia* had its title changed.[30] Despite the brave new world of appeals, none of these films cut by the censor was appealed. Conceivably then, the Board's greatest achievement was not its revolutionary approach but in having the media, film reviewers (and even distributors and exhibitors), who had been starved of representations that were in contradiction to Catholic morality, collude with the state that censorship policy had radically changed, when, in fact, it had only been slightly relaxed. The illusion was also due to the inflexibility of Macken against which the Board seemed to be liberal, but also against whom they struggled until the early 1970s.

Nevertheless, some films did benefit from the regime change. One of the first of these was the latest adaptation of Somerset Maughan's novel *Of Human Bondage*, which had twice previously been adapted for the screen, in 1934, when it was banned by Montgomery, and in 1946, released in Ireland with five cuts.[31] Macken regarded the new version as 'unsavoury' and banned it.[32] The new Board viewed the film in February 1965, only a few weeks after it had been constituted. They issued an over-18s certificate, although only after it was cut in nineteen places, which amounted to about four minutes in total. Besides sixteen dialogue cuts, the film's opening titles were changed because they contained shots of three Auguste Rodin statues that were used as backgrounds. Thus, the statues with 'the back view of a reclining girl, the male and female in which the male is holding the female by the breast, and the male and female in which the male is kissing the female on or about her breast' were cut by the Board.[33] If statues by Rodin were being cut by the new Board, it didn't auger well for the increasing number of films made in the 1960s and 1970s which included scenes of 'real' nudity. If at one level it is a tribute to Rodin's penetrating observation which in his 'The Age of Reason' (1877) resulted in the accusation against him that he cast the sculpture from a real model, it nevertheless remains that both Macken and the Appeal Board were afraid of the image. That the statues of considerable reputation were only artistic representations within film representations did not matter.

The pattern in its first year continued into 1966 as Macken and his equally conservative assistant, Gabriel Fallon, resisted issuing limited certificates and increased by 10, to 52, the number of films banned. These were as various as the horror movies, *The Plague of the Zombies* (John Gilling, 1965, GB)[34] and *Dracula – Prince of Darkness* (Terence Fisher, 1965, GB);[35] the European cinema of *The Silken Skin* (*La Peau Douce*, François Truffaut, 1964, France),[36] *Diary of a Chambermaid* (*Le Journal d'une Femme de Chambre*, Luis Buñuel, 1964, France)[37] and *Viridiana* (Luis Buñuel, 1961, Spain/Mexico);[38] the British films *Morgan – A Suitable Case for Treatment* (Karel Reisz, 1966),[39] *Life at the Top* (Ted Kotcheff, 1965),[40] *Alfie* (Lewis Gilbert, 1966),[41] and *Modesty Blaise* (Joseph Losey, 1966),[42] about a sexy female spy; and the American films *Who's Afraid of Virginia Wolfe?* (Mike Nichols, 1966),[43] *The Group* (Sidney Lumet, 1966),[44] *The Chase* (Arthur Penn, 1966),[45] and *This Property Is Condemned*.[46]

While the Board upheld 9 (or 17 per cent) of these decisions, perhaps only *Jules and Jim* with its *ménage-a-trois* and Russ Meyer's *Fanny Hill* (1965, West Germany)[47] would have been well known. Other films the Board disapproved of were Mario Bava's *Blood and Black Lace* (*Sei Donne per l'Assassino*, 1964, Italy),[48] and *Lilith* (Robert Rossen, 1964), which concerns the relationship between a therapist and a patient in an asylum and includes hints of lesbianism.[49] However, more frequently, the Board disagreed with the Censor (and Fallon), and passed most of the rejected titles with over-16s or over-18s certificates, some of which remained uncut, including *The Haunted Palace, Juliet of the Spirits*, and *I Was Happy Here* (Desmond Davies, 1964, GB), 'the whole tone' of which 'contravenes decency,' according to Macken.[50] Both *Who's Afraid of Virginia Wolfe?* and *Alfie* were awarded over-21s with cuts. Nine over-16s certificates were also issued, including for *Morgan – A Suitable Case for Treatment, Modesty Blaise*, and *Viva Maria!* (Louis Malle, 1965, France/Italy), which features Brigitte Bardot as an Irish revolutionary in Central America.[51] In 2 instances, the Canadian outback film *The Trap* (Sidney Hayers, 1966, GB/Canada),[52] and the British comedy parody, *Carry On Screaming* (Gerald Thomas, 1966),[53] the Board approved under-12s with adult certification, though with five cuts in the latter case, for films banned by the Censor.

As a result of these differences between the two branches of film censorship, there was a vastly increased workload for the Board. Never before was there such disagreement over censorship policy and it would not be until Macken's death in June 1972 that the situation would once again be stabilized. Reluctantly, Macken began to issue limited certificates from February 1966, though the bannings did not stop. Nevertheless, Chairman Judge Maguire, in a newspaper interview in 1966 gave an upbeat assessment of the changes brought about since he took over. The interview, which appeared in the *Sunday Times* of Malta, highlighted the more open attitude towards censorship, and indicated the Board 'were disposed from the beginning ... to issue limited certificates,' the success of which led the Censor himself to follow suit. He added that it was 'more satisfactory' not to have a written code. While acknowledging the existence of 'more adult fare' in the cinema and an 'apparently universal trend to discuss and debate in public subjects which formerly were considered very private,' Judge Maguire suggested that most of the films 'are done tastefully and present sound moral lessons,' as well as displaying 'definite signs ... of maturity and intellectual progression'. He felt that films could not be said 'to have degenerated in a moral sense.' He reported that the Appeal Board took 'a positive approach to what could be a negative task.' Unfortunately, he failed to point out the areas which were still off limits for Irish audiences.[54]

The first limited certificate – over-18 – issued by Macken, seems to have been for *Never Too Late* (Bud Yorkin, 1965), an adaptation of a Broadway play about imminent parenthood featuring Irish-born actress Maureen O'Sullivan as a mother, although he made a cut concerning her preganacy.[55] By the end of the year, Macken had issued at least 22 such certificates, all of which, except the spy romp, *That Man in Istanbul* (Anthony Isasi, 1966)[56] were for over-18s. The Board adjudicated on 10 of these and affirmed the Censor's decision totally on only 2 occasions. It variously changed the cuts or the limitation.[57] For example, in the case of *Torn Curtain* (Alfred Hitchcock, 1966), the cuts were affirmed, but the over-18s was dramatically changed to a general certificate,[58] while with regard to the epic romance *Doctor Zhivago* (David Lean, 1965), the Censor's over-18s certificate was affirmed, but the four cuts – mainly of Lara (played by Julie Christie) and Yuri (Omar Sharif) in bed – were cancelled.[59] Despite Macken's use of limited certificates, his main policy continued to be to issue general certificates, most usually with cuts, especially as he became increasingly obsessed with bedroom scenes, which were cut from films such as *Thunderball* (Terence Young, 1965, GB),[60] *Madame X* (David Lowell Rich, 1965),[61] *He Who Rides a Tiger* (Charles Crichton, 1965, GB),[62] *Ten Little Indians* (George Pollock, 1966, GB),[63] *Our Man Flint* (Daniel Mann, 1965),[64] *The Blue Max* (John Guillermin, 1966),[65] *The Love Cage* (aka *Joy House*, René Clement, 1964, France),[66] and *The Quiller Memorandum* (Michael Anderson, 1966, GB).[67] Moreover, these cuts were not appealed, but in cases such as *The Blue Max*, the cuts – of Ursula Andress and George Peppard about to make love, and a scene in which her arm blocks her naked breast – were ameliorated by the Board, while the general certificate was affirmed by it.

By 1967, the change in policy (as well as relieving a backlog of titles) lead to the Censor banning *only* 23 films, including Joseph Strick's version of James Joyce's *Ulysses* (1967, GB). This film's banning, perhaps the most controversial decision of the period, was upheld by the Board which took three meetings before a consensus was reached.[68] In 9 (or 40 per cent) of the cases, the Board upheld the Censor's banning order; in one instance, *Sleeping Car Murders* (*Compartiment Tueurs*, Costa-Gavras, 1965, France), an over-16s certificate was issued with cuts;[69] while a further 10 films were cut before being issued with over-18s certificates. One such cut film was *The Game Is Over* (Roger Vadim, 1966, France) in which Jane Fonda seduces her husband's son by his first marriage, and was passed with 577 feet cut (over six minutes) and an over-18s certificate, thus eliminating much 'unpleasantness.'[70] By contrast, the Board changed some of the Censor's over-18s limitations to general certificates with cuts, such as the western *Alvarez Kelly* (Edward Dmytryk, 1966)[71] and an under-12s accompanied by an adult certificate with cuts for *The Spy in the Green Hat*. In this latter film, scenes of knife throwing, undressing, and a woman fighting were deleted to achieve the lower rating.[72]

One of the banned films, *Accident* (Joseph Losey, 1967, GB), from a script by Harold Pinter, helps to illustrate the manner in which the Board approached questions of sexual morality, especially extra-marital affairs. In this film, Stephen (Dirk Bogarde), a married university don, develops a fascination with, and lust for, one of his students, an enigmatic foreigner, Anna (Jacqueline Sassard). She has a boyfriend, William (Michael York), but is having an affair with one of Stephen's colleagues, Charley (Stanley Baker). The first cut ordered by the Board after the film was rejected by Macken[73] was of Charley reading statistics concerning the sexual behaviour of university students. Another cut concerned Stephen's visit to an ex-girlfriend, Francesca (Delphine Seyrig), and their being in bed together after love-making. When Stephen arrives home he finds Charley and Anna there, having been at the house while he was away. He is shocked at the discovery of the affair, and during a discussion between the two men which was cut, Charley tells him that he 'can't have enough of' Anna. The fourth cut to the film was after Stephen takes Anna from the wreckage of William's car in which he is killed, to his home. As she lies injured and shocked in a bedroom, Stephen (in a pre-emption of David Cronenberg's *Crash* [1996, Canada], a film cut for release in Ireland in 1997), molests her by 'thrusting his body between Anna's legs,' to use the Board's description of the scene.[74] While *Accident* is a somewhat pretentious, ponderous and very English film, sixties films in general were less coy about sex, nudity, and that quintessential aspect of contemporary youth culture, drugs.

Michelangelo Antonioni's rich meta-cinematic film *Blow-Up* (1966, GB), another Swinging London film with art cinema aspects, contained many of these elements and, as a result, the Board required three viewings of the film between October 1967 and April 1968 to overturn Macken's banning order[75] and then only after six cuts were made. As one might expect, the aspects of the film which the Board objected to were the photo shoot of the female models; the long scene in which two young aspirant models visit the photographer (David Hemmings) and there tear off each other's clothes; the scene in which Vanessa Redgrave tries to retrieve the photographs taken in the park when she is with her lover, and the photographer thinks he has recorded a murder. In these scenes, she walks around topless, but she is seen either from behind or has her hands covering her breasts.

The number of rejects by Macken was up in 1968 to 36 films, 10 of which were upheld by the Appeal Board, including the somewhat amusing *Here We Go Round the Mulberry Bush* (Clive Donner, 1967, GB), which features a teenager obsessed by sex;[76] *The Trip* (Roger Corman, 1967), the controversial drug film;[77] *Belle de Jour* (Luis Buñuel, 1968, France), in which a bored middle-class woman works as a prostitute;[78] *Girl on a Motorcycle* (aka *Naked under Leather*, *La Motorcyclette*, Jack Cardiff, 1968, GB/France), in which lovers Marianne Faithfull and Alain Delon engage in sexual shenanigans;[79] *Barbarella* (Roger Vadim, 1967, France/Italy), featuring naked Jane Fonda in the opening credits and later in sexual reverie;[80] and *Joanna* (Michael Sarne, 1968, GB), in which an innocent becomes corrupted in 'Swinging London'.[81] Three other films banned by Macken, *The Wild Angels*,[82] *Hamburg, City of Vice* (Germany),[83] and *Her Private Hell* (Norman J. Warren, 1968, GB)[84] were not appealed.

Almost half, or 17, of the films banned, were passed with over-18s certificates, but only after they were extensively cut.[85] Two other films were similarly treated but passed with over-16s certificates. However, in the case of one of these, *The Swimmer* (Frank Perry, 1968), to which Macken objected because of its nudity, the Board only ordered one cut, that of a character saying 'Good Christ Ned.'[86] Interestingly, the Board passed one film uncut with an over-18s certificate, *The Yellow Teddybears* (Robert Hartford-Davis, 1963, GB), an exploitation film, but one which has a sympathy for its young protagonist,[87] while another, the action film, *Guns for San Sebastian* (Henri Verneuil, 1967, France/Mexico/Italy), was given a general certificate.[88]

*The Graduate* (Mike Nichols, 1967), banned by Macken[89] but allowed by the Board,[90] albeit with an over-18s certificate and eleven cuts, reveals quite clearly the Board's *modus operandi* and exposes a limitation within its policy when it came to sex. By 1968, the Board, through use of over-18s certificates, was permitting audiences to see consenting unmarried adults having sex with each other, even if the bedroom scenes were brief or non-existent, depending on the passionate intensity of the representations. *The Graduate*, a sort of coming-of-age film in which virginal college graduate Ben (Dustin Hoffman) is persuaded by married Mrs Robinson (Anne Bancroft), a friend of Ben's parents, to have an affair with her. She is mother of grown-up Elaine (Katherine Ross), with whom Ben falls in love and with whom he finally elopes. The Board ordered significant cuts to four crucial scenes, three of which concern the relationship between Ben and Mrs Robinson.

Following a party at his home, Mrs Robinson cajoles Ben into driving her home and when he is there tries to seduce him. The first scene cut is when Ben realizes what she is doing: 'Mrs Robinson – You are trying to seduce me,' a cut which begins when she crosses her legs in a revealing manner. Other lines dealing with seduction, including her 'I am not trying to seduce you' and 'Would you like me to seduce you?' were also removed. Having enticed him upstairs on the (ironic) pretext of seeing a portrait of Elaine, Ben retreats from the bedroom after Mrs Robinson appears before him naked. This exchange ends with Mr Robinson arriving home, but not before his wife has said to Ben, 'If you won't sleep with me this time … you can call me anytime you want and we can make some kind of an arrangement,' adding, 'I find you very attractive.' What an Irish viewer would have understood from the extant scenes stripped of Mrs Robinson's explicit dialogue and her nakedness is only a mildly flirtatious exchange between the two.

Repulsed at first, Ben succumbs to the offer and rings Mrs Robinson, who joins him at a hotel. Realizing that he is nervous and inexperienced, she encourages him to book a room, and starts undressing almost immediately they get there, scenes cut by the Board. 'I'll get undressed now,' she says to him. Unsure what to do, Ben replies, 'I'll watch.' He is in two minds about getting involved with her, but it was this aspect of the scene which the Board allowed. 'I can't do this,' he says, it is 'wrong,' and he asks her to imagine what his parents would say if they knew that he was 'jumping into bed' with his father's partner's wife, while at the same time admitting he finds her desirable. For Irish audiences the scene ends with Ben's line, 'Would you like to go to a movie?' At this point Mrs Robinson realizes that he is a virgin and gets him to admit it. Shortly afterwards, courage renewed, he says to her, 'Don't move,' as he puts out the light, and slams shut the door. However, for an Irish viewer it would have seemed as if they had left the room to go to the movies, rather than, for other viewers, the realization that the affair proper is about to begin.

In this scene, and in the third major cut dealing with the relationship, during one of their regular night-time meetings, any discussion of sex, other than as a seedy, furtive activity, was cut. While in the hotel room scene, the Board allowed Ben's feeling of disgust at what he was doing, in the later scene, long swathes of dialogue were also cut to ensure that any exploration of the relationship, and references to Elaine, were excised. Thus, Ben's request, 'Do you think we could say a few words to each other first this time' because 'for months all we've done is just come up here and leap into bed together,' was removed. Pressed by Ben, Mrs Robinson tells him that she was pregnant with Elaine before she got married and that she and her husband sleep in separate rooms, but none of this, which serves as partial explanation for her behaviour (and alcoholism) and ironically would have provided a cautionary lesson to young girls on the dangers of sleeping around, was allowed. However, Ben's increasingly vicious attacks on her were permitted, 'You think I'm proud of myself ... I am not. I'm not proud I spend my time with a broken-down alcoholic ... This is the sickest, most perverted thing ever that happened to me.' Mrs Robinson responds with her leg extended, 'You don't want me around anymore,' as she puts on her stockings during the famous poster shot from the film with Ben in the background. This is followed by another cut which includes Ben's immediate apology and his admitting that he enjoys their time together ('I enjoy it. The one thing I look forward to.') The affair resumes as she takes off her clothes again. Yet, the Irish viewer would have thought that it ended with Ben's insult as there are no further intimate scenes between the pair.

Cajoled by his parents, Ben takes Elaine out on a date, despite his promise to Mrs Robinson not to do so. They fall in love, but when Elaine discovers his affair with her mother, which has now ended, she dumps him and takes up with a fresh-faced college student whom she plans to marry. When Ben finds out that a quick marriage is being planned by her parents as a means of thwarting him, he rushes to the church. There, he screams for her, and as Elaine leaves the altar to run to him, her parents and the guests try to stop them. Taking a large crucifix from the church wall, Ben uses it to jamb close the church door, a scene, unsurprisingly, given the presence of clergymen on the Appeal Board, cut. An earlier scene, in which a nightclub stripper with little on top comes to Ben and Elaine's table, was also cut, making it a total of eleven cuts to the film. Arguably, it would seem that the new Board was little removed from Montgomery's censorship whereby the narrative is considerably altered, and in terms of gender politics, the morally questionable woman is punished.

By 1968 the censors also had to contend with a series of increasingly incisive films dealing with the most divisive of social topics, abortion, which along with procreation in general, they tried to suppress. The debate around abortion was intense and vitriolic in Britain in the 1960s, and culminated in the legalization allowing for the termination of pregnancy in the Abortion Act of 1967. In Ireland, by contrast, abortion was illegal and remained taboo until the debates of the 1980s when in 1983 Ireland's first referendum on abortion was held. This resulted in the unborn foetus being accorded equal status to the mother. It is still constitutionally prohibited to procure an abortion, though a 1995 referendum permits freedom of information – effectively to procure an abortion in Britain. As a cinematic theme, it has been explored for decades, but given social and legal policy in Ireland, films which treated or even touched on the subject were invariably banned or cut in the country, as discussed in chapters 4 and 5. The 1960s proved no different to other periods, despite the new Appeal Board's liberalism and the fact that thousands of Irish teenage and adult women were going, and continue to go, to Britain for this medical procedure. However, the contrast with Britain was highlighted as was Ireland's own hypocritical position, by the current British debate around abortion, the new legislation and the more lenient policy at the BBFC, which meant that British filmmakers were less constrained in their representations. Between November 1966 and April 1967, Macken viewed three key British realist films dealing with this topic which he banned: *Alfie*, *Georgy Girl* (Silvio Narizzano, 1966),[91] and *Up the Junction* (Peter Collinson, 1968).[92] Subsequently, the Board was called to adjudicate on these films.

Besides abortion, *Alfie* reveals, more than two years after the Board was appointed, what other activities continued to be forbidden. The film was probably cut before being considered by the Board as there is no reference among the twelve 'preliminary cuts' to the long section near the end of the film when the abortion is performed in Alfie's (Michael Caine) flat on Lily (Vivien Merchant), wife of his hospital companion Harry. However, there is the possibility that because of Alfie's contrite and tearful realization after the abortion of the effect his actions had on Lily, that the Board may have viewed it as an anti-abortion moral lesson. This can perhaps be reinforced by the appearance and demeanor of the abortionist (Denholm Elliott) as slovenly and seedy, as well as the absence of any details of the 'induction' itself (except in conversation). Indeed, Alfie's remorseful behaviour is further articulated when he speaks about it afterwards with a friend.

The Board demanded a large section of the opening scenes in which Alfie is making love in his car to a married woman, Siddie (Millicent Martin), to be removed. The first of these lines, 'Ere, you starting all over again?', was an obvious reference to further love-making, and later comments by Alfie about 'your old man,' her husband, were also deleted. Here it seems that the narrative or moral was given arguably more meaning or importance than the image, but then in a cinema that moved towards the literal or the everyday this should be unsurprising. While the Board allowed Alfie to comment on and make love to married and single women, when it got closer to intimacy or anything to do with the sexualized female body, cuts were imposed. For example, when Alfie visits another girlfriend, Gilda (Julia Foster), he notices when he looks at the calendar that she has missed her period, 'She's usually so punctual,' he notes. When he realizes that she is pregnant, he tells her to 'do something about' it. While this less-than-oblique reference to abortion was cut, which in an Irish context hints at a level of knowledge and control over reproduction that was taboo, Gilda's subsequent arguments in favour of adoption – the official Irish solution – and her decision to bring up the child alone – which was not yet socially acceptable in Ireland – were allowed. Alfie plays at being a weekend father for awhile, but Gilda subsequently marries a boring bus conductor who accepts her son as his own.

While in hospital, Alfie carries on his philandering, but the Board cut a scene where he is making love to a nurse in a hospital ward as Harry is being visited by Lily in the adjoining bed. While nothing sexual is seen other than the nurse's legs under the bed screen and noises of love-making, the Board chose to protect the nursing profession from apparent viewer ridicule. Harry's subsequent mildly disapproving comment to Alfie, 'Dirty beast!' was also cut. The one woman with whom Alfie develops a more permanent attachment is Ruby (Shelley Winters), a wealthy older American with an insatiable sexual appetite. The two scenes in Ruby's apartment were cut. The first of these contains Alfie's references to her 'beautiful condition' and that 'she knows what she wants and she's going to get it if there is any going,' which ends in her injunction to him, 'bedroom!' The second visit to the apartment sees Ruby having abandoned Alfie for another man, who is seen in bed in the background as she tells Alfie, 'He's younger than you are,' a line the distributor later sought to have restored as Alfie himself refers to it as he reflects on his life. Despite the cuts of over five minutes (471 feet), the Board issued one of its rare over-21s certificates.[93] What the cuts to *Alfie* show is that the Board was willing to countenance the possibility of sexual activity provided it was only hinted at while suppressing the consequences of and the moral problems which might result from (unprotected) sex. Ironically, in attempting to erase human consciousness or control over sexual activity and the reproduction cycle, to some degree, it cleansed sex of its messier realities.

The banned *Georgy Girl* was also passed by the Board, but with five cuts and an over-18s certificate. While three of the cuts concerned Jos' (Alan Bates) relationship with his wife Meredith's (Charlotte Rampling) flatmate Georgy (Lynn Redgrave), including the first night they sleep together when Meredith is in hospital having a baby, it was Meredith's attitude to pregnancy which would have touched the Board's rawest nerve. After she reveals that she is pregnant, Meredith, a partying, selfish 'Swinging London' hedonist with many boyfriends even while involved with Jos, casually discusses abortion by admitting to him that 'I can easily get rid of it' and 'I've destroyed two of yours already.' This conversation shocks Jos, who wants to keep the baby, but Meredith says, 'You can't stop me.' While this ends the Board's cut, there is a continuation of this scene dealing with abortion to which no reference is made in the cuts report, and must have been removed by the distributor prior to submission. In this, Georgy, a tomboy who has never had a relationship with a man before Jos, tells her that there is 'no use asking me to lend you money this time' and adds that while abortion is a 'middle-class taboo, … the law needs changing.' The issue is resolved when Mededith declares that she is 'having this one,' but she proves uninterested in motherhood, asserting the purely physical side of sex, an 'animal function,' while dismissing Jos' and Georgy's declaration that 'it's a miracle,' by saying they are acting 'as if I were at Lourdes,' a reference to the Catholic shrine which was cut by the Board. After the baby is born and Meredith demonstrates in no uncertain terms her lack of interest in the baby, despairingly, Jos declares, in a further cut dealing with abortion, 'I don't know why she didn't get rid of it like the others.'

*Up the Junction*, a censorship breakthrough film in Britain with the word 'bugger' and a successful abortion allowed by the BBFC, also posed problems for the Irish Appeal Board. Not only did it center on a middle-class woman, Polly (Suzy Kendall), who rejects her background to live, work and have relationships with working-class men and women, but in its presentation of the banter among the women factory workers, presented potentially transgressive moments, with phrases such as 'birthday suit'; 'bun in oven'; 'see your drawers'; 'you're sex mad'; 'dirty cow'; and a reference to a married man, who 'had it off … while his wife was still carrying.' Though such language, would have been forbidden a few years earlier, there is no indication that any of it was cut by the Board. Indeed, one of only three cuts concerned Polly and her relationship with the somewhat diffident working-class lad Peter (Denis Waterman), when he says to her, 'Do me a favour

– seduce me.' While later scenes of the pair making love, him in bed the morning after, and when they go away together for the weekend, were allowed, the major intervention made by the Board was over teenage factory worker Rube's (Adrienne Posta) pregnancy and subsequent abortion. The first cut was of one of her co-workers saying that 'If you ask me – she's up the spout,' meaning she was pregnant. But, in order to ensure that there is no hint of the abortion (and the pregnancy), this line was cut plus the whole section which goes from her admission to Polly that she is pregnant, the factory girls talking about getting 'rid of it,' right through to the abortion itself in a seedy premises, and her distress as she is being cared for at home by her mother and sister. Of course, the treatment of these three British films was similarly reflected in others of the period and represent what was the standard approach to abortion. This continued during the 1970s, effecting (with cuts) such diverse American films as Bob Fosse's 1972 version of the Broadway musical *Cabaret*[94] and the political satire *The Candidate* (Michael Ritchie, 1971),[95] and in the 1980s, as can be seen in relation to the grim and graphic *Pixote* (Hector Babenco, 1981, Brazil)[96] about a young waif who among other criminal (sexual) activities murders three people, and *The Clinic* (David Stevens, 1982, Australia)[97] a non-judgmental comedy-drama which draws on the style of soaps to present, in a series of vignettes, a day in the life of a VD Clinic, from which the line 'it wasn't an abortion' was cut the very year of the abortion referendum in Ireland.

The increase in bannings in 1968 compared to the previous year continued in Macken's final years in office, with 70 films in 1969 (almost double that of 1968), 69 in 1970, and 86 in 1971, a figure which rivals or surpasses (at least in percentage terms) those of Montgomery in the 1920s and 1930s when many more films were submitted to the Censor. Towards the end of his career, Macken's health deteriorated and many decisions were being made either by deputy Censor Gabriel Fallon, or a trio of other deputies. These included from at least 1970, Denis Coakley, an assistant secretary in the Department of Justice; from August 1971, Miss S. Twohig (aka Miss S. Ní Thuathaigh), a higher executive officer in Justice; and later, Mr P. McMahon, another civil servant. With such a huge number of films being banned, and with only 21 of the 225 rejects during 1969–1971 not being appealed or being deferred, the Board was kept extremely busy. There were, also, of course, further appeals against the Censor's cuts or against the category of limitation issued by the Censor.

Many of the films banned by Macken (or his deputy) in 1969 contained what would be regarded as controversial sexual material for mainstream films as it is in this period that soft porn films began to come to Ireland. Exemplary are titles such as *Secrets of a Windmill Girl* (Arnold Louis Miller 1965, GB),[98] set in stripclubs, *Bed without Breakfast* (Natlogi Betalt, Johannes Allen Anker, 1957, Denmark),[99] and *All Neat in Black Stockings* (Christopher Morahan, 1969, GB),[1] all of which were also banned by the Board. In all, the ban on 20 of the 70 films rejected by the Official Censor in 1969 remained. Besides the soft porn films, others where it was confirmed included *The Secret Life of an American Wife* (George Axelrod, 1969), a comedy about an unhappy wife who poses as a prostitute;[2] *Corruption* (Robert Hartford-Davies, 1967, GB), a horror film in which a surgeon kills for pituitary gland fluid in order to restore his wife's beauty, a popular trope within horror;[3] *Les Biches* (*The Does*, Claude Chabrol, 1968, France/Italy), which concerns the *ménage à trois* of two lesbians and an architect;[4] *I Love You, Alice B. Toklas* (Hy Averback, 1968), a comedy about a lawyer (Peter Sellers) who joins 'flower people' and discovers marijuana;[5] *Hard Contract* (S. Lee Pogostin, 1969), about a professional killer (James Coburn) with sexual hang-ups;[6] *Benjamin, or The Diary of an Innocent Young Man* (Michel Déville, 1966, France), a French version of *Tom Jones;*[7] *Justine* (George Cukor, 1969), which is set in 1930s Egypt and adapted from *The Alexandria Quartet* by Lawrence Durrell;[8] *Three in the Attic* (Richard Wilson, 1968), one of the first comedies about the sexual revolution in which three girls lock the university's Casanova in an attic and insist on being serviced by him until he is exhausted;[9] *That Cold Day in the Park* (Robert Altman, 1969, Canada), which is about a lonely spinster who imprisons a young man;[10] *Goodbye, Columbus* (Larry Peerce, 1969), a post-*Graduate* satire of Jewish social class differences with explicit dialogue;[11] *The Best House in London* (Philip Saville, 1968, GB), about a Victorian brothel;[12] and *John and Mary* (Peter Yates, 1969), a sex comedy about a couple (Dustin Hoffman, Mia Farrow) who meet, make love, but cannot decide whether to continue together.[13]

Another 28 of the banned films were passed with over-18s certificates and with cuts, while 4 others,[14] got through uncut with an over-18s limitation.[15] While bed scenes and other scenes of marital and/or extra-marital seduction, or related issues, whether as image, discourse or imagined, variously featuring heterosexuals, lesbians and homosexuals, were excised from the films, below are discussed the treatment of a selection of well-known films of the period, including school-based films, Lindsay Anderson's up-dating of Jean Vigo's *Zero de Conduite* (1933, France), *If …* (1968, GB) for which he won the Golden Palm at Cannes, and *The Prime of Miss Jean Brodie* (Ronald Neame, 1969); the Academy award-winning *Midnight Cowboy* (John Schlesinger, 1969) which along with *Butch Cassidy and the Sundance Kid* (George Roy Hill, 1969) and *Easy Rider* (Dennis Hopper, 1969), set the blueprint of the 1970s buddy genre informed, in the first instance, by the motif of the journey; and Ken Russell's adaptation of D.H. Lawrence's novel *Women in Love* (1969, GB).

In *If …*, the rebellious public school boys, the Crusaders – Travis (Malcolm McDowell), Johnny (David Wood), Wallace (Richard Warwick), Bobby Phillips (Rupert Webster) – and The Girl (Christine Noonan), a waitress at a nearby café, revolt against the strict authoritarianism of a boarding school. In keeping with its acceptance of irreverent topics, and focusing instead on the areas of sexual activity and nudity which were consistently cut, the Board approved the film with an over-18s certificate and six cuts: a 'confessional' conversation between one of the head boys and a clergyman in which 'dirty thoughts' are discussed; Wallace's licking (though interestingly the recorded word in the Board's report is the more acceptable and tame kissing) a naked woman's breast in a photograph; the boys nude while taking showers (though only their rears are visible); the fantasy scene in the café where Travis and The Girl embrace in the nude on the floor; Mrs Kemp (Mary MacLeod), a schoolteacher's wife, as she walks nude through the school's empty corridors and dormitories; and a brief scene in which Wallace and

Phillips are in bed together. Earlier scenes involving the good-looking blonde Phillips were allowed, including where the head boys lust after him and where Phillips himself looks longingly at Wallace as he is practising on the high bar in the gym.[16]

Macken objected to the 'sex theme' involving both teachers and pupils in *The Prime of Miss Jean Brodie* because it was 'subversive of public morality.' In this film, set in Edinburgh in 1932, sexually precocious schoolgirl Sandy (Pamela Franklin) not only engages in speculation with fellow pupil Jenny about the love life of her spinsterly teacher, Jean Brodie (Maggie Smith), but explores in explicit language how Miss Brodie and fellow teacher Gordon Lowther (Gordon Jackson) might engage in love-making. Both of these scenes were cut by the Board before an over-18s certificate was issued. Also cut extensively was the scene in which Sandy, now lover of art teacher Teddy Lloyd (Robert Stephens), with whom Miss Brodie is also in love, is posing nude at his studio while he paints. Not only were all the nude shots of her removed, but all the dialogue indicating the nature of their relationship.[17]

That Fallon should ban *Midnight Cowboy* was only a matter of course as it had been 'X'-rated (over-17s) in America because of its theme and nude scenes. Though he quoted a USA film trade paper saying that its sexual episodes seem 'daring to some even in this permissive day of filmmaking,' in his report to the Board, he added that they would seem so 'even to the most liberal-minded Censor.'[18] Three sequences were excised, though there were other scenes which might also have been cut and, somewhat uniquely, there is no Reserve slip for the film. The offending scenes were of hustler Joe Buck (Jon Voight) making love to Cass (Sylvia Miles), the wealthy older woman whom he wrongly assumes is a client and who humiliates him; his encounter with a first client as a gay prostitute (Barnard Hughes) who, after been serviced by Joe, is unable to pay him; and the love-making with Shirley (Brenda Vaccaro), his first paying client, whom he meets at the infamous party with its drug-taking scenes which could well have been cut. Indeed, other candidates for cutting include Joe's memory of his first love Annie (Jennifer Salt), or the scene with the strange and perhaps gay Mr O'Daniel (John McGiver) with his illuminated statue of Christ, a client of Joe's arranged by his 'partner' the seedy and decrepit turbercular Ratso Rizzo (Dustin Hoffman) with whom he finally travels to Florida to start a new life. However, Ratso dies on the journey.

*Women in Love*, also rejected by Fallon, was passed with six cuts before being issued with an over-18s certificate after appeal.[19] In this celebration of the sensual, the first cut effected by the Board was of Rupert Birkin's (Alan Bates) discourse on fig fruit where he draws a parallel between its shape and texture, and the female 'fissure'. Most of the other cuts were of nudity, including the brief 'full frontal' of Rupert as he rolls around in the forest and discards his clothes. In addition, there were three cuts to scenes of love-making featuring the two couples, of Birkin and Ursula (Jennie Linden) and her sister Gudrun (Glenda Jackson) with the married Gerald (Oliver Reed). However, in this instance, the process of repression remains incomplete as Ursula's breasts can be seen as she is making love to Rupert in a nature setting with the leaves and branches obscuring her body, giving Irish audiences perhaps their first glimpse of female breasts on screen. This partial erosion of censorship did not extend to the film's most celebrated scene which was cut, the 'wrestling' between Rupert and Gerald in which they are completely naked with their private parts clearly visible. The scene ends on the verge of a kiss, but while this does not occur, the two men are thereafter ever more bound together.

Three of the banned films in 1969 were passed with over-16s certificates and cuts,[20] one *The Bed Sitting Room* (Richard Lester, 1969, GB), a black comedy, was given an over-12s certificate (later changed to under-12s) with four cuts,[21] while 2 others, the comedy-drama *Before Winter Comes* (J. Lee-Thompson, 1968, GB)[22] and the historical biopic *Alfred the Great* (Clive Donner, 1969, GB) which attempted to make the subject relevant for modern audiences, were also cut and awarded under-12s with adult certificates, though the latter seems to have been changed to a general certificate.[23] A further 4 were given general certificates, 2 of them without cuts, *The Sadist* (Sweden), about which the Censor complained of 'suspected euthanasia,'[24] and *The Royal Hunt of the Sun* (Irving Lerner, 1969, USA/GB) about Spanish explorer Pizzaro and his hunt for gold in South America.[25] These latter decisions provide further testimony as to the wide divergence of the two branches of censorship at this time. Indeed, the contradiction was made more acute in 1970 with the appointment of a new Appeal Board, and, in fact, some of the banning decisions from 1969 were reviewed by the new Board, one of whose members was Dermot Breen, a public relations consultant who had started the Cork Film Festival in 1956 as a means of promoting tourism, and who became Official Film Censor in June 1972.

Breen's (and the Cork Film Festival's) 'liberal' credentials had been put to the test in 1969 when the Bishop of Cork, Dr Lucey, one of the most conservative members of the Catholic hierarchy, demanded the withdrawal of *I Can't, I Can't* (aka *Wedding Night*, Piers Haggard, 1969, Ireland) from the festival programme. The film, made at Ardmore Studios, concerns the fear of pregnancy by a newly-married Catholic woman. As a result, she wants to use 'artificial' contraception, but is told by a priest of the church's prohibitions on birth control. Her acute anxiety leads her to attempt suicide (another sin) and she is hospitalized. In addition to the film's narrative Bishop Lucey complained that the film's nude scenes would lead to immodest thoughts. The Festival's ruling body met in emergency session and decided to proceed with the screening.[26] When the film, albeit with a scene cut by the distributor, eventually came before the Censor in June 1972, only eleven days before Breen took over, it received an over-18s certificate, though only after two scenes of nudity and the couple in bed were cut.[27] At the time of the Cork controversy, Breen gave a calculatedly evasive interview about the censorship process to *Sunday Independent* film reviewer Ciaran Carty,[28] which did not auger well for his subsequent term as Censor.

In 1970, the Catholic priest Fr Browne was replaced on the Board by Fr Richard O'Donoghue of Avoca, Co. Wicklow, who remained a member until 1985, while the Revd Murray, who had been appointed as the Church of Ireland representative in 1965, also stayed on the Board until 1985. While O'Donoghue is seen as a consistently conservative figure during his period on the Board, Murray was more liberal, often siding with the majority in allowing through films or parts of films which a strict, traditional theologian would have opposed. In addition to Breen and O'Donoghue, Mrs Isobelle Therese Byrne PC, was appointed. Changes to the 1970 Board occurred in 1972 when Breen became Official Film Censor and Judge Maguire resigned from the Board, with John Carroll becoming chairman from December 1972, a position he held until 1997, and Margaret Skehan and Padraic Gearty being appointed as their replacements. With the exception of the selection of Robert V. Kiely in 1975 for outgoing member Helena Ruttledge, the Board remained the same as in 1970. Thus, only Carroll, O'Connor, Murray and Rochford of the 1965 Board remained a decade later.

In 1970 the Board had even more rejects to view than in 1969, 65 (4 were not appealed), compared with the previous year's total of 62. In 19 instances, the ban was upheld, while 28 films were passed with cuts and over-18s certificates; the generational conflict between father and son, *How Do I Love Thee?* (Michael Gordon, 1970) got through uncut with an over-18s certificate;[29] 12 with over-16s limitations, 5 of which were uncut, but at least one – *The Virgins* (*Les Vierges*, Jean-Pierre Mocky, 1963, France) which had received an 'X' rating in Britain and focuses on how five girls lose their virginity – was most probably cut before submission;[30] another, Jean Luc Godard's *Contempt* (*Le Mépris*, 1963) was approved with cuts and given an under-12s accompanied by an adult certificate;[31] the remaining 3 were passed with general certificates with only *The Beat Generation* (Charles Haas, 1959) originally banned in 1959, cut.[32]

From these statistics alone it is clear that the post-1965 liberalization of censorship had been abandoned. However, it was Ciaran Carty in his weekly column in the *Sunday Independent*, the country's largest selling Sunday newspaper, who articulated this and highlighted the extent of the censorship process, and called for reforms in the administration of film censorship. He argued that the single Official Censor should be replaced by a 3-person Censorship Board whose chairperson would have to explain the Board's decisions in public; the censors would be compelled to publish complete information on their decisions; and two types of certificate would be issued: a children's certificate and an over-18s one. In the over-18s category the censors would only have the power to pass or ban films, and not to cut them. In arriving at its decision, he called for 'the Board [to] be obliged to take into consideration the dominant effect of a movie and the reputation and intent of its director.'[33] This was designed to ensure that the work of the 'quality' directors Carty regularly cited would not be cut. In an article entitled 'No censorship for leading directors'[34] in May 1969 Carty suggested, 'why not exempt from censorship movies by certain outstanding directors that are intended for over-18 audiences.' He offered a 'privileged list,' which would be subject to annual revision, of directors of 'outstanding merit' whose films would 'get to screens unmutilated'. This exclusive, but quite lengthy, list included Polanski, Ray, Huston, Chaplin, Bergman, Hitchcock, Hawks, Ford, Godard, Truffaut, Fellini, Penn, Visconti, Welles, Malle, Nichols, Wilder, Cassavetes, Buñuel, Bresson, and many others. Since Carty (as myself many years later), was refused access to the censors' reports, he devised a provocative tactic by gaining the co-operation of film distributors in providing him with details of films banned or cut, and as a consequence made available the most comprehensive information yet published on the censors' decisions.

From January 1971 Carty began publishing monthly lists of films which had been screened in first-run Dublin cinemas during the previous month, including the type of certificate issued and whether or not the film had been cut (the details of the cuts were not given). He also published a list of banned films and later identified those films awaiting a decision by the Appeal Board. This strategy as well as providing much needed information on the films being censored, also helped to keep the issue of censorship on the cultural and national agenda. Notwithstanding his increasingly strong criticism of the film censorship system, which Macken took personally (issuing, for example, a letter through solicitors demanding a 'retraction' of Carty's editorial article of 4 May 1969), the first major salvo in this campaign, it had little immediate impact on the decisions taken. Nevertheless, the 1970 Board did make one important modification of the certification categories by increasing the number of over-16s certificates issued. This pattern continued in 1971 when 14 such limitations were awarded, and in subsequent years as the censors began to broaden the notion of what constituted a teenage audience. However, the Board retained a strict hold on representations of teenage sexuality, upholding in February 1970 the decision to reject Frank Perry's powerful tale of sexual awakening *Last Summer* (1970).[35]

The adult concerns of wife-swapping, and 'swinging' which in a little over thirty years would become the subject of the popular prime-time Irish comedy series on RTÉ television, *Fergus's Wedding*, was, according to Fallon, 'totally impermissible' in *Bob & Carol & Ted & Alice* (Paul Mazursky, 1969), a view shared by the Board.[36] Similarly banned by the Board were the lecherous, though unfulfilled, desire of various men for the eponymous nubile blonde of *Candy* (Christian Marquand, 1968, France);[37] *A Nice Girl Like Me* (Desmond Davies, 1969, GB), in which a repressed young woman (Barbara Ferris) gets pregnant twice by different men,[38] a predicament not uncommon in contemporary Ireland; *Paddy* (Daniel Haller, 1969, Ireland), an adaptation of Irish writer's Lee Dunne's novel, *Goodbye to the Hill*, which features an Alfie-like Dubliner who engages in a *ménage à trios*;[39] and a number of 'sexploitation' films which were submitted to the Irish Censor.[40] However, perhaps the best known film of the period to be banned was Polanski's tightly ploted and disturbing in its ordinariness, hit horror *Rosemary's Baby* (1967). Set in New York, the film looks back to his *Repulsion* in its probing of the psychological or inner world of the central character, who in this instance is the epitome of innocence, but who comes to be mother of the anti-Christ. Though initially banned by Macken in 1969, and viewed by the outgoing Board in December 1969, final adjudication on the film was left to the new Board on the recommendation of the 1965 Board. As no decision was recorded, in effect the rejection was confirmed. In 1977 the film was viewed by Breen, who banned it, a decision which was not appealed.[41] In addition to these, the Board banned *The Killing of Sister George* (Robert Aldrich, 1968) which Fallon had rejected, regarding it as 'existentially LESBIANISM' which made it 'completely impermissible'.[42]

In 1970, in terms of the material that the Board cut from the appealed films before issuing them with certificates, there were no new departures. The familiar scenes of nudity, sex, drug-taking, homosexuality, and violence were curtailed. The suppression of the latter can be seen particularly in relation to Sam Peckinpah's graphic western *The Wild Bunch* (1969) which combines the grand tradition of the Western as epitomized by John Ford and Howard Hawks with a more modern and frenetic stylized violence of George Romero and others. Set in 1913 it tells of a group of aging outlaws led by Pike (William Holden) who plan one final robbery before retirement. Fallon felt he had 'no option' but to reject it 'on the grounds of its sadistic violence' as well as the brothel scene 'in which the wailing of an infant is used to "heighten" the "dramatic" effect.'[43] The Board disagreed, but ordered a series of cuts, including of the film's opening reel centering on a bank robbery during which the gang is ambushed. Also curtailed were the shooting scenes with the deletion of civilians being shot, a woman being trampled on by a horse, the staff being molested and shot, and the close-up of injuries to the face of a badly wounded gang member who is subsequently shot by Pike so that he will not hamper their escape. Likewise, the 'balletic' machine gunning of the soldiers by Pike and Lyle (Warren Oates) was also modified. The effect of these interventions was not just at the level of content, but it seriously disturbed the film's overall balance and rhythm. Prior to the beginning of this last scene, the throat-slitting of gang member Angel (Jaime Sanchez), which precipitates the gang's revenge on the Mexican soldiers, was also cut, as was the earlier scene in which Angel is dragged behind a motor car by the sadistic officer. Other scenes edited were of the 'bawdy' dialogue between the gang members about 'whores' and during the gang's sojourn at the army barracks when they are with prostitutes.[44] The Board also objected to swearing, including the use of 'Christ', references to religion or representations of the sacraments, as well as the less frequent representations of human operations, such as in the Korean War satire *M.A.S.H.* (Robert Altman, 1970),[45] suicide, and paedophilia and incest in *The Damned* (Luchino Visconti, 1969, Italy/West Germany).

*The Damned* is centered around the machinations within a wealthy family during the Nazis' rise to power in Germany. In this film, to which four cuts were made by the Board, the young Baron, Martin (Helmut Berger), is a paedophile who rapes a young girl, Lisa, and she hangs herself as a result. Martin's behaviour is linked to his conniving mother, Sophie (Ingrid Thulin), whom he turns on in the end in a scene of explicit incest. Telling her he will destroy her, he tears off her clothes and the pair make love. Both of these scenes, which serve as a psychotic backdrop to the Nazi state, were cut to ensure that there was no hint of either paedophilia or incest. (Two, more minor, cuts, were of a naked Sophie making love with Frederick (Dirk Bogarde) as they plan to take over the family business, while another scene had cuts of a breast being kissed and a hand being put between legs.)[46] It is a bitter fact that while such material was being censored at the level of representation or the symbolic, the reality of paedophilia (as well as other forms of abuse) was widespread in Ireland, particularly in the context of orphaned or other institutionalized children. Arguably, the denying of such images helped to maintain a silence as well as ignorance of the subject. The lack of language and the invisibility of sex and sexual abuse on the screen contributed to the cultural denial that facilitated the abuse. Of course, while the vocabulary used and created by the contemporary highly sexualized and erotic media whereby children and adults are less segregated, has made both children and adults sexually aware. If this allows positively children to use such knowledge to protect themselves from abuse, it also invites them to partake in the sexual act or associated behaviour at an earlier, and even from a non-'moral' point-of-view, inappropriate age. However, just as the litany of prohibitions remained, so, too, were the inconsistencies. With regard to *Catch-22* (Mike Nichols, 1970), for example, there are no references in the reports to the cutting of a number of scenes, including a reference to rape: 'I only raped her once,' a deranged soldier tells Yossarian (Alan Arkin), the phrases 'Hit him in the balls' and 'You slut', as well as the plane's propeller decapitating a soldier.[47]

Matters only got worse the following year, 1971, with a total of 86 films banned, 9 of which were unappealed.[48] The Board upheld 25 of the Censor's decisions, including that for *What Do You Do to a Naked Lady?* (Allen Funt, 1970), a candid camera film with the emphasis on sex;[49] *The Boys in the Band* (William Friedkin, 1970), an adaptation of the breakthrough gay play;[50] *Myra Breckinridge* (Michael Sarne, 1970), featuring sex changer Raquel Welch and also starring Mae West;[51] *Take a Girl like You* (Jonathan Miller, 1970, USA/GB), in which Hayley Mills tries to stay a virgin until her wedding day;[52] Russ Meyer's soft porn romp, *Beyond the Valley of the Dolls* (1970);[53] *De Sade* (Cy Endfield, 1969, West Germany), a mild version of the Marquis de Sade story;[54] *The Priest's Wife* (Dino Risi, 1971, Italy/France) in which a disillusioned singer (Sophia Loren) tries to convince a priest (Marcello Mastroianni) to disavow celibacy and marry her;[55] *C.C. and Company* (Seymour Robbie, 1970) in which Ann-Margret becomes the object of desire among a motorcyclist community;[56] *Villian* (Michael Tuchner, 1970, GB),[57] an underworld film in which Richard Burton features as a homosexual thug and also starring Michael Caine, whose *Get Carter* (Mike Hodges, 1971, GB), in which he investigates his brother's death in a North of England town, was likewise banned;[58] *Summer of '42* (Robert Mulligan, 1971) about a teenager with a crush on a young war bride; *Dorian Gray* (aka *The Secret of Dorian Gray*, Massimo Dallamano, 1970, Italy/ Germany/ Lichenstein), an adaptation of Oscar Wilde's novel;[59] *Joe* (John G. Avildsen, 1970), featuring blue collar bigot Peter Boyle;[60] *The Queer ... The Erotic* (*L'a Altra Faccia del Peccato*, Marcello Avallone, 1968, Italy);[61] *A Touch of the Other* (Seymour Robbie, 1970);[62] *Percy* (Ralph Thomas, 1971, GB), about the world's first penis transplant, which the Board considered 'bawdy, indecent and immoral,'[63] a sequel of which, *Percy's Progress* (Ralph Thomas, 1974, GB), was banned in 1974;[64] the sex comedy *Up Pompeii* (Bob Kellett, 1971, GB);[65] *Bloody Mama* (Roger Corman, 1970), about real-life gangster Ma Barker;[66] *Making It* (John Erman, 1971), which features a 17-year-old with sex on his mind;[67] *Panic in Needle Park* (Jerry Schatzberg, 1971), the breakthrough film about drug-addiction in which a crook (Al Pacino) and a nice girl (Kitty Winn) get hooked on heroin;[68] *The Marriage of a Young Stockbroker* (Laurence Turman, 1971), in which, following a marital breakdown, the separated husband has affairs;[69] *The Novices* (*Les Novices*, Guy Casaril, 1970, France/Italy);[70] and *She'll Follow You Anywhere* (David C. Rea, 1971, GB) about the discovery of an aphrodisiac.[71] A total of 32 of the banned films were subsequently passed with over-18s certificates, 30 of them with cuts,[72] a further 14 were given over-16s certificates, 10 of them with cuts,[73] while

4 over-16s were passed without cuts;[74] 3 of the rejected films were awarded under-12s with adult certificates, only one of which was uncut,[75] while the remaining 3 were given general releases, but only after 2 of these were cut.[76]

When Gabriel Fallon viewed the counter-cultural film *Five Easy Pieces* (Bob Rafelson, 1970), made by the same production company (BBS) which produced Dennis Hopper's 1969 road movie *Easy Rider*, seen by many as the key counter-cultural expression of postclassical cinema – which although not representing a clearly defined or even complete break with American classical filmmaking, reflects the fundamental changes in the Hollywood system and product both in terms of content (and the representation of the hero) and form (largely influence by European art cinema) – his latent reviewing talents were in evidence. Writing to the Board, he commented that it may possibly have a relevance for what is known as 'the American way of life,' but, he added, 'I doubt if as yet it has any relevance here.' He went on to say that it was 'a sordid, depressing piece of entertainment, *and though not without an inverted moral content*,' it 'might (even with cuts) have the opposite effect to that which *may* have been intended.' (Emphasis added.) Artistically, he pompously and erroneously concluded, 'it has a low rating.' The Board overturned Fallon's ban and confined its cuts (with an over-16s certificate) to two 'Jesus Christs' and two 'shits', while also deleting the passionate love-making of Bobby (Jack Nicholson) and Betty (Sally Ann Struthers), with whom he has a brief affair.[77] Another 'adult' film, *Sunday, Bloody Sunday* (John Schlesinger, 1971, GB), was also given an over-16s certificate, though the cutting of that film was more extensive. Scenes of love-making involving the triangle of Glenda Jackson, Peter Finch, and Murray Head, including the latter pair kissing and in bed together, were among the film's eleven cuts, though the limited certificate seems to have been deferred, and it was eventually passed uncut (in the undetermined version submitted) with an over-18s certificate in 1978.[78]

In 1972, in the months prior to Dermot Breen taking over as Censor, 13 films were banned. The Board upheld 7 decisions, including 2 films rejected by relief Censor Twohig: the mainstream black comedy *Pretty Maids All in a Row* (Roger Vadim, 1971)[79] and *Carnal Knowledge* (Mike Nichols, 1971), which follows the sexual trials and tribulations of two men (Jack Nicholson, Art Garfunkel) from college days to middle-age and featuring an acclaimed performance by Ann-Margret as Nicholson's mistress. (This film was eventually passed with an over-18s certificate in 1979 by Frank Hall.)[80] Those remaining were *Brotherhood of Satan* (Bernard McEveety, 1971), a horror in which a witches' coven takes over a town;[81] and the 'sex' films *Curious Female* (Paul Rapp, 1969),[82] *Fun and Games* (aka *Bed Games*; *1000 Convicts and a Woman*, Ray Austin, 1971, GB),[83] which concerns the sexual activities of a prison governor's daughter, *Sex of Angels* (*Il Sesso degli Angeli*, Ugo Liberatore, 1968, Italy/West Germany),[84] and *Angels Who Burn Their Wings* (Zbynek Brynych, 1970, West Germany).[85] There were 3 other banned films which were passed with over-18s certificates and cuts: *The Queens* (*Le Fate*, aka *Les Ogresses*; *Sex Quartet*; *The Fairies*, Luciano Salce, Amrio Monicelli, Nauro Bolognini, Antonio Pietrangeli, 1966, Italy/France), made up of four episodes satirizing Italian women and from which a sequence referring to homosexual conduct was cut;[86] *Where's Poppa?* (Carl Reiner,

1970), in which a Jewish mother interferes with her son's sex life and from which some expletives and a rape scene were cut;[87] and *Straw Dogs* (Sam Peckinpah, 1971, GB) with its anti-liberal value system privileging (regressive) male violence, which was submitted in its complete length in January 1972, and passed with cuts (though the slip is not in the Reserve book) and an over-18s certificate. In 1981 another version was passed with just one cut, that of the scene of rape and buggery of Susan George.[88] Three other films were not appealed: *The Sisters* (aka *Sisters*, Brian de Palma, 1972),[89] and two 'sexploitation' films: *School for Virgins* (*Josefine Das Liebestolle Katzchen*, Geza Von Cziffra, West Germany/Italy),[90] about the sexual adventures of a 16-year-old girl, and *The Libertines* (*Les Libertines* aka *The Versatile Lovers; L'intreccio; Las Bellas del Bosque*, Dave Young, 1969, France/Italy/ Spain).[91]

With Macken seriously ill in early 1972, and Twohig largely in charge of film censorship, many films were being passed with none or minor cuts, including Robert Altman's *Images* (1972, Ireland); *The Ruling Class* (Peter Medak, 1972, GB); *The Hospital* (Arthur Hiller, 1971); *Never Give an Inch* (aka *Sometimes a Great Notion*, Paul Newman, 1971); *Macbeth* (Roman Polanski, 1971, GB); *Dirty Harry* (Don Siegel, 1971); *The Ballad of Joe Hill* (aka *Joe Hill*, Bo Widerberg, 1971, Sweden); and *Cool Breeze* (Barry Pollack, 1972). These films were enthusiastically cited by Ciaran Carty in his column of 11 June 1972 as evidence that the civil servants, acting, he believed, as the type of 'Censorship Board' he advocated, were liberalizing Macken's strict regime. Indeed, a month earlier, Carty had reported a distributor telling him that 'a great deal of rethinking' of film censorship was going on in the Department of Justice,[92] perhaps in anticipation of Macken's imminent retirement, which occurred in June 1972 only three months before his death. Dermot Breen was appointed Official Film Censor, and after six and a half years of chaos, the Appeal Board was finally relieved of the huge backlog of work and its role quickly receded once again into the background. The Board considered only thirteen films during the July-December 1972 period, though some of the appeals were the legacy of Breen's predecessors, including Coakley and Twohig. This was the same number of appeals as in both 1973 and 1974, and dropped to 11 in 1975 and 1976, 5 in 1977, 6 in 1978, and only 2 in 1979 – Frank Hall's first full year as Censor – and 3 in 1980 and 1981. A further 21 appeals occurred during the remainder of Hall's tenure in office to September 1986. During the years in office (1986–2003) of Hall's successor, Sheamus Smith, the Board considered 48 theatrical films, but most of these were for limitations of the certificate, and some were for cuts. In summary, therefore, the Board's role declined from 1973 onwards, assessing only 137 films (and post 1994, 14 videos) from January 1973 to April 2004 inclusive, a figure which can be compared with the 90 films viewed by the Board in 1971 alone, the last full year before Breen became Censor. The crisis caused by the divergence between the two branches of film censorship was ended.

Breen, a member of the Board for two and a half years, was appointed to the post by the Fianna Fáil government of which fellow Corkman Jack Lynch was Taoiseach. This change of personnel did not signal a significant liberalization of film censorship: as we will see below, he upheld traditional Catholic values in a way James Montgomery

would have been proud of, though, at the same time, he loosened up the previous suppression of all matters relating to the body and, in effect, formalized during his tenure
the approach which the Board had been taking in recent years. As Breen put it to
Ciaran Carty in 1969, 'The emphasis is too much on sex and not enough on violence,'[93] though in practice, Breen was very much concerned with sex as well as violence. Indeed, Carty and Breen became something of a double act as they frequently
debated film censorship in various forums around the country after his appointment,
which, in itself, was a major departure from the secretive, even paranoid, approach
to the job of his predecessors.

Breen was the first person to be appointed Film Censor who had a background in
film, and he retained his post as Director of the Cork Film Festival during his six years
in office. (Smith, incidentally, while serving as Censor, was appointed to the Board of
the now-defunct Dublin Film Festival in 2000.)[94] As evidence of his open approach to
the task he gave a wide-ranging and discursive interview to Carty five weeks after
taking up office. Though Breen declared that there were some words he was 'vehemently opposed to' in film, he suggested that in certain contexts they might be retained.
As an example, he said that the use of the Holy Name might not always be blasphemous, though this issue became one of his major preoccupations. Nevertheless, such
a comment, which now may appear somewhat naive, represented a major break from
the decades when any word or action that might offend the Christian religions was
invariable cut or the film banned. However, in a warning of the limits of his 'liberalism', he said that he interpreted films through what his children aged 10 to 19 should
see. This approach was to become a more refined form of the bludgeon of the chil-
dren-first policy of previous decades. He also acknowledged that he had to operate
within certain guidelines laid down by the Department of Justice and he tried to follow
these as best he could while being 'as flexible' as possible, but, he added, 'there are
limitations.'[95] He also agreed to check Carty's monthly censorship lists for accuracy.[96]

Breen's relative flexibility was confirmed in the rapid fall in the number of films
banned, and to a lesser extent, cut to achieve over-16s and over-18s ratings. One of
the public debates in which Breen engaged with Carty was at University College
Dublin's Economics and Commerce Society. He replied to Carty's argument in favour
of allowing the work of 'major' directors to be passed uncut for over-18s with a revealing and ultimately disappointing outburst. He said that 'many of them are perverts.'[97]
Two months later Carty declared that 'censorship changes but doesn't change.'[98] It
was, perhaps, an acknowledgment by a liberal, whose arguments had been couched
in the high art language of individual special talent, rather than a more general critique of film censorship, that the limits of Irish liberalism had been defined and reached,
at least for that decade. The emphasis seemed to have changed according to Carty from
a film's imagery to its language. While this was perhaps an incomplete assessment of
the shift in film censorship policy heralded by Breen's appointment, it nevertheless
pointed to a more general cultural shift which finds expression in the internet and text-
based culture from the 1990s onwards. It is ironic that the transition as understood
by Carty begins with Breen given his unique cinematic rather than literary background,

and, that during his period in office, cinema returned to a cinema of attractions in which more attention was drawn to form and visual effects than characterization, dialogue or affect. However, even Carty himself declared, as his interest began to shift a few months later, that 'with censorship becoming less of an issue, it may now be possible to focus attention on the abysmal lack of support given to [Irish] cinema by the State.' Ironically, within six months of Breen taking over as Censor, Carty was complaining that Breen's more liberal approach was not being emulated by the Board and he called for a new Board more in keeping with Breen's 'liberalism'.[99]

## SEX FILMS AND THE IRISH EXPERIENCE

It was not until the early 1970s that there was anything remotely resembling sex films, or soft pornography, screened in Irish cinemas. The post-1965 'liberal' regime while passing slightly more explicit dialogue still cut all manner of sex scenes and nudity, even of a most circumscribed kind. Nevertheless, enterprising film exhibitors sought to develop at least the modicum of an Irish 'soft-porn' film experience.

Modern sex films in the Anglo-Saxon countries, arguably began with the American nudist camp film *Garden of Eden* (Max Nosseck, 1954). Like most films dealing with this most sanitized and asexual form of nudity, together with the endless series in the 1960s of films with 'nudist' or 'bare' in their titles,[1] it was never submitted to the Irish Censor. Indeed, as noted in the previous chapter, when the mainstream *I'm All Right, Jack*, which features nudist camp scenes at the beginning and end, was submitted it led to what is perhaps the first major controversy challenging an Irish Censor's decision when these scenes were cut. Prior to this, the first nudist camp cut identified in the censors' reports was in a 1945 *Pathé Pictorial* newsreel (no. 61).[2] However, as late as the 1970s, documentaries including *Naked England*[3] also had such scenes curtailed, while in the pre-1965 general certificate environment, Irish distributors did not bother to submit the many mainstream films featuring nudity, such as topless Jayne Mansfield in *Promises! Promises!* (King Donovan, 1963) or Mamie Van Doran as a stripper in *Three Nuts in Search of a Bolt* (Tommy Noonan, 1964). By the end of the 1960s, 'simple nudity no longer had the power to shock,'[4] at least in Britain and the USA, but pseudo-documentaries with a voyeuristic anthropological character had already been established as a popular genre. Unsurprisingly, the original of these, *Mondo Cane* (1961, Italy), albeit in a 'drastically cut' version, was banned by Liam O'Hora in 1964, a decision upheld by the Board.[5] Its sequel, *Mondo Cane 2* (aka *Mordo Pazzo*, Gualtiero Jacopetti and Franco Prosperi, 1963, Italy) was banned by Macken, though after appeal it was passed with cuts and an over-18s certificate,[6] while a spin-off by the same directors, *Women of the World* (1963, Italy), was also banned,[7] but on this occasion there was no appeal. However, an American clone, *Mondo Bizarre* (Manfred Durniok, 1965) was passed,[8] as was the banned Italian film *This Shocking World* (*Il Mondo del Notte*, aka *The World at Night*, Gianni Proia, 1963),[9] which runs the gamut from black magic to strippers, but both were almost certainly cut prior to submission. *The Queer ... The Erotic*, which fea-

tured sex education for children in Germany, an orgiastic wake in Sweden, and a homosexual marriage in Rotterdam,[10] unsurprising was banned.[11] If these films were voyeuristic and exploitative, they were nonetheless 'mild' not just by later standards, but with
regards to the contemporary films produced and screened outside Ireland. Films such as
*Pornography in Denmark* (Alex de Renzy, 1970) and *Pornography: Copenhagen 1970*
(1970) included 'blue-movie' footage and sex show activity 'on the pretext they were
essential "informational" elements of the documentary.'[12] Needless to say, these films
were never submitted in Ireland, and even failed to pass the British censors.

The related sex education documentary genre made a major impact in Ireland in
the late 1960s following the release of the German film *Helga* (Erich F. Bender, 1967,
West Germany), which explored the sexual repression of a young German woman as
it reinforced the need for courtship rituals, marriage, and childbirth. Offering a glimpse
of what repressive Irish Catholicism denied, it proved a hit with Irish audiences, as it
had with the British. However, unknown to Irish viewers, the section dealing with abortion had been cut by Macken.[13] Two years later in 1970, its sequel, *Michael and Helga*
(*Helga und Michael*, Erich F. Bender, 1967, West Germany)[14] was banned by him, while
another sex education film, *The Cure of Patty Switl*, had references to legalized abortion cut, and its title tellingly morally negativized: *Cure* was replaced with *Shame*.[15]
Many other such films with doctors and 'experts' discussing sexual problems, including coital positions, contraception, impotence, frigidity, use of vibrators, and oral sex,
were not submitted to the Irish Censor. Even in 1976, three years before 'bona fide'
family planning legislation allowed married couples to be legally prescribed 'artificial'
contraceptives for the first time in fifty years, *The Right to be Born* (*Der Arzt Stellt
Fest...*, aka *The Doctor Speaks...*, Aleksander Ford, 1966, West Germany/Switzerland)
had dialogue advocating birth control as well as references to abortion cut.[16]

In Britain, as in other countries, the subterfuge of the cinema club had allowed
exhibitors to by-pass state or industry-imposed film censorship regulations. However,
in Ireland, commercial exhibitors did not dare to defy the Department of Justice and
introduce members-only cinemas, thus leaving it to 'art' cinemas to show, in any sustained or acceptable way, any form of alternative or, in Irish terms, morally or artistically challenging films. (Middle-class dominated 'art' cinemas from 1976–1977
onwards catered in part to the more risqué tastes – something, of course, which was
an unacknowledged aspect of the film society movement since its establishment in
Ireland in 1936 – as is discussed below.) As a consequence, those few exhibitors who
wished to show films of a more prurient kind for the 'dirty mac brigade' in a commercial environment were confined to a few small independent central Dublin outlets in the 1970s. Despite being marketed in Ireland as sex films, many of these not
only arrived years after they were made, but had the 'sex' removed. Thus, *Danish
Dentist on the Job* (*Tandlaege Pa Sengekanten*, John Hilbard, 1971, Denmark) had
seven cuts, including of frontal nudity, a girl being molested in the dentist's chair, references to masturbation, and girls in bed,[17] while *Do You Want to Remain a Virgin?*
(*Willst Du Ewig Jungfrau Bleiben?*, Hubert Frank, 1968, Germany) had eight deletions of references to the 'Pill,' words such as penis and vagina, 'orgiastic activity,'

and male frontal nudity.[18] None of the 'King of the Nudies,' Russ Meyer's early sex films, including the astoundingly successful and profitable *Vixen* (1969) were submitted to the Irish Censor, while his somewhat milder *Beyond the Valley of the Dolls*,[19] and his parody of *Valley of the Dolls*, *The Seven Minutes* (1971)[20] were banned. Both of these were made for 20th Century-Fox in order to boost their flagging fortunes and, like *Vixen*, brought Meyer's reputation (if not always his earlier more explicit sex–violence aesthetic) and the genre into the mainstream. In Ireland, the tease still substituted for the real thing so that exploitation sex films or 'skin flicks' and commercial features alike were cut to conform to a rigid puritanism which had been discarded in mainland Europe in the 1950s and in the USA and Britain in the 1960s. Video, which facilitated a more 'democratic' distribution of film and one which remained unregulated in Ireland until the 1990s, ended the brief flurry of 'sex' cinemas in Dublin, as consumers moved to under-the counter trade in forbidden tapes. Neither in the past nor in the present has Ireland had a pornography industry, notwithstanding the abandon with which the term was later used in the video and internet debate, as is discussed in the next chapter.

While 'pornography' was not of great concern to Irish censors, they still had to adapt to the increase in soft porn and the more explicit treatment of sex in mainstream cinema of the 1970s and 1980s. Dermot Breen's initial decisions were important with regard to defining his parameters. The first film he banned, in June 1972, was *Sexy Susan Knows How* (*Frau Wirtin Blast Gern Trompete*, Franz Antel, [François Legrand], 1969, West Germany/Austria/Italy/Hungary, 1969),[21] which set the pattern for his and his successor, Frank Hall's, terms in office. Though a few soft porn films had been submitted to the Censors prior to Breen's appointment – *Strip Poker* (aka *The Big Switch*, Pete Walker, 1968, GB) for example, in which a man is blackmailed by a gangster into posing for pornographic photographs, had been passed by Macken with cuts of nude girls and bedroom scenes for over-18s, but on appeal it was cut further and granted an over-16s certificate[22] – it is not surprising that *Sexy Susan* was submitted early in his tenure, given that distributors often seek to push the boundaries of acceptability. *Kama Sutra* (Raj Devi, 1971)[23] and *The Sextrovert* (*Desirella*, Jean-Claude Dague, 1970, France)[24] were two other such films banned by him by the end of 1972. In the Irish context, the censors' treatment of mainstream films and European 'art' cinema might be a better measure of the extent of censorship. That the second film Breen banned was Pasolini's *The Decameron* (1971)[25] followed shortly afterwards by Ken Russell's *The Devils* (1971),[26] which deals with possession in a seventeenth-century convent, seems to indicate, nothwithstanding the extreme nature of both the films and notoriety of the two directors, that he did not intend to make any radical changes to Irish censorship. Indeed, he banned a total of 12 films in his first six months in office, and in 1973, his first full year in the job, 18, two by his deputy, Frank Hall. The titles of most of these reveal their content, such as the first film banned by Hall, *Sex Artist*,[27] and others including *Swedish Fanny Hill* (aka *Fanny Hill*, Mac Ahlberg, 1968, Sweden),[28] about a poor prostitute who rises in society through her relationship with men, the American short *Anatomy of a Pin-Up*[29] and *Sex Service* (aka *Sexy Show*, Elio Balletti, ca. 1972).[30] Once again, though, a number of the films banned were at the center of contemporary social and cultural discourses, such as the comedy about a Catholic couple in which the woman goes on the pill, *It's a 2' 6" above the Ground World* (aka *The Love Ban*, Ralph Thomas, 1972, GB),[31] Woody Allen's 1972 comedy of sexual neuroses, *Everything You Always Wanted to Know about Sex (But Were Afraid to Ask)*,[32] low-life criminal betrayal in *The Friends of Eddie Coyle* (Peter Yates, 1973),[33] and one of the most controversial films of the decade dealing with sex and violence, Stanley Kubrick's adaptation of Anthony Burgess' novel *A Clockwork Orange* (1971).[34] In this case, the decision was not appealed.

While the number of films (excluding trailers) banned by Breen actually increased, in 1975 to 34, thereafter there was a decline in rejects: 25 in 1976, 16 in 1977, and in 1978, 18 rejects until Hall took over in October. Most of these were 'soft porn', though an important minority were mainstream commercial or 'art' films. These included *Blume in Love* (Paul Mazursky, 1973);[35] *Percy's Progress*;[36] the sequel to the 'X'-rated animated feature *Fritz the Cat* (Ralph Bakshi, 1972) based on Robert Crumb's infamous underground comic character, *Nine Lives of Fritz the Cat* (Robert Taylor, 1974);[37] *The Groove Tube* (Ken Shapiro, 1974);[38] two films by Pasolini, *Arabian Nights* (1974, Italy/France),[39] and *The Canterbury Tales* (1971, Italy/France),[40] banned on successive days in March 1976; the commercially successful voyeuristic comedy *Alvin Purple* (Tim Burstall, 1973, Australia)[41] about a young man who is a hit with the opposite sex and which featured full frontal nudes; *Casanova* (aka *Fellini's Casanova*, Federico Fellini, 1976, Italy), which was later passed by the Board with an over-18s certificate and cuts;[42] *Next Stop, Greenwich Village* (Paul Mazursky, 1975);[43] *Looking for Mr Goodbar* (Richard Brooks, 1977),[44] a decision upheld by the Board; and *The Hills Have Eyes* (Wes Craven, 1977);[45] while at least 2 films submitted under the 'seven year rule' were rejected again: *Rosemary's Baby* and *Ulysses*. Breen also continued the practice of changing film titles, the last Censor to do so, but these were largely confined to sex films. Thus, Breen ordered changed *Sex Seekers* (*Jeux pour Couples Infidelites*, Georges Fleury, 1972, France) which became *Hot and Blue*;[46] *Sex with a Smile* (Sergio Martino, 1976, Italy) became *The Bodyguard* (while also having the first of the film's five episodes cut, a total of 1,232 feet, or over fourteen minutes);[47] and *Sextasy* (Max Pecas, France) was retitled *The French Lovers*.[48]

With the widespread banning of mainstream films, a feature of Macken's term, which had hugely increased the workload of the Board, now a thing of the past (the Board considered 58 films [excluding trailers] during the period Breen was in office), the focus quickly shifted to the treatment of those films that were passed cut for public exhibition, and following precedent, sexuality in the broadest sense, including nudity, came under scrutiny. When Ciaran Carty remarked that 'censorship changes but doesn't change' he was perhaps most obviously referring to the continuing cutting of films and, indeed, the repression of representations of the body and sexuality which seemed only to be emphasized by American cinema's more forthright representations of all aspects of (adolescent) sexuality, and the screen's new explicitness as regards sexual practices more generally.

The category of coming-of-age films was one which the Irish censors were very wary of and while not a new phenomenon, the genre began to draw on some of the more permissive and sexually explicit themes of 'adult' cinema. Ireland, of course, did not have such a cinema of its own, and when it did emerge in the 1980s, and more particularly in the 1990s, it was characterized by a nostalgic tweeness which barely scratched the surface of teenage sexuality. Nevertheless, films such as *The Miracle* (Neil Jordan, 1991 GB), *The Last of the High Kings* (David Keating, 1996, Ireland/ Denmark), *Circle of Friends* (Pat O'Connor, 1995, USA/Ireland) and *About Adam* (Gerard Stembridge, 2001, Ireland/GB/USA) did explore adolescent and young adult sexuality in a more frank way which was reflective of current behaviour. As a result, American cinema's treatment of the same subject, inevitably caused problems. Thus, it is not surprising that *Summer of '42* was banned in 1971, as it is a coming-of-age film set during World War Two which focuses on the sexual desire of young Hermie (Gary Grimes), who, with his friend Osky (Jerry Houser) develops an intimate interest in girls. While Osky loses his virginity to Miriam (Christopher Norris), Hermie becomes fascinated with the older Dorothy (Jennifer O'Neill), but it is only when she receives a telegram informing her that her boyfriend has been killed in the war that she seduces Hermie out of grief, but also out of pity for the inexperienced boy. When re-viewed by Breen in 1978 under the 'seven year rule,' it was passed, albeit with ten cuts, all but one of which was of 'Christ,' further evidence of Breen's strict suppression of the 'Holy Name'. The other cut was of a conversation between Osky and Hermie about 'rubbers,' or condoms, as the pair try to come to terms with the nature of sexual activity. Nevertheless, it is most likely that the film was cut prior to submission, because there are no references to other forbidden words such as 'boobs,' 'shit,' 'crap,' and 'son of a bitch,' as well as conversations about 'getting laid,' and Hermie, worried about the consequences of intercourse, telling Osky that he doesn't want to be a father. There are three other scenes which should have offended Breen. As part of his plan to lose his virginity, Hermie, egged on by Osky, eventually succeeds in buying condoms in a chemist's shop; there is a beach scene in which, off-screen, Osky and Miriam have sex; and, finally, the long seduction scene in which Dorothy and Hermie make love after they slowly, sensuously, remove their clothes.[49] While such films, moreover concerning the teenage male's focus on losing his virginity, were being treated more leniently by the 1980s, this was invariably cut or even banned by Hall. Ironically, by the beginning of the next decade the Censor passed without cuts and with an over-18s certificate an Irish coming-of-age oedipal tale, Jordan's understated *The Miracle* which has its central character Jimmy (Niall Byrne), who is a virgin, actually pray to God in a church that he might 'get laid' by the end of the summer. When he does, though with his mother, he returns to the church and waits for another miracle.[50]

*Porky's* (Bob Clark, 1982, Canada), which is set in Florida in the early 1950s, sees a group of teenagers attempt to lose their virginity through gaining entry to a local brothel and bar, Porky's. A huge box office hit in the USA in the tradition of *American Graffiti* (George Lucas, 1973), it is a coming-of-age movie American style with crude, lecherous humour, sexually explicit dialogue by both boys and girls, a liberal sprinkling of expletives, as well as a comic love-making scene in which the over-sexed girl's groans are heard in the gym as a class is in progress. This form of male adolescent humour, not to mention the explicit topless striptease scene at Porky's, was, naturally, banned by Hall. What is perhaps surprising is that it was passed uncut albeit with an over-16s certificate by the Board.[51] This was also the case with *Porky's II* (Bob Clark, 1983, Canada).[52]

The Board passed many such films banned by Hall including *Fast Times at Ridgemont High* (Amy Heckerling, 1982),[53] with one lengthy cut in reel 9 and an over-18s certificate, and an uncut *The Last American Virgin* (Boaz Davidson, 1982),[54] a teen comedy-drama, with an over-16s certificate. In the 1990s this more liberal attitude to teen movies may also be seen in the reduction of age certification of *National Lampoon's Loaded Weapon I* (Gene Quintano, 1993) from over-15s to under-12s accompanied by an adult.[55] This was one of a highly successful series of eight films – mostly displaying the same (tasteless) humour to that of *Porky's* – which began with *National Lampoon's Animal House* (John Landis, 1978), set in an American college fraternity, and was passed with five cuts and an over-18s certificate.[56] Also passed was *National Lampoon's Class Reunion* (Michael Miller, 1982)[57] though a confession scene was cut, as was a line about the 'time of month'. Undaunted, Hall continued with his particular sensibility, banning many of this sub-genre, or cutting entire scenes. For example, the 'Girls in Trouble' sketch in the teenage-oriented *The Kentucky Fried Movie* (John Landis, 1977) was cut by him, as were other sequences, including the final love-making scene, even though it was rated over-18s.[58] Elsewhere, Hall cut five sex scenes from *My Tutor* (George Bowers, 1982), in which a teenager tries to lose his virginity;[59] a drive-in movie scene from *Screwballs* (Rafal Zielinski, 1983),[60] also rated over-18s; and a love-making scene from *Risky Business* (Paul Brickman, 1983), in which a teenager in charge of his parents' house fills it with pimps and prostitutes.[61]

Both male and female full frontal nudity (as well as breasts) remained a preoccupation of the censors during the 1970s, with films as varied as the pro-Indian Western *Soldier Blue* (Ralph Nelson, 1970),[62] Hammer's *Lust for a Vampire* (Jimmy Sangster, 1970, GB),[63] *Puppet on a Chain* (Geoffrey Reeve, 1970, GB),[64] and *Walkabout* (Nicolas Roeg, 1970, Australia) being cut. This latter film about two school children lost in the Australian desert and befriended by an Aborigine was awarded an over-16s certificate, had a total of eleven cuts made to the scenes where Jenny Agutter swims nude and dresses afterwards.[65] Jack Nicholson's directorial debut, *Drive, He Said* (1970), was given an over-18s certificate and cut in sixteen places. These were mostly dialogue cuts of forbidden words (shit, fuck, 'For Christ's Sake'), but one concerned pubic hair and another was of male frontal nudity.[66]

Male frontal nudity was also a problem for director Ken Russell in *Women in Love*, while female frontal nudity was one of four deletions from his *Savage Messiah* (1972, GB), a decision of the Censor upheld after appeal.[67] Similarly cut was Yoko Ono's 'frontal nude scene' in the documentary *Imagine* (John Lennon, Yoko Ono, 1972),[68] while male and female nudity, as well as love-making between Lucia (Charlotte Rampling) and Max (Dirk Bogarde), was cut from *The Night Porter* (Liliana Cavani, 1973, Italy),[69] which explores the masochistic relationship between a concentration camp inmate and a Nazi guard. The award winning *The Devil's Playground* (Fred Schepisi, 1976, Australia) set in a Catholic monastery and exploring issues around both the boy students' pubescence and adult brothers' relation to the body and their desires, featured not just 'male frontals' which were cut, but a reference to the forbidden topic of masturbation.[70] Other films featuring masturbation which were cut ('Induced by narcissistic and permissive self-abusive practices') were *Up the Down Staircase* (Robert Mulligan, 1967),[71] *Malizia* (aka *Malicious*, Salvatore Samperi, 1973, Italy),[72] *Amarcord* (Federio Fellini, 1973, Italy),[73] *The Apprenticeship of Duddy Kravitz* (Ted Kotcheff, 1974, Canada),[74] the soft porn, *Danish Dentist on the Job*,[75] *Macon County Line* (Richard Compton, 1973),[76] *The Reincarnation of Peter Proud* (J. Lee-Thompson, 1974),[77] *The Sailor Who Fell from Grace with the Sea* (Lewis John Carlino, 1974, GB),[78] *Valentino* (Ken Russell, 1977, GB),[79] and in the 1980s, Hall cut the line 'Have you finished masturbating?' from *The Clinic*.[80]

Other, more adult-orientated, films of the 1970s and 1980s in which love-making scenes were curtailed included *Thieves like Us* (Robert Altman, 1974),[81] *The Reincarnation of Peter Proud*,[82] and *The Man Who Fell to Earth* (Nicolas Roeg, 1976, GB).[83] Indeed, the very title of Woody Allen's *Everything You Always Wanted to Know about Sex* (1972) was probably enough to ensure Breen banned it, a decision not appealed, but in 1979 a slightly shorter version of the film was passed with two cuts and an over-18s certificate.[84] These were of the 'What is Sodomy?' scene in which the Armenian shepherd goes to see the doctor (Gene Wilder) and tells him of his love for a sheep. His account of falling in love with the sheep one night while in the mountains, and the description of it being 'the greatest lay I ever had,' was cut, though the doctor's subsequent love affair with the same sheep was allowed. The second cut was in the sex researcher's 'Frankenstein' scene in which a man is having intercourse with a large rye bread. *Bolero* (John Derek, 1984), featuring a frequently nude Bo Derek, was suppressed by Hall, but re-considered by him nine months later and passed with four sex scenes cut and with an over-18s certificate.[85]

One of the features to emerge in the 1970s was not just more explicit foreplay and sexual intercourse scenes, but the aural expression of orgasmic pleasure. Indeed, the discomfort at the embarrassment of the body's noises as an expression of its unrestrained animal physicality is most succinctly explored in Charlie Chaplin's *Modern Times* (1936), though in this case Chaplin confines it to digestion. Fittingly, the scene takes place in the prison warden's office in the presence of the officer's bourgeois wife. When confronted by such scenes, the censors, alert to the notion that polite society demands the body to be a closed repressed system,[86] cut them to suppress the sounds, whether on- or off-screen. 'Orgasm' does not enter the Reserved book until 1972 when Vanessa Redgrave has an orgasm in *A Quiet Place in the Country*, a scene cut by the Board after the film had been rejected.[87] Other films where similar sounds were deleted were from *Macon County Line*,[88] *Murder Inferno* (aka *Le Trio infernal/The Infernal Trio*, Francis Girod, 1973, France)[89] featuring Romy Schneider, *Jackson County Jail* (Michael Miller, 1976),[90] and the media satire, *Network* (Sidney Lumet, 1976),[91] which, though rated over-18s, was cut by Breen so as to remove a bed scene with Diana (Faye Dunaway) moving on top of Max (William Holden) and orgasmically exclaiming her pleasure, while simultaneously undercutting it with talk about her work. Such sexual pleasure continued to be cut throughout the decade, with, for example, the line, 'An orgasm a day keeps the doctor away' cut from the soft-porn film, *Strip First then We Talk* (*Amore Mio Spogliali ... Che Poi Ti Spiego!* Fabio Pittorru, 1975, Italy).[92] (Ironically, the adage from which the phrase is adapted – 'an apple a day keeps the doctor away' – is also rooted in the physical, though, like Chaplin's *Modern Times*, in terms of digestion and bowel motions!) Another, less jocular comment was also removed from the film, 'Why don't we castrate him.'[93] However, Hall modified this blanket ban on orgasm sounds when he ordered cut 'substantially,' rather than deleting in its entirety, an orgasm scene in *Winter Kills* (William Richert, 1979).[94] The only other cut scene of an orgasm was of a lesbian in 1981 in *The Blood Splattered Bride* (aka *La Novia Ensangrentada/ The Bride covered in Blood/'Til Death Do Us Part*, Vicente Aranda, 1972, Spain).[95]

Male and female prostitution continued to be cut into the 1980s, including that of lead Richard Gere in *American Gigolo* (Paul Schrader, 1980). Though rejected by Hall, it was subsequently passed with cuts by the Board, but not before it divided with 4 in favour of an over-18s certificate (Carroll, Liddy, Ryan, Skehan) and 3 against: (Fr O'Donoghue, McCarthy, O'Neill). On re-view, the vote was 5 in favour of an over-18s with cuts, mainly dialogue about 'fucking,' and sex scenes, with the Revd Murray, McCarthy, Jennings and Liddy voting for it along with Carroll, while the other 4 members were absent.[96] Another film featuring prostitution which was edited by Hall was *Number One* (Les Blair, 1984, GB),[97] while the last film he banned was Ken Russell's *Crimes of Passion* (1984),[98] which was not appealed. Similarly, Hall continued to cut 'adult' sex such as in the mainstream, but seedy and exploitative, *Nine and a half Weeks* (Adrian Lyne, 1986) which was given an over-18s certificate with one cut of the 'sex in train' sequence reduced substantially.[99] Clearly, given such prohibitions, rape also remained a difficult subject for the censors, with Breen cutting such scenes (always for over-18s) in *Lipstick* (Lamont Johnson, 1976);[1] *Jackson County Jail*[2] and *The Centerfold Girls* (John Peyser, 1974);[3] while Hall cut rape scenes in *Young Warriors* (Lawrence D. Folder, 1983)[4] and *Flesh + Blood* (Paul Verhoeven, 1985),[5] which was, in fact, the last film cut by him.

When the extraordinarily successful if controversial European 'Art' film, *Last Tango in Paris* (Bernardo Bertolucci, 1973, France/Italy) brought sodomy into mainstream cinema (through its famous 'butter' scenes with Marlon Brando and Maria Schneider), the distributors chose not to test Breen's liberalism and decided against even submitting the film, knowing full well what the response would be. However, when viewed by Hall in 1981, eight years after its international release, it was banned, a decision upheld by the Board. Nevertheless, the decision was not unanimous with 3 in favour and 2 calling for an over-18s certificate. At a reviewing of the film, the Board divided 4 to 2 in favour of banning it.[6] Sodomy (or 'buggery' as it is sometimes referred to) continued to be removed from films, including *The Mountain Men* (Richard Lang, 1980);[7] the re-submitted *Straw Dogs*;[8] *Blue Belle* (aka *The End of Innocence; La Fine dell Innocenza*, Massimo Dallamano, 1975, GB/Italy),[9] about the sexual experiences of a 17-year-old who has just left convent school; and *Pixote*, a film from which scenes of love-making, masturbating and urination were also deleted.[10] Likewise, *The New Barbarians* (aka *Warriors of the Wasteland*, Enzo G. Castellari, 1983, Italy), had a sodomy rape cut.[11] Homosexuality also remained taboo with, for example, a scene in a 'queer bar,' as Hall so insulting called it, removed from *Hussy* (Matthew Chapman, 1980, GB),[12] while, the graphic *Caligula* (Tinto Brass, 1980) was banned by both Hall and the Board with only Noel Ryan favouring its release.[13] Thus, as each nudge of liberalism was forthcoming from the censors, commercial cinema was always racing ahead of it. This is as true of the forbidden lexicon of 1980s cinema with words such as masturbation, fucking, and the like which was a far cry from the more innocent, but, nonetheless, forbidden words of the earlier eras.

## FORBIDDEN WORDS

As belies his reputation as a devout Catholic, it is perhaps to be expected that Richard Hayes cut (infrequent) allusions to Jesus Christ in reverent, exclamatory or swearing contexts during his term as Censor. In his first such decision, one month after taking office, he ordered cut the 'sacred name' from *Maryland* (Henry King, 1940),[14] a rather innocent children's film. This clearly fits within his predecessor's sensitivity to *all* representations of Christianity. However, the difficulty facing the Censor on this issue and other problematic or swear words such as shit and fuck was only to increase given their entrance into common currency in Britain especially during World War Two (as had happened briefly during World War One), as the closer proximity of all classes to each other in the context of war led to the upward mobility of words previously anathema, at least in public discourse, to the bourgeoisie. Nevertheless, it was another two decades, and the broader context of 1960s liberalization, before such utterances became generalized in artistic usage.

Yet prior to this shift, the somewhat acceptable substitute for Jesus Christ, Jeepers Creepers, was cut from *Seeing Red*[15] in 1940, by Hayes, two months after he took office. While Jeepers, or variants such as as Jumping Jeepers or Holy Jeepers, was cut from at least eight films during the following five years, all versions, reverent or otherwise, of Jesus Christ were certain to be cut. Thus, the 'Holy Name,' Jesus Christ, was cut twice from *The Nelson Touch* (aka *Corvette K22*, Richard Rosson, 1943) providing a neat juxtaposition of Hayes' Catholicism and nationalism.[16] During the following fifteen years, the words Jesus Christ do not seem to appear among those films cut, and when they make an appearance in the 1960s, they were usually only part of films which were deemed objectionable in other ways as well. Thus, *Wild in the Country* (Philip Dunne, 1961), an Elvis Presley vehicle set in hillbilly country, had the word 'Jesus' cut on two occasions,[17] *The Trial* (Orson Welles, 1962, France/Italy/West Germany),[18] in common with other films such as *Who's Afraid of Virginia Wolfe?* used it as an exclamation, such as 'Oh Jesus' which was cut.[19] While 'Christ' and 'Jesus' were the least of the censors' problems in *The Graduate*, they were cut along with much else by the Board after the Censor had banned it.[20] Similarly, the much-cut *The Lion in Winter* (Anthony Harvey, 1968, GB), in which the line, 'In the name of bleeding Jesus,' was one of eight excisions ordered by Macken, and one of two maintained by the Board despite its over-18s certificate.[21] 'Eh Jesus' was the only cut to *Oh! What a Lovely War* (Richard Attenborough, 1969, GB) to allow it to qualify for an over-16s certificate.[22] As variations on the words began to appear, such as 'Bejesus' and 'For Christ's Sake' in *The Reckoning* (Jack Gold, 1969, GB),[23] these, too, were removed, the latter expression was also cut from the adaptation of the Irish-American drama, *The Subject Was Roses* (Ulu Grosbard, 1969).[24] An occasional variation, 'Jeez,' was also cut from *Evel Knievel* (Marvin Chomsky, 1972).[25] Cutting of Jesus and Christ continued through the 1970s, with films such as *Jaws* (Steven Spielberg, 1975) having the words cut, in this case to qualify for an under-12s with adult certificate.[26] The breakthrough film of the Irish cinema renaissance, the formally complex *Caoineadh Airt Uí Laoire* (*Lament for Art O'Leary*, Bob Quinn, 1975), had Jesus, Christ, 'fucked up' and 'shit' cut from its subtitles to qualify for a general certificate.[27] In fact, the censors' reports in the 1970s reveal an obsession with the word, such as when the Censor hears 'Jesus' on the soundtrack in a washroom scene in *One Flew over the Cuckoo's Nest* (Milos Forman, 1975) and demanded the film's only cut in order for it to qualify for a general certificate.[28] Similarly, the sexually violent *An Unmarried Woman* (Paul Mazursky, 1978)[29] also had 'Jesus Christ' cut so as to warrant an over-18s certificate.

While aspirations to heaven were encouraged by the Catholic church and use of the word has been universally positive ('Heaven help us,' etc), the other place, hell, has had an altogether more negative connotation, though, interestingly, it has only infrequently bothered Irish censors. 'Hell' was allowed to remain in the title of a great many films, but the word, or its later version, 'bloody hell,' was often cut within films. From *Drôle de Drame* (Marcel Carné, 1937, France), for example, even though the Censor in this instance, Martin Brennan, viewed it seventeen years after it had been released elsewhere, the line, 'You're sure to go to hell and me with you,' was removed.[30] Yet, after initial hesitation, in the same year, 1954, two cuts of 'go to hell' were restored to *On the Waterfront* by Brennan.[31] Once again, this is indicative of a more general inconsistency within Irish film censorship practice and displays the problem of the Act's vague terms of reference. Arguably because the word had been combined with 'bloody' in *A Kind of Loving* in 1962 it was a matter of course that Liam O'Hora cut it.[32]

Other swear words to become more commonplace during World War Two were 'bastard,' and more offensively, 'pox,' a slang term for venereal disease. The one example of the latter seen in the censors' reports was the only cut to the adventure story *Captain Kidd* (Rowland V. Lee, 1945) from which the insult 'You pox-riddled villain' was removed.[33] The usage of 'bastard' in war films was not an issue for Hayes until these films were released from May 1945 onwards. Thus, Hayes cut 'persistent bastards' from *In Which We Serve* (Noel Coward, David Lean, 1942, GB)[34] and 'Bloody lot of bastards' from *Flying Fortress* (Walter Forde, 1942, GB).[35] In the 1950s, the word began to appear more often in mainstream commercial productions, though, despite the censors proclivity for high art, the articulation of Shakespeare's language when it contained such words was forbidden. In this regard, Laurence Olivier's version of *Richard III* (1956, GB) was passed with five cuts, which included the words 'harlot,' 'strumpet' and 'bastards'.[36] While, narratively, all allusions to prostitution were cut by the censors, even the word, when used as an analogy, such as already referred to in *The Blackboard Jungle*, 'Even a prostitute makes more than we [teachers] do,' was cut.[37] Brennan's list of forbidden words also included tramp and trollop which were removed from *The Big Knife* (Robert Aldrich, 1955),[38] though the contemporaneous Disney animation film, *The Lady and the Tramp*, with its 'inter-class' dog relationship was allowed to keep its title presumably because it did not refer to a person.

British New Wave cinema brought working-class patois to the screen, though many of these films, as previously discussed, were banned. Even when eventually released, a key film, *Room at the Top* had a line cut, where Elspeth (Hermione Badderley) says, 'you filthy northern bastard,' from a version of the film re-edited by the distributor and passed by the more 'liberal' post-1965 Board, which issued an over-18s certificate.[39] The expletive, one of a series of 'bastards', is directed at Joe (Laurence Harvey) for his discarding of Elspeth's married friend Alice (Simone Signoret), who subsequently dies in a car crash, so that he can marry Susan (Heather Sears) the industrialist's daughter. The word 'bastard' was also cut from *Spare the Rod* (Leslie Norman, 1961, GB),[40] *The Hustler* (Robert Rossen, 1961),[41] and *Knife in the Water*.[42] By 1967, 'bastard' was allowed, with the Board approving *A Man for All Seasons* (Fred Zinnemann, 1966, GB) uncut with a general certificate after Macken had ordered an under-12s with adults certificate and the line, 'why Bishop Fisher says that in this country every second bastard born is fathered by a priest,' deleted.[43] By 1972, *A Town Called Bastard* (Robert Parrish, 1971, GB/Spain) was approved with four cuts and an over-18s certificate by the Board after it was banned by Macken. Interestingly, the Board chose not to order the film's title to be changed.[44] Nevertheless, in the 1970s, even under Dermot Breen's stewardship, the less offensive swear words or sexually specific comments were age restricted. Thus, when he passed *Monty Python and the Holy Grail* (Terry Gilliam, 1975) with thirteen cuts and an under-12s with adults certificate, words such as 'shit,' 'you stupid bastard,' 'fart,' and 'buggered off' were cut.[45] Later, the film was passed uncut with an over-15s certificate indicating how limited certificates had specific cut off points.[46] Indeed, it was the term upon which adaptation of Alan Sillitoe's *Saturday Night and Sunday Morning* almost floundered. By contrast, *Alfie*, as noted, released in 1966, contained a range of 'language' hitherto not allowed in British films. While *Saturday Night and Sunday Morning* was banned in Ireland and not released until 1972, *Alfie* was passed with an over-21s certificate and extensive cuts, including of the offensive dialogue.[47]

'Shit' had entered the censors' lexicon in the mid-1960s with Orson Welles' *The Trial*[48] and again with Roman Polanski's *Cul-de-Sac*, from which the post-1965 Board insisted it be removed despite an over-18s certificate being issued.[49] The line 'you're all full of shit' (repeated twice) and signaling a more generalized use of such vocabulary by Hollywood was cut by the Board from *Five Easy Pieces*, after having intially been banned by Macken.[50] Indeed, there are few films of the decade, well known or otherwise, which do not contain the word or its variant, bullshit. As a consequence, films from *Don't Look Now* (Nicolas Roeg, 1973, GB)[51] to *Deliverance* (John Boorman, 1972);[52] *Duel* (Steven Spielberg, 1971)[53] to *The Exorcist* (William Friedkin, 1973);[54] *Blazing Saddles* (Mel Brooks, 1974)[55] to *The Towering Inferno* (John Guillermin, 1974);[56] which all featured it were cut. Nevertheless, while such censorship continued throughout the decade, there was an apparent loosening towards the end of Breen's tenure. This aspect of 1970s censorship can be summarized through the example of *Sunday, Bloody Sunday*. As noted, it was banned by Macken, but passed by the Board with eleven cuts, including of the words shit, fucking and Jesus Christ. The film was not released, but seven years later, in one of Breen's last decisions, it was passed uncut with an over-18s certificate,[57] indicating that, at least as regards language, few restrictions remained for adult audiences.

'Bitch,' always more degrading than its literal meaning, which made its appearance for Irish censors in Jack Clayton's *The Innocents* where the line 'A dammed dirty-minded bitch [*sic*]' was one of many cuts ordered so as to allow the film to receive a general certificate,[58] was another in the vast litany of prohibited words. Similarly, the word, along with bastard, was one of the milder cuts to *The Night of the Iguana* (John Huston, 1964).[59] To qualify for a general certificate, *Behold a Pale Horse* also had the word removed.[60] The new Board, which came into office a few months later, seems to have largely ignored the term, as they had to contend with far more explicit and socially-divisive locutions.

Although Kenneth Tynan is credited with articulating 'fuck' for the first time on British radio in 1965 and Peregrine Worsthorne on BBC Television in 1973 (both within the broadcasting signal overspill range of most of Ireland), the vocable in its various manifestations was already common currency. While British commentators tend to cite the successful defence trial in 1960 of D.H. Lawrence's *Lady Chatterley's Lover* as signaling the acceptance of 'crude' language by the public, such was not the case in Ireland where Irish publications' censorship was not liberalized until 1967. (James Joyce's *Ulysses* was an exception within Irish censorship as it was never banned even though it contained many taboo words. Yet, the same respect was not given to the film adaptation which was banned by Macken in 1967, a decision upheld by the Board, and re-affirmed in 1974, not because of its visual content, one suspects, but because of its sexually explicit and highly erotic language.)

Arguably, 'fuck' is perhaps the most charged and forbidden, if also highly prominent, of all English language swear words. Though its origins can be traced to the German verb 'to dig,' its connotations of penetration or even rape were in evidence by the eighteenth century. Even though the Victorians attempted to suppress the word, it found a broad-class usage during both world wars. Therefore, like bastard before it, it is fitting that the first cut of the word should be from a war film, *The Bridge at Remagan* (John Guillermin, 1969), rated over-16s, in which the line 'Go fuck yourself,' along with four cuts of 'Jesus,' accounted for the film's five deletions.[61] However, it was not until usage by (middle-class) counter-culturalists in the 1960s that the term became more broadly accepted. The key moment of this paradigmatic shift was when Country singer Joe McDonald boomed out the beginning of his anti-Vietnam War song with 'Give me an F …' etc. to the huge crowd at Woodstock in 1969. Thus, Michelangelo Antonioni's *Zabriskie Point* (1969), a key film dealing with America's counter-culture, had its ban reversed and awarded an over-18s certificate by the Appeal Board provided three fucks were cut, two of which were that most provocative of 1960s/70s insults, 'mother-fucker'.[62] Later, the word came to be used primarily in crime films, often with an African-American background, such as *Shaft* (Gordon Parks, 1971),[63] *Shaft's Big Score!* (Gordon Parks Jnr, 1972),[64] *Across 110th Street* (Barry Shear, 1972),[65] *Superfly* (Gordon Parks, 1972),[66] and *Lady Sings the Blues* (Sidney J. Furie, 1972),[67] while the number of expletives: 3 Jesus Christs, 2 'fuckin', 1 'mother-fucker', and 1 'balls' in *The Long Goodbye* (Robert Altman, 1973) qualifies it as one of the most cut films of the period, despite it receiving an over-18s certificate.[68] The use of the word as an adjectival addition to a sentence was arguably the most common insult of the 1970s, such as 'You fucking bitch' in Irish writer Edna O'Brien's *Zee and Co* (aka *X, Y and Zee*, Brian G. Hutton, 1971, GB). Well before Booker Prize winner Roddy Doyle gave to Irish writing 'fucking' by the hundred and the colourful, swear-ridden language of working-class Dublin suburbia, O'Brien, whose work ran into difficulties with both book and film censors, gave the film 3 'fuckings', 2 of which were merely as adjectives, 'fucking frauds.'[69] Unlike in the 1960s where a single objectionable word might be found in a film, by the mid-1970s mainstream commercial cinema was so sprinkled with such language that the censors' reserved reports became dominated by their attempts at containment. Two films censored by Dermot Breen, *Serpico* (Sidney Lumet, 1973) and *American Graffiti* help to illustrate how the blanket banning of the forbidden words began to break down.

*Serpico* was cut by Breen in thirty-eight places, all of which were words such as Jesus, fuck, bullshit, mother fucker, tits, and perhaps the most insulting (from the macho male perspective and, ironically, given that it allows for a 'transgressive' active female by the female) term, cocksucker.[70] However, with the film's rating changed from general to over-18s, fifteen of these cuts were restored, including 'shit'; 'fucking weird'; 'fucking nut'; 'fucking thing'; 'fuck him'; and 'he's no fucking good.'[71] Likewise to *American Graffiti*, which Breen ordered twenty-three cuts of 'bullshit', 'Jesus,' 'Jeez,' 'shit,' and 'chicken shit,' three of these were restored (Jeez once, and shit twice), while eight others were masked by bleeps to enable it to qualify for an over-15s certificate.[72] Despite this apparently more 'liberal' attitude, the range of words from 'Jesus Christ' to 'fuck yourself,' 'you fucking bitch' and 'You bastard' were cut from the over-18s certified *Next Stop, Greenwich Village*.[73] Otherwise, the over-18s rated *Carrie* (Brian de Palma, 1976), an adaptation of Stephen King's novel about a girl reaching puberty, was cut in fourteen places, almost all of which were the words fuck, fucking, fucked up, shit, and Jesus Christ.[74] In an earlier period, *Carrie*'s powerful combination of religion and sex would have ensured its banning; by the late 1970s, the Censor was only concerned with a few swear words.[75] Nevertheless, while Breen ordered four cuts of shit and Jesus to *The Sunshine Boys* (Herbert Ross, 1975) in order to qualify it for a general certificate, he later restored the line, 'The songs he wrote were shit,' suggesting something other than a blanket ban on such words even for children.[76]

Another locution which emerges in 1970s mainstream cinema is cunt. Among the three cuts to *Harry and Tonto* (Paul Mazursky, 1974) to allow it receive an under-12s with adult certificate was, besides 'bullshit' and 'Christ Almighty,' the line, 'but I think you're a cunt.'[77] The word is used twice in *Death Wish* (Michael Winner, 1974), as is 'mother-fucker'. In this unpleasant and repulsively sexist film, it is interesting to note that, somewhat uniquely during this period, the Censor felt obliged to write that he had 'been lenient with some language' in the film, though once again he issued an over-18s certificate.[78] Two years later, the word was removed (along with Jesus Christ, fuck, and mother-fucker) from Martin Scorsese's *Mean Streets* (1973),[79] while the following year it was deleted, along with mother-fucker, from the post-Vietnam War film, *Coming Home* (Hal Ashby, 1978).[80] While cunt remains arguably one of the most insulting expressions, nevertheless, feminism has, in part, allowed for its repositioning in much the same way as bitch, for example – a word most often seen in a farmyard context, such as 'a bitch in heat' – could be deemed a badge of assertiveness and defiance of patriarchal authority. Such refiguring or reclaiming of language is not limited to women but is an essential strategy of all minority groups, and is most apparent in the use of 'niggers' as self-description by modern African-Americans. Thus, as with *A Town Called Bastard*, the name of the film *The Bitch* (Gerry O'Hara, 1979, GB), with Joan Collins in the title role, was allowed unchanged with an over-18s certificate, no doubt because it purports a positive use of the word, though there were nine cuts to the film itself.[81] Finally, that most Irish of swear words, 'bollocks' (or the variation 'bollix,' a reference to an unpleasant person, but also meaning testicles), rarely made the cinema screen. The Board cut 'bollix' from the horror film *Gorilla at Large* (Harmon Jones, 1954),[82] while 'bollocks' was cut from *The Alf Garnett Saga* (Bob Kellett, 1972, GB), Breen's only cut to the film, even though he issued an over-18s certificate.[83] Thirty years later, the nature of public discourse had changed so much that such a mild, dismissive word is almost innocent. Indeed, Roddy Doyle capturing a most natural speech pattern of a particular class in Dublin, has often put it in the mouth of his characters including loveable Jimmy Senior. Like other, so-called expletives, it has come to be so fully incorporated into everyday, particularly working-class, language that its literal meaning is secondary, or even denied and subverted and is alternatively used as a floating noun, adjective, exclamation, and, of course, a pronoun.

Ironically, given the desired state of all characters (even married ones) by Irish censors, 'virgin' as a word was forbidden in the era of general certificates, but the term necessarily points to the reality of its opposite, something which outside of marriage could not be countenanced and within deemed to be most private. Of course, all discussions of sex and sexuality were culturally taboo, such that when Mary Kate in *The Quiet Man* wishes to seek advice on the non-consummated state of her marriage, she uses the Irish language to express herself. Tellingly, this hints at the private and more complete language of the native culture which as well as celebrating or looking to a form of (semi-Christianized) paganism, seems to have enjoyed a more bawdy and comfortable relation to the body as is evident, for example, in Peig Sayers' 'memoirs'. Furthermore, the (past) use of Irish as a means to transgress, frustrate or otherwise evade the colonial English-speaking authority is arguably relevant and might suggest that official Ireland took on board – much more than it could care to admit – at least some of the characteristics and governing strategies of its once (at times paternalistic) oppressor.

The first of seven cuts to the musical *High Society* (Charles Walters, 1956) was the description of a character as a 'virgin goddess'.[84] Other films where use of the word or reference to virginity were cut included *This Could be the Night* (Robert Wise, 1957);[85] *The Third Voice* (Hubert Cornfield, 1960)[86] in which a girl is referred to as a 'professional virgin'; *The Entertainer* (Tony Richardson, 1960, GB);[87] *Wild Strawberries*;[88] *The Dock Brief* (aka *Trial and Error*, James Hill, 1962, GB)[89] in which the line 'Don't tell us you're a virgin' was deleted; *The Wild and the Willing* (aka *Young and Willing*, Ralph Thomas, 1962, GB)[90] from which the 'Inverness virgins' was cut; *Rendezvous at Midnight* (Christy Cabanne, 1935) which had songs cut that made reference to losing one's virginity, because, as O'Hora put it, 'virginity is not a laughing matter to me';[91] *Smiles of a Summer Night* which had references to the young bride's virginity curtailed;[92] *The Pink Panther* (Blake Edwards, 1963) which featured a joke about the 'Virgin Queen';[93] and *Night of the Big Heat* (Terence Fisher, 1967, GB) from which the words virgin and slut were removed in order for it to gain an under-12s with adult certificate.[94]

By the late 1960s/early 1970s films could retain their titles even if they included the word virgin, such as the gangster film *The Amorous Virgin* (*Una Virgine per un Bastardo/Sweet Smell of Love/Das Bett Einer Jungfrau*, Ubaldo Ragona, 1966, Italy/West Germany);[95] *The Virgin Soldiers* (John Dexter, 1969, GB);[96] *The Virgins*;[97] and the adaptation of D.H. Lawrence's novel, *The Virgin and the Gypsy* (Christopher Miles, 1970, GB);[98] all of which were passed with cuts by the Appeal Board after having been banned by the Censor. However, during the 1970s, the word was still excised from films such as *Never Mind the Quality, Feel the Width* (Ronnie Baxter, 1972, GB) where the lines 'You've just ruined another virgin' and 'Another virgin up the spout,' were deleted;[99] *You Can't Run Away from Sex* (Bickford Otis Webber, 1971) from which the line 'You are a virgin' as was 'all dialogue relating to this subject' cut;[1] the mainstream *Drum* (Steve Carver, 1976);[2] soft porn films including *Naughty Girls* (aka *Gymslip Lovers/Naughty Schoolgirls*, Jean Paul Scarido, 1976)[3] and *Strip First then We Talk*;[4] while *The Reluctant Virgin* (*No … Sono Vergine*, Norman Schwartz [Cesare Mancini], 1973, Italy)[5] was banned in 1976. As one would expect, when the Blessed Virgin Mary's virginity was commented on, the censors were clearly nervous, as in the case of *The Forbidden Christ* (*Il Christo Proibito* aka *The Strange Deception*, Curzio Malaparte, 1950, Italy), a story of the partisans, from which the following lines were deleted: 'They say the Madonna is a virgin. She cannot be, she's had a child. Don't you believe in miracles? The sun can penetrate a window without breaking it.'[6] Necessarily then, the description of the other side of the dominant representation of women – the whore/prostitute – was also forbidden for Irish audiences. Therefore, both virgin and

whore were removed from *Expresso Bongo*,[7] while the only cut to *China Gate* (Samuel Fuller, 1957) was 'and lived *like* a prostitute.' (Emphasis added.)[8]

## DERMOT BREEN, FRANK HALL AND CATHOLICISM

Interestingly, the word heresy does not appear among the millions of written words by Montgomery, Hayes, Brennan, O'Hora, and Macken, the first five censors. All five in their devout Catholic manner complained about paganism, materialism, and the representation of non-Catholic, indeed non-Christian ways, but none accused the cinema of apostasy. Yet, heresy is the term used by the Censor who is regarded as the first, true modernizer of Irish film censorship, Dermot Breen, in 1977 to describe *Audrey Rose* (Robert Wise, 1977). This reincarnation thriller has a stranger (Anthony Hopkins) telling a happily married couple (Marsha Mason, John Beck) that their 12-year-old daughter (Susan Swift) is in fact his own daughter returned to life. As the film deals with 'the transmigration of the soul' (including the views of an Indian guru), Breen held that it was 'totally unacceptable to all Christians who believe in the existence of Heaven and Hell.' (Of course, this theme had been central to the horror genre not least as figured through the physical, even after death, being seen as the site for a person's soul or personality.) Acknowledging that 'heresy may be a strong word to use,' nevertheless it summed up why he was rejecting the film. He added that there were many sequences expounding support for the 'theory' of transmigration of the soul, even though the family in the film has a Christian background, and 'the mother contributes to this by her recital of the Act of Contrition in an early sequence.' He concluded that 'at the end of the film we witness a complete reversal of her thinking' as she rejects 'the main fundamentals of Christianity'. The Board (of whom seven were in attendance, including the Catholic priest, Fr O'Donoghue) disagreed, and passed the film uncut with an over-16s certificate.[9]

By 1977, Breen had been Censor for more than five years, and while issues of 'soft porn' and 'bad language' were major preoccupations of his period in office with such films invariably cut or banned, it is perhaps as the last truly conservative Catholic wishing to protect the declining influence of the church in an increasingly secular Ireland which is of most interest. Certainly, he allowed previously banned or cut scenes dealing with personal relationships and the body to be screened without the intervention of the Board (thus considerably reducing its workload), although even in this regard he was perhaps more conservative than is popularly imagined. However, when it came to the sanction of the use of the words Jesus Christ or its variants as already discussed, and more particularly, dogmatic certainties of Catholic ideology, he embraced them as the previous more conservative generation had done.

By the early 1970s the authoritarianism of the Catholic hierarchy had been severely shaken, if not overthrown. While at least some of the new generation of middle-class Irish youth, influenced by 1960s social and political radicalism, refused uncritical allegiance to the church (or, indeed, other institutions), it was not until the 1990s that the full extent of the abuse of power by the church in Ireland was exposed to public scrutiny as the scandals involving clerical sexual and physical abuse of children emerged in what appeared an unending stream in the media. Breen then can be seen to occupy a transitional position in Irish society.

As noted, early in his career as Official Film Censor, Breen banned the first of Pier Paolo Pasolini's medieval trilogy, *The Decameron*, which provided an early opportunity for him to express his views on such a bawdy approach to the church. In his report to the Board, which upheld his decision, Breen said that some of the short stories which make up the film were 'completely objectionable and would have to be entirely removed.' These included the convent scene, the confessional, and the priest with the mare, as well as scenes of 'male and female pubic hair, vulgar expressions and suggestive conversations and dialogue.' The suggested cuts totaled 2,500–3,000 feet (twenty-nine to thirty-six minutes) or almost one-third of the film's 9,900 feet.[10] After this treatment of *The Decameron*, unsurprisingly, neither Passolini's *Arabian Nights* or *The Canterbury Tales* were appealed.

In this context, *The Devils*, dealing as it does with witchcraft and political intrigue in the seventeenth century, and featuring nuns with sexual desire, was banned, a decision not appealed. A few months later, in December 1972, *Pope Joan* (aka *The Devil's Impostor*, Michael Anderson, 1972, GB) was viewed by Breen. This legendary tale of a ninth-century German woman prostitute who becomes a preacher and ends up Pope was banned, but notwithstanding Breen's strong attack on the film as being 'entirely based on a gross deception' which was 'most objectionable' as it concerns 'the Holy Office of the Pope,' it was subsequently passed by the Board with cuts of prostitution and rape, and with an over-18s certificate.[11] A decade later, Hall also came to the papal rescue in *Joystick* (aka *Video Madness*, Greydon Clark, 1983), in which the Pope and a bishop 'discuss beans and farting' and quote St Paul to support their views. These offensive scenes were cut.[12] Breen imposed eight cuts on *Fellini's Roma* (Federico Fellini, 1972, Italy), including two and a half minutes of the parades of sacristans (later restored), and men wearing chasubles and cassocks – right through to the death figure.[13] A story of intrigue in a nunnery, *Nasty Habits* (Michael Lindsay-Hogg, 1977), was cut in six places to ensure, among other matters, the deletion of a novice nun arising from bed and meeting with a Jesuit student priest, a comment about the Jesuit 'screwing' Sister Felicity, and a conversation referring to a 'whore' and a priest,[14] while a 'long obscene prayer,' as Breen called it, was cut from the Vietnam War drama *The Boys in Company C* (Sydney J. Furie, 1978).[15]

As part of the broader social engagement with the church, the issue of 'defrocked' or laicized priests was incorporated into European cinema. While Italian, French and Spanish directors could be seen to follow in the wake of the irreverent, though Jesuit educated, Luis Buñuel, whose films were invariably banned in Ireland or not even submitted, when critiques of the church appeared within mainstream cinema the attack seemed potentially more dangerous, not just because as a more democratic medium it had been stripped of an artistic, intellectual, middle-class content which could provide some detachment and protection, but that it clearly pointed to a more obvious and generalized erosion of belief and respect, and hence highlighted the growing impossibility of the Censor's job. While arguably secularization was in itself less problematic to the Censor than the broader cultural transformation, it nevertheless was the filter through which it could be most clearly seen. Shortly after Breen's appointment one such film presented itself which contained sufficient theological ambiguity to make him nervous.

*The Wrath of God* (Ralph Nelson, 1972), set in a Central American country, features a thief masquerading as a priest, Van Horne (Robert Mitchum), an Irish informer on the run, Keogh (Ken Hutchinson), and a gun runner, Jennings (Victor Bruno), all of whom are blackmailed by the military into overthrowing local tyrant Tomas De la Plata (Frank Langella). Breen made nine cuts to the film, mostly of scenes concerning the three men, including after they have survived a mock execution when Jennings comments, 'It's – it's the Resurrection – and I didn't even wait three days.' As the three leave to confront De la Plata, Colonel Santilla (John Colicos) says, in a scene cut, 'God bless you, Father,' to Van Horne, who replies with a blessing which converts in his hands to, as Breen puts it, the 'Italian sign'. It was this confusion of Van Horne's role as a real priest from Boston on a fund-raising trip for his parish, and his use of clerical garb as a masquerade for robbery, which caused most difficulty for the Censor. Thus, when Van Horne appears to take on genuine spiritual elements, saying mass and administering the sacraments, clearly Breen was concerned, not least perhaps because it necessarily negatively impacts on the cultural importance and relevance of the priest within the community. Whether or not he is real (or good or bad) does not change the people's relationship to God or their faith. As such, the priest is shown only to be a functionary within the ritual in which *appearance*, not interiority or meaning, matters. It is fitting then, if also ironic, that Breen attacks or attempts to destroy the image so as to maintain (ideological) meaning but also the illusion of interiority and the priest's status as being beyond ordinary humanity with all its flaws and desires. Consequently, he cut a scene in which Van Horne says mass, breaks bread at communion, and distributes it to the villagers, ending on a shot of the crucifixion. Other scenes cut included a brief one in which Jennings baptizes himself with a mimicry of the real sacrament, and an argument between Van Horne and Keogh about the priesthood. In this exchange, Keogh says that 'once a priest, always a priest,' to which Van Horne replies that the church sides with the wealthy. Ending the argument, which takes place in the church, Van Horne drinks from a whiskey bottle and delivers a line cut by Breen, 'It should be blessed, don't you think.'[16] At this time the idea of a priest finding solace in alcohol let alone in a church or offering it as a subject of blessing was outside representation at least within an Irish context. That a comic incarnation of this, the foul-mouthed, perpetually drunk Fr Jack of BBC television's *Father Ted*, became such an icon in the 1990s gives some indication as to its previous repression.

The day after his decision on *Wrath of God*, Breen cut completely the priest's commentary near the end of *Harold and Maud* (Hal Ashby, 1972),[17] while *Fellini's Casanova* had a section cut in which girls discourse on St Augustine and the Virgin Mary, though the eight cuts to this were later changed to a banning order.[18] Breen rejected all criticism of the church, or à la carte Catholicism, and he objected to a section in *The McCullochs* (aka *The Wild McCullochs*, Max Baer, 1975) in which the philosophy expounded between Mrs McCulloch and her daughter lead to the conclusion that you 'do what you think is right.' For Breen 'the suggestion that one is free to ignore Church teaching if one finds it inconvenient,' was objectionable.[19] Equally, in a further throwback to earlier censorship policies, he complained, ignoring the reality of injustice, about the ending of *Bootleggers* (aka *Bootleggers' Angel*, Charles B. Pierce, 1974), which he regarded as unacceptable as 'murderers escape the law.' He demanded a moral ending in conformity with his conservative views. As a result, 'the ending has therefore been removed to indicate that murder is punished by the law.'[20] Nevertheless, adults, as well as children know that the world, even as represented in nursery rhymes and fairy tales, can be a vicious and unkind place. Seeing a cinematic representation does not give them this or indeed other difficult or immoral and amoral ideas, or necessarily alters their perception of reality, but, driven by a paternalistic responsibility, Breen denied or severely curtailed those aspects that did not show man at his best or were contrary to the law or Catholic morality.

*The Exorcist* might be thought to be a film which would have caused censors fundamental difficulties. It includes a doubting priest-psychiatrist, Fr Karras (Jason Miller), a 12-year-old girl, Regan (Linda Blair), who expresses herself when possessed by the Devil in the most sexually violent ways, and an horrific exorcism. Overarching the film, though, is the religious belief that good will triumph over evil, that the Devil will be defeated, and this will be done in spite of the failure of medical science to cure the possessed child on the brink of puberty. To clean up the film, Breen made seven cuts which took out all the expletives Regan/Demon shouts ('Fuck me'; 'Let Jesus fuck you – lick me, lick me,' which includes the section where Regan is bloodily smashing the crucifix as a penis substitute into her vagina until stopped by her mother Chris [Ellen Burstyn], and when she says to the exorcist, Fr Merrin [Max von Sydow], 'Stick your cock up your ass, you mother-fucking worthless cocksucker'). The scene in which Regan/Demon gets sick on Fr Karra was also cut to ensure that the vomit was not seen on the priest, as was an earlier scene in which Chris tries to contact her estranged husband by telephone in which she uses three expletives. Finally, Regan's medical blood extraction was shortened. Indicating his sensitivity to the film, Breen gave the distributor a warning about the trailer: 'Any infringement' of it being shown with any programme other than an over-18s 'will necessitate the withdrawal of the film as well as the trailers.'[21]

The association of sex, or, more usually sexual fulfillment, with supernatural/unnatural forces, or the impregnation of women by a demon was an established feature of horror films before the 1970s. One of the many imitations of *The Exorcist* was the sexually-explicit Italian film, *The Anti-Christ* (*L'Anticristo*, aka *The Tempter*, Alberto de Martino, 1974), viewed by Breen two years later. He ordered just three cuts (to achieve an over-18s certificate) including 'the Devil entering [a] girl and [her] subsequent orgasm,' a vomiting scene in which a man licks it, and an early scene in which a picture of the Sacred Heart is juxtaposed 'with [the] prominent depiction of [the] pinus [*sic*]'.[22] Other such films were the re-released and extensively re-cut (by the producers) version of Mario

Bava's *Lisa E Il Diavolo* (aka *Lisa and the Devil*, Mario Bava, 1972, Italy) and *The House of Exorcism* (*La Casa dell'Esircismo*, 1975, Italy) which was given a further five cuts by the Censor, probably to eliminate its *Exorcist*-like new scenes, as well as elements of necrophilia.[23] Since *Rosemary's Baby*, banned by Macken in 1969 and again by Breen in 1977, cinema remained interested in the idea of a human having a baby with the Devil, with the conception often happening during a sexual orgy. One of these was *To the Devil a Daughter* (*Die Braut des Santes*, Peter Sykes, 1976, GB/West Germany), which was cut in three places to ensure deletion of orgy and copulation scenes; the pregnant Margaret (Isabella Telezynska), who gives birth to the 'Creature'; and Fr Michael's role in the affair.[24] Another film featuring an Anti-Christ was *Holocaust 2000* (aka *The Chosen*, Alberto De Martino, 1978, Italy/GB) to which Breen ordered cut a perhaps theologically sound line by a priest, 'This is God's will. You must be strong.'[25] A spin on this theme was contained in *The Nun and the Devil* (*Le Monache Di Sant'arcangelo*, Paolo Dominici [Domenico Paolella], 1973, Italy/France). Though edited prior to submission, Breed additionally cut scenes of a nun and a man in bed, as well as a suggested lesbian relationship between two nuns.[26] In the same vein, the 'sacrilegious' *Don't Deliver Us from Evil* (*Mais ne Delivrez pas du Mal*, 1970, France) given the dubious honour by Breen of being the most immoral picture he had seen, which concerns two young girls who 'at their own behest sell themselves to the devil' was banned, a decision upheld after appeal.[27]

Unlike in earlier decades, representations of church sacraments were allowed from the 1960s, but, nonetheless, censors still scrutinized any 'irreverent' scenes set in churches. Thus, the children's film, *The Spikes Gang* (Richard Fleischer, 1974), which features a gunfighter who helps three children become bank robbers, had a scene deleted in which the boys are seen in church eating Communion breads and drinking altar wine.[28] Similarly, Ken Russell's *Mahler* (1974, GB) had eight and a half minutes cut of Mahler's religious conversion because Breen regarded it as 'grossly offensive' to the Jewish and Catholic faiths. In this scene, Mahler cynically converts from Judaism to Catholicism in order to gain a position at the Vienna Opera and is seen cavorting with a scantily-clad 'Nazi' woman, who joins him dancing on a cross. During this long episode, symbols of both religions are inter-mingled and burnt in a manner typical of Russell and designed to cause offence. After this sequence, the film cuts to a convent where Mahler declares to his sister in lines allowed that 'Man is his own God' and makes other irreverent and anti-religious comments, but a further shot of the Nazi woman 'gyrating' on a cross was cut.[29] However, the cuts were restored by the Board with a vote of 5 to 2. The dissenters were Jack O'Connor, who, in recorded votes, is seen as one of the most conservative members of the Board in the 1970s, and Fr Richard O'Donoghue.[30] While Breen regarded *The Rebel Nun* (*Flavia La Monaca Musulmana*, Gianfranco Mingozzi, 1974, Italy/France) as blasphemous, and despite twelve minutes being cut from it prior to submission (including an orgy scene in a convent) banned it, the Board unanimously disagreed ordering just two cuts, one of a cross, the other a decapitation.[31] What Breen called 'obscene representations of [the] crucifixion' were cut from the jackets of motor cyclists in the biker movie, *Born Losers* (Tom Laughlin, 1976),[32] while Ingmar Bergman's *A Lesson in Love* (*En Lektion i Karlek*, 1953,

Sweden), which had been banned in 1960, had the sub-title, 'You men have cooked up the Immaculate Conception,' deleted by Breen.[33]

Though *The Exorcist*, ultimately, endorsed the 'goodness' of the Catholic clergy when faced by the 'Devil,' other films of the 1970s were far more skeptical of the church as an institution, and focused on celibacy as an aberration. Thus, while *Lipstick* was cut in five places, as much for its use of forbidden words as anything else, it was the combining of these with reference to Catholicism, such as 'Do you fuck priests too?' and 'Catholic education can't do a damn thing about [sex],' ensured the deletions, even though this film, like most of the other films dealing with religion, was rated over-18s.[34] Even the Robin Hood adventure, *Robin and Marian* (Richard Lester, 1976) was not immune from any hint of secular love being more powerful than allegiance to God. Thus, Marian's line at the end of the film, 'I love you more than God,' was cut, even though the film was for over-18s.[35]

As noted, central within cinematic representations from the 1960s onwards were secular concerns including birth control, contraception, the highly charged subject of abortion, and a new topic of the 1970s, surrogate births. In all these areas, Breen and Hall were no more liberal than their predecessors in their attitude. Breen universally cut or banned films dealing with such material, including, for example, the sex comedy about a Catholic woman who want to go on the Pill, *It's a 2' 6" above the Ground World*, which, as noted, he banned.[36] Similarly, *The Baby Maker* (James Bridges, 1970), which focuses on the opposite of birth control, infertility and surrogacy, was banned by Breen, who explained in his report to the Board, which upheld his ban, that the film was 'contrary to the moral standards of all Christian peoples.' While the fact that the unmarried young woman, due to have a baby for a childless couple, is living with a man, 'could be overlooked,' the surrogacy itself was 'contrary to the whole concept and sanctity of marriage.'[37] Such a view of the family (not withstanding his acceptance of the representations of unmarried people co-habiting or extra-marital affairs) also informed his attitude to 'counter-culture' films. Thus, *Made* (John Mackenzie, 1972, GB) was banned because in its exploration of its theme as Breen saw it – 'the conflicts between the Christian way of life and the theory of "free-living"' – free-living 'appears to triumph'. It was 'therefore contrary to the feelings and beliefs of the vast majority of the Irish people.'[38]

Notwithstanding the legislation in 1979 allowing for bona fide family planning, Hall consistently removed from films all references to condoms. Thus, *Chicane* had a lengthy sequence in a repair shed deleted because there was a prominent sign for Durex condoms.[39] Likewise two years later, the short *Test Rider* was cut because it, too, had a scene with a Durex advertisement.[40] (Both films were rated general.) Among the scenes trimmed in *That Summer!* (aka *Torquay Summer*, Harley Cokliss, 1979, GB) were those where condoms are purchased, and later when a boy is seen throwing away condoms and returning to pick them up.[41] A lecture on 'sex hygiene' (to quote Hall's phrase to describe birth control) was cut from *Cracking Lip*,[42] while a scene in a sex shop was cut from the black comedy satire *Eating Raoul* (Paul Bartel, 1982) because of its references to 'cock rings, penis lubricants, stay hard creams,' but a customer who says he wants a vibrator as a novelty cocktail stick was allowed perhaps because it was not explicitly sexual or understood.[43] Another comic scene, in which a condom is blown up and zooms around a room before landing on a mother's head, was cut from *Baby Love* (Alastair Reid, 1968, GB), as well as a simulated fellatio scene.[44]

Considering the prevailing attitudes towards sex and the family, naturally incest remained one of the most forbidden topics with Hall ordering such scenes cut from the gory *The Crazies* (aka *Code Name: Trixie*, George Romero, 1973)[45] and the cinematically stylish *Luna* (Bernardo Bertolucci, 1979), in which a mother-son relationship is explored.[46] While even under Sheamus Smith's more liberal regime, *Bliss* (Ray Lawrence, 1985, Australia), a rather fragmented if stylish film about a man who, after a heart attack and out-of-body experience, changes his life, had an incest scene cut from it.[47] Subsequently, films that treated such themes were passed uncut, including the Irish films *The Miracle* and *November Afternoon* (John Carney, Tom Hall, 1996), which concerns an on-going relationship between an adult brother and sister. Indeed, such has been the transformation of Irish society that by 2003 the incestuous relationship between a brother and (half) sister was a lead story line in Ireland's premier soap-opera, *Fair City*.

Homosexual acts between consenting adults (over-17 years) remained a criminal offence in Ireland until 1993.[48] Consequently, censors until the mid-1980s seem to have maintained the view that since these acts were illegal, they should not be allowed on the screen. However, this restriction was further limiting as one of the developments in 1970s mainstream cinema was the regular representation of homosexuality. Interestingly, such relationships seem to have been represented more often between women than between men. For example, Claude Chabrol's lesbian art film, *Les Biches*, was banned by Gabriel Fallon in 1969, before eventually being passed by the Board in 1972 with one cut, a bed scene.[49] Macken, like his predecessors, suppressed such scenes throughout his career, including banning, for example, *Sunday, Bloody Sunday*.[50] Similarly, Breen cut homosexual and lesbian scenes from films, including such diverse ones as *Savages* (James Ivory, 1972);[51] the sanitized biopic of New York Madame Xavier Hollander, *The Happy Hooker* (Nicholas Sgarro, 1975);[52] *Vampyres* (aka *Daughters of Darkness*, Joseph (Jose) Larraz, 1974, GB),[53] in which two female vampires fall in love; action-packed, violent and sexy *Cleopatra Jones and the Casino of Gold* (Chuck Bail, 1975);[54] and the horror film *Shivers* (aka *They Came from Within*, David Cronenberg, 1975, Canada) in which the residents of an apartment block become infected by a sexually liberating parasite.[55]

Frank Hall was no more sympathetic to representations of homosexuality, or indeed to any questioning of Catholic teaching (of which homosexuality is an anathema). While, as noted, the first film he banned was the soft porn *Sex Artist*, his attitude to such material was revealed a few months later in July 1973 when he described the 'undisguised record of homosexual relationships, prostitution and promiscuity' in *Some of My Best Friends Are* (Mervyn Nelson, 1971) as 'complete moral squalor,' a view shared by the Board.[56] The first film he cut after his appointment as Official Film Censor on 25 October 1978 was another soft porn film, *A Young Emanuelle* (*Neá*, Nelly Kaplan, 1976). Besides cutting a lesbian scene, he also deleted a girl masturbating[57] which as all expressions of female sexuality seems less culturally permissible than their male counterparts, references to 'fucking,' and instances of female voyeurism, even though, arguably, male voyeurism is the largest single aspect of mainstream (classical) cinema. Two weeks later, he banned *Seven Women for Satan* (*Les Weekends Malifiques de Comte Zaroffi*, Michel Lemoine, 1974, France) a film he described as 'pornography thinly disguised as [a] horror film.'[58] But, then, both genres are undeniably rooted in the visceral experience.

Both Breen and Hall were sensitive to any criticism of the priesthood, or representations of priests in an 'unfavourable' light. Hall, for example, was on high alert when he viewed *Pieces of Dreams* (aka *The Wine and the Music*, Daniel Haller, 1970) as it dealt with the 'delicate subject' of a man who is leaving the priesthood. While 'not deliberately offensive,' there were nevertheless several scenes which 'seem likely to cause grave offence to Catholic audiences.' In order to justify his decision to ban the film, he stated that there were certain scenes which inaccurately represented the 'processes of leaving the priesthood.' The overall effect of the film, he concluded, was 'to glamorize the situation rather than to cast a light upon it,' while it tended 'to mislead and to misrepresent the dilemma of a priest in such a situation,' and, in this regard, 'it must follow that it is contrary to accepted moral norms.'[59] The Board was less certain when it viewed the film as it divided evenly between the eight members present. The Board, albeit consisting of different members, reviewed the film two weeks later, but again split evenly.[60] In such a circumstance, the 1923 Act declares that the Censor's original decision stands. Another film dealing with the priesthood, this time the topic of celibacy, *Intimacy* (*Il Prete Sposato*, Marco Vicario, 1970, Italy/West Germany/Spain) was banned by Breen, who complained that the topic was treated too flippantly and since it was 'much too sensitive a situation to be treated with such lightness,' adding that scenes in a confessional, conversations among the seminarians, and 'even suggested homo-sexuality' in the back of a car, which cause embarrassment to a priest, were enough to reject it. When viewed by the Board eight months later, 2,160 feet (over twenty-five minutes) had been cut from it, but it, too, rejected it, with just two, Skehan and Kiely, of the eight present voting for the film.[61] Similarly banned were the third *Omen* film, *The Final Conflict* (Graham Baker, 1981), because Hall regarded it as 'blasphemous,' but the Board reversed the decision;[62] *The Visitor* (Michael J. Paradise [Giulio Paradisi], 1979, Italy), a supernatural thriller in the tradition of *The Omen* (Richard Donner, 1976) with an Anti-Christ;[63] and *Monsignor* (Frank Perry, 1982), which features the Vatican's Irish Cardinal business manager in an outrageous parody of the church. Again, in this instance the Board, though without Fr O'Donoghue, unanimously passed the film uncut with an over-16s certificate.[64]

The unique, zany, irreverent humour and satire of the Monty Python team is both instantly recognizable as it is popular, if not so for those with delicate sensibilities, but ironically Frank Hall, himself a well-known satirist with his own television show, *Hall's Pictorial Weekly*, was blind to the humour when he viewed *Monty Python's Life of Brian* (Terry Jones, 1979, GB) in 1980. In a style typical of the outrageous ensemble, the film – arguably their most sustained feature – tells the story of Brian who throughout his life is mistaken for Jesus and is, in a case of swapped identities, inserted into the Jesus narrative. The film concludes with his hanging on a crucifix, singing 'Always look on the bright side of life.' Though the film if taken literally is clearly blasphemous or at least offensive to all religions, the riotous manner by which the material is presented demand that it should be viewed as an intelligent, amusing satire. Nevertheless, Hall banned it, a decision upheld by the new Appeal Board in its first decision since its appointment three months earlier. Those supporting its release with an over-18s certificate were chairman John Carroll, and Noel Ryan, who was consistently the most liberal member of the Board during his tenure (at least of the votes recorded), but they were out-voted by Fr O'Donoghue, Margaret Skehan, Michael McCarty, primary schoolteacher Kathleen O'Neill, and the Board's most conservative voice, Cormac Liddy. When re-submitted under the 'seven year rule' in August 1987, the film was passed uncut with an over-18 certificate by Sheamus Smith, who was appointed Official Film Censor the previous September.[65] Hall also banned, in a decision likewise upheld by the Board,[66] *Monty Python's The Meaning of Life* (Terry Jones, 1983, GB), their fourth feature in which through a vignette structure, the various aspects of life – birth, work, education, sex, eating, philosophy and death – are explored though often in an uneven and at times tasteless fashion.

If such clearly humorous work was rejected, it should come as no surprise that Hall regarded a scene in *Hair* (Milos Forman, 1979) in which a hippie distributes LSD sugar cubes in imitation of Holy Communion as a 'travesty' of the sacrament and he cut it,[67] while *Odds and Evens* (*Pari e Dispari*, Sergio Corbucci, 1978, Italy), had the following dialogue deleted: 'Why didn't you marry?' 'How about you?' 'Oh, I married Christ.' 'You mean I should marry the Boss? He's not my type.'[68]; while the one cut from the Bette Midler film *The Rose* (Mark Rydell, 1979) was the line, 'The Virgin Mary's coming off the bench to fill in for us.'[69] Hall was no more sympathetic to secular satire. When he viewed *Lenny* (Bob Fosse, 1974) in 1979 he acknowledged that it was 'a compelling account of the life and times of Lennie [*sic*] Bruce,' but he found some of the dialogue 'obscene and arguably tending to corrupt' and as a result he banned it,[70] a decision not appealed. Similarly, *Richard Prior Live on the Sunset Strip* (Joe Layton, 1982), with its explicit sexual content, was banned by the long-serving deputy Censor, Jerome Hegarty. When the distributor appealed the cuts, the ban was upheld by the Board in a vote of 3 to 2.[71]

Other instances where Hall cut films which contained, from his viewpoint, negative references to religion were *S.O.S. Titanic* (William Hail, 1979),[72] from which the lines at the end of the film: 'No God either. God went down on the Titanic,' were removed; *Fame* (Alan Parker, 1980), where a scene in a church was cut in which a little girl is being blessed by a priest, but her brother enters and 'abuses' the priest: 'She needs a doctor, not the goddam Holy Ghost';[73] *Absolution* (Anthony Page, 1981, GB) was cut where a priest kills a boy;[74] while *Scrubbers* (Mai Zetterling, 1982, GB) had a sequence edited in which rosary beads are broken, spat out by a woman, and used in ping-pong.[75]

When Hall viewed *Catholic Boys* (aka *Heaven Help Us*, Michael Dinner, 1985) in 1985, and cut a 'Holy Communion' scene, he still allowed material, albeit for over-18s only, which a decade earlier would have been cut or ensured the film's banning.

Both *Catholic Boys* and *The Devil's Playground* concern the effects Christian Brothers' education had on teenagers. While Breen seems to have allowed a brother inquiring as to a pupil's experience of 'wet dreams' in *Devil's Playground*, and a somewhat embittered and drunken discourse on celibacy by another brother, nevertheless, an elderly priest's reference to masturbation was cut, as was the drunken brother's comment about another, 'What a prick!'[76] *Catholic Boys* contained not just many derogatory comments by the boys about the brothers, but graphically articulated adolescent sexuality. Indeed, the film opens with a shot of a Monstrance (once a forbidden image in Irish cinemas) as a priest says mass to the school congregation, during which one of the boys displays a condom to his sniggering companions. At home, the film's main protagonist, Michael Dunn (Andrew McCarthy), hears his grandmother offer an irreverent comment about the Pope, while one of his friends later says, 'Shit. I could do the Goddamn Rosary standing on my head.' Most of what would have been previously problematic material concerned adolescent sexuality. For example, among the banter of the boys, Rooney (Kevin Dillon), a bully and show-off, replies to the dismissive word 'Nuts,' with the bravado, 'What about my nuts?' while the scene goes on to involve Dani (Mary Stuart Masterson), who tells Michael that after Rooney assaulted him, he should have 'kicked him in the balls.' In another scene, Rooney assessing the extent of the 'sins' to be confessed by his schoolmates, is told by one boy that he plans to say that he 'jerked off 168 times.' For this, Rooney tells him, the priest will 'cut your balls off.' The film's one cut was of the same lustful student who, serving as an altar boy, becomes overcome with desire on seeing the girls put their tongues out to receive Holy Communion, and collapses.[77]

It is ironic in this context that Irish filmmaker Cathal Black's drama-documentary about the Irish Christian Brothers and their contribution to education, *Our Boys*, made four years earlier in 1981, should be effectively banned from RTÉ television until a decade later, by which time the scandals surrounding the Irish church were being exposed. The revelation in 1992 that Bishop Eamon Casey had a teenage son, as had media friendly Fr Michael Cleary, was only a mild distraction from the plethora of more serious scandals featuring paedophile priests and brothers which first surfaced on Ulster Television's *Counterpoint* in 1995 about Fr Brendan Smyth. Thereafter, the number of allegations of sexual, physical, emotional and intellectual abuse against the religious, particularly those under state care with religious orders, spiraled to alarming proportions such that no defence could be made for holding back any film that dealt with the church and containing the most damning images not just of priests and brothers but of the beliefs and practices of the church itself.

While films such as Bob Quinn's *Budawanny* (1987, Ireland) and his revisiting of it in *The Bishop's Story* (1994), both centrally concerned with clerical celibacy, and Colin Gregg's *Lamb* (1985, GB) in which a sensitive brother 'saves' a troubled inmate from the harshness of the residential religious-run school by drowning him, allowed for a growing debate to emerge within the media, such that RTÉ could show in 1996 the ground-breaking documentary, Louis Lentin's *Dear Daughter*, none of these films came close to the sheer bleak brutality of *The Magdalene Sisters* (Peter Mullan, 2002)

or *Song for a Raggy Boy* (Aisling Walsh, 2003).[78] The latter, passed with a 15PG (over-15s on video/DVD) certificate, features for example a brother brutally kicking a boy to death. However, when the detailed horror as re-constructed from state records and personal testimony of those abused were published in 2004,[79] these graphic cinematic testimonies may also seem somewhat mild.

### SHEAMUS SMITH: IRISH FILM CENSORSHIP'S FIRST LIBERAL?

With the exception of James Montgomery and Liam O'Hora, all Censors prior to Sheamus Smith had been appointed by Fianna Fáil governments. According to Smith, a friend, knowing that he had been a media adviser to Fine Gael leader Garret FitzGerald, who was elected Taoiseach in 1983, asked him to recommend him for the post of Censor as Hall was nearing retirement in 1986. While the friend had considerable audio-visual experience, he was deemed to be too old for the appointment, and Smith himself was then approached and offered the position as the eighth Official Film Censor. While the position is a political appointment, Smith had little official contact with his ministers, and though he liaised with senior civil servants when issues, often financial rather than policy, emerged, he never viewed himself as a civil servant, but someone whose office happened to be serviced by civil servants from the Department of Justice. Measured against his predecessors, he has also been the most open of all Censors and regularly granted interviews to the media (and eventually, as noted in the Introduction, in 1998, twelve years after taking office, deposited the censors' reports going back to the 1920s in the National Archives).

In a 1994 interview, Smith revealed that in the sixteen years prior to his appointment in September 1986 as Official Film Censor, a total of 4,976 films were cut by Irish film censors.[80] He explained in another interview that the extensive cutting of films by his predecessors was often at the insistence of distributors in order to get a wider certificate (though the evidence presented in earlier chapters of this book disputes this):

> I don't approve of [cutting]. I think that a film is a director's work and he is the only one really entitled to cut it. Therefore I avoid it. I won't do it on request and I rarely do it anyway.[81]

In this context, Smith offered a redefinition of his task similar to the renaming of the BBFC in the 1980s. Accordingly, his job was not to censor, but to classify films. Smith argued[82] that 'if you look not just at the UK but at other countries around the world, by and large most films tend to have the same classification and the same would apply to video.' As a result, he encouraged his mentors at Justice to consider changing the title of his office, though he was well aware that should such an amendment be put before the houses of the Oireachtas, a far broader and perhaps less desirable range of changes to film censorship might be put forward by those from the left as much as from the right, something the experience of video censorship shows, as is discussed in the next chapter.

Smith's desire to change the nomenclature of his office to reflect a more liberal regime, however, did not indicate any lessening of the importance of film censorship.

The Censorship of Films Act, 1923, Smith told a journalist in 1995, was 'marvellous' because it had stood the test of time,[83] a view he reiterated during an interview in 2000.[84] With this support for the subjective criteria of the Act and a reconceptualizing of his own role, it was hardly surprising that Smith sought to claim that he was not ultimately responsible for any censorship affecting a film; in effect, he was not a censor. In an interview[85] he placed the blame for banning films on the Appeal Board.

> It's really the Appeal Board who ban a film ... Every distributor has the right to appeal, so while I refused to give [*Bad Lieutenant*, Abel Ferrara, 1992] a certificate that doesn't mean it's banned. It then [went] to the Appeal Board and they looked at it and they decided in their wisdom that it was unsuitable for general consumption in Ireland.

Despite such blatant (if playful) obfuscation of his role, clearly intended to emphasize his liberal credentials, he was by far the most consistently liberal of all Irish Censors, banning *only* ten theatrically-released films and cutting *only* sixteen others during his almost seventeen years in office, 1986–2003. Additionally, he reduced the over-16s category to over-15s, and in 2001 created the 12PG and 15PG categories, allowing a degree of parental involvement in cinemagoing decisions hitherto forbidden, but, simultaneously, creating the anomaly of there being no over-15s or over-16s certificates, unlike in the UK. As central to his policy was the avoiding, as much as possible, the cutting of films, the approaches by Smith and his deputies, Jerome Hegarty and Audrey Conlon, need to be scrutinized on this score.

Besides the feature films he cut, he also cut two trailers: *Romero* (John Duigan, 1989), and *Men in Black* (Barry Sonnenfeld, 1997), from which the word 'shitometer' and a dog saying 'Kiss my furry little butt' were taken out.[86] Indeed, that he did not cut the film is important in that it clearly shows his understanding of the importance of context, something which many of his predecessors did not. All except four of the films were cut between 1986 and 1991, or during his first five years in office. The cuts are not too dissimilar to those of his predecessor, with, for example, a 'bathtub copulation' scene 'reduced' in the first film he cut, *About Last Night...* (Edward Zwick, 1986),[87] which is based on David Mamet's play *Sexual Perversity in Chicago*. A few days later he cut the distasteful poor live-action comic book adaptation *Howard the Duck* (William Huyck, 1986) so as to remove erotic scenes in a health club, any nudes, and 'all suggestion' of a sexual relationship between the duck and the female character Beverly.[88] In 1987, the Australian Academy Award winner, the satire *Bliss* was edited to conform to the over-16s category. This required that a 'fornication' scene on a restaurant table was cut, as were a fish falling between a woman's legs, and, as already noted, an incest scene in which the central character's daughter performs oral sex on her coke-dealing brother for drugs.[89] The other film cut that year was *Playbirds* (Willy Roe, 1978, GB), a soft porn film, from which scenes of models being photographed, including of a nude policewoman with 'explicit poses,' and a sequence in a massage parlour, were cut so as to achieve an over-18s certificate. Also cut were scenes of girls astride a man on a table, and a burning girl in front of a cross.[90] The following year, 1988, thirty-two, mainly dialogue cuts, were excised by Hegarty from *A Night on the Town* (aka *Adventures in Babysitting*, Chris Columbus, 1987). However, this last major intervention which sought to suppress words such as Jesus, bitch, pissed, shit, ass, scum, sucker, and jeez, was cancelled after appeal.[91] Another film cut in 1988 was *Prince, a Sign of the Times* (Prince, 1987) from which a scene was cut featuring rock star Prince and the Cat ascending the stairs, divesting their clothes as they do so, and meeting at a rising heart under a neon sign with the words, 'Love' – 'Sex'. Cat lays back as he comes down on her and she embraces his body with her leg. 'Amputate leg,' the Censor humorously ordered.[92]

The first recorded comment Smith made about any of his decisions concerned the next film he cut, the children's feature, *Big* (Penny Marshall, 1988), since adapted as a Broadway musical and possibly the most enjoyable and best of the body switching sub-genre which includes such films as *Freaky Friday* (Gary Nelson, 1977) remade by Mark Waters in 2003, *Like Father, like Son* (Rod Daniel, 1987) and *Vice Versa* (Brian Gilbert, 1988). (This film also is somewhat similar to *Vice Versa* [Peter Ustinov, 1948, GB], the first father-son comedy.) Justifying cutting the line by Tom Hanks – 'Who the fuck do you think you are?' – in order to award the film an under-12s with adult certificate rather than an over-15s which the word 'fuck' would have required,[93] he told an interviewer that he regarded the line as 'totally gratuitous and unnecessary'.[94] Yet, arguably the word, whether gratuitous or not, is less problematic than the boy-man discovering sexual pleasure with his new woman-friend, even if their union is figured only in terms of his leaving childish things behind, drinking coffee and acquiring a new urgency about being a grown man. In 1989 Smith cut only one film, *Pet Sematary* (Mary Lambert, 1989), a Stephen King adaptation, which had two cuts imposed on it.[95] Concern over imitative knifing behaviour must have prompted the cutting of two rather different films in 1990, *The Krays* (Peter Medak, 1990, GB),[96] based on the infamous London gangster twin brothers, and the action-packed *Die Hard 2* (Renny Harlin, 1990),[97] from which such scenes were reduced or deleted. The extensive sex scenes in the triangular story, *Zandalee* (Sam Pillsbury, 1991), featuring Nicolas Cage and Erika Anderson, were too much for the Censor, who cut four scenes amounting to just over three minutes of the film. These included in a brothel, a 'copulation' scene, a woman's bottom being rubbed with olive oil and cocaine, the line, 'We'll fuck like animals,' and a confession box scene which was totally removed.[98]

The next year, 1992, almost seventy years after national film censorship had been introduced in Ireland, was the first year in which no film was either cut or banned for theatrical release. There were only two appeals, and those were against the certificates awarded to *Wayne's World* (Penelope Spheeris, 1992), which had its over-15s certificate reduced to under-12s accompanied,[99] and *Far and Away* (Ron Howard, 1992), which had its over-15s certificate upheld by the Board.[1] No other films were cut until 1995 when *Highlander 3, The Sorcerer* (Andy Morahan, 1994, Canada/France/GB) had a sex scene cut which opens with a man sucking a woman's nipple in order to achieve an over-15s rating.[2] The following year, scenes of mutilation, a man falling on a fire accompanied by the line 'We'll be smelling that all night,' knife throwing, and a man's intestines exposed after contact with helicopter blades, were cut from John Woo's *Broken Arrow* (1996),[3] while the only feature film cut in 1997 was David Cronenberg's *Crash*, in which the director completes his obsession with the transforming or mutilating body, the focus of much of his *oeuvre*. In this instance, the single cut, as is discussed in the next chapter, was designed to inhibit its video rather than theatrical release. During the next three years, only one further film was cut, *The Honest Courtesan* (aka *Dangerous Beauty*, Marshall Herskovitz, 1998) in 1999, but that was by the Board for lower certification purposes. Deputy Censor Audrey Conlon had awarded the film an over-18s certificate without cuts, but the distributor appealed the rating. The Board then ordered cut a scene near the beginning of the film where a mother with the aid of a male model is teaching her daughter the ways of a courtesan, a total of 71 seconds, thus, rating it as over-15s.[4] Rather than cut the film, the distributor accepted the higher certificate as Conlon had originally proposed. This was the first and only film cut by the Board appointed in June 1997 (and the last cut made by the Appeal Board as of April 2004), chaired for the first time by a woman, Barbara Culleton, though it varied the certificates on four other films, three of them from over-18s to over-15s: *The Object of My Affection* (Nicholas Hytner, 1998), *Kevin and Perry go Large* (Ed Bye, 2000, GB/USA), and *Any Given Sunday* (Oliver Stone, 1999), while one certificate, *Wild Wild West* (Barry Sonnenfeld, 1999), was reduced from an over 15s to an over 12s.

The Appeal Board, chaired by John Carroll until 1997, made its first and only serious divergence from Smith's approach to censorship within eight months of his appointment. According to Smith[5] early in his tenure he was searching for a film to test the Board's mettle and so decided to ban *Personal Services* (Terry Jones, 1987, GB). It was the only banning decision during Smith's time in office to be reversed by the Board, which passed the film without cuts and with an over-18s certificate by a vote of 6 to 2.[6] Indeed, the Board had not met for almost three years before viewing *Personal Services*. Smith or Hegarty banned a further nine films during the following decade: the feminist film *Working Girls* (Lizzie Borden, 1986) which de-eroticizes the sex industry and presents it as a mundane alternative to traditional forms of work was banned by Hegarty, in 1987;[7] next banned was *Whore* (Ken Russell, 1991) which highlights the 'profession's' more sordid and negative aspects in 1991;[8] in 1993 Smith banned the dark uncompromising cult film *Bad Lieutenant*, a decision upheld by the Board, though two of its members favoured an over-18s certificate;[9] in 1994 *U.F.O. – The Movie* (Tony Dow, 1993, GB)[10] and *Lake Consequence* (Rafael Eisenman, 1992) were banned in decisions which were not appealed,[11] as was *Natural Born Killers* (Oliver Stone, 1994), in the most controversial banning of his tenure in office;[12] in 1995, the partly-pornographic *Showgirls* (Paul Verhoeven, 1995) was rejected;[13] in 1996, *From Dusk till Dawn* (Robert Rodrigues), which delights in the grossest of visceral experiences, suffered a similar fate, a decision not appealed;[14] and in 1997, *Preaching to the Perverted* (Stuart Urban, 1997, GB),[15] was banned, a decision not appealed. This latter film concerns a British MP (played by Tom Bell) who, in order to bring a prosecution against sado-masochistic clubs, recruits a young computer salesman (Christian Anholt) to infiltrate a club run by an American dominatrix.[16]

While the Board upheld all Smith's banning orders except for *Personal Services*, appeals against cuts or age limitation were treated much more liberally. Of the 42 theatrical film appeals against the category of limited certificates from September 1986 to April 2003, the Censor's decision was upheld only in 18 instances. Nine over-18s certificates were changed to over-15s or 15PG; one of Hegarty's over-16s was altered to a general (*A Night on the Town*), one of only 2 films where cuts were appealed; 5 over-15s were amended to over-12s; 5 over-15s were altered to under-12s accompanied by an adult; while *Return of the Jedi* (Richard Marquand, 1983) originally awarded a parental guidance was given a general rating. This period also saw one of those rare instances, at least in recent decades, where the Board altered a certificate but demanded a cut as a result. Thus, in *Look Who's Talking Too* (Amy Heckerling, 1990), the Board reduced the over-15s certification to under-12s accompanied, but deleted a scene that featured the cutting of an umbilical cord and the accompanying blood.[17]

*Personal Services* concerns the kinky sexual practices provided for her clients by real-life brothel keeper and prostitute 'Madame Cyn,' Cynthia Payne, played by Julie Walters. While Smith did not comment publicly at the time on his decision and only retrospectively stated that he banned *Personal Services* to assess the Board, the reason that he might have rejected this particular film is no doubt due to issues around the appropriate representation of women. A theme running through his tenure as Censor has echoes of the proto-feminism emanating from the BBFC in the 1980s and 1990s. Thus, films were occasionally banned or cut to conform to a feminist agenda asserting infringement of civil or human rights because certain representations were deemed 'pornographic,' a position discussed in the next chapter in relation to the 'video nasties' controversy of the 1980s. It is all the more ironic, therefore, that the censors misread, or refused to accept, the representational complexities of *Working Girls*. Despite it being set among female prostitutes, they are sympathetically portrayed as the film places their work in an economic context while refusing the voyeurism which is a feature of even short scenes set in brothels within mainstream cinema. Indeed, there was a rare defence of a film in the Oireachtas when Senator David Norris singled out *Working Girls* as an 'excellent film' which

> has some images that would be disturbing to comfortable middle-class people because it shows the involvement of comfortable middle-class people in the exploitation of women through prostitution. It is precisely because those images are disturbing that it gets banned.[18]

Less problematic then was *Showgirls*. Representing women working as strippers in Las Vegas, it was banned, because, according to Michael Dwyer, Smith 'objected to the exploitative treatment of women throughout the film and, in particular, to a rape scene.'[19] *U.F.O.*, on the other hand, concerns a sexist comedian, played by the infamous, crude and often misogynistic Roy 'Chubby' Brown, who is kidnapped by twenty-fifth-century feminists while he is performing in Blackpool, England. In an increasingly popular trope of the male as mother or as maternal vessel such as in the very different films *Junior* (Ivan Reitman, 1994) and *The Fly* (David Cronenberg, 1996), he returns home to find himself pregnant and gives birth. Dwyer commented that 'it is most likely that the consistent vulgarity and lavatorial humour of the film caused it to be banned.'[20]

Like his predecessors, Smith was obliged to rule on more than one film that could be interpreted as blasphemous or profane, and like those before him, he assumed an air of extreme caution when doing so. *Life of Brian*, banned by Hall in 1980, presumably on grounds of blasphemy, was re-submitted to Smith in 1987 under the 'seven year rule' when he gave it an over-18 certificate.[21] It was eventually screened in Dublin in June 1988, when, one assumes, its alleged blasphemy and notoriety no longer carried the subversive and controversial edge it once had.[22] The most prominent film censorship controversy of the 1980s, both internationally and in Ireland, concerned blasphemy. The American and British campaigns against Martin Scorsese's *The Last Temptation of Christ* (1988) were monitored closely in Ireland. In a triumphant expansion of the moral crusade which had been such a feature of the Catholic church's victories in the anti-abortion and divorce referendums in 1983 and 1986, respectively, the recently-appointed Archbishop of Dublin, Dr Desmond Connell, denounced the film, sight unseen, and called, indirectly, for its banning.[23] A fundamentalist/charismatic group, the Dublin Inter-Denominational Christian Churches, took up the clerical cudgels with all the intensity of that displayed against *From the Manger to the Cross* in 1913. Unlike on that occasion, though, opposition to a ban on the film was loudly articulated. The *Irish Times*, for example, in an ironic reversal of its role in the earlier controversy, carried a number of articles favouring the release of the film, and its letters page featured a lively debate on the topic.[24] Perhaps symbolically, the moment when the 'popular will' was most clearly displayed was following a debate on RTÉ's *The Late Late Show* in September 1988. The presenter of the show, Gay Byrne, asked the audience to vote on whether the film should be allowed in Ireland. By a majority of about ten to one the audience indicated support for its Irish release. The reasons for such a response may be complex, not least of which may be the antipathy in Ireland to the state and its institutions instructing people how to act. On the other hand, it could be interpreted as a sign of cultural maturity, even a further whiff of liberalism. Such a deduction was both premature and misleading.[25]

While Smith certified *Last Temptation* uncut with an over-18s rating, the banning five years later of *Bad Lieutenant* was unsignalled. The film focuses on a corrupt and degenerate policeman (Harvey Keitel), who is a cocaine and gambling addict, as he investigates the rape of a nun by two young men. The trajectory of the film follows Keitel, a lapsed Catholic, who uses this to seek redemption for his waywardness. Meanwhile, the nun refuses to identity the rapists whom she has forgiven. The film was banned because Smith regarded it as blasphemous and profane.[26] The Board agreed, with 6 (Ms Phil Brady, Eugene Phelan, Joe Mulrooney, the Revd John Dardis, the Revd Cecil Faul and John Carroll) against the film, and 2 (Ed McDonald and Mona McGarry) in favour of awarding it an over-18s certificate.[27] The film's only Irish public showing was at the 1993 Dublin Film Festival, but as the *Sunday Independent*'s Ronan Farren commented,[28] it was hard to discover where Smith or the Board found the blasphemy, though the Censor did tell Colum Kenny that 'it was such a nasty piece of work that I did not think anyone would benefit from seeing it in Ireland.'[29] Such a misreading of the film belies the film's redemption of its anti-hero. After allowing the two rapists leave town with his gambling money so that they can start a new life, he is himself shot dead by the gangsters to whom he owes the money. The censors' approach was a case of isolating certain images or sections of scenes out of the film's overall context. Even if the film's texture owes more to Ferrara's earlier gritty dark work such as *Driller Killer* that Smith thought to censor a work on aesthetic or tonal grounds clearly goes beyond the role of the Censor. Indeed, there might be few films released if the measure for certification was whether or not an audience might benefit from seeing it. *From Dusk Till Dawn*, an unresolved generic hybrid that is ostensibly a vampire film mainly set in Mexico, was also banned because of 'gratuitous violence and profanity,'[30] but by the end of the 1990s, such apocalyptic and millenarian religious features as *End of Days* (Peter Hyams, 1999), *Stigmata* (Rupert Wainwright, 1999), and *Dogma* (Kevin Smith, 1999), which would probably have been banned even in the 1980s, were now allowed as part of the uninhibited exchange of discourses in Irish society which had been fought for, but resisted, for so long. It is noteworthy that Smith gave *End of Days* and *Stigmata* over-15s certificates, whereas the BBFC certified them as over-18s, while in 2004, *From Dusk Till Dawn* was certified over-18s for video/DVD release by new Censor John Kelleher.

While *Natural Born Killers* offers a critique of the media's exploitation of real-life crime, it disturbed many people not just in its failure to mete out a traditional narrative retribution to its protagonists, but in its mixing of fictional and non-fictional elements (which is typical of Oliver Stone such as in *JFK*) in a 'post-modern' representation of extreme 'mindless' violence. The film was screened at the Dublin Film Festival some months before Smith banned it in October 1994, a decision upheld by the Board with a vote of 6 to 1 three months later. The controversy that surrounded the film continued until April of the following year when a two-month run of the film was planned under club conditions at the Irish Film Centre (now the Irish Film Institute). The response by the state apparatus to these proposed screenings was to be a salutary experience for many, myself included as a member of the board of the Irish Film Institute at the time, when the full legal and administrative system was employed by the Department of Justice to stop the screenings.

By the time *Natural Born Killers* was viewed by the Irish Censor it was already the subject of considerable controversy internationally not least because of allegations of copycat killings in France and the USA and the likelihood of more to follow. This concern was fuelled by hysterical tabloid media in Britain and the USA which cited murders which could be blamed on the film. In the American case, a teenager couple, one with mental difficulties, were arrested in March 1995 in connection with murder and attempted murder, and when the girl's father claimed they had watched *Natural Born Killers* more than twenty times the connection was established between their actions and the film. This particular case became a *cause célèbre* when writer John Grisham declared that there was 'overwhelming evidence to link the film to the crime' because the perpetrators had no history of violent crime, and he threatened to sue production company Warner Bros and director Oliver Stone under product-liability law. Perhaps more pertinently, the French case occurred on 4 October 1994, exactly one week before Smith banned the film. In this instance, a couple shot dead 3 policemen and a taxi driver and the press characterized the couple responsible as 'France's natural born killers'.[31] One of the few balanced accounts in the Irish media of this and other such controversies was Ian O'Doherty's article 'Copycat Killings Scare Top Film Men' in the *Irish Independent* in 1998.[32] O'Doherty recounted the events in Japan following the release there of *Scream* (Wes Craven, 1996) after which a series of murders were blamed on the film. (*Scream 2*, [Wes Craven, 1997], based on a copycat killer trying to emulate his predecessor in *Scream*, incidentally, had its Japanese release postponed as a result.) O'Doherty also mentions the false link made between the killing of toddler Jamie Bolger and the *Child's Play* video series. Other films in which 'deranged' people have drawn energy from cinematic representations include the cases in 1983 of John Hincklie, who became obsessed with Jodie Foster's persona in *Taxi Driver* (Martin Scorsese, 1976) and 'stalked' her, and the case of 14-year-old Michael Carneal, who killed 3 of his schoolmates in 1997, ostensibly influenced by *The Basketball Diaries* (Scott Kalvert, 1995), a biographical account of New York junkie-poet Jim Carrol (played by Leonardo DiCaprio), in which a dream sequence features him shooting his teachers and classmates.[33] Another copycat story highlighted by Bernadette Murphy was of two men who in 1995 sprayed flammable liquid into a New York subway token booth, flicking in a match and setting fire to the booth clerk, in a scene replicating one in *Money Train* (Joseph Ruben, 1995). The scene in the film, however, was itself based on real-life events that occurred in 1988 and before.[34] Finally, in 2000, three Mersyside teenagers were found guilty of the killing the previous year of another teenager in a way which the media regarded as paralleling a scene in *Reservoir Dogs* (Quentin Tarantino, 1993), released six years earlier. As two of the *Irish Independent's* headlines put it after the verdict was announced, 'Schoolboys guilty of *Reservoir Dogs* murder' and 'Movie's sick torture scene recalled in horror killing'[35] An earlier article[36] declared that the boys 'acted out' a scene from the film as they beat, stripped, doused with petrol, and stabbed the boy to death in a playground at night, one of them reprising the song from the film sung by the criminal-torturer as he dances and inflicts pain on his captive, scenes which, in the film, happen indoors. That there were extenuating circumstances: the boys were drinking vodka and cider; there was jealousy over the dead boy's relationship with one of their ex-girlfriends; and the claim by the defendants that the dead boy had asked to be beaten up as part of a compensation scam to buy a motorbike; were sidelined in favour of references to the film's most controversial scene.[37]

Rather than enter the philosophical mirrors of Jean Baudrillard's simulacrum and celebrate the continuity between reality and image, it is important to understand the difference 'normal' people make between the two. Public and private fantasy is not somehow identical with real actions, nor can it be said that a publicly articulated fantasy, such as a novel or a film, is more dangerous or (personally) motivating than a private one. In short, while Murphy may note research which concludes that 'depicted violence can feed the inclinations of an already violent nature,' the important point must be the already pathological tendencies within the viewer. Notwithstanding her attempt to offer a critique of real-life violence on television, the very topic of Stone's film, she joyously declared that *Natural Born Killers* was 'quickly relegated to the bin' by the Irish Censor.[38]

A similar attitude to film and the media was displayed sometime later in the *Independent*'s articles on *Resevoir Dogs* in which the Censor's verdict was accompanied by a contemporaneous statement from four US *medical* bodies claiming that there was a link between violence in television, music, video games and films and increasing violence among children. However, yet again, it is not a fixed or fully determined relationship. The statement went on to say that 'prolonged viewing of media violence *can* lead to emotional desensitization towards violence in real life,' (emphasis added) although no methodology or details of the studies were included in the report.[39] An Irish contributor to the debate was Olive Braiden, director of Dublin's Rape Crisis Centre, who took issue with an article by Steve MacDonagh which asserted that 'the cause of sexual violence goes deeper than pornography.'[40] While she agreed that it was wrong to lay the blame for all violence against women at the door of pornography, nevertheless, she favoured 'the elimination of pornography by censorship' which 'would remove one pernicious form of human degradation.' But, she went on, 'it would not alter the ideology of a society which produces and tolerates it,' adding, in a positive move, that the way forward was through 're-education'.[41] In an interview in 1999, Braiden re-stated her view that pornographic films were contributing to the increasingly sadistic nature of sex crimes, though she accepted that 'a right-minded person' would not act out a pornographic scene they had seen, and that pornography was just *one* factor in the growth of sex attacks. (She also drew attention to the 'addiction' of porn-watchers and their escalating appetite, which is explored in the following chapter.)[42] As such, these conclusions hardly warrant every adult being denied access to representations of violence.

The origin of the modern copycat panic can be traced from the allegations which surrounded the killing of a man in England by thugs who claimed they were influenced by *A Clockwork Orange*.[43] This was accepted by director Stanley Kubrick who withdrew the film from circulation in Britain. However, in 2000, the film was released uncut in Ireland and Britain following Kubrick's death the previous year. Republican Senator Bob Dole, among many other right-wingers, attacked *Natural Born Killers* as evidence that Hollywood was producing 'nightmares of depravity'.[44] In this way, the copycat crime was re-born, and this was the reason given by Smith, the Appeal Board, and Department of Justice officials for the decision to ban the film, though in a 2000 interview, Smith claims to have been unaware of this controversy when he banned it. Of course, what even this cursory glimpse offers is a highlighting of the motivation behind censorship: fear that the audience is unable to think for themselves and belief that they are unable to generate (dangerous) ideas on their own and hence the notion that all immoral, illegal or otherwise odious actions – directly or indirectly through a process of naturalization – derive from public (media) articulations. As one horror writer flippantly replied when asked about assuming responsibility for copycat actions, such people should be sued for plagiarism!

*Natural Born Killers* had been viewed by the British Board of Film Classification in autumn 1994 just as the tabloid print media called for its banning. Perhaps as a means of deflecting the intensity of the media pressure, the BBFC postponed any decision until after an investigation it had requested was completed by the Federal Bureau of Investigation to ascertain the veracity of the allegations of copycat murders. Subsequent to an inconclusive report, a certificate was issued in early 1995. As Oliver Stone put it in an interview with the *Irish Times* after Smith banned the film, 'There's not one single instance of any murder directly linked with my film, and that is the view of the FBI, too.'[45] Even if there was a directly imitative crime, the crucial issue of cause or motivation would also have to be examined as well as the broader context of social and familial formation and responsibility. However, Smith had a different notion of copycat killings in mind when he banned the film.

Declaring that he was not influenced by any outside commentary or agency, he stated that it was the reality of IRA violence which lead him to ban the film.

> I was certainly very aware that one was living in the context of a violent society. The IRA were riding rough shot over the country with ... two or three [bank robberies] a day. People were being shot right, left and center. In the context of that, and the fact that we were living in a violent society in Ireland. ... (I would be very violently anti-IRA, so I would be influenced by that).[46]

He added that the film's 'wall to wall violence' made 'light of the fact' that such behaviour was seen to be acceptable 'or even amusing,' and pointed out that most of the people 'didn't have any reason to be killed ... It was gratuitous violence.' When this attitude was extended to actual representations of Irish political violence, it led to strange anomalies. These include *In the Name of the Father* (Jim Sheridan, 1993, GB/Ireland/USA) which successfully adapted to a neat and dramatic Hollywood structure the 'awkward' political history of the Guildford Four's wrongful imprisonment by the British justice system being awarded an over-18s certificate even though it received an over-15s in Britain; and the hunger-strike film *Some Mother's Son* (Terry George, 1996, Ireland, also co-scripted by Sheridan) similarly been given an over-18s certification, but which was unanimously reduced by the Appeal Board to over-15s.

Whatever about Smith's awareness of the political and cultural environment into which a film is released and which undeniably necessarily affects the text, his argument about the killings as undeserved or 'gratuitous' deserves some discussion, in that it points up a particular 'realist' aesthetic that, despite his refreshing liberalism, links him to his predecessors. Indeed, there is the implicit and dangerous suggestion that if those murdered were like the 'victims' of the serial killer in *SE7EN* (David Fincher, 1995) – guilty of sin – it would be okay. That the killings are at times arbitrary is central to the project of *Natural Born Killers*. But then, like many cultural texts that move beyond the literal into a space that 'slips' and blurs otherwise distinct categories and (moral) structures and causes one to think critically or differently, state or institutional reception is necessarily challenged and moreover tries to stifle the voice. This seems to be supported in any number of highly visceral graphic and violent films which have been approved, but which are clearly coded in terms of fantasy, or at least beyond the mundane and everyday, or are mindless and do not require the viewer to think. As Stone put it, 'the film is intended to make people think about their own relationship to violence, and their own relationship to television.'[47] The film, though, was to have a further profound impact on Irish film institutions.

The Appeal Board agreed with Smith's assessment of *Natural Born Killers* after he made a strong recommendation that his ban should be upheld. Viewing the film after the media hype has died down, it is hard not to conclude that Smith was panicked into his decision to ban it, or he failed to read the film with any degree of sophistication. It is difficult to imagine how anyone could seriously believe that the film, with its myriad of distancing devices and its critique of the cynicism of the media, could induce any socially adjusted or 'normal' individual, especially politically-motivated activists, to kill.

In a grand tradition of censors, Smith placed great emphasis on the 'dignity' of the office. As he put it – even if somewhat ironic – in an interview shortly after his appointment, the Film Censor's job is 'one of the few honours we have in Ireland.'[48] Such accrual of power and prestige to the position of Film Censor is designed on the one hand to disguise what is essentially a repressive job, and on the other hand, to frighten critics of film censorship into believing that the limits of permissiveness have been reached. Thus, when the Irish Film Centre (IFC, now IFI) cinemas included in its April–May 1995 programme a total of 240 screenings of the film, Smith felt that his 'dignity' as Film Censor and the relevance and authority of the 1923 Act was being undermined. The IFC was able to justify such apparent flagrant breach of the law, with recourse to the practice – established by the Irish Film Society (IFS) founded in 1936, and accepted by the state since 1939 – whereby films screened under club conditions could be screened without having to submit them for Irish certification. This practice was continued by the IFS's successors, the Federation of Irish Film Societies and Access Cinema, which even in the 1940s could get away with showing banned films, and film (club) festivals such as, among others, Dublin, Galway and Cork. In the 1970s a new element was introduced into the uncensored films equation. During the time of the Project Cinema Club, 1976–1978, and the Irish Film Theatre, 1977–1985, regular screenings of films were run under club conditions. Whereas Film Society members bought a ticket for a season of films, once people became members of the Project or IFT film clubs by paying an annual fee, they were free to attend any screening and even bring along a guest who was not a member of the club and simply pay at the box office. (This remains the operational procedure of all film clubs, though film festivals operate slightly differently in usually not allowing guests to be admitted.) The Project Cinema Club – a 16mm alternative cinema mainly showing contextualized film seasons – received the attention of the authorities on only one occasion, when the banned film *Ulysses* was screened. A visit and a warning from detectives was not followed up with a prosecution, if even such was possible.⁴⁹ The IFT, a company set up by the Arts Council, was more cautious in its dealing with the authorities. Before opening the cinema, the Arts Council approached the Department of Justice to enquire whether it had any objection to the IFT being established under club conditions. While not opposing the proposal, Justice warned that it could withdraw its benign attitude to the venture at any time. Following the demise of the IFT in 1985, the film club void was not filled until the opening in 1989 of the Lighthouse Cinema in Dublin's Middle Abbey Street. This joint venture between the Irish Film Institute and exhibitor Neil Connolly was viewed by the Institute as a forerunner of the planned Irish Film Centre. Showing a mixture of art house films with the Censors' certificates and non-certified films under club conditions, Sheamus Smith gave his endorsement to the project when the cinema's opening film, Peter Greenaway's *The Cook, The Thief, His Wife & Her Lover* (1989, France/Holland) was passed by him uncut with an over-18s rating. As Smith told me,⁵⁰ had the film been destined for a mainstream commercial cinema it would not have been treated so leniently, since the Lighthouse, like all other art cinema institutions, was patronized in the main by a middle-class (informed) clientele, and, as a result, such screenings were left largely untouched by the state apparatus, at least until the *Natural Born Killers* controversy.

The Irish Film Center had opened in 1992 as the national center for film in Ireland. Supported by the Arts Council and other state institutions, it is, nevertheless, an independent organization with an elected board. That independence was seriously compromised during the events surrounding *Natural Born Killers*. Smith was quite willing to 'turn a blind eye,' as he described how the authorities viewed the bypassing of film censorship by the IFC and other organizations, if the IFC showed the film for a few days to 'people who cared for cinema as opposed to treating it as pure entertainment,' but he objected to it being used as a 'vehicle for making money,' an important part of the cash-strapped IFC's motivation for showing it for such an unusually long run. Of course, should *Natural Born Killers* have been a commercial success, the IFI, as a non-profit distributing body, would have been in a strong position to fulfil its remit to bring culturally important or interesting films, as well as its education and archive programmes, to the widest possible constituency. While Smith did not regard the screenings as defying his office as such, he thought they were 'against the spirit' of the state's benign attitude to film clubs. However, as in all such things, a degree of black propaganda was in evidence with the view held by him that the membership fee at the IFC was being reduced to 'virtually nothing' to encourage a mainstream audience to visit the IFC. While this was untrue – the IFI's policy has always been the fostering (and encouraging) of a film culture and film appreciation, therefore pricing policy has never been on the basis of excluding certain categories of people – it served to colour how the institution was viewed by Smith and the Department of Justice.

The first screening of the film at the IFC was scheduled 1.00 p.m. on April Fools' Day 1995. Despite the long run of the film, it was contextualized with a public forum exploring film censorship and accompanied by a season of films which had been the subject of censorship debates in Ireland and elsewhere. These films fall into two categories: Those that were submitted to the Irish Censor, which have already been mentioned in this study – *Don't Look Now*, *Straw Dogs*, *Viridiana* and *The Devils*, the latter two banned, the others cut – and those which were never submitted. This latter group of films included the highly controversial *Salò, or The 120 Days of Sodom* (Pier Paolo Pasolini, 1975, Italy), which is an adaptation of the Marquis de Sade's novel re-set in Italy during World War Two when fascists abuse adolescents in a myriad of sexually perverse ways; *In the Realm of the Senses* (*Ai No Corrida*, aka *L'Empire des Sens*, Nagisa Oshima, 1976, Japan/France), an intensely erotic film in which a sexually-obsessive couple make the ultimate commitment; *La Béte* (Walerian Borowczyk, 1996, France); and the erotic *WR – Mysteries of the Organism* (Dušan Makavejev, 1971, Yugoslavia), some of which had been shown at the Irish Film Theatre under club conditions in the early 1980s. What is most ironic about the events which were to follow is the attitude taken by the Department of Justice to these films. While *Natural Born Killers*, like *The Devils*, had been banned, the other, and much more sexually and violently explicit films, which had not been submitted to the Censor, could be screened because they had not been refused a certificate and, thus, in the warped logic of Justice, did not present a challenge to Irish film censorship.

Anticipating annoyance from the authorities, the Film Institute had sought to defuse criticism of its proposed screening of the film by writing to the Minister for Justice, Nora Owen, on 15 March 1995 pointing out that the IFC regularly showed films which had not been certified and stated that the cinemas operated under strict club conditions in such circumstances. It was acknowledged that Sheamus Smith had 'expressed his anxiety' that people under the age of 16 might gain access to the film, though he, too, was written to by the Institute assuring him that such would not be the case. (Why he chose this age category was never explained as the IFC operates an over-18s policy for unclassified films.) Smith subsequently told me he had initiated the response by Justice by drawing their attention to the screenings and declaring that he regarded them as 'high-handed' and driven by 'commercial exploitation'. While he was willing to ignore a few screenings of the film for those with a 'genuine interest in *odd* movies,' he would not countenance such a blatant affront to his office. (Emphasis added.)[51]

Following Smith's approach, the department made enquiries and the Garda Siochana were asked to check up on the IFC cinemas' criteria for membership. The minister did not respond to the letter from the Film Institute, but on 31 March 1995, the day before the first screening of the film, one of the minister's advisers, Pat Murray, was phoned by the Director of the Film Institute, Sheila Pratschke, who expressed concern that members of the Serious Crime Squad had visited the IFC twice during the previous week. Later that day, an Assistant Secretary of the Department of Justice, Diarmuid Cole, phoned Pratschke to express concern that if the film was shown it would make it appear as if the office of Film Censor and the Appeal Board were irrelevant. He added, menacingly, that the Institute's action was calling into question the whole existence of film clubs, and he threatened to take procedures which would be to the detriment of all clubs, while also repeating the allegations about copycat killings. Cole stated that they would be driven to take extreme measures if the screening went ahead and added that film clubs would be tolerated as long as they catered for *minority* audiences. Later it was revealed that the Department of Justice had been in contact with the Attorney-

General's office, which in turn was taking Counsel's opinion on the matter. Though then, and subsequently, it was never made explicit, what was behind the threat was the fear that the screenings at the IFC would bring in a mainstream commercial cinema audience, namely a working-class audience believed to be without any sophistication in reading films and which in the main did not frequent film clubs such as the IFC.

With this threat directed against the Institute, an emergency board meeting was called for the following morning only three hours before the first scheduled screening. As the debate shifted back and forth on the relative merits of proceeding with the screenings, it is probable that had a vote been taken a majority of the board would have been in favour of defying Justice. That was until a further phone call from Cole, the essence of which was the direct threat that an injunction would be served on the Institute if the film was exhibited. With such an explicit threat to the viability of the Institute, then, unlike now, in some financial difficulty, and the broader attack on film clubs which could affect film festivals and others, the board decided to withdraw the film. *Natural Born Killers* was replaced by *Pulp Fiction* (Quentin Tarantino, 1994) in the programme.[52]

There was a finale to this sorry tale. A couple of weeks later following a request from the Institute, a delegation (myself included as a member of the Film Institute Board), met the Minister for State with responsibility for film censorship, Fine Gael's Austin Curry. The minister was accompanied by a civil servant from central casting. The minister refused to allow even a short run for *Natural Born Killers*, and, as a result, the film was not screened at the IFC until February 1998 when it was shown twice as part of a Quentin Tarantino season that also included the then-banned *From Dusk till Dawn*. *Natural Born Killers* was eventually certified for video and DVD release in 2001. One of the issues which the Institute's delegation wished to explore was the lack of legal certainty for film clubs. While the minister was willing to entertain the idea of the possible regulation of such (il)legal entities, he also enquired of the Institute whether in fact this was in its best interests, and, more broadly, of the type of screening practices for clubs and societies going back to the 1930s. Aware, perhaps, that its middle-class constituency had been reasonably well served by the legal space available to it, the Institute has not pursued the issue of regulating film clubs. It has accepted, at least for now, the limits to which it can defy the state while being able to strengthen its own organization and membership base.

### JOHN KELLEHER AND CONSUMER CHOICE

Following his retirement as Film Censor in April 2003, Smith was succeeded by John Kelleher, whose formation, like Smith's, was in television and film production. A barrister with a master's degree in drama, Kelleher worked in RTÉ for many years, producing a range of programmes including (political) news and current affairs programmes *Newsbeat*, *Seven Days*, *The Politics Programme*, and the satirical review *Hall's Pictorial Weekly*; documentaries, including Cathal O'Shannon's award-winning *Even the Olives Are Bleeding* (1976) on the Spanish Civil War; and dramas such as *Strumpet City*, an adaptation of James Plunkett's widely acclaimed 1969 novel of Dublin life and trade unionism in the early part of the twentieth-century. He was appointed Controller of Programmes, RTÉ 1 Television in 1980 and launched the *Today Tonight* programme in the same year. In 1983 he left RTÉ to become managing director of the *Sunday Tribune*, and subsequently established his own film and television production company, Fastnet Films. He has produced six cinema films, including Mike Newell's *An Awfully Big Adventure* (1995, GB/Ireland), which, set in late 1940s Liverpool and based on Beryl Bainbridge's novel, is indebted to J.M. Barrie's *Peter Pan*. In addition, he co-wrote and produced the commercial Irish indigenous film, *Eat the Peach* (1986), in which the central characters, recently made redundant, are motivated by an engagement with American culture in the guise of an Elvis Presley film and subsequently build a 'wall of death' so they might defy gravity and all that it entails; produced six television drama series; and was executive producer for four years of TV3's weekly current affairs programme *Agenda*. He has also served on the board of Bord Scannán na hÉireann/Irish Film Board and is a member of the Royal Television Society; Film Makers Ireland; the Irish Film and Television Academy; and is chairman of the Programme Advisory Committee of the Media Production Unit of the Dublin Institute of Technology.

The only film Kelleher banned during his first year in office was *Spun* (Jonas Åkerlund, 2002, GB/France/USA), which (in an often frenetic and self-conscious style most associated with music videos of rapid editing, jump cuts, and other visual and aural techniques such as the extreme close-up), follows the fortunes of a series of characters during three days of sex and drug-taking in Las Vegas.[53] Later, the film was unanimously passed without cuts and with an over-18s certificate (also the BBFC's decision) by the Appeal Board. In a letter to Paul O'Higgins, the chairman of the Appeal Board, Kelleher – in a welcome development of explaining his actions following four decades of relative silence on the decision-making process – argued that 'because it depicts graphic and pervasive hard drug misuse, contains an unacceptable level of gratuitous violence and obscenity, contains scenes of sexual cruelty *and, for the most part, is devoid of any moral or redeeming value*' (emphasis added) he felt that he had to ban the film.[54] While he later explained in an interview[55] that he would have had no difficulty in certifying the film for the 'controlled conditions' of the cinema, its availability on video and DVD for home use made it incumbent on him to ban it because of the specific and detailed prohibitions contained in the Video Recordings Act, 1989, which also state that a film awarded a certificate for public exhibition automatically (and without further cuts) is given a video/DVD certificate, issues which are discussed in the next chapter, particularly with regard to David Cronenberg's *Crash*. The Board took a contrary view and unanimously reversed Kelleher's ban. Nevertheless, six months earlier, the same Board in its first consideration of a banned film or video, upheld, in a majority decision, Smith's decision to ban (for video distribution) the graphic rape/revenge film *Baise-Moi* (*Fuck Me*, Virginie Despentes, Coralie Trinh-Thi, France, 2000), and interestingly one which like the ever-controversial *I Spit on Your Grave* (aka *Day of the Woman*, Meir Zarchi, 1977) banned most recently in 2000 and discussed in the next chapter, could be described as a feminist text.[56]

In common with his predecessor, Kelleher invited two professionals experienced in the area of illegal drug misuse to view *Spun* with him, and they concurred with his decision. This use of those involved in healthcare and social problems was repeated with regard to another controversial sado-masochistic highly-charged French film *Irreversible* (Gaspar Noé, 2002, France) featuring graphic violence against women and sado-masochism, which was viewed by professionals in the area of rape-counselling and were used to support the Censor's decision to award, without cuts, an over-18s certificate.[57] Indeed, the making available of explicit, if also mainstream, material in Irish cinemas has extended such that Jane Campion's *In the Cut* (2003, GB), starring Meg Ryan which, uniquely for a Hollywood film, features an erect penis, was not only approved uncut by Kelleher with an over-18s limitation, but, even more surprisingly, not a single complaint about his decision ensued. Nevertheless, as with all censors, there are certain representations which remain 'taboo'. For the most part, these are not dissimilar to those observed by Smith and largely concern images of 'sexual violence,' followed by violence in general.

Having completed his first year in office, Kelleher signalled the introduction of a series of reforms within his office, all in the name of openness and the transformation of the 'service' to that of a 'consumer guide' to film. In that regard, plans were being laid for a two-way grid to be displayed on video/DVD boxes akin to that already pertaining to certain computer/playstation games where the four areas of Violence, Drugs, Sexual Content and Language would be categorized according to the range: None, Mild, Moderate and Strong. Additionally, he has commissioned a nationwide survey to ascertain what people want from the Censor's office. As part of these initiatives, Kelleher announced that explanations of his decisions would be made available on a website. He has also questioned the limited range of certificates available under the current regime – general, 12s, 12PG, 15PG and 18s – and has highlighted the absence of an over-15s (or similar) category under which it would be illegal for under-15s, even with parental guidance or permission to access the material. Consequently, many films which have been awarded a 15s certificate in the UK, have received an 18s certificate in Ireland.

Nevertheless, it is not expected that a 15s or 16s certificate will be re-introduced. Examples he cited of this anomaly are the prison drama *Animal Factory* (Steve Buscemi, 2000), *The Mother* (Roger Michell, 2003, GB) which features a 60-something widow in a relationship with her daughter's married lover, and *Ripley's Game* (*Il gioco di Ripley*, Liliana Cavani, 2002, USA/Italy/GB), a modern reworking of Patricia Highsmith's third Ripley novel.[58] 'Hard-core' pornography is unlikely to find its way into Irish shops and homes any time soon, at least via the Film Censor's office, though a potentially explosive legal challenge is in the process of being assessed by the High Court where affidavits have been lodged arguing that it is unconstitutional to deprive adults of the right to watch (any legal) representations of sex. Kelleher's view is that hard-core is 'unacceptable' because of its representation of women, with *Baise-Moi* described as 'totally gratuitous and exploitative'.[59]

Ironically, it was not *Spun* or a perception of censorship as repressive or overly restrictive which led to the only major controversy of Kelleher's first year in office, but his decision to award a 15PG certificate – rather than, as in the UK, an over-18s – to *The Passion of the Christ* (Mel Gibson, 2004). Many, including proponents of a liberal film censorship regime for adults, questioned the wisdom of allowing 15-year-olds, not to mention (irresponsible) adults bringing younger children, to such a relentlessly violent and gory film which fits within horror rather than the religious generic tradition.[60] Beyond criticism of the film's alleged anti-semitism, the general thrust of news reports and comment has been that the film reflects a fundamentalist Christian – especially Catholic – perspective of the last twelve hours of Christ's life.

Some Irish reviewers were not too kind to the film. Pat Stacey, echoing many others, called it a 'repellent film – crude, narrow, simplistic and self-serving,' and revelling in violence – that he summed up as 'a religious snuff movie,' offering 'visceral spatter,' and devoid of spiritual content.[61] Likewise, Hugh Linehan placed it within the horror genre, but also as part of a tradition of provocative filmmaking, in which the film's 'vulgarity' gives it a 'visceral, unsettling force'.[62] 'Schlock horror' was the title of Eddie Holt's article, and he went on to call it 'a "shock and awe" gore-fest and a disturbing example of technology as religion,'[63] while Michael Dwyer wrote, somewhat ironically: 'this is jolting screen violence that is so explicit and deeply disturbing that it firmly confounds the theory that cinema audiences may become desensitised to images of violence.'[64] Much of the non-specialist film comment surrounded either the film's alleged anti-semitism, with, for example, the Chief Rabbi for Ireland calling on the Catholic church to denounce the film,[65] while the comments attributed to Pope John Paul II in support of the film, 'it is as it was,' an 'unofficial *imprimatur*,'[66] was an echo of the 1913 *From the Manger to the Cross* controversy as discussed in chapter 2. However, on this occasion it was not simply the Catholic church against the others, as the film came to be used by many Christian churches as a means of engaging their congregations in religious ceremonies. Indeed, a number of Catholic parishes block-booked a screening for their parishioners, while one held a raffle for free tickets to the film at the end of a Novena, adding a prayer for the film in the hope that it 'will bring back many from the cul-de-sac of secularism and materialism.'[67] All of this led to the film emerging as one of the greatest box office successes of all time in Ireland, as well as worldwide, with some projecting that the €25 million *Passion* could become one of the few films to take a billion dollars.[68]

In her *Irish Times* column, Breda O'Brien drew attention to how *Passion* had apparently changed perceptions of cinema. It had led to Hollywood itself complaining about the film's violence, while Catholics claimed such graphic depictions of Christ's suffering were necessary, even Protestant evangelists, traditionally suspicious of Catholic actions, who transpired to be supporters of the film. Nevertheless, by acknowledging that the film owes more to Hollywood than religious norms, O'Brien[69] accepted that all cinema is representation, not reality. After all, *Passion* is a made thing, a representation, even if, in this case, it touches people at deeply visceral, physical and emotional levels, something, of course, which is common to much mainstream cinema. Despite all the censorship and all the controversy, powerful cinema – no matter how conservative or liberal, regressive or progressive – will still find its audience with a visceral thrill that might even transcend its often limited and limiting ideology.

# CHAPTER 7

# Electronic media and film censorship in Ireland

Is a video nasty a very bad horror film ... or a film about Vietnam?

Senator Denis Cregan, 1987.[1]

## TELEVISION

In anticipation of the new television service, the Department of Posts and Telegraphs, with responsibility for broadcasting, prepared a memo for government on 'Censorship of Television Films'.[2] This followed a cabinet meeting of 8 December 1959 when it was decided that the issue of censorship be excluded from the Broadcasting Act. It nevertheless proposed that while it was up to the Board of the television authority 'to apply proper [censorship] standards' consideration should be given by the Minister for Posts and Telegraphs Michael Hilliard as to the inclusion of a provision in the regulations providing for liaison with the Official Film Censor. Subsequently, he, together with the Minister for Justice Oscar Traynor, concluded that such a statutory provision 'need not be made,' with Hilliard assuring his colleagues that the Authority would be 'very glad' to avail of the Censor's advice 'without being placed under a statutory duty to do so.' Despite this agreement, the Minster for Justice was concerned at the anomalies that might arise, not least when films that had been denied a certificate by the Censor, and hence unavailable for mainstream theatrical release, were shown on television. The spill-over signals from British and Northern Ireland television channels, which by the end of the 1950s was available to 40 per cent of the population, already allowed for the circulation of material beyond the remit of the Irish Film Censor. This issue had been addressed when the Television Committee expressed concern about the programme content of the BBC when it reported to government in 1956, also the year the commercial British broadcaster, Independent Television (ITV), started. Declaring that the station was 'governed by ideas that are wholly alien to the ordinary Irish home,' it went on to describe some of them as 'brazen' and '"frank" in sex matters,' though it was equally agitated by the station's 'desire to exalt the British royal family and the British way of life.' The report characterized the BBC's representation of sexuality as 'quite alien' to Ireland and noted that the station featured 'semi-nudity,' '"blue" jokes in comedy shows, documentaries ... of the unmarried mother' and plays 'hinging on the theme of adultery,' while films screened included 'in detail the sex activities of animals!'³ (This issue of the spill-over signal was aired regularly in the Dáil during the 1960s.) In the 1960 memo to government, the minister did not think it possible to find a solution by way of permitting cinemas to show uncensored films, or ones already broadcast on Irish television, something which necessarily would have meant a loss of revenue for the government. Furthermore, there could be no guarantee as to the version of the film shown on television and the extent or otherwise of the cutting, while 'informal' arrangements between the television authority and the Official Film Censor would inevitably lead to an additional cost which would have to be recouped by increasing the fees on films submitted for theatrical release. This 'will not be easy to defend,' the Minister for Justice warned his colleagues, and he thought that the government should be prepared for some loss of the £7,000 per annum censorship fees, which would be 'an incidental cost' of the establishment of the television service.⁴

Notwithstanding the Minister for Justice's concerns, the Minister for Posts and Telegraphs informed the Senate in January 1960 during the debate on the Broadcasting Authority Bill that 'the Bill deliberately says nothing about censorship' as it was the government's wish 'that the Authority should act as its own censor, recognising the absolute importance of safeguarding truth and of preserving intact the moral integrity of our people.' Nevertheless, it was intended that the Authority would maintain a close liaison 'on a common standard' with the Film Censor and that there would be a provision to establish advisory committees and advisers.⁵ At the Committee stage of the Bill in the Dáil, the minister said that the Authority would have 'the maximum freedom' with no provision for any formal censorship in the matter of programmes. He added that he was confident the Authority would respect 'proper moral standards' in its programmes and with regard to filmed material would 'in practice … maintain a fairly close liaison' with the Film Censor.⁶ In a further contribution, he suggested that 'in the last analysis, the public will be the censors,' a position distinctly different to that obtaining for the cinema. However, in a barely veiled warning and in terms reminiscent of the Censorship of Films Act, 1923, he said that if a television programme was not 'up to our standards' it would be necessary for the government 'to take immediate cognisance of that' and for the Authority to 'do something about it to make certain that there would not be a repetition of shows that were sub-standard, so far as our ideas of good shows are concerned.'⁷ In short, the Authority would be given 'freedom' so long as it operated according to the narrow limits of the defined status quo and ideological boundaries of the government.

Film Censor Liam O'Hora in his annual report for 1959 to the Minister for Justice, written while the Broadcasting Bill was being debated in Cabinet and in the Oireachtas, warned that 'the duel with television' was already responsible for an emerging 'moral vacuum' evident in 40 per cent of the films submitted to his office. He continued that 'if such films are now refused certificates for theatrical exhibition, they will eventually be seen through the medium of television.'⁸ The following year, O'Hora returned, though less pessimistically, to 'the struggle between television and the screen.' He felt that given the steadily increasing viewing population in Ireland during the 1950s for 'spill-over' signals from British and Northern Ireland television, 'the new medium [would] not cause the same disruption … as it [had] in other countries.'[9] By the time of his 1961 report, the Irish television service, Telefís Éireann (TÉ), had begun broadcasting and formal liaison had been established between the television authority and the Censor's office. It was, O'Hora told Charles J. Haughey, appointed Minister for Justice following the October 1961 general election, 'operating most amicably and no television material – I mean of a filmed kind only – has so far transgressed the general standards that we try to maintain here.'[10] While this statement came five weeks after TÉ commenced broadcasting, less than four months later, the first public controversy erupted concerning the content of an American drama series from NBC, *Medic*, screened late night on Fridays, which focused on different diseases and biological problems. The offending episode, entitled *Candle of Hope*, made under the supervision of the American Medical Association, was broadcast on 25 May at 10.30 p.m. Dealing with infertility and sterility and illustrating the methods used to help childless couples to conceive, it followed the dramatized attempts of a recently married Greek Orthodox couple to have a child. After a year the couple are unsuccessful and seek medical advice. Following tests, the husband – anxious for a son to inherit the vineyards – is surprised to discover that the source of their difficulty lies, not with his wife, but with himself. The doctor advises a course of injections which will, over a period, have the effect of bringing about in him 'the positive capacity necessary'. In the end there is hope that the treatment will result in the wife's pregnancy.[11]

Following a Dáil question put down by the Labour Party leader, conservative Catholic Brendan Corish, concerning the programme, it emerged in a letter from TÉ's Head of Management, T.A. Irvine, to civil servant Mr A. Ingoldsby of Posts and Telegraphs' Telecommunications Branch that prior to the series' transmission, advice had been taken from the Irish Medical Association. Irvine also outlined TÉ's practice concerning all films screened:

> Every piece of film is previewed and passed before being shown [a practice which continues to the present]. Censorship is the [Television] Authority's own responsibility but a close liaison has, in fact, been established with the Censorship of Films Office and this has been found to be of benefit in cases of difficulty.

He concluded his letter by saying that the station 'had virtually no public reaction against the *Medic* programme' in question.[12] The next day, S. Ó Seaghdha of Posts and Telegraphs wrote to Irvine stating that the programme 'was probably embarrassing to quite a number of people.' In gathering information for his minister, Ó Seaghdha wanted to know (a), who approved the programme?; (b), was the Censor consulted?; (c), would the Censor have approved it for cinema release?; and (d), was the Censor's advice obtained frequently on individual programmes or were there 'some common rules to ensure that a common standard' was maintained?[13] In his reply of the same day, Irvine expressed concern that the criticism which might emanate from the department in reply to Corish's question would be that the film was unsuitable for transmission. Reiterating his point concerning medical advice, he stated that consideration was also given as to whether there might be objections 'from the point of view of Catholic teaching in relation to medicine.' He went on to quote the Censorship of Films Act's criteria for public exhibition and asserted that the *Medic* programme could not be held to be unfit for public exhibition, and that 'a close liaison' had been established with the Censor's office. He also reminded his correspondent that – beyond what appears in the 1923 Act – it all 'boils down to good taste and judgement' since 'there is no written code of rules for judging films and … interpretation can vary.' Criticizing the administration of the Act, Irvine bluntly stated that 'it would scarcely be claimed that there has been absolute consistency [by Official Censors] down the years.' He pointed out that 'as a rule' TÉ did not submit individual programmes to the Censor, but in the case of feature films which had received a theatrical release in Ireland it was practice to ask for the list of cuts demanded by the Censor 'so that we would have the benefit of this in forming our judgements.' Such judgments, he said, are made 'at an appropriate level' and in this case, TÉ's Controller of Programmes was consulted. However, the Film Censor was not asked his opinion in this instance.[14] In his memorandum outlining the programme's storyline written the following day, Irvine concluded by saying that the film was regarded as 'a responsible adult study of a serious problem' and TÉ as a Public Service Broadcaster 'would feel that if it avoided serious subjects involving life, human relations and problems of disease it would be evading its responsibility.'[15] The contrast with film censorship could hardly be more stark.

Similarly, Hilliard responded to Corish's question later that day, by stating the close liaison between TÉ and the Film Censor, and that the *Medic* programme had been previewed in the normal way. He refused to be drawn by Corish who enquired whether these American films were a method whereby TÉ could give sex education to the Irish people.[16] In its report of the parliamentary discussion, the *Irish Times* honed in on the key issue of the 'TV authority act[ing] as its own censor.'[17] The report in the *Leinster Leader* offered a factual account of the Dáil proceedings, although a commentary by Fr Brophy supported Corish's criticism of TÉ arguing that the programme was 'an intrusion into the intimacy of the family' and as such was 'disturbing'. He opinioned that what goes into the cinema was not an acceptable standard when it 'enters the intimacy of the family circle.'[18] While such a distinction and recognition of the viewing space is important, it should be accompanied by an understanding of the different viewing practices associated with the two mediums. If television had not yet developed the distracted viewing patterns of contemporary spectatorship, defined in part (thanks to multi-channels, VCRs and DVDs) by synchronic and diachronic choice as well as by familiarity and busyness (with the medium just one among many simultaneous activities such as looking after children, eating, housework, reading), its place within the (lit) living room as opposed to a darkened auditorium together with a distancing effect of black and white and a small screen image, clearly presented a radically different context which would have facilitated critical discussion. Of course, the official cultural environment both repressed such a discussion and acted to deny it when it did emerge. O'Hora, on the other hand, was also very unhappy with TÉ and how Hilliard had characterized the relationship between his office and the station.

The first formal opportunity afforded to O'Hora to respond to the public controversy on this relationship was in his 1962 annual report to the Minister for Justice. In this he complained that the liaison with Telefís Éireann was 'not working as smoothly as it might.'[19] In a reply to a query from the minister,[20] he outlined the history of the relationship, reporting that prior to the station's establishment 'it was decided ... that the standards observed would be those obtaining in this office and that a liaison should be set up with the Official Film Censor.' To this end, he had met the Director-General and the Controller of Programmes of Telefís Éireann prior to the commencement of broadcasting on 31 January 1961. He went on to say, in a reversal of his positive comments within his earlier report, that while tentative schemes had been agreed, 'that was the last ... heard of the suggested liaison.' Although from time to time the Head of Film at the station rang him to suggest a meeting, this never materialized. Telefís Éireann obviously wanted to keep the Censor happy without entering into any formal arrangements with him. O'Hora was concerned that there was 'an idea abroad' that he 'vetted all contentious material emanating from Telefís Éireann,' and it seemed to him the station itself and the Minister for Posts and Telegraphs, who had responsibility for the station, were perpetuating this idea even though the contrary was fact. He cited an *Irish Press* report[21] in which the minister told the Dáil the previous May during the *Medic* controversy that while Telefís Éireann previewed all programmes before transmission, it had established 'a close liaison with the film censors.' O'Hora concluded that 'if a liaison is not soon established the anomalies and misinterpretations will increase and multiply as time goes on.'[22]

These exchanges led, on Haughey's instructions, to Peter Berry – the powerful Secretary of the Department of Justice who, as discussed in chapter 5, had been carefully gauging film censorship during O'Hora's tenure – writing to the Secretary of the Department of Posts and Telegraphs, Leon Ó Broin. The communication pointed to the absence of the close liaison which Posts and Telegraphs seemed to think was occurring, and which TÉ publicly affirmed stating that with 'the single exception' of the weekly programme dealing with films currently on cinema release, the Censor had 'never been consulted'. Although the document acknowledged the legal right of TÉ to act as its own censor, it nonetheless noted that because the Oireachtas and Government 'were given to understand' that there would be a liaison, the Minister for Justice wanted the matter raised with the station so that the impression given by Posts and Telegraphs would not be repeated. Haughey wanted to avoid a public disagreement between the Censor and TÉ, but unless TÉ changed the perception it was creating, 'a public repudiation on behalf of the Film Censor would become necessary.'[23]

Such a public disagreement did not occur as the wily Secretary of the Department of Posts and Telegraphs, Leon Ó Broin, who had overseen the introduction of the Irish television service,[24] took up the issue with TÉ's Director-General, Kevin C. McCourt, by sending him a copy of Berry's letter.[25] In his reply to Ó Broin, McCourt said that TÉ personnel 'held consultation with the Film Censor for the purpose of gaining practical knowledge of the policies and operating procedure' employed by him. He further stated that while TÉ intended to maintain, even intensify, this relationship, the Authority did not want to convey the idea that 'this informal liaison, useful and desirable as it is, does in any way relieve the Authority of its statutory responsibilities vis-à-vis its own filmed programmes.' The Authority regretted 'any wrong impression that may unintention-ally' have been formed and stated that steps would be taken to ensure this would not recur.[26] Six months later, in February 1964, McCourt wrote again to Ó Broin telling him that he had met the Minister for Justice, Charles Haughey, to discuss the matter. He reported that he had raised with Haughey 'the possibility of a practical working arrangement' than had hitherfore obtained, and it was agreed, rather amazingly, that O'Hora would act as 'a special consultant' to TÉ outside of official office hours. Following discussions with O'Hora, it was decided that he would (a), do 'a reasonable amount' of home-viewing of TÉ programmes 'giving special attention as required to particular programmes' about which TÉ would give him advance notice of; (b), he would prepare a monthly report for the Programme Controller, commenting on his viewing and 'making such criticism and constructive proposals as he thought fit'; (c), attending TÉ's regular monthly previewing sessions each of 'several hours' duration; (d), attend quarterly meetings with the Director-General 'for a general exchange of views on standards of propriety, taste and suitability in television programmes'; and (e), pro-vide ad hoc consultation with the Head of TÉ's Film Department or other office instructed by the Progamme Controller 'on general or specific problems'. McCourt added that the previous arrangement whereby the Film Department consulted with the Censor's office and had access to his records in regard to feature films was to continue.[27]

O'Hora died six weeks later so the detailed after-hours consultation work would hardly have begun; the new Censor, Christopher Macken, was also appointed a paid consultant. As a result, the issue of the relationship between the Censor and Radio Telefís Éireann (the new name for the combined national public service radio and television stations) does not appear again in the Censors' annual reports. Thus, the arrangement with regard to feature films continued, it seems satisfactorily, as a 1971 RTÉ memo reported that the organization paid the Film Censor an annual retainer of £300 'for advice and consultation,' though this does not appear to be as wide-ranging as outlined in McCourt's 1964 letter. The procedure involved RTÉ's Head of Film sending the Censor a form enquiring as to whether the particular film had received a certificate, and if so whether it was subject to any limitations, or cuts, all of which were to be detailed. Subsequently, the Head of Film decided whether these or other cuts should be made to the film before transmission. 'If in his opinion the cuts should not be made he may call in the censor for consultation before reach-ing a final decision.' However, the Censor refused to provide information on films released during the previous five years, as, for whatever reason, he felt this would be 'unfair to the film distributors.' (Arguably, film distributors were happy to collude with the Censor on the matter of silence, for marketing purposes. Clearly, if the extent of the Censor's intervention was made known, it is highly probably that the film's appeal might be diluted.) As a result, the memo reported, 'in the case of such films

... the Head of Film must use his own judgement and knowledge of the standards currently applied.'[28]

In the meantime, the issue was raised in the Dáil in 1967 by Fine Gael's Oliver J. Flanagan. The then Minster for Justice, Brian Lenihan, who, as outlined in chapter 6, liberalized film censorship in 1965, responded to a query concerning censorship at RTÉ by saying that he was satisfied with the internal arrangements, and the 'informal consultation' with the Film Censor. He added that RTÉ followed 'the same yardstick' as the Film Censor.[29] Three years later in 1970 the subject of film, television and censorship resurfaced during the debate on the amendment to the Censorship of Films Act to allow for the re-submission of a film to the Censor seven years after it was banned, cut, or given an unfavourable rating. The Minister for Justice, Micheal Moran, opened the discussion arguing that if there was not some kind of flexibility, there would arise the 'wholly indefensible position [of] films ... being shown on television [which] cannot be shown in cinemas because the application for a film censor's certificate was made several years earlier and was judged by the standards of the day.'[30] While Opposition politicians supported the measure, some speakers warned against a 'lowering of standards' of film censorship and complained about film and television violence. One contributor, for example, said he had to leave the cinema on a number of occasions because of the amount of violence on screen, to which the minister replied by referring to the 'public morality' clause in the 1923 Act.[31] Much of the concerns expressed by members of the Oireachtas were not focused on the 'seven year rule' as it became known, or even the standards and processes of censorship, but on what Senator Rory Brugha so graphically described as, the need to 'prevent filth and dirt that might tend to deprave youngsters,'[32] that according to cultural protectionists was emanating from the 'spill-over' signals of British television. Likewise, Senator Tomás O'Maoláin suggested in connection with the development by RTÉ of a cable television system that 'somebody will have to do something if we are not to be completely brain-washed and subverted as a result of the filth, dirt and distortion of history that is created night after night on these foreign channels.'[33] These comments, together with the criticism of television (foreign and native) and film, were largely ignored by the minister. Nevertheless, they have continued to have a currency.

During a poignant funeral service for a (Roman Catholic) father who drove with his two young daughters into the River Shannon in 1987, the parish priest of the Co. Limerick parish of Athea, the Revd Fr Thomas O'Donnell, chose to shift the focus away from a considered analysis or sympathetic understanding of the suicide and murder which might have taken on board issues around the family, society and (personal) mental health and even refigure the murder as a misguided though logical expression of fatherly duty. Instead, his homily displaced responsibility on to the media and specifically on to RTÉ. He stated that the dead man, John Joseph White, had spoken to a few people about the film *Lamb* (Colin Gregg, 1985, GB) which had been shown on RTÉ on 27 December 1986, though it had received an Irish cinema release in September 1986. In the film, a Christian Brother, played by Liam Neeson, drowns the boy he has sought to save from the harsh life at an orphanage, believing that he is positively releasing the boy from misery. Fr O'Donnell declared that

> While we cannot accuse RTÉ of being guilty of [John Joseph White's] death, we can point a finger at them under many other headings, especially for the type of film they are showing night after night, which include scandal, crime and murder. Surely many of these films were corrupting the young and innocent and it is time for RTÉ … to show itself as being more responsible.

He added that the fact viewers were advised in advance that certain films were only suitable for adults 'did not excuse them.' In a complaint echoing James Montgomery's arguments against limited certificates, he said that these notices 'only entice young people to pay more attention.'[34] Since it was an adult, albeit one who was suffering from 'grave depression' who had seen the film, the target seems to have been the whole medium itself, and the public screening of adult material. Such displacement of painful internal realities on to film has been moreover extended from the 1960s onwards to the electronic media and the internet. Too often societal, familial, parental and most of all personal responsibility is lost in the discussion.

Although *Lamb* had been passed by the Censor, RTÉ has consistently shown films which have been banned or cut,[35] yet controversies surrounding their transmission have been rare. One exception was the dropping of a proposed screening of Joseph Strick's banned *Ulysses* on Bloomsday, 1979. RTÉ asserted at the time that they were not swayed by protests from the League of Decency, a right-wing Catholic group, but a spokesperson for RTÉ did acknowledge that 'it was station policy not to rush on the screens a recently banned movie.'[36] As noted in chapter 6, *Ulysses* had been banned in both 1967 and 1974. RTÉ eventually screened it in 1984, and Strick successfully re-applied for a certificate in 2000 when it was awarded a 15PG. Similarly, British television stations have made available to Irish viewers a wide range of films which have been banned or cut in Ireland. This has varied from Channel Four's screening of *Whore* in 1995 to its showing of *Caligula* in 2000, both of which remain banned in Ireland, to BBC2's 'Forbidden Weekend' in May 1995 which featured along with a number of contextualizing documentaries, such controversial films as Peter Jackson's cult gross-out comic body horror/ science-fiction film *Bad Taste* (1988, New Zealand); Ken Russell's *The Devils*; Donald Cammell's and Nicolas Roeg's psychological X-rated melodrama featuring Mick Jagger, *Performance* (1970, GB); Liliana Cavani's masochistic *The Night Porter*; and Edmond Greville's *Beat Girl*. Subsequently, Ireland's only commercial (and entertainment-driven) television station TV3 attempted to show a *cut* version of *Natural Born Killers* in 2000. However, it met with legal threats from the state,[37] and it was not shown on the station until 26 August 2001, almost four months after it was passed for video/DVD release.

It was not film, but the restrictions on RTÉ broadcasting paramilitary republican and loyalist views under ministerial directive through Section 31 of the Broadcasting Act, 1960, which became the main preoccupation of anti-censorship campaigners from the 1970s to the mid-1990s, certainly as regards television.[38] (This is discussed in the next chapter.) Nevertheless, a number of controversies have surrounded RTÉ's covering of questions of sexual morality and representations of sexuality. Certainly, the *discussion* of sexuality, and reproductive 'technology' was frequently the subject of controversy on both television and radio in the 1960s and 1970s. While the Catholic church took the view that such topics as contraception should not even be discussed, perhaps the moment when the chasm between different experiences of sexuality entered the public sphere was in 1966 as part of a game of Mr & Mrs. A guest on *The Late Late Show* – RTÉ's long-running flagship programme which mixes topical events and issues with discussion and light entertainment – was asked the colour of his wife's nightie on their honeymoon, and though he answered 'transparent,' she said that she had not worn a nightie at all, but realizing the cultural threshold she had crossed, replied that it was white. Such a public articulation of sexuality even with regard to honeymooners, outraged the Bishop of Clonfert who attacked the programme's immorality and asked his congregation to send protests to RTÉ, thus giving birth to the affair that became known as 'The Bishop and Nightie'.[39]

As regards RTÉ's drama output, one high-profile moment was its withdrawal in 1978 of the vocational school-based television series *The Spike*, which showed, however crudely, the nature of working-class education in Ireland, following the controversial featuring of a nude model in the fifth episode.[40] While in retrospect the affair was mild, it may have contributed to the ensuing long period of caution during which RTÉ made few dramas dealing with contemporary Ireland. When seen in the context of the domestic video cassette recorder (VCR) introduced at the end of that decade, it indicated that the apparent gains made from the mid-1960s in liberalizing censorship were being rowed back. Indeed, more broadly, the 1980s and 1990s saw attempts to redress the balance between individual liberty and the state and other institutions which was central to the changes in Irish society heralded by the 1960s 'revolution.' However, the audio-visual battleground was neither television nor the cinema, but video, which confirmed that the cinema was giving way to more 'democratic' and home-based entertainments. In due course, the domestic VCR, and later digital technologies and widespread access to the internet, would fundamentally challenge and undermine the state's capacity to maintain its tight surveillance of audio-visual material.

VIDEO

While September 1979 may be remembered as the month in which Pope John Paul II visited Ireland, the cultural effects of video distribution in the Republic of Ireland which began the same month had decidedly longer and more important impact on the social fabric. Although video offers a more democratic distribution system than theatrical film release, in that it allows for greater control on the part of the viewer in terms of choice of material, viewing time, and more generally viewing practices and environment, in its wake a new and highly restrictive form of censorship followed which rad-

ically undermined Censorship of Film Appeals Board Chairman John Carroll's observation that film censorship was likely to wither away in the 1980s. Nevertheless, the
serendipitous nature of his comment (he gave the interview to *Film Directions* magazine in autumn 1979), indicates that Irish film censors were no more prepared for the
video revolution than their predecessors were for the coming of sound, the one technological precedent, from a film censorship perspective, with which it can be usefully
compared. The first salvo in the 'moral panic' campaign that was to mirror the 'video
nasty' hysteria in Britain during the early 1980s came only four months after domestic videos were introduced to Ireland.

In a *Sunday Press* article entitled 'Censor is Beaten by Video; Banned Film Sold
for Home Viewing' published in early January 1980, Frances O'Rourke reported the
availability on video of uncut versions of a number of films which had been either
banned or cut by the Irish Film Censor.[41] Titles mentioned included the mainstream
cinema sexual journey to middle-age of two college friends, *Carnal Knowledge*,
banned in 1972 but passed with an over-18s certificate in October 1979, and the
adaptation of Jackie Collins' cult porn novel, *The Stud* (Quentin Masters, 1978, GB),
which had been cut by the Censor before being released in 1979, and its sequel, *The
Bitch*, which had been passed with nine cuts of fornication, lesbianism, and other
sex scenes just two weeks before the article appeared.[42] These were among the titles
imported by Video Entertainments which had begun selling them through music and
hi-fi stores at wholesale prices of between £35 and £40 each four months earlier. By
January 1980 in Dublin alone there were twelve such outlets selling videos, while
nationwide there were around 4,000 to 5,000 video cassette recorders. According to
O'Rourke, prior to importing the videos, the company had checked the legal position with the Film Censor's office, the police, and the Revenue Commissioners, who
had powers under Section 42 of the Customs (Consolidation) Act, 1876 to impound
imported 'indecent' or 'obscene' prints, books, magazines and other material. The
Film Censor, it transpired, had no such jurisdiction, while according to the Revenue
Commissioners it was up to the individual examining officer 'to decide whether or
not the material was obscene and should be let in.' The company had formed the
view that the videos had been allowed in because they were for home use. The article went on to quote an assistant manager of the major book and magazine retailer
and wholesaler, Eason's, who stated that while they were selling videos bought from
a London company which also offered 'Adults Only' titles, no such videos would be
imported 'any more than [they would] … sell pornographic books and magazines.'
Thus, from the beginning the association of video with pornography was established.
Ironically, Eason's reported that its best-selling video was of the Pope's Irish visit,
produced by RTÉ.

The article seems to have prompted the *Irish Independent* to focus on video ten
days later. Under the top front page story, 'Pornographic videos – TD to raise issue in
Dáil,' Jim Farrelly reproduced the bulk of O'Rourke's text but gave it a more dramatic
spin with the opening sentence, 'Legal defects facilitating the sale of pornographic films
and records free from scrutiny by the censors are [to] be raised in the Dáil.' He went

on to suggest that complete versions of films which had been cut by the Irish Censor were available through Video Entertainments. The 'pornographic' titles which he cited included the fast-moving crime film *The French Connection* (William Friedkin, 1971) which won five Oscars about a successful drugs bust in New York, the western *Soldier Blue*, and the quirky musical spoof of prohibition gangster films, *Bugsy Malone* (Alan Parker, 1976, GB) which featured a child-only cast. He mentioned just one of 'hundreds' of records which he claimed could be deemed 'subversive of public morality': the soundtrack of the banned film *Monty Python's Life of Brian*. According to Farrelly, Fine Gael TD Michael Keating, the party's spokesman on Law Reform, intended to raise the issue in the Dáil. For Keating, 'the technological revolution [meant] that data and information [was] now being communicated in ways not envisaged by the censorship statutes,' and thus an 'urgent examination' of censorship law in relation to videos and records was needed. Keating added that his primary concern was that 'young people be protected from soft and hard porn, in every form. The laws should be such that it should not be available to them, *or anybody*.' (Emphasis added.)[43] However, he did not raise the issue in the Dáil until 1986[44] and it was almost fifteen years before video censorship was fully introduced to Ireland.

Eighteen months after these articles appeared, the *Irish Times* published a two-part investigation by Deaglán de Bréadún demonstrating how Irish film censorship laws were 'being undermined by technology,' with the first of these tellingly entitled, 'Show Your Own Blue Movies,' accompanied by a still of Joan Collins in *The Bitch*. According to de Bréadún[45] pornography, which would not have even been submitted to the Censor, was now 'easily available,' even though the Customs and Excise service of the Revenue Commissioners had 'from time to time' seized videos. As part of his research, he viewed an 'adult video' and reported that films such as Gerard Damiano's *Deep Throat* (1972), *Sex Tour* and *Teenage Fantasy*, standard fare produced by the European and North American pornography industries, were being rented and sold in Dublin. Also highlighted was the widespread showing on large video screens in pubs and hotels of films (which later became associated with the collective viewing of sport), of recently released or soon-to-be released films, which had been illegally copied. In this regard, Tralee, Co. Kerry, where up to ten pubs were showing videos, often in uncut versions a week or two prior to their cinema release, was cited as typical within provincial towns. For example, *Dressed to Kill* (Brian De Palma, 1980) cut by the Film Censor, was screened in a number of pubs several weeks before its Dublin opening. Such screenings undermined not just censorship but the profits of the film industry. As a result of this piracy, the major distributors found themselves in alliance with pro-censorship campaigners, something, of course, which had previously happened. Together with Catholic groups such as the Knights of St Columbanus, and certain feminists, they sought to pressurize the state into introducing controls over video. There were few dissenting voices.

The purchase of VCRs accelerated during the 1980s. The first official survey reported that by August 1980, 20,000 VCRs had been imported, with demand, despite the then high cost of £550, remaining well ahead of supply. In 1986, by which time

there were about 500 video outlets, the number had risen to 200,000,[46] ten times the
1980 figure, but well below 600,000 or 700,000 which had been predicted by the
industry in 1981.[47] Compared to the growth of the British market, this relatively slow
pace of sales can be explained by the severe economic recession in Ireland during the
first half of the 1980s and may have contributed to the tardy way the legislature
responded to pressure for censorship of videos. Consequently, in the absence of controls on either video content or the licensing of retail outlets, it was left to the industry to use the Copyright Act, 1963 so as to enforce its will on pirates who were selling or renting mainstream videos. However, it took a number of years for the industry
to prove effective in bringing some of these to heel given the relatively high cost of pre-
recorded videos and digital video disks, DVDs, but the elimination of all piracy is never
likely to be fully successful.

The police raid on 27 May 1981 on a Dublin video outlet, Home Video Club,
Rathmines, which led two months later to a court case under the Copyright Act, was
almost certainly prompted by the major distributors. When it reached the High Court
in July 1981, the defence claimed that the raid was unlawful.[48] Nevertheless, the distributors continued in their attempt to contain the burgeoning video club business
and to stamp out video piracy by campaigning for state control of the business. This
they carried out through an umbrella body, the Irish Videogram Association (IVA,
ironically, carrying the same acronym as its 1910s Catholic counterpart). In the meantime, they established the Irish National Federation Against Copyright Theft (INFACT)
which began using the legal mechanism of an Anton Pillar, which, with the permission of the courts, allows for a surprise raid. In this way they could gain evidence and
under the Copyright Act achieve prosecutions. Indeed, the first time video was raised
in the Dáil was in a 1982 question addressed to the Minister for Industry, Commerce
and Tourism Desmond O'Malley, in connection with the use of this. The minister
noted the 'effective action' being taken in court by the industry under the Act, which
he did not propose to amend.[49] Thereafter, most Oireachtas questions and debates on
video concerned 'video nasties' and pornography, even though Sean Doherty, the
Minister for Justice in 1982, was quite dismissive of the need for legislative change,
correctly reporting that the Gardaí were not aware of any problem regarding pornography on video.[50]

The IVA reported in 1985 that while the legitimate video industry was worth £16
million per annum, it estimated the loss through piracy at £14 million.[51] Two years
later, it told the *Irish Times* that while the legitimate business had risen to £28 million
per annum, piracy was siphoning off a further £14 million.[52] Unsurprisingly, in defence
of its members' commercial interests, INFACT intensified its activities in the early
1990s, seizing 44,392 pirated videos in 1992 alone,[53] while in 1993 it led 156 raids
on pirates, and 100 in the first half of 1994 as piracy was apparently being rapidly
ended.[54] However, a Garda raid in Co. Louth in April 1998 led to the seizure of over
10,000 pirated videos, the largest haul ever in Ireland, including copies of the unreleased blockbuster *Titanic* (James Cameron, 1997). According to INFACT, piracy was
costing the industry £30 million annually at this time, and this particular operator had

netted between £4 and £6 million per annum from the business. Those caught were arrested under the Trademarks Act, 1997, a modernization of the Copyright Act, which carries penalties of up to £150,000 and five years in jail.[55]

Just as video sales were, by comparison with Britain, slow, so, too, as noted was the Irish political response to the industry and to pro-censorship campaigners. In Britain, Mary Whitehouse and her Festival of Light Movement, supported by sympathetic Conservative MPs succeeded, after initial hesitation by the free-marketeers of the Thatcher government, in having included in the Tories' 1983 general election manifesto a commitment to legislate against 'video nasties'. This vague all encompassing and highly emotive term is used to refer to a broad range of films that employ bad taste, moreover in the areas of violence, obscene or perverted (sexual) behaviour, gratuitous or pornographic representations and unethical or immoral practices such as the filming of real acts of death (the so-called 'snuff' movie), cannibalism, or other taboos. In real terms, much of what qualifies is at one extreme no more than exploitative 'X'-rated material, and, at another, mainstream (horror) as well as European cinema rated 15s or over. Though some voices in the British national press, such as Nigel Andrews in the *Financial Times* and Derek Malcolm in the *Guardian*,[56] placed the 'video nasties' – generally 1970s and 1980s horror – within a generic framework, the 'moral panic' hysteria generated by the *Sun*, among other tabloid newspapers, ensured the passage of the British Bill, which resulted in the Video Recordings Act, 1984. In Ireland, however, despite the Minister for Justice, Fine Gael's Michael Noonan, telling the Dáil in November 1983 that he was having the law in relation to videos examined 'as a matter of urgency,'[57] no action was taken. Indeed, his successor, Alan Dukes, erroneously told the Dáil in March 1986 that the Censorship of Films Act, 1923 applied to video, though he also said the UK video legislation was being studied by his department.[58] By then, the Select Committee on Crime, Lawlessness and Vandalism had initiated an investigation into the area and during the first half of 1986 held hearings on 'video nasties' after its members

> expressed concern at … a tendency towards a higher tolerance for violence in [Irish] society. The presence of violence and sexual abuse on videos, films and television was considered to contribute to a lowering of standards in society generally and to the unconscious conditioning of people to accept such standards.[59]

The Committee ensured that its report would have a populist and predominately right-wing bias, notwithstanding the by-now standard sop to a feminist agenda by incorporating them into the pro-censorship camp. Chaired by Fianna Fáil's Michael Woods, the Committee also included other party stalwarts Bertie Ahern (Taoiseach 1997–), Brian Cowen (later a Minister for Health and Minister for Foreign Affairs), Vincent Brady and Willie O'Dea (later a Junior Minister at Justice); right-wing Fine Gael members Liam Cosgrave (who later admitted accepting bribes from property developers), Joe Doyle and Alice Glenn; the Progressive Democrats' Mary Harney (a future leader of the party, and Tánaiste [Deputy Prime Minister] from 1997); and Labour deputies, Frank Prendergast from Limerick, and Mervyn Taylor from Dublin. Overall, the bias of the 9 men and 3 women members was on the conservative side of Irish politics at the time.

The Committee held five meetings with invitees, the more balanced of which was probably the delegation from RTÉ. Led by the station's Director-General, Vincent Finn, and including Bob Collins, Finn's successor, audience researcher Tony Fahy, Mr A. Burns and Mr Vercoe-Rogers, it reported that RTÉ employed 'film acceptance viewers,' who viewed imported films and programmes to assess them for their portrayal of violence. Any 'gratuitous or purely sensational' violence was not broadcast.[60] Nonetheless, the delegation commented that it was extremely difficult to establish any causal relationship of the effects of televisual violence on young people, noting a major US government-sponsored 1972 study which 'could only conclude ... a preliminary and tentative relationship between violence and television viewing.'[61] Such nuances were soon lost in the debate and most other contributors preferred assertion to research or argument. As a later Minister for Justice, Maire Geoghegan-Quinn, put it in 1994, 'Scientific evidence *or not* ... Ireland must have a system of sensible censorship.' (Emphasis added.)[62] Needless to say, like the terms of the 1923 Act, 'sensible' was not defined in this context.

While no other people working in film or television, let alone academic researchers or educators, were asked to contribute, the Committee on Crime, Lawlessness and Vandalism did invite the Campaign Against Sexual Exploitation (CASE). The organization articulated a position familiar from the work of Andrea Dworkin in particular, that pornography was an infringement of women's civil rights. Pornography, the CASE advocates Antoinette Farren and Linda Kavanagh stated, should be rejected 'for its exploitative and degrading sentiments,' rather than on grounds of 'obscenity' and 'indecency,' which, they suggested, maintained the view that 'sex is something shameful in itself.' Developing the link between pornography and prostitution on the one hand (the word pornography, from the Greek, means prostitute/writing, or as another advocate of this ideology, Clodagh Corcoran, rather crudely put it, 'to write about whores'),[63] and sex education and sexual freedom on the other, the pair argued that the long-term effects of exposure to pornography was socially harmful to men, women and children. Though it was not discussed in this forum, Kavanagh, and Corcoran of the Irish Council of Civil Liberties (ICCL), sought to establish the distinction between soft and hard-core pornography, or between erotica and pornography. Corcoran also wrote a polemical pamphlet, *Pornography: The New Terrorism*, expounding the Dworkin thesis and relating it to the upset she felt after viewing what she regarded as a 'snuff' movie.[64]

The issue of 'snuff' movies, or films in which real people are allegedly killed, was one of the main propaganda weapons used in the 1980s by pro-censorship campaigns. The origin of this particular sub-genre of horror was the cheap and crudely-made *Slaughter* (Michael and Roberta Findlay, 1971, USA/Argentina). Having been initially shelved as unmarketable, it was retitled *Snuff* in 1975 by exploitation pioneer Allan Shackleton, and promoted not so as to cash in on the new interest in the 1969 Charles Manson 'Family' murders due to Lynette Alice Fromme's assassination attempt of President Ford, but the emerging public interest in 'mondo' or documentary atrocity. To this end, Shackleton highlighted the film's appalling quality, and, cutting the opening sequence and film credits, passed it off as *ciné-vérité*. Furthermore, he added a four-minute 'film-within-a-film' sequence in which a woman film crew member is brutally killed, dismembered and disemboweled. This sequence underpinned the film's 'authenticity' for many pro-censorship campaigners, though many failed to notice the impossibility (for a *vérité* film) of some of the shots filmed. Attendant with the American release of the film, he organized a protest campaign fuelled by self-created fictitious decency groups. The publicity trick worked and the film which was a commercial and notorious success – in a post-modern play – came to provide the evidence for the existence of a genre.[65] So far, there has been no reported seizure of a (real) snuff movie in Ireland, or that said, any evidence that one exists even if it is safe to assume that such a criminal activity like the sexual abuse of children as well as adults, has been recorded for the camera and circulated (for obvious reasons) in private. (Of course, the internet broadcasting by Islamic militants of the beheading of prisoners in 2004 could be characterized as 'snuff movies' though they more easily fit into mondo film.)

Jennifer Wicke notes that while pornography is associated with mass culture, erotica's reference points are within art, thus legitimizing certain forms of pornography for bourgeois consumption.[66] As Pamela Church Gibson and Roma Gibson suggest, pornography 'is a hidden partner of the high art/mass culture conflict.'[67] Or, put another way, erotica is about desire and titillation; pornography is concerned with the physical, and, as such, the *emptying* of desire. No such field of discussion was opened by those Irish parliamentarians concerned with 'video nasties'. Indeed, by focusing on the relatively unproblematic exploitation of children they operated at the extreme, and as such beyond debate. Central to this limiting approach were the invited contributions of Dr J. Robins, Child Care Services, Department of Health, and Dr Maire Woods of the Sexual Assault Unit, Rotunda Hospital, who reporting on their work with sexually-abused children, noted, rather interestingly, that in an Irish study of sixteen abusers of children, 'half of those involved were considered by their families to be excessively religious.'[68] A 1985 Dutch survey confirmed the Irish finding of the link between abuse and 'extreme religious orthodoxy'. The relevance of, or reason as to this interrelationship was not explored, but it was asserted that 'the combination of sex and violence in some material available at present has a very significant effect on young people.' This effect was stated to be 'the identification of the viewer' with 'the person committing the violent acts, rather than with the victim.' However, while it is true that audiences get involved or identify with the hero or strong characters, it remains the case, as has been noted within film theory and analysis that attraction is moreover motivated by goodness but also by a vulnerability or softness. As Robin Wood, discussing Alfred Hitchcock's *oeuvre* argues, 'there is a "natural" (read: endemic to our culture) tendency to identify with the character who is threatened'[69] and where danger is extreme, as in the roof scene in *Vertigo* (1958), identification is immediate. When the subject is attractive (female), identification is intensified.[70] Indeed, if we measure the group's conclusion and analyze how it operates in relation to one of the most noto-rious video nasties (along with *Snuff* and Abel Ferrara's 1979 *The Driller Killer* ) – *I Spit on Your Grave* – we find a surprising reading which perhaps explains why this particular film was elevated to such heights of opprobrium by male and unsuspecting female critics who had not seen the film.

*I Spit on Your Grave*, of which John Boorman's *Deliverance* and Sam Peckinpah's *Straw Dogs* are important prototypes, is a rape/revenge film. One of the first films to stage such a story on a city/country axis,[71] it concerns the brutal and graphic though detached rape, by four men of city-dweller Jennifer Hills (Camille Keaton) who has rented a house in the countryside in order to finish writing her novel. Seeking revenge, Jennifer kills the four men in the most gruesome, though similarly detached, ways. The first one – a simpleton, who is a virgin and despite a number of attempts fails to suc-cessfully rape her – she lures into a trap, where, as he is reaching sexual climax, is strung up by a rope and hanged. The ringleader of the rapists finds his comeuppance when he is enjoying sex in a bath with Jennifer and she cuts his penis off, which leads to his bloody death. The two remaining men, one who had anally raped her, she kills with an axe, while the fourth – a psycho who put a bottle in her vagina and demanded oral sex – she fatally mutilates with a boat's outboard engine.

The film's status in Ireland is clearly illustrated by the *Evening Herald's* front page reproduction of the video cover on 7 October 1987, the day when the Video Recordings Bill was published. The cover carries a description of the motivation of the video's female protagonist: 'This woman [seen from behind after being raped] cut, chopped, broke and burned four men beyond recognition ... But no jury in America would con-vict her!' This description alone indicates why the video was targeted for special atten-tion by male politicians and commentators. Marco Starr offers an interpretation of the film in which he shows how distorted even liberal critics had been in their (mis)read-ing of the film. He suggests that although the film makes male viewers uncomfortable and insecure in that 'a castration scene ... is performed with such realistic anguish ... that it should make even the most unconverted male viewer think twice about even considering committing rape,'[72] the film should not be seen as representing the rapists' points-of-view. He argues that far from being the anti-female film which its critics claimed, it could be read as being sympathetic to its female protagonist as its ultimate point of identification is with the original victim. Carol Clover, who offers a detailed analysis of the film, has a similar position. According to her, while it presents a cine-matically 'rare expression of abject terror on the part of the male'[73] and 'which for all its disturbing qualities at least problematizes the issue of male (sexual) violence,'[74] *I Spit on Your Grave*, with its too simple structure of rape and revenge stripped of deeper intellectual motivation or context, 'shocks not because it is alien but because it is too familiar, ... we recognize ... the [repressed or culturally unacceptable] emotions it engages [and which are] almost never bluntly acknowledged for what they are.'[75] In contrasting the film with the commercial feature *The Accused* (Jonathan Kaplan, 1988), in which group rape also takes on the aspect of a sport, Clover suggests that what is disturbing about *I Spit on Your Grave* 'is the way it exposes the inner workings of *The*

*Accused* and films like it – the way it reminds us that lots and lots of the movies and television dramas that we prefer to think of in higher terms are in fact funded by [primitive] impulses we would rather deny.' *I Spit on Your Grave* is, in effect, 'the repressed' of *The Accused*. 'I suspect,' Clover concludes, 'that it is for this reason as much as any other that it has met with the punitive response it has.'[76] While the film was characterized by critics 'in tones of outrage in the name of feminism, as the ultimate incitement to male sadism,' Clover says that

> there is something off here: something too shrill and too totalizing in the claim of misogyny, something dishonest in the critical rewritings and outright misrepresentations of the plot required to sustain that claim, something suspicious about the refusal to entertain even in passing the involvement with the victim's part, something perverse about the unwillingness to engage with the manifestly feminist dimensions of the script, and something dubious in the refusal to note its debt to *Deliverance* and the critical implications of that debt.[77]

Interestingly, in Ireland *I Spit on Your Grave* continues to be banned as the prohibition order of 1994 when video censorship was introduced was re-confirmed in 2000.[78]

Of course, from the perspective of right-wing Irish legislators, the ability to co-opt feminists for a censorship measure was a bonus. The Council for the Status of Women, which represents a very broad church of women's organizations, at their annual conference on 12 April 1986 had passed an emergency resolution which stated that it was

> seriously alarmed at the widespread availability of 'video nasties' in this country. Pornographic, often extremely violent, films seem to be readily accessible, even to young children. The Council believes that this *could* be a contributory factor in the growing incidence of rape and other forms of violence against women and children. (Emphasis added.)[79]

The national newspapers, liberal and otherwise, played their roles in support of the video censorship measures by echoing the misrepresentations of *I Spit on Your Grave*, *Snuff* and other such titles in the horror/slasher genre.

At the Committee on Crime, Lawlessness and Vandalism, the child abuse workers stated that 'the combination of sex and violence has a greater influence on young people than hard-core pornography,' but there was no questioning of point-of-view; it was always assumed that the oppressors were positively represented. The other two invited contributors to the Committee's deliberations were the Film Censor, Frank Hall, and the IVA. Hall, who largely confined himself to outlining the operation of the Censorship of Films Act, 1923, said he favoured censorship of videos as their widespread availability was affecting the censorship of films. He also explained that 'the main criteria in examining films was to look at the *overall purpose* and if it is to excite sexual violence then such a film will be banned or cuts will be made if appropriate.'

(Emphasis added.)[80] The IVA restated their by-now familiar pro-censorship arguments whereby videos would be classified and video retail outlets would be licensed. For obvious financial and administrative reasons, the body favoured adopting the BBFC video classification system, or some other international code. However, it displayed its more repressive approach by suggesting that there should be included in the legislation a provision to prosecute anyone found viewing or possessing an unclassified video. Such people, they stated, should be liable to 'stiff prison sentences and heavy fines'.[81] Although this draconian proposal was not included in the Committee's recommendations, the industry was generally happy with its conclusions.

The Committee stated that 'the widespread availability of videos depicting unrestrained violence, sexual abuse, mutilation and murder ... was a rapidly growing social problem' which was arousing 'wide public concern'.[82]

> Such videos can have a damaging and disturbing effect on many people who see them. Some videos depict dreadful rape scenes and physical abuse which have the effect of dehumanising women. Others deal with unrestricted physical violence. The combination of brutal sex and violence is extremely dangerous and cannot but have a corrupting influence on some viewers, especially young people.[83]

Consequently, it concluded, there was an immediate need to introduce controls regarding video. It recommended that videos be classified for audience suitability; that the Film Censor's terms of reference be extended to allow the Censor to consider an appeal against classification of a video; that retail outlets be licensed; and that the legislation include heavy penalties, including imprisonment, for anyone trading in unclassified videos. What the Committee shied away from was the crucial aspect of defining the criteria under which videos should be classified, though, by then, committee member Mervyn Taylor had published a Private Member's Bill proposing censorship of videos. Taylor didn't look too far for his Bill as he simply reproduced parts of Britain's 1984 Video Recordings Act, while also proposing restrictions more oppressive than those within that document.

The British Act states that a video is not allowed if it depicts to any significant extent (a), human sexual activity or acts of force or restraint associated with such activity; (b), mutilation or torture, or other acts of gross violence towards humans or animals; (c), human genital organs or human urinary or excretory functions; or is designed to any significant extent to stimulate or encourage anything falling within paragraph (b). Similarly, Taylor's Video Recordings Bill (No. 20 of 1986), proposed that a video be prohibited if it depicted to any significant extent (a), acts of force or restraint associated with sexual activity; (b), mutilation or torture, or other acts of gross violence towards humans or animals; (c), human urinary or excretory functions, or is designed to any extent to stimulate or encourage anything falling within paragraph (a) or (b), or could reasonably be regarded as so doing. Taylor excluded nursing, medical and psychiatric training videos, and perhaps reflecting his Judaism, added a final exclusion of videos which disseminated information relating to crimes of genocide as defined in the Genocide Act, 1973.[84] However, Taylor's Bill did not progress to the second stage (of parliamentary debate) because the Minister for Justice, Alan Dukes, told the Committee on Crime, Lawlessness and Vandalism on 16 June 1986 that his department was examining the law in relation to videos. When this review was completed he intended to bring proposals to government. Almost eighteen months later in October 1987, Fianna Fáil's Gerard Collins appointed Minister for Justice eight months earlier, published the Video Recordings Bill (No. 38 of 1987), but it was another two years before the Video Recordings Act became law and a further five years before video censorship was fully activated on 1 September 1994.

The Video Recordings Bill, 1987 proposed a system to be administered by the Film Censor's office of censoring videos prior to release by which videos would be approved for general viewing or banned. Under Section 3 (1), certification was to be prohibited if the Official Censor considered that the viewing of it, (a) (i), 'would be likely to cause persons to commit crimes, whether by inciting or encouraging them to do so or by indicating or suggesting ways of doing so or of avoiding detection'; (a) (ii), 'would be likely to stir up racial hatred against any group of persons in the State on account of their race, nationality or religion'; (a) (iii), 'would tend, by reason of the inclusion in it of any obscene or indecent matter, to deprave or corrupt persons who might view it'; or (b), 'it depicts acts of gross violence or cruelty (including mutilation and torture) towards humans or animals.'

These clauses were a significant development of the criteria in the Censorship of Films Act. For example, in the areas of representations of crime, humans and animals, new concepts of censorship were being introduced. Also, the mere depiction (or representation) of violence or cruelty (rather than as in Britain's 1984 Act where it was the depiction to *any significant extent*) was to be forbidden for the first time, a point forcefully made by David Norris during the debate in the Senate, where the Bill was introduced, when he gave a graphic description of King Lear having his eyes gouged out in Shakespeare's play.[85] A film with such images, he argued, could very well be banned under the Bill while sub-clause (a) (ii) of Section 3 (1) in which the phrase 'would be likely to stir up' could be deemed as giving too wide political latitude to a future censor. Brendan Ryan and David Norris proposed,[86] with the strong support of Irish National Teachers Organization General-Secretary Senator Joe O'Toole, an amendment to include 'sexual orientation' in the list of minorities to be protected. Rather than accept the amendment, with its implied reference to homosexuality, the government withdrew the whole sub-section. Later in the Dáil they relented and an extended sub-section was introduced. As a result, it now reads, 'would be likely to stir up hatred against a group of persons in the State or elsewhere on account of their race, colour, nationality, religion, ethnic or national origins, membership of the traveling community or sexual orientation.' Otherwise, the criteria for prohibition were approved as originally published. In both the Senate and the Dáil, where all sides of the House welcomed its provisions, there was little reflective questioning of its wide-ranging provision – exceptions were (from the Left) Proinsias de Rossa and (from the Right) Michael

McDowell (appointed Minister for Justice following the 2002 general election). As the
Bill made its way through the Oireachtas between November 1987 and December
1989, most of the contributions were marked by the familiar impressionistic, unin-
formed and prejudiced assertions concerning 'video nasties' which had characterized
the debate in Ireland (and Britain) throughout the 1980s. In practice, few 'video nasties' came to the attention of the video censorship authorities after the activation of
the legislation; the vast majority of videos prohibited have been 'hard-core' and 'soft-
core' pornography, not the horror/slasher genre.

While the Bill did not include a provision for cutting of films or the classification
of videos, it did allow for the release on video of films which had already received a
theatrical release. Had this proposal become law it would have created the anomaly
of films with limited certificates being given a general release on video without further cutting. Though about 10 per cent of films for video submitted to the BBFC are
cut, in Ireland, film distributors lobbied against cutting on the basis that the country
offered too small a market to justify the effort and expense.[87] An appeal to the
Censorship of Films Appeal Board was, however, proposed. After all parties in the
Senate came out in favour of video classification, and later many others in the Dáil
debate, the government conceded and introduced (later given effect by ministerial
order from 1 September 1994) four classification categories: over-18s, over-15s, under-
12s with adult, and general. (On 1 January 1997, video classification was amended
by ministerial order such that under-12s with adult was renamed 12PG ['parental guidance'], describing material 'fit for viewing generally, but in the case of a child under-
12 years, only in the company of a responsible adult,' and a new category of 'fit for
viewing by persons aged twelve years or more' was introduced, bringing video in line
with film censorship, though the changes in film classification with the replacement
in 2001 of the over-15s certificate with 15PG, and the over-12s with 12PG, were not
introduced for video classification. Thus, film classification currently has five categories: general, parental guidance, 12PG, 15PG and over-18s, while video classification has general, under-12PG, over-12s, over-15s and over-18s.) Another amendment
to the Bill accepted by the minister was that all video outlets be licensed, a proposal
long advocated by the IVA. Their not-so-hidden hand was evident throughout the
debate with many senators promoting the IVA's case and reporting on the intensity of
the group's lobbying. By way of illustration, the minister said that the organization
had met his officials on a number of occasions to discuss the Bill. Unsurprisingly, such
interference disturbed a number of senators, most especially Ryan and Norris.
According to the latter, 'quite a substantial amount of the energies behind the Bill
[were] orchestrated by [this] very strong commercial lobby.'[88] Given that, among other
issues, 'no convincing evidence was adduced of a casual relationship between crime,
corruption and videos,'[89] Norris remained opposed in principle to the Bill, the only
senator to do so. While the IVA was undoubtedly a major influence in the debate,
other sometimes diverse organizations also supported the introduction of the new
measures to control film on video, including the Irish Housewives' Association, the
Rape Crisis Centre, the Women's Rights Committee of the Oireachtas, the Children's

Protection Society, the Community Standards Association, and the teachers' unions, though the support of the INTO's Joe O'Toole's was qualified. The minister also revealed that officials from his department involved in drafting the Bill had held consultations with the British Videogram Association, the Home Office, and the BBFC.[90] Additionally, the Bill proposed that there would be at least one woman member of the Appeal Board in future, something which had been operating in practice since the first Board was appointed in 1924. Usually there were two women members, but it was not until 1997 that it had its first chairwoman, Barbara Culleton; its first clergywoman, the Church of Ireland's the Revd Canon Virginia Kennerley; and a third woman, Mary McEvaddy, among its members.

The Bill was supported in principle by the two main opposition parties, Fine Gael and Labour. Fine Gael's Philip Hogan, displaying the same social class bias against popular culture as his parliamentary predecessors, expressed his 'serious concern' not just about the availability of 'video nasties' but that 'teenagers are being lured to engage in the manufacture of video nasties.'[91] In the course of his speech with its tone of moral outrage, Hogan managed to criticize 'the lower socio-economic' groups on four occasions:

> The rampant corruption of attitudes and minds, particularly in urban areas and in the lower socio-economic areas, is very worrying at the moment. It is indefensible that any society should tolerate this for so long.[92]

Senator McEllistrim quoted favourably the since discredited report which influenced the British Houses of Parliament in passing the 1984 Act.[93] He went on to express 'shock and deep concern at the horrific content' of films such as *The Driller Killer* (a rather tedious film, poorly scripted, badly acted, and with low production values, which made a name for itself with its electric driller/artist who kills all and sundry without much motivation) and *I Spit on Your Grave*. Only independent Senators Ryan and Norris offered any resistance to these prejudices. However, despite pronouncing his liberal credentials as an opponent of censorship, Ryan conceded to the Bill's principle in the second sentence of the first of his many contributions to the debate.[94] Thereafter, he proposed numerous amendments with the intention of ameliorating the Bill's more extreme elements, before finally describing it as 'reasonably liberal'.[95] The *Irish Press* also was unimpressed with the Bill, especially following Minister for Justice Gerard Collins somewhat incoherent second stage speech in the Senate. The *Press'* editorial, 'Get Tough on Nasties,' argued that the proposals were 'half-baked'.[96] The *Press* called for a three-pronged approach: censorship, licensing outlets, and tougher piracy regulations,[97] though there was no mention of the grading of videos.

While the Irish Council of Civil Liberties (ICCL) expressed concern at the Bill's provisions this was tempered by a split within the organization with anti-pornography feminists supporting it on the basis of the 'civil rights' issue affecting women. Tom Cooney, the organization's chair and law lecturer at University College Dublin, told the *Irish Times* that although the ICCL acknowledged the need for legislation to protect children from certain videos, it opposed the Bill,[98] ICCL member Clodagh Corcoran responded in a letter to the *Irish Times* expounding the view that pornography ('video nasties') was 'anti-social'. The presence of 'video nasties' in our midst 'constitutes a societal tolerance for sexual abuse of all women and children. Those who defend their continued existence are complicit in this.'[99] Consequently, anyone who opposed the Bill or her ideological certainties was constituted as a supporter of abuse against women and children. The issue erupted again when the ICCL released a statement attacking the Bill as being so broad it could lead to the banning of *Moby Dick* or *The A-Team*, a popular family, if more male-oriented, American television series in which a group of four men operating outside the law, though always to serve justice, concoct and carry out various madcap plans that result in violent spectacles but during which no one is shown to be fatally injured or killed.[1] In early May 1988, by which time the Bill had been approved by the Senate, a press conference was held by some women members of the ICCL, including executive committee members Pauline Beegan and Odile Hendriks, and former executive member Bernie Dwyer, who cited the 'snuff' movie scare as a further motivation to support censorship.[2] Among the speakers at the conference were Ailbhe Smith of UCD's Women's Studies Centre, who described the ICCL's official position as 'unthinking and disgraceful'. Cooney responded by simply stating that 'in a liberal democracy adults can differentiate between fact and fantasy.'[3]

In the meantime, a group at the Irish Film Institute organized a seminar in December 1987 to explore the implications of the Bill. This event was addressed by Tom Cooney, and cultural and media academics Luke Gibbons, Stephanie McBride and myself in the capacity as the IFI's chair.[4] A summary of the main concerns of the seminar was communicated to the Minister for Justice, with the emphasis placed on amending the criteria for censorship in a manner not dissimilar to that proposed by Senators Norris and Ryan. Section 3 (b) of the Bill concerning depictions of violence and cruelty was discussed at considerable length and was found to be objectionable on a number of grounds. It was argued in the submission to the minister that

> This provision greatly extends censorship as it has applied to films. The mere depiction or representation of any acts of gross violence or cruelty will lead to automatic banning of a video film. If, for example, a single frame of mutilation or torture in any video film is objected to the whole film may be banned. Since the Bill makes no provision for suggested cuts of video films, then, as with book censorship in the past when a single sentence or paragraph taken out of context could lead to a banning, so, too, may the same approach be applied to video films. What was deemed most objectionable in this paragraph was that this banning will apply irrespective of whether it will have any effect on a viewer.[5]

Although the submission was acknowledged,[6] the key issues concerning representations raised by the ICCL and the IFI seminar were ignored and no amendments to the Bill followed. For example, cutting of videos is not offered as an option to the censors. They are either classified according to age groups or prohibited entirely 'due to the [commercial] impracticality of making separate versions for the Irish market.'[7] As a *Film Ireland* editorial noted, 'distributors seldom go to the trouble and expense of having [a] cut [made for a cinema release] replicated on tapes which would be released solely in the Irish market.'[8] As a result, one of the most productive areas in assessing the history of Irish film censorship policy in earlier chapters – the ability to explore the thinking behind particular decisions when a list of cuts is available – is unavailable under the Video Recordings Act. This provides the censor with a further piece of administrative artillery.

As films certified for theatrical release are automatically given a video certificate, the Film Censor, when viewing a theatrical film, may have an eye on what will happen to that film on video. There is at least one example of this, David Cronenberg's *Crash*, to which Film Censor Sheamus Smith ordered a cut in the hope that it would scupper its video release (something he confirmed in an interview with me).[9] To Smith's surprise the film was subsequently, if not immediately, released on video and DVD in Ireland with a cut of about thirty-five seconds acceded to by the distributors. The offending material was in the scene in which James (James Spader) and his wife Catherine (Deborah Unger) are naked and having sex on their bed, while she fantasizes out loud about her husband having sex with Vaughan (Elias Koteas), a man with whom they both are infatuated and who organizes car crashes as a type of sexual and life-enhancing sport. Though the film 'delights' – if, in a strangely cold and clinical way – in the body, often fetishizing the combination of metal and the injured or 'mutated' body which opens further sexual possibilities. The choice of this particular scene was hardly casual or accidental as it describes a homosexual encounter fantasized by Catherine, one which is more explicit than usually heard in commercial cinema:

> Is he circumcised? Can you imagine what his anus is like? Describe it to me. Would you like to sodomize him? Would you like to put your penis right into his anus, thrust it up his anus? Tell me, describe it to me. Tell me what you would do. How would you kiss him in that car? Describe how you'd reach over and unzip his greasy jeans, then take out his penis. Would you kiss it or suck it right away? Which hand would you hold it in? Have you ever sucked a penis? Do you know what semen tastes like? Have you ever tasted semen? Some semen is saltier than others. Vaughan's semen must be very salty …

As the published script puts it at this point, 'they both have huge orgasms within moments of each other,' and the cut continues to the interior of Helen Remington's (Holly Hunter) car where she says, 'Have you come?' as she and James (who earlier in the film crashed into her) are having sex in the back seat until she dismounts him 'and touches his shoulder with an uncertain hand, as though a patient she had worked hard to revive.'

While the cut removed one of the longest verbal exchanges between characters in the film, for a sex scene, as the editorial in *Film Ireland* noted, 'it's not particularly graphic.'¹⁰ As it happened, the film was only shown (uncut) in Ireland in 1997 under club conditions at the Irish Film Centre and at the Dublin and Cork film festivals. Criticizing the Censor's approach to the film, the *Film Ireland* editorial concluded that no one would censor *Crash* if it was shown at the Irish Museum of Modern Art (IMMA), 'but because it might be ... at the Savoy or UCI cinemas, or ultimately, on a VCR in your home, then it needs a licence to be seen.' Such a benign view of the immunity of art galleries from film and video censorship was rudely shattered when in August 2002 the Butler Gallery, Kilkenny, was raided by police investigating a complaint from a member of the public that the gallery was showing uncensored performance art videos, mostly from the 1970s, featuring often naked American artist Paul McCarthy. Following consultations with the Film Censor's office, the videos were allowed to be shown, but the exhibits were confined to over-18s, who had to sign in, ergo creating a mock membership for the event, before the work could be seen.¹¹ According to censor Audrey Conlon, had the gallery, even if informally, shown the videos to the video censors, as seems to be the practice even at IMMA if videos are being shown, then they would get a form of official endorsement without a video certificate being issued.¹²

Prior to the full activation of the Video Recordings Act, and following criticism of the delay by Workers Party TD (and now Judge) Pat McCartan in enacting the legislation, sections of the Act were implemented. Under a ministerial order with effect from 1 May 1991, wholesalers and retailers were licensed to sell videos. By April the following year, 10 of the former had paid £4,000 each for licences, while 1,418 retailers had paid £100. These numbers have remained fairly constant, with, for example, 8 wholesale, 1,437 retail and 45 vehicle retail licences issued in 1999; and in 2003, 9 wholesale, 1,351 retail and 22 vehicle retail licences, at a cost of €220,040 to the trade. From July 1991, the Film Censor was empowered to prohibit videos under the terms defined in the Act, and by the end of the year, 34 such videos had been banned, including Ken Russell's *Whore*, a film which has the distinction of being the first video banned in Ireland as its prohibition order is 1/1991; *Slaughter/Snuff* whose notoriety is confirmed by being the number 2 banning of 1991, but on whose history Ciaran Carty accurately reported;¹³ and *The Texas Chainsaw Massacre* (Tobe Hooper, 1974) was number 3 in 1991. As further staff resources were needed to censor videos, it was necessary to introduce separate legislation – the Censorship of Films (Amendment) Act, 1992 – to empower the Minister for Justice to appoint assistant censors to certify the newly-released videos. By 1994, one full-time chief assistant, Audrey Conlon, in practice the deputy Film Censor, together with six assistants were employed, initially, to systematically censor all newly-released videos. In this first phase, largely without training or guidelines, although Conlon spent a week at the BBFC observing their classification system, the censors assessed pornographic and other videos seized by the Gardaí and customs officials. It was a baptism of fire for a group with little or no familiarity with how different straight-to-video can be from theatrical films.

Choosing a somewhat random selection of videos from the more than 3,200 prohibited (PO) during 1991–2003, one characteristic of the early banning is how many date from the 1970s, or even earlier, such as *Debbie Does Dallas* (Jim Clark, 1978;

PO 6/1992), *Deep Throat II* (Joseph W. Sarno, 1974; PO 9/1994), *The Devil in Miss Jones* (Gerard Damiano, 1973; PO 203 1996), Jayne Mansfield in *Promises! Promises!* (PO 595/1994), *Russ Meyer's Up!* (Russ Meyer, 1976; PO 153/1999), *Russ Meyer's Beneath of the Valley of the Ultra Vixens* (Russ Meyer, 1979; PO 157/1999), *Sex and the Married Woman* (Jack Arnold, 1977; PO 22/ 1991), *Straw Dogs* (PO 597/1994), and *Trash* (aka *Drug Trash*, Paul Morrissey, 1970), which failed the 'deprave and corrupt test' because of two long scenes of injecting drugs, a 'sex scene [with a] girl using [a] beer bottle and lots more' (PO 452/1995; video censor Olga Bennett, 17 October 1995). In this selection, horror is well represented (as befits a censorship law that sought to repress its more extreme productions) with titles such as *Blood Sucking Freaks* (Joel M. Reed, 1976; PO 27/1994), *Zombie Creeping Flesh* (*Inferno Dei Morti-Viventi*, Vincent Dawn [Bruno Mattei], 1981, Italy/Spain; PO 12/1992), *Zombie Flesh Eaters* (Lucio Fulci, 1979, Italy; PO 702/1994), and *Zombie Holocaust* (*La Regina dei Cannabali*, Marion Girolami, 1980, Italy; PO 110/1993) all banned. There is a further category, perhaps somewhat amusing, but often hard-core sexually pornographic films which seek (often in their weak punning ways) to echo mainstream commercial cinema titles, as well as popular songs: *A Prayer for the Fucking* (PO 115/1999), *Booberella* (GB, 1997; PO 55/1998), *Bang Cock* (PO 256/1995), *Bonnie Does Clyde* (PO 139/1992), *Cum All Ye Faithful* (PO 118/1998), *Driving Miss Crazy* (PO 90/1992), *Educating Nina* (Juliet Anderson, 1984; PO 307/1996), *The Erotic Adventures of Bonnie & Clyde* (PO 9/1991), *First Fuck Instinct* (PO 117/1994), *Great Balls for Hire* (PO 340/1994), *House of the Licking Sun* (PO 174/1997), *Jane Bond Meets Golden Rod* (PO 212/1994), *Looking for Mr Goodsex* (PO 7/1992), *Love Me Tender* (PO 623/1994), *Miss Adventures at Megaboob Manor* (PO 274/1994), *Nightmare on Porn Street* (PO 32/1991), *Read My Lips* (PO 142/1995), *Roman Holiday* (PO 68/1995), *Secrets of My Sexcess* (PO 628/1994), *Terms of Endowment* (PO 382/1994), *The British Are Coming* (PO 763/1994), *Total Reball* (PO 302/1994), *Twin Cheeks 3 – Behind Closed Doors* (PO 386/1994), *Very Dirty Dancing* (PO 49/1994), and *Whole Lotta Fucking Goin' On* (PO 158/1995). Many others simply have sexually explicit descriptive titles: *American Fuckathon* (PO 357/1994 ), *Anal Partners* (PO 18/1992), *Animal Fucking* (8/1993), *Boys Who Do It All* (PO 58/1995), *Boys Will be Girls* (PO 219/1992), *Chinese Kama Sutra* (PO 63/1995), *Cocks in Frocks* (PO 122/1999), *Dog Fuckers* (PO 541/1994), *Gagged and Bound* (PO 20/2000), *Girls for Hire* (PO 302/1993), *Hot Lesbo* (PO 320/1994), *Lady Lust* (PO 51/1996), *Lesbian Lovers* (PO 219/1993), *Lust Italian Style* (PO 649/1994), *Naughty Nurses* (PO 186/1994), *Nothing But Sex* (PO 178/1997), *Porno Painting* (PO 27/1993), *Sexcapades* (PO 79/1994), *Slave for Rent* (PO 741/1994), *Stiff Competition* (PO 115/1995), *Teenage Dog Orgy* (PO 162/1993), and *Who Wants to be an Erotic Billionaire?* (PO 7/2002). The irony, of course, as is discussed in the next section, is that it is perfectly legal for an Irish citizen to access any of this adult pornography on the internet. It is only child pornography which is illegal, and even then it seems, it is illegal only if the viewer downloads it to his/her computer.

The video classifiers reports overwhelmingly are made up of specific references to the 1989 Act, such that usually there is no social or cultural commentary offered. However, on these one-page reports, there are categories for recording the classifier's view on the following areas: Theme; Audience; Language; Sex/Nudity; Drugs; Copycat Techniques; Horror; and Violence. While few videos exercised the classifiers to assess the video beyond quotations from or references to specific sections of the 1989 Act, a few required more considered articulation of the decision. Thus, in a rare commentary on a banned video, the two video censors, Violet Ennis and Ger Connolly, defended their 1999 decision to prohibit Tod Browning's, 1932 *Freaks* (a box-office failure discussed in chapter 5), by declaring it to be 'grossly offensive' not just to 'those in society who may suffer from the afflictions portrayed,' but because 'it assumes that all members of this group would exact a dreadful punishment on those who ridiculed or looked down on them.' The 'inclusion of so many abnormalities,' the censors suggested, was for 'the purpose of horrifying the viewer' and 'to create a feeling of revulsion,' something which was quite explicit in the film's original publicity campaign by MGM, although it was tempered with recourse to sentimentality and the 'human' aspect of these 'freaks'. Additionally, because the film suggested that society had no place except a circus for anyone who is not 'normal,' the film, which, even at the time of the film's initial release against a background of the (dying) freak-show, could be regarded as an exercise in unsettling exploitation, 'offends not only the people who are affected but also the general public,' who, the censors argue, 'are, by implication, unable to cope with' physical difference, as well as confirming the social 'prejudice and fear of those who do not conform to our idea of the norm.' (Video report, 7 February 1999; PO 134/1999.) Unfortunately, but as is to be expected within the limitations of the censoring process, in John Keith's censor's report on *The Annabel Chong Story* (1999), shown initially at the 1999 Dublin Film Festival, and about a young woman's attempt to set a world record by having sex with 250 men in a ten-hour period, he confined himself to a literal description void of cultural commentary. He offers an inventory of various aspects of the 'World's Biggest Gang Bang': 27 uses of the 'F' word and 'several males having sex with woman,' etc., yet there is no attention drawn to the (somewhat ridiculous) spectacle of the men lining up publicly to have sex with Annabel. The relentless focus on sex, leads not to an erotic or pornographic voyeurism, but to a potentially distancing examination of the relationship between the sexes. (Viewing, 21 March 2000; final decision, 31 March 2000.)

While there were an estimated 10,000 different video titles in distribution in Ireland in 1992, a figure that was increasing annually by as many as 4,000,[14] as table 3 indicates (excluding trailers) an average during 2000–2003 (inclusive) of 965 videos were certified for the rental market and a further 3,183 for the sell-through market, or just over 4,000 per annum.[15] From 1 September 1994, only new video releases were legally obliged to carry the Irish Censor's classification. Back catalogue titles, it was decided, would be certified later. In practice, the censors may not still have caught up with the backlog due to the number of new videos being submitted by distributors, as well as their having to adjudicate on the thousands of tapes (mainly pornographic) seized by customs officers and the Gardaí. Consequently, some pre-1992 videos in circulation

**57** *Gilda* (Charles Vidor, 1946, USA)

Gilda (Rita Hayworth) performs 'Put the Blame on Mame'. 'A sinister unpleasant film. Sex, passion right through but without moral considerations. There are numerous sensual scenes and several murders. I have considered cutting but find that it would have to be so drastic, that it would leave the picture meaningless.' (Banned by Richard Hayes, 1946; passed with cuts after appeal.)

**58** *Rear Window* (Alfred Hitchcock, 1954, USA)
Sports' writer L.B. Jeffries (James Stewart) and fiancée Lisa Freemont's (Grace Kelly) kissing had to be 'drastically' curtailed while his comment 'Sure, like staying here all night uninvited' was removed. Additionally Martin Brennan imposed on this meta-cinema narrative a number of cuts concerning the revealing Miss Torso, and the attempted assault in the flat.

'Complaints are pouring in from all parts of this State regarding kisses shown on the screen that would not be attempted even on the stage. As a matter of fact a prolonged kiss on the stage provokes ridicule, but the cinema, to the accompaniment of the most sensuous music, lavishes miles of celluloid on this unsanitary salute.' (James Montgomery, 1928)

59 *Camille* (Fred Niblo, 1927, USA)
Norma Talmadge as Camille with one of her lovers, Armand (Gilbert Roland), in this adaptation of Alexandre Dumas, fils, *La Dame aux Camelias*. Montgomery rejected the film in 1927 as undesirable: 'A year ago exactly I rejected another screen version of "La Dame" and wrote ... "Stripped of its sentimentality, it is the unhealthy and immoral story of a consumptive courtesan".'

60 *Sunset Boulevard* (Billy Wilder, 1950, USA)
Norma Desmond (Gloria Swanson) draws Joe Gillis (William Holden) into her bed. 'This picture centres round the infatuation of a wealthy middle-aged ex-film star for a young man. She loads him with favours and finally seducing him she becomes his mistress ... certificate refused.' (Banned by Richard Hayes, 1950; passed with one cut after appeal.) Surely, it is he who becomes *her* plaything.

**61** *The Postman Always Rings Twice* (Tay Garnett, 1946, USA)
Lovers Frank (John Garfield) and Cora (Lana Turner) plan the murder of her husband (Cecil Kellaway). 'The usual triangle – but in this case without a relieving feature ... It is a base, sordid picture into which moral considerations of any kind do not even faintly enter. Certificate refused even for adult audiences.' (Banned by Richard Hayes, 1946; ban upheld after appeal.) 'I have to be particularly careful about this picture ... I doubt the validity of my passing it at all.' (Passed with five cuts by Liam O'Hora, 1962.)

**62** *Brief Encounter* (David Lean, 1945, GB)
Platonic lovers Laura (Celia Johnson) and Alec (Trevor Howard) leave a cinema. 'This film dealing with the entanglement of a married man and married woman has numerous seductive and indelicate situations. The woman lies to her husband regarding her intrigue. Moral considerations are completely ignored ... and only circumstances part them at the end. At the end, too, the woman hesitates about suicide, and the pair part with regret and without remorse. The intriguing pair as presented tend to arouse a certain sympathy in their amorous relationship.' (Banned by Hayes, 1946; ban upheld after appeal. Released with cuts in 1962.)

**63** *Les Enfants du Paradis* (aka *Children of Paradise*, Marcel Carné, 1945, France)
Mime artist Baptiste (Jean-Louis Barrault), loves the enigmatic Garance (Arletty, above), who has several lovers including Lemâitre (Pierre Brasseur, above). Hayes 'regret[ted]' banning this 'outstanding film. Its central character is a lady without moral sense and with many lovers. The dubious situations are delicately done, and I would have little hesitation in granting a certificate for adult audiences ...' (1947)

**64** *Room at the Top* (Jack Clayton, 1958, GB)
Socially-ambitious Joe (Laurence Harvey) and married Alice (Simone Signoret) continue their love affair in this key film of the British New Wave. 'I have seen three different editions of this picture. Much of the adulterous overtones, the erotic love-making and all the crude dialogue have been removed but I still felt that I could not pass the film for general exhibition.' (O'Hora, 1961. Banned in 1959, 1960, 1961, 1962, 1964; released 1967.)

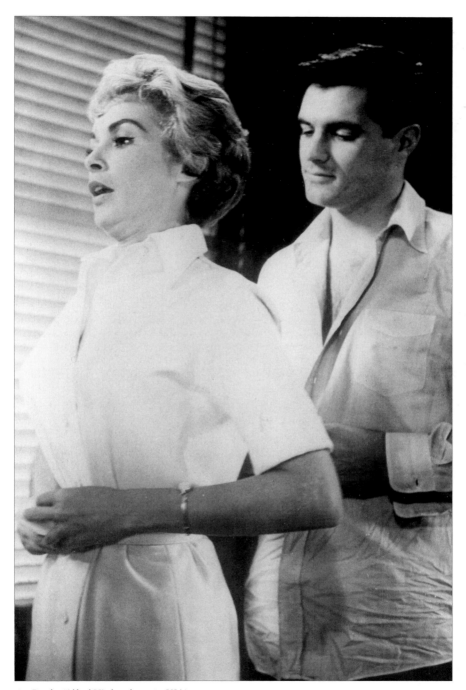

**65** *Psycho* (Alfred Hitchcock, 1960, USA)
In a hotel room, Sam (John Gavin) and Marion (Janet Leigh) get dressed after having made love. O'Hora in his 1960 banning report 'doubt'[ed] its suitability for exhibition even to adults, never mind children. 'It is horrific in the most sadistic manner and there is too much sex. The straightforward sex scenes might be coped with, but I would find the deviational ones impossible to handle.' The film was later released with cuts.

**66** *The Public Enemy* (William A. Wellman, 1931, USA)
Enjoying the good life as wealthy gangsters, Tom Powers (James Cagney) and Matt Doyle (Edward Woods) meet glamorous Gwen Allen (Jean Harlow). This classic melodramatic gangster film, based in part on real-life Irish criminals, the 'Bugs' Moran gang of Chicago, was cut by James Montgomery in 1931, who noted that it had already been cut prior to submission.

**67** *The Wild One* (Laslo Benedek, 1954, USA)
Cathy (Mary Murphy) is repulsed by yet simultaneously attracted to, motorcycle gang leader Johnny (Marlon Brando). 'This is a story of thirty or forty irresponsible, law flouting, sadistic motor cycle riders who terrorise a town for a day and a night. It has no merit and there is not, with possibly one exception, a single scene worth viewing. Certificate refused.' (Martin Brennan, 1954; passed with cuts, 1956.)

**68** *Dr Strangelove; or, How I Learned to Stop Worrying and Love the Bomb* (Stanley Kubrick, 1963, GB)
This nightmarish satire about global nuclear war, driven by 'neurotic' males starring Peter Sellers, was one of
the films that forced a change in the general certificate policy. In one of three cuts demanded by Macken and
upheld by the Appeal Board in 1964, bikini-wearing Miss Scott (Tracy Reed) and her lover General 'Buck'
Turgidson (George C. Scott) were excised.

**69** *Girl with Green Eyes* (Desmond Davies, 1964, GB)
Adapted from an Enda O'Brien novel, in this scene, ill-fated lovers Kate Brady (Rita Tushingham) and Eugene
Gaillard (Peter Finch) who is separated from his wife but with whom he has had a child, walk through Dublin.
'I do not consider this unsavoury picture to be fit for exhibition here.' (Banned by Macken, 1964; ban upheld
after appeal; re-confirmed by Macken in 1970; passed after appeal.)

70  *King Creole* (Michael Curtiz, 1958, USA)
Elvis Presley as Danny Fisher with the singer (Carolyn Jones) of the cut 'Banana Song'. 'This picture is a tough one for me, particularly so because it features the controversial Presley who has such an appeal for uneducated adolescents.' (Passed with eight cuts by Liam O'Hora, 1958, but banned on appeal. Re-submitted in 1961, passed with further cuts after the renter submitted a cut version, 1961.

71 *Mädchen in Uniform* (aka *Girls in Uniform*, Leontine Sagan, 1931, Germany)
Boarding school teacher Fraulein von Bernburg (Dorothea Wieck) comforts her 'favourite' pupil Hertha Thiele (Manuala von Meinhardie). 'This is one picture that rather puzzles me and I am more than pleased to have the guidance of the Appeal Board. I am worried about theme, i.e. the friendship between a female teacher and one of her charges. I feel that somehow the picture is not fit for youngsters at any rate. Perhaps I am rather harsh but no picture of this particular kind has ever come in here before.' (Liam O'Hora, 1960; passed after appeal.)

72 *Oscar Wilde* (Gregory Ratoff, 1960, GB)
Robert Morley as Oscar Wilde (left) in one of two films released in 1960 on the Irish-born wit, dramatist and aesthete. 'The theme of this picture is the downfall of Oscar Wilde, which is eventually due to his being convicted of sexual misconduct with other men.' (Banned by Liam O'Hora, 1960; ban upheld after appeal.)

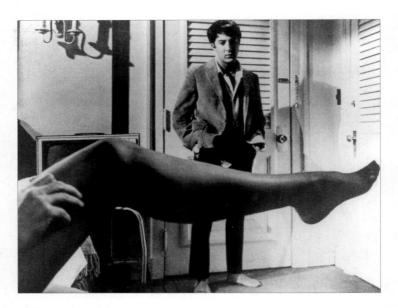

**73** *The Graduate* (Mike Nichols, 1967, USA)
Ben Braddock (Dustin Hoffman) is once more seduced by Mrs Robinson's (Anne Bancroft) outstretched leg, in this at times comic coming-of-age critical hit which won the director an Academy award, and made Hoffman a star. Ben eventually rejects the furtive affair and runs away with Mrs Robinson's daughter. (Banned by Christopher Macken, 1968; passed with cuts after appeal.)

**74** *Paddy* (aka *Goodbye to the Hill*, Daniel Haller, 1969, Ireland)
In this adaptation of Lee Dunne's novel *Goodbye to the Hill*, carefree Dubliner Paddy (Des Cave, right) and Breeda (Judy Cornwell) make love, after which Breeda invites Tony (Clive Geraghty) to join them in bed. A cross between *Alfie* and *The Ginger Man*, according to deputy Censor Gabriel Fallon in 1970, 'this would necessitate so much cutting in both sight and sound that … it is best rejected.' (Ban upheld after appeal, 1970.)

75 *Bob & Carol & Ted & Alice* (Paul Mazursky, 1969, USA)
Elliott Gould, Natalie Wood, Robert Culp and Dyan Cannon share a bed in this hit wife-swapping comedy. '"What the world needs now is love." Is sex just physical fun? Is the truth always beautiful? The working out of … these questions makes this film, in the opinion of the deputy Censor [Gabriel Fallon] totally impermissible. Cutting … would hardly improve it.' (1970; ban upheld after appeal).

76 *Come Play with Me* (George Harrison Marks, 1977, GB)
Popular soft porn comedy romp whose narrative, ostensibly about money forgers and gangsters who end up in a country health farm where the emphasis is on 'massage', is almost by the way. Banned by Dermot Breen (1977), it was passed with five cuts of massage sequences, nudes, and sex scenes and awarded an over-18s certificate by Frank Hall, 1983.

**77** *Juno and the Paycock* (Alfred Hitchcock, 1930, GB)
During the Irish Civil War, as Mary (Kathleen O'Regan, left) watches her lover Bentham (John Longden) read the details of a supposed legacy, her parents, Juno (Sara Allgood) and the 'Captain' (Edward Chapman) look on. Montgomery passed without cuts the 'cleaned up' version of the first Abbey Theatre play to be adapted for the screen, whose American title, *The Shame of Mary Boyle*, reflects Mary's transgressive sexual behaviour. When shown in Limerick, local Catholic activists seized and destroyed the film.

**78** *The Informer* (Arthur Robison, 1929, GB)
Gypo Nolan (Lars Hanson, right) turns informer in the first adaptation of Liam O'Flaherty's novel. 'This [is a] sordid show of Chicago gunmen, armed police and prostitutes at gunplay and soliciting in the standard slum of movieland. It is offered as a realistic picture of the underworld of Dublin. It is a pity that the citizens cannot take an action against the producers for a libel on our city. I refuse to grant a certificate for the exhibition of this impudent and mischievous distortion.' (James Montgomery, 1930).

79 *The Fighting 69th* (William Keighley, 1940, USA)
In this celebration of the fighting Irish, rebel Jerry Plunkett (James Cagney, left) joins his Irish regiment colleagues, including Fr Francis Duffy (Pat O'Brien, standing, centre) in 1917 to honour the 69th's war dead. It was cut by James Montgomery in 1940 as it infringed Irish neutrality policy during World War Two.

80 *A Yank in the RAF* (Henry King, 1941, USA)
In London, mercenary Tim Baker (Tyrone Power) meets up with old flame Carol (Betty Grable) during World War Two. It was cut in thirty places by Richard Hayes in 1943 to make it conform to Irish neutrality policy. The film subsequently had its certificate withdrawn, causing controversy within film distributors and exhibitor circles. It was re-released in 1945 after war-time restrictions were lifted.

**81** *The Spy in Black* (aka *U-Boat 29*, Michael Powell, 1939, GB)
During World War One, British undercover spy Schoolmistress (Valerie Hobson) infiltrates a German plot led by Captain Hardt (Conrad Veidt) to blow up warships anchored at Scapa Flow, the Orkneys. The certificate was withdrawn after the start of the war as it was deemed to infringe Irish neutrality.

**82** *Confessions of a Nazi Spy* (Anatole Litvak, 1939, USA)
Fast-paced, unashamedly anti-Nazi propaganda film in which a vast Nazi spy operation is investigated by the FBI led by Ed Renuard (Edward G. Robinson). This landmark film from Warner Bros (banned by James Montgomery in 1939 just before the outbreak of war) was one of a number of such films to remain suppressed in Ireland during World War Two. (Ban upheld after appeal.)

at the time of the Act's implementation were not censored and, according to the censors, an excuse as late as 2000 for avoiding censorship scrutiny of certain video retailers was that the offensive videos were pre-1992. However, it was obvious to anyone
who frequented video retailers in Dublin at the end of the 1990s or even later that
there were post-1992 videos, including soft-porn titles, on sale and for hire which had
not been certified.[16] Under-the-counter uncensored hard-core porn tapes continue to
be seized by the Gardaí and customs, but these are usually destined for sex shops (and
are seized as they arrive in the country more often than through police raids on shops)
where they are just another commodity. Another anomaly, which the two-tier introduction of the legislation threw up, was the industry's concern with UK imports into
Ireland. Under the first phase of the Act, UK video certificates were accepted, but by
1994 all new tapes had to carry the Irish Censor's classification. As a result, in 1996
Warner Home Video's Irish managing director attacked the failure to enforce the Video
Recordings Act, complaining about the volume of imports, even of mainstream films,
into the country. As a result, during the period 1992 to 1995 inclusive under the Act
there were 176 seizures of videos representing a total of 29,521 tapes (as opposed to
the larger numbers seized because of piracy), while the number of prosecutions was
498, of which 211 were convictions.[17]

While one of the early videos banned by the specialist video unit was Abel Ferrara's
mainstream *Dangerous Game* (1993), featuring Madonna and Harvey Keitel,[18] as indicated above, most of those banned throughout the 1990s were pornographic. Occasional
controversies emerged in the media, such as when 1970s British sex comedies *Come
Play With Me I* (George Harrison Marks, GB, 1977; PO 671/1994; PO 17/1997),[19]
*Emmanuelle in Soho* (PO 679/1994)[20] and *Confessions from the David Galaxy Affair*
(aka *Star Sex*, Willy Roe, GB, 1979, PO 25/1997),[21] were banned.[22] In March 2003,
shortly before he retired, Sheamus Smith's banned the video and DVD of *Baise-Moi*,
the sexually-explicit rape/revenge film which brought the conventions of hard-core
pornography into a mainstream film.[23] The film, regarded by many as a more grim and
graphically explicit version of *Thelma & Louise* (Ridley Scott, 1991), had initially been
restricted to sex cinemas in France, but following a public campaign initiated by direc-
tor-writer Catherine Breillat (who made the intelligent, if overly detached, disturbing
and complex essay on human sexual relations, *Romance*), and backed by other filmmakers, including Jean-Luc Godard, it was given an over-18s release. Four weeks after
its Australian release *Baise-Moi* had its R18+ (the most restrictive category) withdrawn.[24]
Ironically, it was screened at the Irish Film Centre in June 2002, where the much milder
*National Born Killers* had *not* been allowed to be shown seven years earlier. Of course,
*Baise-Moi* had not been submitted to the Censor at the time of the IFC screenings.[25] By
the end of 2003, in all 3,284 videos had been banned since 1991. However, the vast
majority of these were seized (pornographic) videos, with, for example, only 3.5 per
cent of the prohibitions in 1996 relating to the video rental and sell-through markets,
but a significant drop-off in prohibitions was evident by the early 2000s. This seems to
have been largely the result of a change in practice by the Gardaí. Prior to then, all
seized videos were sent to the Film Censor's office, but with the volume of such mate-

rial steadily increasing, the staff resources were not available to view every seized video. As a result, a sample, maybe only 3 or 4 videos from a consignment of 1,000, are viewed by the video classifiers and their reports are made available to the Gardaí, who then decide on whether to prosecute the importer/distributor/retailer of the seized videos/ DVDs. Additionally, uncertified material continued to be removed from retail outlets (there were 40 such cases notified to the Film Censor by the Gardaí in 2003) (see table 3). Despite, or maybe because of, the very high number of bannings, there have been only fourteen video/DVD appeals, most of which concerned the rating given to a main-stream commercial feature,[26] but also including *Baise-Moi*, the banning order for which was upheld by a majority decision of the six members who attended.[27] The other video appeals emanating from a video prohibition order were *Secret Games 3*, which had the ban upheld;[28] the narratively uncomplicated allegorical journey set in Latin America, which for all its darkness is a politically-informed redemptive tale, *Men With Guns*, from independent American writer/director John Sayles (1998) had its initial ban upheld;[29] and *Pariah*[30] also had its ban confirmed. During 2000–2001, 7 violent wrestling videos submitted under the label WWF (World Wrestling Federation) were banned, and of the 3 appealed, only one, *'No Way Out'*, was passed (with an over-18s certificate).[31] Only 3 films on video: *Texas Chainsaw Massacre*,[32] *Natural Born Killers*[33] and *Retroactive* (Louis Morneau, 1997),[34] had their prohibition orders revoked; in all instances an over-18s certificate was granted.

Sheamus Smith, who was consulted with regard to the Bill's contents, welcomed the Video Act,[35] and outlined his approach to videos in an illuminating interview prior to the Act's introduction:

> all censors or classification boards are stricter on video, for obvious reasons. One is that cinema is controlled in the sense that if a film is rated over 15 then only people over 15 can get in. Video can be taken out by an over 15 and left around the house, so you need highly-responsible supervision in the house, whether that be from parents or older children or social workers or whatever the family situation happens to be.

In practice then, while classification according to age limitation operates, it, neverthe-less, implicitly acknowledges the original proposal that videos be given a general cer-tificate or be banned altogether. In addition, pointing to the control a viewer has over the video image (freeze-frame, slow-motion, rewind, fast-forward), he said that 'the dangers of video [and DVD] need much more control. Something that flashes by on a cinema screen can be stopped in freeze-frame on a video by anyone.'[36] While Smith did not offer a reason as to why a freeze-frame should be any more potentially pernicious than a moving picture, one could perhaps revert to cinema's prehistory and the 'pornog-raphy' of Eduaerd Muybridge's images of men, women and animals, for an answer.[37] Indeed, one might return to the wording of the British Video Act, 1984 'to any signif-icant extent'. Clearly, the technology of a VCR or DVD player can make an insignifi-cant or brief image significant by prolonging its screen-time, or in others by taking a sequence out of context, something (film) censors have arguably done for decades. Conlon, who was in charge of video censorship until her resignation in 2002, also articulated concern with freeze-framing, but in the context of a copycat technique, where, for example, a 'live' hairdryer might be thrown into a mother's bath following a row. She also has pointed to the difficulty in assessing films and videos for 12- to 14-year-olds, where physical as well as emotional development can vary enormously. Though she has suggested that familiarity with developmental psychology is often more useful to the censor than film/media analysis, she has acknowledged the importance of the cultural/media environment, such as the generality of viewing (from soaps to horror to music videos) which shapes or influences their development. Another issue for this age group is whether or not they should be allowed access to adult themes. An example she cited in an interview with the author is *The Cider House Rules* (Lasse Hallstrom, 1999), which includes abortion and incest. Smith gave it an over-18s certificate, but Conlon (similar to the BBFC), advocated an over-15s on the basis abortion was a subject that this age group should be discussing.[38] Arguably, such material should provide a starting point for critical dialogue or contextualized discussion rather than been seen as a taboo especially when these issues may be starting to affect their lives.

There might be merit in linking the limitation (as guidance rather than as the current legal fiction) not to age, but to particular institutional or other contexts. For example, it seems unacceptable that an independent working 16-year-old who has left the relative shelter of the family home and school, or a teenage unmarried mother, cannot view adult material when their circumstances mean that with few exceptions they live adult lives. Of course, if protection was really the motivation, other limitations – even affecting gender (unsustainable politically) in the face of crude democracy and equality which fails to recognize difference – might be fruitfully considered. To this end, one possible and, in terms of regulation and administration, relatively unproblematic avenue is the introduction of education certificates for fiction films. (An education category already exists for documentary or informational film.) Films, which might be rated over-18 for commercial release, but which feature subjects that might be relevant for teenagers or young adults, if given an education certificate could be usefully integrated to a contextualized (responsible) debate. Instead of a single general education certificate, limitations could apply such that they could be subject and (school/college) year/stage appropriate. Under such a system, even banned films might be passed exclusively for third-level (or higher) educational material, particularly with regard to disciplines such as feminism, film studies, cultural or media studies, sociology and history. (Indeed, already there is a certain difficultly in screening over-18 material to first-year film or media university students as a significant number of them might be under-18.) The failure to provide such certification will continue to hamper the awareness of film and the ability to decode film and related material. Anything that may help to educate young people and lead to a critical engagement with (visual) texts and social, moral, and political issues is necessarily always superior to censorship and restriction.

Whether adults or children should be allowed to view these films in Ireland may become redundant as new distribution systems emerge via the internet, which enable subscribers to tap into a global (market) system via their telephone line, television set or, increasingly, wireless technology. In this context, even the question of classification is irrelevant as many parents (or other adults) permit their children and teenagers to view over-18s videos in their homes. Indeed, the Irish censors are now arguing that classification should only be regarded as a consumer guide to film and video and not be treated as a punitive, repressive apparatus, thus acknowledging the emerging reality of new viewing practices. Conlon went so far as to say that she would 'throw out the whole legislative basis' of film and video censorship and go the route apparently favoured by the Irish state in the self-regulation of the internet with its codes of practice, discussed below. Although this view was not shared by Smith, it is one, if not in such direct language, being promoted by the current Film Censor, John Kelleher, who introduced the 'consumer's guide' to film in 2004.[39] More broadly, this helps to put into relief the relationship between the state and the family, or, more particularly, the extent to which surveillance of the public sphere should be extended into the private sphere. After all, if an exhibitor or a video retailer can be prosecuted for providing an 'under-age' child or teenager access to a film or video/DVD, why should adults, including parents, not suffer sanctions if they commit the same offence. Whatever protection should be afforded to a parent showing or allowing their *own* child to view what the state has deemed inappropriate material, it is difficult to extend this to *other* people's children, where the offence of 'corruption of minors' could apply. As James Montgomery might say, it brings the law into disrepute.

Table 3: Videos/DVDs prohibited by Official Film Censor, 1991–2003

| | Rental | | Sell-through | | Seized | *Total banned* |
|---|---|---|---|---|---|---|
| | *Submitted* | *Banned* | *Submitted* | *Banned* | | |
| 1991 | | | | | 34 | |
| 1992 | | | | | 253 | |
| 1993 | | | | | 304 | |
| 1994 | 349 | 3 | 262 | 1 | 927 | 931 |
| 1995 | 541 | 11 | 592 | 5 | 430 | 446 |
| 1996 | 525 | 9 | 839 | 9 | 529 | 547 |
| 1997 | 511 | 6 | 1057 | 8 | 184 | 200 |
| 1998 | 526 | 5 | 1326 | 8 | 198 | 211 |
| 1999 | 579 | 7 | 1504 | 16 | 142 | 166 |
| 2000 | 840 | 13 | 2425 | 16 | 93 | 134 |
| 2001 | 825 | 10 | 3058 | 11 | | 26 |
| 2002 | 1043 | 10 | 3421 | 5 | | 16 |
| 2003 | 1152 | | 3830 | | 16 | |
| Total: | 6,891 | 74 | 18,314 | 79 | 2,503 | 3,284 |

*Source*: Annual Reports of the Official Censor of Films.

MORAL PANIC IN THE 1990S – THE INTERNET, CHILD PORNOGRAPHY AND
THE COMMODIFICATION OF CHILDHOOD – AND CONCLUSIONS

Ironically, the issue that dominated Irish film censorship in the 'pre-liberal' era – the leveling of the audience to children – was revisited in the 1990s, but in a radically different social, cultural, and technological context. While the focus of censorship in the 1980s was the seemingly ubiquitous 'video nasty,' 'child porn on the internet,' or, more generally, the child under threat either from seeing too much or becoming embroiled in or consuming pornography, characterized the debate from the 1990s onwards. Though the current media discourse centers on the fear of real physical harm to minors that may result from internet usage, the underlying issue of moral or intellectual corruption or the loss of childhood innocence through (over) exposure to adult (sexual) experience and fantasy is similarly relevant to film censorship, particularly with regard to video/DVD, and computer games[40] not least because the internet operates in a way that had not been anticipated by the legislators. This is because the internet makes available a vast global distribution system through e-commerce,[41] while the actual content of the internet, including games which can be freely downloaded, throws film censorship into relief and, it would seem, serves to produce anomalies in a more extreme way than television did from the 1950s onwards. Indeed, the internet delights in the global network of undifferentiated bodies where geography, biology and age are unimportant and where what appears to be only virtual effects or (mistakenly) becomes the real, such as in the much discussed phenomenon of MUD (on-line fantasy) rape, violence, and murder.[42]

Unfortunately, within discussions of censorship, the idea of childhood, and more specifically its particular contemporary configuration formed by the evolving institutions of the family, education, the church and more broadly by society is frequently lost or marginalized. Likewise sidelined is the crucial role played by technology itself, as opposed to its content. For example, how do we employ the fundamental conjoined issues of context, ethics and personal responsibility if the internet and related technology has effectively made these obsolete or at least problematized them? After all, this virtual world, where the concept of the unique original self is an anachronism, is defined by its transcendental abstraction from the physical even though it offers an inhabitable first person 'sensory' world which trades in the language and secret desire of the (often highly sexualized and gendered) body, and, as such, is necessarily emptied of social or material context.[43] It is not that certain on-line or computer-based actions do not produce consequences, but they are of a different order than those carried out in the 'real' world where the subject's identity (excepting schizophrenics) is known or fixed. Beyond the multiplication of identity which the internet and gaming so readily offers, further emptying of context occurs, most apparently in computer-generated graphics of war as evidenced in the Gulf War technology and its reporting, and, more generally, in video and computer games. Nevertheless, the assertion that such technology is 'bad' (because it dehumanizes or desensitizes or, in other words, causes a decline in affect as all is reduced to a spectacle) is too simple a formulation and fails to look at other issues around the social context in which the technology is placed and the use to which it is put.

Within this debate it is important to understand that the categories of childhood and adolescence owe in large part to (modern) capitalism's commodification or reification of all human experience in order to better serve the market, and, as such, should not be viewed as unchanging age-determined monolithic states of physical, intellectual and emotional growth before moving into the distinct sexually and otherwise mature category of adulthood. As cultural and social historians such as Philippe Aries have argued, childhood as a heightened period of vulnerability emerged as late as the seventeenth century, and as such the 'concept of youth as a time of sexual innocence is a relatively recent historical phenomenon.' It is from this time onwards that a discourse on the possibilities of literature leading to indecent or sexual thoughts, which might lead to masturbation or worse, arose, and subsequently led to various forms of suppression and censorship in the nineteenth century.[44] Even the most cursory look at children's and teenagers' television illustrates not only the many sub-categories of group identity which reflect the constantly shifting, multiplying, socially-specific and gendered patterns of experience of children and teenagers (created as much as reflected by the media), but provides a microcosm of popular culture which it would seem has lucratively locked in on the often repressed fantasy of minors to be sexualized adults. If this can be seen as early as 1959 with the creation of Barbie (and subsequently boyfriend Ken which were followed by British teenage dolls Sindy and Paul), or the male action hero counterparts for boys who later became Meccano 'trained' engineers, the 1990s has intensified this fantasy and made, particularly for young girls, its sexual aspect more explicit such that there developed a new growth sector of the precocious 'tweenager'. It is this category that is problematic for Breda O'Brien of the Family and Media Association, a pressure group, who argued that there used to be 'a period of latency just before puberty where they were still quite innocent,' now 'market forces are moving to sexualize them prematurely.'[45] Neither children nor teenagers, these increasingly independent, sexually 'aware' 8 to 12-year-olds represent a fresh target market which is most obviously exploited by Saturday morning television, its presenters and pop idols, including *the* girl band of the 1990s, The Spice Girls, which gave a 'new' if ultimately problematic meaning to 'girl power', boy bands, Take That, Boyzone and Westlife, and other groups such as S Club 7, and singers, not least of which is Britney Spears. This phenomenon accelerated in the late 1990s in Ireland with the increase in wealth of Irish parents; two-income families, often relying on and welcoming their children's (relative) independence; and the emergence of specialist services, such as children's hair salons (which offer party make-overs) and the increasing availability of designer and street-based fashion clothing for children and even toddlers. If parents clearly encourage such dress and behaviour, seeing in the child a miniature 'doll' model of the ideal girl-woman – or to a lesser extent, action-man-boy – the difficulty arises when the child's sexuality begins to be articulated, such as when the body changes at the onset of puberty or when the signifiers come more clearly attached to the signifieds either from within or without.[46] In this new cultural context (of the dance mat, the make-over, and the midriff) childhood sexual 'innocence' has become destabilized and has allowed for the public acknowledgment (to the distress of many adults) of access by 'children' to sexual fantasy, the supposed exclusive preserve of adults, but a condition reluctantly though increasingly conceded to teenagers. Ironically, a certain layer of guilt or sexual knowledge is prematurely placed on children who at 8 or 12 do not fully comprehend the significance of, or, in any meaningful way, relate to much of the music they listen to, the programmes (including American sit-com *Friends*) they watch, or see in their dress, dance or make-up any of the elements that contribute to the rituals of animal sexuality. This is not to say that they are 'innocent'.

The attempt to suppress the idea of children as sexual beings (whose sexuality is polymorphous rather than genitally focused) or to characterize such obstinate displays of sexual behaviour or even knowledge of the sexual act as perverse or demonic, as in *The Turn of the Screw* or *The Exorcist*, in favour of an adult constructed image of idealized and innocent purity is a peculiarily modern western idea, and one which is symptomatic of a broader social regulation and management of sex which serves a rational instrumental order of use-value.[47] If the infantalizing of the Irish people by both the colonial and post-colonial authorities was done, as referred to in chapter 3, by way of theological, social and cultural protectionist arguments and supported by notions of decency and reticence, which were observed to a significant extent by the media through self-regulation and the work of the various publications and film censors, as a means to control the general population, most especially the working-class, the effect of this project was clearly very different in 1980s and 1990s Ireland. Following the liberal and secular gains from the 1960s onwards, the emergence of an adult explicit media, and what could be described as a generalized postmodern malaise or distrust of institutions, including most notably the Catholic church whose scandals were coming to the fore in the 1990s, the previous levels of repression were impossible to maintain. Consequently, the cultural project of the political and moral right, a feature not just of Ireland, but Reganite America and Thatcherite Britain,[48] and driven by a certain (religious) fundamentalism, was necessarily more hysterical and moreover resorted to provocative and deliberately emotive strategies, most especially that of the innocent child. While the scurrilous campaign slogans such as 'Hello Divorce, Goodbye Daddy' of the anti-divorce lobby during the heavily defeated referendum (1986) are exemplary, so, too, were many of the tactics used by the pro-life groups in the on-going abortion debate. However, the public nature of the debates surrounding the abortion and divorce referendums in the 1980s, the much publicized and related cases of the Kerry Babies Tribunal in which the mechanics of reproduction and a woman's sexual behaviour were held up for scrutiny,[49] and the death of a teenager giving birth in front of a statue of Our Lady in Granard; together with the political H-Block campaigns in the North in which, as Fintan O'Toole puts it, 'excrement became a weapon of war,'[50] meant that despite, and, often as a direct result of, those who sought to deny the body and row back the cultural tide of openness, that the physical and sexual body, complete with all its intimate secrets and fantasies, was turned into a 'family spectacle'. (over-18s material, as it were, became universal in an attempt to bring into line over-18s behaviour and moral and legal entitlements with that of asexualized children.) Of course, in all of these debates and beyond, the difficult or problematic cases are sidelined and treated without the subtlety they demand. For example, the current debate around childhood and independent teenage sexuality, and one which provides a context for censorship laws and decisions, seems to pivot between those who encourage 'responsible' behaviour with regard to sexual activity which they view as a natural, ergo morally neutral, practice so as to prevent disease and pregnancy, and those who deny the reality of such activity or condemn it as morally wrong. The more reasonable voice that accepts that children or teenagers have real desires and sexual fantasy but nonetheless argues that, in the main, even apart from the possibility of pregnancy, they are not ready for the emotional and other consequences of having these fantasies made real, even if acting within their own cohort, would appear to be absent. Furthermore, what is lost or at least partially silenced in such debates is the hidden agenda such as the opposition to the separation of church and state, secular versus religious freedom, or even rationalism versus theological certainty. Additionally, another feature that became evident from the 1980s onwards was how secular 'experts,' social workers and psychologists in particular, and, to a lesser extent, the legal establishment, began to fill the 'moral' void left behind by the Catholic church.

It was in this context that 'child porn on the internet' became the focus of moral panic in the 1990s. But then, all new mediums, such as the novel, vaudeville, early popular press, comics, cinema, television, and video games, have, in their beginnings, been associated or engaged with the erotic or sexual, or other dangerous subjects, and in each instance, the threat they posed to the child or woman was invoked by those moral watchdogs intent on bringing in broader ranges of moral and social control. That the particular reprehensible spin given to the internet has been the marriage of this with children, arguably says more about contemporary awareness of, and sensitivity to child abuse and the need for protection than indicating a rife subculture of paedophiles. It may also point to a cosy cultural fantasy that, like in 1950s Cold War paranoia, the danger is external or 'out there' rather than in the domestic or familial environment, where, in fact, the majority of such abuse occurs.[51] Further, the image of an invading, pervasive and ultimately mocking technology is a convenient one through which to displace parental or, indeed, personal responsibility. In much of the discourse it would seem that pornographic sites are lying in wait so as to trap and infect the unsuspecting and innocent internet-user, who then becomes a porn addict or is lured into paedophilic or other 'non-normative' behaviour. The reality, of course, is that the majority of such sites accessed are done so consciously, particularly with regard to Bulletin Board Services (BBS) in which contact is made by direct-dial-up and generally requires a credit card.

To help ground the discussion of the internet, it is important to outline how it operates and its cultural significance.[52] At its most basic, the internet allows a computer to communicate vast quantities of information including text, sound and (moving) image based data (such as for example an entire film), via a telephone line (and increasingly wireless technology) with any other number of similarly connected computers regardless of their location, time-zone differences, and legal or other restrictions that govern a particular state. While the ultimate expression of this new technology is the poetic merging of man and machine in the figure of the cyborg (such as those in the *Terminator* films) or the creation of a *virtual* reality (a computer created environment that appears to be, or is approximate with the real in that it offers an immersive, cause-effect based inhabitable space),[53] it is only a continuation of the radical reshaping of society already begun by the internet. Consequences of this apparently simple coupling of the computer with the phone mean that one can, in effect, work anywhere or be virtually everywhere; be an affective global citizen with a voice that can readily establish connections with others to create new virtual communities and non-hierarchal networks, so that the small or local has a presence within the dominant capitalist discourses; self-publish free from governmental or institutional interference, censorship or bureaucracy and in so doing cross international, economic and other boundaries; share in a democratic celebration of a multiplicity of views, unencumbered by physical or other barriers that may cause prejudice, such as gender, age, colour or physical disability; trade in or access information at the relatively cheap cost of a phone call; and, more generally, move away from a passive spectator culture to one of inter*action* and communication.

Nevertheless, even without getting into issues around downsizing, deskilling, the decline of free-play and creativity or the related topic of the technologization of entertainment and pleasure, many of these can be *re*interpreted negatively. Accordingly, information is not free and democratic, but exists within a techno-apartheid in which some people (and entire countries) as a consequence of their 'developmental' position within the global corporate capitalist world, education, biology, and geography are excluded or are limited in their access. Similarly, the virtual communities are not so nearly utopian as is imagined in that they lack the same sense of sensory engagement as real life communities and yet, by offering physically and intellectually non-threatening environments, may isolate further the internet-user from social interaction, and hence can be seen to fragment rather than to connect. Arguably, this feature of the internet as 'safe tourism' is not just central to the popularity of virtual sex in an era of awareness about the increasing instances of STDs and AIDS, but should be considered in regard to internet (exploitive and criminal) pornography, where the user can feel at a remove from the actual crime by reasoning that they are only subsequent witnesses or collectors of images.[54] Such feelings of being an invisible voyeur and the need to access the material away from prying eyes (or traceability) led to much-hyped concern in libraries and other institutions over persistent porn surfing with, for example, one newspaper reporting in 2000 that public library staff had banned use of the internet until there were staff available to police it.[55] In addition, though the technology promises a place where things such as gender, appearance and age do not matter, the on-line narratives that have emerged and language used would seem to suggest such things have been magnified.[56] While a sizeable amount of cyborg fiction tends to represent the extreme appearance of masculinity or femininity so that Laura Croft of *Tomb*

*Raider* may be far from the classical damsel in distress and allow for male identification, but her body is grotesquely female, other on-line material such as the shared fantasy rooms resort to expressions of violence and abuse. Indeed, if initially the internet
was synonymous with free speech and potentially offered a genuinely democratic environment, increasingly this has given way to capitalism and e-commerce whose trade
in part consists of offensive and sometimes illegal material, such as is relevant to this
chapter – erotica and pornography.

Although the internet as a valuable resource for industry and business (including
marketing and retail) as well as education is undeniable, too often, particularly with
regard to the latter, confusion is made between, on the one hand, the use of it as a *tool*
in order to source academically creditable information or texts, and to consult on-line
library or other reference databases and catalogues, and, on the other, aimless 'surfing' through poorly written, uncritical and often inaccurate material which serves entertainment more than the pursuit of genuine (academic) knowledge. Unfortunately, while
many of the reputable specialized sites are to some degree membership or fee based,
the other more 'subjective' or dubious ones which, like advertising sites and SPAM
(suspect, problematic or annoying mail),[57] are rapidly multiplying and are largely free.
However, even with regard to 'quality' material, and especially such things as e-pub-
lished books or music, on-screen reading or listening can hardly compete with the pleasures of holding a book or the convenience of listing to a compact disk on a (fully
portable or high quality) music system.

It is, therefore, under these negatives that we may consider the availability not so
much of (adult) pornography which, after all, is a valid expression of adult sexuality,
whatever about personal or national morality, but criminal-based forms of it, especially as it impacts on children. That it seems to have found a home so readily in internet technology is unsurprising. Not only does the internet operate without regard to
legal and national borders, but the medium fits perfectly the message and mocks the
user in his/her compulsive downloading of images. Each image is as empty as the next
or fails to satisfy desire, which, as noted, can never be satisfied, yet like the next generation of processors and computers, the next image promises something more, or in
other words, the pleasures of transcendence. Of course that this 'more' is not realized,
as evidence in the sheer obsessive collecting of images of up to 22,000 is already written in the language used to refer to the human body in discussions of computers and
related technologies: meat. This splitting of the subject into mind and meat which has
philosophical antecedents in Descartes, La Mettrie and others, brings us back to the
earlier point of context. How can the body as meat deliver a sustainable pleasure (even
if through legitimate porn) if it is stripped of the social context of emotional and intellectual engagement and empathy? In a sense, the user's relationship to the victim in the
image is not of the order of person-to-person contact where the abuse might actually
offend the moral or legal framework of the collector, but is pathological. Such a suggestion is supported by the fact that many of collectors limit their paedophilic encounters to viewing representations of same, while Dennis Howitt in his book *Paedophiles
and Sexual Offences Against Children*[58] argues that most paedophiles have little or no

interest in such sites. As O'Toole explains, 'to see child-porn imagery and child sexual abuse as inextricably linked is a mistake.'[59]

The availability of this and other pornographic material has led to calls both from the right and left for state control of the internet. Others (including various governments and their police forces) have suggested that service providers – those local companies which connect individual subscribers to the internet – should police the system so as to stop their clients from gaining access to such material. This move, ironically, given the general 1960s free-wheeling anti-authoritarian ethos of those who developed the 'rules' and 'highways' of cyberspace, is increasingly being taken on board by the industry, who have begun to self-regulate and introduce voluntary classification of sites, as well as the development and promotion of filtering software, and, in tandem with state watchdog bodies, recommend to parents that they keep a responsible eye on their children's on-line activities. Whatever the policy in Ireland (and more generally in the Europe Union) will finally be, it will have an impact not just on the suppression of child pornography, but perhaps more importantly on the surveillance and control of all forms of electronic communication and therefore raises issues around privacy, state regulation and censorship.

The title of an *Irish Times* article in 1997, 'Someone who'll watch over you; Children surf while parents worry,'[60] was an early instance within the mainstream Irish media of coupling surfing – the dominant practice of younger users and those using it largely as a pleasure tool for info-tainment – with pornography, itself moreover erroneously grouped with child pornography and other forms of abusive and illegal sexual-based activities. The article articulated concern as to whether parents could put software in place to block their children's access to certain internet sites. Already, though, in 1996, Irish Member of the European Parliament, Fianna Fáil's Niall Andrews, had called for tough laws to be introduced to crack down on child pornography on the internet,[61] while Irish Internet Service Providers announced plans to block 'obnoxious' content from getting to their customers.[62] The Irish legislative response came in 1997 when the issue was taken a stage further by linking the internet with child porn and sex tourism, a practice outlawed in the Child Trafficking and Pornography Bill which, published in December 1997, became law in 1998. (The Act provides for a maximum sentence of fourteen years for production and distribution of child pornography, while possession carries more lenient sentences.) Relating to persons under-17, the Irish age of consent for sexual relations,[63] this broadly drafted legislation, as was pointed out by one rare dissenting voice, Paul O'Brien of the National College of Art and Design, in a letter to the *Irish Times*,[64] could be potentially used to suppress countless art books. The first time it was used in connection with video censorship was when *Another Day in Paradise* (1998) directed by Larry Clark who had made the controversial *ciné-vérité* style film *Kids* (1995) which explored the sexual hedonism of a group of New York teenagers[65] was submitted in 1999. Starring Melanie Griffith and James Woods, the film is set in the 1970s which is richly evoked in the film's overall aesthetic. Like Gus Van Sant's *Drugstore Cowboy* (1989), which in part was influenced by Clark's photographs of junkies in his collection *Tulsa* (1971), *Another Day in Paradise* presents in a matter-of-fact way the world of a small time junkie 'family'. However, a scene of 'rough sex', as Audrey Conlon described it, between under-17s was deemed to infringe the Act. The video was later passed after it was re-submitted by the distributor with nine minutes cut.[66]

Simultaneously, a broad-based government commission, the Department of Justice, Equality and Law Reform's Working Group on 'Illegal and Harmful Use of the Internet,' were working on a report. Established in 1997 with representatives from the Departments of Health and Education, internet service providers, as well as Professor Max Taylor of the Child Studies Unit, University College Cork, and among others, the executive directors of UNICEF Ireland and the ISPCC, the group had previously been consulted with regard to the formulation of the section of the 'Child Pornography Bill' dealing with the internet. Also, they had encouraged the establishment in July 1997 of the Internet Service Providers' Association of Ireland (ISPAI).[67] This organization in its first public outing announced that it was already blocking access to some Usenet newsgroups in anticipation of being compelled to do so under the Child Pornography Bill then being drafted and suggested that Web access might also need to be blocked 'if it becomes illegal to store or transmit child porn.' One industry professional commented that, despite such restrictions, 'any serious Web user would still be able to locate [child pornography] without much time or effort.'[68] While there were dissident voices within the service provider sector such as Dave Walsh of Electronic Frontier Ireland, a promoter of the internet and bulletin boards, who argued that service providers should be no more responsible for what is sourced by customers than are the post and telephone companies for their's,[69] nevertheless, managements within these organizations, in tandem with the general thrust of the recommendations which later emerged from the Working Group report published in 1998, favoured self-regulation of the industry.[70] An issue which was not resolved satisfactorily by the Working Group was the extent to which a service provider is responsible for the content of material downloaded by a subscriber. This had been deliberated on in the German courts from 1995 when an American service provider, CompuServe, was charged with responsibility for what their customers received through the internet. Subsequently, access for its 4 million users worldwide to 200 electronic message boards was denied, but in 1996, with the exception of 5, these were restored. While initially the courts rejected the company's defence of shifting responsibility on to their subscribers,[71] following the commencement of the case proper in May 1998,[72] CompuServe was exonerated in 2000.

The consensual bid for self-regulation was a significant departure from the state's censorship of films, videos and text, especially in light of the fact that the Working Group's membership included film censor Audrey Conlon, whose main responsibility until her resignation in 2002 was video classification. Nevertheless, despite this position, she has voiced misgivings regarding existing laws governing video and film censorship, and, as noted in chapter 6, favoured a non-statutory classification system, ironically, a throw-back to film industry attempts in the 1910s in Britain and in the

1920s in the USA when industry 'watchdogs' were established as filter-protectors for children in a successful bid to stave off state-regulation of film content. Another development that emerged from the Working Group was the establishment in 2001 of the Internet Advisory Board. Chaired by ex-Director of Public Prosecutions Eamonn Barnes, it was to operate in parallel to the Working Group with which it shared many of the same members. Among the Advisory Board's members were Conlon, Professor Taylor, child-psychologist Marie Murray, representatives from government departments, the police, and children's agency Barnardos.

Arguably, the main issue that concerns the authorities in Ireland as elsewhere is the possession and transmission of still and moving images of children and pre-pubescent teenagers for sexual gratification, and the related fears over paedophile use of the internet to make contact with victims in what is referred to as 'net seduction' whereby an on-line relationship is developed which leads to real life physical engagement (or abduction).[73] These images, often of children in the nude, may vary from wholly-legal representations taken from advertisements, the media in general, family photos or other such innocent sources as art books, as well as from nudist and pornographic/erotic publications; the covert filming of children by an individual but where no contact with the subject occurs, for which an admitted paedophile was jailed for eighteen months in October 2000,[74] and which in the era of the camera-phone is an increasing issue; fake or digitally enhanced and otherwise created montage images for which there is no original moment; and, most disturbingly, photographic or film material of minors given 'voluntarily' by the subject, or recorded as part of the abuse and in which the subjects are seen to be in sexually compromised acts with peers or adults. It is this latter area that has received most attention.

Notwithstanding that these (latter) records of sexual and exploitative crimes against children clearly exist, given the scarcity of evidence produced by customs and police worldwide, and the number of prosecutions, it may only represent a minor element of the whole. Considering that possession and trade in child pornography is illegal in Ireland, as it is elsewhere in Western Europe and North America, and the necessarily secret culture that it inhabits, one has to pose the question as to how extensive the internet based paedophile subculture actually is, and whether the panic surrounding the internet as a conduit for paedophilic activity is fully justified. The uncovering of rare instances of rings or paedophile networks have largely been represented in the media, as Linda Williams and others, such as Laurence O'Toole, author of *Pornocopia* (1998), have argued in terms of representing the tip of the iceberg.[75] Yet, the major risks to children still lie within the family and its extended circle or its substitutes (foster or institutional homes),[76] while a 1992 study in which two Dutch academics examined the scale of child pornography found that 'virtually no new' material had been produced on a global commercial scale since the time when it was legal in Denmark to do so (1969–1979).[77]

The first Irish prosecutions for the possession of internet pornography were noteworthy not least for their sensational reporting and the seeming coincidence that they were not Irish nationals. Thus, a German computer programmer working for the

American transnational Gateway was charged in Dublin in late 1998 with possessing child pornography from the internet and convicted the following year under the 1998 Pornography Act.[78] Likewise, in 1999, a Scottish radiologist had to quit his job in Cork after it became known that he had a conviction in Scotland for possessing child pornography downloaded from the internet. By then, police were investigating nine people for downloading child pornography. The first case in which internet child 'pornography' was found to have been distributed from an Irish base, though not produced or sourced in Ireland, was in 2000 when Thomas Muldoon, who was living in Dungarvan, Co. Waterford, was discovered with over 700 images of babies, young children and pre-teens, including ones of children being sexually abused. Muldoon was caught after sending the images to a German undercover police detective and he was sentenced to two and a half years in jail for advertising and possessing child pornography.[79]

Arguably, the clearest lesson which the history of censorship teaches is the impossibility of determining what constitutes indecency and how such a vague term necessarily shifts not just according to context – both with regard to a text's integrity and its relation to other similar texts – but in relation to individual consumers and the tools and baggage they bring to bear on a text. This is not to say that texts are entirely free-floating signifiers, indeed, images by their nature tend to be more grounded in a physical reality of meaning than words, but they are nonetheless open to negotiation. If, for example, a woman's shoe even without intentional encoding by the photographer through lighting or other such techniques, can be easily read in terms of the highly-charged image of the stiletto-heeled phallic-woman of *film noir* or seduction, or that in the context of *manga*, a stiletto-heel signifies bar hostess,[80] it is hardly surprising given the sensitivity to paedophile activity, that *all* images of children are treated with caution. There have been a number of cases including Northern England businessman Lawrence Chard (1989) and British newsreader Julia Somerville and her partner Jeremy Dixon (1995) in which photographs taken with innocent intent were wrongly interpreted as indecent.[81] Such instances, in which the state in the name of protecting the children, destroyed the family's privacy and innocence, indicate not just the difficulty in dealing with vague criteria, but point to the importance of intention and motivation. Consequently, it illustrates that censorship does not treat of the image in isolation whether in terms of its content, levels of explicitness, and/or its self-conscious and publicly understood allusion to the forbidden or the socially/morally dangerous, but at times, acts to censor or curtail indecent thoughts that certain non-explicit and non-intentionally coded texts might produce, and then, in relation to the internet, only when these are downloaded or purchased; it is not an offence to view an 'indecent' image on screen, only to acquire it. It is at this extreme of censorship where its limitations as well as its unsustainable oppressive nature are most obvious. However, no such doubts as to the 'indecent' content or viewer motivation could be voiced with regard to many other cases.

In Ireland, 2000 witnessed an exponential rise in the number of police investigations into internet-based child pornography. Although no Irish study has yet been produced detailing the profiles of those who collect such images, from various reports, it seems as if they fit the blueprint as has been established in other jurisdictions, of respectable white middle-class and, moreover, married males. According to one FBI examination of 413 paedophiles caught during an internet operation, the 'overwhelming majority' of them were middle-class, white and well educated.[82] Why this should be, conceivably owes less to the sexual proclivities of class than the social placing and use of the technology. For example, such internet activity can be easily accommodated by professional work patterns, income, and levels of privacy both within the home/study and office, as well as offering the detachment – so they can remain safe and respectable – that the computer allows.

An early 2000 article entitled 'Internet porn images seized in house swoop' reported that Irish police, following an allegation that a businessman married with a child had sexually assaulted a 5-year-old girl, raided his home where they found 'pornographic images of girls as young as eight' that had been downloaded from the internet.[83] When the case came to trial in May 2001, it was revealed that the Gardaí had discovered 22,000 'paedophile images' stored in the man's computer, including three photographs of the 5-year-old 'in overtly sexual postures with the man.' After the trial in which he was sentenced to nine years in prison, the girl's parents, neighbours of the abuser, expressed their shock because prior to this he appeared to have been 'a normal, genuine and nice man'.[84] Though this represents just 'one of a small number of such seizures in Ireland,'[85] and typifies the 'respectable' profile of the criminal and the volumes of images collected, this is nevertheless unusual within a context of known Irish internet collectors of paedophile imagery as reported on in the media, as he was engaged in *active* abuse. This is not to suggest that viewing and collecting such images is not a form of abuse and is a victimless crime, though a Scottish judge did describe it thus.[86] Even if the original abuse or recording of the child happened (legally or otherwise) in the distant past, it is revisited on the subject continuously, effecting issues around the right to personal dignity and control over one's own image. But, to equate *all* subjects of 'pornography', which can be so broadly defined by people such as Andrea Dworkin, Catherine MacKinnon and others to include almost all media representations of the *female* body,[87] with victims of exploitation and abuse, ultimately insults those who have been subjected to *real* rather than *symbolic* abuse, particularly if that symbolic abuse is of a relatively mild nature, such as in beauty contests or pageants and nonexplicit advertising.

While other cases came before the courts, it was the Irish police's 'Operation Amethyst' which yielded not only the most prosecutions, but on-going media attention and confirmed the relative wealth and status of the collectors. These cases developed from an FBI investigation in 1999 of a Texas-based internet company, Landslide Productions, which was trading in offensive material, including child pornography. Sifting through the records of the company's 250,000 subscribers, the FBI found at least 100 Irish consumers who subsequently became the subjects of police raids in May 2002.[88] Among those named were the high profile chef Tim Allen of Ballymaloe, Cork – an awarding-winning restaurant, country house hotel, and cookery school – whose computers were found to contain almost 1,000 images of children, some as young as 5 and including representations of oral sex and rape.[89] When, in early 2003, he was convicted, to some considerable outrage, he was given the Probation Act and ordered to serve 240 hours of community service. The perceived leniency of his sentence was popularly presumed to be related to his €40,000 charity donation rather than to his admission of guilt and his undergoing of therapy for his addiction. However, most other such offenders, both before and after Allen, received non-custodial sentences, a view confirmed by the Granada Institute, an independent treatment center for child sexual abusers and those caught in possession of child pornography.[90] Another similarly respectable offender was Alan Robinson, an ex-Dublin City Councillor for the right-wing political party, the Progressive Democrats, and, ironically, at the time of his arrest, director of the Junior (or child-orientated) Dublin Film Festival. He was found to have had three 'sexually explicit' images of children, one of which featured an 8-year-old performing sex. He was given 'one of the tougher sentences' by comparison to other such cases of six months in prison, though this was later appealed. Another Amethyst catch, a former teacher, received a nine-months custodial sentence; a South Korean student was sentenced to two years, suspended for five years, provided he left the country; an Irish student was given a nine-months suspended sentence; while a Galway electrician was given a six-months suspended sentence for similar offences of possessing child pornography under Section 6 of the 1998 Act.[91] Other Amethyst arrestees included a married man (40) with two children, who was charged in July 2003 with the possession of 500 images of child pornography, 11 of which featured children being subjected to sexual acts including oral intercourse, full intercourse or fondling;[92] a fun-park founder (63), jailed for six months for possession of 1,000 child pornography images;[93] a Kilkenny engineer (43), married with one child;[94] a college lecturer (48), who was given a three-month suspended sentence after he was found guilty of downloading 12 child pornographic images, which according to a sex addiction councilor who gave evidence at his trail, he used so as to pretend to other internet-users that he was the girl in the photographs although he had no sexual interest in minors;[95] Circuit Court Judge Brian Curtin, who allegedly had been found in possession of 280 images of child pornography, but who was acquitted on the technical issue of the search-warrant being a day out-of-date;[96] a Dutch national, but County Cork resident, who was charged with the possession of 11,534 images of child pornography;[97] and two Navan men who were found with images of girls aged 3 to 16 in different poses with adult naked males.[98] Unusually, when this case came up for sentencing, District Court Judge John Brophy stated that he may not record a conviction against one of them because he pleaded guilty to possessing child pornography.[99] Other, non-Amethyst, cases include a married Limerick man with a young family who was caught with more than 500 child pornographic images;[1] a 34-year-old man who was found guilty of distributing and possessing child pornography in 1999, but whose sentencing was postponed while he underwent counseling, and was eventually given a two-year suspended sentence;[2] in January 2002 a Church of Ireland cleric was charged with possession of child pornography;[3] a member of the Gardaí was arrested on 9 May 2003 when he was found to be in possession of child pornography;[4] and an unemployed, but well-educated man, aged 40, was found with 3,500 child pornography images, 400 of which showed young semi-naked girls in sexual activities with adults, after he was observed spending twelve hours at a cyber-café. Like many other arrestees, his sentence was postponed while he was treated for his addiction.[5]

Before these cases occurred, the Working Group's first report in 1998 on 'Illegal and Harmful Use of the Internet' stated that the internet was being used for illegal purposes with evidence that Irish paedophiles were using it to access child pornography, but the problem was seen to be 'limited'. This assertion was based on research carried out for the report by an internet monitoring group at the Child Studies Unit, University College Cork, run by Psychology Professor Max Taylor. Part of the Combating Paedophile Information Networks in Europe (COPINE), and funded by Interpol, the Irish Department of Justice, and police forces in Britain and Holland, this leading Irish research body which has accumulated a comprehensive searchable reference database on child pornography, identified 31 internet channels with 'titles relating to child sex' which had 281 participants. It also found at least one Irish website with links to paedophile sites, and 40 Japanese websites containing child pornography. Of course, in Japan, notwithstanding prohibitions on representations of pubic hair and the penis, (heteroerotic) pornography is not only big business and possibly is the fastest-growing area in the publishing industry there, but is considered 'normal' fare for adult males (and, more recently, females) such that 'adult' *manga* comics which emerged in the 1970s are openly read by men within the public sphere.[6] The study concluded that the internet was 'a major, if not the major, focal point of child pornography and information about paedophile behaviour.' This concern was later foregrounded in 1999 when the Child Studies Unit hosted a COPINE conference aimed at co-ordinating a crackdown on internet child porn. Speaking at the time, Taylor reported that there was 'now evidence that paedophiles are using the Internet to solicit young child victims.'[7] The following year, this was reiterated by Rachel O'Connell (an expert in the area who had worked at the Child Studies Unit on the internet porn project) in a warning about an expansion in the use of the internet by paedophiles.[8] Nevertheless, such a conclusion must be placed in perspective and problematized. Put simply, the internet and on-line camera mobile phones are only the latest medium through which a paedophile may extend his means of operating, but as a British policeman working in this area put it, 'Children are far more at risk of falling prey to a paedophile whilst standing at the school gates [or indeed in their own home] than they are surfing the net.'[9] That said, by the end of 2003, Taylor's unit was seeing an exponential growth in sexually-explicit images of children, and was analyzing 100,000 such images per month, most of which were among the 600,000 held in the unit's archive, though 20 new images of child rape per month were appearing.[10]

Like much of the media debate around pornography and related activities, the Working Group report failed to offer a detailed graded distinction of the various forms of 'pornography'. These may include images of teenagers posing as adults or masquerading as children in erotic, sexual or innocent situations; minors (up to age 17) engaging in sexual activity with their peers or in abusive relations with a paedophile; images of children and infants naked and otherwise in isolation or engaging in non-sexual relations with an adult; and the many genres within adult erotica and pornography: soft, hard, hetero-, gay, lesbian, bi-, group, straight and fantasy. Instead, it simply reported that of the 40,000 newsgroups examined by UCC, only 0.07 per cent contained 'major elements of child erotica and child pornographic pictures' and of these 6,058 pictures, two-thirds depicted child erotica while the remainder 'could be described as pornographic.' The UCC research went on to report that in its examination of Internet Relay Chat (IRC) services, 'there was no evidence of any active or consistent Irish involvement,' and while 'accidental access' to child pornographic pictures on the World Wide Web was deemed 'unlikely,' the number of child pornography sites appeared to be growing, particularly Japanese commercial sites.[11] While this growth pattern is grotesquely mirrored in other sex related sites and SPAM, such that access to this material ranging from classified type advertisements for cosmetic surgery including for penis enlargements or lingerie, to trailer or teaser images of credit-card-access-based pornography, to chat rooms or computer versions of phone-sex and dating type advertising are not just easily available without cost, but can (unsolicited) attach themselves to one's browser page or electronic address, nevertheless, the much-hyped accidental hitting on 'sexual' sites is often overplayed by teenagers whose search words may be carefully 'carelessly' keyed in! But then, the danger that such sites may represent must be placed in the context of the average user's everyday experience.[12] Children, from an increasingly young age, are endlessly exposed to sex by the media, while much, if not all, of the free material is no more extreme, and in most cases, less so, than top-self magazines in their local newsagents. However, the combination of internet technology and sex, is, it would seem, culturally regarded as more highly furtive, actively-engaging and libidinally exciting than the print medium, or even film and video. While the eroticization of technology, explicit in the figure of the vamp android in Fritz Lang's 1927 *Metropolis*, is not by any means a new thing, the internet's relative newness as well as the vastness of cyberspace, allows for an 'unexplored quality that can add frisson to the mundane.' Likewise, it offers 'the arousing combination of anonymity and omnipotence that is the fruit of the human-machine interface.'[13]

While acknowledging that the internet was 'a development which cherishes freedom of speech above content quality,' the Working Group report published in July 1998 recommended that an internet monitoring centre be established along the lines of the Film Censor's Office with 'an active function, which would include scanning of internet material, reporting to and discussing abuses with the Gardaí and raising public awareness of undesirable activity.' As part of the conditions of the licensing of service providers, a licensee would undertake not to carry certain proscribed material, while a permanent advisory board was also recommended.[14] In November 1999, eighteen months after the report was published, a 'hotline on child porn,' one of the Working Group's proposals, to be run by the ISPs, was set up in co-operation with the

Department of Justice, which is funding the initiative along with the European Community. Working closely with the Internet Advisory Board, it was the eighth such national service to emerge within the EU; by 2001 there were 16 hotlines in 12 countries, part of the INHOPE Association (the Internet Hotline Providers in Europe), which was established in November 1999, of which Ireland was president in 2001. In addition, there were three associate members, including from the CyberTipline of the US National Centre for Missing and Exploited Children (NCMEC). According to the hotline's director and ISPAI Chairman Cormac Callanan, they do not see themselves as 'policing the Internet as a global activity, but child pornography is something that affects all of us and we are doing our part.' Just as he drew on the extreme emotive issue of child pornography, which represents a 'tiny, hard to access and resolutely amateur corner' of the pornography market,[15] he also played on a central fear of the internet porn scare by saying that the 'most difficult operations to uncover are those set up by rings of paedophiles using passwords and other ways of escaping notice.'[16]

Although, as already acknowledged, there is evidence to show that these rings exist, such as Britain's Wonderland Club,[17] the international Shadowz Brotherhood,[18] and the German Operation Marcy case which had a global reach and involved thousands of internet-users,[19] it is not of the scale that the 'conspiracy theorists' and other subscribers to moral panic who call for *all* questionable sites, news groups and other BBSs to be removed would have us believe.[20] Ultimately, it serves another agenda to that of (a) protecting children from abuse or from accidental exposure to these moreover self-advertising sites, or (b) even apprehending paedophiles as such sites have already provided vital evidence and leads in a number of criminal cases.[21] Ironically, a policy of surveillance and closing down of sites may lead to sites relocating and becoming less obvious to the user such that the 'offensive items [might] become harder to monitor, [with] any records of illegal acts ... more difficult to track, or act upon' or being accidentally stumbled upon and read by a child.[22] This broader agenda, though moreover lost in the popular, most especially tabloid media, was noted at least by Karlin Lillington writing in the *Irish Times* who argues that it is made to serve the more generalized suppression of other ideologically or morally difficult information. As she puts it, 'they would like to limit what other people see, talk about, and look for. They take an offensive issue, child pornography, and use it to forward other agendas.'[23] While the Irish hotline's first report, in line with INHOPE policy, explicitly ruled out the archiving of any internet material,[24] surprisingly, Callanan, despite his statement that they did not want to 'police' the internet as a global activity, was relatively upfront when he said that although the 'hotline' was designed to encourage internet-users to report sites featuring child porn, which would, in the short term be very clearly its focus, nevertheless, 'the procedures and systems ... put in place *can be adapted to different issues as appropriate.*' (Emphasis added.) Indeed, this suggestion of extending internet surveillance and ultimately censorship was quickly taken up, with, for example, the National Parents' Council seeing the Working Group's proposals as 'a start' and calling on the United Nations' Convention on the Rights of the Child to become involved.[25]

Similarly, the Minister for Justice, John O'Donoghue, commenting after the launch of the 'hotline' said that he saw the project as 'ultimately becom[ing] one of the biggest international co-operative projects which has so far been undertaken.'[26] Clearly this contrasts with the co-operative, hands-off approach proposed in the 1998 report, but was in line with discussions going on at European expert level since 1997. By 2001, in the wake of the G8 Summit riots in Genoa and the illegal detention there of Irish nationals, the extent of the co-operation between European police forces emerged, itself not a remarkable revelation, but what underpinned their liaison was access to a very broad range of personal and commercial electronic data relating to particular individuals. Unsurprisingly, this intensive surveillance, done in the name of national security and combating criminal activity, has intensified as a consequence of 9/11 and the American-led 'war on terror'. However, the Irish Council for Civil Liberties and more importantly, the European Parliament, rejected in September 2001 a European Union Directive requiring telecommunications and internet companies to keep data transmitted by their subscribers for up to seven years,[27] and the Irish Internet Advisory Board, accepting the inevitable impossibility of effective internet surveillance and censorship, recommended in its proposals, published in October 2001, self-regulation. In the meantime, the international social and cultural landscape had changed dramatically in the wake of the 9/11 atrocities in the USA which occurred a few days after the European Parliament vote, with resistance to the surveillance of personal communications subsequently weakening. As a result, when an international treaty on cybercrime was adopted in late 2001 by the European Council of Ministers, not only did the Irish government agree to sign up to it, despite the serious reservations of the Department of Enterprise, Trade and Employment as well as the Data Protection Agency,[28] but the European Parliament accepted the new data surveillance measures as they became increasingly enshrined in western national government laws.[29] In 2003, the new Minister for Justice Michael McDowell announced, in contradiction to the existing and continuing policy of self-regulation, that Irish telecommunications transmitters, including ISPs, would be required by law to retain all voice and data communications for a period of three years, making Ireland the only western democracy with a mandatory data retention regime. However, the Irish Data Protection Commissioner threatened to initiate High Court proceedings against the minister following his secret ministerial direction to telecommunications operators because of the unconstitutionality of the proposal to store citizens' phone, fax and mobile call data.[30] Immediately following the March 2004 Madrid bombings, such measurers became generalized throughout the European Union.[31] Simultaneously, as part of the post 9/11 monitoring of visitors, entry to the USA now requires travellers to provide detailed personal data in forty-three categories (soon, perhaps, to include DNA profiles) which may be retained for up to seventy-five years, a US Government demand which was acceded to in 2004 by the European Commission despite the overwhelming opposition to it by the democratically-elected European Parliament.

Despite the media hype and concern over internet pornography – subsequently, successfully used as the thin edge of the wedge so as to monitor and control the internet –

as well as the extensive publicity surrounding the launch of the hotline, there were less than ten complaints during the hotline's first week, many of which were 'very general' while none of the material in question had originated in Ireland.[32] Similarly, despite the ISPCC campaigns on behalf of children, the ISPCC's 1998 report of its Childline calls indicated 'very little evidence of forced participation in or exposure to child pornography' by children calling the service,[33] while its 2003 report, analyzing 760,000 calls from children, makes no mention of child pornography.[34] The reality of the limited threat posed was also seen in the first report of the hotline which covered the period November 1999 to June 2001. The report outlined its operational procedure whereby with regard to offending material hosted on Irish sites, the relevant ISP was requested to remove it and the police informed, while with material hosted outside of Ireland, the complaint was passed on to the appropriate international body, in practice, to INHOPE. Though there was a total of 671 complaints received, of which 567 (84.5 per cent) were alleged child pornography, and 18 (2.6 per cent) alleged adult pornography, on investigation only 39 (5.8 per cent) were actually deemed to be child pornography while 2 (0.3 per cent) related to child abuse, 48 (7.1 per cent) to child erotica (and presumably not illegal under the 1998 Act), and a much increased 69 (10.2 per cent) to adult pornography. Indeed, for the whole period only 2 reports of internet child pornography and of adult pornography were forwarded to the Irish police. Such disparity between the two sets of figures makes clear the slippage in perception and the difficulty inherent in subjective, vague and loaded language. What one regards as offensive and criminal imagery another sees as morally acceptable adult pornography and, as such, perfectly legitimate on the internet, although it would be banned automatically under the Video Recordings Act if strictly interpreted. (Soft porn in various forms is clearly available on video/DVD). Notwithstanding the inclusion of these more refined statistics, when the junior minister with responsibility for Health and Children, Mary Hanifin, launched the report, she chose to highlight the number of such complaints: 'a complaint a day about child pornography on the web.'[35]

Also included in the report were four sample investigations. The first concerned an unauthorized use of an Irish domain address in which a 14-year-old male stated he was available for sex with any adult males located in Ireland. Another focused on university students exchanging images of popular family cartoon characters participating in family sexual activities, which included animated images of young children having sex with parents and with each other. While such images were deemed to be strictly legal under the 1998 Act, the concern expressed was that this may have been part of a validating procedure for 'grooming' children into believing sexual activity with adults is acceptable. Ironically, this fantasy of the child with his mother, central to the Oedipal narrative (or daughter with father in the Electra Complex) arguably is at the root of much classical cinema, and refigured in so much of children's or young people's texts including the highly successful movie, *Big*, discussed in the previous chapter. The third example was of an Irish language domain which had a link to a site offering adult sex toys. When the owner of the website was made aware of the connection, the offending material was removed. The final investigation was of a report concerning an American website that featured compressed, password-protected activities that contained large volumes of child pornography including representations of pre-pubescent children participating in sexual relations with each other and with adults. In this instance, the information was relayed to US Cybetipline via INHOPE.[36]

Sadly, the popular media rather than confront the more complex social issues and reality of actual abuse, focus on the relatively few *representations* of child pornography and condense the viewers of such representations with the producers of them and those who engage in criminal and abusive relations with minors. This is despite the fact that Max Taylor, writing in the wake of the Amethyst police raids, pointed out there is no evidence to suggest that such behaviours are necessarily linked or interchangeable and that abuse in general is largely of a domestic nature with 'perpetrators having legitimate access to the child.'[37] Such slippages and misunderstanding also occurs within the political and professional discourse. Many of the social workers and psychologists who as a body of professionals have been influential commentators, just as they were with regard to 'video nasties,' have often lacked the cultural sophistication to analyze such representations, or failed to provide an adequate context for their research. For example, the editor of *Irish Social Worker*, Kieran McGrath, writing in the *Irish Independent*, used a very rare piece of footage featuring a Polish boy being 'sold' to some paedophiles, and being tied up and sexually abused, as the centre-piece of an article calling for more restrictions on the internet. The material, which he had seen at a conference on domestic violence in Amsterdam, by its nature could only have had an extremely small circulation.[38] What is perhaps most interesting is not the interlinking of the technology with abuse but the root of the abuse in the family; in a sense the technology is irrelevant. A 2004 report, *Just One Click*, from the children's charity Barnardos, confirmed the 'selling' of children on-line by relatives and friends, who used 'indecent' photographs of pre-pubescent boys and girls, with the settings for such abuse becoming more 'everyday'. In its survey, Barnardos found that 83 UK children had been abused via the internet or cameraphone, of whom seven had been sold on-line and one who had been abused live on the world wide web. The availability of digital camera technology was, it appeared, causing an 'explosion' in the number of child abuse images on the net.[39] The use of cameraphones for the recording and distribution of (pornographic) images emerged as an Irish national issue in January 2004 when an allegedly pornographic image of a 15-year-old girl was distributed throughout the mobile phone network.[40] This totally mobile wireless technology, usually in the hands of teenagers, led to calls for their banning in schools,[41] and their use prohibited in Parliament, while a swimming pool banned them after a 12-year-old girl took a camera picture of a woman in the pool's dressing room.[42]

Undeniably, the cultural anxiety surrounding internet child porn is fuelled by an attraction/repulsion aesthetic whereby one is helplessly sucked into a world that disgusts, evident in much of the vicarious and sensationalist reporting as well as fictional accounts of this subterranean world, such as in *Mona Lisa* (Neil Jordan, 1985, GB), or more recently *8mm* (Joel Schumacher, 1999, USA/Germany). If, in the first instance, it seems to speak of the fear of the abusive act itself, and the desire to extend the legal structures supporting the ideological and moral status quo, other factors may be more powerful. These include fear of the reality of the breakdown of the family unit; the untenability of idealized notions around childhood; the recognition that the domestic environment is the primary site of abuse; and that sex is not bound by instrumental rationality and goes beyond confines of consensual and pleasurable expressions of adult (heterosexual) encounters. Additionally, that the internet refuses to observe rigid categories is, without doubt, anxiety-producing, at least for the state and those who have a vested interest in concepts such as truth, certainty, and who wish to protect the ideological status quo. If at one level this 'messed up' aesthetic is evident in the often cited analogy of the internet as the most vast and diverse library imaginable, but with its books randomly scattered on the floor, or in the quality or otherwise of material which ranges from highly specialized, researched and accurate information to that which is misleading and incorrect, it is likewise present with regard to on-line identity. There is no easy way to determine whether a young girl, for example, is really a young girl or an adult (male) masquerading as such. Though a man taking on the persona of a young girl is not in itself inherently wrong, the boundaries crossed are nonetheless problematic even when the man in question is not doing this in order to form an abusive or sexual relationship with a child. Put another way, it confuses and fundamentally goes against the established social grammar of interaction. For many cultural theorists such boundary breaching is a feature of the contemporary postmodern world and is directly reflected in the phenomenon of the child as adult, or, the commercialization and sexualization of the child, but it is also evident in its flipside: the infantalization of the adult. In Ireland, given prohibitive property costs, adult offspring are increasingly staying in the parental home, but without radically modifying their behaviour from when they were legal dependents. Complaints from parents about their adult children's refusal to grow up and take on adult responsibility and commitment and their levels of spending, drinking and engagement in 'child' oriented pursuits (i.e. reading the likes of *Harry Potter*, or gaming) for short-term pleasure gain, frequently erupt in the media. A corollary issue, which is also destabilizing the 'traditional' nuclear family occurs when a son or daughter brings home his/her partner to live with the family.

Nevertheless, perhaps the single most potent factor in all of the moral panic about the internet and visually reliant mediums such as the cinema and television is centered on the image *itself* and owes to the cultural dominance that vision and sight have enjoyed in Western thought and philosophy since the Greeks.[43] With regard to images of pornography, even the odious subclass of child pornography and images of paedophilic abuse, the suggestion is made that they are toxic or invidious. As such, beyond impacting on the viewer's innocence in the case of a child, or sensibility in the case of an adult, they lead to libidinous or indecent thoughts that cause them to see the acts depicted as 'normal,' and/or become additive consumers of such material, or engage in the represented practices. As a result of this, the market grows and more images have to be produced and therefore more abuse occurs. This simplistic paradigm of exposure to material leading to acceptance and ultimately to imitative behaviour employed by James Montgomery, particularly in relation to children and the working class, is one that is outlined in much of the media and sociological work of the 1970s and 1980s and ultimately is a reiteration of Plato's thesis in his *Republic: Book*

*II* that 'a young person cannot judge what is allegorical and what is literal; anything that he receives into his mind at that age is likely to become indelible.'[44] Such a position is inflexible and fails to appreciate that often the fetishizing of the image *itself* and the act of collecting, as is supported by the quantities of images in the possession of the various internet offenders, is almost as important as the actual content, and that, more importantly, the images might also lead to the somewhat unfashionable notion of catharsis. Similarly, the genetic disposition of a person, which at least in scientific circles has come out on top within the nature versus nurture debate, is ignored, as are individual and family background and other social and economic factors. In other words, while televisual, filmic and computer images may be the most 'visible', easily namable and accessible forms of expression, they to do not operate within some moral or cultural void but are part of a broad social texture. It is this point of context that is central to understanding and going beyond censorship, in its crude form, in favour of pedagogical and artistic discretion, and classification. However, censorship, so as to protect the social order from *real* rather than potential moral, ideological or symbolic harm, is something different. As Heins argues, 'If speech is proven to cause *direct harm* – to personal privacy, to a fair trial, to physical safety, to the right to work, study, or vote – there is a good argument for suppressing or punishing it.' (Emphasis added.)[45]

Notwithstanding existing legislation and the current trends in Irish and European law to affect increasing control and surveillance over its citizens, a significant strand of Irish government policy and practice has been precisely towards this more open attitude and the displacement of responsibility, in the case of minors, on to the family, as is evident in the Film Censor's decision making, and which in effect is turning the office from that of censor to classifier. While this has implications, not least in terms of parental absence during working hours which means that children (and their friends) are often left alone and unsupervised for extended periods of time, this is partly motivated by the recognition of the impossibility and futility of fully controlling the internet. A 2002 Internet Advisory Board survey found that 40 per cent of children usually access the internet alone, though the relatively small proportion of 14 per cent said they accessed unsuitable material on-line.[46] A 2002 European study, with the Irish input from the National Centre for Technology in Education, reported that one in every four 8- to 17-year-olds 'accidentally' accessed porn websites, while it said that 48 per cent of Irish children were unsupervised on-line.[47] This will only intensify with the international pay-per-view to follow in the wake of reductions in the cost of international telecommunications whereby people will be able to bypass Irish regulators and directly watch films and access other material including games – some of which deemed by the Irish state to be unsuitable – on their computers. While there is no specific Irish legislation regulating games, the Department of Justice in 1999 instructed the Film Censor to begin regulating and classifying the content of computer games in 1999 by interpreting the Video Recordings Act, 1989 to include video computer games.[48] Another factor is the protection of the economy and the technology sector. After all, the technology/computer industries (together with the return of mothers to the work place, and general standards of education) largely contributed to the successful 'Celtic Tiger' economy. In short, overly restrictive measures or excessive moral questioning might impact on e-commerce, a central plank of Irish economic planning into the future. For example, in the late 1990s the government went to extraordinary lengths and expense to entice America's MIT Media Lab, a corporate 'education' body, to set up its European facility in Dublin.

Consequently, perhaps the real debate should not be one of censorship per se, but of the relevance of the Censor's classifications, and the ways in which we, as a society, can define and create a 'safe' space in which young people can access, assess, and enjoy material even if it sometimes raises difficult and challenging issues such as unwanted pregnancy, abortion, sexuality, racism, or terrorism, without being exploited or otherwise being endangered. Such ways necessarily include a more revolutionary education system from a very young age which provides children with the critical tools of language and analysis by which, in media terms, they can 'decode' or 'deconstruct', or contextualize and evaluate a text, and come to see that even what appears as Plato's 'literal' (fact) is always ideological or, in some sense, a fiction. For example, it is crucial children (and adults) understand that documentaries, news reportage and other 'reality'-based forms do not give unmediated access to reality, but involve human agency and selection both in terms of 'creating' and receiving/interpreting the text. Likewise, they should appreciate that a piece of art or fiction can offer culturally pertinent and 'truthful' insights. While media, visual literacy and computer studies have been incorporated into the curriculum, generally, it is not of a sufficiently specialized, culturally theoretical, or sophisticated standard. For the most part, texts tend to be safe or canonical rather than representing or being selected from within the current popular texts that the children consume on a daily basis, or, more importantly, those that directly challenge society and its taboos. Similarly, subjects such as film or media studies too often only begin to be taught within second-level education where they are treated as an offshoot of English instead of being treated as independent, at times, interdisciplinary subjects which should be available from early primary grades.

If education is the first element that allows for a contextualized viewing practice to emerge, parental or other adult engagement before, during or after viewing, is the second. This is not simply the acquiring of blocking internet filters or locking the video/DVD cabinet, or in other words, closing down or denying debate, but in actively being aware of and seeking to discuss the content or significance of particular sites, films, music,[49] television or games. As an article in the *Sunday Tribune* suggested, the way to counteract 'the damage' that videos or television 'might do' is to ensure more parental involvement in what is being viewed[50] while an *Irish Times*' piece advised that 'supervising your child's time online is the best protection they can have from inappropriate matter, misleading information and malevolent strangers.'[51] Perhaps, surprisingly, it is not just 'dangerous' adult material that has given rise to media controversies and moral panic, but material, often promoting positive qualities, specially targeted at children, and the attendant advertising of children's products.[52] In this regard, *Pokemon*, a children's animated series with various spin-off products including trading cards detailing the various pocket monsters, is exemplary. In Ireland, its popularity reached craze proportions during 1999–2000 such that it led to a series of anguished articles in the press about child addicts or even 'junkies' dealing in Pokemon cards and trinkets on street corners, with 'secret transactions well away from prying adult eyes.'[53] What is noteworthy is that in such instances a secret world is invoked. If this draws on notions of forbidden or criminal activity, it also points to the fear of parents and, more generally, society and the state, that they do not know, own, or control their children who may be the ultimate enemy to their system of values. Essentially, it is yet another instance of the old struggle for children's hearts, minds, souls and sexual bodies, that is always best won when there is openness and dialogue. Typically, the *Pokemon* debate was not broadened to include a consideration of the commercialization of childhood and the irony that the majority of Irish children enjoy an unprecedented freedom and independence and relative economic wealth (on the one hand), and are subjected to intense commercial exploitation by an uncontrollable and rampant capitalism, as well as being limited by (knowledge of) a more violent, predatory and dangerous society in which innocence is often condemned as ignorance (on the other).

The extent of the lack of control over children's and teenagers' viewing habits (as well as pictorial representations of them) in the 1990s was brought home in a report by clinical psychologist Marie Murray and consultant psychiatrist Nuala Healy of St Joseph's Adolescent and Family Service, which is attached to St Vincent's Psychiatric Hospital, Fairview, Dublin, which was given extensive media coverage from 1995 onwards. Based on responses by 1,000[54] 12- to 17-year-olds to a 57 item questionnaire assessing the type, frequency and certificate of 120 listed videos that were categorized into different ratings, unknown to the children. The object of the research was to measure the extent to which Irish schoolchildren had seen over-18s certificated films 'containing scenes of graphic violence.' It found that 96 per cent of first year students had seen such videos, while 70 per cent claimed to have seen 'blue' or sexually explicit movies. However, the top three over-18s films viewed were *The Terminator* (James Cameron, 1984), *Boyz 'n the Hood* (John Singleton, 1991) and *GoodFellas* (Martin Scorsese, 1990) hardly films which were likely to corrupt 13- or 14-year-olds. The report concluded that there was 'a significant increase in low self-esteem among video watchers and it made a clear connection between poor verbal reasoning and increased use of videos.' However, based on media accounts of the report, it would seem that key factors such as the video user's social-class, family environment, relationship with parents and/or siblings, gender and age profile, academic or other achievement, and position within the peer group, as well as the viewing practice within the home, were not (sufficiently) explored, and as a result the conclusions are not fully justifiable or verifiable.[55]

It is this type of 'sociological'-based research of the social worker/psychologist which lacks a media or cultural sophistication, and usually fails to appreciate the difference between reality and representation, that is placed center stage by the state (and media), which is then used as a legitimizing tool in the call for restrictions on the media. For example, in this instance, some media took the opportunity to give the findings the most lurid spins such as the *Irish Independent's* 'Trading Porn behind the School Sheds'.[56] The same newspaper again resorted to tabloidesque sensationalism with regard to another study, with a headline declaring that 'Internet Porn was "big factor" in rape of students.'[57] This was an account by a Norwegian speaking to the annual conference of the Irish primary school's National Parents Council about his own country, though no details of the research carried out was included in the report. Others commented on the Murray/Healy report, including Cian Ó Tighearnaigh, the then-Chief Executive of the Irish Society for the Prevention of Cruelty to Children (ISPCC).[58] Expressing concern that mainstream television (*Power Rangers*, *The A-Team*) sanitizes violence, Ó Tighearnaigh dragged up the different social-class readings of moving images reminiscent of James Montgomery. He suggested that if a boy or girl from Darndale or Ballymun (two 'deprived' areas in Dublin) were to see in a film a person of the same age who was 'sexually active, wealthy and with mobile phones,' it could 'create a lot of confusion'.[59]

Marie Murray's subsequent assertions that exposing children to 'unsuitable' television scenes was 'a form of child abuse' and that television 'can be very insidious, very toxic'[60] while having a certain, if unquantifiable, validity, evident alone in the viability and importance of advertising,[61] is nonetheless a gross misunderstanding of how meaning is produced. If this hypothermic model of passive spectatorship whereby the viewer is 'injected' with a media message is less than useful to current debate, it also shows up the limitations of her understanding of the media, even though she is frequently used by the media when seeking out negative views on pictorial representations of sex and violence, as well as being a member of the Censorship Review Group of the Department of Justice. (Of course, to be fair, arguably it is the media's obsession with simple polarities and sound bytes stripped of context and subtleties, that has crudified her position.) Criticism of such a position is not limited to those involved in cultural and media analysis as is evident in the comments of another psychiatrist, Peader O'Grady, who has called attention to the way videos are used as cultural scapegoats.

> Portraying videos as the harbinger of doom is a handy way for adults to shrug off their responsibilities and make excuses for our society. What videos reflect is that violence is a necessary part of life when the State wants it to be. But, when children get out and start stealing and committing acts of vandalism or getting into drugs, then it is the fault of videos.[62]

Complementary to a visual culture and media literacy education, and parental interaction and engagement with the viewing process, both of which act to place the texts in a wider context, is the provision (by the industry and state) of comprehensive ratings information so that adults might assess not just particular internet sites – which as a site of panic and fear has already begun to recede in the face of concerns over the growth in *real* teenage and young adult drinking and violence – but also videos, DVDs, computer games and, of course, cinema films. The challenge for parents and guardians in the twenty-first century is whether they are willing to take on this responsibility through informing themselves of all these media, including understanding the nature of representations, or, instead, to abdicate such responsibility and allow the state to make decisions for them, or with regard to the internet, remain helpless in the face of the few who will always be able to find a technical solution to overcoming censorship measures.[63] Whatever the society's decision will be, it should be remembered that 'irresponsible indifference and unsubstantiated moral panic are the greatest enemies to ensuring that vulnerable users are adequately protected.'[64]

# CHAPTER 8

# *Film censorship and Irish politics*

The authorities may [have been] made to look ridiculous if challenged as to
why a particular film was rejected.
Thomas Coyne, *Controller of Censorship, 1945.*[1]

Although the narrative of Irish film censorship is predominantly a 'moral' one, it has,
nonetheless, a political dimension both with regard to film production and exhibition. While this aspect has direct relevance to the World War Two period when the
policy of Irish military neutrality was imposed on all media, it is not its exclusive
reserve. Certainly, the first Film Censor, James Montgomery, objected to stories set
during the Irish War of Independence, some of which his British counterpart, J.C.
Hanna, sought to stymie during the script-vetting procedure operating at the British
Board of Film Censorship during the 1930s and 1940s. The flip-side of such 'politics' was the direct action of the Irish Republican Army (IRA) from the 1920s to the
1950s against cinemas screening films which they deemed as promoting or celebrating British imperialism. However, in keeping with the Irish state's official reception,
exemplified in its endorsement of *Man of Aran* (Robert Flaherty, 1934, GB) as a
depiction of raw reality in which the 'resourcefulness and fortitude of the Irish family'[2]
was affirmed, the IRA, unaware of the interrelationship and continuity of actuality,
fiction and ideology, largely confined itself to newsreels, documentaries and representations of 'real' events. Of course, even before the 1923 Censorship of Films Act,
the IRA had been involved with the cinema at least through their unconventional
means of ensuring exhibition for a film promoting the Dáil Loan Bonds in 1919 when
they ordered cinema projectionists at gunpoint to put on the (banned) film. By the
time the authorities had been alerted they had left.[3] More extensive censorship in the
Irish state occurred primarily to ensure internal civil stability rather than confirm
Irish neutrality per se during World War Two. In the modern era, this political censorship has been most associated with the, at times, controversial use made by Irish
governments of Section 31 of the Broadcasting Act, 1960 to deny 'subversives' access
to the Irish national radio and television service, RTÉ.

IRISH REPUBLICAN RESPONSES TO 'IMPERIALIST' FILMS

The first skirmish between the IRA and the Irish Free State Government concerning the cinema was during the Civil War, when in 1922 the IRA issued a statement stating that cinemas should close down during the hunger strike of anti-Treaty activist Mary MacSwiney. The government promptly responded with a directive to cinema owners instructing them to keep their premises open[4] and no further action ensued. Subsequent IRA campaigns were more pointed and tended to focus on British newsreels which, in the absence of consistently-produced Irish newsreels, were a regular feature of Irish cinema programmes, and around which most controversies centered. That there was such a void owes in large part to the state's failure to invest in film. While there was a certain, but very limited, support given to documentaries in the 1920s and 1930s, reflecting the aesthetic preferences for realism evident in Film Censor Richard Hayes' promotion of 'educative' or 'propaganda' films as the direction an Irish cinema should take (or, indeed, one of his successors, Christopher Macken's, preference for didactic and realist films: ones 'which teach a lesson')[5] there was no investment in fiction filmmaking.[6]

Nevertheless, as the censorship narrative thus far shows, the state was acutely aware of the power of cinema, and if the Cosgrave or de Valera governments were not fully appreciative of the importance of newsreels, this was not so by the early sound era when in late 1930 President Cosgrave made direct camera statements for Pathé and, in early 1931, for Movietone. Although he gave his approval to the brief statement he had made on camera for Gordon Lewis, First National Pathé's Dublin Editor, after viewing the item prior to release on 3 December 1930, he had difficulty with his piece for Movietone. In February 1931 the company had made a request for a substantial piece to camera which the government viewed as 'a very good [opportunity] from the propaganda angle.' However, Movietone's intention was for Cosgrave to place less emphasis on commercial trade with Britain, or the presentation of the Irish Free State as a separate and individual country to that of Britain, in favour of positioning Ireland within 'the Commonwealth group and closely linked in co-operation with other Dominions.' Items on world peace, Ireland's international policy, and Yeats and the Irish literary revival were also planned for inclusion. Though two versions of the newsreel were made, one for Britain and Ireland, the other for America, because Cosgrave would not approve the American version, an indication of his sensitivity to Irish-Americans, only the British/Irish version from which a reference to world peace was cut, was released in all countries.[7]

The problem with the newsreels was not just this unsubtle attempt to pressurize President Cosgrave into declaring support for the Commonwealth but the juxtaposing of the item on Ireland with celebratory images of English nationality, royalty and English institutions. Equally critical was that the English-originating, if occasionally American-owned, newsreels only periodically included items on Ireland. This was so even in the case of *Irish Movietone News* where the 'national' prefix was used moreover as a marketing tool. One such example of the questionable 'contextualization' and limited analysis of Ireland can be seen shortly after de Valera became President of the Executive Council when *Movietone* reported on his trip to London in summer 1932 to determine the end of the Land Annuities and the Oath of Allegiance. The item, *De Valera in U.K. but Fails to Agree with the British Cabinet*, was presented without background or reference to the issues under negotiation, while the only aspects considered noteworthy of comment were that de Valera had not been in England since 1921 and that he was not smiling. This piece was sandwiched between items on golf, the Royal Horse Show and an air pageant with martial music. By way of small compensation at least, de Valera was spared a billing with one of the previous week's items on 'the Little Royal Lady,' Princess Elizabeth, the future Queen, with music and guns at the Aldershot Tattoo.[8] It was such footage of British royalty that most irritated Irish republicans because until 1949 and the declaration of the Republic of Ireland and its withdrawal from the Commonwealth, the British king or queen was more than a foreign if near symbol of (colonial oppressive) power, but was also head of the Commonwealth. The hated oath of allegiance to the English monarch had been the principal stumbling block to the entry into the Dáil in the 1920s of the main bulk of the anti-Treaty IRA and Sinn Féin, including de Valera and his followers. Therefore, any representations of England's military power or of royalty were understandably and undeniably anathema to Irish republicans.

One of de Valera's closest lieutenants prior to their departure from IRA/Sinn Féin and subsequent formation of Fianna Fáil in 1926 was the organization's Minister for Defence, Seán Lemass. At the 1925 Sinn Féin ardfheis a resolution was passed instructing members to take direct action against British propaganda in cinemas. Speaking in support of the motion, Lemass 'echoed strongly held current views about the effectiveness of the new medium as a political and ideological weapon when he warned that "the principles of Irish nationalism were in danger of extinction among a large section of people as a result of this propaganda".'[9] A few days earlier, armed men had held up the management of the Masterpiece Cinema, Talbot Street, Dublin and disrupted the screening of the First World War British commemorative film *Ypres* (Walter Summers, 1925)[10] which was one of a number of factual-based war reconstruction films, including *The Battles of the Coronel and Falkland Islands* (also directed by Walter Summers, 1927) produced by Bruce Woolfe and which gained considerable prestige for British films and as Rachael Low states, cinema itself.[11] In Galway on 30 November, a few days after the Sinn Féin ardfheis, another of Woolfe's productions, the 1924 film *Zeebrugge* (H. Bruce Woolfe and A.V. Bramble) was seized and burned.[12] According to Lemass' biographer John Horgan,[13] 'the ardfheis resolution had the dual function of providing a retrospective justification for the earlier military action (presumably carried out on Lemass' orders as Minister for Defence, or at least with his approval) and a mandate for the subsequent one.' Cinema managers were warned by the IRA that if such films were shown they would be 'drastically dealt with'.[14] This action by Lemass can be seen in a somewhat ironic light as he was to become the single most influential figure in the formulation of Irish film production policy from the 1930s to the late 1950s. In his capacity as Minister for Industry and Commerce during those decades he almost totally neglected indigenous Irish cinema in favour of encouraging foreign film producers to make films in Ireland. The culmination of this policy was his support for the anachronistic establishment of Ardmore Studios in 1958, which, in the main, served the British film industry and was, as veteran documentary filmmaker Louis Marcus put it, an 'irrelevance' to Irish cinema and, indeed, it proved to be a handicap.[15]

In 1927, a pragmatic, not loyalist, approach to the oath of allegiance was adopted by Fianna Fáil and as a result, 'speaking empty words,' they took their seats in the Dáil. On Fianna Fáil's accession to power in March 1932 there was a temporary resurgence of radical nationalism by the anti-Treaty, anti-English republicans. Indeed, one of Frank Aiken's first acts as Fianna Fáil's Minister for Defence in de Valera's first Cabinet was to visit imprisoned IRA leader George Gilmore (Lemass' secretary at the time of the 1925 ardfheis) on the day Fianna Fáil assumed office. The following day, all political prisoners were released and within another few days the IRA's banned newspaper, *An Phoblacht*, was re-established while the ban on the IRA itself, which was due for renewal shortly afterwards, was left lapse, and military drilling and recruitment commenced immediately. Though the accommodation between Fianna Fáil and the IRA and other republicans was short lived, it was sufficient to allow for an upsurge of activity against symbols of English nationality. As far as the cinema was concerned this proved to be images of English royalty. The first and most obvious expression of republican attitudes emerged in 1934 with newsreel footage of the marriage of the Duke of Kent and Princess Marina.

A few days after the wedding, on 3 December 1934, the Savoy, Dublin showed the film. Half way through the screening, a number of people – 500 according to *An Phoblacht*,[16] 400 according to the *Irish Press*,[17] and a mere 50 according to the pro-monarchist *Irish Times*[18] – rushed into the cinema shouting 'Up the Republic,' 'Stop British Propaganda' and other anti-imperialist slogans. Rotten eggs and other missiles were thrown at the screen and some of the demonstrators 'wearing slouch hats and trench coats,' the IRA's 'uniform,' 'clambered on to the front of the proscenium and began to tear the screen down.' In a few moments the whole lower portion had been destroyed. The Irish national anthem, 'The Soldier's Song,' was then sung. When the film had ended, the audience applauded the film, at least as reported by the *Irish Times*. The paper also noted that during the disturbance several women had 'fainted through sheer fright,' and complained that there was 'a noticeable absence of police,' who only arrived when 'the trouble was nearly over.'[19] By then the youths had left by the emergency exits to back lanes and no one was arrested. When the lights went up the Savoy's organist sought to impose a degree of national melancholic harmony by playing 'My Dark Rosaleen'. The police rushed to the Grafton Cinema where the film was also being shown, but no incidents occurred there.

The raid on O'Connell Street's Savoy had been organized by republican bodies, especially the IRA and the left-wing breakaway group from the IRA, the Republican Congress. The demonstrators had assembled in Cathal Brugha Street, scene of many republican meetings, and which also happens to be just around the corner from the Savoy. They marched from there to the cinema where they were met by a contingent which had assembled at Nelson's Pillar, also quite close to the Savoy. Police and commissioners on duty at the cinema were swept aside by the superior numbers of the demonstrators. The reasons for the attack on the Savoy were given in the Republican Congress newspaper[20] a few days after the raid. It also warned cinema managers against continuing to show the film:

> There is no film industry in Ireland. Our cinemas are just branch shops of English companies which control our supplies of films. Hence it is natural that Imperialist news reels dominate Irish screens. And it is natural, too, that cinemas are occasionally smashed up, as was the Savoy ... If cinema managers will insist on showing news reels to which the majority of the audience object, they must be prepared to take the consequences.

During the Savoy disturbance some of the republicans shouted 'Remember Casement' as they reminded the audience of Roger Casement's execution in 1916, and of the BBFC's hostile attitude to a film script about Casement (discussed below). This provoked a letter to the *Irish Times*[21] from Roger Casement's brother Tom who denounced the demonstrators as 'fanatics'. Obviously missing, or at least deliberately refusing to acknowledge the nature of the Monarchy/Republican clash over the film, he noted that his brother 'gave his life for the rights of minorities – in the Congo, in Putamayo and in Ireland.' He added, with unconscious irony, that his brother 'would have been the first to condemn last night's exhibition of tyranny.'

The *Republican Congress* replied[22] to Tom Casement through the device of an anonymous letter-writer who accused him of having sympathy for 'a select and traitorous minority Master [to whom he] is so anxious to ingratiate himself,' while *An Phoblacht* warned cinema managers that 'British propaganda films would not be tolerated in Dublin.'[23] *An Phoblacht*[24] also attacked the *Irish Times*, which, it said,

> should understand that there are other sources for obtaining 'brilliant photography' and that the Irish people are not interested in any form of English 'pomp and pageantry'. The action of the citizens of Dublin which the *Irish Times* describes as 'blackguardism', is in no way different from the action which would be taken by citizens of Berlin if shown during the war; or by the citizens of Paris, Brussels or London if German propagandist films were shown.

The writer ended with a warning to the newspaper which was deemed to have 'consistently insulted Ireland' to change 'the tone of its leading articles if it intends to continue in circulation.' Though the paper survived this and other threats during the 1930s, it was another decade before it toned down its unionism and began to more fully enter an accommodation with the majority of the Irish people.

The royal film was immediately withdrawn from the Savoy 'in the interests of their women patrons,' while a number of other Dublin cinema managers followed suit. In Cork the film was cancelled following a visit to a manager by a young man who requested that the film not be shown again as it was 'British propaganda'. In Waterford, the Savoy and Theatre Royal both withdrew it. In Limerick where it was due to be shown in three cinemas, the Civic Guards took the film 'as a precautionary measure' to William Street Barracks. When it was subsequently exhibited at Limerick's Coliseum a group of youths shouted for its withdrawal and began singing 'The Soldier's Song' and 'Legion of the Rearguard'. Regardless, the picture continued to the end 'with the approval of the audience generally,' at least according to the biased *Irish Times*.[25] A few days later in Sligo, after a request by an IRA deputation, the Savoy decided to remove the film from the programme. The IRA men told the manager that they regarded the film as imperialist propaganda and that it was offensive to the nationalists of Sligo.[26] On 17 December when it was being shown in Kilkenny the film was kept at the Garda Station for safe keeping, while in Ballinrobe, Co. Mayo, the Garda Superintendent requested the cinema not to show the film 'in the interests of peace'. The manager agreed and the film was not screened.

There was a curious disparity in the 1930s between the hostile reception given to English newsreels and the more muted response to the cycle of royal costume dramas. The first of these films was *The Private Life of Henry VIII* (Alexander Korda, 1933, GB). Immensely successful both in Britain and internationally, it grossed an unprecedented for a British film, £500,000 before it had finished its first run,[27] and led to a new, but short-lived, era in British film of big-budget films intended to compete with American product. In Ireland, the film had a well-received three-week run at the Metropole, Dublin in January 1934, but then the film, which delights in the conceits of theatrical farce, is not overly concerned with politics. The *Irish Times*, which given its political leanings and its aesthetic and ideological partiality to newsreels and costume drams of royalty, stated that 'the claims that it was the best film yet produced by a British studio are justified.' It added, however, that 'we find ourselves a little disgusted by [Henry's] sensuality and cruelty.'[28] This view reflected the concerns about 'immoral' films which were to the fore in the *Irish Times* as much as in the Catholic press in the 1930s. Despite these qualifications, the film did not raise a controversy and as evidenced in its Dublin run, proved extremely popular with Irish audiences, such that it was revived at Dublin's Metropole and DeLuxe cinemas in 1938. While this particular film, self-consciously aimed at an international market, was set in the relatively distant past, treated its subject with a light touch and did not display its nationalism too jingoistically, other quintessentially British royalist or imperialist fiction films and newsreels, particularly if concerned with more recent subjects, demanded that film renters in Ireland had to thread very carefully so as to avoid nationalist or republican reaction.

No doubt many cinema managers became subscribers to *An Phoblacht* to see whether they were planning any more actions against cinemas. In March 1935 the newspaper published a lengthy attack on an *Irish Press* campaign against immoral films which had been initiated in January and led to some Dublin cinemas withdrawing advertising from the *Press*, a policy which backfired on the exhibitors as the *Press* mobilized national support in its favour.[29] *An Phoblacht*[30] was not interested in the

*Press'* 'manufacturing [of] one of those carefully calculated Indignation Campaigns' since the original article 'did not go to the roots of the cinema evil' in Ireland.

> The Cinema in Ireland is, in the opinion of many, the greatest Anglicising force in the country. Apart from its representation of shady, alien modes of life, its continued depictions of British imperialist functions and British War Office propaganda displays is designed to make Irish youth in particular 'sensible' of the British connection.

*An Phoblacht* complained that the *Irish Press* failed to

> protest at the attempt to link up this country with a recent British Royal wedding by showing on the screen the crazed adulation of foolish English people. And when Irish Republicans showed in no uncertain terms their determination to prevent these Imperialist film displays there was no note of approval sounded by the *Irish Press*.

Against this background cinema managers sought to anticipate republican anger. Potential trouble was looming on the horizon only four months after the Savoy incidents. In April 1935 Paramount's *Lives of a Bengal Lancer* (Henry Hathaway, 1934), a hymn to British imperialist policy in India, was screened in Dublin. It was, as the *Daily Mail* described it, 'a powerful and popular argument for the continuance of that rule.'[31] The distributors of the film in Ireland, therefore, thought it prudent, given the events at the Savoy and other cinemas, to cut or change two particularly provocative sections. The recitation of Rupert Brook's poem, 'England, My England' was taken out, and at the end, 'Land of Hope and Glory' was substituted for 'God Save the King,'[32] though James Montgomery's only subsequent problem with the film was a scene of torture.[33]

A week after the opening of *Bengal Lancer* George V's Royal Jubilee Procession took place. Already it had been deemed wise not to screen the Jubilee film *Royal Cavalcade* (Herbert Brenon, Norman Lee, Walter Summers, Will Kellino and Marcel Varnel, 1935, GB) which was 'very much the official version of the reign, with the stress laid on tradition, pageantry, service and unity.'[34] Indeed, if Irish republicans had heard the comments of John Maxwell, managing-director of ABPC, the parent company of Dublin's Savoy cinema,[35] in which he suggested that the film could allow 'the British millions who throng to the cinema … find expression for their loyalty and devotion to the king,'[36] it might have been more than the cinema's screen which would have been torn down. The *Irish Times* observed[37] that every cinema proprietor who shows such films must be aware of the 'serious risk' involved. Subsequently, the distributors decided not to attempt to show the film of the royal procession on 6 May and the *Irish Times*[38] castigated the 'ignorant behaviour' of those who were preventing Irish audiences from seeing 'many pictures of real interest such as *Royal Cavalcade*,' described by Rachael Low as 'a long pedestrian, episodic survey of the [preceding] twenty-five years.'[39]

In May 1937 a more orthodox approach was taken to prevent the screening of a film featuring the coronation of George VI. Letters had been addressed by republicans to film renters 'requesting' them not to show the film. This led to what the *Irish Times*[40] described as 'an unusual conference'. Representatives of four renting organizations – General Films, Fox, Pathé and Paramount – met republicans and others on 6 May, the day of the coronation. They agreed that while items on the coronation in the regular newsreels could be shown, there would be no special film of the royal event. This clearly disappointed the *Irish Times* which was looking forward to footage from Movietone's thirty-four cameras at the coronation. Gordon Lewis, who attended the meeting in his capacity as Editor of Pathé's Dublin offices, tried to convey the impression that the decision had been voluntary. He said they would have reviewed the copy in the usual way, implying an organized approach to cut out offensive material, and they had always removed 'partyism and sectarianism'.[41] Nevertheless, the agreement between the republicans and the renters did not satisfy Sinn Féin, and it disassociated itself from 'any pact or agreement made for the display of British coronation films.' There was, however, no repetition of the events of December 1934. (In 1953 the issue of Coronation films was once more in the news. Sinn Féin visited cinema managers warning them not to show that year's coronation films.[42] When this approach failed in Northern Ireland, direct action was initiated. In Banbridge, Co. Down, a cinema showing *A Queen is Crowned* was damaged by a bomb explosion. The British press sought to characterize the deprivation of coronation films in the South at this time as a shock for the population, with the *Manchester Guardian*[43] even discovering a Belfast cinema-manager who expected 30,000 people from the South – 'they are falling over themselves to come here'! – some traveling by a special train to see the coronation film.

The celebratory royal films of the 1930s reached their apotheosis with *Victoria the Great* (1937) and the sequel shot in full Technicolor, *Sixty Glorious Years* (1938), both of which were directed, ironically enough, by Cork-born Herbert Wilcox. These films, as Jeffrey Richards noted,[44]

> represent the definitive hagiographical account of Queen Victoria. It is a picture of Victoria the mythic Great White Mother, the living symbol of the British Empire, divine source from which all the benefits of that empire are seen to flow.

For an Irish nationalist audience films about Victoria or George V were likely to bring to the fore rather different memories than these, as between them they had been on the throne for 70 of the 120 years of the Union of Great Britain and Ireland. No matter how much the films concentrated on domestic matters, or in these instances, displayed little or 'no interest in the England or the Empire behind the pomp, or the real people behind the royal façade,'[45] Irish nationalists could recite a series of often traumatic and violent events, including famines, which took place in Ireland when it was under the rule of the British Empire during those years and before. Nevertheless, these events did not stop the submission to the Irish Censor of the two 'imperialist' films in the late

1930s. Both *Victoria the Great*[46] and *Sixty Glorious Years*[47] were passed uncut by Montgomery. The latter film was given a release in January 1939 in one of the smallest of Dublin's city-centre cinemas, the 233-seat Astor, and it had a surprisingly long seven-week run. The *Irish Times*[48] loved it, and congratulated the script-writers, noting that the film deals with its subject with 'delicacy' whereas it 'could easily have provided a jingoistic story of Britain's growth in power during Queen Victoria's reign.' It added that it was a film 'to which the highly emotional well might take an extra handkerchief.' The less emotional writer on films for the most nationalist of all the national newspapers, the *Irish Press'* Liam MacGabhainn, an ex-editor of *An Phoblacht*, grudgingly accepted the film for what it was:

> This film recalls a period of time which is of little interest to a new Ireland, except to recall what might have been under different circumstances. It is, nevertheless, directed with much pomp, and majesty, and will, I am sure, appeal to those monarchically inclined.[49]

Why there should be this muted response to *Sixty Glorious Years* may be traced to the changing fortunes of radical republicans by 1939. The most militant left-wing members of the IRA and the Republican Congress had gone to fight in the Spanish Civil War. The traditional nationalist, anti-imperialist mainstream of the organization had begun to embark on a bombing campaign in England which alienated it from popular support in Ireland and led to many of its members being imprisoned and two hanged in England.[50] This change in the IRA was affected in parallel with its total alienation from the Fianna Fáil government which had grown from the organization and incorporated many of its members and followers. By 1939, the government had a formidable array of repressive laws to use against the IRA as well as against the proto-fascist Blueshirts. Other neutralizing tactics were the provision of pensions for IRA Civil War anti-Treaty fighters and the establishment of a new Volunteer Force which was set up as a branch of the Irish army and where commissions were given to ex-IRA men. This also led to a reduction in the IRA's strength. By 1939 de Valera also had a popular new Constitution which was a further step towards a Republic. Seán MacBride, who had been IRA Chief of Staff in 1936, was one of the most prominent gunmen to accept constitutional politics with the new Constitution. Even the Economic War with Britain had ended in April 1938. Thus, by the time the film was screened radical republicans not yet incorporated into the state were dispersed and split as well as otherwise occupied. They also probably thought that the issue of filmic images of royalty was, at least at this juncture, irrelevant to their struggle. However, during World War Two, Martin Quigley Jnr, an American spy whose cover was as a film trade representative, sought out the IRA's views on film censorship. In October 1943, Quigley met an ex-IRA man who had participated in the 1939 English bombings and had been released shortly before from the Curragh Internment Camp having given up the 'armed struggle'. He told Quigley that the IRA had no film policy 'except that it would object to any picture deemed extremely pro-British.'[51]

THE BRITISH BOARD OF FILM CENSORS AND IRELAND

Though Irish republicans took direct action against offending British and American films of English royalty and the imperialist past, which, it must be remembered were passed already by the Irish Film Censor, and/or had jingoistic or provocative images of English nationality, including the British flag, 'discreetly' removed by the Censor or were otherwise cut prior to submission, there were many more provocative films from a nationalist point-of-view not submitted. Contrawise, the employees of the British Board of Film Censors sought to ensure that offending images of Ireland from a British viewpoint were not even produced. While Britain retained a military presence in Ireland it could and did restrict or ban fiction, documentary and news films sympathetic to Irish republicanism.[52] After independence this process had to be done at one remove. As has been noted in chapter 3, the first drama film about the Irish War of Independence, *Irish Destiny* (1926), was banned by the British Board of Film Censors in 1926, one of only six films banned that year. Through its process of vetting scripts prior to production the BBFC sought to remove any elements which could be considered offensive to British interests. As James C. Robertson notes, 'potentially the greatest source of friction between the BBFC and American and British studios from 1919 to 1939 was Ireland.'[53]

In the 1920s and 1930s there were a number of people in senior positions at the BBFC who had direct experience of Ireland. The best known of these was Irish-born T.P. O'Connor, President of the BBFC from 1916 to 1929. He was the only member of the Home Rule-Irish Parliamentary Party at Westminster to sit for an English constituency (the Scottish division of Liverpool, 1880–1929) and might have been disposed to the Irish cause had he a more direct involvement with the film censorship decision-making process. Certainly, he contrasts with the other two key BBFC personnel – Edward Shortt and Colonel J.C. Hanna – who helped to maintain the British presence in Ireland. Shortt, who succeeded O'Connor as the BBFC's President, a position he retained until his death in 1935, had been Chief Secretary for Ireland during 1918 to 1919 and Home Secretary from 1919 to 1922. According to Robertson, he was 'more reactionary in general outlook than O'Connor' and was 'over-inclined to bend to Home Office views.'[54] During the 1932–1935 period when radical republicans were in the ascendant in Ireland, and a serious Economic War was being waged between the two countries, sympathy towards Irish politics and history was unlikely to emanate from such a person. Nevertheless, it was Hanna's role as the BBFC's Chief Censor from 1930 to 1946 and his involvement in the vetting of film scripts, which was most influential. Hanna, having served with British military forces in Ireland during the final four years of the British presence of the twenty-six counties, 1918–1922, after which he immediately joined the BBFC, was determined to carry over his experience of Ireland to his work at the BBFC where he sought to ensure that nothing offensive to British colonial designs slipped through his pre-production censorship net.

Both Arthur Robison's stylish 1929 version of Liam O'Flaherty's novel *The Informer* (1925), which, unlike John Ford's 1935 version, concentrates on Dublin's criminal underworld, and Alfred Hitchcock's less successful 1929 adaptation of Sean O'Casey's play *Juno and the Paycock* were passed by the BBFC despite having the events of 1916–1923 in the background or being indirectly related. However, in both instances neither Shortt nor Hanna occupied the Board's two most senior positions. Thus, when the first of twelve scripts on Ireland submitted during the 1930s and 1940s arrived in 1933, three years after script-vetting had been introduced, it was likely to be carefully scrutinized.

*The Man with the Gun* was based on a yet-to-be produced play and was submitted by Temple Thurston whose first wife was the Irish novelist Katherine Cecil Thurston. Set in 1921, it concerned the IRA/Black and Tan War in the South of Ireland. Early scenes were to be set in London when an IRA leader, Madden, visits the city and meets unofficially with a British cabinet minister. Madden falls in love with Jane Carroll, wife of the man at whose house the meeting takes place. She is also attracted to the IRA man and persuades her husband to return to Ireland with Madden. In Ireland the military conflict was to be depicted and a summary execution of an IRA man by the Black and Tans was to be shown. Meanwhile, Madden 'makes open love' to Jane and seeks to encourage her to go away with him. However, Madden is abducted by three masked men who accuse him of being a traitor. Jane escapes but Madden is killed. Though the film might have been objectionable on grounds of sexual morality, comment was confined to the story's political-military aspect and the fact that it was 'in the opinion of the Board too recent history to be a suitable subject.' He added that 'no matter how the subject is treated, one side or the other will be angered and much harm might result.'[55] Such a negative assessment of the script seems to have caused the project to be dropped.

The following year a script by Julian Klein for Universal Pictures was submitted to the Board about the life of Dublin-born Sir Roger Casement 'from his first appointment in the [British] Consular Service in 1895 to his trial for High Treason and execution in 1916.' In recognition of his work as a public servant, especially in Africa, where he wrote an acclaimed report on white abuse of natives in the Belgian Congo, and in Peru where he exposed to international outcry white traders' cruelty towards natives, Casement was knighted in 1911, the year prior to his retirement from public life. Despite his relationship with the Empire, he remained a dedicated Irish nationalist, such that he went to Germany during World War One to secure help to win Irish independence. In April 1916, a German ship, the *Aud*, set sail for Kerry with a shipment of arms which were to be used in the Easter Rising, but it was intercepted by British warships and its crew scuttled the ship. Casement, who was following in a submarine, landed in Kerry, and was subsequently captured and taken to England where he stood trial for treason. He was sentenced to death and hanged in Pentonville Prison in August 1916. Casement's trial and its aftermath were particularly seedy and unpleasant. Held a few months after the Easter Rising, he was also affected by the virulent anti-German feeling in Britain. Additionally, Black Diaries as they became known (whether written by Casement or a British forgery remains in dispute despite recent scholarship), were widely publicized as proof that Casement was a practising homo-

sexual. The effect of this disclosure was to dilute the international campaign, particularly in America, to have Casement's sentence of death commuted to a jail term.

Given this context, it is hardly surprising that a British military figure from that
period should react strongly to the script. 'He is held up to admiration as an Irish patriot
dying for his ideals,' Hanna disdainfully remarked, 'rather than as an insignificant traitor to his country who paid the ordinary penalty for his offence.' He continued that he
'had no hesitation in reporting that a film of this subject would be extremely undesirable in this country and would be most unlikely to receive our Certificate.'[56] The BBFC
report had been written only five weeks before the disturbances at the Savoy cinema
when newsreel of the wedding of the Duke of Kent was screened and which was referred
to during the controversy. The script seems not to have been produced, but such was
not the case with the film of the script of Sean O'Casey's play *The Plough and the Stars*
which was submitted in May 1935 and came in the wake of the hugely successful John
Ford version of *The Informer*. Although no script of Ford's film, which won four
Academy awards, was submitted to the BBFC prior to its production, 'extensive indirect consultations' with the BBFC had been undertaken by the film's producers, RKO.
Nevertheless, when the BBFC viewed a 'modified version' of the film on 6 June 1935 it
cut 376 feet, or just over four minutes screen time.[57] In Ireland, the film initially suffered
a more severe fate when Irish Censor James Montgomery, after describing it as 'a sordid
and brutal libel', banned it. Among Montgomery's complaints was about Gypo, the
'"brothel bully" who turns informer in order to use the reward to bring a prostitute to
America,' suggests that the Board, at least in this one instance, was willing to overlook
the normally forbidden character of the prostitute because of the film's status or theme.[58]

Hanna's summary alone of *The Plough and the Stars* displays a warped, even racist,
view of Irish politics and history, according to which 'Young Covey' is

> spouting labour propaganda which he doesn't understand, and the others
> drunk with their own verbosity spouting about rebellion and freedom ... The
> brave talking officers of the I.R.A. are not nearly as brave when bullets are
> flying, but prefer to get gloriously drunk and help in looting shops.

He went on to offer more general opinions of the script such as commenting on the
play's cleverness, and its bitter cynicism, and complaining that the coarse and swear-
word-ridden language 'is impossible from a film standard.' No less problematic were
'most of the political speeches [which] would be prohibitive from our point of view.'
While he complimented the 'excellent character studies of unpleasant characters,' he
biasly suggested that 'the Corporal and Sergeant are not well drawn types, and rather
tend to discredit the English army, or at any rate to give a false idea of it'. After noting
the 'good deal of drunkenness, and quite a bad scene of Rosie, with Fluther Good very
drunk,' he concluded with a reference to his personal relationship to Irish history: 'The
rebellion of Easter week 1916 evokes many sad and painful recollections and will
always prove highly controversial. I am strongly of [the] opinion that it is undesirable
to rouse these feelings.'[59]

The following day Shortt, Brooke Williamson and Hanna interviewed Mr Leishman and Mr Reisman representing RKO and though they agreed that the 'theme could not be considered prohibitive,' the BBFC personnel insisted that 'the language … went far beyond what had been allowed.' As a result, it was suggested that the scenario should be submitted to the Board prior to the commencement of shooting.[60] When the completed film was submitted to the Board the following year (without it seems another script being submitted) it was passed.[61]

Another proposed War of Independence script with the alternative titles *Covenant With Death* and *Love Your Enemy* was submitted by United Artists in April 1936. With some parallels to the later life of Michael Collins it tells how an IRA leader, Dennis Riordan, becomes involved with Lord Athleigh and his son-in-law, Ned Barlowe, who come to Ireland to collect information on the situation on behalf of the British government. Lady Helen, Ned's wife, meets Dennis, not knowing him to be a rebel leader, and he falls 'violently but honourably in love with her.' Later, when Dennis is sent to London to negotiate for a Republic, he is persuaded by Lady Helen, who is induced to do so by Lord Athleigh, to accept a 'Free State'. After she succeeds in this task Dennis signs the Treaty on behalf of the Irish party and returns home knowing that anti-Treaty forces have pronounced a death sentence on him for 'betraying the cause'. He is then reluctantly shot by his old friends. Lady Helen and her husband who have been estranged for some time come together again, 'and after tragedy comes Peace.'[62] While Reardon was based on Michael Collins, Lady Helen, it would seem, was probably based on Lady Lavery and the exaggerated relationship between herself and Collins when he was in London negotiating the Anglo-Irish Treaty, something also invoked in *The Man with the Gun*. Hanna, noting that 'the love interest is the main theme,' advised that 'if no details of the conflict between the two forces are shown,' he did not foresee any objection, while Lord Tyrrell, the new president of the Board, personally approved the project. 'Seldom' during the 1930s was the president called upon for a decision at script stage, but as James Robertson suggests, it indicates a 'likely split' within the BBFC over films on Ireland, one that 'is tentatively confirmed by the comments of Hanna and Mrs Crouzet [another censor] on the scenario for *Parnell* in May 1936 when Hanna favoured rejection but Mrs Crouzet recommended acceptance.'[63] That film, produced and directed by John M. Stahl, was passed uncut in June 1937 in large measure because the film concentrates on Parnell's relationship with Kitty O'Shea.[64] Such was not the case with *Love under Fire* released as *Beloved Enemy* (directed by H.C. Potter) in December 1936 in America and in 1937 in Britain and Ireland. The main difference between the script and the finished film is that in the film Lady Helen is the unmarried daughter of diplomat Lord Athleigh, who favours a negotiated peace, while Dennis Reardon is the charismatic Scarlet Pimpernel IRA leader. Though Hanna's strictures about leaving out details of the conflict were ignored, such that the film opens with a bloody raid by the British army on the IRA's Dublin headquarters,[65] the American version of the film re-wrote a significant 'detail' of the conflict in favour of the love story and a happy ending whereby Reardon survives the assassin's bullet and looks forward to a happy life with Lady Helen.

A script entitled *The Rising* by Myrtle Johnson on the 1848 and 1867 Rebellions was submitted in 1938. This was a story concerning a 14-year-old boy, Wolfe Darragh, who with his parents, is forced to emigrate to America after the 1848 Rebellion. In America, Darragh fights in the Irish Brigade during the Civil War where he is influenced by James Stephens to help the Fenians in Ireland. Darragh finds an ill-disciplined and inadequately-armed Fenian army when he returns to Ireland. He has to shoot an informer and to contend with a priest who refuses to marry him to Cathy unless he gives up his allegiance to the Fenians. The objective of the Rising is to capture Chester Castle in England but this 'fails hopelessly' with Darragh leading his intransigent men against the English soldiers led by a friend of his, Corporal Trunk. Mrs Crouzet commented that she did not think that 'the political element is sufficient to cause offence.'[66] The summary of the story given by Hanna when he submitted his report two days later indicates a better knowledge of Irish history and geography than that displayed by Mrs Crouzet. The emphasis in this synopsis is on the events in Co. Tipperary where the one significant action of the 1867 Rebellion took place. The castle in this version is a local one (though, militarily, the Fenian 'Rising' was based around a dramatically uninteresting farmhouse) with Darragh leading 'a desperate charge' against the soldiers to end the film. Hanna, too, could find nothing objectionable in the story.[67]

While the distant events of 1848 and 1867 were acceptable to Hanna, a script submitted by Warners Bros, *Irish Story*, in 1939 on events in Ireland immediately following the 1921 Treaty was not. This was a story set in the Irish Free State where the anti-Treaty forces are seen carrying on the fight against the Free State soldiers. Hanna declared that *Irish Story* would prove 'quite unpopular with the Irish Government' as it dealt with the Civil War.[68] Mrs Crouzet and another BBFC staff reader took a contrary view. She described the story as similar to two or three recent films dealing with the Troubles, presumably *The Informer*, *Ourselves Alone* (Brian Desmond Hurst, 1936, GB) and *The Plough and the Stars*, and suggested that from 'the censorship point of view [there was] no serious objection.' Nevertheless, she wondered whether 'it would be advisable to publish a film on this subject while the recent outbreak of I.R.A. outrages in Great Britain persist.'[69] This 'Bombing Campaign' by the IRA in England had begun the previous January and by July there had been 127 attacks, 57 of which occurred in London. Sixty-six members of the IRA had been captured and convicted and a huge amount of bomb-making equipment had been uncovered. In one incident at Coventry in August 1939, 5 people were killed and 2 IRA men were subsequently executed for the explosion.[70] With such events continuing during 1940 when not just the IRA, but Ireland as a whole, was on the receiving end of the opprobrium of the British government in particular for its stance of neutrality between the belligerents, American, much less British film production companies, would have regarded films about the IRA as improbable ventures. And, indeed, so it was. It was not until the release in 1947 of *Odd Man Out* (directed by Carol Reed) that British cinema came to represent the IRA for the first time, since its single previous effort, *Ourselves Alone*, and unlike the latter film, a War of Independence drama, *Odd Man Out* is set in Northern Ireland during World War Two. (Frank Launder's 1946 film *I See a Dark*

*Stranger* can hardly be regarded as one featuring the IRA, despite the sympathies of its main Irish protagonist and its World War Two setting.) These films were not submitted at script stage to the BBFC but, since they concentrate on emotional and humanist interaction of the characters rather than politics or history, the BBFC would have been unlikely to question their approach. However, four further Irish-theme scripts were submitted to the BBFC during the war.

Two of these four scripts were almost identical and submitted under the same title, *Meet the Enemy*. In 1942, Associated British Picture Corporation submitted a story set in Ireland about the activities of German spies and their Irish collaborators who are being pursued by British agents.[71] Again, Mrs Crouzet could find nothing problematic in the script with the exception of an 'Irish peasant' making the Sign of the Cross. Two years later, when the script was re-submitted by R. Bernauer in substantially the same form, J.C. Hanna also could see no political or other objections to the story.[72] Though this film does not seem to have been produced, the closest parallel to it was *I See a Dark Stranger* which featured Deborah Kerr as an Irish nationalist willing to collaborate with German spies until she meets and falls in love with an English military officer played by Trevor Howard.

The last script with even a partial IRA background was submitted in 1944 before the practice of script-vetting was discontinued in the late 1940s. *Twilight on the Border* by GN [Grand National] Film Productions was mainly a cross-border cattle smuggling story with a remorseful IRA man who deserts the organization rather than participate in a train-wrecking operation. Similar to *Meet the Enemy*, Hanna found nothing objectionable in the script with the exception of the utterance of a religious sign, 'In the Name of the Father, the Son and the Holy Ghost.'[73] This script bears a very close resemblance to the British film *The Voice Within* (aka *Crime on the Irish Border*, Maurice J. Wilson), which was released by Grand National Pictures in 1946.[74] The final Irish-theme script to be vetted by Hanna and the BBFC was *Banshee Harvest*, which had been submitted by Film Sales Ltd. Based on a novel by Jim Phelan published in New York in 1944, it centered on the Land League of the 1870s and 1880s, events which are depicted in *Captain Boycott* (Frank Launder, 1947, GB). In *Banshee Harvest* the police are shown to be on the side of the landlords but an English police officer, who is visiting his uncle, a landlord with a private army, ends up as leader of the peasants. Hanna did not find it objectionable, which is hardly surprising when one considers the distorted representation of the Land War being suggested, nevertheless, he was concerned that the Irish government might find it unacceptable. He wrote that 'perhaps the accuracy of the story is a matter for Mr de Valera's government to consider.'[75] Few British filmmakers even paused to consider that the films they made on Irish history and politics might have been offensive in Ireland. As John Hill shows, *Odd Man Out* was only the beginning of a forty-year history of British commercial cinema's distorted representations of Ireland's past and present,[76] which, subsequently, informed other cinemas, including Ireland's.

THE 'EMERGENCY' AND IRISH FILM CENSORSHIP, 1939–1945: NEWSREELS

After rejecting *Mademoiselle from Armentiéres* (Maurice Elvey, 1926) in which a French girl acting as a spy meets her captured British lover and which followed the vogue for nostalgic and unrealistic war films started by *The Big Parade* (King Vidor, 1925) and *What Price Glory* (Raoul Walsh, 1926),[77] James Montgomery wrote: 'I conscientiously believe such pictures are a menace to peace, and I feel that the admission of Germany to the League of Nations should not be made to coincide with the exhibition of this and similar films.' The Germans in *Mademoiselle from Armentiéres*, the Censor declared, 'are held up to odium in a manner that might have been justified as recruiting propaganda.'[78] Although the film, which became a British box office success, was subsequently released with cuts after its submission to the Appeal Board, Montgomery remained consistent in banning or cutting films which he regarded as inciting racial hatred either against Germans or the French, who were deemed to have been insulted in *Beau Geste* (1926), directed, incidentally, by Irish-born Herbert Brenon, and in the romantic melodrama *Devil's Island* (Frank O'Connor, 1926). (Such a liberal extension of his censorial powers or even breaching of the actual criteria of the 1923 Act resulted in similar restrictions over images which he deemed to be 'stage Irish'.) 'Just think of the outcry in Great Britain or USA,' Montgomery wrote after banning *Beau Geste*,

> if this film dealt with their armies. The French Foreign Legion is shown as the refuge of the world's dregs. The picture inspires feelings of horror, contempt and hatred for the country that would allow such things to exist ... The burning of a man (no matter how brutal he may have been) in the uniform of France at the feet of the English hero ... [is] positively revolting.[79]

Likewise, he banned *Devil's Island*, a decision upheld after appeal, which tells the story of a once-great Parisian surgeon, Jean Valyon, who is forced to spend seven years on the eponymous penal colony before he is moved to the prison city of Cayenne where he is allowed to marry. The couple's son grows up to be a surgeon and following Jean's death he arranges that his mother be released.[80] In his report on the film, Montgomery wrote that he considered the film

> subversive of public morality as it is calculated to inflame hatred and contempt for a nation with such a prison system, but is it true that a convict's wife and family are also doomed to live their lives in such a Hell: if it is a lie is it fair to France and if so is this censorship to countenance a libel on a country that is out of favour at present in Hollywood?[81]

Of all the nationalities, it was the representations of Germans which most agitated Montgomery, and thus presaged the close scrutiny of films released during World War Two. Indeed, in his account of the war melodrama *Convoy* (Joseph C. Boyle, 1927), which was passed with cuts after appeal, he reported to the Appeal Board that since

Irish censorship was a 'State Censorship' the German government had made 'formal protests' to the Irish government regarding these pictures. As a result, Kevin O'Higgins, a close friend of Montgomery, who in addition to his responsibilities of overseeing film censorship as Minister for Justice, was also Minister for External Affairs, 'promised to introduce legislation against films offensive to friendly states.'[82] However, O'Higgins was murdered before he could introduce such legislation and no additional powers were given to the Film Censor until after the outbreak of World War Two in September 1939. Consequently, he used the all-embracing provision from the 1923 Act, 'subversive of public morality,' to restrict films he regarded as anti-German. Among the films banned or cut by Montgomery or the Appeal Board with such a bias were *Whom the Gods Would Destroy* (aka *Whom the Gods Destroy*, Frank Borzage, 1919) which featured 'anti-German propaganda calculated to inflame popular sentiment';[83] *Dangerous Days* (Reginald Barker, 1920), in which there was 'crude anti-German propaganda, calculated to influence racial hatred and contempt';[84] *Butterfly Nun* 'contains anti-German propaganda calculated to inflame racial hatred';[85] *Four Sons* (John Ford, 1928), from which 'all scenes and incidents showing German officers as brutes and cads [were] eliminated ... They are most offensive to a friendly nation, and they are likely to inflame racial hatred and contempt ... We are never shown officers of other armies in such contemptible guise';[86] *Hearts of the World* (D.W. Griffith, 1918): 'Apart from a scene of attempted rape – one of the most disgusting and realistic I have seen – the Germans are shown as such brutes that the picture is calculated to provoke racial hatred.'[87] Little real war footage in Europe ended up in Griffith's film which recalls the basic narrative structure of his *The Birth of a Nation*, complete with the attempted rape of Lillian Gish, though in this instance a German is substituted for the African-American rapist. In his report on the war drama *Mare Nostrum* (1926), directed by Irish-born Rex Ingram, which recommended the film be banned, Montgomery was more expansive:

> An unsavoury story of conjugal infidelity in which a sea captain surrenders his honour to the sex appeal of a beautiful German spy. The picture is one of a class that is a menace to the peace of the world. The Germans are shown as hellish brutes – Its exhibition would inflame racial hatred, so I reject, not only as sexually immoral, but as subversive of public morality.[88]

Another film, the popular World War One aerial-spectacle drama *Hell's Angels* (Howard Hughes, 1930), was cut because parts of it were regarded as 'holding up Germany to hatred and contempt.'[89] This film was one of many to be released between the wars whose certificate was revoked after the outbreak of World War Two. However, one of the most influential of the cycle of World War One films, *All Quiet on the Western Front* (Lewis Milestone, 1930) was found to be transgressive in the most mundane and familiarly moral way such as in the scenes when the three soldiers fantasize in front of the poster of a beautiful woman in a bar, and later when they visit at night the hungry French girls, which, Montgomery recorded, 'no matter how reticently conveyed, it is swapping food for fornication.'[90]

While World War One had served as a catalyst for action among those seeking a separate Irish nation-state, World War Two helped to reinforce independent Ireland's isolation from the rest of the world. The economic, social and cultural policies of both the Cumann na nGaedheal and Fianna Fáil governments during the 1920s and 1930s gave expression to the narrow protectionism which was as much a feature of the ruling parties' psyche as was their approach to business and trade. With the outbreak of war in September 1939 the Fianna Fáil government adopted a policy of neutrality between the belligerents, in practice the Irish state embarked on what the Minister for the Co-ordination of Defensive Measures, Frank Aiken, described as a form of 'limited warfare,'[91] which allowed the Irish government to steer a middle-course between conflicting strains within Irish society. To have sided with Britain would have implied acceptance of Partition, a policy which not only Fianna Fáil but a majority of the Irish people would have rejected and almost certainly would have led to serious internal violence with many people opposed to giving any aid to England. As de Valera put it in 1941:

> We can only be a *friendly* neutral: Our circumstances, our history, the incompleteness of our national freedom through the partition of our country, made any other policy impractical. Any other policy would have divided our people, and for a divided nation to fling itself into this war would be to commit suicide. (Emphasis added.)[92]

Consequently, despite Ireland's official declaration of neutrality, it was a 'friendly' one that favoured the Allies with, for example, Allied warplanes which had landed in Ireland, and their crews, being quietly spirited out of the country while servicemen from the Axis countries were interned. Nevertheless, and to the great offence of the Allies, Taoiseach Éamon de Valera visited the German Legation to sign the book of condolences upon the death of Adolf Hitler.

When it came to applying internal controls on information pertaining to the war there was no ambiguity and little favouritism shown towards the Allies. When the war broke out, the Emergency Powers Act, 1939 was passed by the Oireachtas on 3 September. It amended Article 28 of the Constitution and allowed for the Dáil to declare a state of emergency. In this way 'the Emergency' was born. The Act did not specify a policy of neutrality but merely facilitated the securing of public safety and 'the preservation of the State in time of war.' Clause (i) of the Act, entitled 'supervision of propaganda,' permitted for the censorship of newspapers and periodicals, but Aiken felt obliged to be forthright: 'In our own interests and according to our declared policy we must suppress propaganda against the nearest belligerent and are thus led naturally to prevent propaganda against the other.'[93] Such was the extent of the suppression of all shades of public opinion on the war, including criticism of the censorship itself, during the following almost six years, that, as Robert Fisk comments,

> it called into question the very nature of neutrality. If Éire's policy of non-intervention was intended to preserve the freedom and parliamentary democ-

racy of the twenty-six county state, then how far could the Government go in restricting the democracy in order to strengthen its neutral shield? ... For censorship was not only intimately associated with the policy of non-intervention. It became neutrality's backbone and had to be defended as forcefully as neutrality itself.[94]

To give effect to the Emergency Powers Act, statutory instruments were applied to particular areas. In the case of cinema films, Article 52 of Emergency Powers Order, 1939 (Statutory Rules and Orders, 1939, No. 224) was the mechanism used to amend the Censorship of Films Acts, 1923 to 1930 by introducing from 3 September additional censoring criteria. Films were not to be given a certificate for public exhibition if the Censor was of the opinion that the screening 'would be prejudicial to the maintenance of law and order or to the preservation of the State or would be likely to lead to a breach of the peace or to cause offence to the people of a friendly foreign nation.' These powers were to be administered by the Official Film Censor and not, as in the case of the restrictions on the print media and other sources of information, by the specially-appointed Controller of Censorship, Joseph Connolly. Powers of appeal with regard to the criteria under the new film censorship order were not accorded to the Censorship of Films Appeal Board, but to the Minister for Justice, Gerald Boland, who was appointed to that post on 8 September. The clause also gave the Minister for Justice power to nominate a person to hear an appeal against the Film Censor's decision.

Connolly and his assistant Thomas G. Coyne, who became Controller in 1942, were based in the office of the newly-created Department for the Co-Ordination of Defensive Measures. Even though they had no direct say in the censorship of films under Article 52 they visited the Film Censor's offices on 15 September to discuss film censorship. They wanted to explore the 'general classes of film and film matter that would in the present emergency be objectionable and should not be passed by the Censor.' Connolly identified five areas under which films should be scrutinized:

1. All films dealing with war preparations, parades, troop movements, naval and aircraft movements, Defence preparations, pictures of shelters, sand-bagging, etc.

2. All references for or against any of the countries involved as belligerents either in regard to war propaganda or propaganda for or against peoples – their mode of living, culture etc.

3. All films dealing with Imperial, Colonial, or Dominion activities which tend to glorify the empire or British rule – White man's burden – spreading the benefits of white (British) civilisation – Kipplingesque – Gunga Din – Bengal Lancer – Four Feathers type of stuff.

4. All news films – Pathé Gazette – Movietone etc must be free from war news or anything of a propagandist or partisan nature.

5. References such as 'Our King and Country' – 'This Little Island of Ours' (meaning Great Britain). 'We' (meaning the British people) – 'Our troops' and the like must be eliminated.[95]

It is clear from this list that they had come with a very precise understanding of the nature of British colonial ideology as it existed in 1930s cinema. While at the Censor's office they viewed three newsreels and ordered cut material with British Prime Minister Chamberlain, air raid preparations, and other defensive measures.[96] The following day Connolly and Coyne complaining in a memo to Aiken that film censorship did not fall within their remit and proposed that the Minister for the Co-Ordination of Defensive Measures be given the 'final word' in censoring war films. In a memo on the amendment to Article 52 Coyne drew attention to an anomaly in the wartime film censorship. While the Military Censor was under the direct control of the Minister for the Co-Ordination of Defensive Measures, wartime film censorship still remained the responsibility of the Department of Justice. Coyne pointed to a potentially awkward situation: 'in theory, if the Official Censor wants to pass a film he cannot legally be compelled to do otherwise.' Similarly, Coyne declared, appeals to the Minister for Justice may not coincide with the requirements of his office. While Coyne did not anticipate such difficulties arising, he was arguing, indirectly, for powers of film censorship to be accorded to his department.[97] This was resisted by Justice, which did not wish to have two types of certificates issued.[98] Aiken and Boland met to discuss the impasse and on 20 September Connolly conceded in a memo that the Department of Justice would have sole responsibility for the censorship of films.[99] In practice, as we will see, there was close liaison between the Official Film Censor and others interested in wartime film censorship. It was not until 1942 when appeals to the Minister for Justice were ended, and any minister could direct the Film Censor to cut or ban a film, that Justice's monopoly on the wartime censorship of films was extended to other ministries. After that, Coyne was generally appointed by the Minister for Justice to hear appeals of films rejected under the Emergency Powers Order (EPO).

Within a few days of the EPO being published another loophole was identified in the amendments to the Censorship of Films Act by the Department of Justice and by Coyne. Previously certified films, which were likely to infringe the new policy of neutrality, could legally still be re-issued by the distributors and as a result additional restrictions needed to be introduced. As Coyne observed,

it has come to notice that film renters and distributors are contemplating reissuing, and releasing a number of old films which have been previously passed for exhibition, which it might be undesirable to allow to be shown now in view of the changed circumstances resulting from the present emergency.[1]

*The Spy in Black* (Michael Powell, 1939, GB) starring Conrad Veidt was the first such film to be re-issued. This stylish expressionist-looking film is a World War One story set in 1917 and concerns the attempt by a German naval captain to destroy fifteen British Naval warships in Scapa Flow, the Orkneys. The film which presents a less than flattering image of Germany with food shortages and unpleasant sexual advances towards a British undercover spy, was at least in part designed, like many other British films of the 1930s, to alert the public to the dangers of German militarization through the vehicle of the World War One narrative. During its London run at the Odeon the war broke out which gave the film a contemporary significance. However, when a 'submarine did get into Scapa Flow and torpedoed one of [Britain's] best battle ships, ... it just made people go more ... It was such a success that it was immediately retitled *U Boat 29* and sent to America, where it cleaned up.'[2] Similarly, it was the outbreak of war which led its distributors to re-release the film on 8 September at the Carlton Cinema, Dublin, having initially been screened in Dublin in July. This 'dramatically topical' film, as the *Irish Press*' Liam MacGabhainn described it,[3] was seen in a somewhat different light under the emergency provisions. It was now deemed capable of causing 'offence to Germans'. Montgomery, who had passed the film, contacted the exhibitors who voluntarily agreed to re-submit it for examination and it was re-released only after the Censor cut it.[4] As this anomaly had not been anticipated when the EPO was enacted, a new regulation allowing for the revoking or cutting of previously certified films, Emergency Powers (No. 6) Order, 1939 (No. 260 of 1939), was introduced on 26 September. *The Spy in Black* continued its run at the Carlton for two weeks, at which point it transferred to the Grafton until 5 October. It was re-released in July 1941. Meanwhile, other cinemas re-issued what they regarded as relevant films once war had broken out.

The Grand Central re-issued *M*, the 1931 Fritz Lang film about a German child murderer played by Peter Lorre. The Adelphi responded with a counter-espionage story, *Smashing the Spy Ring* (Christy Cabanne, 1938),[5] while the Green Cinema re-issued the 1938 re-make of Howard Hawks' 1930 World War One story, *The Dawn Patrol* (Edmund Goulding) starring Errol Flynn. Another 'patriotic' theme was to be found in the pre-war African adventure, *The Sun Never Sets* (Rowland V. Lee, 1939), whose title alone was enough to set alarm bells ringing. Though suffering only minor cuts on its initial submission, on recall it had its first five reels cut, as well as its title changed to *Passport to Glory*.[6] *The Charge of the Light Brigade* (Michael Curtiz, 1936), another re-issue, was an obvious target for the Censor as it shows the heroism of an army officer (Errol Flynn), though most of the film is set in colonial India.[7] The 1935 film *Clive of India* (Richard Boleslawski) was also revisited to ensure Union Jacks and the National Anthem were cut.[8] *Mutiny on the Bounty* (Frank Lloyd, 1935) was recalled because of its references to England's sea-power in the introduction, two renditions of 'Rule Britannia' and shots of the Union Jack, one which Hayes regarded as 'rather blatant,' and the trial speech lauding England 'sweeping the seas'.[9] Perhaps in anticipation of difficulties which a wide range of re-issues could create, Joseph Connolly wanted to discourage appeals when a previously issued certificate was revoked or suspended. He argued in a memo to Justice that such appeals be made *de novo*.[10] Justice rejected this proposal, and appeals against revocation of certificates were to be treated as appeals, though now, of course, it was the Minister for Justice who was the final arbiter of a film restricted under the EPO, something agreed between Aiken and the Minister for Justice, Gerald Boland.[11] For example, when the distributor sought to re-issue in June 1940 the British-made Irish War of Independence drama *Ourselves Alone*, which had been banned in Northern Ireland upon initial release,[12] Montgomery withdrew the certificate under the EPO even though it had been passed uncut by him in 1936, on the basis that now it would be 'prejudicial to the maintenance of law and order or would be likely to lead to a breach of the peace.'[13]

Following the issuing of the EPO the Film Censor, James Montgomery, circulated a notice to the film distributors alerting them to the new censorship regime. As it would be some time before fiction films made under wartime conditions would come before him he confined his strictures to newsreels and documentaries. This brief communication set out the twin elements of the film censorship policy:

> In order to avoid demonstrations prejudicial to the maintenance of law and order, or the creation of scenes likely to lead to a breach of the peace – films showing pictures of the rulers, statesmen, warriors and flags of the belligerents must not be shown. In order to avoid offence to the people of a friendly foreign nation, war news must not be accompanied by titles or commentary of a propaganda nature.

Images of war would be permitted provided (a), commentary was 'objective,' or conformed to the later preferred word, 'technical'; and (b), little or no indication was given of the identity of the protagonists.[14]

The Film Censor lost no time in using the new powers to impose his will on the film trade. In September 1939 alone, five editions of *Movietone*, *Gaumont* and *Pathé* newsreels were cut. Movietone's edition seen by the Censor on 9 September had all allusions to Hitler removed, as well as a cheering Cockney crowd. Additionally, 'the entire episode' was deleted of the sinking of the British passenger liner *Athenia*, which had been sunk north-west of Donegal on the first night of the war with the loss of 112 people (the survivors were brought ashore at Galway).[15] Later in the month, Pathé, Gaumont and Movietone had to cut the 'Duke of Kent's horse' and an item on gasmasks. 'Do not import war news. The above items are all due to the war,' the Censor sternly told the distributors.[16] Even though the United States was not in the war, references to the American Navy, 'second only to the British navy,' were cut from a *Movietone* edition in November 1939.[17] By the end of the year he had cut references to the breakthrough on the Siegfried Line,[18] demonstrating that even information on the progress of the war could be forbidden, and the 'Empire's fight for freedom,'[19] while Montgomery's successor, Richard Hayes, also kept from Irish screens newsreels of events which took place in Ireland.

In January 1941, when German aircraft dropped bombs on Rathdown Park, Dublin, Pathé Gazette produced an item on the bombing. When the newsreel was submitted to Hayes it was extensively cut, including sections of the commentary such as 'They have since proved to be of German origin'; 'Murderous attack from sky';

'Shocking attack'; and 'Strong protests have been sent to Berlin by the Irish government.'[20] Such treatment clearly went beyond a reasonable interpretation of what it meant to be neutral and suggests an almost hysterical fear of informing cinemagoers of the reality of war and its devastating impact in Ireland, as elsewhere. Less than six months later the most destructive German bombing of the South during the war was of the North Strand Road, Dublin in the early morning of 31 May 1941: 34 people were killed and 200 were injured. When newsreels of the events were submitted to the Film Censor a fortnight later, such as *British Movietone News* 'Bombs on Dublin' extensive cuts were ordered.[21] Hayes remained sensitive to the issue of the North Strand bombing even after the EPO was lifted. In an edition of *Pathé Gazette*, submitted in June 1945 after the war had ended, there was what Hayes described as 'remarks of a sarcastic nature to the effect – "Éire was forcibly reminded there was a war on. Dublin sent protests to Berlin which were considered a huge joke by Berlin (or Hitler)."' He ordered the item to be removed as it would undoubtedly have caused offence.[22]

The censors were also overly-sensitive to any items which even hinted at Irish popular support for Britain, or commercial dealings with the country. A newsreel item, *Irish News 648*, was passed only after the cutting of the 1940 Liverpool St Patrick's Day Parade that included a British Army display. 'The exhibition [was] likely to lead to a breach of the peace,' Montgomery wrote in his report.[23] The following year a complete item on Irish cattle exports to Britain, a consignment of 750 cattle following a government-to-government agreement, was suppressed.[24] Deemed equally problematic was an item in 1942 of 'Soldiers at Mass for Fallen Comrades,' where the words 'Who fell on [the] French coastline near Dieppe' were cut, as was a priest drinking from a chalice at mass.[25] Irish people fighting for the Allies were not to be publicly acknowledged.

During the only major Oireachtas debate on the wartime censorship, which took place in the Seanad in late January 1941, Frank Aiken responded to criticisms which were then being voiced about the wartime restrictions on *information*. A large number of senators contributed to the lengthy discussion on Censorship and Constitutional Rights which generally supported the wide-ranging restrictions. While the debate mainly centered on the print media, Aiken was also questioned on wartime film censorship. One issue raised was the newsreel of the bombing by German aircraft of Dublin's South Circular Road in December 1940, only a few weeks earlier. While even the government acknowledged that the bombs were German, the newsreels were not allowed to state their origin.[26] It was what Senator Professor Alton of Trinity College called 'the paucity of depicted events' in the newsreels which was of most concern. Aiken was unrepentant. He declared, in a revision of the earlier more flexible policy outlined by Montgomery to the renters, that

> it has been agreed that newsreels showing war pictures will be stopped for the duration of the war. The reason is that we do not want any trouble in the picture houses. If a newsreel is shown in which one belligerent or the other is prominent, somebody may start to 'booh' and somebody may start to cheer, and we do not want that sort of competition to start.[27]

Aiken went on to differentiate between newspaper images of the war and those on cinema screens, according to which cinema represented a threat not from the working class uneducated sector, a staple concern of Irish censorship, but as a result of the aesthetic communal experience of the cinema theatre:

> We allow war pictures to appear in the newspapers simply because they are in cold print, and if a man gets a newspaper in the morning he will not start either cheering or booing the paper.

It was such attitudes towards film censorship that infuriated the British press who regularly ridiculed the restrictions in Ireland on newsreels in particular. One instance highlighted by the *Daily Telegraph* and magnified by the film trade publication *Kine Weekly*[28] illustrated how the restrictions could be easily caricatured. 'Neutrality has become such a fetish,' declared *Kine Weekly*, that even newsreel footage in which children were seen feeding animals in a zoo was cut because it showed the children carrying gas-masks. This was despite the fact that a great many Irish households had gas-masks and were constantly reminded of war, not least by their ration books (introduced in June 1942). Such criticism, of course, was not permitted in Ireland, as Aiken told the Senate: 'We do not allow, or do not propose to allow … the newspapers to criticize the censorship department from day to day.'[29] Consequently, newsreel companies, while ostensibly producing Irish editions, in fact tended to compile innocuous items on sport, social activities, or other non-contentious events, sometimes imported from America. Ó Drisceoil[30] provides one telling example from May 1940 in which the war dominates Gaumont's British edition, but in which items on Italian royalty meeting the Pope, an Australian boat race, the Kentucky Derby, and Dublin's Spring Show were featured in the Irish edition for the same week. The only hint of war was a remote event in China when Madame Chiang Kai Shek inspected air-raid damage at Chunking. With pressure on film stock as a result of the war, newsreel companies discontinued the Irish editions in May 1943.

Martin Quigley Jnr, son of one of the key figures in the Irish-American campaign to impose strict censorship on Hollywood from the late 1920s onwards and publisher of the American film trade newspaper, *Motion Picture Herald* (*MPH*), was resident in Dublin during May to November 1943. His book, *A U.S. Spy in Ireland* (1999), tells of his work as an OSS (the forerunner of the CIA) agent while posing as a representative of the film trade organization, the Motion Picture Producers and Distributors of America, and as a contributor to *MPH*. The only American spy in Ireland to retain his cover throughout the war, Quigley's front was to gather information on wartime film censorship, and in this capacity he befriended Richard Hayes, who himself worked with Irish military intelligence because he was an accomplished code-breaker.[31] Quigley offers one of the most succinct descriptions of Hayes, as 'a gentleman of the old school in the very best sense of the term … serious and soft-spoken … As the film censor he was meticulous and conscientious,' the latter observation based on Quigley's frequent viewing of films with him, as often as four mornings per week during his stay. In the only recorded instance where a censor responded to the 'observation' of another, Quigley reports that 'on a few rare occasions ... he eliminated or shortened a few of the cuts.'[32] However, Quigley's main preoccupation was not 'moral' censorship, but while ostensibly studying wartime restrictions on American films, he tried, 'not very successfully,' to have allowed in films 'as much about the war as was regularly permitted in the press.' He instances an occasion when Hayes wanted to cut a whole scene from a New York City office because of an offending 'Buy War Bonds' poster on the wall, while on another occasion a line objected to, 'While you know there is a war on,' was cut. Nevertheless, when Abbey Theatre actor Michael J. Dolan, Hayes' substitute during holiday leave in July 1943, was briefly in charge of censorship, distributors, according to Quigley, held back films until Hayes' return because of Dolan's 'very strict' application of the EPO, citing his cutting in all films of the word 'war,' irrespective of context.[33]

In his reports to his OSS handler in Washington, Quigley argued for the submission of more war films, rather than operate the widespread policy of withholding films which distributors felt would be rejected. Following his detailed discussions with the most senior personnel in American film companies in Britain and Ireland, Quigley wrote that while over thirty American films were rejected by the Censor during the previous year, 'at least a dozen others' were not submitted 'because rejection was deemed certain.' In addition, half a dozen or more shorts were rejected, but 'an equal number not imported'.[34] According to Quigley it was not so much that this unsubmitted material might be passed even though Irish 'censorship is not very consistent, and, in advance, it can never be known exactly what will be rejected,' but that it might provide a broader context and facilitate the passing of other items. When the 'censor realises how powerful some of the anti-Nazi films are, he may be inclined to pass over some little things in other films which might appear to him to be important as he has no other standard of comparison.'[35] Following a meeting with John Betjeman of the British government's Ministry of Information's film division, Quigley wrote a report on the newsreel service in Ireland. In this, he noted that until spring 1943 three of the newsreel companies distributed a joint newsreel composed in part of scenes taken by a cameraman in Ireland and in part of non-war general subjects. This newsreel was discontinued on grounds that there was no raw film stock available for the special reel, but the decision was welcomed by Irish exhibitors according to Quigley, 'who had long since tired of the many zoo and other animal scenes which comprised much of the issues.'[36] However, some war scenes had been passed by Hayes – 'the Irish public rushed to see these newsreels' – before distribution of the special newsreel was halted. Consistent with the Censor's more benign attitude to film representations of the war in the (remote) Pacific, a number of such films were approved, these included the Japanese attack on Pearl Harbour and an attack on an aircraft carrier in the Pacific.[37] In his memo to Betjeman, Quigley argued for a special newsreel to be produced for Ireland, and suggested a series of subversive measures in order to infiltrate newsreel of the war through the Irish Censor. These measures were: 1. Avoiding pictures which could be criticized as 'un-neutral'; 2. Stressing American, Canadian and Australian participation in the war and 'play[ing] down British participation (at first)'; 3. Realizing that the Irish Censor will be less sensitive about Pacific War scenes; 4. 'Avoid[ing] United Nations personalities, as Winston Churchill would be regularly cut,' while Theodore Roosevelt, 'sometimes'; 5. 'Remember[ing] that the British flag has regularly been cut' in Ireland, while the American one 'has never' been cut; 6. Recognizing that 'National anthems of belligerents will be cut'; 7. 'Using 'an entirely objective commentary – probably the less spoken the better'; and 8. Having 'a speaker who at least will never mispronounce an Irish name or place.'[38]

Besides advising British propagandists on how to infiltrate their views on to Irish cinema screens, Quigley was even more keen to get American product through the Irish Censor. As a result, he arranged for five editions (61–64 inclusive) of the American-produced *United Newsreels* to be sent to Ireland. This was an American government propaganda newsreel targeted at sixteen neutral and 'doubtful' countries. It was compiled through the co-operation of the five major American newsreel companies and co-ordinated by the film arm of the Office of War Information, for which Quigley had previously worked. When seen (unofficially) by Hayes in September 1943, he said that he would pass almost all of them, if the spoken commentary was removed,[39] although when Quigley met Frank Aiken on 24 September 1943, mainly to discuss Aiken's revocation of the certificate for *A Yank in the RAF* (Henry King, 1941, discussed below), he was less than favourable.[40] By this time, Quigley had begun to detect a tightening of EPO censorship, perhaps in reaction to his own encouragement of protests to the minister following the withdrawal of the certificate for *A Yank in the RAF*, though he attributed the changed atmosphere[41] to the possibility of an imminent general election in spring 1944 and that the hyped-up 'external threat' factor could benefit Fianna Fáil. Within a few weeks another American film, *Army Chaplain* – a twenty-minute short in RKO's 'This is America' series, profiling Harvard University's special school for army chaplains of all denominations, which follows a Catholic chaplain into battle in the Pacific where he helps a Jewish soldier as he dies, passed by Hayes on 14 May 1943 – was suddenly ordered stopped after having already being screened for about six weeks in five separate Dublin venues where it was seen by about 70,000 people.[42] Quigley complained to the Papal Nuncio, Archbishop Pascal Robinson, about the banning,[43] but the decision was not rescinded. As a result of these setbacks, Quigley's own usefulness was quickly receding, such that he told his secret service handler that, for some unknown reason, in late September 1943, the Irish authorities decided to tighten up on film censorship, as a result of which his mission in that regard was 'largely a failure'.[44] When he tried to apply pressure on Aiken, and then indirectly on the government by encouraging Fine Gael and 'labour interests' (presumably the Irish Transport and General Workers Union, ITGWU, which represented workers in film exhibition and distribution) to take up film censorship with the minister, 'it was not surprising that my name became unpopular with Aiken,' who according to one trade union leader 'saw red' when Quigley's name was mentioned.[45]

This more entrenched position is evident in the treatment of *United Newsreel 1* and 2 which were submitted to the Irish Film Censor a year later. In October 1944 Hayes wrote of them[46] that 'this effort to make a newsreel presentable in a neutral country has been only partially successful.' Two of the items, 'News Flashes from Italy' and 'Return to France,' about Charles de Gaulle's return after D-Day, were deleted in their entirety, while 'Penicillin and Plasma Save Lives' was permitted only if a scene depicting injured soldiers being brought back to England was cut. 'The part of the item shown,' Hayes wrote, 'is to be solely of scientific interest.' Cuts were also demanded in 'Saipan Offensive,' on the war in the Pacific, 'Riviera Landing,' on Allied landings in the Mediterranean, and 'Flying Bombs,' which was about the flying bomb attacks on Southern England. Of the total of eight items, only three: 'Guam Landing,' about American forces re-taking the island from the Japanese, 'New Volcano in Mexico,' and 'His Holiness Blesses Troops,' were passed uncut. As a result of the Irish state's policy, it was not until May/June 1945 that the scale and devastation of the war was seen in Irish cinemas.

The pressure for an alternative Irish-originating newsreel had been constant during this period and afterwards. Thus, Fr Richard Devane called[47] for an educational and propaganda arm of government as part of a more general programme for film in Ireland. Oliver J. Flanagan,[48] an occasional commentator on film issues in his first years in the Dáil, asked in 1944 that all news films regarding Ireland produced and shot in the post-War period be under the direction of a board set up by the Oireachtas in view of the misleading and often anti-national nature of the news films which were formally exhibited as reviews of passing events in Ireland. The Minister for Industry and Commerce, Seán Lemass, replied that the production and exhibition of cinema films, including newsfilms, was one of the issues for consideration in connection with post-War control of the film industry.

In 1950, Clann na Poblachta deputy Con Lehane, complained[49] in the Dáil that newsreel screened in cinemas throughout the country contained little or no matters of interest to Irish people and include 'the pirouettings of British royal personages,' and that much of the fare is of an anti-national propagandist nature. He asked the Parliamentary Secretary to the Taoiseach, Fine Gael's Liam Cosgrave, whether he would consider taking steps to ensure that in future newsreels would aim primarily at screening Irish-related items of news and events. Some months previously Lehane had already suggested to Cosgrave that he seek powers 'to compel the showing by exhibitors of a certain percentage footage of news films filmed and processed in Ireland,' to which he had replied[50] that this would be borne in mind as part of the proposals under consideration and intended to assist in the development of an Irish film industry. In February 1951 Lehane pressed the Minister for Justice, General MacEoin, about the distribution in Ireland of films that he saw as 'vehicles of pro-British propaganda ... being used for the glorification of the British armed forces with a view of recruiting young Irishmen.' MacEoin pointed out[51] that such a censorship of so-called propaganda is neither constitutional nor feasible, except in time of war. The following month, Lehane questioned the newly-appointed Minister for Justice, Daniel Morrissey, on the constitutional restriction relating to these films, and he responded[52] that the first part of Article 40 of the Constitution would be infringed. This provision was designed to limit the power of the state to impose censorship. Nevertheless, he said that harmful anti-national propaganda would be unconstitutional if such propaganda was calculated to undermine public order or morality or the authority of the state, and as such was provided for in the Censorship of Films Act, something which allowed a cavalier Richard Hayes to gleefully tell an interviewer in 1949 that 'anything advocating Communism or presenting it in an unduly favourable light gets the knife.'[53]

Despite the reactivation of an idea from the 1930s of an Irish News Agency,[54] no State newsreel emerged. Privately, what was promoted as the first in a planned series of Irish newsreels, *Mirror of Ireland*, turned out to be a one-off amateur effort, and was released in April 1946.[55] The previous month, one of the makers of the film, M.W. O'Reilly, had written to Taoiseach Éamon de Valera with a proposal to establish an Irish newsreel service. O'Reilly's associates in a recently-formed company, Hibernia Pictures, were Desmond Egan, Michael Scott, Edmund Mahony and George Fleischmann. The company had also completed a documentary, *Michael Davitt*, about the Land League leader the centenary of whose birth was in 1946, though it, too, seems to have received only limited distribution. The Draft Proposal for a Cinema Newsreel Service noted that due to the comparatively small number of cinemas in Ireland, a ban on the import of newsreels or a prohibitive import duty would be necessary.[56] It was anticipated that a minimum of ten copies of each edition would be required and that production costs would be at least £200 per week. It was planned to develop the newsreel service on a strict exchange basis with foreign companies. Thus, European and Anglo-American newsreels would be channelled through Hibernia Pictures in exchange for newsreel items from Ireland. Consequently, Ireland could have access to foreign newsreel items, but equally crucial, Irish events and issues depicted in a favourable manner could find an audience abroad and act as a corrective to the dominant practice of external representations of Ireland and its people, history and events while simultaneously promoting Ireland as an independent nation, something which might bring economic and other benefits. Hibernia Pictures also held out a very attractive propaganda carrot to the government by explicitly stating that it would be 'invaluable as Government publicity in presenting important information to the public.'[57] In this context, it cited the current fuel shortages and suggested that

> pictorial presentation of present situations would help the public to realise the need of restrictions in gas and electricity supplies and to appreciate the transport position ... [and] would go far towards [both] easing the public mind and expel[ling] existing doubts as to the efficiency of fuel supply.

It also added that 'pictorial comparison of conditions (1) At home (2) Abroad particularly in Continental Europe, would give a proper perspective on our domestic problems and show the value of the help we have sent to Europe at such small, individual sacrifice.' Similarly, labour, management and economic problems pictorially reviewed, they argued, would help the public to understand these difficulties. Also suggested were short documentary-type items on industry and agriculture as well as a periodical review, *The State of the Nation*, in which it was envisaged that government and civil service personnel would detail new plans and proposals in various fields. State and semi-state organizations, sport and social events, State receptions, personalities of state, religion, and national and of international importance would also be covered. Despite the progressive nature of the ambition to establish such a service, what is most disturbing about the Draft Proposal is the apparent acceptance that Fianna Fáil and the state were one and that no oppositional voice is even hinted at. Indeed, it could be said that having been in power for fifteen continuous years many Irish people thought of Fianna Fáil in this manner. It is possible, of course, that those involved in the report understood quite well the politics of the government and were merely strategically promoting film as a tool of the state, even if that was not ultimately the limit of their vision. Equally surprising is that neither the Taoiseach, Éamon de Valera, nor the Minister for Industry and Commerce, Seán Lemass, were interested in the proposal. John Leydon, Secretary to the Ministry of Industry and Commerce, replied to O'Reilly's letter,[58] pointing out that another private group had submitted proposals in relation to the establishment of a small film studio and the production of newsreel and documentary films but without the proposed prohibition of imports of newsreels or a penal import duty.[59] Leydon informed O'Reilly that his minister was not disposed to restrict the private distribution of newsreels. Lemass was, at the time, working on his own comprehensive proposals for an Irish film industry and probably regarded the Hibernia Pictures' proposals as of minor importance to his grand design, which finally led to the opening of Ardmore Studios eleven years later. Hibernia Pictures itself was more successful in the production of documentaries, while George Fleischmann did, in fact, work as the main supplier of Irish newsreel items to foreign companies, especially *Universal News* and *Movietone News*. However, it was not until 1956 when Gael Linn[60] produced their newsreel, *Amharch Éireann* (A View of Ireland), that the first regular Irish newsreel since *Irish Events* of 1917–1920 was established. This series of three minute items in the Irish language was attached to the end of the *Universal* cinema newsreel and ran for thirty-six items until the *Universal* newsreel ceased in 1958. Gael Linn then continued the series with more regular items until 1964 at which point 267 editions had been produced. The Irish news content had by then been superceded by Telefís Éireann.

## THE 'EMERGENCY' AND FICTION FILMS

The rather tame version of the war that was permitted in actuality films differed little to that in fiction films. As a result of the EPO, during 1939 to 1945 the Censor was obliged to give a two-tier report of many feature films – one of which focused on infringements concerning the war and the other on the traditional concern of 'indecency'. With regard to preserving Ireland's neutrality, Busby Berkeley's 1939 loose adaptation of the Rodgers and Hart musical *Babes in Arms*, which pits opera against swing, had one of the song numbers cut because it included the lines, 'We've got no Duce, we got no Fuerher' and 'Got no goosestep.'[61] Shortly afterwards, *Jailbirds* (Oswald Mitchell, 1939, GB), a comedy set among jewel thieves, was extensively cut as it included words such as 'Mein Kampf,' while the 'Nazi gesture' and a joke about

Hitler were also removed. Montgomery included in a further report on the film that owing to the imperfect British script being submitted 'a gross breach of the Emergency Powers Order' had escaped his notice when viewing the film. When complaints were made 'regarding the breach of neutrality,' he re-called the film and on re-viewing, he cut a song which had not been in the script, plus a Nazi salute. Chastened by the experience, the Censor wrote, 'This is a lesson to me. I shall never view a British film again if the script is not verbatim.'[62] Even indirect references to Hitler and Mussolini were deleted, such as from Frank Capra's *Mr Smith goes to Washington* (1939) in which the NBC radio reporter outside the Senate chamber says that the 'envoys of two dictator powers' had come to watch the proceedings in which James Stewart challenges the corruption of his fellow senators.[63]

As early as January 1940 Montgomery was reporting that such films left unchecked might lead to 'a breach of the peace,' in this case *French without Tears* (Anthony Asquith, 1939, GB), which included the playing of 'Rule Britannia' (twice) and the English flag unfolding and waving in the breeze, followed by saluting to the flag.[64] Likewise he cut 'Rule Britannia' from Alfred Hitchcock's *Foreign Correspondent* (1940),[65] while a song was excised from the western *The Lady from Cheyenne* (Frank Lloyd, 1941) because the censor, sensitive to British 'national' tunes, noted that it had 'an air identical' with the English anthem, 'God Save the King,'[66] which was cut from John Ford's Academy award-winning *How Green Was My Valley* (1941).[67] Needless to say, the patriotic film *Lady Hamilton* (aka *That Hamilton Woman*, Alexander Korda, 1941, GB), co-incidentially Churchill's favourite film from this period, was extensively cut.[68] It is a surprise that this version of the relationship of Lord Nelson and Lady Hamilton was allowed at all as the censors were atuned to the parallels being drawn cinematically to earlier periods, especially Napoleonic Europe with contemporary Europe. As Hayes put it when ordering seventeen cuts to Carol Reed's *The Young Mr Pitt* (1942, GB):

> This picture which is entirely historical, does, intentionally or otherwise, draw a parallel between Napoleonic Europe and the Europe of today. It expresses opinions and sentiments which (under E.P.O.) must be deleted to make it presentable in a neutral country.[69]

Similarly, the struggle between England and Spain in the sixteenth-century, culminating in the defeat of the Spanish Armada, offered another contemporary parallel. For example, *Fire over England* (1937, GB), directed by American William K. Howard, son of Irish immigrants, had originally been released in Ireland in 1937, but was recalled to conform with the EPO, though Hayes also wanted to cut scenes concerning the Inquisition.[70]

Prior to America's entry into the war in December 1941, its cinema began to produce a wider variety of war films and intensified its treatment of the current war particularly through the increased production of espionage thrillers. Moreover, the placing of war-related subjects and imagery within established genres had already been a dominant cinematic practice. If Griffith's *Hearts of the World* is one such example, the list as Thomas Schatz in his book *Boom and Bust* suggests,[71] also includes among others, Alfred Hitchcock's *Foreign Correspondent* which 're-hashed' *Espionage Agent* (Lloyd Bacon, 1939),[72] as well as Hitchcock's quasi-political 'chase' films *The 39 Steps* (1935)[73] and *The Lady Vanishes* (1938); *The Mortal Storm* (Frank Borzage, 1940) and *The Man I Married* (aka *I Married a Nazi*, Irving Pichel, 1940) which register the Nazi takeover of Germany through family melodramas; and *Arise, My Love* (Mitchell Leisen, 1940), a romantic comedy featuring two war reporters. Notwithstanding the relative leniency with which Pacific or distant events of the war were treated with regard to newsreel footage, fiction films dealing with the war in the Pacific against the Japanese were cut. This category includes *Guadalcanal Diary* (Lewis Seiler, 1943) detailing the recent American victory, banned in 1944, but in which shots of bayoneting of Japanese lying on the ground were removed on re-submission after the end of the war;[74] *China* (John Farrow, 1943), set during the Japanese-Chinese war from the Chinese perspective, but in which Alan Ladd takes on the Japanese army, was banned in 1944 under the EPO even though 538 feet (over six minutes) was cut, and after the war had scenes of garroting and knifing removed, while a shot of the clubbing of a wounded Japanese with a rifle was also deleted;[75] and *The Whistler* (William Castle, 1944), which had a telegram cut concerning a wife's death in a Japanese Internment Camp. This latter film was also issued with an over-16s certificate, probably Hayes', indeed any Irish Censor's, first limited certificate, though this condition was reversed by the Appeal Board.[76]

Perhaps the most extensive cutting of any film by an Irish censor, sixty-three to make it conform to the EPO, was of *The Life and Death of Colonel Blimp* (Michael Powell, Emeric Pressburger, 1943, GB), which was the subject of considerable controversy in Britain due to official opposition to it. The government regarded it as 'defeatist' and Churchill sought to have it suppressed as it depicted the cartoon character 'Colonel Blimp' as typical of official lethargy and backwardness. After being viewed at 'rough cut' stage by British government officials it was released, but its foreign distribution was delayed for a number of months.[77] In Ireland, the Censor removed any material from the film which indicated even indirect support for the war right through to the playing of the national anthem at the end of the film, with only one of the film's eighteen reels escaping cuts. Because of the extent of the intervention, it appears that the film was not released during the war, and, as a result, a certificate was not issued until after the EPO had been repealed, by which time the cuts were cancelled.[78]

As noted, the Irish censors' concerns were primarily motivated by the possibility of films encouraging internal dissent. Though the Censor had 'moral' difficulties particularly with the lead couple in the gangster film *The Roaring Twenties* (Raoul Walsh, 1939) which was 'decidedly anti-social,' and narrowly escaped rejection, the Censor pointed out that the showing of 'methods of raiding Government stores [a bonded liquor warehouse], and the cold-blooded murders are most dangerous items for public exhibition just now.'[79] Similarly, in his report on *Penn of Pennsylvania* (aka *Courageous Mr Penn*, Lance Comfort, 1941, GB), which includes a speech in which the king makes a statement regarding America's possible aid to Europe, Montgomery wrote that it 'would surely lead to a demonstration in the theatres.'[80] While the censors honed in on openly racist remarks made about the German people in many British and American films of this period (for example, derogatory comments about 'Bosches' and 'Heinies' in William Keighley's 1940 *The Fighting 69th* were removed),[81] also cut were the some-times 'innocuous' scene-setting voice-overs at the beginning of films. This happened with regard to such diverse films as the World War One love story of a soldier (Robert Taylor) and a ballet dancer (Vivian Leigh), *Waterloo Bridge* (Mervyn LeRoy, 1940),[82] and the showcase of African-American entertainers, *Stormy Weather* (Andrew L. Stone, 1943).[83] In the case of *Waterloo Bridge*, although a much sanitized version of the 1931 (pre-Hays Code) James Whale film, the Censor's cutting otherwise largely concerned the representations of prostitution and the film's final scene in which the dancer, now a prostitute, commits suicide.[84]

While only 3 films (including *The Lion Has Wings*, Michael Powell, Brian Desmond Hurst and Adrian Brunel, 1939, the first major British propaganda film)[85] which featured a 'rude opening scene denigrating Nazism'[86] were rejected under the EPO by the end of 1939, the following year, as noted, saw a tightening of censorship: 22 fiction and 5 'interest,' or non-fiction, films were banned, while 64 fiction and 73 non-fiction films were cut under the EPO. These restrictions were further intensified during 1942 when 52 films were banned and 231 were cut under the EPO. In all, as the table below illustrates, 265 films were banned and another 1,171 cut during 1939–1945. Despite the severity of the administration of the EPO, there were only 20 appeals during the first twenty-two months of the EPO's operation, of which 8 were successful, with the Minister for Justice, acting on the advice of the Controller of Censorship, reversing the Censor's decision in whole or in part.[87]

This information came to light when a change was made to Article 52 of the EPO in July 1942 which ended all official avenues of appeal against the Film Censor's deci-sions. There were a number of possible reasons why the EPO was amended. With an increasing number of wartime fiction films being submitted by 1942 the number of appeals was steadily increasing from 3 in 1939, 6 in 1940, 8 in 1941, and 3 to mid-1942 until the abolition of the appeals' procedure. Thus, concern may have been mount-ing about a growth in appeals against the EPO. Perhaps more importantly, was the confidence which the two relevant Fianna Fáil Ministers, Boland and Aiken, would have had in the Film Censor, Richard Hayes. Though Montgomery had been associ-ated with the Cumann na nGaedheal government in the 1920s, Hayes, by contrast, had been an IRA colleague of both ministers during the War of Independence, as well as being a friend of de Valera's since childhood.

The terminology for a banning order was altered at this time through the substi-tution of the phrase 'prejudicial, directly or *indirectly*, to the public safety or to the preservation of the State' (emphasis added)[88] for the earlier more detailed clause. The benefit of such a catch-all phrase was that not only did it incorporate the provisions of the 1939 Order, but that it was almost beyond challenge. Nevertheless, any challenge was now impossible since the right of appeal even to the Minister for Justice was terminated. The Official Censor could now revoke *any* certificate already awarded including, but not exclusively, those issued prior to 3 September 1939. Additionally, *all* ministers were granted powers of film censorship. Any minister who now regarded a particular film as being prejudicial to the state or its policy of neutrality could order the Official Censor not to grant a certificate to that film or have suspended a certificate if it had already been issued. Only the minister in question could lift such a suspension order. In this way, Aiken's department gained equal censorship powers to Justice over films affecting neutrality. Likewise, if a particular government department objected to a film, it could order it cut. Indeed, External Affairs, one the departments most interested in film censorship, almost certainly on foot of a complaint from the German Minister, complained to Justice about the line 'Adolph Hitler casts covetous eyes on Dutch East Indies,' featured in a 1941 *March of Time* edition entitled 'Dutch-East Indies' which had already references to Japan and Germany cut when submitted to the Censor. James Montgomery, by then acting as the deputy Censor, phoned distributor Walter McNally who undertook to further cut it immediately.[89] Other instances of complaints against cinematic representations of their countries or leaders, include a Swiss objection to dialogue in the Rodgers and Hart musical comedy *Too Many Girls* (George Abbott, 1940) in which a man tells how his daughter was expelled from Switzerland after her boat hit a pontoon on which the Swiss president was speaking about safety;[90] the Italian minister complained that *Sundown* (Henry Hathaway, 1941), in which a native girl assists British troops in Africa during World War Two, insulted the dignity of the Italian army;[91] while the Spanish minister expressed concern over the adaptation of Ernest Hemingway's Spanish Civil War novel *For Whom the Bell Tolls* (Sam Wood, 1943), which was severely cut by Hayes. On foot of this representation, Aiken wanted to ensure that 'nothing derogatory to General Franco and Spain' was retained. A total of nineteen cuts were made to the film, the last of which – following a second viewing, and ministerial intervention – concerned the scene in which the Spanish Nationalist soldiers refuse to advance on their captain's order.[92]

Even before the 1939 EPO had been amended in July 1942 the film trade, especially the renters representative body, the Kinematograph Renters Society (KRS), was becoming seriously agitated about the administration of Article 52. In March 1942, the KRS wrote to the Irish High Commissioner in London, John Dulanty, protesting about the number of films being banned and cut in Ireland. They delivered a barely disguised threat that unless the situation was modified the 'economic data line' would be reached whereby the extra costs in Ireland would make it economically unviable to continue Irish distribution.[93] Through the trade press they let it be known that as a consequence of the level of Irish censorship 'a withdrawal of films from Éire might have to be undertaken.'[94] When the KRS met the High Commissioner on 26 March, they asked him to try to secure 'a standard of censorship less oppressive and restrictive,'[95] while in June a KRS delegation visited Dublin to press their case directly.[96] However, there is no evidence that their demands had any bearing on wartime censorship. On the contrary, as noted in the previous section, Aiken in particular wished to see Article 52 strictly enforced.

The Achilles' heel of the amended Article 52 was the lack of an appeals' procedure. This deficiency had been acknowledged in a memo from the Department of the
Taoiseach to the Controller of Censorship after de Valera signed the new Order. The
document argued that as there had been 20 appeals to the Minister for Justice since
September 1939, 8 of which were in whole or part successful, there was a case to be
made for an appeals' procedure. It suggested that the 'difficulty' posed in abolishing
a right to appeal could be overcome by an 'administrative arrangement' whereby the
Minister for the Co-Ordination of Defensive Measures or a member of his staff 'would
see every film which the Censor considered within the scope of the Order and would
advise (or direct) the Censor as to the line which he should take.'[97]

It was not long before the KRS instituted representations on behalf of their members to Aiken on the issue. In a letter dated 14 September 1942 the solicitors representing the Irish Advisory Committee of the KRS wrote to Aiken declaring that the
new EPO was 'unreasonable and ... constitute[d] a serious restriction in the pursuit of
our Members' legitimate business.' They complained that it was an 'injustice' that their
members, who represented 95 per cent of the film rental business in Ireland, had no
appeal, while *any* minister, could revoke *any* film certificate. Additionally, they pointed
out that the Censor, 'in his anxiety to avoid items which may contravene' the EPO,
curtailed or rejected items which 'may otherwise be passed and which actually give no
cause for complaint.' Consequently, and with the evidence of previous successful
appeals, they urged for the retention of the appeals' system. Their request for a meeting with Aiken was granted and on 18 September the minister, with Coyne in attendance, met four renters – Robert C. McKew from General Film Distributors, J. Gordon
Lewis of Pathé, Neville of MGM, Livingston of Fox Films – and O'Riordan, a representative of the KRS's solicitors, Taylor and Robinson.

When O'Riordan and McKew re-stated the case for the right of an appeal along
the lines outlined in the letter, Aiken responded conciliatorily. He declared that although
the right of appeal had been abolished, 'if any renter felt aggrieved ... he would ...
consider any representations which were made to him ... and, if necessary, ... see the
film himself.' He also indicated that 'he was in the closest touch with the Official Censor
on the policy to be pursued with regard to the rejection of films on emergency grounds.'
Nevertheless, Aiken cautioned that this unofficial and indirect appeal procedure be
reserved for 'a case of real hardship,' or when a renter feels 'substantial grievance'. If
representations were made to him too frequently, 'they would be likely to be less successful.' Consequently, Aiken, recommended that for the most part, renters enter discussions with the Censor directly. This type of slippery logic, that there remained in
effect an appeal to the minister, must have confused and confounded the renters.[98]

The difficulties faced by newsreel companies was referred to by Livingston, Lewis
and McKew. While they sought to add an 'objective commentary' to current news items,
some of this additional information or small sections (twenty to thirty feet) of the item
itself rendered the entire item (200–300 feet) objectionable. Aiken advised that the pieces
and accompanying commentary should favour 'technical information' and not be 'purely
propagandist'. He added that he might go further than the Censor in a particular case,

but 'this was understandable as a member of the government would naturally feel freer than an official in deciding a matter where purely political considerations were involved.' Upon leaving, and notwithstanding the delegation's failure to affect actual legal gains, they declared themselves 'well satisfied' with Aiken's assurances.

One case in which Aiken's intervention overturned the Film Censor's decision under the revised EPO is *San Demetrio, London* (Charles Frend, 1943, GB). Set in 1940, it concerns a crippled Merchant Navy ship brought home by its survivors despite hardship and death. According to *To-Day's Cinema*, the film which was released in Britain in late 1943, offered a 'patriotic exaltation ... [to] stir the heart of every Britisher.'[99] Regarding it as 'provocative,' the Film Censor was aware of its potentially problematic reception in Irish cinemas and, as a result, banned it.[1] Despite the lack of an appeals' procedure since 1942 for such bannings, Michael Balcon, head of Ealing Studios, which produced the film, appealed to Aiken to have the ban reversed. Stating that he 'could not believe this decision at first,' Balcon went on to complain that 'the only explanation offered to our representative was that the film glorifies the British Merchant Navy. I would merely say it shows the Merchant Navy as it is.'[2] In response to Balcon's appeal, Aiken viewed the film on 9 February and agreed with Hayes' rejection, but also allowed the renter to cut and re-submit it to him. Aiken viewed the cut film on 20 March and agreed to pass it subject to three additional cuts. Thus, *San Demetrio* was allowed to be shown in Ireland with eighteen cuts, which included the introductory dedication to the men of the British navy and thanks to the Admiralty, numerous references to U-Boats, displays of the Union Jack, a comment about (neutral) Norway, and non-EPO deletions of the forbidden word 'Jeez'.[3]

By autumn 1943 it was not just the renters who were feeling the effects of wartime film censorship. On 1 October Aiken met representatives from the main exhibitors' body, the Theatre and Cinemas Association (TCA): Gerald Ellis, Savoy Cinema and the TCA chairman; Leonard Ging, Drumcondra and Fairview Cinemas and the TCA vice-chairman; Joe Stanley, Drogheda and Dundalk Cinemas; Mr G. Kirkham, Provincial Cinemas; and Colman Conroy, managing-director of the Savoy Cinema, Dublin. Ging presented the TCA's chief worry, which was a shortage of product due to the EPO. The exhibitors 'hardly knew from week to week whether or not a picture was available' as the number of first-run films was 'severely restricted,' while, as Stanley pointed out, films released could, without warning, be withdrawn.

Stanley instanced the case of *A Yank in the RAF*, among the top grossing films at the American box office in 1941. The film tells the story of Tim (Tyrone Power) a mercenary pilot who meets up with old flame Carol (Betty Grable) who has joined the RAF as a Wren and likewise enlists. Although he does this only to impress her, during the course of his many flying missions he is 'converted' to the Allied cause. Hayes ordered twenty-nine cuts to the film, all except three, that were deemed 'suggestive,' infringed the EPO. These included (inevitably) the Union Jack flying on the USA/Canada border at the film's beginning; references to Dutch and Belgian neutrality; bombing Berlin and Dortmund during military briefings; part of a lecture concerning a downed German aircraft; the German invasion of Holland; indeed, the whole section where Power crash lands in Holland following a bombing raid over Germany was removed, including where he and fellow flyers are being pursued by German soldiers; and one-off comments such as Carol to an English suitor: 'From what I read in the papers the church is one thing [the Germans] never miss.' As the major event of the war contemporaneous with the film's production – the British retreat and evacuation of 325,000 men at Dunkirk – features at the end of the film, this caused problems for the Censor. Wishing to highlight optimism during England's 'darkest hour' by focusing on the struggle to 'wrest control of the air' from the Germans, the retreating soldiers' perspective from the ground is that of British aircraft successfully re-taking the skies and thus allowing the evacuation to proceed. The Censor, maintaining his policy of de-nationalizing and cleansing the war, cut out references to German aircraft, including their insignia, 'the enemy,' and the joyous cry from an evacuee, 'Look sir, over the Channel, spitfires, spitfires, spitfires,' and the subsequent shots of 'Nazi planes' and a 'Nazi pilot bleeding' after engaging the British planes. The final montage of shots of the evacuation from Dunkrik was also edited.[4] Thus, while direct references to the combatants were cut, it would not have taken much imagination to work out the main thrust of the (military) narrative, as the bombers and fighter planes were seen on combat missions, something which was brought to Aiken's attention and led to his revoking of the certificate.

The film had been withdrawn, Stanley alleged during his meeting with Aiken, after 'pressure [was] brought to bear on the authorities.' He said that such a claim was being made by Ailtire na h-Aiséiríghe (Architects of the Revolution), a short-lived nationalist organization which contested the 1943 and 1944 general elections. Aiken declared that it was the first he had heard of this suggestion but in a meeting a month later with representatives of the ITGWU, General Secretary William O'Brien and Secretary of the Theatre and Cinema branch Frank Robbins, Aiken said that the certificate for *Yank* had been withdrawn 'because I received a letter from Old IRA men objecting to its exhibition here.'[5] While Aiken did not acknowledge to the TCA delegation that he had been party to its banning, he did offer a detailed account of the state's attitude to the film. When submitted to the Official Censor 'all demonstration parts' were cut, but, 'even so, when people went home after seeing the film there was a certain resentment and dissatisfaction at the exhibition of a film of this type.' It was the film as a whole, Aiken said, to which objection was taken and 'not to any scene or incident.' No doubt what was most objectionable from an anti-British or Irish nationalist perspective was the film's implicit political or propagandist interventionism and its validation, even glorification, of Britain by a (cynical) American played incidentally by the great grandson of the famed Irish stage actor Tyrone Power (1797–1841) and who, for example, in his introductions to the three sections of John Ford's *The Rising of the Moon* (1957), advertised his Irish roots. In reply, Ging argued that there was no demonstration at the Savoy where *Yank* was seen by 40,000 people before the certificate was revoked. Aiken also informed them that it was only the second film to be withdrawn after a certificate had been granted. (The other suspended film, discussed below, was the Soviet film *A Day in the Life of Soviet*, Russia (1941), which seems to have precipitated the introduction of the amended EPO in 1942. Another Soviet film known to have been rejected was the short musical *Russian Revels*, which had been submitted to the Censor by the mainstream General Film Distributors, and was regarded as 'a subtle form of propaganda' for the USSR, but, it was approved after the war ended.)[6] At the meeting, Kirkham, a provincial exhibitor, reminded Aiken that the film trade operated 'a kind of pre-censorship [policy] and restrained from submitting a very large number of films which they themselves regarded as undesirable or little likely to be passed by the censor.' Stanley added that only half the 500 films produced annually were available to Irish exhibitors due to such restrictions. He estimated the needs of the seven first-run cinemas in Dublin at 350 films per annum, considerably more than the 250 features he claimed were available to them.[7] Aiken retorted that of the 252 films submitted during the previous twelve months *only* 29 had been banned and 88 cut.

Likewise, at the ITGWU meeting already referred to, in which Aiken gave his neutrality policy a marked nationalist tinge, O'Brien and Robbins voiced their concern that a shortage of product could effect their members' livelihoods. They also, in perhaps a strategic error, conveyed views attributed to Martin Quigley in the *Motion Picture Herald*[8] in which he outlined film censorship difficulties and the moderately serious product shortage being experienced by exhibitors.

> The basic aim of the war censorship of films is to keep off theatre screens any audience disturbance. This makes the censors stricter in many respects than in other neutral countries ... There is a tradition in Ireland of violent action even in such a matter as the showing of motion pictures which were considered objectionable by persons in audiences. The actual cases of serious audience trouble, even over a period of twenty years, are few in number. But exhibitors and distributors who have been in the business any considerable length of time can recall cases when the objectionable film was taken out and publicly burnt. Most of these occurrences were concerned with pictures held to be pro-British.

If that article gave a reasonably temperate account of the EPO's impact on the cinema and placed it in a context not normally accorded to it in the film trade press, elsewhere, Quigley was less circumspect, and in a meeting with O'Brien and Robins told them that if the current policy continued there was a danger that *no* pictures would be sent to Ireland. When O'Brien and Robbins put this implied threat to Aiken, he responded that

> our policy regarding the exhibition of pictures here was one to be thrashed out between ourselves; that I resented very much Mr Quigley's threat which in fact amounted to one to starve the Irish film operatives unless we agreed to allow foreigners to dictate our policy.

An obviously angry Aiken declared that he 'resented interference from any outsider' and likened the threat to the British opium war against the Chinese! In defending the decision to withdraw the certificate for *A Yank in the RAF* he said that the policy was 'not directed to please foreigners or to prevent their ill-will, but for the purpose of keeping our own people together to resist attack from abroad.' In a parting salvo Aiken advised the ITGWU men to tell Quigley 'where to get off.'[9] Of course, had any of them known that Quigley was in fact an OSS agent a somewhat different complexion would have been put on the meeting.[10] US Minister David Gray tried to get financial compensation from the government for the losses incurred by 20th Century-Fox, the film's distributor. The film industry, Gray told de Valera, was subject to Aiken's 'unpredictable mental processes'. Coyne ended the exchanges with the observation to Gray that 'for barefaced audacity I know of no parallel for such a claim in the history of international relations.'[11]

War films made by Warner Bros prominently featured in Quigley's complaints against the Irish Censor. The hugely profitable *Sergeant York* (Howard Hawks, 1941), based on a true story about a hillbilly farmer played by Gary Cooper who, despite being an instinctive pacifist, comes to understand the moral right of the Allies and the necessity to fight, ends up becoming a World War One hero.[12] It was banned in Ireland on the basis that, although its first seven or eight reels were 'practically unobjectionable,' when the scenes move to France in order 'to make the picture presentable it would be necessary to cut so extensively that it would leave the picture of little value.' The Appeal Board agreed and upheld Hayes' decision.[13] This point was reiterated by Coyne as he advised the Department of Justice following a complaint from Warner Bros' Irish representative, Mr Nash. It would be best, he said, not to make 'ourselves ridiculous and to expose the whole institution of censorship to ridicule and contempt' by issuing a certificate. 'Just imagine what the trade papers and the public press would have to say about us.' He recommended the rejection of the film *in toto*.[14] Aiken was also alert to Warners' films and he told the ITGWU delegation that only 6 of the 13 films submitted by the company had been passed, as Warners had produced 'virulent war propaganda pictures long before America was pulled into the war.' Indeed, as Thomas Schatz points out, before 1940 only that particular studio which had in the 1930s been closely associated with the gangster genre and produced films with a critical social conscience, endorsing the politics of Roosevelt and the New Deal, 'seemed willing to treat political conditions in Europe directly in feature films,' and in the process invoke American patriotism and critique isolationism, pacifism and fascism or Nazism. This, Schatz suggests, was largely due to Harry Warner's 'virulent anti-Nazism,'[15] but, as Edward Buscombe notes, it was directly related to the studio's relative financial independence from Wall Street.[16] Though the studios regarded such material and the promotion of the US military build-up as bad business, this clearly changed in 1941 with Pearl Harbour and America's entry into the war.[17]

Columbia Pictures also suffered from the vagaries of emergency censorship. When *Community Songs No. 61* was submitted in January 1944, Hayes cut the whole song 'When the Lights Go On Again,' which looks towards war's end. He also cut from the song 'Rosie the Riveter' the second and seventh verses, which talked of working for victory, as well as two lines in the eight verse which refer to the red, white and blue (the 'British' colours).[18] Columbia were 'amazed' at the Censor's decision and their

Irish representative appealed to Aiken. The minister caused 'further astonishment' to them when, after he and Coyne viewed it, not only did he uphold the Censor's decision, he cut another song, 'Bless 'em all.'[19] Columbia wrote to say that not only were the songs widely known in Ireland but that Irish soldiers had recently sung 'Bless 'em all' at the Theatre Royal, Dublin.[20] However, this was not the first time that a censor disallowed something which had appeared unproblematically on the Dublin stage.

Clearly, not all films dealing with the war were banned. A case in point was Warners' *The Fighting 69th*, which, ironically, given its Irish reception, 'enhanced Hollywood's general shift to war-related features.'[21] The film, starring Irish-American actor James Cagney, who converts to a team player and finally sacrifices himself for his fellow soldiers, depicts the heroic exploits of this Irish-American US Army regiment during World War One, which included, interestingly enough, Martin Quigley's OSS boss, General William ('Wild Bill') Donovan, who in 1917 was a major in the 69th, and is played in the film by Irish-born (and reputably ex-IRA man) George Brent. Released in Dublin in June 1940 its Irish (and European) première was attended by the US Minister, David Gray, and other distinguished guests, including ex-members of the regiment.[22] As Coyne wrote in a comment on the very close attention being accorded by the government to a *March of Time* edition being made in Ireland in 1943 'certainly if we have to choose between being depicted as the Fighting 69th or the Irish Japs I am all in favour of the Old 69th.' Coyne went on to say that 'I feel no great harm would be done if a reference were made to the fact that Irish neutrality has not prevented many Irishmen from achieving distinction in the war.'[23] Neutrality, as most Irish people, even the censors, agreed was in favour of the Allies. The only difficulty in terms of Irish history and politics was that it included the British, and American films more often than not focused on the British war effort, perhaps partly because of the Hays office curtailing of the excesses of anti-fascism, and Hollywood used Britain in peril to incite American sympathy for the war.

### THE IRISH FILM SOCIETY AND THE 'EMERGENCY'

It was not just American or British films that exercised the minds of the censors during World War Two. While contemporary German films were unavailable in Ireland there were pre-war German films as well as contemporary and pre-war Soviet films in distribution. Even though Irish exhibitors never displayed much enthusiasm for Soviet cinema, the Irish Film Society (IFS) already had a tradition of screening such films. Of the 60 films shown by the IFS during its first eight years (1936–1943), no less than 6 had come from the USSR,[24] though none had dealt with contemporary events. During their meeting with Aiken, the ITGWU representatives, O'Brien and Robbins, had enquired about a 1941 Soviet film, *A Day in the Life of Soviet Russia* (the film, directed by Mikhail Slutsky and Roman Karmen, is also referred to in the censors' reports as *One Day in Soviet Russia* and *A Day in Soviet Russia*) which, like *A Yank in the RAF*, had its certificate subsequently revoked. Unlike *Yank*, *A Day in the Life*[25] and a 1941 musical short, *Russian Salad* (aka *Kino-Concert*, Adolf Minkin, Herbert Rappaport, Semyon Timoshenko, Mikhail Tsekhanovsky and Mikhail Shapiro, USSR)[26] both viewed by Hayes on 2 June 1942, had their certificate suspended[27] *prior* to their release which seems to have been planned for 1 August 1942.[28] These suspensions seem to have precipitated the introduction of the revised EPO Order as no provision existed in the 1939 Order to have a film withdrawn after it was certified by the Censor. Aiken told the ITGWU representatives that the reference in *A Day in the Life of Soviet Russia* to the Tinashenko war had led to its banning, though Hayes had already cut out five references to the alliance between the USSR and western democracies, Russia's fight against Nazism, including numerous comments about Hitler, praise for the Russian army, and the sacrifice the Russian were making to defend their country. According to David Gray,[29] Aiken's attention had been drawn to the film by Eduard Hempel, the German minister. It was, though, an Irish distributor who first brought the issue of Soviet films to the forefront.

In its 1943/44 season the IFS included four Soviet films in its programme. These were an animated film, *A New Gulliver* (*Novyi Gulliver*, Alexsander Ptushko, 1935); *Russian Salad*, shown on 9 October at the Olympia, Dublin and thereafter in provincial centers, including Cork and Limerick; the historical epic *General Suvorov* (V.I. Pudovkin, 1941), screened four weeks later, which 'emphasized [the general's] forgotten victories over Napoleon ... accomplished in spite of his sovereign, Paul I, the Tsar's trusted advisers, and his two-faced allies';[30] and *We from Kronstadt* (*My iz Kronstadt*, aka *We are from Kronstadt*, Efim Dzigan, 1936), set in 1919 during the Civil War, which became the principal target of the censors' campaign against the IFS. Two days after the screening of *General Suvorov*, distributor Irish Photoplays wrote to Aiken drawing attention to the Soviet films in the IFS programme and enquiring whether there had been a change in film censorship policy regarding such films, as they later told Aiken it had been their intention to distribute *Suvorov* in Ireland.[31] They reported that they had submitted *Russian Salad* to the Censor, but it was rejected, but, as the knowledgeable Martin Quigley knew, Hayes actually passed the film, and only subsequently was it 'stopped before it had been shown in a cinema.'[32] When Aiken met a delegation from the distribution company on 24 December 1943 he informed them that there was 'no question' of relaxing the government's attitude with regard to propaganda films. Irish Photoplays pointed out that they did not oppose the IFS's screening policy as indeed some of them were members, but, nevertheless, they had set in train a process which was to cause considerable difficulty for the society. Aiken told them that he proposed to 'get after' the IFS.

Prior to meeting Irish Photoplays an enquiry into the IFS's programme was initiated by the censorship authorities and one of the Controller's own staff, Mary Davoran of its Postal Censorship section, who was also a member of the IFS, provided a commentary on the society's programme and on the organization. In this report it was stated that another IFS programmed film, *Soviet Songs and Dances*, had been banned,[33] while neither *General Suvorov* nor the documentary *Soviet Paintings and Sculpture* had been submitted to the Official Film Censor. (Such an approach to Soviet films was not uncommon, going back in particular to the pre-IFS screening in Dublin in 1936 of Sergei Eisenstein's *Battleship Potemkin* [*Bronenosets Potemkin*, 1952, USSR].[34]) However, as a membership-only society it was not obliged to submit films to the Censor, and its status as such had been recognized in the 1939 Finance Act when it was exempted from paying excise duty on imported films, thus facilitating it to initiate 35mm screenings in large cinemas and to greatly expand its exhibition activities. Its trustees included Mrs Jim Ryan, wife of the Minister for Agriculture, and Ernest Blythe, the ex-Minister for Finance, Gaelic League supporter, and by then running the Abbey Theatre having succeeded W.B. Yeats. As Davoran pointed out, neither Mrs Ryan nor Blythe were 'likely to overdo this type of propaganda.'[35]

A debate had already been going on within the IFS concerning the screening of war films, and in the first issue of its newsletter, *Fioru* (Realization or Fulfillment) in October 1943, the IFS published two views on wartime film censorship. The most prominent of these argued that to exclude war films from the programme was in effect to impose a voluntary censorship. The writer, who displayed a pro-British bias, castigated 'the more enthusiastically isolationist' members of the organization and recommended the inclusion of British Ministry of Information films, but also 'enemy films'. It was also pointed out that *49th Parallel* (aka *The Invaders*, Michael Powell, 1941), partly-funded by the British Ministry of Information, and described by Mary Davoran in her report as 'definitely pro-British,' had been banned by Hayes.[36] The film, which was an enormous financial success, is a World War Two narrative of Nazi servicemen whose U-boat is sunk off the Canadian coast, was shown as the final film of the 1942/43 season, and seems to have precipitated the debate among the IFS's members. A subsequent response in *Fioru* argued that no war films should be shown if only British ones were available. Because of protests from some IFS members, it was decided not to screen 'controversial' films.[37] The 9-film 1943/44 season, however, included not just British and American films, but early German and, as we have seen, Soviet ones as well.

The single American film in the programme was a Disney short, *Dances of the Waves*, while there were two British documentaries: the Ministry of Information's *Listen to Britain* (Humphrey Jennings, 1942), with its emphasis on a diverse but united Britain, which was not submitted to the Irish Censor, and Paul Rotha's *World of Plenty* (1943), 'a comparatively rare example of a political film which refuses to be celebratory.'[38] Perhaps because it was a documentary (or 'interest' film) and thus not subject to censorship fees, *World of Plenty* was submitted to Hayes in April 1944 (on 16mm.) for a certificate. Hayes banned it on the grounds that it was 'full of propaganda talk, treats of the co-operation of the Allies at present-past war, gives speeches of Roosevelt and other leaders of United Nations with their photographs.' He concluded by saying that it 'would require such drastic cutting that little of interest would be left.'[39] The German-directed films were all from the pre-war era: G.W. Pabst's *Le Drame de Shanghai* (1938, France), Fritz Lang's *Metropolis* and Josef von Sternberg's 1930 *The Blue Angel*, with Marlene Dietrich as *femme fatale* Lola Lola, which had been banned by Montgomery in 1930. While two pre-war films directed by two[40] of the 'Big Five' of French cinema, were included: Jacques Feyder's *Les Gens du Voyage* (1937), the

French version of *Fahrendes Volk*, and Julien Duvivier's poetic realist *La Belle Equipe* (aka *They Were Five*, 1936), presumably in its director's preferred darker version,[41] it was the remaining film from the Soviet Union, *We from Kronstadt*, which most interested the censorship authorities. It was scheduled to be screened on 12 February 1944, less than two months after Irish Photoplays met Aiken.

In early February, Thomas Coyne's deputy, Jack Purcell, met Liam O'Laoghaire (later O'Leary), the honorary secretary of the IFS and one of those who founded the Society in 1936. At the meeting, Purcell told O'Laoghaire that 'for the present' it was not proposed to take any action against the IFS, but that it wished to be kept informed about its activities. When Coyne saw the IFS's programme he expressed particular interest in the imminent screening of *We from Kronstadt* and requested more information about the film. O'Laoghaire submitted a memo, 'Notes on Russian Films Shown by the IFS' on 3 February.[42] He explained that the film was chosen based on favourable reviews from Catholic writers: one from *Sight and Sound* by Arthur Vesselo and another by Graham Greene for whom the film 'full of last charges and fights to the death, heroic sacrifices and narrow escapes' had taken 'a firm hold of the imagination'.[43] O'Laoghaire added that the film had also received a positive review in the *Catholic Herald* in 1936. He asserted that since the subject matter was not contemporary, but set in 1919, 'its effect cannot be reasonably expected to be subversive or objectionable.' He stated that the propaganda of 'Russian' and American films was similar and, in an echo of his defence against Catholic critics of the screening of *The Battleship Potemkin* eight years earlier, said that these 'outstanding films' were 'concerned with universal human values.' He went on to outline the IFS's approach to war films. He said that 'since the commencement of the present war its difficulties have been very great in trying to preserve a balance in its programme.' Despite this, programmes were kept representative, with, for example, the present programme including films from Germany, France, England, Sweden, Holland and Russia. Equally important, they had 'deliberately avoided spurious publicity in selecting films which would help to foster international hatreds though many of the war films were of such high technical interest that it might reasonably be expected to include them.'[44]

Convinced perhaps by the Catholic writers cited by O'Laoghaire, a week later Coyne wrote to Aiken to declare that *We from Kronstadt* was 'all right'. He added that newspaper publicity should not be allowed for these films: 'The mere fact that a film was of Continental origin often led to tendentious comment in the press on matters not really relevant to the film itself but rather to the political conditions prevailing in the country of origin.' According to Coyne, O'Laoghaire had no difficulty with such a condition, 'and would, indeed, be glad to be saved from it if the effect of such publicity was likely to lead to a restriction of their activities.' Aiken was dissatisfied with Coyne's recommendation that *We from Kronstadt* be allowed and in a note on Coyne's memo wrote 'I am not happy about this. There is a great difference between films displaying the heroic defence of an "ism" and other types.'[45] Nevertheless, the screening took place as scheduled on that very day, 12 February, but the press censors issued a notice that *all* IFS notices and reviews were to be prohibited in future.[46]

Despite O'Laoghaire's reasoned explanation and presentation of the IFS policy, once Coyne and Aiken had been alerted to the IFS programme as a source of potential difficulty their 1944/45 season was certain to be closely scrutinized. Once again Mary Davoran provided details of the planned screenings while Coyne later took out membership of the society in his wife's name! The new season included Pabst's classic *Kameradschaft* (aka *La Tragedie de la Mine*, 1931, Germany/France). Davoran, who had obviously seen the film, which calls for the solidarity of all workers regardless of national or other politics, as it had been previously screened by the IFS, described it as 'a fine piece of propaganda for the brotherhood of man à la Trotsky.' Coyne offered comments on two other films: *Les Otages* (aka *Hostages*, France, 1939), a World War One satire, which 'looks doubtful to me,' and *Der Spiegel* (*Spiegel der Lebens* aka *The Mirror*, Gela von Bolvary, Austria, 1938), which was regarded as 'tendentious'. When Aiken appended a note to Coyne's report he made a much broader challenge to the institution: 'I would not allow them to show pictures which the Commercial Cinema would be anxious to show and which they are prevented from showing by Emergency Powers. Neither would I allow *stuff* on the ground of its artistic merit.' (Emphasis added.)[47] Such a crude position clearly left little negotiating room for the society.

Coyne met the IFS's secretary Kevin O'Kelly (who later became an Irish radio and television journalist). In a letter to O'Kelly the following day Coyne sought information on three films: *Les Otages*, due to be shown on 11 November, *Lone White Sail* (*Byeleyet Parus Odinsky*, Vladimir Legoshin, USSR, 1938) and *Fear and Peter Brown* (1940), scheduled for 25 November.[48] The IFS sent reviews of *Fear and Peter Brown* and *Les Otages* to the censors, and pointed out that all of the films of their 1944/45 season, except for *Les Otages*, *Lone White Sail* and *Land of Promise* (Paul Rotha, 1945), had been censored. While the comedy *His Girl Friday* (Howard Hawks, 1940), a remake of *The Front Page* (Lewis Milestone, 1931), had been passed after two references to Hitler had been deleted,[49] the parts of *Les Otages* dealing with the German invasion of France were to cause particular concern. According to Purcell, who, without having seen *Les Otages*, wrote to Aiken on 13 October depicting it negatively and inaccurately, argued that 'it may well be that the invading German forces are shown in anything but a favourable light.'[50] Such a position can be compared with a positive review in *Monthly Film Bulletin*[51] which was made available to the censors and in which the Germans are described as being represented as 'natural human beings' while the war is regarded as not 'introduced for propaganda purposes'. As for *Fear and Peter Brown*, Purcell opinioned, 'it all depends upon the slant given to such war scenes.' Aiken was adamant. He simply wrote STOP in his familiar red pen, adding only his initials to Purcell's letter. Informed that *Les Otages* had been banned, the IFS desperately tried to convince both Coyne and Aiken as to why the film should be screened. It was, they wrote, 'a fine example of cinematic art' that 'utilises an historical event merely as a background, [and not to] make any propaganda, and ... therefore [is] not likely to arouse political passions.'[52] Of course, the film was unavailable for viewing by the censors so such assertions could not be assessed. When Aiken replied to the pleas of the IFS's Honorary Secretary, Peter G. Sherry, on 19 October he was unapologetic about banning the film:

> As a nation we have had, since the beginning of the war, deliberately to forego certain pleasures and conveniences, not because we haven't a right to them, but because the exercise of that right might have been misunderstood to the detriment of our unity and ability to defend ourselves, or of our relations with other peoples.

'I feel,' Aiken added, 'we will have to postpone the pleasure of seeing *Les Otages* until the war is over.'[53]

Eventually, the modest but commercially-successful British social comedy *Storm in a Teacup* (Victor Saville, 1937) replaced *Les Otages*.[54] Coyne and Aiken also expressed an interest in the proposed screening of *Millions like Us* (Frank Launder, Sidney Gilliat, 1943),[55] a British film banned under the EPO about life on the 'home front' (women factory workers in South Wales) during the war made especially as a tribute to 'ordinary' people with support from the Ministry of Information. According to Roy Armes, the film 'is a key document of the period, posing questions about class and the durability of national unity.'[56] Sherry sent Coyne a review of the film, again from *Monthly Film Bulletin*[57] which praised the film. Unimpressed, in a memo to Aiken, Coyne gave a distorted impression of the film's content: 'I suspect that this is *pure* and *unadulterated propaganda* of the stiff upper lip' kind. (Emphasis added.)[58] Once more, Aiken wrote the word STOP on the memo. Coyne confirmed to Sherry within a few days that *Millions like Us* remained banned and could not be screened.[59] In a more general comment a month later, Coyne, reiterating Aiken's position, declared that the IFS should not seek 'to show films which the commercial cinemas have been prevented from showing' on EPO grounds.[60] Thus, the Irish Film Society was being put on a par with the commercial cinemas, at least as far as the Emergency was concerned. Other, more influential groups, succeeded, partly in connivance with the authorities, to hold more private screenings of war films.

While the right to import for a private screening the highly popular *Target for Tonight* (Harry Watt, 1941), a British Ministry of Information film which tells the 'almost' fictional story of a British bombing raid on Germany through largely focusing on a single British pilot, was denied in 1941,[61] in early 1945, with the war nearing its end, a number of private presentations of American feature films about the war were held in large Dublin cinemas.[62] Additionally, war films had already been screened under the auspices of the Voluntary Defence Services in late 1944 and early 1945 in schools and halls throughout the country. These events, Aiken told the Dáil, were organized for their 'technical' interest and 'cannot be said to have had a propagandist effect on the members.' As these were private affairs, they were not subject to censorship and he would not amend the EPO 'unless the situation regarding the exhibition of such films required it.'[63] Coyne commented at the time that the authorities had no power to restrict private screening of even 'propagandist' films. He added that they had been able 'to carry on to the present simply because the matter has not become a problem. In the case of the Film Society, it was really the threat to take further and better powers, if necessary, which induced them to meet our point of view.'[64] When the file is opened on the cancellation by the Irish Film Institute of screenings of *Natural Born Killers* in 1995, which is discussed in chapter 7, no doubt it will emerge that the language of 'threats' will not be dissimilar to that of Coyne's.

Within a few months the war ended and the EPO was lifted from 11 May 1945. Almost immediately, Dublin cinemas were flooded with war films. The American air force melodrama *Winged Victory* (George Cukor, 1944) was released on 13 May, though it had been passed with two EPO cuts earlier in the year, including the line 'that's the Gestapo with bloomers,'[65] while another US air force film, *March of Time's The Unknown Battle*[66] and *Battle for Italy*, both banned during the war, were released the following week. Pathé Gazette's *Liberation of Stalingrad* and Cecil B. DeMille's biopic *The Story of Dr Wassell* (1944),[67] about the war in Java, were also released by the end of the month by which time an avalanche of war films was being submitted to the Film Censor. While the *Irish Times* enthusiastically welcomed these films – 'It is a great relief to see films that are publicly and shamelessly belligerent'[68] – other commentators were more restrained, even hostile. Indeed, the experience in Dublin cinemas at least indicated that as far as the war was concerned the EPO on the cinema may have been justified.

The Film Censor's primary concern had been to exclude from Ireland all war newsreels and fiction films which might lead to cinema disturbances between militant nationalists and those pro-British elements in Ireland who would have regarded 'our army' as the British Army. This approach was confirmed by Richard Hayes when he was questioned about the decision to ban Charlie Chaplin's undisguised satire on Hitler, *The Great Dictator* (1940), the number 2 film at the American box office in 1941. In his interview with *The Bell* Hayes described the film as 'blatant and vulgar propaganda from beginning to end,' and characterized it as being 'about as vulgar as Gillray's cartoons of Napoleon.' He added more somberly, 'if that picture had been shown in this country it would have meant riots and bloodshed.' For Hayes, the same argument applied to newsreels. 'We simply couldn't risk these things with the sort of mixed audiences you get in this country.'[69] *The Great Dictator* did not escape the Censor's more traditional concerns in 1945 when he cut an 'indecent suggestive' scene featuring Hitler (Chaplin) and his secretary.[70]

When this material was finally screened Irish cinema audiences divided along pro- and anti-British lines, but there were no reports of major disturbances. As Benedict Kiely put it in the (Catholic) *Standard* in the course of a review of *Five Graves to Cairo* (Billy Wilder, 1943), which – set in North Africa during the war and featuring German Field Marshall Rommel (Erich von Stroheim) 'in a sinister light' – was banned in 1944, but subsequently passed:[71] 'To judge from the ludicrous applauding and counter-applauding heard nowadays in Dublin cinemas there are some subnormals among the indomitable Irishry.'[72] In the *Irish Catholic* T.J.M. Sheehy asked[73]

Will some public benefactor please rent a medium-sized Dublin cinema and exhibit a continuous film consisting of four shots repeated 'ad nauseam' and depicting (a) a Union Jack, (b) a Swastika, (c) Churchill, (d) any Axis individual; and will the same benefactor please allow our fanatical West Britons and equally enthusiastic anti-West Britons to watch the performance and clap and counter-clap to their hearts content. And will he please go one step further and provide all his patrons with rubber truncheons and mutual opportunities during regular intervals of complete darkness.

Sheehy added that

Such films as *In Which We Serve*[74] and *Tunisian Victory* [Roy Boulting, 1943, GB/USA],[75] which are sincere tributes to fighting men ... we can appreciate; but those naive diatribes which attempt to pass as entertainment or propaganda are no more welcome here than they are in England, where they long ago wearied even the least intelligent of British audiences.

Writing in the *Irish Press* Liam MacGabhainn lamented the loss by the Film Censor of his emergency powers, although he did not 'blame the film censor for having to allow these crude propaganda films, the dregs of the slander war.'[76]

When the previously banned or cut war films came before the Censor, he generally dealt with them in the context of the 'morality' provisions of the 1923 Act, such as in the case of *Casablanca* discussed in chapter 4. Hayes had cut 'stage-Irish' sections from films during the war, citing the EPO in *The Fighting 69th* (the scene with the mule),[77] and a stage-Irish song in *Follow the Band* (Jean Yarbrough, 1943).[78] As noted above, after the war he ordered cuts to a *Pathé Gazette* about the 1941 North Strand bombing.[79] 'Anti-Christian outbursts' by Nazi leaders were also cut from John Farrow's *The Hitler Gang* (1944).[80] All the key films from the war were released by the end of the year, including the British hits *49th Parallel*[81] and the home front drama *In Which We Serve*,[82] and the enormously successful American film *Mrs Miniver* (William Wyler, 1942) starring Irish-born Greer Garson.[83]

In his report on the effectiveness of wartime censorship, Coyne stated that 'the authorities may [have been] made to look ridiculous if challenged as to why a particular film was rejected.'[84] This is a somewhat ironic point in the context of the study of Irish film censorship. The draconian and sometimes heavy-handed wartime censorship had at least an underlying and consistent logic in contrast to the almost totally subjective and shifting criteria of moral censorship, and was arguably in part, if not on the scale that occurred, warranted. Interestingly, it has been for many years the most accessible area within Irish film censorship to research. It was easier to discover until 1998 the inner workings of the Ministry for the Co-Ordination of Defensive Measures than the process of cutting or banning of films for 'moral' reasons, itself a telling comment on the formation of post-colonial ideology.

Table 4: Film censorship decisions under Emergency Powers Orders, 1939–1945

| | Films banned[1] | | Films cut[2] | | Certificates revoked[3] | | Appeals to Minister[4] | |
|---|---|---|---|---|---|---|---|---|
| 1939 | 10 | (3) | 36 | | 16 | (8) | 3 | (3) |
| 1940 | 27 | (22) | 137 | (64) | 6 | (6) | 6 | (2) |
| 1941 | 33 | (28) | 157 | (85) | N/A | | 8 | (2) |
| 1942 | 52 | | 231 | | 4 | (3) | 3 | |
| 1943 | 77 | | 275 | | 3 | (3) | – | |
| 1944 | 57 | | 269 | | N/A | | – | |
| 1945 | 9 | | 66 | | 1 | | – | |
| TOTAL | 265 | | 1,171 | | 30 | | 20 | |

*Note*: James Montgomery administered the first year of the EPO until Richard Hayes became Official Film Censor in October 1940. During the period of the EPO the two Censors banned a total of 265 films and cut 1,171 films.

[1] Includes newsreels and documentaries. The bracketed figures refer to the numbers of fiction films banned.
[2] The bracketed figures refer to the numbers of fiction films cut.
[3] The bracketed figures refer to the number of films whose certificates were revoked and were then resubmitted to the Censor.
[4] The bracketed figures refer to the number of films in which the Censor's decision was confirmed. In only one instance in 1940 and one in 1942 was the Censor's decision reversed. The other films were approved with cuts. Appeals to the minister ceased from 24 July 1942, though *San Demetrio, London* was approved with cuts by the minister in 1944 after a private appeal (see above).

*Source*: Official Film Censor's Annual Reports to the Minister for Justice.

## POLITICAL CENSORSHIP OF IRISH BROADCASTING

Interference by politicians in the running of Irish broadcasting and the sometimes subsequent censoring by management goes back to the 1920s. In a Dáil debate on the 1928 government estimates for broadcasting, the case of a contract-employee of the then two-year-old 2RN was raised. Under the pseudonym 'Mrs John Brennan' (Mrs Sidney Czira) a presenter of programmes on political ballads, had a letter published in the *Irish Times* in 1927 criticizing a senator who, in a potentially prejudicial statement, had linked the killers of Justice Minister Kevin O'Higgins, awaiting trail, to the Irish Volunteers. The following day she had her contract terminated by the Director of Broadcasting who informed her that she would not be re-employed, a situation which remained until Fianna Fáil took power in 1932.[85] The only other major controversy prior to the modern era also resulted from behaviour outside the radio station. In 1946 broadcaster Noel Hartnett was sacked after he attacked the government for its treatment of prisoners accused of illegal activities during World War Two, although he too resumed broadcasting following the change of government in 1948.[86] What is of greater interest, though, is what happened within the studio.

While during World War Two as part of the Emergency Powers Order the script for Radio Éireann (as 2RN was then known) news was cleared in advance by the head of the Government Information Service, and all radio discussions were scripted in order to avoid controversial subjects, including criticism of government departments, even while such debates were on-going elsewhere. This came to an end in 1951 when the newly-appointed Minister for Posts and Telegraphs, Erskine Childers, introduced unscripted debates on Radio Éireann on heretofore sensitive topics. A result of this new 'air of reality' within Irish broadcasting was the establishment of the first major Irish political programme, *The week in Leinster House*, presented by *Irish Times* journalist Brian Inglis.[87] However, it was not until 1953 that the government lifted the ban on members of the Oireachtas taking part in radio discussions and debates.[88] As would happen later, it proved difficult for the station to get 'balanced' discussions as the political parties frequently scuppered programmes by ordering their TDs and senators not to participate, a precedent which subsequently affected early Irish television. Nevertheless, by 1954, agreement was reached with the political parties which lead to party political broadcasts during that year's general election. The first major political attack on Radio Éireann came when, in 1957 the minister in charge of broadcasting, Neil Blaney, made intemperate and inaccurate comments about the station and claimed that its programmes had deteriorated in recent years. Though a crisis between the government and Radio Éireann was avoided as Blaney was moved to another ministry in a cabinet reshuffle a week later,[89] it was a sign that the station's semi-independent status would be continually under threat from its political masters.

The Wireless Telegraph Act, 1926 established 2RN on a statutory basis within the Department of Posts and Telegraphs, while the Broadcasting Authority Act, 1960, which superceded the earlier Act, detached broadcasting from the department, notwithstanding the minister's retention of an on-going supervisory role, and effectively created a public service broadcaster with a remit to inform, to educate and to entertain. (The national broadcasting service was renamed Radio Telefís Éireann [RTÉ] later in the 1960s.) Similar to the 1923 Censorship of Films Act, the 1926 Act prohibited broadcasters sending messages 'of an indecent, obscene or offensive character,' as well as material deemed 'subversive of public order'. With the passing of the 1960 Act, this prohibition was refined such that broadcasters were now required (under Section 18) to ensure that

> when it broadcasts any information, news or feature which relates to matters of public controversy or is the subject of current public debate, the information, news or feature is presented objectively and impartially and without any expression of the Authority's own views.

Under Section 31, the Minister for Posts and Telegraphs was empowered to 'direct the Authority in writing to refrain from broadcasting any particular matter or matter of any particular class, and the Authority shall comply with the direction,' a directive designed in particular to restrict RTÉ from broadcasting material which could promote the aims of a subversive organization. Notwithstanding the powers vested in the minister under this section, the 1960 Act was regarded by many as an enlightened piece of legislation – writer and broadcaster Desmond Fisher called it 'a remarkably liberal piece of legislation'[90] – which gave a great degree of autonomy to the Authority, such as is discussed in chapter 7 with regard to their relationship with the Film Censor. Indeed, Section 31 did not become an issue until after the eruption of conflict in Northern Ireland from 1969 onwards, and even the on-going, but low-intensity, IRA 'Border Campaign,' which did not end until 1962, was not mentioned during the Oireachtas debate

Ironically, in light of how Section 31 was subsequently used, Taoiseach Seán Lemass had considered using it to instruct RTÉ to be careful in its presentation of Ireland's 'image,' so as to avoid 'stage Irishisms,' and to treat social problems objectively and constructively, though he was persuaded from formalizing these proposals in a directive.[91] While the government had no official channel to influence broadcasting policy, beyond a directive under Section 31 or by dismissing the Authority, nevertheless, Lemass in particular often lobbied the station's Director-General in order to try to ameliorate what he regarded as unfair criticism of the government, in particular in the politics programme *Broadsheet*.[92] Furthermore, in an outspoken statement in the Dáil in 1966 at the time of a major confrontation with the National Farmers' Association, Lemass was clear about his interpretation of the relationship between the government and RTÉ: It was, he said, 'an instrument of public policy and as such is responsible to the Government.' Additionally, 'the Government have over-all responsibility for its conduct and especially the obligation to ensure that its programmes do not offend against the public interest or conflict with national policy as defined in legislation.' The government 'reject the view that Radio Telefís Éireann should be, either generally or in regard to its current affairs and news programmes, completely independent of Government supervision.' Since it receives public funds and operates under statute, Lemass continued,

> it has the duty, while maintaining impartiality between political Parties, to present programmes which inform the public regarding current affairs, to sustain public respect for the institutions of government and, where appropriate, to assist public understanding of the policies enshrined in legislation enacted by the Oireachtas.[93]

While many within and beyond RTÉ interpreted Lemass' remarks as implying that 'public policy' and 'Government policy' were the same, and RTÉ itself responded with a week of programmes focusing on freedom of expression, this did not deter the government, led by Lemass' successor, Jack Lynch, from intervening the following year to stop an RTÉ film crew from traveling to North Vietnam to cover the war there, some-thing, of course, which would have annoyed the Americans, one of Ireland's 'allies'. Likewise, in early 1968 another RTÉ crew was forbidden from traveling to Biafra, an area of Nigeria which was seeking to secede from the Federal Government, and a con-flict in which many Irish Catholic missionaries were intimately involved. Also of note was a 1969 RTÉ current affairs investigation into illegal money-lending which alleged that Garda inaction was a significant factor in the continuation of the activity. Subsequently, a judicial enquiry was established not so much to consider the alleged criminal activity and the role of the Gardaí, but the accuracy of the programme itself, which was found to be legally-flawed by the tribunal, something that satisfied the gov-ernment who had been made uncomfortable by the programme.

1969 was also, of course, the year in Northern Ireland when paramilitary violence began to supercede the earlier, non-violent Civil Rights' Movement. For the next twenty-five years, it was the reporting of events in Northern Ireland, and in particular those who spoke on behalf of or in support of republican and loyalist paramilitaries, which presented the greatest challenge to RTÉ, as well as to their Northern Ireland and British counterparts, though the British state did not introduce statutory controls on broad-casters until 1988.[94] In 1970, the Republic of Ireland was plunged into further politi-cal crisis when two cabinet ministers, Finance Minister Charles Haughey and Neil Blaney, were dismissed by Taoiseach Jack Lynch from government and charged with attempting to use state funds to import arms for use by Northern nationalists. However, it was not until June 1971 that the first major dispute emerged between the govern-ment and RTÉ when IRA men were interviewed by the station's Northern reporter, Liam Hourican, and the Taoiseach called into question the suitability of interviewing members of illegal organizations.[95] RTÉ refused to change the item and stated that it would only do so if issued with a Section 31 directive, but the government chose not to do so. Three months later, on 28 September 1971, RTÉ's current affairs programme *Seven Days* included interviews with prominent members of the two ideologically dis-tinct IRAs: the Official IRA and the Provisional IRA. On 1 October, the government responded with the first directive under Section 31, instructing the RTÉ Authority to 'refrain from broadcasting any matter … that could be calculated to promote the aims or activities of any organization which engages in, promotes, encourages or advocates the attaining of any particular objective by violent means.' Renewed annually, it remained in force until January 1994. As John Horgan notes, during the years Section 31 was in force, there was no Oireachtas debate on it. If 'such a lack of concern with a major restriction of speech is difficult to understand,' as he notes, the historical con-text provides the reasons. These include

> a fear among politicians of all parties that the Northern conflict might spill
> over the border into the republic; strict party discipline; and an unwillingness
> on the part of any elected representative to take an action which could be
> interpreted as supporting the IRA.[96]

Since the directive was far from clear, or as the RTÉ Authority complained at an RTÉ operational level, it was 'imprecise,' the Authority, unsuccessfully, sought clarification from the government. However, it was no doubt intentionally drafted and as Horgan suggests, its 'studied ambiguity ... may well have been designed for intimidatory effect.'[97] While the directive prohibited the transmission of interviews with paramilitaries, it did not stop RTÉ reporting or analyzing paramilitary or terrorist events, or discussing the policies of the proscribed organizations, provided the Authority could assure its staff, 'reasonable people' would not interpret so as to be sympathetic to such organizations.[98] However, in June 1972 RTÉ showed a silent film featuring IRA members. A meeting between the government and the RTÉ Authority was subsequently called as the Authority sought to retain its relative independence. Five months later in November 1972, RTÉ radio broadcast an interview conducted by news feature editor Kevin O'Kelly with the IRA's Chief of Staff, Seán Mac Stiofáin, who was arrested after leaving O'Kelly's house. The interview was designed to explore IRA policy following a statement the previous week by British Prime Minister Edward Heath. Confronted by the government, the Authority, while accepting that the interview should not have been broadcast, stated that it was a matter internal to RTÉ. Furious, the Fianna Fáil government dismissed the 9-member Authority on 24 November, five days after the interview was broadcast, and appointed a new one. The following day, O'Kelly was sentenced to three months imprisonment for contempt of court when he refused to identify Mac Stiofáin as the person he interviewed, a sentence reduced to a fine on appeal.[99] The new Authority issued a revised and very strict set of staff guidelines, including the prohibition on radio and television interviews with members of the two IRAs, while reporters had to receive advance clearance from the Head of News, or in the case of current affairs, the Director-General, if such personnel were being filmed. Though these events fuelled a public debate on the relationship of RTÉ to the government, especially in the areas of news and current affairs, worse was to come for RTÉ when the combination of Fianna Fáil's defeat to a Fine Gael/Labour coalition government at the 1973 general election, the first since 1954, and the appointment of the intellectually-combative Conor Cruise O'Brien as Minister for Posts and Telegraphs with responsibility for broadcasting.

Cruise O'Brien occupies a contradictory position in relation to censorship. Notwithstanding his truculent denouncing of the decision to dismiss the RTÉ Authority,[1] he was also a severe critic of modern Irish republicanism. In this latter regard, he became even more extreme and seemed to abandon his previous republican ethos and instead came to advocate a 'two-nations' policy, rejecting the role of the Republic of Ireland in the affairs of Northern Ireland, and accepting that the previously endemically-corrupt majoritarian unionists should be allowed to govern alone in Northern Ireland. These views found expression in his belief that the editor of the *Irish Press* should be prosecuted for publishing letters which supported the IRA. His additional comment that 'any coverage of Sinn Féin [the IRA's political front] activity is too much,'[2] revealed, in effect, that Sinn Féin were the primary target of the Section 31 directive. By the time of his appointment as minister, the Provisional IRA was waging a destructive terrorist war against the British presence in Northern Ireland. In that context, he responded in 1974 to the difficulties RTÉ was facing in trying to achieve a balance between news coverage and not wishing to infringe the directive by issuing a more detailed one. Nevertheless, Cruise O'Brien introduced in the 1976 Broadcast Amendment Act a certain liberalization of the 1960 Act, especially in the area where political 'balance' could be achieved across a range of programmes rather than being confined to an individual item. Another amendment was a modification of Section 31 such that the RTÉ Authority could not be dismissed by ministerial edict without it first being passed by a majority of both houses of the Oireachtas, while an existing directive can be overturned by the Oireachtas.

The 1974 directive actually named the Provisional IRA, Provisional Sinn Féin and the Official IRA (and later, the loyalist Ulster Defence Association) whose spokespersons could not be interviewed on radio or television, while adding an extraordinary provision by which Irish sovereignty was being conceded to the dictates of the British Parliament in that organizations banned by the British government would be automatically denied access to Irish airwaves. (This coupling of British and Irish broadcasting law which, despite its ideological and political implications, was again invoked when Cruise O'Brien in 1977 attempted to counter the effect of spill-over signals in Ireland by calling for censorship in Britain.)[3] As a consequence, RTÉ issued its staff with revised guidelines for programme making in which the 1974 directive was interpreted 'with considerable rigidity,'[4] such that members of Sinn Féin even when talking on topics unrelated to politics or Northern Ireland were to be excluded. This led to the situation when in 1981 the RTÉ/BBC co-produced Irish historical series *The Troubles* had to receive special permission from the government to include interviews with members of proscribed organizations. In 1982, the contradictory policy was further exposed when Sinn Féin, a registered political party with seven candidates, the number required to qualify for a party political broadcast, enquired of RTÉ whether it would be given a broadcasting slot for the up-coming general election. When the RTÉ Authority decided in favour of Sinn Féin, a new directive was issued by the government prohibiting Sinn Féin from *all* broadcasts, and an unsuccessful Sinn Féin Supreme Court case seeking to overturn as unconstitutional the election broadcast ban ensued, with the court ruling that the IRA and Sinn Féin were one and the same body, a view still widely held in Ireland despite Sinn Féin's official argument to the contrary. (Similarly, Sinn Féin's involvement in the 1981 and 1983 British general elections and the 1982 Northern Ireland Assembly election were reported on RTÉ without interviews with the party's candidates.) The result, as Horgan notes, was that while the Irish public was reasonably well served by newspaper reports of the Northern Ireland conflict, 'the overall picture available to the public from the electronic media was an inadequate one,' with a 'yawning gap in the electronic media archive for more than twenty of the most politically significant years in twentieth-century Ireland.'[5]

Section 31 had the overall effect, one journalist wrote in 1977, of creating an 'ultra-cautious atmosphere' whereby enquiries into controversial areas were not encouraged while there was 'a general anxiety about tackling stories which might embarrass the government on the issue of security.'[6] Events in Britain paralleled the RTÉ experience, though the BBC and ITV operated less under strict statutory directive, at least until 1988, than self-censorship.[7] Indeed, in both jurisdictions self-censorship largely accounted for the minimal number of public controversies. As RTÉ producer Betty Purcell records of her experience in seeking to interview those who might have similar or approximate views to members of proscribed organizations, a quiet prohibition pervaded RTÉ. Such sensitivity extended to coverage of items on drug abuse, housing, employment, industrial relations, or other social topics if Sinn Féin members were associated with the events.[8] More serious was RTÉ's failure in this self-censorship climate, as the anti-censorship group Let in the Light argued in a submission to the minister, to investigate, as British television had done, the wrongful convictions of the Birmingham Six, Guildford Four and Maguire Seven.[9] This 'climate of fear,' as the NUJ described it, inhibited broadcasters' ability to investigate state-sanctioned crimes, as in these cases, a point also forcefully and repeatedly made by journalist Mary Holland.[10]

RTÉ's implementation of Section 31 received close scrutiny following an incident in 1988 when reporter Jenny McGeever, who was covering the journey from Dublin Airport to Northern Ireland of the funeral cortège of three IRA members shot dead in Gibraltar by SAS soldiers, had her contract terminated when comments by Sinn Féin's Martin McGuinness on the arrangements made with the RUC were included in her report.[11] A subsequent case by the National Union of Journalists against Section 31 to the European Court of Human Rights proved unsuccessful. It was clear that Wesley Boyd, RTÉ's Director of News from 1974 to 1990, was interpreting Section 31 in such a strict manner that the High Court declared it illegal, and even Conor Cruise O'Brien, by now a newspaper commentator, made the extraordinary claim that RTÉ's rigidity in administering Section 31 was designed to bring the directive into disrepute. Boyd replied that Cruise O'Brien himself approved RTÉ's internal guidelines,[12] which Justice O'Hanlon found to be 'bad in law, a misconstruction of the law and null and void,' a decision upheld by the Supreme Court (decision, 31 March 1993) after RTÉ told it that it would not allow a Sinn Féin actor to advertise a bar of soap![13]

The irony was that the guidelines did not mention a ban on Sinn Féin members, but, in practice, the self-censorship processes meant, as Purcell also recounts, that Sinn Féin members were barred from speaking on any topic on RTÉ, as no distinction was made between spokespersons for the party and its membership. The circumstances which led to the spat in court was the case taken by Sinn Féin member and trade unionist Larry O'Toole who claimed that Section 31 was being used to exclude him from the airwaves even when he was speaking solely in his capacity as a member of the executive of the Bakers' trade union, especially citing events during a 1990 strike at Dublin's Gateaux factory. RTÉ issued new guidelines in October 1993 following the court defeat in which reference was made to a Sinn Féin member's 'status' as justifying his/her exclusion from RTÉ, a factor which may explain the banning of an advertisement for a book of short stories by Sinn Féin President Gerry Adams, even though no mention was made of his Sinn Féin activities. As the *Irish Times'* Michael Foley queried at the time, 'Could the [new] guidelines simply be a blanket ban by another name?'[14] In any case, the Section 31 directive's days were numbered.

Niall Meehan[15] drew attention to the contradictions in RTÉ's and Cruise O'Brien's positions. Pointing to the vagueness of the RTÉ guidelines, which he characterized less as guidelines than explanatory day-to-day broadcasting practice and contrasted them with the BBC's 'Advice to Editors' (dated 26 October 1988) following the British government censorship restrictions. In the British case, reports of interviews were allowed, including an actor's voice-over of interviews with Sinn Féin leaders, and the ending of censorship at election times. Additionally, in relation to the spokespersons versus members argument, the BBC document made it clear that a distinction was to be made between Sinn Féin members acting as spokespersons for the party and carrying out their functions as elected representatives discussing, for example, county council business: 'It is accepted that such people are not always representing their organisation even when speaking about their public duties.' Prior to the court case, O'Toole had argued that RTÉ could take a similar approach to Section 31.[16] Indeed, even more ridiculous earlier incidents had occurred featuring Sinn Féin members. Two may be mentioned. The first concerns a 1987 RTÉ Radio 1 *Liveline* programme which would not allow a speaker talk about making wine from mushrooms because he identified himself as a Sinn Féin member.[17] Another incident was when in 1988 housewife and mother Lydia Comiskey spoke at length on the morning radio *Gay Byrne Show* on the same station about the strains her husband's emigration was putting on her family. When it later transpired that she was a member of Sinn Féin, RTÉ announced that this was a breach of Section 31 even though Sinn Féin was not mentioned during the discussion.[18]

Another element of RTÉ's treatment of potential breaches of Section 31 was its general omission in informing its listeners that any particular item was produced under the censorship regime, such that the public remained largely unaware that Sinn Féin or others were being excluded from a report to which they would normally be expected to contribute. While there was nothing in the Section 31 directive, or in RTÉ's own guidelines, to justify this, Director-General Vincent Finn and Head of News Wesley Boyd told an International Federation of Journalists fact finding team on Section 31 that it was 'impractical' to mention the restrictions on all occasions, but that, 'when appropriate' a 'health warning' was broadcast.[19] This issue came into acute focus in the reporting of what became known as the Hume/Adams talks. Beginning in 1988 SDLP leader John Hume and Sinn Féin President Gerry Adams had engaged in an extended dialogue in an attempt to find a way for Sinn Féin/IRA to enter more completely the democratic process, which eventually led to a new political dynamic in Northern Ireland. However, when this major story broke publicly in September 1993, RTÉ covered it without an interview with Adams (or, for that matter, Hume who was in the USA at the time), but it failed to tell the audience that Adams was censored.[20] As a result, very cursory representations of the Sinn Féin position was all that was reported, ironically, undermining both state policy and even, it might be thought, those in RTÉ who would have wished to see an end to IRA violence. Yet, a strange alliance existed in RTÉ between conservative senior management and many programme makers who, while giving their allegiance to the left, so hated Sinn Féin that it overrode any concern with free speech.

As the Hume-Adams talks progressed, it became increasingly anomalous that the subtleties and nuances being signaled by Adams could not be seen and heard through the electronic mass media in Ireland or Britain. As noted, one British television solution was to engage an actor to speak the words being spoken by Adams or other Sinn Féin personnel, thus by-passing the prohibition on interviews with spokespeople of proscribed organizations. In this context a new dispensation was required, and less than four months after the Hume/Adams talk were revealed (and RTÉ's revised guidelines were produced), the progressive Labour TD Michael D. Higgins, the Minister for Arts, Culture and the Gaeltacht with responsibility for broadcasting policy, secured government agreement not to renew the Section 31 directive when it came up for annual review in January 1994. Almost simultaneously, suggesting co-ordination between the two governments, British television restrictions were similarly eased. When shortly afterwards Gerry Adams was invited to be a guest on RTÉ's flagship television programme *The Late Late Show*, and notwithstanding the open hostility displayed towards him by host Gay Byrne, who refused to shake his hand, and other panelists, nevertheless a new plateau in Irish politics had been reached. In August 1994 the IRA called a ceasefire in its military campaign against the British presence in Northern Ireland, and though it broke down in 1996, its renewal eighteen months later, ensured that the tentative steps being taken to achieve a political settlement in Northern Ireland would continue and that the electronic media would be permitted to represent the diversity of views.

Farrell Corcoran gives a telling account of the post-Section 31 RTÉ environment as he experienced it in his capacity as chair of the RTÉ Authority to which he was appointed in 1995. According to him, the ingrained and often secretly-coded self-censorship of programme makers who remained hostile to the emergence of Sinn Féin as a legitimate political force in Ireland and who resented their access to the airwaves remained,[21] even though the state's strategy was to ensnare Sinn Féin in constitutional politics as expressed in the Belfast Agreement (1997). Often commentators from the right and left (the latter usually within RTÉ) continue to prefer suppression of uncomfortable and awkward opinions rather than to accept that even the most marginal views and groups have a right to be heard, especially when moving from politically-inspired violence towards constitutional politics. The lifting of Section 31 in 1994 was one of those moments when constitutional politicians calculated that the greater benefit was to be achieved in hearing the points-of-view of Sinn Féin/IRA than in suppressing them. By the early 2000s, the Irish state was sufficiently confident of the new direction in Irish politics and broadcasting that Section 31 was repealed in the Broadcasting Act, 2001.

# Appendix

**Official Film Censors**

| | |
|---|---|
| James Montgomery | 1 November 1923 to 31 October 1940. |
| Dr Richard Hayes | 8 October 1940 to 15 January 1954. |
| Dr Martin Brennan | late January 1954 to 25 June 1956. |
| Liam O'Hora | 1 August 1956 to 22 March 1964. |
| Dr Christopher Macken | 13 April 1964 to 20 June 1972. |
| Dermot Breen | 21 June 1972 to 5 October 1978. |
| Frank Hall | 25 October 1978 to 13 September 1986. |
| Sheamus Smith | 14 September 1986 to 6 April 2003. |
| John Kelleher | 7 April 2003 to present. |

Deputy Censors (not an official title) have included (apart from civil servants) Joseph Holloway, Liam O'Leary, Michael J. Dolan, Gabriel Fallon, Jerome Hegarty, and Audrey Conlon. After retirement, James Montgomery was deputy Censor at least until 20 November 1942.

**Censorship of Films Appeal Board**

*1. Appointed 29 February 1924*
Professor William Magennis TD (chair)
E.H. Alton FTCD, TD
Máire Ní Chinnéide (Bean Mhic Ghearailt) MA
Revd T.W.E. Drury MA
Senator Oliver St John Gogarty MD
Dr Myles Keogh TD
Revd Luke Sheehan CC
Senator Jenny Wyse Power
Senator W.B. Yeats

Senator J.T. O'Farrell (appointed December 1924 following Senator Yeats' resignation)
Canon Michael Cronin PP, VG, MA, DD (appointed January 1926; replaced Fr Sheehan)
Walter F. Starkie MA, FTCD, Litt.D (appointed November 1927 following Senator Gogarty's resignation)

*2. Appointed 14 April 1929*
Senator J.T. O'Farrell (chair)

Senator Jenny Wyse Power
Dr Walter F. Starkie
Máire Ní Chinnéide
Canon Michael Cronin
Canon T.W.E. Drury
Dr E.H. Alton TD
Dr Myles Keogh TD
Arthur Cox

Mr T.C. Murray (appointed April 1933)

*3. Appointed 16 April 1934*
Senator J.T. O'Farrell (chair)
Senator Jenny Wyse Power
Máire Ní Chinnéide
Canon T.W.E. Drury
Dr Myles Keogh TD
Monsignor Michael Cronin
Dr Walter F. Starkie
Mr T.C. Murray
Mr R. Caulfield-Orpen

Replacing Senator Jenny Wyse Power and Mr R. Caulfield-Orpen:
Mrs M.J. McKean (appointed April 1938)
Mr T.F. Figgis LLD (appointed April 1938)

*4. Appointed May 1939*
Senator J.T. O'Farrell (chair)
Máire Ní Chinnéide
Canon T.W.E. Drury
Dr Myles Keogh TD
Monsignor Michael Cronin
Dr Walter F. Starkie
Mr T.C. Murray
Mrs M.J. McKean
Dr T.F. Figgis

Revd Thomas O'Donnell BD (appointed October 1941; replaced Monsignor Cronin)
Mr J.A. Cooper-Walker (appointed March 1942)
Dr Angela G.C. Russell MB, BCH (appointed 5 January 1943; replaced Mrs M.J. McKean who resigned)

*5. Appointed 7 November 1944*
Senator J.T. O'Farrell (chair)
Máire Ní Chinnéide
Mr T.C. Murray
Canon T.W.E. Drury
Dr Myles Keogh TD

Revd Thomas O'Donnell
Mr J.A. Cooper-Walker
Dr Angela Russell
Thomas P. Waller

Geraldine Fitzgerald MA (appointed May 1946)
Seán Ferns (appointed July 1947)

6. *Appointed 1950*
Mr J.T. O'Farrell (chair)
Canon T.W.E. Drury
Revd Thomas O'Donnell
Dr Angela Russell
Geraldine Fitzgerald
Senator Seamus O'Farrell
Mr J.M. Flood
Mr E.P. McCarron
Thomas King Moylan

Revd W.W. Rooke BA (appointed July 1953; replaced Canon Drury)
Thomas O'Reilly (appointed July 1953)
John Joseph Irwin (appointed October 1953)

7. *Appointed January 1955*
Mr J.T. O'Farrell (chair)
Canon Thomas O'Donnell
Dr Angela Russell
Geraldine Fitzgerald
Mr E.P. McCarron
Thomas King Moylan
Revd W.W. Rooke
Thomas O'Reilly
John Joseph Irwin

Eibhlín Bean Mhic Giobuin (appointed February 1958)
Mrs J.J. Stafford (appointed January 1959)

8. *Appointed Janaury 1960*
Mr J.T. O'Farrell (chair)
Revd Thomas O'Donnell
Dr Angela Russell
Geraldine Fitzgerald
Revd W.W. Rooke
Thomas O'Reilly
John Joseph Irwin
Eibhlin Bean Mhic Giobuin (Mrs Gibbons)
Mrs J.J. Stafford

Samuel Stephenson (appointed April 1964)

*9. Appointed January 1965*
Judge Conor Maguire (chair)
Revd Michael Browne BA, DCL, CC
John F. Carroll PC
William Coyne MD, FRDI, DPH, DPM
Fr J.C. Kelly SJ
Revd John Desmond Murray MA
John A. O'Connor
Justice Alfred A. Rochford
Helena Ruttledge

Samuel Stephenson (appointed September 1965; replaced the Revd J.C. Kelly, who resigned)

*10. Appointed January 1970*
Judge Conor Maguire (chair)
John F. Carroll (appointed chair, December 1973 following Judge Maguire's resignation)
Revd John Desmond Murray
John A. O'Connor
Justice Alfred A. Rochford
Helena Ruttledge
Dermot Breen (appointed Official Film Censor 21 June 1972)
Isobelle Therese Byrne
Revd Richard O'Donoghue CC

Margaret Skehan (appointed 10 March 1973; replaced Dermot Breen)
Padraic Gearty (appointed 10 March 1973; replaced Judge Maguire)

*11. Appointed 25 July 1975*
John F. Carroll (chair)
Revd John Desmond Murray
John A. O'Connor
Justice Alfred A. Rochford (deceased 9 October 1979)
Isobelle Therese Byrne
Revd Richard O'Donoghue
Margaret Skehan
Padraic Gearty
Robert V. Kiely

*12. Appointed 27 March 1980*
John F. Carroll (chair)
Revd John Desmond Murray
Revd Richard O'Donoghue
Margaret Skehan
Kathleen O'Neill NT
Cormac Liddy
Michael J. McCarthy

Noel Ryan
Michael Doherty

Nancy Jennings (replaced Michael J. McCarthy)

*13. First meeting new Board 12 May 1987*
John F. Carroll (chair)
Monsignor O'Doherty
Revd David Woodworth
Revd Cecil Faull
Seamus Finn
John Brennan
Eileen Silke
Paul Keane
Una Deeling

*14. Appointed May 1992*
John F. Carroll (chair)
Revd Cecil Faull
Fr John Dardis SJ
Joe Mulrooney
Mona McGarry
Eugene Phelan
Ed McDonald
Phil Brady, solicitor
Mary Burke-King

*15. Board appointed 13 June 1997*
Barbara Culleton (chair)
Revd Canon Virginia Kennerley
Fr John Dardis SJ
Ms Fran McVeigh
Mary McEvaddy
John O'Shea
Frank O'Daly
Joe O'Callaghan
Con Kelleher

*16. Board appointed 6 December 2002*
Paul O'Higgins SC (chair)
Anne Walsh, solicitor
Cathy Herbert, former RTÉ journalist
Dave Tyndall, retired public servant
Sara Moorehead, barrister
Kevin Myers, *Irish Times* journalist
Ann Mooney, Cork journalist
Revd Damien McNiece, a spokeman for Cardinal Desmond Connell
Canon David Pierpoint, representing the Church of Ireland

# Notes

ABBREVIATIONS

MA      Military Archives, Dublin.
NAI     National Archives of Ireland, Bishop Street, Dublin
OFC     Office of the Official Film Censor, 16 Harcourt Terrace, Dublin
OCC     Office of the Controller of Censorship (1939–1945)

INTRODUCTION

1. Record 27198, 11,632 feet; Reserve 8243, Censor's decision, 6 May 1952; review, 8 May 1952; certificate issued on 8 May 1952; distributor: Republic.
2. See Richard Falcon, 'Reality is too shocking', *Sight and Sound*, vol. 9, no. 1, January 1999:10–13, for an account of how contemporary European cinema still seeks to challenge established norms in the cinema.
3. Letter from the Private Secretary of Alan Dukes TD, Minister for Justice, to Kevin Rockett, 10 July 1986.
4. A more expansive letter from B. O'Neill, Secretariat, 30 January 1990, to Kevin Rockett, reiterated the earlier refusal.
5. I had a letter published in the *Irish Times* in 1997 suggesting these reforms, including the publication of the rationale for censorship decisions. Appropriately, perhaps, the letter from Sheamus Smith informing me of this decision was dated 16 June, Bloomsday, 1998. Smith released the information publicly to long-time anti-film censorship journalist Ciaran Carty, *Sunday Tribune*, 5 July 1998:3, whose late 1960s/early 1970s *Sunday Independent* campaign articles against film censorship are collected in his *Confessions of a Sewer Rat* (1995).
6. *Film Directions* censorship issue, vol. 3, no. 9, 1980.
7. Cheryl Herr, *Joyce's Anatomy of Culture*, Urbana and Chicago: University of Illinois Press, 1986:36.
8. Record 30547, 6,808 feet; Reserve 9134, Censor's decision, 15 November 1955; distributor: Elliman. This was one of two cuts to reel 3, which were later cancelled, 25 November 1955.
9. Record 16028, Reserve 4757, Censor's decision, 25 April 1941.
10. Record 36942, Reserve 10769–70, Censor's decision, 15 July 1963; Appeal Board decision, 4 February 1964; distributor: United Artists.

CHAPTER 1

1. Quoted, *Irish Times*, 15 February 1943:1.
2. W.B. Yeats, 'The Fisherman' from *The Wild Swans at Coole* (1919), in A. Norman Jeffares (ed.), *W.B. Yeats Selected Poetry*, London: MacMillan, 1967:71–72.
3. Margaret Ward, *Unmanageable Revolutionaries: Women and Irish Nationalism*, London: Pluto Press, 1993:51.
4. The issue of watching, more particularly voyeurism in artistic representations, is explored by Katherine Mullin in a discussion of an 1897 mutoscope, *Kicking Willy's Hat*, which features in the 'Nausicaa' chapter of James Joyce's *Ulysses*. See Katherine Mullin, 'Making a spectacle of herself: Gerty MacDowell through the mutoscope', in *James Joyce, Sexuality and Social Purity*, Cambridge: Cambridge UP, 2003:140–170.

5. Elizabeth Bowen, 'Why I Go to the Cinema', in Charles Davey (ed.), *Footnotes to the Film*, London: Lovat Dickinson, 1938:213–214.
6. James Joyce, *Ulysses*, quoted Herr, 1986:102.
7. Liam O'Flaherty, *Mr Gilhooley*, Dublin: Wolfhound Press, 1991:6; orig. 1926.
8. Ibid. 24–25.
9. Ibid. 26–27.
10. Ibid. 29.
11. Indeed, it must be remembered that such (mis)behaviour and more particularly its strict policing was not unique to Ireland. For example in May 1908, Walter Tyler introduced 'daylight projection' to Britain so that, for the sake of morality, films could be screened in a non-darkened auditorium. See *The Chronicle of Cinema 1: The Beginnings, Sight and Sound*, 1995:19.
12. Department of Justice File H265/11, NAI.
13. Raymond Williams, *The Country and the City*, London: The Hogarth Press, 1985; orig. 1973.
14. As Donald Theall reports, Wyndham Lewis 'attacked Joyce's assigning a primacy to time in ... *Ulysses*, for this sharply divorced space from time, allegedly resulting in a loss of the spatial. In *Time and Western Man*, Lewis identifies Joyce as the leading exemplar of this new "time-mind" which reveled in this new space-time culture that bridged the elite and popular.' ('Joyce's Techno-Poetics of Artifice: Machines, Media, Memory, and Modes of Communication in *Ulysses* and *Finnegans Wake*', in R.B. Kershner (ed.), *Joyce and Popular Culture*, Florida: UP of Florida, 1996:141.
15. Herr, 1986.
16. Margaret Cohen, 'Panoramic Literature and the Invention of Everyday Genres', in Leo Charney and Vanessa R. Schwartz (eds), *Cinema and the Invention of Modern Life*, Berkeley/Los Angeles: University of California Press, 1995:231.
17. Quoted, Luke Gibbons, *Transformations in Irish Culture*, Cork: Cork UP, 1996:165.
18. Joseph Lee, *The Modernisation of Irish Society*, Dublin: Gill & Macmillan, 1973:138.
19. Quoted Colm Lincoln, 'City of Culture: Dublin and the Discovery of Urban Heritage', in Barbara O'Connor and Michael Cronin (eds), *Tourism in Ireland: A Critical Analysis*, Cork: Cork UP, 1993:205.
20. Quoted, Kevin B. Nolan, 'The Gaelic League and other National Movements', in Seán Ó Tuama (ed.), *The Gaelic League Idea*, Cork, Dublin: The Mercier Press, 1972:47.
21. Gearóid Ó Tuathaigh, 'The Irish-Ireland Idea: Rationale and Relevance', in Edna Longley (ed.), *Culture in Ireland: Division or Diversity?*, Belfast: Institute of Irish Studies, 1991:59.
22. O'Tuathaigh, ibid. 60.
23. Gibbons, 1996:167.
24. Ben Singer, 'Modernity, Hyperstimulus, and the Rise of Popular Sensationalism' in Leo Charney and Vanessa R. Schwartz (eds), *Cinema and the Invention of Modern Life*, Berkeley/Los Angeles: University of California Press, 1995:75 ff.
25. For an overview of the representation of the Irish in American cinema in particular, see Kevin Rockett, 'The Irish Migrant and Film', in Patrick O'Sullivan (ed.), *The Creative Migrant*, vol. 3, *The Irish World Wide* series, Leicester: Leicester UP, 1994:170–191.
26. Pastoral read out in all diocesan churches on 2 February 1937, quoted in the trade paper, the *Cinema*, 16 February 1937.
27. B.G. MacCarthy, 'The Cinema as a Social Factor', *Studies*, vol. 33, 1944:46.
28. Sean Rothery, *Ireland and the New Architecture*, Dublin: Lilliput Press, 1991:109.
29. Ibid. 193.
30. Ibid. 194.
31. Alan Hope, 'Cinema Interiors', *Irish Cinema Handbook*, Dublin: Parkside Press, 1943:134.
32. Gabriel Fallon, *Capuchin Annual*, 1938:248–260.
33. Elizabeth Bowen, in Davey (ed.), *Footnotes to the Film*, 1938:205.
34. Helen Byrne, 'Going to the Pictures: The Female Audience and the Pleasures of Cinema', in Mary J. Kelly and Barbara O'Connor (eds), *Media Audiences in Ireland*, Dublin: UCD Press, 1997.
35. For the motivation behind and a consideration of Joyce's involvement with the cinema, see Kevin Rockett, 'Something Rich and Strange: James Joyce, Beatrice Cenci and the Volta', *Film and Film Culture*, 2004. Of course, Joyce no doubt wanted to make money out of the venture, and was also motivated by his interest not just in popular culture and cinema's temporal, spatial, and aesthetic play with and juxtapositions of the image, but its ability to resist the dominant native monolithic culture, which ironically Hollywood later came to epitomize.

CHAPTER 2

1. *Irish Monthly*, vol. XLV, February 1917:74–75.

2. This is the contemporary euphemism quoted by Bowser 1994:201 used to describe Johnson.
3. See Musser 1994:193 ff. for a discussion of early cinema genres.
4. There is sometimes confusion in accounts of early cinema between the 'peep-hole' mutoscope machine using the 'flicker-book' effect, and the projected films of the Mutsocope Co. The mutsocope machine was manufactured from 1895 onwards by the American Mutsocope Co. (later American Mutoscope and Biograph Co.), and at which a single person could view up to 150 feet of film after putting a coin in a slot and hand-cranking the machine. Mutoscope parlours quickly spread throughout the USA and Europe, such that by 1898 there were at least two in Dublin: one at 24 South Great George's Street, and another at 14 College Green. The charge in Dublin was one penny. The same footage could also be projected on to a 'cinema' screen for a paying audience, and thus early reference to the mutoscope, such as those by James Joyce, sometimes do not distinguish between the two methods of viewing the footage, though in Joyce's case the reference to 'Peeping Tom' suggests the coin-in-the-machine mutoscope.
5. The 1890s saw a huge growth in physical fitness movements in the industrialized countries of the USA and Europe. Ireland, with its predominantly rural population, did not have such a movement per se, but the thrust of nationalist ideology well into the twentieth century was to exhort Irish people to follow healthy outdoor sports and recreations, rather than the commercialized entertainments of the cities.
6. Musser 1994:198.
7. One of the debates that surrounded the fight film concerned the illegality of attendance at a real or actual fight and the legitimate attendance at the fight film, or a 'reproduction'. The issue was further complicated by the filming of facsimiles or reconstructions of the fights.
8. *Limerick Leader*, 19 December 1900:2.
9. Musser 1994:202.
10. See Miriam Hansen, 'Early Cinema: Whose Public Sphere?' in Thomas Elsaesser (ed.), *Early Cinema: Space, Frame, Narrative*, London: BFI, 1990. Drawing on the writings of Jürgen Habermas, and of Oskar Negt and Alexander Kluge, Hansen argues that the cinema allowed for the possibility of an oppositional 'proletarian public sphere' to develop in relation to the bourgeois public sphere which had seen since the mid-nineteenth century the modern mass media turn 'the raw material of human experience into an object of capitalist production.' (p. 231.) Early cinema had provided a 'social space, a place apart from the domestic and work spheres, where people of similar background and status could find company [and] where young working women would seek escape from the fate of their mothers.' (p. 233.) See also Miriam Hansen, *Babel & Babylon: Spectatorship in American Silent Film*, Cambridge, Mass./London: Harvard UP, 1991.
11. *Boston Herald*, quoted Musser, 1994:200.
12. The New Woman, indicating economic and personal freedom, was sharply different to the stereotyped and subjugated Irish woman confined to a life of drudgery in the home. Representations of the independent New Woman became a prime target for Irish film censors from the 1920s onwards, as is discussed in subsequent chapters.
13. Musser, 1994:200.
14. *Irish Times*, 16 November 1897:6. This review was written the day after the insensitively newly-named Empire had opened following renovations after having been integrated into the English-owned Moss & Thornton Group of Provincial Empires. Three months earlier, Dan Lowrey, owner of the theatre for almost twenty years, died, and his duties passed to a booking manager from the Moss organization. Shortly afterwards, the Moss company was amalgamated with the Stoll circuit, creating the powerful Moss & Stoll Empire of Empires chain. One of the immediate consequences of this change was that the 'free and easy rowdyism of sing-songs which has lingered in certain sections of Music Hall' was toned down. (Watters and Murtagh, 1975:171.) To consolidate the bourgeoisification of the venue, queues were organized to avoid crushing at the doors, and thus encourage middle-class clientele, women as well as men, who would have avoided Lowrey's theatre because 'there was a backstreet flavour about the name "Dan Lowrey's", a whiff of male tavern delights, and the tone was a bit too "common" for the respectable new regime.' (Ibid. 174.)
15. *Irish Times*, 22 August 1910:6.
16. By contrast, admission prices to the Volta ranged from six pence to one shilling, with matinees at two pence. Even though James Joyce sought a middle-class clientele for his cinema, 'The Most Elegant Hall in Dublin' according to its advertisements, with the two-tiered pricing designed to attract 'fashionable' people to the cinema, the fact that the cinema was located at the edge of a poor district, and that the screenings did not begin until 5.00 p.m., indicates that the cinema's actual constituency was workers, not women with leisure time.

17. Referred to in *Irish Times*, 22 August 1910:10.
18. The film was shown at the Theatre Royal, Limerick, 2 November 1909; Empire Palace Theatre, Dublin, 21 March 1910; Rotunda, Dublin from 11 April 1910; and re-released, 18 April 1910. Another fight film seen just prior to the Johnson–Jeffries fight was Walsh (or Welch) v. Daniels (Limerick, 26 June 1910). Fight films seen in provincial Limerick during the twelve months following the Johnson–Jeffries contest were Lewis v. Summers (27 April 1911); Sam Langford v. Sam McVey (4 May 1911); and Hague v. Chase (9 May 1911). Also, in March 1910 the then retired boxer John L. Sullivan combined his autobiographical monologue with three rounds of boxing with Jake Kilrain at the Theatre Royal, Dublin without public protests being voiced against it.
19. For accounts of the Johnson–Jeffries contest, and more broadly, Johnson's career, see Randy Roberts, *Papa Jack: Jack Johnson and the Era of White Hopes*, London: Robson Books, 1986; orig. 1983; and Patrick Myler, *A Century of Boxing Greats*, London: Robson Books, 1999; orig. 1997.
20. For listings of African-American and other ethnic groups in the cinema, see *American Film Institute Catalog, Within Our Gates: Ethnicity in American Feature Films, 1911–1960*, Berkeley: University of California Press, 1997. For a discussion of the Irish in this context, see Rockett, 'The Irish Migrant and Film', 1994.
21. Because of its explicit racism, by the time *The Birth of a Nation* was screened at Dublin's Gaiety Theatre from 18 September 1916, one year after its American première, it was already a controversial film. Public commentaries in Ireland displaced the offensive depiction of African-Americans in the South after the Civil War and during Reconstruction on to the film as spectacle. As advertisements for the film put it: 'The Mightiest, Most Astonishing Spectacle ever known, The Human Mind Falters and Gasps with Amazement at the Marvels Revealed by this – The 8th Wonder of the World: 18,000 people; 5,000 horses; £100,000 cost; and eight months to produce.' The film's racism was ignored in Irish reviews of the film: The 'most thrilling scenes' in the film occur when the 'ghostly garbed ghouls' of the Klu Klux Klan, 'an institution of chivalry, humanity, and patriotism ... ride madly to the rescue of the women and children of the South' at the film's climax. (*Dublin Evening Mail*, 16 September 1916:4.)
22. See Hunnings, 1967:50.
23. *Irish Times*, 22 August 1910:10.
24. Ibid.
25. Ibid.
26. Ibid.
27. *House of Commons Debates*, vol. 9, cols. 2260–66, 25 August 1909.
28. Robertson 1985:3.
29. Butler reported to Dublin Corporation that after initially experiencing 'great difficulty' and resistance by exhibitors to the construction of 'substantial' fireproof projection boxes and other safety devices, cinema-owners complied with the new regulations. See *Reports and Printed Documents of the Corporation of Dublin* (hereafter *Reports*), vol. 3, 1 October 1910:668.
30. This account of the difficulties being experienced by Jameson in acquiring a licence is taken from the *Freeman's Journal*, 22 August 1910:8, to whom Jameson released the details of his dealings with Butler. The *Journal* also carried a long and generally favourable review of the film in the same issue.
31. *Irish Times*, 22 August 1910:10.
32. Ibid.
33. Musser, 1994:195.
34. Ibid. 53.
35. Ibid. 195.
36. *Reports ...*, vol. 1, 1912:287.
37. Robertson, 1985:4.
38. For a comprehensive account of how the Cinematograph Act was extended and used to impose restrictions on cinema licences see, in particular, Hunnings, 1967.
39. *Reports ...*, vol. 1, 1912:288.
40. Ibid. The cinema as a counter-attraction to the pub and brothel was well recognized by this time. The Dublin Total Abstinence Society ran its own cinema at its Coffee Palace, Townsend Street, while the Dublin Central Mission held screenings at its George's Hall, perhaps as a means of making its proselytizing more attractive. Later in the decade when an intense debate raged in Rathmines over Sunday opening of cinemas one of the strongest counter-arguments to those favouring Sunday closure was that it would keep working-class men out of pubs and 'clubs', a euphemism for brothels. Indeed, it is hardly an accident that all of the early cinemas on O'Connell Street were opened on its 'respectable' west side, as prostitutes were confined to the east side of the street. It was only after the closure of Dublin's Red Light district, the Monto, in the early 1920s, following a campaign by the Legion of Mary, that the Savoy Cinema opened on the east side of the street, the only

cinema that was ever built on that side of O'Connell Street. For the American discourses on cinema as a substitute for the saloon see Gunning 1994:163ff.

41. Joseph V. O'Brien, *"Dear Dirty Dublin": A City in Distress, 1899–1916*, Berkeley/Los Angeles/London: University of California Press, 1982:149.

42. For a discussion of cinematic representations of urban Ireland see Kevin Rockett, '(Mis) Representing the Irish Urban Landscape', in Mark Shiel and Tony Fitzmaurice (eds), *Cinema and the City: Film and Urban Societies in a Global Context*, Oxford: Blackwell Publishers 2001.

43. Mary Daly, *Dublin: The Deposed Capital: A Social and Economic History 1860–1914*, Cork: Cork UP, 1984:272.

44. Ibid. 319.

45. 'Recorder and Cinema Licences; Not Enough Conditions on Them', *Dublin Evening Mail*, 21 February 1913:3.

46. Kinnard and Davis 1992:27–31.

47. As there is no film of this title, it was probably the 1898 Eden Musée-Edison film, *The Passion Play of Oberammergau*, based on the play by Salmi Morse, a film in *twenty-three* scenes, rather than Lubin's production of the same year, *The Passion Play*. Both films were shot in America using professional actors. Following a dispute over patent rights to the film won by Edison, the film was broken up and sold as individual scenes, thus allowing only twelve scenes to be shown in Dublin. Meanwhile, two theatrical producers, Klaw and Erlanger, made a documentary, *The Passion Play* (1897), on location in Europe. However, this was a record of the annual passion play at Horwitz, Bohemia, rather than the once-a-decade Oberammergau spectacle.

48. Filmed on 30 July 1905, it was screened a week later on 7 August 1905. Filming of local religious events was not uncommon: Screenings in Limerick, which would have been replicated locally in other provincial centres, included, for example, 'Congregations Leaving Jesuits' Church and St Michael's Church, Limerick' (Theatre Royal, October 1900); 'Arch-Confraternity of the Holy Family leaving the Redemptorist Church on the morning of the General Communion,' winding up the recent retreat (Theatre Royal, May 1913); the 'First National Pilgrimage to Lourdes' (Rink Picture Palace, November 1913). Catholic religious events in other countries were also screened, such as 'The Pope's Legate – Cardinal Vannutellis' Official Visit to Paris for the Festivities of the Centenary of "Ozaman"' (May 1913).

49. *Irish Catholic*, 1 February 1913:6.

50. Writing of the American experience, Bowser (1994:133) notes that 'the appeal to religion and church people was important, because they were the respectable society in most small towns, and often in the cities as well. On the other hand, films on religious subjects often fell afoul of interdenominational sensibilities.' Bowser goes on to observe that 'after years of the film industry's using religion as uplift, it was now asked whether religious films were suitable for showing in a theatre for entertainment purposes, reviving the troubles the passion plays had encountered at the end of the previous century.' (Ibid.) See also Musser 1994:208–221.

51. Bowser 1994:133.

52. Ibid. Ironically, by the time *From the Manger to the Cross* was released, many of the elements of the transition period from primitive to classical cinema, such as the refinement of parallel editing, or cross-cutting, by D.W. Griffith and others, were in place. These developments, from around 1908 onwards, laid the formal groundwork for the development of classical cinema's defining element of narrative suspense and tension (will the hero rushing to the scene rescue the heroine before she is run over by the train, or she is assaulted by her abductor? etc.), while the static format of the earlier 'cinema of attractions' was superseded by the classical cinema style which was to remain dominant until the 1960s. See Gunning, 1994 for a discussion of the transition period, and Bordwell et al., 1985 for a consideration of the classical period.

53. Kinnard and Davis 1992:22.

54. 'From Manger to Cross', *Irish Times*, 30 January 1913:6.

55. *Dublin Evening Mail*, 24 February 1913:4.

56. *Irish Catholic*, 15 February 1913:5. The *Irish Catholic* does not seem to have objected to the representations as such, but to their showing for money in a cinema which was 'composed to some degree ... of the wayfarers of the streets.' Cinema-patrons were, the newspaper alleged with references to three contentious issues – alcohol, prostitution, and anti-national collaboration – 'semi-intoxicated English soldiers, with their female companions.' With a characteristic rhetorical flourish, the *Irish Catholic* concluded that it 'regarded the performance with which we are now threatened as an outrage on all the canons of public decency which should be held sacred in a Catholic city.

57. *Dublin Evening Mail*, 24 February 1913:3–4.

58. *Irish Times*, 25 February 1913:4.

59. Ibid. The (Catholic) vigilance committees are discussed in the next section.
60. 'Cinema Films; A Protest Meeting', *Irish Independent*, 1 March 1913:5–6. Just below its report of the meeting the *Independent* published a letter from 'An R.C. [Roman Catholic]' looking forward to seeing the film, an indication, perhaps, that the Catholic proprietors of the *Independent* did not share the Protest Committee's viewpoint.
61. *Irish Times*, 1 March 1913:6.
62. Ibid.
63. Since the early 1880s many Protestants had 'escaped from a City whose political tone was becoming increasingly unpalatable to live in a more congenial atmosphere where the Protestant conservative ascendancy had not yet been challenged.' (Mary Daly, *Dublin: The Deposed Capital*, 1984:202.)

    In the first volume, *Dublin Made Me*, Dublin/Cork: The Mercier Press, 1979, of his autobiography, C.S. (Todd) Andrews (born 1901), gives a telling account of a central Dublin childhood at the beginning of the century in which Protestants only featured as alien beings with whom there was little or no contact: 'From childhood I was aware that there were two separate and immiscible kinds of citizens: the Catholics, of whom I was one, and the Protestants, who were as remote and different from us as if they had been blacks and we whites. We were not acquainted with Protestants but we knew that they were there – a hostile element in the community, vaguely menacing us with such horrors as Mrs Smylie's homes for orphans where children might be brought and turned into Protestants. We Catholics varied socially among ourselves but we all had the common bond, whatever our economic condition, of being second-class citizens.' (pp. 9–10.)

    Andrews goes on (pp. 10–13) to give a detailed description of class differentiation among Dublin Catholics but, for him, this was secondary to the city's religious divide.
64. *Reports ...*, vol. 2, 1913:273. It can only be speculated as to whether the visit to the planned venue was coincidental with the court case or a response to the pressure against the film being screened.
65. *Irish Independent*, 4 March 191:5.
66. 'A New Phase of Sacred Art', *Freeman's Journal*, 4 March 1913:10.
67. Ibid.
68. *Irish Catholic*, 8 March 1913:5.
69. *Freeman's Journal*, 4 March 1913:10.
70. *Dublin Evening Mail*, 4 March 1913:3.
71. *Irish Catholic*, 22 March 1913:1. The pattern of highlighting clerical support for the film was followed outside Dublin, when, for example, it was screened in Limerick from 19 April 1913 with an unusually large half-page advertisement on the front of the *Limerick Chronicle*. Only the 'epic' *Quo Vadis?*, which received a full-page advertisement the following month, surpassed it. (*Limerick Chronicle*, 24 May 1913:1.) For a discussion of that particular film, with its struggle of the Christians against the 'licentious and pagan' Roman court, see Marcia Landy, *Italian Film*, Cambridge: Cambridge UP, 2000:29ff. Its range of taboo subjects – drunken orgies, cruelty to animals, female 'wantonness,' and suicide – suggest that Irish audiences in the pre-censorship period had access to a range of transgressive representations which soon would be eliminated from Irish cinemas.
72. As an advertisement in the *Irish Times* declared, 27 March 1913.
73. *Reports ...*, vol. 2, 1913:274–5. For an account of the origins of the BBFC see Robertson 1985:4 ff.
74. Robertson 1985:185–87.
75. *Reports ...*, vol. 2, 1913:275. Despite such support for local authority film censorship, by the end of 1915, as Robertson 1985:7 reports, only 36 of the hundreds of local authorities so empowered in Britain and Ireland introduced film censorship regulations.
76. *Reports ...*, vol. 2, 1913:275.
77. Correspondence and memos concerning this controversy are preserved in Dublin City Council's Archive. While the campaign against Sunday opening in Rathmines was initiated by the Protestant and Jewish churches, some Catholics were equally vehement in their opposition to Sunday cinema. Writing in the *Irish Catholic* (15 March 1913:9) Francis P. Carey declared that Sunday cinemagoing was a 'pagan practice' and should be prohibited. This view, though, is exceptional among Catholics, who, in general, took a more relaxed view of recreations on Sundays. There was one important exception. In keeping with its conservative Catholic ethos, in 1927 Limerick Corporation banned Sunday cinema. In congratulating the city on this action, the *Leader* (vol. LIII, no. 24, 15 January 1927:566) contrasted the 'doubtful-quantity' of films with the 'clean amusement in hurling, football, handball and country tramping,' and the indoor recreations of reading and billiards. It went on to say that 'anybody who knows anything about cinema pictures knows that they are not uniformly clean.'
78. *Reports ...*, vol. 1, 20 January 1914:102; *Minutes of the Municipal Council of the City of Dublin*, hereafter *Minutes ...*, 1913:477. Dublin Corporation asked the PHC on 6 November 1913 to report

on the LCC Elementary Schools circular on the use and abuse of the cinematograph. The PHC reported on 20 January 1914.
79. *Reports ...*, vol. 1, 1914:102.
80. *Reports ...*, vol. 1, 1914:101. A copy of the licence was attached to this report as an appendix.
81. Twenty-two grounds on which films were cut or banned were reported by the BBFC in 1914. See Robertson 1985:7–8.
82. *From the Manger to the Cross* was eventually viewed by the BBFC in 1918 when it was passed uncut with a 'U', or universal/general, certificate.
83. Their influence, of course, can be easily detected in the Rathmines and Rathgar Urban District Council agitation against Sunday opening during 1916–1917.
84. Like many other campaigns which developed a national profile in Ireland there was an important pre-history of the issue in Britain. Since the production of more explicit sexual writing from the 1890s onwards consideration gradually began to be given to introducing restrictions on this material. During 1908–1909 in particular a national debate had raged over the possibility of imposing statutory or other controls on such material. One outcome of this debate was the re-invigoration of the National Vigilance Association and the establishment in 1910 of the National Council of Public Morals. In 1913 further intense debate ensued in Britain on the subject.
85. The most detailed account of the vigilance committees' campaign in Ireland during this period and later is contained in Louis Cullen's study of Ireland's premier booksellers, *Eason & Son: A History*, Dublin: Eason & Son, 1989. Cullen includes a chapter, 'The Problem of "Evil Literature"', which makes use of contemporary correspondence to and from the company, as well as newspaper reports, to sketch the progress of the campaign.
86. *Irish Times*, 2 July 1912:8.
87. Cullen, *Eason & Son*, 1989:252.
88. Ibid. 256.
89. Ibid. 257.
90. *Limerick Leader*, 6 November 1911:3. This support was reiterated less than eighteen months later. (*Irish Catholic*, 15 March 1913:1) Despite the lifting of the ban on the AOH, the organization continued to be viewed with deep suspicion by many members of the Catholic hierarchy, especially Cardinal Logue, due in large measure to the inability of the church to control it or, at least, to have a strong influence over it. In 1909, for example, Logue had described the AOH as 'a pest, a cruel tyranny, and an organised system of blackguardism.' (David W. Miller, *Church, State and Nation in Ireland 1898–1921*, Dublin: Gill and Macmillan, 1973:245.) As Miller puts it (ibid. 214), the AOH 'threatened to become an established institution clearly labelled "Catholic" in everyone's mind but remaining effectively outside clerical influence.' Thus, the AOH's search for acceptance among the Catholic clergy may have been as strong a motivation in its involvement in the 'evil literature' campaign as the issue itself.
91. 'Immoral Literature', *Sinn Féin*, vol. 2, no. 93 (new series), (no. 285, old series), 11 November 1911:5.
92. *Irish Catholic*, 12 April 1913:5.
93. Ibid.
94. Cullen, *Eason & Son*, 1989:253, declares that from the 'start' the vigilance committees were 'heavily clerical' and cites the case of the Limerick priest, Fr Gleeson, director of the 5,000 strong Holy Family Sodality (p. 250), who started the anti-'evil literature' agitation there and used that organization, whose membership included many of the city's newsboys, to block the distribution of the English Sunday newspapers to which objection was made.
95. *Irish Catholic*, 1 March 1913:4.
96. Report dated 20 January 1914, *Reports ...*, vol. 1, 1914:101. Considered by council, 9 March 1914, *Minutes ...*, 1914:148–9.
97. *Minutes...* no. 271, 20 April 1914, 1914:184. In 1913 the United Confraternities of Dublin had made such a call, which was endorsed in a letter to the *Irish Catholic*, though it does not appear to have been presented to the Corporation. That letter also revealed the broader political concerns about cinema and cinemagoers six months before the Lock-Out began: 'Their patrons are mostly the half-instructed youths – if even they be half-instructed – of both sexes; it would be better to see them flock to the churches to hear good sermons ... The times are very dangerous, and these half-educated people are the most likely to become, first the dupes and then the victims of the false but plausible and seemingly attractive doctrine of the Socialist orators.' (*Irish Catholic*, 15 February 1913:6.)
98. *Reports ...*, vol. 2, 26 May 1915, 1915:59. The Committee of the Whole House was chaired by J.J. Farrell.

99. Cosgrave had presided over a DVC meeting as early as 1912 (*Irish Catholic*, 21 December 1912:5). Peter Tierney, a businessman, who later played a prominent role in the anti-cinema campaign, seconded a motion at that meeting on the pledge, and said that the DVC's 'eyes' were on theatres and cinemas.
 1. *Minutes ...*, no. 597, 9 August 1915, 1915:361.
 2. *Irish Catholic*, 28 August 1915:8. See also, editorial, ibid. 4 September 1915:7–8.
 3. *Irish Catholic*, 11 September 1915:1.
 4. Ibid. 4.
 5. Ibid.
 6. *Minutes ...*, no. 669, 6 September 1915, 1915:407. The other members of the delegation were Fr M.H. MacInerney OP, one of the original activists in the vigilance committees; Peter Tierney; Mr O'Malley-Moore; and Mr McHugh.
 7. *Irish Catholic*, 11 September 1915:4.
 8. *Dublin Evening Mail*, 6 September 1915:3.
 9. *Irish Catholic*, 11 September 1915:4.
10. Ibid.
11. *Irish Times*, 7 September 1915:8.
12. During the course of his Mansion House speech Fr Paul had called for a loud protest from cinemagoers if anything 'improper' appeared on the screen. A person named Frank Larkin, who may have been a relative of William Larkin, or alternatively may have been misnamed in the article, had addressed the overflow meeting at the Mansion House on 6 September. The *Irish Catholic* (11 September 1915:8) described him as the 'hero of so many prosecutions for making vigorous public protests that drew on him the attention of the law.' In 1917 Fr Paul gave a paper on 'The Vigilance Movement' in which he compared the vigilance committees' campaigns with the leprosy scares in Dublin in the nineteenth century: 'When the plague of 1867 and 1872 attacked our capital, the health authorities did their duty, and were acclaimed as saviours of Dublin from the leprosy of foreign ships which had to be kept out of our harbours. The Vigilance Committee has preserved our capital from "a plague that cuts deeper than the skin or flesh and goes to the marrow of the soul".' (*Irish Catholic*, 24 February 1917:3.) It was not the last time such a metaphor was applied to literature or popular culture.
13. *The Bioscope*, 29 July 1915.
14. 'Cinema Scene; Stampede in City Theatre', *Dublin Evening Mail*, 15 September 1915:3–4.
15. *Dublin Evening Mail*, 11 November 1915:3–4.
16. See *The American Film Institute Catalog: Feature Films 1911–20*, Berkeley/Los Angeles/London: University of California Press, 1988:628.
17. At the resumed trial, defence counsel Patrick Lynch KC claimed that the version of the film brought especially from London to be viewed by Swifte contained only a small part of the scene deemed offensive. This was strongly denied by Sparling who declared that the print was identical to the one exhibited at the Bohemian. See '"Faked Film"', *Dublin Evening Mail*, 19 October 1915:4.
18. The Dublin Vigilance Committee at least was a male organization though it had a women's auxiliary section involved in fund-raising and other activities. Even at the Mansion House meeting on 1 July 1912 women, including the Lord Lieutenant's wife, Lady Aberdeen, were not admitted. Of course, it was not unusual even for so-called 'progressive' or 'revolutionary' organizations to impose gender apartheid at this time. See, for example, the way women involved either in land agitation or the nationalist military struggle were treated, in Margaret Ward, *Unmanageable Revolutionaries: Women and Irish Nationalism*, London: Pluto Press, and Dingle, Co. Kerry: Brandon, 1983. There were 31 members of the Dublin Vigilance Committee at this time. They can be divided into two groups: a core of 14, half of whom were priests, and 17 representatives of various city organizations. The members were: Thomas J. Deering, president; the Revd Joseph McCabe, OCC; Michael Comyn KC; the Revd B. MacMahon CP; Dr Michael Walsh; the Revd Anthony Doherty CP; the Revd Joseph Smith, CP; the Revd Fr Paul OSFC; Mr F.J. Little, solicitor; the Revd H. MacInerney OP; Fr Berthold ODC; Mr O'Malley-Moore, honorary treasurer; Laurence O'Dea and Mr J. Bradley, joint-honorary secretaries; Mr Gallagher and Mr Larkin representing the Confraternities Central Council; Robert Keely PLG, representative, Ancient Order of Hibernians; Michael Gorevan, representative, Catholic Young Men's Society (at whose premises, 35 North Great George's Street the DVC met); James Flynn, representative, St Agatha's local committee; Mr Nolan, representative, St Saviour's local committee; and representatives of other unnamed city organizations: Messrs J. Hynes, Michael Nolan, Graham, Dunphy, Brennan, O'Mahoney, Nolan, J. Fintan Lalor, Hayes, W.J. Nolan, and Purcell. (*Irish Catholic*, 11 December 1915:10.)

19. *Reports* ..., vol. 2, 1916:410. Report dated 15 August 1916.
20. Ibid. 415. One of the first moral panics associated with the cinema was the concern as to what went on in the darkened cinema. D. Drennan 1917:77, cites 'The Darkness of Cinemas' as one of the evils to be guarded against even in a 'decent cinema': 'This is often a cover for evil. The remedy here is obvious, as there is no necessity for the darkness. Local authorities can insist upon reflecting lamps of such power being used that a well-lighted hall need not interfere with the picture on the screen.'
21. *Reports* ..., vol. 2, 1916:413.
22. Ibid. 414.
23. *Irish Catholic*, 11 December 1915:10.
24. *Irish Catholic*, 22 January 1916:5.
25. *Irish Catholic*, 24 June 1916:5.
26. *Minutes* ..., no. 441, 5 June 1916, 1916:271.
27. *Reports* ..., vol. 2, 1916:412, 15 August 1916. The only known occasion when a film was referred to the archbishop of Dublin for consideration was in 1918 when *The Garden of Allah* (Colin Campbell, 1916) was imported by N. Ormsby-Scott of National Films Ltd, and Canon O'Connell was nominated to view it: 'Much concern was expressed over the hero being referred to as Father Antoine, implying that he was an ordained priest. It was requested that the film's titles be changed to "Brother", thus making the leading man only a renegade monk.' (Anthony Slide, *The Cinema and Ireland*, Jefferson, North Carolina/London: McFarland & Co., 1988:15.) Indeed, this is a mild rebuke for a film adapted from a novel by Robert Smythe Hichens (London, 1904) set in an oasis in the Sahara desert in which Antoine (Thomas Santschi) in disguise as Boris is revealed to be 'a priest whose irrepressible lust forced him to leave the monastery.' After making love to Domini (Helen Ware) his previous identity is uncovered, and she urges him to return to the monastic life, which he does, and she raises their son Boris in the Garden of Allah. (*The American Film Catalog of Motion Pictures Produced in the United States: Feature Films, 1911–1920*, Berkeley/ Los Angeles/ London: University of California Press, Film Entries 314.) A 1927 version of the same novel was banned after independence; see chapter 3.
28. *Irish Catholic*, 24 June 1916:5, published the letter from the IVA's O'Dea and Hayes, dated 20 June, and the letter from C.A. Cameron, the PHC's secretary and the Chief Medical Officer, dated 9 June, informing the IVA of the PHC's decision.
29. *Reports* ..., vol. 2, 1916:412.
30. Letter dated 13 September 1916 from Laurence O'Dea and James J. Hayes, joint secretaries, IVA, to councillors, published *Irish Catholic*, 23 September 1916:6.
31. *Irish Catholic*, 30 September 1916:5.
32. *Minutes* ..., no. 688, 2 October 1916, 1916:428.
33. *Minutes* ..., no. 704, 9 October 1916, 1916:438–9.
34. *Irish Catholic*, 14 October 1916:1.
35. *Reports* ..., vol. 2, 1916:415.
36. *Reports* ..., vol. 3, no. 182, 1917:288, for 2nd quarter.
37. *Reports* ..., vol. 3, no. 244, 1918:548, for 4th quarter 1916.
38. For a discussion of the American cinema reform movement, see chapter 4 in Lary May, 1983. Unlike in Ireland, though, the Urban Progressives in the USA hoped to move the cinema's audience as well as filmmakers beyond seeing films as a release from work or sexual experimentation, and sought to utilize the cinema to spread family values in civic society, as well as being an alternative for working-class males to the saloon. (Ibid. 59.)
39. *Reports* ..., vol. 3, no. 272, 1918:753, for 1st quarter 1917.
40. *Irish Limelight*, vol. 1, no. 2, February 1917:14.
41. *Irish Monthly*, vol. XLV, February 1917:82.
42. T.P. O'Connor (1848–1929) was perhaps a surprising choice as president of the BBFC. Born in Athlone, Co. Westmeath he was a journalist before being elected Parnellite MP for Galway in 1880, and in 1885 to the Scotland electoral district of Liverpool, a seat he held until his death. Throughout his parliamentary career he continued his journalistic work, founding in 1902 a literary paper, *T.P.'s Weekly*. Appointed to the BBFC in 1917, he held the position until his death, by which time he was also 'Father' of the House of Commons. O'Connor's appointment had been reported in the Irish national newspapers on 11 December 1916, though the *Irish Catholic* chose to ignore it, perhaps as a result of the fact that 'O'Connor, though nominally a Catholic, wore his Catholicism rather lightly' (Miller, *Church, State and Nation in Ireland*, 1973:149) and was not a mass-goer (ibid. 348). For an account of O'Connor's career as a censor, see Robertson 1985.

43. *Irish Catholic*, 13 January 1917:6. It has been argued that there were important Irish Catholic voices other than such as the *Irish Catholic* which have not been given due prominence in Irish cultural debates. Brian Murphy has suggested ('The Canon of Irish Cultural History: Some Questions', *Studies*, vol. 77, no. 305, spring 1988) that the sophisticated intellectual debates published in the *Catholic Bulletin* are a case in point. Indeed, at the time of O'Connor's appointment to the BBFC, the *Bulletin* (vol. 7, no.1, January 1917:6) declared that 'faith and morals are at last safe in the picture house.' The writer added, somewhat gingerly, that 'the Dublin Vigilance Committee – if we venture to whisper – may proceed to a voluntary winding up.' Such hesitancy was a feature not just of the *Catholic Bulletin* but of the national media in general when issues of censorship were in dispute. The restrained Catholic intellectuals of the *Bulletin* rarely addressed themselves to questions of cinema, or popular culture, and allowed by default the more extreme positions of the *Irish Catholic* and the Irish Vigilance Association to hold sway. Fr Peter Finlay SJ, Professor of Catholic Theology, University College, one of the neglected Catholic intellectuals cited by Murphy (p. 73), regularly wrote front page articles for the *Irish Bulletin* during the period under review here, yet never, it seems, engaged with the questions of urban popular culture raised by the vigilance committees' agitation.

Nevertheless, when cinema was addressed by the *Catholic Bulletin* its position was often reactionary. Following the 1915 Budget, when excise duty on film imports was introduced, an editorial in the *Bulletin* declared: 'Patent medicines and cinema films have been severely taxed: we only regret the vile things have not been taxed out of existence.' (Vol. 5, no.10, October 1915:722.) It supported the vigilance committees' campaign (vol. 5, no. 12, December 1915:885) despite its qualification of this support after O'Connor's appointment. It also supported the appointment of a Dublin Corporation film censor and called for action on film posters (vol. 6, no. 4, April 1916:193). It added that 'so long as the Irish Vigilance Association sticks closely to its programme, such happenings will only bring it support from what is best in the nation.' (Ibid. 193.) And, in an impatient editorial in 1923 shortly before the appointment of the first national film censor, the *Bulletin* called for 'early and energetic action' to implement film censorship. (Vol. 13, no. 11, November 1923:740.)
44. *Irish Limelight*, vol. 1, no. 3, March 1917:1.
45. Editorial, 'The Cranks' Campaign Against the Cinema', *Irish Limelight*, vol. 1, no. 7, July 1917:1.
46. Frame, an early associate of J.J. Farrell as chairman of the Dublin Electric Theatre since 1911, had by 1917 been involved in the establishment of the Coliseum, Cork, the Curragh Picture House, Kildare, and he was chairman of both the Dame Street Picture House and the Phoenix Picture House, Ellis Quay. He also applied for a licence to operate a cinema in the Town Hall, Clontarf. (*Irish Limelight*, vol. 1, no. 3, March 1917:8.)
47. 'Cinema Notes', *Irish Times*, 8 October 1921:9.
48. Hunnings, 1967:69.
49. W.A. Magill, Secretary, Chief Commissioner of Police, 29 May 1917, to Commission, *The Cinema: Its Present Position and Future Possibilities; Report of the Cinema Commission of Inquiry*, London: Williams and Norgate, 1917:372.
50. Cardinal Logue to secretary, Irish Vigilance Association, 13 February 1917, *Irish Catholic Directory*, 1918:507.
51. Editorial, 'Sunday Night Cinemas', *Irish Catholic*, 7 April 1917:5.
52. *Reports ...*, vol. 3, no. 272, 1918:753, for 1st quarter 1917.
53. In his Lenten Pastoral Archbishop Walsh had called for the complete closure of cinemas on Sunday evenings, *Irish Catholic*, 7 April 1917:5.
54. *Minutes ...*, no. 261, 1918:157. Letter from Confraternities Central Council dated 1 April 1917.
55. Ibid. 157–8.
56. *Reports ...*, vol. 3, no. 173, 1917:181–2.
57. Ibid. 182.
58. *Reports ...*, vol. 1, 1919:238.
59. 'Smut From Theatres Must Go', *Evening Herald*, 12 January 1918:3.
60. 'Our Cinema Censors', *Evening Herald*, 31 January 1918:2.
61. *Reports ...*, vol. 3, no. 207, 1919:20.
62. Ibid.
63. *Irish Limelight*, vol. 2, no. 2, February 1918:5.
64. Ibid., vol. 2, no. 5, May 1918:11. Unfortunately, this list, or any details of the films banned by the PHC's censors, has not survived in Dublin Corporation's Archives.
65. *Reports ...*, vol. 3, no. 232, 1919:154–55.
66. Ibid., vol. 3, no. 243, 1919:254.

67. Ibid.
68. *Reports* ..., vol. 3, no. 284, 1919:560, for 2nd quarter 1919. At this time an IVA delegation sought PHC assistance in compiling information which would support the case to have legislation enacted for the transfer of the jurisdiction over stage productions from the police to the Corporation (ibid. 559).
69. *Irish Times*, 8 October 1921:9.
70. For 1917–1919 see the quarterly Breviates of the Public Health Committee, Dublin Corporation, printed in Dublin Corporation *Reports* ... The details for 1921 are given in *Reports* ..., vol. 1, 1922:728.
71. Undated Irish Vigilance Association statement, 'Cinema, Theatres & Music Halls', perhaps circulated to members of the Dáil in early 1922.
72. *Irish Times*, 8 October 1921:9.
73. *Irish Catholic*, 17 February 1917:6.
74. *Thom's Directory*, 1919:1438.
75. *Thom's Directory*, 1920:1438 and 1921:1438.
76. *Thom's Directory*, 1922:1438.
77. *Reports* ..., vol. 1, no.124, 1922:738.
78. See Table 1.
79. *Reports* ..., vol. 1, no. 124, 1922:739. An almost complete list of Honorary Film Censors is given in *Thom's Directory* 1923 and 1924, p. 1438, covering the period from January 1922 to January 1924, at which time national film censorship was introduced. These include: Aldermen Mrs K. Clarke, T.P. O'Reilly, Sir Andrew Beattie PC, DL, JP, William O'Connor, Seán T. O'Kelly; Councillors Patrick T. Daly, J.R. Stritch JP, Jenny Wyse-Power, Mrs E.A. Ashton, Robert Rooney, Sir J.M. Gallagher JP, Michael Brohoon, Thomas F. Nolan, P.S. Doyle, J.N. Briscoe, Dr Myles Keogh TD, Patrick McDonnell, Seán O'Callaghan, M.J. Maxwell-Lemon, William McCarthy JP; Irish Vigilance Association: A.J. Murray, Andrew F. Clancy, Joseph Cleary, Lady Beattie, Mrs M. McKean, Miss S.R. Stritch; Archbishop Gregg's nominees: the Revd T.W.E. Drury, the Revd H.B. Dobbs, Mr J.W.P. Pope; Priests Social Guild: Fr Tomkin SJ, Fr Wrafter SJ, the Revd L. Sheehan CC, the Revd J. Dempsey. Other nominees of Archbishop Gregg were Mrs Florence Kennedy, The Deanery, St Patrick's Close, and the Revd A. Chamberlain, making a total of thirty-five film censors.
80. *Irish Times*, 3 January 1922:6.
81. *Reports* ..., vol. 1, no. 124, 1922:739.
82. Ibid.
83. Ibid. 740.
84. Ibid.
85. Ibid. 741.
86. *Dáil Éireann: Minutes of Proceedings 1919–1921*, Dublin: Wood Printing Works, undated, p. 215. At its session on 17 September 1920 the Secretary for Home Affairs reported that 'it was thought that the setting up of a National Film Censorship could be undertaken by An Dáil. The latest suggestion was that the Municipal Bodies should be asked to appoint a Central Censor in Dublin. It would be well to have one recognised authority for the whole country as it sometimes happened that pictures passed in Dublin were not approved of in the country. He did not, however, intend to introduce legislation on the subject at the present Session.' There was no further discussion of film censorship in the Dáil until May 1923.
87. *Irish Times*, 22 October 1921:9.
88. *Irish Times*, 7 January 1922:9.
89. Anon., 'The Question of Film Censorship', *Irish Times*, 7 January 1922:9.
90. *Irish Times*, 4 March 1922:9.
91. Ibid.
92. *Irish Times*, 18 March 1922:9.
93. *Irish Times*, 25 March 1922:7.
94. *Minutes* ..., no. 328, 1 May 1922, 1922:250–51.
95. *Minutes* ..., no. 606, 1 November 1922, 1922:454–55. The deputation consisted of Fr Flanagan, Fr Lawrence OSFC and Fr N.J. Tomkin SJ, representing the Priests' Social Guild, Thomas J. Deering and A.J. Murray of the Vigilance Association, the Revd T.W.E. Drury, representing the Church of Ireland, and Mr B. Delahunty.
96. *Minutes* ..., no. 629, 1922:483.
97. *Minutes* ..., no. 53, 1923:38–39.
98. *Minutes* ..., no. 145, 1923:97.

CHAPTER 3

1. Quoted, Thomas P. Gallagher, 'Our First Film Censor,' in *Irish Cinema Handbook*, 1943:93.
2. 'Statement of the Irish Vigilance Association Re Cinema, Theatres & Music Halls', undated, but prepared in 1922 or early 1923.
3. *Dáil debates*, vol. 3, col. 587, 3 May 1923.
4. Ibid. col. 751, 10 May 1923.
5. Ibid. col. 586, 3 May 1923.
6. These eight men were the signatories to the statement which was presented to O'Higgins during the course of the meeting. (File S3026, National Archives of Ireland, [NAI].) Phrases from that statement re-appeared in O'Higgins' introductory speech on the Bill in the Dáil. Ernest Blythe (*Seanad debates*, vol. 1, col. 1127, 6 June 1923) described Fr Tomkin as Fr Tomkins, and the Revd Drury as the Revd J.W. Drury, Professor of Pastoral Theology, TCD.
7. *Seanad debates*, vol. 1, col. 1127, 6 June 1923.
8. Section 10, sub-section 1, Censorship of Films Act, 1923. During the debate Senator Jenny Wyse-Power spoke of her experience as a Dublin Corporation censor and admitted that there were too many film censors in the Corporation. (*Seanad debates*, vol. 1, col. 1128–30, 6 June 1923.)
   Many local authorities continued to attach conditions to the licence, especially relating to the hours children could attend cinemas. When Dublin Corporation, for example, amended its licence after the passage of the Censorship of Films Act it retained the ban on children attending the cinema between 9.00 a.m. and 3.00 p.m. unless accompanied by a parent or guardian. Additionally, it changed the clause which forbade children under-12 years of age from attending cinema after 7.00 p.m. unless accompanied by an adult, to excluding under-14s from the cinema after 9.30 p.m. unless accompanied by an adult.
   Two decades later during the autumn and winter of 1944/45 a number of local authorities adopted resolutions calling for additional restrictions on children's attendance at cinemas. In 1945 the proprietor of The Picture House, Bray, Co. Wicklow, Maurice Baum, and Associated Picture Houses (1941) Ltd, owners of the Royal Cinema, Bray, were charged with the offence of allowing under-14s to enter their cinemas after 7.00 p.m. on Saturday and on Sunday evenings in contravention of the local authority licence. Another condition forbade entry to a cinema after 6.00 p.m. on a weekday on which the National Schools were open. In this instance the judge dismissed the case under the Probation of Offenders Act. He said that 'the amount of harm commonly said to have been done to young children [by the cinema] was greatly exaggerated.' (*Wicklow People*, 19 January 1946:2.)
   The most revealing amendment to Dublin Corporation's licence was the alteration of the clause which stated that 'no known prostitutes or thieves shall be admitted into or shall be permitted to remain on the premises.' By 1924 this had changed to 'No known improper character, reputed thief, or other disorderly person, or any person in a state of intoxication, shall be admitted into, or permitted to remain on, the licensed premises.' (*Dublin Corporation Reports*, no. 277, 1924:457.) Prostitution, it would seem, was to be banished from the lexicon of the new state, while drinking was to become the (un)acceptable public face of social evil.
9. *Dáil debates*, vol. 3, col. 587, 3 May 1923.
10. Censorship of Films Act, 1923 (no. 23 of 1923), Dublin: The Stationary Office.
11. *Dáil debates*, vol. 3, col. 762, 10 May 1923. In 1919 when Magennis was Lecturer in Moral Psychology at University College Dublin he played some form of advisory role to the Dublin Corporation censors. In that year he was asked to adjudicate on the split decision among the four censors who had divided three to one in favour of allowing the film *When a Woman Sins* (J. Gordon Edwards, 1918) to be shown. Magennis sided with the majority view. (*Reports ...*, vol. 3, 1919:425.) The film concerns a young divinity student, Michael (Albert Roscoe), who falls in love with his father's young nurse, Lillian (Theda Bara). When Michael's father dies while sexually assaulting Lillian, Michael blames her for his father's death. She abandons nursing and becomes a degenerate dancer and the object of affection for Michael's cousin Reggie (Jack Rollens), who subsequently commits suicide when she and Michael are reconciled. Following a further estrangement between the couple, she offers herself to the highest bidder at a party, but, she is won by Michael with a bunch of lilies. The decision to pass this film is surprising in light of the severe restrictions imposed with the introduction of national film censorship. The film's central themes – rape, the abandonment of religious vocations, cabaret dancing, and suicide – would all be considered taboo or at best dangerous subjects from 1923 onwards.
12. *Dáil debates*, vol. 3, col. 762, 10 May 1923.

13. Ibid. col. 753.
14. Ibid. col. 755.
15. Ibid. col. 753–54.
16. Ibid. col. 755.
17. Walter Benjamin, 'The Author as Producer' (1934), in *Understanding Brecht*, London: New Left Books, 1973:95.
18. *Dáil debates*, vol. 3, col. 760, 10 May 1923.
19. Ibid. col. 752.
20. Ibid. col. 753.
21. Ibid.
22. Ibid. col. 1178, 28 May 1923.
23. Ibid. col. 1001, 17 May 1923.
24. Richard Hayes in John Gerrard, 'Irish Censorship – or Fighting for Cleaner Cinema', *Sight and Sound*, vol. 18, no. 70, summer 1949:82.
25. *Seanad debates*, vol. 1, col. 1127, 6 June 1923.
26. Ibid. col. 1128.
27. Ibid. col. 1146–48, 7 June 1923.
28. *Dáil debates*, vol. 3, col. 587, 3 May 1923.
29. *Seanad debates*, vol. 1, col. 1147, 7 June 1923.
30. Ibid. col. 1148.
31. Ibid. cols. 1143–44.
32. Ibid. col. 1149.
33. *Dáil debates*, vol. 11, cols. 725–26, 1 May 1925.
34. Official Film Censor's annual reports.
35. *Dáil debates*, vol. 11, col. 1638, 15 May 1925. The Censorship of Films (Amendment) Act, 1925 (no. 21 of 1925). An amendment was also passed at that time reducing the quorum of the Appeal Board from four to three members in attendance for a decision to be made. The debate between O'Higgins and Magennis is of interest as both men were keen not to have included in the Amendment Act any censorship pertaining to written text within cinema's publicity material. Indeed Magennis proposed an amendment in which the word 'pictorial' would precede the word 'advertisements' in the Amendment Act. This was accepted after Magennis argued that 'a censorship of reading matter would be very bold and would, doubtless, create a great amount of discussion, would produce perhaps endless controversy, and I do not believe that the country is ripe, or, it is possible, would ever be ripe, for a drastic proposition of this kind to meet with general approval.' (*Dáil debates*, vol. 11, col. 1635, 15 May 1925.) However, four years later (by which time O'Higgins was dead) the Censorship of Publications Act, 1929 was passed. Considering Magennis' subsequent role as a member, and later as chairman, of the Censorship of Publications Board, it would seem that he no longer held this view.
36. Ibid. col. 1639.
37. Ibid. col. 1646.
38. Editorial, 'Film Censorship', *Freeman's Journal*, 9 May 1923:4.
39. Editorial, 'Censorship of Films', *Irish Independent*, 9 May 1923:4.
40. Editorial, 'A Censor of Films', *Irish Times*, 11 May 1923:4.
41. Editorial, 'The Bane of Evil Literature', *Irish Catholic*, 12 May 1923:5. In an editorial the *Catholic Bulletin* (vol. 8, no. 3. 1923:131) also welcomed the Act as helping to restrict the 'interlaced "business" interests engaged in this unwholesome and degrading traffic.'
42. *Dáil debates*, vol. 3, cols. 755–56, 10 May 1923. The full list of censors can be found in Appendix 1.
43. Memorandum S120938, Department of Justice to Department of the Taoiseach, 23 April 1948 (NAI). According to the Minister for Home Affairs, Kevin O'Higgins, a friend of James Montgomery, the first Censor was employed at a salary of £250 per annum in an office projected to cost £2,070 to run in 1924. The costs were based on viewing 50,000 feet of film per week at a cost of one-fifth of a penny per foot for all films except interest, topicals and educational films which were one-tenth of a penny per foot. (*Dáil debates*, vol. 6, col. 1644, 5 March 1924.) For a discussion on the qualifications cited by the British Board of Film Censors in the 1970s as suitable for its examiners see Phelps 1975:101–2. The BBFC did not seek specialists, or representatives of organizations, or of the professions. It usually sought a person with a university degree, a person with a sense of humour, someone with the ability to work well with others, and a love of films. The post of examiner of the BBFC was advertised for the first time in 1972.

44. In 1926 the *Irish Independent* (John Brennan, 'Peep at the Film Censor', 5 April 1926:5) in an interview with Montgomery, reported that the Censor was debarred from giving interviews on matters concerning his job. Later, though, Montgomery and some other censors broke this guideline. Montgomery himself contributed articles anonymously to the *Irish Statesman*, as he revealed after his retirement. (*Studies*, vol. 31, no. 124, December 1942:420.) An article entitled 'The Los Angelesation of Ireland' (*Irish Statesman*, 15 January 1927:446–447), while not apparently penned by Montgomery – there is no writer credit – reported on a paper given by the Censor in which he warned of 'the danger of the Los Angelesation of the world.'

45. The Revd Monsignor Michael Cronin, *Primer of the Principles of Social Sciences*, Dublin: M.H. Gill, 1956, fourth edition, revised, 1955.

46. *Seanad debates*. vol. 13, col. 1014, 7 May 1930.

47. Ibid. col. 1008.

48. James Montgomery to Monsignor M.J. Curran, Rome, 18 December 1936, OFC.

49. James Montgomery, 16 December 1924. The film was *In a Monastery Garden* (1924).

50. Report of the Official Film Censor for 1927 to the Minister for Justice, dated 18 January 1928:2, OFC.

51. One of O'Leary's decisions was to approve with eight cuts a certificate for Howard Hughes' *The Outlaw* (1943). (Record 21349; 10,451 feet, Reserve 6978; Reject 1862, Censor's decision, 24 January 1947; Appeal Board decision, 4 March 1947; distributor: United Artists. The film was re-submitted in 1952: Record 26912; 9,343 feet, Reserve 8173–4; Censor Richard Hayes' decision, 28 January 1952, ten cuts, but no certificate was issued; distributor: RKO Radio.) O'Leary gave a sympathetic account of the film, but under pressure from producer Hughes the distributor refused to accept the cuts and the film was sent to the Appeal Board. However, the Board banned the film. O'Leary was appointed as a deputy Film Censor not so much due to his film activities in the Irish Film Society, of which he was one of the founders in 1936, but because at the time he was employed as a producer with the Abbey Theatre. A tradition already existed whereby Abbey Theatre personnel deputized for the Censor, and M.J. Dolan most frequently filled this role in the 1940s. Film Censor Richard Hayes was a Government-appointed director of the Abbey Theatre from 1933 until his death in 1957. There is no official title of deputy Film Censor, but a practice emerged in the 1990s with the appointment of video classifiers that the full-time assistant in charge of video is often described as deputy Film Censor, the first of whom was Audrey Conlon.

52. Hugh Hunt, *The Abbey: Ireland's National Theatre 1904 – 1979*, Dublin: Gill and Macmillan, 1979:88.

53. James Montgomery to Monsignor M.J. Curran, Irish College, Rome, 18 December 1936, OFC.

54. *Dáil debates*, vol. 6, col. 1658, 5 March 1924.

55. Report of the Official Film Censor to the Minister for Justice for the period 1 November 1923 to 31 October 1924, dated 13 November 1924, OFC.

56. Quoted, Thomas P. Gallagher, 'Our First Film Censor', in *Irish Cinema Handbook*, 1943:93.

57. Report of the Official Film Censor for 1927 to the Minister for Justice, dated 18 January 1928, OFC.

58. Censor's decision, 9 January 1925.

59. Censor's decision, 8 September 1933.

60. The 1923 Act does not set down any criteria for the re-submission of films to the Film Censor, but a practice seems to have developed whereby the Censor allowed distributors to re-submit films on an ad hoc basis when he thought that the distributor would cut out the objectionable parts of a film, thus relieving him of much work, and then re-submitting the cut version. This practice is different from the Censor viewing a film at a 're-show,' which is when the distributor has cut a film after receiving the list of cuts specified by the Censor and prior to the certificate being issued. The question of re-submission was not formalized until 1970 with the passage of the Censorship of Films (Amendment) Act, 1970 which states that a film can only be re-submitted for a certificate after a period of seven years has elapsed. The 'seven-year rule' allows for a film to be considered anew by the Censor.

61. Report of Official Film Censor to the Minister for Justice for the period 1 November 1923 to 31 October 1924, dated 13 November 1924, OFC. The key sentence in the undated draft of this report reads: 'These undesirable parts dealt principally with indecent dancing, riotous scenes of drunkenness and debauchery and the habits and customs of the "divorcing classes" in England and America.' Montgomery amended it before sending it to the Minister.

62. Ibid. There is a discrepancy of four between the sum of the totals of films banned, cut, and passed without cuts in the reports and the total number of films viewed.

63. Report of the Official Film Censor for 1925 to the Minister for Justice, dated 11 January 1926, OFC.
64. Film Censor's Annual Reports. The Film Censor did not include a statistical breakdown in his first annual report, and the reports for 1926 and 1928 are unavailable. As a result, the statistics for these years are taken from the figures listed by the Film Censor in a summary prepared in 1936, 'Film Censorship in the Irish Free State,' (unpublished) and from figures supplied to the author by the Film Censor's office. The figures include 'short subjects,' that is, films of less than 2,000 feet, which are listed separately from 1929 onwards. The Censor's separate decisions for 'short' and 'long' (feature) films are recorded only from 1930 onwards. During the period 1930–1940 inclusive, 'short' films accounted for 386, excluding results of appeals, or one-third, of the 1,163 films banned by the Censor during those years. While a few of these short films were trailers, almost all of them, as with the 'long' films, were dramas. Appeals against cuts, which appear for the first time as a category in the Censor's annual report for 1932, when 7 such appeals were lodged, are included in the passed with cuts figure. A total of 39 such appeals during 1932–1940 inclusive were recorded in the annual reports. In one instance, in 1936, a film was banned after the distributor lodged an appeal against the cuts. As Montgomery retired in October 1940, though he stayed on as deputy Censor, the numbers banned by his successor for the last quarter of 1940 are unknown. In 1939–1940, 8 films were banned for infringing the Emergency Powers Order relating to the cinema, see chapter 8, but these are not included in the above figures.
65. Adams, 1968:243.
66. Film Censor's Annual Reports.
67. Report of the Official Film Censor for 1927 to the Minister for Justice, dated 18 January 1928, OFC.
68. Handwritten draft of Report of the Official Film Censor for 1931 to the Minister for Justice, dated 11 January 1932:2–3. The typed report is dated 14 January 1932, but does not include this section, OFC.
69. 6,870 feet; Reject 188 (Reject Book 2), Censor's decision, 1 November 1928; ban upheld after appeal, 20 November 1928. The last sentence of this critique was 'for Board only', indicating his desire to keep his policies private, or at least not explicitly stated to the distributors.
70. Record G2995 (Reject Book 2), 9,078 feet; Reject 104, Censor's decision, 5 July 1927; distributor: Wardour.
71. Record 11696; 9,867 feet, Reserve 3815 and 3860; Reject 1301; Censor's decision, 10 April 1937 and 22 June 1937. Montgomery had initially banned the film, but the distributor was allowed to cut it and re-submit it without the offending parts. It was then passed by the Censor. An earlier version of *Camille* (Fred Niblo, 1927) was also banned by Montgomery, who repeated at that time his comment about another version of the Dumas story viewed a year before: 'Stripped of its sentimentality, it is the unhealthy and immoral story of a consumptive courtesan.' (Record G2935 (Reject Book 2), 8,898 feet; Reject 101, Censor's decision, 16 June 1927; distributor: First National-Pathé.)
72. Record 80245 (Reject Book 1), 4,600 feet; Censor's decision, 10 February 1925; distributor: Fox Film Co.
73. Record C1291 (Reject Book 1), 5,731 feet; Reject 84, Censor's decision, 12 December 1924; no appeal; distributor: MGM.
74. Censor's decision, 1 September 1923.
75. Record 6628 and 8226, 5,600 feet; Reserve 3115; Censor's decision, 31 October 1934; review, 2 November 1934; certificate issued on 3 November 1934; distributor: Universal.
76. A germinal study of ideology and the cinema is a 1969 *Cahiers du Cinéma* editorial by Jean-Louis Comolli and Jean Narboni who divided films into seven categories, 'a'–'g'. Category 'e' covers films that seem to conform to the status quo, but on closer examination reveal social or political contradictions. 'An internal criticism is taking place which cracks the film apart at the seams. If one reads the film obliquely, looking for symptoms, if one looks beyond its apparent formal coherence, one can see that it is riddled with cracks: it is splitting under an internal tension which is simply not there in an ideologically innocuous film.' Examples include the excessive melodramas of Douglas Sirk who stretched the limits of the genre and forced a questioning of ideological values which the films only seem to reinforce. Sirk has spoken of the classical Hollywood resolution as an 'escape exit,' a term which coincides with Montgomery's opinion. Comolli and Narboni, 'Cinema/Ideology/Criticism', in Gerald Mast, Marshall Cohen and Leo Braudy (eds), *Film Theory and Criticism: Introductory Readings*, fourth edition, New York, Oxford: Oxford UP, 1992: 687.
77. Record 14438; 5,767 feet, Reserve 4237, Censor's decision, 17 July 1939; distributor: Warner Bros.

78. Reject 1381, Appeal Board decision, 10 October 1939.
79. Record 11148 and 14698; 16,166 feet, Censor's initial decision, 6 November 1936; review 17 November 1936; Appeal Board Reserve 3738–9, 3743 and 3746; decision, 9 December 1936; certificate issued on 9 December 1936; distributor: MGM.
80. Record 8705 and 14039, 6,762 feet; Reserve 3229; Censor's decision, 14 February 1935 and 3 May 1935; review, 8 May 1935; certificate issued on 10 May 1935; distributor: Warner Bros.
81. See Helen Hickey, *Images of Stone: Figure Sculpture of the Lough Erne Basin*, Fermanagh, Co. Tyrone Fermanagh District Council in co-operation with the Arts Council of Northern Ireland, second edition, 1985, orig. 1976. Though many of these figures were collected for preservation by the National Museum of Ireland they were not put on public view until the 1980s.
82. Record C759 (Reject Book 1), 6,164 feet; Censor's decision, 13 Sept. 1924; distributor: First National.
83. Record 7422 and 36041; 8,307 feet, Reserve 2740; Censor's decision, 7 March 1934; review (Joseph Holloway), 24 March 1934; certificate issued on 26 March 1934; trailer: Record 7422; distributor: Warner Bros. Most readers would not expect the pairing of Montgomery with textual theorist Christian Metz, but in a pertinent comment Metz records: 'I am at the cinema, attending a film show. ATTENDING. Like a midwife who attends at a birth, and thereby also helps the woman, I am present to the film in two (inseparable) ways: witness and helper; I watch, and I aid. In watching the film I help it to be born, I help it to live, since it is in me that it will live and it was made for that.' Metz, 'History/Discourse: A Note on Two Voyeurisms,' in John Caughie (ed.), *Theories of Authorship*, London, Boston: Routledge and Kegan Paul/BFI, 1981:227. Ironically, and as Montgomery himself implicitly acknowledged in his discussion of the different audiences for theatre and cinema, even when a film does not feature a birth scene, he, like all viewers, becomes a *midwife* to meaning.
84. Record 15253; 9,704 feet, Reserve 4465 and 4476; Censor's decision, 21 May 1940 and 29 May 1940; certificate issued on 5 June 1940. Trailer: 211 feet; Censor's decision, 4 June 1940; distributor; Warner Bros.
85. Record C1076, 8,244 feet; Reject 53, Censor's decision, 4 November 1924; passed with cuts after appeal; distributor: Gaumont.
86. Record 7696 and 13275; 6,368 feet, Reserve 2848; Censor's decision, 28 May 1934; review, 5 June 1934; distributor: Paramount.
87. Record 13120; 8,188 feet, Censor's decision, 16 June 1938 and 27 July 1938; certificate issued on 9 August 1938.
88. Record 10900; 8,267 feet, Reserve 3710, Censor's decision, 30 September 1936; review, 6 October 1936; certificate issued on 13 November 1936; distributor: 20th Century-Fox.
89. Record 5437 and 5539; 6,391 feet, Reserve 1585 and 1659; Censor's decision, 6 June 1932 and 25 July 1932; review, 16 August 1932; certificate issued on 10 September 1932; distributor: First National Pictures/Warner Bros. Montgomery could also have been worried about the theme of incest, with Karl in love with his foster sister Lottie (Marian Marsh) while masquerading as her brother. Karl eventually abandons medicine, marries Lottie, and they return to the family farm.
90. Record 5563 and 7540; 6,926 feet, Reserve 2815, Censor's decision, 26 April 1934 and 27 April 1934; review, 18 September 1934; certificate issued on 26 September 1934; distributor: RKO Radio. Montgomery described the version of the film seen by him as an 'emasculated remnant' which suggests extensive pre-submission cutting by the distributor. For an account of the struggle over the making of the novel into a film, see Black 1994. Another title changed by Montgomery was *Madonna of the Streets* (John S. Roberston, 1930) which became *The Slum Angel*, probably because the word 'Madonna' was associated with the Virgin Mary. (Reserve 1377, Censor's decision, 4 May 1931.) There is a 1924 film directed by Edwin Carewe of the same title and which is also based on Wm Babington Maxwell, *The Ragged Messenger* (1904).
91. The exact cuts are not fully clear from the Censor's reports as the combination of two screenings and the unrecorded modfications agreed with Neville and with Gray were not always written down. Record 15272, 19,793 feet; Reserve 4474 and 4561–62 and 4573; Censor's decision, 28 May 1940, 3 June 1940 and 7 September 1940; review, 15 May 1942; certificate issued on 18 May 1942; distributor: MGM. The film opened at Dublin's Savoy cinema on 4 September 1942, almost three years after its American release. Ironically, the *Irish Times* commented (7 September 1942:3) that 'the whole tragedy of a nation's birth-pangs are in this picture.'
92. Record 10632 and 28975; 7,817 feet, Reserve 3651; Censor's decision, 6 July 1936; review, 14 August 1936; certificate issued on 14 August 1936; distributor: Warner Bros.
93. Record 4601 and 10302; 8,529 feet, Reserve 1925; Reject 555; Censor's decision, 28 October 1931; review, 14 November 1931; certificate issued on 28 November 1931; distributor: Paramount. The renter received permission to amend the film and re-show it on 28 October 1931, as a result of which the rejection was suspended.

94. Record 7989 and 19666; 7,652 feet, Reserve 2968; Censor's decision, 8 August 1934; review, 22 October 1934; certificate issued on 22 October 1934; distributor: G B Distr. Co.

95. Record 2852 and 33741; 8,599 feet, Reserve 917; Censor's decision, 16 July 1930; review, 22 July 1930; certificate issued on 23 July 1930; distributor: Lasky.

96. James Montgomery in the report on *Holy Ghost Fathers*. Record 12344; Reserve 3933; 393 feet, Censor's decision, 6 November 1937; review, 23 November 1937; Appeal Board viewing, 25 February 1938; distributor: Pathé.

97. Record 13911; 8,400 feet, Reserve 4169; Censor's decision, 27 January 1939; review, 8 February 1939; certificate issued on 3 March 1939; distributor; Warner Bros. Montgomery also cut Cagney being dragged to the electric chair: 'His screams are more than enough.'

98. Record H4018 (Reject Book 2), 8,002 feet; Reject 168, Censor's decision, 22 May 1928; passed with cuts after appeal; distributor: MGM.

99. Record C1409 (Reject Book 1), 7,624 feet; Reject 86, Censor's decision, 16 December 1924; no appeal; distributor: MGM.

1. Record 8092 (Reject Book 1), 7,664 feet; Reject 115, Censor's decision, 21 January 1925; distributor: Express Film Agency.

2. Record C289 (Reject Book 1), 9,023 feet; Reject 155 and 158, Censor's decision, 12 May 1925 (re-submitted, 8,121 feet); distributor: J.F. Boland.

3. See Umberto Eco, *Art and Beauty in the Middle Ages*, New Haven and London: Yale UP, 1986, especially chapter 1, 'The Medieval Aesthetic Sensibility'.

4. Censor's decision, 12 May 1925.

5. Record H4658 (Reject Book 2), 12,763 feet; Reject 198, Censor's decision, 13 December 1928; passed with cuts after appeal, 18 December 1928; distributor; P. D.C.

6. Record 1896 and 34668; 8,742 feet, Reserve 680, Censor's decision, 30 October 1929; review and certificate issued, 14 November 1929; distributor: Lasky.

7. Record 3494 and 8088; 9,112 feet, Reserve 1215, Censor's decision, 8 January 1931; review, 12 February 1931; distributor: MGM. The Censor also ruled that the title of the film had to be changed to be *Singer of Seville*.

8. Censor's decision, 24 August 1933; *Movietone News* item 220a.

9. Record 12344; Reserve 3933; 393 feet, Censor's decision, 6 November 1937; review, 23 November 1937; Appeal Board viewing, 25 February 1938; distributor: Pathé.

10. Censor's decision, 7 January 1935. The newsreel was *Super Sound* 35/2.

11. Censor's decision, 30 December 1937.

12. Record 12662, 3,600 feet, Reserve 3982, Censor's decision, 1 February 1938; reviewed and certificate issued on 2 March 1938.

13. Record 9194 and 19684; 7,414 feet, Reserve 3374; Censor's decision, 24 June 1935; reviewed, 26/27 June 1935; certificate issued on 2 July 1935; distributor: 20th Century-Fox.

14. Record 12662, 3,600 feet; Reserve 3982, Censor's decision; review and certificate issued, 2 March 1938; distributor: the Revd Fr Horgan. Montgomery view this film with Monsignor Cronin and Fr Horgan on 1 February 1938, and it was deemed 'unsuitable for public exhibition' and asked Fr Horgan 'not to show it'. At Fr Horgan's request Montgomery 'gave permission for two reels dealing with Minor Orders to be shown. A Special Cert. was issued with this endorsement: Reels 1 and 2 dealing with Minor Orders may be shown to Special Audiences at exhibition where '"The Call" is also shown.' Exception was also taken to 'The Host' in reel 4. A slightly cryptic additional note states that the Provincial (or Head) of the CSSP Order called and said that 'as the film was intended for a Catholic audience – it altered matters,' suggesting non-theatrical exhibition to Catholics only of this dubbed French film.

15. Record 11869; 6,252 feet, Reserve 3858; Censor's decision, 17/18 June 1937; review, 19 June 1937, when Monsignor Cronin attended the screening; certificate issued on 16 July 1937; distributor: British Lion.

16. The observation was made in the report of the musical drama *I am Suzanne* (Rowland V. Lee, 1933). Record 7673 and 16606; 7,847 feet, Reserve 2871; Censor's decision, 9 June 1934; Appeal Board decision, 22 June 1934, passed with cuts; review, 26 June 1934; certificate issued, 5 July 1934; distributor: Fox Film Co. With the 'materialisation of Christ,' nudity was the other prohibition introduced by the BBFC in 1913, as discussed in chapter 2.

17. Stephen Heath, 'Narrative Space', in *Questions of Cinema*, London: Macmillan, 1981. For a collection of stimulating essays on the subject of challenging the dominant scopic regime, see Dia Art Foundation, Discussions in Contemporary Culture, Number 2: Hal Foster (ed.), *Vision and Visuality*, Seattle: Bay Press, 1988.

18. Walter Benjamin, 'The Work of Art in the Age of Mechanical Reproduction' (1935), in Gerald Mast, Marshall Cohen and Leo Braudy (eds), *Film Theory and Criticism*, 1992.

19. Male nudity in Hollywood is, and has always been under-represented. The crude, if not entirely accurate, formulation is that the female is the bearer of the look, and the male is the looker. The germinal intervention in this debate was Laura Mulvey's 'Visual Pleasure and Narrative Cinema' (1975), in *Visual and Other Pleasures*, Bloomington: Indiana UP, 1990, which since then has been developed by other feminists film theorists such as Kaja Silverman, Gaylyn Studlar, and Linda Williams. This issue of the 'scopophilic look' is explored in chapter 7 in a discussion of the relationship between 'video nasties,' pornography, and mainstream commercial cinema.

20. Record 1716 and 6871; 7,770 feet, Reserve 642; Reject 265; Censor's decision, 11 September 1929; review, 2 December 1929; Appeal Board viewing, 6 December 1929; distributor: Wardour.

21. Record 2452 and 22548; 7,528 feet, Reserve 812; Censor's decision, 24 March 1930; review, 31 May 1930; Appeal Board viewing, 31 May 1930; distributor: Allied Artists.

22. Record 10632; 7,817 feet, Reserve 3651; Censor's decision, 6 July 1936; review, 14 August 1936; certificate issued on 14 August 1936; distributor: Warner Bros; Censor: AB.

23. Record H3560, 6,045 feet; Reserve 1; Censor's decision, 4 January 1928; review, 13 June 1928; distributor: Ivvy Metro. Montgomery recorded that the film 'barely escapes rejection'.

24. Record 3146 and 24570; 9,243 feet, Reserve 1039; Censor's decision, 6 October 1930; review and certificate issued on 1 November 1930 (James Holloway); distributor: Paramount.

25. Record 6718 and 14568, 8,394 feet; Reserve 2462; Reject 948; Censor's decision, 4 August 1930; Appeal Board decision, 21 November 1933; certificate issued on 6 December 1933; distributor: Warner Bros.

26. Record 7334 and 16967, 6,350 feet; Reject 994; Censor's decision, 13 February 1934; no appeal lodged; no certificate issued; distributor: Paramount.

27. Record F1590 (Reject Book 2), 9,661 feet; Reject 38, Censor's decision, 24 June 1926; distributor: Fox Film Co.

28. Record 8805 and 12893; 8,927 feet, Reserve 3263; Censor's decision, 11 March 1935; Appeal Board decision, 17 May 1935; certificate issued on 25 May 1935; distributor: Warner Bros.

29. Record 10609; 6,710 feet, Reserve 3650; Censor's decision, 2 July 1936; Appeal Board decision, 15 September 1936; review, 13 October 1936; certificate issued on 2 November 1936; distributor: Elliman.

30. Record 5795 and 6667; 1,733 feet, Reserve 2444 and 2494; Censor's decision, 21 July 1933 and 28 August 1933; Appeal Board decision, 19 September 1933; certificate issued on 21 September 1933; distributor: MGM.

31. Record 9826 and 12267; 7,655 feet, Reserve 3502; Censor's decision, 29 November 1935; review, 4 and/or 11 December 1935; certificate issued on 31 December 1935; distributor: Empire.

32. Record H3718; 8,344 feet, Reserve 41; Censor's decision, 20 July 1928; review, 27 July 1928; distributor: Fox Film Co. Montgomery wrote of this highly influential film, 'I have never ordered cuts with greater reluctance.'

33. Record 4186; 8,340 feet, Reserve 1458; Censor's decision, 26 June 1931; review, 9 July 1931; certificate issued on 10 July 1931; distributor: Wardour.

34. Record 11969 and 34326; 5,857 feet, Reserve 3876; Censor's decision, 19 July 1937; review 27 July 1937; distributor: MGM.

35. Record 11793; Reserve 3835; Censor's decision, 19 May 1937; review, 14 December 1937; certificate issued on 15 December 1937; distributor: RKO Radio.

36. Record 12751; 9,995 feet, Reserve 3998; Censor's decision, 25 February 1938; review, 19 March 1938; certificate issued on 21 March 1938; distributor: 20th Century-Fox.

37. Record C1076, 8,244 feet; Reject 53, Censor's decision, 4 November 1924; passed with cuts after appeal; distributor: Gaumont.

38. Censor's decision, 22 June and 23 June 1936.

39. Censor's decision, 1 August 1933; Interest certificate 6712; distributor: Paramount.

40. Ibid.

41. The idea that the more one increases the size of an image, the more it reveals, is treated in *Blow-Up* (Michelangelo Antonioni, 1966, GB/Italy), a film a later Censor banned.

42. Record 3146 and 24570; 9,243 feet, Reserve 1039; Censor's decision, 6 October 1930; review and certificate issued on 1 November 1930 (James Holloway); distributor: Paramount.

43. Benjamin, 'The Work of Art in the Age of Mechanical Reproduction', 1935.

44. Thekla J. Beere, *Journal of the Statistical and Social Enquiry Society of Ireland*, 89th session, 1935–36:97.

45. 'Stars Get in Your Eyes', *Framework*, no. 25, 1986; 'Aspects of the Los Angelesation of Ireland', *Irish Communications Review*, vol. 1, 1991.

46. See, for example, the Lenten Pastorals issued by Irish bishops during the 1920s and 1930s.

47. Declan Kiberd, *Inventing Ireland: The Literature of the Modern Nation*, London: Vintage, 1996:103.

48. Record 15253; 9,704 feet, Reserve 4465 and 4476; Censor's decision, 21 May 1940 and 29 May 1940; certificate issued on 5 June 1940. Trailer: 211 feet; Censor's decision, 4 June 1940; distributor: Warner Bros.

49. *Dáil debates*, vol. 3, col. 757, 10 May 1923.

50. Robertson 1985:186–88.

51. Record H3633; 7,465 feet, Reserve 20; Censor's decision, 26 January 1928; review, 7 January 1929; distributor: Express.

52. Robertson 1985:59. *King Kong* was certified 'A' rather than 'H' in Britain. For a more extended discussion of the censors treatment of horror see chapter 5.

53. Record 6428 and 18458; 9,236 feet, Reserve 2336; Censor's decision, 29 April 1933; review, 5 September 1933; certificate issued on 10 October 1933; distributor: RKO Radio.

54. Record 14939; 10,430 feet, Reserve 4417; Censor's decision, 2 April 1940; review, 9 April 1940; certificate issued on 10 April 1940; distributor: RKO Radio. A 1936 article in *Kine Weekly* entitled 'Running Times in Irish Cinema; Films "Hacked" by Censor' (15 October 1936) reported on what the trade paper characterized as 'an increasing amount of protests from Irish cinemagoers' at the cutting of films. It added that there was 'a considerable body of public opinion in favour of the introduction of the 'A' and 'U' system of classification which obtained in England, while another issue 'which has been the subject of vigorous letters' in the Irish press was that the single Censor should be replaced by a 3-person Censorship Board, a proposal which was also promoted over thirty years later by Ciaran Carty (see chapter 5).

55. James Montgomery, 'Film Censorship in the Irish Free State', 9 December 1936:2. This report was prepared at the request of Monsignor M.J. Curran, Irish College, Rome for presentation at a Catholic Cinema Congress due to take place in Rome on 17–19 December 1936, which according to a letter from Curran to Montgomery dated 27 November 1936, was 'to bring about an exchange of views as to the best ways to carry out the views expressed' by the Pope in the Papal Encyclical on the cinema, *Vigilanti Cura*, published the previous April. The Congress was postponed until January 1937 due to the illness of the Pope, as Curran stated in a letter to Montgomery on 14 December 1936. (Correspondence, OFC.)

56. Reserve 4561–2; James Montgomery, 22 August 1940.

57. See Kevin Rockett, Luke Gibbons, and John Hill, *Cinema and Ireland*, London: Croom Helm, 1987; London: Routledge, 1988 for the history of film production in Ireland and for discussion of the representations of the Irish in British and American cinemas. See also, Kevin Rockett, *The Irish Filmography: Fiction Films 1896–1996*, Dublin: Red Mountain Media, 1996, for entries on a comprehensive range of fiction films produced worldwide about the Irish.

58. In his report to the Minister for Justice for 1935, he stated wearily that 'there are the usual vague rumours of production being started in Ireland.' (8 January 1936.)

59. This comment was included in the Censor's report on *Outside of Paradise*. Record 13178; Censor's decision, rejected, 30 June 1938; passed with 'slight cut' by Appeal Board, 14 July 1938; distributor: British Lion.

60. Record G3237 (Reject Book 2), Reject 121, Censor's decision, 14 September 1927; distributor: Whelan.

61. Record 1872 and 5012; 10,285 feet, Reject 257; Censor's decision, 23 October 1929; Appeal Board decision, 29 October 1929; distributor: Lasky.

62. Irish-American groups picketed cinemas where the film was being shown and threatened to boycott those associated with it. See Joseph M. Curran, *Hibernian Green on the Silver Screen: The Irish and American Movies*, New York/Westport, Connecticut/London: Greenwood Press, 1989:34–35.

63. Record G3317 (Reject Book 2); Reject 124, Censor's decision, 10 August 1927; distributor: MGM.

64. Censor's decision, 14 March 1928.

65. Record G3049 (Reject Book 2), Reject 122, Censor's decision, 26 September 1927; distributor: Warner Bros.

66. Record 3852 and 18197; 7,160 feet, Reserve 1397 and 1418/19; Censor's decision 13 May 1931; review, 2 June 1931, 6/7 July 1931; distributor: RKO Radio.

67. Record 17406; 6,338 feet, Reserve 5299 and 5300; Censor's decision 21 October 1942; review, 4 November 1942; certificate issued on 12 November 1942; distributor: Paramount.

68. *Bioscope*, 13 February 1929:45.
69. Record 1501; Reserve 598 and 601; 6,117 feet, Censor's decision, 30 July 1929; review, 28 February 1930; certificate issued on 12 March 1930; distributor: Wardour.
70. Reserve 2677; 7,927 feet, Censor's decision, 27 January 1934; reviewed, 1 February 1934 and 10 February 1934; certificate on 3 May 1934.
71. 'A very good first attempt,' Report of the Official Film Censor for 1936 to the Minister for Justice, dated 12 January 1937.
72. Record 2372 and 16883; 7,922 feet, Reject 284; Censor's decision, 18 March 1930. There was no appeal. No certificate was issued; distributor: Wardour.
73. Record 9270 and 16988; 8,481 feet, Reject 1218; Censor's decision 28 June 1935; Appeal Board decision, 7 or 9 July 1935; certificate issued on 22 July 1935; distributor: RKO Radio. 'Nest-fouling' was Montgomery's description of Liam O'Flaherty's novel. See also chapter 8.
74. See Burns-Bisogno, *Censorsing Irish Nationalism*, 1997: 67–77. The film was banned in British Malaysia, Guatamala, Hungary, Palestine and Peru, ibid. 72.
75. In the *Limerick Chronicle* (12 November 1930:5) there is a report on the events surrounding the storming of the Athenaeum Hall, Limerick on 10 November when about a dozen men forced their way into the hall during the screening of *Juno and the Paycock*. Two reels of the film were taken from the projection box and destroyed in the street. It was understood, the report stated, that the film 'contained scenes which were considered objectionable and were the cause of the destruction of a considerable portion of the film.' The lessee of the hall, John Cronin, appealed to the 'large audience' to resume their seats, but the screening was subsequently cancelled. At the weekly meeting of the Arch-Confraternity of the Holy Family prior to the attack on the hall, Fr Murray CSSR made reference to the film which he said 'contained objectionable features, and advised the men not to patronise it, and to see it was not witnessed by their children.' He added that 'this was the best way of showing disapproval and not in violent methods, which could not be condoned.' As the prayer meeting took place before the attack on the cinema, Fr Murray seems to have planted the seed of the action in the attackers' minds. A shopkeeper, Stephen Kennedy, was charged with destroying the film. At a court hearing later in the month it was reported that the film had been withdrawn in Derry and Waterford, and that there were protests in Dublin. (*Chronicle*, 25 November 1930.)
76. Record 1832; 8,501 feet, Censor's decision and certificate issued, 9 October 1929; distributor: Universal. For an account of that controversy see Rockett et al., 1987:53–55.
77. Record 13178; Censor's decision, rejected, 30 June 1938; passed with 'slight cut' by Appeal Board, 14 July 1938; distributor: British Lion.
78. Report of the Official Film Censor from 1 November 1923 to 31 October 1924 to the Minister for Justice, dated 13 November 1924, OFC.
79. Report of the Official Film Censor for 1927 to the Minister for Justice, dated 18 January 1928:2, OFC.
80. Report of the Official Film Censor for 1929 to the Minister for Justice, dated 8 January 1930, OFC.
81. *Seanad debates*, vol. 13, col. 1014, 7 May 1930.
82. *Irish Cinema Handbook*, 1943:94.
83. *Dáil debates*, vol. 34, col. 987, 11 April 1930.
84. Ibid. col. 988.
85. Ibid. col. 992–93.
86. Ibid. col. 994.
87. *Seanad debates*, vol. 13, col. 1008–9, 7 May 1930.
88. Report of the Official Film Censor for 1931 to the Minister for Justice, dated 14 January 1932, OFC. One of the areas of concern as regards brutality was 'All-in Wrestling,' a genre which made a reappearance in the late 1990s when extremely violent wrestling videos were banned or rated over-18s by the censors. Rather dramatically, Montgomery warned a distributor as he rejected a *Fox Newsreel* with 'All-in Wrestling' ('all out'): 'Don't import – forbidden by police.' (Edition 218A, Censor's decision, 25 October 1934.) The same warning was given to *Pathé Newsreel* shortly afterwards (Edition 34/94, Censor's decision, 22 November 1934), while feature films such as *Swing Your Lady* (Ray Enright, 1938), which included 'even a glimpse' of 'all-in wrestling,' were cut. (Censor's decision, 31 October 1938 and 1 December 1938.) 'All-in Wrestling' remained an issue throughout the 1930s. In his report for 1935 he declared that 'unfortunately the growing taste for brutality has even reached the news and interest films, where murderous gladiatorial displays of "All-in Wrestling" are becoming common.' (Report of the Official Film Censor for 1935 to the Minister for Justice, dated 8 January 1936, OFC.)

89. From undated handwritten draft of the Censor's report for 1931 as page 2 of the typed report is missing from files; dated 11 January 1932, OFC.
90. Report of the Official Film Censor for 1931:3, to the Minister for Justice, dated 14 January 1932, OFC.
91. Ibid. 1.
92. Record 4763 and 25832; 6,125 feet, Reserve 1961; Censor's decision, 8 December 1931; review, 3 March 1932; certificate issued on 4 March 1932; distributor: Warner Bros. Montgomery made six cuts to the film, but it should also be noted that in the USA local censorship boards cut this and other gangster films even after their approval by the Hays Office. For example, in New York, American cinema's most important market, censors cut the scene in *The Public Enemy* where 'Putty Nose' hands Tom and Matt a gun, removed all scenes of the warehouse robbery, cut the scenes showing the boys being paid off after the government liquor robbery, edited out most of the scene of Tom killing 'Putty Nose,' and dropped the seduction of Tom by one of Paddy's 'girls' and Tom's slapping her around. See Gregory D. Black, *Hollywood Censored: Morality Codes, Catholics, and the Movies*, Cambridge: Cambridge UP, 1994:121.
93. Report of the Official Film Censor for 1931:3, to the Minister for Justice, dated 14 January 1932, OFC.
94. Record 4208 and 5520; 9,117 feet, Reserve 1476; Reject 498; Censor's decision, 8 July 1931; review, 24 July 1931; Appeal Board ban after appeal against cuts, 24 July 1931. No certificate issued; distributor: Paramount. Of the 127 films banned by Montgomery in 1929, 53 were comedies, as he notes in his Report of the Official Film Censor for 1929 to the Minister for Justice, dated 8 January 1930:1.
95. Reserve 2190; 6,050 feet, Censor's decision, 3 January 1933; reviewed, 19 January 1933; certificate issued on 24 January 1933; distributor: Paramount.
96. Scott Siegel and Barbara Siegel, *American Film Comedy: From Abbott & Costello to Jerry Zucker*, New York: Prentice Hall, 1994:188.
97. Mikail Bakhtin, 'Epic and Novel', in *The Dialogical Imagination*, Austin: University of Texas Press, 1981:23.
98. French psychoanalyst Jacques Lacan (1901–1981) uses the term Symbolic to describe the social structures within society – such as family relations, language, law – into which a child enters (after it has passed from the realm of the mother, and the pre-language Imaginary).
99. See Robert Stam, *Subversive Pleasures: Bakhtin, Cultural Criticism, and Film*, Baltimore and London: John Hopkins UP, 1989; pb:1992.
 1. Record G2864 (Reject Book 2), 6,658 feet; Reject 98, Censor's decision, 27 May 1927; distributor: Lasky.
 2. See Black, 1994.
 3. See ibid. 1994:84 ff.
 4. Jack Vizzard, *See No Evil: Life Inside a Hollywood Censor*, New York: Simon & Schuster, 1970:207–8.
 5. Black, 1994:37.
 6. Ibid. 39.
 7. Ibid. 39–40.
 8. William Halsey in *The Survival of American Innocence: Catholicism in an Era of Disillusionment, 1920–1940*, Notre Dame: University of Notre Dame Press, 1980:107–11, quoted Black 1994:41.
 9. As is discussed in the next chapter, Censor Richard Hayes gave explicit support for such a 'realist' cinema.
 10. The full Code is reproduced in Leonard J. Leff and Jerold L. Simmons, *The Dame in the Kimono: Hollywood, Censorship, and the Production Code from the 1920s to the 1960s*, New York: Anchor Books, Doubleday, 1990: 283–92.
 11. Ibid. 284.
 12. Will H. Hays, *The Memoirs of Will H. Hays*, New York: Doubleday & Co., 1955:449–50.
 13. For a comprehensive account of the activities of the Legion of Decency, see Black, 1994 and Black, 1998.
 14. Evelyn Bolster, *The Knights of Saint Columbanus*, 1979:53. The National Film Institute of Ireland issued film ratings from 1948 until the 1970s.
 15. Report of the Official Film Censor for 1932 to the Minister for Justice, dated January 1933:1, OFC.
 16. Montgomery was not impressed. In his report on *G-Men*, he wrote that 'this has really all the ingredients that made the gangster film such a menace. Gun play is a horror no matter who pulls the trigger. It is part of the cheapness of human life for which gun play films are blamed ... Deal with

the final shooting with great restraint, remembering the outcry in the [Irish Free State] about these scenes.' (Record 9362 and 14279; 7,694 feet, Reserve 3411; Censor's decision, 24 July 1935; passed with six cuts after appeal; Appeal Board decision, 3 September 1935; certificate issued on 19 September 1935; distributor: Warner Bros.)

17. Report of the Official Film Censor for 1935 to the Minister for Justice, dated 8 January 1936, OFC.
18. Report of the Official Film Censor for 1932 to the Minister for Justice, dated January 1933, OFC.
19. Report of the Official Film Censor for 1933 to the Minister for Justice, dated January 1934, OFC.
20. Report of the Official Film Censor for 1934 to the Minister for Justice, dated 7 January 1935, OFC.
21. Record 8291 and 21153; 6,343 feet, Reserve 3113; Censor's decision, 29 October 1934; reviewed, 28 November 1934; certificate issued on 29 November 1934.
22. Report of the Official Film Censor for 1935 to the Minister for Justice, dated 8 January 1936: 1.
23. Letter to W. Cresswell Reilly, dated 18 May 1936. Besides his contact with the Australian Film Censor, Montgomery was also in regular contact with the BBFC, as is demonstrated by a friendly exchange of letters in 1932 between Montgomery and J. Brooke Wilkinson, Secretary of the BBFC, enclosing their respective annual reports. Montgomery to Brooke Wilkinson, 19 January 1932, in which he refers to his report to the minister as 'a privileged comment,' something which, of course, has not been published until now; Brooke Wilkinson wrote to Montgomery, 22 January 1932, in which he commented that Montgomery's report 'bears out, in great measure, the difficulties we have also had to contend with.' Brooke Wilkinson again wrote to Montgomery, 16 February 1932, in which the BBFC's report for 1931 was enclosed. (Correspondence, OFC.)
24. Robertson 1985:180–82.
25. Record 11704; 6,941 feet, Reject 1302; Censor's decision, 13 April 1937; Appeal Board viewing, 20 April 1937; review, 15 June 1937; certificate issued on 27 August 1937; distributor: GFD.
26. Report of the Official Film Censor for 1937 to the Minister for Justice, dated 12 January 1938, OFC.
27. Report of the Official Film Censor for 1938 to the Minister for Justice, dated 11 January 1939, OFC.
28. Ibid.
29. Report of the Official Film Censor for 1939 to the Minister for Justice, dated 10 January 1940, OFC.
30. Quoted, Thomas P. Gallagher, 'Our First Film Censor', in *Irish Cinema Handbook*, 1943:94–95.
31. There is a copy of the booklet in the National Library of Ireland. The subscribers to the booklet are headed by Douglas Hyde, President of Ireland, and included literary, legal, academic, political and film trade persons. A surplus of £646 was sent to Montgomery, who was unable to attend the function held in his honour due to illness. On 14 January 1941, Montgomery wrote to J.T. O'Farrell, chairman of the Appeal Board, who chaired the Presentation Committee, to thank him for the souvenir programme and the cheque.
32. T.C. Murray, *Irish Press*, 17 March 1943:3. Murray also reported him as describing Anglo-Irish fiction with 'its exploitation of the unsavoury element of life,' as 'the new lecherature'.
33. Anon., 'Death of Film Censor', *Irish Times*, 15 March 1943:1.
34. Montgomery, 1942:420.
35. 'It will be necessary to keep carefully in mind in reaching a decision,' de Valera wrote to the Minister for Finance, Seán MacEntee, 'the type of film which will be produced. We must guard against the danger of the enterprise being used for the production of plays which would be regarded as hurtful from the national point of view.' Letter dated 25 November 1937, in file S13914A, 'Film Production in Ireland: Proposals by Outside Peoples and Bodies,' NAI.
36. Fr Cormac had been in contact with de Valera's private secretary, Ms O'Connell, on 2 October 1946. Archbishop McQuaid had also been in communication on the matter with de Valera's office. These proposals originated from the peculiar alliance of writer George Bernard Shaw and film producer Gabriel Pascal, who had produced an adaptation of Shaw's *Pygmalion*, for which the Irishman won an Academy Award for best screenplay in 1938. Correspondence and memos concerning the protracted studio affair during 1946–47 are in file S13914A, NAI. Fr Cormac was the brother of the fourth Official Film Censor, Liam O'Hora, who took up the post in 1956.
37. Montgomery, 1942:424–25.
38. Ibid. 423.
39. Record 6890 and 30461; 9,255 feet, Reject 346; Censor's decision, 16 September 1930; no appeal; distributor: Wardour.
40. Montgomery, 1942:424.

41. Ibid. 425.
42. J.H. Whyte, *Church and State in Modern Ireland, 1923–79*, Dublin: Gill and Macmillan, second edition, 1980:60–61; orig., 1971.
43. *Seanad debates*, vol. 13, cols. 1009–10, 7 May 1930.
44. At least according to William Magennis. (*Seanad debates*, vol. 11, col. 1647, 15 May 1925.) There is an extensive popular and academic literature on film censorship, especially in the two countries, Britain and the USA, whose film production and film censorship policies most affected Ireland. See the bibliography for a selection of these studies. Unlike in Ireland, in the film production centres of those countries there was, at least for a while, resistance to film censorship.
45. Magennis, 1944:55.

CHAPTER 4

1. The Bellman, *The Bell*, vol. 3, no. 2, November 1941:109.
2. Hugh Hunt, *The Abbey: Ireland's National Theatre*, Dublin: Gill and Macmillan, 1979:161.
3. Dublin: Sinn Féin, February 1918.
4. Official Film Censor's report to Minister for Justice, 21 January 1941, OFC.
5. Phelps, 1975:39.
6. Montgomery, 1942:422.
7. *Dáil debates*, vol. 98, col. 306, 17 October 1945:21. It can be noted in passing that Boland, along with others who had a direct influence on film censorship, including William Magennis and Kevin O'Higgins, were members of the secretive and conservative Knights of St Columbanus (Evelyn Bolster, *The Knights of Saint Columbanus*, Dublin: Gill and Macmillan, 1979:117). Indeed, the first chairman of the Catholic body, the National Film Institute of Ireland, Dermot J. O'Flynn, was a Supreme Knight of St Columbanus.
8. Record 18177, 5,211 feet, Reserve 5669, Censor's decision, 12 August 1943; review, 3 December 1943; certificate issued on 6 December 1943; distributor: 20th Century-Fox.
9. Record 18512 and 18542, 6,227 feet, Reserve 5905, Censor's decision, ten cuts, 18 February 1944; Reject 1712, 2 March 1944; review, 2 March 1944; ban upheld after appeal, 21 March 1944; distributor: Columbia.
10. Record 19122, 6,353 feet, Reject 1769, 29 November 1944; passed after appeal, 12 December 1944; certificate issued on 1 January 1945; distributor: GFD.
11. Record 19245, 10,070 feet, Reject 1777, Censor's decision, 20 December 1944; passed after appeal, 16 January 1945; Reserve 6325, passed with four cuts under Emergency Powers Order, 18 January 1945; review, 23 January 1945 and 10 April 1945; certificate issued on 2 February 1945; distributor: Warner Bros.
12. Record 20617, 5,700 feet, Reserve 6778, Censor's decision, 14 May 1946; review, 23 May 1945; certificate issued on 27 May 1946; distributor: Egan Film Service.
13. *Dáil debates*, vol. 143, col. 2019, 10 December 1953.
14. Record 21680; 14,653 feet; Reject 1870, 4 June 1947; Appeal Board decision and Censor's report, 15 July 1947; certificate issued on 12 August 1947; distributor: British Lion. Four of the Appeal Board's cuts remain unknown, but almost certainly concern Garance's promiscuous life and Baptiste's unfaithfulness. The version of the film submitted to the Irish Censor, 14,653 feet, is slightly longer than the British release version, 14,500 feet (161 minutes), listed in *Monthly Film Bulletin* (1946:173), but still considerably shorter than the original version, 17,039 feet (188 minutes).
15. Despite this comment Hayes passed the film with cuts two years later. Record 27846; 9,154 feet, Reject 1943, Censor's decision, 23 May 1951; Ban upheld after appeal, 5 June 1951; re-submitted in 1953, 9,153 feet, Reserve 8403, passed with five cuts, 5 February 1953; certificate issued, 9 February 1953; distributor: Warner Bros.
16. Reject 1962, Censor's decision, 30 May 1952; ban upheld after appeal, 10 June 1952; Distributor: Paramount.
17. Record 24123; 9,704 feet, 'revised version,' 9,063 feet, Reject 1910, Censor's decision, 25 March 1949. The film had received an over-16s 'A' certificate in Britain, with *Monthly Film Bulletin* (1948:102) commenting that 'though the subject is terrible it should not be avoided.'
18. Appeal Board decision, 10 May 1949.
19. Reserve 7601–03, Censor's decision, 7 September 1949; review and certificate issued, 26 October 1949; distributor: 20th Century-Fox.
20. Reject 2132, 11,014 feet, Censor's decision, 12 November 1956; ban upheld after appeal, 8 January 1957; Re-submitted in 1962: Record 35827, Reserve 10460, Censor's decision, 4 January 1962;

certificate issued on 7 February 1962. In Britain it received an 'X' certificate. For a synopsis of the story see *Monthly Film Bulletin*, 1956:112.

21. However, almost simultaneous with this interview, Hayes passed uncut the prestigious but controversial *Citizen Kane* (Orson Welles, 1941), even though the narrative is based on the real-life relationship between newspaper tycoon Randolph Hearst and his mistress, actress Marion Davies. (Record 16463, 10,736 feet; Censor's decision, 16 October 1941; certificate issued on 17 December 1941; distributor: RKO Radio.)

22. The Bellman, *The Bell*, vol. 3, no. 2, November 1941:112.

23. *The Standard*, 27 August 1943:3.

24. Record 17783; Reserve 5467–68, 10,540 feet, Censor's decision, 11 March1943; review, 12 July 1943; certificate issued on 10 August 1943; distributor: B. McNally. When the film was re-submitted for a certificate in 1969, these cuts continued to be demanded; Letter to Elliman Films, 16 September 1969. (Correspondence, OFC.)

25. The Bellman, *The Bell*, vol. 3, no. 2, November 1941:108.

26. For Claire Johnston, Arzner's films represent women determining their own identity 'through transgression and desire' as they search for an independent existence 'beyond and outside the discourse of the male.' Claire Johnston, 'Dorothy Arzner: Critical Strategies', in *The Work of Dorothy Arzner: Towards a Feminist Cinema*, Claire Johnston (ed.), London: BFI, 1975:4. For a detailed analysis of *Dance, Girl, Dance*, see Pam Cook, 'Approaching the Work of Dorothy Arzner', in ibid.

27. Record 15593, 8,014 feet, Reject 1448, Censor's decision (Montgomery), 23 October 1940; Censor's decision (Hayes), 18 January 1941; ban upheld after appeal, 18 February 1941; distributor: RKO Radio.

28. Record 15797, Reserve 4631 and 4646, Censor's decision, 17 December 1940; review, 7 January 1941 (Reserve 4646); review 5 February 1941 (4631); review and certificate issued, 28 January 1941; distributor: MGM.

29. Record 15769, 872 feet, Reserve 4625, Censor's decision, 11 December 1940; certificate issued on 30 December 1940; distributor: Columbia.

30. *Road to Zanzibar* (Victor Schertzinger, 1941), Record 16176, Reserve 4780, Censor's decision, 28 May 1941; *Road to Morocco* (David Butler, 1942) 17579, Reserve 5364, 17 December 1942 and 25 January 1943; *Road to Utopia* (Hal Walker, 1945), Record 20057, Reserve 6605, Censor's decision, 26 October 1945; *Road to Singapore* (Victor Schertzinger, 1940), Record 28434, Reserve 8537, Censor's decision, 1 September 1953. The cuts were often of dancers.

31. Record, 18487, 6,826 feet, Reserve 5873; Censor's decision, 14 January 1944; review, 21 January 1944, 15 February 1944; certificate issued on 27 January 1944; distributor: 20th Century-Fox.

32. Record 19046, 10,084 feet, Reserve 6213; Censor's decision, 6 October 1944; review, 17 October 1944, 10 November 1944; certificate issued on 13 November 1944; distributor: Warner Bros.

33. Record 19985, 10,165 feet, Reserve 6594; Censor's decision, 17 October 1945; review, 26 October 1945; certificate issued on 30 October 1945; distributor: Paramount.

34. Record 27214, 9,238 feet, Reserve 8251, Censor's decision, 19 May 1952; review and certificate issued on 20 June 1952; distributor: MGM.

35. The Bellman, *The Bell*, vol. 3, no. 2, November 1941:109.

36. Record 16271, 8,277 feet, Reserve 4815, Censor's decision, 3 July 1941; review, 3 September 1941; certificate issued on 4 September 1941; distributor: Paramount.

37. Record 16131, 6,708 feet, Reserve 4764, Censor's decision, 1 May 1941; review, 14 May 1941; certificate issued on 15 May 1941; distributor: Warner Bros.

38. Record 16643; 7,308 feet, Reserve 4949; Censor's decision, 27 November 1941; review, 9 January 1942; certificate issued on 13 February 1942; distributor: MGM.

39. Record 17223; 6,016 feet; Reserve 5175 (Emergency Powers Order), 30 July 1942; certificate issued on 8 October 1942. The following year he ordered *Striptease Lady* (William Wellman, 1943) to be changed to *Lady of Burlesque*. (Record 18220; 8,214 feet, Reserve 5706, Censor's decision, 7 September 1943; review, 14 September 1943; certificate issued on 5 October 1943; distributor: United Artists.)

40. Record 16027, 5,820 feet; Reserve 4737, Censor's decision, 2 April 1947; certificate issued on 23 April 1941; distributor: Pathé.

41. The Bellman, *The Bell*, vol. 3, no. 2, November 1941:113.

42. Record 16544, 5,528 feet; Reject 1498, Censor's decision, 29 October 1941; review, 15 November 1941; certificate issued on 19 November 1941; distributor: 20th Century-Fox. Note in Register says, 'Suspend 1498; film cut by renter' (no date), which suggests that after the 29 October rejection, the distributor re-submitted a cut version without Hayes issuing a formal cuts list and this was subsequently viewed and approved on 15 November.

43. Record 16575, 8,421 feet, Reject 1500, Censor's decision, 7 November 1941; Appeal Board decision, 18 November 1941; distributor: Paramount.
44. Record 25838, 8,069 feet, Reject 1933, Censor's decision, 9 March 1951; Reserve 7928, Censor's decision, 15 March 1951. Passed with cuts after review of re-edited version; certificate issued on 16 March 1951; distributor: Republic.
45. Record 28074, 8,792 feet, Reject 1984, Censor's decision, 29 April 1953; no appeal; distributor: 20th Century-Fox. Re-submitted in June 1964: passed with cuts.
46. 7,499 feet, Reject 1917, Censor's decision, 11 May 1949; distributor: GFD.
47. Record 17081, 6,696 feet, Reject 1540, Censor's decision, 18 June 1942; passed after appeal; certificate issued on 1 July 1942; distributor: 20th Century-Fox.
48. Record 17397, 8,701 feet, Reject 1573, Censor's decision, 30 September 1942; Appeal Board decision, 1 December 1942; certificate issued on 14 December 1942; distributor: Warner Bros.
49. Record 21296, 11,111 feet, Reserve 6993, Censor's decision, 13 February 1947; review, 2 April 1947; certificate issued on 11 April 1947; distributor: MGM.
50. 9,921 feet, Reject 1886, Censor's decision, 19 April 1948; ban reversed after appeal, 27 April 1948; certificate issued on 30 April 1948; distributor: British Lion.
51. The Bellman, *The Bell*, vol. 3, no. 2, November 1941:109.
52. Record 26412, 7,041 feet, Reject 1948, Censor's decision, 31 August 1951; ban reversed after appeal and certificate issued, 9 October 1951; distributor: International Film Distributors.
53. Record 26415, 7,140 feet, Reject 1950, Censor's decision, 28 September 1950; ban upheld after appeal, 30 October 1951; distributor: British Lion.
54. Record 20249, 8,164 feet; Reserve 6739, Censor's decision, 1 April 1946; review, 4 April 1946; certificate issued on 5 April 1946; distributor: GFD.
55. Record 20740, 11,085 feet, Reject 1842, Censor's decision, 8 July 1946; Appeal Board decision and Censor's report, 17 September 1946; distributor: Paramount.
56. Record 20509, 10,216 feet, Reserve 6741–42, Reject 1930 after renter refused to accept fourteen cuts in reels 4–6, Censor's decision, 3 April 1946; Appeal Board decision, cuts confirmed, 30 April 1946; review, 7 May 1946, cuts 'were not in accordance with instructions'; review, 22 May 1946; certificate issued on 23 May 1946; distributor: Warner Bros.
57. Record 22060, 7,469 feet, Reject 1880, 22 October 1947; Appeal Board decision and Censor's report, 11 November 1947; certificate issued on 19 November 1947; distributor: Pathé.
58. Record 26412, 7,041 feet, Reject 1948, Censor's decision, 31 August 1951; ban reversed after appeal and certificate issued, 9 October 1951; distributor: International Film Distributors.
59. Record 16578; Reserve 4923, Censor's decision, 6 November 1941, 14 November 1941; certificate issued on 18 December 1941; distributor: MGM.
60. Record 24464, 8,788 feet, Reserve 7655, Censor's decision, 22 December 1949; review and certificate issued, 13 February 1950; distributor: MGM.
61. Record 25910, 5,700 feet, Reject 1935, Censor's decision, 14 March 1951; Appeal Board decision, 3 April 1951; distributor: Egan Film Service. In Britain, *Street Corner* was given an 'A' London certificate only with 'a didactic sequence showing the technique and biological effect of an abortion' excised. (*Monthly Film Bulletin*, 1950:88.) As the version submitted to the Irish Censor was the same length, 5,700 feet, as the film released in Britain, this abortion sequence seems not to have been seen by Hayes.
62. 6,844 feet, Reject 1940, Censor's decision, 2 May 1951; no appeal; trailer also banned; distributor: Warner Bros.
63. 9,289 feet, Reject 1949, Censor's decision, 20 September 1951; Appeal Board decision and Censor's report, 2 October 1951; re-submitted 'revised version,' Reserve 8160, Censor's decision, 4 January 1952; no certificate issued; distributor: Warner Bros.
64. Record 27380, 9,846 feet, Reserve 8296, Censor's decision 23 July 1952; certificate issued on 28 July 1952; distributor: Warner Bros.
65. Record 20051, 8,382 feet; Reserve 6634, Censor's decision, 26 November 1945; passed with cuts after appeal, 11 December 1945; review, 8 January 1946; certificate issued on 10 January 1946; distributor: GFD.
66. Record 25351, 8,870 feet, Reserve 7816, Censor's decision, 15 September 1950; review and certificate issued on 20 October 1950; distributor: United Artists.
67. Record 23441, 9,023 feet, Reserve 7461, Censor's decision, 28 February 1949, 3 March 1949; certificate issued on 25 March 1949; distributor: Paramount.
68. Record 26643, 6,733 feet; Reject 1953, Censor's decision 28 November 1951; ban was upheld after appeal, 15 January 1952; distributor: RKO Radio.

69. Feminist film critic Barbara Koenig Quant is far from impressed by Ida Lupino's work, commenting, for example, that the representation of the traumatic effects of the rape in *Outrage* is 'counterbalanced by the embarrassment of the miracle-working god-like hero that the heroine turns to for comfort, and by the film's extreme deference, obeisance, to male wisdom and authority.' (Barbara Koenig Quant, *Women Directors: The Emergence of a New Cinema*, New York/Westport, Conn./London: Praeger, 1989:26.) Commenting on *The Bigamist* (Ida Lupino, 1953), a 'sordid story' according to Hayes' deputy, E.C. Powell, who banned it (7,200 feet, Reject 2006, Censor's decision, 18 December 1953), a ban upheld by the Appeal Board (12 January 1954; distributor: Irish Film Agency), Quant claims that in this film Lupino 'again allows full expression of [her] profound sympathy for men,' with the man becoming a bigamist 'out of his goodhearted caring about women.' (Ibid. 27–28.) 'One is struck,' Quant (p. 28) observes, 'by the almost excessive goodness Lupino bestows on the male characters, especially the hero.' Notwithstanding these representations of sympathetic males, Hayes judged the films on their subject-matter alone, while accepting Lupino's *Hard, Fast, and Beautiful* (1951) with one cut of 'semi-nude pair' (Record 26510, 7,023 feet, Reserve 8111, Censor's decision, 25 October 1951; review and certificate issued, 13 November 1957; distributor: RKO Radio), probably because, as Quant (p. 27) puts it in contrast with a film with a similar theme, *Mildred Pierce*, in *Hard* 'the ambitious mother, associated with career ... [is] far more viciously ... denounced,' while her glamorous daughter gives up her career for marriage. Lupino's first film as producer, *Not Wanted* (Elmer Clifton, 1949), which concerns a teenager 'who picks up men in bars and becomes pregnant,' (Quant, p. 26) was banned by Hayes because of its theme even though it 'is worked out with a good deal of restraint and delicacy,' and as a consequence of the general certificate policy which would mean that 'young people and adolescents' would see it. (Record 25015, 8,136 feet, Reject 1926, Censor's decision, 5 June 1950; distributor: International Film Distributors.)

70. Record 19481, 9,888 feet, Reserve 6438; Censor's decision, 27 April 1945, review, 24 May 1945; certificate issued on 26 May 1945; distributor: MGM.

71. Record 15309, 11,660 feet; Reserve 4486, Censor's decision, 7 June 1940; review, 10 June 1940; certificate issued on 12 July 1940; distributor: 20th Century-Fox. In a comment after viewing the trailer, Montgomery said that the film was 'not entertainment,' and went on to observe, in relation to the Dust Bowl's disposed farmers and their dependency on both bankers and the vagaries of the weather, that 'America fought the Civil War to abolish slavery.' (16 August 1940.)

72. Record 16499, 8,917 feet, Reserve 5093, Censor's decision, 30 April 1941, 7 January 1942; certificate issued, 6 November 1941, 10 January 1942; distributor: RKO Radio. Other dates listed include review, 30 April 1942 and 15 May 1942, when reels 6, 7 and 8 (2,406 feet) were censored. Also viewed by Censor, 29 April 1958.

73. Booklet with the reissued De Luxe commemorative boxed video set, The Walt Disney Co., 1990:16.

74. Record 17653, 318 feet, Reserve 5402, 25 January 1943; certificate issued on 9 February 1943; distributor: Kodak (16mm).

75. Record 33180, Reserve 9841, Censor's decision, 15 October 1958; review and certificate issued, 25 October 1958; distributor: United Artists.

76. Record 33340, 7,217 feet; Reserve 9844, Censor's decision, 17 December 1958; review and certificate issued, 1 January 1959; distributor: Columbia.

77. Record 17890, 6,772 feet; Reserve 5521, Censor's decision, 29 April 1943; review, 3 May 1943; certificate issued on 6 May 1943; distributor: 20th Century-Fox. The title was also changed to *Strange Incident*.

78. Reserve 6751; Censor's decision, 10 April 1946; review, 2 May 1946, 29 June 1946; certificate issued on 8 May 1946; distributor: RKO Radio.

79. Record 20700, 9,626 feet; Reserve 6792; Censor's decision, 4 June 1946; review, 25 June 1946; certificate issued on 27 June 1946; distributor: MGM.

80. Record 21669, 9,049 feet; Reject 1871, Censor's decision, 12 June 1947; certificate issued on 9 July 1947; distributor: GFD. The film was later passed with undetermined cuts by the Appeal Board, 24 June 1947.

81. Record 18629, 14,043 feet; Reserve 5938; Censor's decision, 14 March 1944; review, 21 March 1944; certificate issued on 22 March 1944; distributor: 20th Century-Fox. There were two other cuts to the film. One was a shot of children with their clothes drawn up as they cross a stream. The word 'bottom' was also cut from the same scene. The film was reissued in 1945, 1946, 1949 and 1958 when the Censor also reviewed copies of the film.

82. Record 27374, 15,337 feet; Reserve 8293-94, Censor's decision, 17 July 1952; review, 4 September 1952; certificate issued on 24 October 1952; distributor: MGM.

83. Record 36122, 8,623 feet; Reject 1986, Censor's decision, 7 May 1953; distributor: Warner Bros. The information on Warner Bros cutting prior to submission is outlined in a letter dated 18 July 1956 from Warners' Dublin office to Miss Gleeson at the Film Censor's office when it was planned to re-release the film. This version of the film was passed by the Appeal Board on 24 July 1956.
84. Appeal Board decision, 3 June 1953. The Board divided with only three present when the film was first seen by them on 26 May 1953, thus necessitating a second viewing on 3 June.
85. See E. Ann Kaplan (ed.), *Women in Film Noir*, London: BFI, 1980.
86. For a discussion of such characters see Frank Krutnik, *In a Lonely Street: Film Noir, Genre, Masculinity*, London/New York: Routledge, 1991.
87. After initially demanding cut a choking scene in reel 2, this was later cancelled. Record 19335, 8,907 feet, Reserve 6375, Censor's decision, 15 February 1945; certificate issued on 21 March 1945.
88. Record 23688, 7,063 feet, Reserve 7511, Censor's decision, 12 May 1949; review, 30 June 1949; certificate issued on 24 August 1949; distributor: MGM.
89. The cuts mainly concerned Dix's (Humphrey Bogart) use of graphic language to describe murder. Record 24881, 8,365 feet; Reserve 7741, Censor's decision, 19 May 1950; review and certificate issued on 23 October 1950; distributor: Columbia.
90. The cuts were of a man being kicked while on the ground (in reel 9) and of a kiss in the following reel. Record 21157, 9,227 feet; Reserve 6948, Censor's decision, 22 November 1946; review, 25 November 1946; certificate issued on 28 November 1946; distributor: GFD.
91. Choking shots in reel 10 had to be toned down. Record 20291, 8,985 feet; Reserve 6714, Censor's decision, 28 February 1946; certificate issued on 15 March 1946; distributor: Paramount.
92. The end of the fight involving Richard Widmark and the communist (reel 9) had to be cut. Record 28198, 7,230 feet, Reserve 8483, Censor's decision, 8 June 1953; review and certificate issued , 12 June 1953; distributor; 20th Century-Fox.
93. A long strangulation scene involving Mansfield and Vendig had to be curtailed. Record 23190, 9,429 feet; Reserve 7411,Censor's decision, 11 January 1949.
94. A blow to the head from behind had to be cut from reel 9. Record 24836, 7,289 feet; Reserve 7719, Censor's decision, 1 April 1950; review and certificate issued on 3 May 1950; distributor: MGM.
95. A kiss had to be cut from reel 9. Record 23287, 8,562 feet, Reserve 7437, Censor's decision, 2 February 1949; certificate issued on 9 February 1949.
96. In reel 9 a choking shot had to be curtailed, while a scene shortly before between Debby and Stone had to be toned down. Record 28523, 8,052 feet; Reserve 8570, Censor's decision, 20 October 1953; certificate issued on 23 October 1953; distributor: Columbia.
97. Record 22530, 7,858 feet; Reserve 7243–45, Censor's decision, 31 March 1948; review 14 April 1948; certificate issued on 27 April 1948; distributor: Columbia. When a cut version of the film was viewed in 1960, the Censor ordered eight cuts, Reserve 7245, 27 July 1960.
98. The cuts were designed to ensure 'the elimination of any scenes or dialogue which suggest marital infidelity on the part of the heroine.' Record 23633, Reserve 7504, Censor's decision, 4 May 1949.
99. Record 20664, 8,922 feet; Reserve 6783, Censor's decision, 20 May 1946; review, 15 July 1946; certificate issued on 18 July 1946; distributor: 20th Century-Fox.
1. Record 25678, 7,856 feet, Reserve 7869, Censor's decision, 20 December 1950; certificate issued on 4 January 1951.
2. However, the cuts were made as they were deemed to have infringed the Emergency Powers Order, 1939. Set during World War Two, this film mainly concerns John Garfield returning to New York having fought in the Spanish Civil War and being pursued by undercover Nazis. Record 18432, 8,432 feet, Reserve 5847–49, Censor's decision, 20 January 1944; certificate issued on 20 January 1944.
3. Record 19027, 9,683 feet, Reject 1749, Censor's decision, 28 September 1944; passed after appeal, 10 October 1944; certificate issued on 13 October 1944; distributor: Paramount.
4. Record 17408, 7,654 feet, Reject 1585, Censor's decision, 13 November 1942; reviewed by Hayes and Montgomery on 20 November 1942 when rejection was confirmed; passed after appeal. According to Hayes, the 'sordid story of gangster life has not a single redeeming feature – physical brutality, murder, suicide and low intrigue succeed each other.'
5. Reject 1477, 8,964 feet; Censor's decision, 16 July 1941. The main objection was the 'sympathy' aroused for the main gangster (Humphrey Bogart) through his generosity towards the 'afflicted child,' while the gangster methods were shown in too much detail.
6. Reject 1943, 9,154 feet; Censor's decision, 23 May 1951. According to Hayes, 'scene follows scene of murder, blackmail, crooked deals, double-crossings and free love.'

7. Record 20670, 9,960 feet, Reject 1834; Censor's decision, 30 May 1946.
8. Record 20579, 10,153 feet, Reject 1832, Censor's decision, 28 May 1946; Appeal Board decision, 28 May 1946. Re-submitted in 1962: Record 35917, 9,837 feet, Reserve 10484, Censor's decision, five cuts, 14 February 1962; certificate issued on 7 March 1962.
9. Record 19467, 8,572 feet, Reserve 6429; renter refused cuts, Reject 1796, 19 April 1945.
10. *Monthly Film Bulletin*, 1953:109.
11. Record 22567, 9,157 feet, Reserve 7246, Censor's decision, 20 April 1948; certificate issued on 22 April 1948; distributor: 20th Century-Fox. Hayes ordered three cuts, two of which concern violence, including part of the scene where the wheelchair is pushed down the stairs.
12. Record 21126, 10,237 feet, Reject 1852, Censor's decision, 4 November 1946; ban was upheld after appeal, 12 November 1946.
13. Record 20670, 9,960 feet, Reject 1834; Censor's decision, 30 May 1946.
14. Record 17816, 9,222 feet, Reserve 6470; Censor's decision, 15 June 1945. This film had originally been banned under the Emergency Powers Order, Reject 1609, Censor's decision, 19 March 1942.
15. Film Censor to RTÉ, 16 July 1974. The relationship between RTÉ and the Film Censor is discussed in chapter 7. It may be that this scene is still forbidden by the Irish Censor, though, of course, if the film was re-submitted now it would be passed uncut.
16. Record 24290, Reserve 7635, Censor's decision, 3 November 1949.
17. 9,926 feet; Reject 1927, Censor's decision, 29 June 1950; Appeal Board decision, 4 July 1950.
18. Record 20726, 9,852 feet; Reject 1835, Censor's decision, 12 June 1946; Appeal Board decision, 25 June 1946.
19. As Richard Dyer notes (p. 96), 'no other *femme fatale* dances,' and he goes on to point up, as he draws on Laura Mulvey's germinal essay, 'Visual Pleasure and Narrative Cinema', the cinematic opposition between statis, which 'fixes or contols the object of desire for the pleasureable gaze of the specator,' and movement, where the objectified (woman) 'escapes' this control (p. 97). Richard Dyer, 'Resistance through charisma: Rita Hayworth and *Gilda*', in E. Ann Kaplan (ed.), *Women in Film Noir*, London: BFI, 1980.
20. Record 5671 and 27974; Reject 740; Censor's decision, 19 August 1932; Appeal Board ban, 30 September 1932; distributor: United Artists. Re-submitted under title *Gang War* in 1941: Reject 1479; Censor's decision, 29 August 1941 (eleven cuts); Appeal Board rejection, 7 October 1941. Re-submitted as *Scarface* in 1953: Reject 1983; Censor's decision, 24 April 1953; no appeal.
21. Record 19467, 8,572 feet, Reserve 6429; renter refused cuts, Reject 1796, 19 April 1945.
22. Record 23688, 7,063 feet, Reserve 7511, Censor's decision, 12 May 1949; review, 30 June 1949; certificate issued on 24 August 1949; distributor: MGM.
23. Record 30249, 7,200 feet; Reserve 9005, Censor's decision, 7 July 1955; certificate issued on 22 July 1955.
24. Record 20530, 9,114 feet; Reject 1833, 7 May 1946; no appeal. Re-submitted in 1961: Record 35841, Reserve 1046, Censor's decision, 23 January 1962.
25. Record 20579, 10,153 feet, Reject 1832, Censor's decision, 28 May 1946; Appeal Board decision, 28 May 1946. Re-submitted in 1962: Record 35917, 9,837 feet, Reserve 10484, Censor's decision, five cuts, 14 February 1962; certificate issued on 7 March 1962.
26. Record 20392, 7,733 feet; Reject 1828, Censor's decision, 9 April 1946; Appeal Board decision, 9 April 1946. Re-submitted in 1962: 7,777 feet; certificate issued on 4 January 1962.
27. A rare voice of criticism of the Irish film censorship process was offered by writer Aidan Higgins, who in a long letter to the British Film Institute's journal *Sight and Sound* described Irish censorship as 'strict, stupid and pernicious' because it functioned on the assumption that 'if one takes care of the ethics, the aesthetics will take care of themselves.' (Vol. 19, no. 9, January 1951:381.) Citing the banned *Brief Encounter*, and what he called the 'attempted banning' of *Sunset Boulevard*, he felt that Hayes had 'an unholy fear of films that take their immorality seriously.' Higgins went on to attack the lack of film criticism in Ireland (the Irish critic is 'like a dog who eats someone else's vomit'), with the exception of the unnamed reviewer of the (unnamed) *Irish Times*. Like the Censor, the Irish film critic 'is painfully conscious of his duty as protector of adolescent morals. His watchword is the Sanctity of the Family.' (p. 382.) He concluded his attack on the Irish film environment by complaining that cinema managers were unadventurous in their programming, saying that Thorold Dickinson's adaptation of Pushkin's *The Queen of Spades* (1948) and Robert Flaherty's *Louisiana Story* (1948) were not released because they were not 'box-office,' and he reported that the specialist cinema, the Astor, Dublin, had been converted into an ice-cream parlour. (p. 382.)
28. Geoffrey M. Shurlock, successor to Joseph Breen as administrator of the American film industry's Production Code Administration, quoted Schumach 1975:72.

29. Ibid. 190–91.
30. In 1999, the Irish Supreme Court heard the first blasphemy case since 1855 (when a case was taken concerning bible-burning and the ruling related to the privileged position in law of the 'Established' Church of Ireland) and ruled that it 'is impossible to say what the offence of blasphemy is, despite its prohibition in the Constitution.' This 'landmark judgment' arose out of an appeal by a Dubliner against a 1996 High Court decision which rejected his attempt to pursue a case of 'criminal blasphemy' against the *Sunday Independent* for publishing a cartoon in November 1995 which showed a priest in vestments holding a chalice and host pursuing Taoiseach John Bruton and ministers Ruairi Quinn and Proinsias de Rossa, who had led the Government campaign in favour of the divorce referendum. The cartoon's caption, 'Hello progress – bye-bye Father' mocked the infamous slogan of the anti-divorce campaign. While acknowledging that the Constitution accepts the crime of blasphemy, there is no legislation defining it on the statute books, with the judgment stating that 'the State is not placed in the position of an arbiter of religious truth.' Ironically, given the perception of the role of religion in the respective societies, the Irish position can be seen as more liberal than Britain's. In 1979, media campaigner Mary Whitehouse won a blasphemy case in the House of Lords which found that 'there was no need to prove a specific intention to blaspheme, only an intention to publish what was held to be blasphemous matter.' The Supreme Court commented that such a case would not be successful in Ireland, and added that if there was a secular constitution in Britain, with the Church of England disestablished, an outcome similar to the Irish one was likely. See, Carol Coulter, 'Court unable to state what blasphemy is' and 'State no arbiter of religious truth, Supreme Court rules', *Irish Times*, 31 July 1999:4. Former High Court Judge Rory O'Hanlon, a prominent activist in the anti-divorce campaign, strongly attacked the judgment. See, 'Why it's open season for blasphemy', *Sunday Business Post*, 21 November 1999:9.
31. The first figure is the Irish submitted length; the second is taken from *Monthly Film Bulletin* 1954:21. The treatment of *The Moon is Blue* by British and Irish censors parallels its problems in America as 'the supposedly "outspoken" nature of the dialogue ("seduction", "virgin", "mistress", etc.) explains the film's difficulties with various censorship organizations in the United States.' (Ibid.)
32. Record 30685, 8,962 feet; Reject 2010, Censor's decision, 10 February 1954; ban upheld after appeal, 16 February 1954; re-submitted in re-edited form (8,880 feet), Censor's decision, Reject 2091, 5 January 1956, 'still some objectionable scenes and suggestive dialogue'; renter refused further cuts; ban upheld after appeal, 6 March 1956.
33. Record 30844, 10,144 feet; Reserve 9211, Censor's decision, thirty (mainly dialogue) cuts, 29 February 1956 and 1 March 1956; renter refused cuts; ban upheld after appeal, 10 April 1956. For an account of the controversy in 1957 surrounding the first Irish performance of the play, the English-speaking European première, and the subsequent court case against the play, see Carolyn Swift, *Stage by Stage*, Dublin: Poolbeg, 1985:240 ff., and Gerard Whelan with Carolyn Swift, *Spiked: Church-State Intrigue and the Rose Tattoo*, Dublin: New Island, 2002.
34. Record 31654,10,301 feet, Reject 2136, Censor's decision, 28 January 1957; no appeal.
35. Record 34263, 10,267 feet; Reject 2296, Censor's decision, 2 February 1960; ban upheld after appeal, 23 February 1960. Re-submitted 'unofficially' to Christopher Macken in June 1964; Appeal Board decision, over-16s certificate, and Censor's report, 18 August 1966; distributor: Columbia (1960); British Lion (1966).
36. Record 34502, 10,927 feet; Reject 2307, Censor's decision, 12 May 1960; ban upheld after appeal, 31 May 1960; distributor: United Artists. O'Hora erroneously referred to this film as D.H. Lawrence's autobiography. Ban upheld after appeal, 31 May 1960.
37. Record 35990, 10,624 feet; Reject 2390, Censor's decision, 22 March 1962; ban upheld after appeal, 10 April 1962; distributor: Paramount. This 'typical offering of Tennessee Williams [who is] obsessed with sex … is utterly unfit for exhibition here.' (Censor's report to Appeal Board, 10 April 1962.)
38. 9,270 feet, Reject 2391, Censor's decision, 18 April 1962; no appeal.
39. 10,800 feet; Reserve 37434, Reject 2397, Censor's decision, 17 May 1962; no appeal. Re-submitted in 1964: 10,781 feet; Reserve 10871–72; passed with cuts, 2 June 1964; review and certificate issued on 21 August 1964; distributor: MGM.
40. 9,907 feet, Reject 2586, Censor's decision 19 December 1966; passed with one cut and Over 18s certificate after appeal, 3 January 1967; Appeal Board Reserve 11224, 9 January 1967.
41. It was approved, even though Censor Liam O'Hora declared that, in parts, it was 'absolutely unfit for children,' he still refused to give it an adult certificate. Record 36664, 10,015 feet; Reserve 10687, Censor's decision, 7 March 1963; review, 6 February 1963; certificate issued on 6 August 1963; distributor: MGM.
42. Record 26960, 10,936 feet; Reserve 8187–88, Censor's decision, 14 February 1952; and Reserve 8197, 22 February 1952; certificate issued on 25 February 1952; distributor: Warner Bros.

43. *Irish Times*, 8 December 1952:6. Incidentally, in a review of *Cat on a Hot Tin Roof* in 1959, the *Times*' correspondent (13 April 1959:8), commented incorrectly that 'rather surprisingly,' the film did not share the same fate as *Streetcar*, *Rose Tattoo* and *Baby Doll*, by being banned.

44. Record 33310, 9,710 feet; Reserve 9888; Censor's decision, 9 December 1958, 5 January 1959; review, 18 February 1959; distributor: MGM.

45. The scene in which Big Daddy says to his son, 'I'm contemplatin' pleasure,' and that he will 'pick me a choice woman,' even though his wife, Big Mama (Judith Anderson), is still alive is more straightforwardly an affront to Catholic morality and the sanctity of marriage and was cut. For a review of the film, see Ken Gray, *Sunday Independent*, 12 April 1959:21.

46. *Irish Times*, 13 April 1959:8.

47. Record 28571, 10,610 feet; Reserve 8599, Censor's decision, 9 December 1953; review and certificate issued, 14 December 1953; distributor: Columbia.

48. Ciaran Carty, 'Confessions of a Sewer Rat', *Film Directions*, vol. 3, no. 9, 1980:16–17.

49. 8,913 feet; Reject 2008, Censor's decision, 21 January 1954; no appeal; distributor: National Film Agency. The film seems to have been cut by the British Board of Film Censors, as the version submitted to the Irish Censor was 393 feet longer than the one released in Britain. (*Monthly Film Bulletin*, 1952:170.)

50. Record 29024, 7,436 feet; Reject 2013, Censor's decision, 22 April 1954; distributor: National.

51. During Hayes' term in office, Powell also deputized as censor. His style of commentary is as extreme as any of the full-time censors, and can be seen in the case of *Thy Neighbour's Wife* (Hugo Haas, 1953), a melodrama of adultery, murder and revenge, when he banned it: 'A squalid, immoral story with no relieving feature.' (Record 29153, 6,820 feet; Reject 2019, Censor's decision, 1 June 1954; distributor: 20th Century-Fox.) Powell deputized for Hayes from at least 1951 when he banned *Strictly Dishonourable* (Norman Panama, 1951). (Record 26359; 8,490 feet; Reject 1947, Censor's decision, 20 August 1951; no appeal; distributor: MGM.)

52. These included a shot of the Sacred Host cut from a documentary about Sister Maria Goretti (Record 28864, 16mm, Reserve 8622, Censor's decision, 3 February 1954, distributor: Fr Simoni); Holy Communion in *Universal News* (Reserve 8629, Censor's decision, 11 March 1954); and the Monstrance in *Universal News*, No. 270 (Censor's decision, 26 August 1954).

53. Record 30244, 7,525 feet; Reject 2066, Censor's decision, 8 July 1955; Appeal Board decision, 9 September 1955; review and certificate issued, 30 September 1955; distributor: British Lion.

54. Record 30570, 8,319 feet; Reject 2081, Censor's decision, 25 November 1955; Appeal Board decision, 6 December 1955; distributor: United Artists.

55. Record 30012, 9,459 feet; Reject 2049. Censor's decision, 4 April 1955; ban upheld after appeal, 19 April 1955.

56. *National Film Quarterly*, 1955. The *National Film Quarterly*, the publication of the NFI, had already favourably reviewed the film (vol. 5, no. 1, 1954), even putting a still from the film featuring Marlon Brando (rather than of the priest played by Karl Malden) on the magazine's cover. It did warn, though, that the film's violence, already cut by the Censor, was not suitable for children.

    In his address to the Congress, Archbishop McQuaid offered an extremist position on the moral classification of film, the subject of the event. These comments are of importance as not only did he have a close relationship with influential civil servant Peter Berry, who oversaw film censorship (see chapter 5), but (unofficially) he nominated Catholic clergy to the Appeal Board: 'By moral [classification], I mean, doctrinal classification, for morality is based on the doctrine that is the deposit of Faith, entrusted to her Divine Founder to the Church.' He went on to make a critique of cinema-scriptwriters. According to him they 'have never undergone the discipline of being taught the theory of dramatic structure and the differences between the different types of literature' – while cinema was often only a collection of costumes and 'an unrelated juxtaposition of incidents.' He also attacked the awarding of an international prize to the film *Cielo Sulla Palude* (Augusto Genina, 1949, Italy), which was based on the life of the Catholic saint, Maria Goretti, who, rather than succumb to sexual assault, killed herself. True to form, McQuaid described it as 'a debasing film whose inspiration is insanity of lust.' (*Evening Herald*, 4 July 1955.) (This may be a reference to the film about Maria Goretti passed with one cut (Record 28864, Reserve 8622, Censor's decision, 3 February 1954), discussed above.

57. Record 29231, 9,678 feet; Reserve 8687, Censor's decision, 30 June 1954; review and certificate issued on 1 October 1954; distributor: Columbia. Interpreting a cut earlier in the film is not so straightforward. When Edie tries to keep her distance from Terry he goes to her home, breaks in when she won't open the door, and says, 'Edie you love me,' as he forces a kiss. She replies: 'I didn't say I didn't love you. I said stay away from me,' lines which were cut by the Censor, perhaps because there is a crucifix in the shot.

58. The editor, 'A Brutal Film: Our Attitude', *Sunday Independent*, 10 October 1954:11. Refusal to review films to which it objected to on moral or other grounds seems to have been part of the newspaper's policy at this time, and even into the early 1960s. Ironically, the *Sunday Independent's* film reviewer in the 1950s, Noel F. Moran, was perhaps the first writer arguing in favour of issuing limited certificates, as is discussed in chapter 5.

59. Record 29014, 3,498 feet; Reserve 8644, Censor's decision, 7 April 1954; review and certificate issued, 22 May 1956; distributor: National.

60. Record 30260, 12,150 feet; Reserve 9009, Censor's decision, 15 July 1955; certificate issued on 9 August 1955; distributor: United Artists.

61. Record 30129, 8,706 feet; Reserve 8957, Censor's decision, 16 May 1955; passed with two cuts after appeal, 8 July 1955; review and certificate issued, 15 July 1955; distributor: British Lion.

62. Record 29028, 8,251 feet; Reserve 8652, Censor's decision, 21 April 1954; review and certificate issued, 6 May 1954; distributor: GFD.

63. An item on bathing fashions was cut from *News Reel No. 257*, Reserve 8694; Censor's decision, 12 July 1954.

64. Record 29266, 9,294 feet; Reserve 8698, Censor's decision, 19 July 1954; review 6 August 1954; certificate issued on 7 August 1954; distributor: Paramount.

65. Record 28917, 9,860 feet and 9,900 feet; Reserve 8626, Censor's decision, 1 March 1954; certificate issued on 7 April 1954; distributor: MGM.

66. Record 29891, 7,381 feet; Reserve 8889, Censor's decision, 7 March 1955; review and certificate issued, 23 March 1955; distributor: Pathé.

67. Record 29939, 10,535 feet; Reserve 8888, Censor's decision, 25 February 1955; review, 25 March 1955; certificate issued on 19 April 1955; distributor: 20th Century-Fox.

68. Record 30079, 8,299 feet; Reserve 8939, Censor's decision, 27 April 1955; review and certificate issued, 19 May 1955; distributor: Paramount.

69. Record 30122, 8,926 feet; Reserve 8952, Censor's decision, 13 May 1955; certificate issued on 31 May 1955; distributor: RKO Radio.

70. Record 30199, 7,303 feet; Reserve 8989, Censor's decision, 14 June 1955; review and certificate issued, 5 July 1955; distributor: JAR; GFD.

71. Record 30826, 10,360 feet; Reserve 9208, Censor's decision, 20 February 1956; certificate issued on 5 March 1956; distributor: Columbia.

72. Record 29182, 8,079 feet; Reserve 8682, Censor's decision, 17 June 1954; review and certificate issued, 24 June 1954; distributor: Warner Bros.

73. Record 29408, 9,156 feet; Reserve 8726, Censor's decision, 17 August 1954; certificate issued on 27 October 1954; distributor: 20th Century-Fox.

74. Record 30852, 6,043 feet; Reserve 9219, Censor's decision, 6 March 1956; review and certificate issued, 2 July 1956; distributor: United Artists.

75. Record 29606, Reserve 8782, Censor's decision, 26 October 1954; review and certificate issued, 18 November 1954; distributor: Warner Bros.

76. Record 30332, 7,967 feet; Reserve 9044, deputy Censor E.C. Powell's decision, 25 August 1955; review and certificate issued, 1 September 1955; distributor: J.A. Rank.

77. Record 19283, 9,565 feet; Reserve 6327–29, Censor's decision, 19 January 1945; certificate issued on 24 May 1945; distributor: United Artists.

78. Record 20744, 8,988 feet; Reserve 6823–24; renter refused cuts, Reject 1837, Censor's decision, 19 June 1946; renter appealed cuts; passed with one cut (the silhouette dance) after appeal, 2 July 1946; certificate issued on 31 July 1946; distributor: United Artists.

79. Record 30255, 7,590 feet; Reject 2067, Censor's decision, 18 July 1955; Appeal Board decision, 16 September 1955; certificate issued on 16 September 1955; distributor: J.A. Rank.

80. See Mary Douglas, *Natural Symbols*, London: Pelican, 1978.

81. Record 29765, 10,069 feet; Reserve 8832, Censor's decision 15 December 1954; review and certificate issued on 23 December 1954; distributor: Paramount.

82. Record 29129, 9,063 feet; Reject 2016, Censor's decision, 27 May 1954; no appeal; distributor: National.

83. 6,925 feet; Reject 2051, Censor's decision, 20 May 1955; no appeal. Re-submitted in 1956 (5,936 feet); banned again, Reject 2127, Censor's decision, 26 October 1956; ban reversed after appeal, 20 November 1956.

84. Record 29982, 10,423 feet; Reject 2044, Censor's decision, 14 March 1955; certificate issued on 14 March 1955; distributor: MGM.

85. Record 30773, 7,362 feet; Reserve, 9196, Censor's decision, 6 February 1956; review and certificate issued, 20 February 1956; distributor: Pathé. Commenting on the version of the film released

in Britain, *Monthly Film Bulletin* (1956:18) said that 'some cuts have obviously been made' (though the film submitted to the Irish Censor was only twenty feet longer than the British release version). It was most likely the cut British version that was cut further by the Irish Censor, notwithstanding the slight discrepancy in lengths recorded.

86. Record 30415, 8,913 feet; Reject 2078, Censor's decision, 20 September 1955; Appeal Board decision, 25 October 1955; distributor: 20th Century-Fox.

87. Record 30698, 9,340 feet; Censor's reject decision, 17 January 1956; Appeal Board decision and Censor's report, 17 February 1956; certificate issued on 27 March 1956; distributor: 20th Century-Fox. Nevertheless, the Board demanded cut 'all kisses and embraces between Edwina and Dr Softi' as well as Softi's phrase, 'while you were so energetically trying to seduce her.' (Reel 5.)

88. Record 30777, 10,630 feet; Reject 2090, Censor's decision, 8 February 1956; Appeal Board decision, 28 February 1956; review and certificate issued, 6 March 1956; distributor: United Artists. The Board, chaired that day by Canon O'Donnell, was only concerned with 'semi-nude ladies' in reel 2.

89. Record 30099, 7,918 feet; Reject 2057, Censor's decision, 2 May 1955; Appeal Board decision and certificate issued, 24 May 1955; distributor: British Lion.

90. Record 30388, 9,444 feet; Reject 2071, Censor's decision, 9 September 1955; Appeal Board decision, 24 May 1955; distributor: 20th Century-Fox. Re-submitted in 1961: Record 35309, Reserve 10345, Censor's decision, passed with five cuts, 16 May 1961. *The Seven Year Itch* contains perhaps the 1950s most iconic image when Marilyn Monroe's dress is 'inflated' over a pavement vent as Tom Ewell looks on. Hayes had cut two precedents of this image: in *Hellzapoppin'* (H.C. Potter, 1941) where a girl's dress is blown aloft by a wind machine (Record 16858, 7,564 feet; Reserve 5078, Censor's decision, 30 March 1942; passed with cuts after appeal, 21 April 1942; certificate issued on 29 April 1942; distributor: GFD), and in *The Set-Up* where a young woman's dress is blown up as she walks over a vent as a group of boys laugh. (Record 23847, 6,449 feet; Reserve 7566, Censor's decision, 26 July 1949; certificate issued on 22 August 1949; distributor: RKO Radio.) As regards *Seven Year Itch*, Hayes commented that he found himself 'incapable of cutting [it] without destroying its continuity.'(Martin Brennan to Appeal Board, 19 September 1955.) Nevertheless, in 1961 Liam O'Hora passed it with five cuts, including the reference to underwear in the refrigerator and the plumber episode.

91. Record 29505, 8,281 feet; Reject 2027, Censor's decision, 27 September 1954, ban upheld after appeal, 11 January 1955. When re-submitted in 1959 in a cut version, 8,006 feet, the ban was maintained: Reject 2279 (20 November 1959). Undetermined version viewed on 21 January 1963; certificate issued on 7 October 1963; distributor: Abbey Films.

92. Record 30968, 8,743 feet; Censor's reject, 20 April 1956; Appeal Board decision, 15 May 1956; distributor: International Film Distributors/Elliman.

93. Record 36613, 8,379 feet; rejected in 1956; ban upheld after appeal, 5 June 1956; distributor: Paramount. Re-submitted in 1963: Reserve 10670, Censor's decision, four cuts, 24 January 1963; certificate issued on 31 January 1963.

94. Record 31021, 9,881 feet; Reject 2101, deputy Censor E.C. Powell's decision, 10 May 1956; ban upheld by Appeal Board in majority decision, 12 June 1956; distributor: Columbia.

95. Record 23615, 8,163 feet; Reserve 7507, Censor's decision, three cuts of 'brutalities,' knifing and kicking, 9 May 1949; certificate issued on 23 September 1949; distributor: GFD.

96. Thomas Doherty, *Teenagers and Teenpics: The Juvenilization of American Movies in the 1950s*, Boston: Unwin Hyman/London, 1988:7–8.

97. Ibid. 37.

98. Ibid. 14.

99. Record 30959, 9,564 feet; certificate issued on 13 April 1956; distributor: Warner Bros.

1. Doherty, 1988:76.

2. Schumach, 1975:17.

3. Robertson, 1989:116.

4. Record 30164, Reserve 8976, Censor's decision, 26 May 1956; review and certificate issued, 22 July 1955; distributor: MGM. In 1964, *Blackboard Jungle* was re-submitted and the cuts were reduced to three by Christopher Macken, but the 'entire bedroom scene' was eliminated by him. (Reserve 9115, 17 September 1964.) In 1961 there was a British *Blackboard Jungle* dealing with homegrown juvenile delinquents, *Spare the Rod* (Leslie Norman, GB), O'Hora ordered five cuts, one which was of an insolent student calling a teacher, 'You bastard.' (Record 35454, Reserve 10378, Censor's decision, 18 July 1961.)

5. Noel F. Moran, *Sunday Independent*, 6 November 1955:13.

6. Record 28996, 7,114 feet, Reject 2012, Censor's decision, 9 April 1954; ban upheld after appeal, 27 April 1954. Re-edited version, 6,390 feet, submitted with new ending, Reserve 9164, Censor's decision, 6 January 1956, passed with cuts; review and certificate issued, 10 January 1956; distributor: Columbia.

7. Robertson, 1989:105.

8. *Irish Times*, 6 February 1956:6. The *Times* also reported that two days earlier the Irish Film Society had shown to its members both the original and the new ending of the film.

9. Record 32612, 7,003 feet; Reserve 9657, Censor's decision, one cut, 28 February 1958; review and certificate issued on 17 April 1958; distributor: Abbey Films.

10. Record 43097, 7,650 feet; Reject 2617, deputy Censor Gabriel Fallon's decision, 29 March 1968. Re-submitted in 1976: Reserve 12595, passed with cuts and over-18s certificate, 18 May 1976; review, 28 July 1976; distributor: Abbey Films.

11. 6,749 feet; Reject 1981, Censor's decision, 25 March 1953; no appeal. Re-submitted in 1958: Record 32521, 5,960 feet; Reserve 9635, Censor's decision, 22 January 1958; review and certificate issued on 22 April 1958; distributor: British Lion.

12. Record 23287, 8,562 feet; Reserve 7437, Censor's decision, 2 February 1949; certificate issued on 9 February 1949.

13. Record 25678, 7,856 feet; Reserve 7869, Censor's decision, 20 December 1950; certificate issued on 4 January 1951.

14. Record 32229, 7,213 feet; Reject 2166, Censor's decision, 23 September 1957; Appeal Board decision and Censor's report, 22 October 1957; distributor: Pathé.

15. Doherty, 1988:132.

16. Record 33510, 9,270 feet; Reserve 9899, Censor's decision, 2 March 1959; review and certificate issued on 23 April 1959; distributor: 20th Century-Fox.

17. Of course, O'Hora was not concerned with such subtleties, and concentrated on cutting entirely the bedroom scene between Tony and Marie, while the later scene of a boy being thrown on a girl was also cut. Record 36118, Reserve 10569, Censor's decision, 15 June 1962.

18. Quoted, Doherty, 1988:73.

19. Record 31037, 6,749 feet; Censor's decision and certificate issued, 24 May 1956; distributor: Columbia.

20. His call for restrictions on children attending night-time cinema shows was not acted upon. Anon., 'Rock 'n' Roll takes Sligo by Storm', *Sligo Champion*, reprinted in *Sesquicentenary 1836–1986* issue, p. 87. For an account of American and European responses to the film, see Doherty 1988:79–82.

21. Record 31631, Reserve 9389, Censor's decision, 16 January 1957.

22. One of the cuts was during the rendition of 'Hook Line and Sinker' where 'the girl in tights commences to corkscrew her hips to the end of the dance.' This description replaces one crossed out, which described her actions thus, 'where the girl in tights commences to wriggle her bottom so tortuously.' (Record 31632, 7,606 feet; Reserve 9390, Censor's decision, 17 January 1957; review and certificate issued on 23 January 1957; distributor: Columbia.)

23. Record 31704, 8,750 feet; Reserve 9412, Censor's decision, 19 February 1957; review and certificate issued on 25 March 1957; distributor: 20th Century-Fox.

24. Record 31572, 8,050 feet; Censor's decision, 13 December 1956; distributor: 20th Century-Fox.

25. Record 34127, 10,011 feet; Reserve 10051–52, Censor's decision, 15 December 1959. Re-submitted in 1962: Record 36154, Reserve 10590, Censor's decision, 4 July 1962; distributor: British Lion.

26. Record 32163, 6,749 feet; Censor's decision and certificate issued, 29 August 1957; distributor: Abbey Films.

27. Anon., *Irish Times*, 10 March 1958:6.

28. Noel Moran, *Sunday Independent*, 3 February 1957:13.

29. Noel Moran, ibid., 1 December 1957:15; Noel Moran, 'Fans Say "I'm Square"... but I stand firm', ibid. 15 December 1957:15.

30. Record 32543, 8,687 feet; Reserve 9640, Censor's Decision, 31 January 1958; certificate issued on 13 February 1958; distributor: MGM.

31. Doherty, 1988:97–98.

32. Record 31493, 8,465 feet; Reserve 9341, Censor's decision, 18 November 1956; Record 314493, Censor's decision, 8 November 1956; review, 15 November 1956; certificate issued on 5 December 1956; distributor: 20th Century-Fox.

33. Record 33081, 10,381 feet; Reserve 9775, Censor's decision, 8 September 1958; Appeal Board decision and Censor's report, 7 October 1958; distributor: Paramount.
34. Record 34949, 9,337 feet; Reserve 10248, Censor's decision, 25 November 1960; review and certificate issued, 25 January 1961; distributor: Paramount.
35. Record 35421, 9,268 feet; Reserve 10374, Censor's decision, 14 July 1961.
36. Record 35476, 10,070 feet; Reserve 10382–83, Censor's decision, 31 July 1961; review and certificate issued, 18 September 1961; distributor: 20th Century-Fox.
37. Record 35796, 9,109 feet; Reserve 10449, Censor's decision, 13 December 1961; Appeal Board decision and Censor's report, 23 January 1962; distributor: Paramount.
38. Doherty, 1988:195.
39. Record 35308, Reserve 10348, Record 35308, Censor's decision, 19 May 1961.
40. Record 33833, 8,583 feet; Reject 2260, Censor's decision, 21 July 1959; Appeal Board decision and Censor's report, 1 September 1959; distributor: Columbia.

CHAPTER 5

1. Record 34376, 8,661 feet; Reserve 10106, Censor's decision, 10 March 1960; review and certificate issued, 23 March 1960; distributor: Hibernian.
2. See Rockett et al., 1988, chapter 4, for details of the Shaw/Pascal proposals.
3. *Irish Trade Journal and Statistical Bulletin*, vol. 35, no. 1, March 1960:40–41, traces the decline in Irish cinema audiences from 1956, a decade after a similar fall-off in Britain. In Ireland, the number of admission in millions per annum were: 54.1 in 1954, the highest of the decade; 50.9 (1955); 52.1 (1956); 49.8 (1957); 45.6 (1958); 43.8 (1959); and 41.2 (1960), representing a 31 per cent drop on the 1954 figure. By 1976, the Irish cinema audience had shrunk to five million admission per annum, or less than one-tenth its 1954 peak. (*Report of Enquiry into the Supply and Distribution of Cinema Films*, Dublin: Stationary Office, 1978:17.)
4. Film Censor's report to the Minister of Justice, 21 January 1957, OFC.
5. Film Censor's report to the Minister of Justice, 22 January 1958, OFC.
6. Record 29412, 6,700 or 6,725 feet; Reserve 8,730, Censor's decision, 23 August 1954; Appeal Board decision, 14 September 1954; distributor: United Artists.
7. Record 32143, 7,979 feet; Reserve 9524, Censor's decision, 23 August 1957; no certificate issued; distributor: Hibernian.
8. Record 35675, 9,071 feet; Reserve 10419, Censor's decision, 25 October 1961; review and certificate issued on 7 November 1961; distributor: Elliman.
9. Record 32149, 8,403 feet; Reserve 9527–28, Censor's decision, 23 August 1957; certificate issued on 7 November 1957; distributor: MGM.
10. See Dermot Keogh, *Ireland in the Twentieth Century*, Dublin: Gill and Macmillan, 1996. This amendment to the 1929 Censorship of Publications Act resulted in the immediate unbanning of thousands of books. See also Adams, 1967. In his capacity as Secretary of the Department of Justice, Berry later made an appearance as a central figure in the 'Arms Crisis' of 1971 (see Keogh, ibid.), and he may have been responsible for altering a key statement implicating Defence Minister Jim Gibbons in arms importation for Northern Ireland nationalists in 1970, as a controversial RTÉ *Primetime* documentary suggested in April 2001.
11. Film Censor's report to the Minister of Justice, 16 January 1959.
12. Record 33464, 10,900 feet; Reserve 9906, Censor's decision, 6 March 1959; review and certificate issued, 19 March 1959; distributor: United Artists.
13. As the *Sunday Independent* reported, 3 May 1959:23.
14. Record 33617, 8,015 feet; Reserve 9940, Censor's decision, 15 April 1959; review and certificate issued, 5 May 1959; distributor: Elliman.
15. Film Censor's report to the Minister of Justice, 1 February 1960, OFC.
16. Liam O'Hora to Mr Toal, Department of Justice, 6 May 1961, OFC.
17. Record 29429, 8,103 feet; Reject 2028, Censor's decision, 7 September 1954; Appeal Board decision and Censor's report, 12 October 1954; certificate issued on 12 October 1954; distributor: National. Despite these cuts, the Board seems to have taken a more lenient approach to the film than their British counterparts because the version submitted to the Irish Censor was 718 feet longer than the one released in Britain, and the cut demanded was only a fraction of this. Perhaps it was the film's well-meaning didacticism (and, of course, Continental European origins) that persuaded the Board to approve a film which dealt not only with illegitimacy, but also with suicide. (*Monthly Film Bulletin*, 1952:129.)

18. 6,914 feet, Reject 2048, Censor's decision, 25 March 1955; Appeal Board decision, 17 May 1955.
19. Record 30370, 7,372 feet; Reject 2082, Censor's decision, 29 August 1955; Appeal Board decision, 7 October 1955; distributor: Irish International Film Agency.
20. Record 32079, 9,411 feet; Reject 2152, Censor's decision, 8 July 1957; Appeal Board decision, 16 July 1957; distributor: Paramount.
21. Record 34151, 6,738 feet; Reject 2287, Censor's decision, 29 December 1959; Appeal Board decision and certificate issued, 21 January 1960; distributor: Warner-Pathé.
22. Record 34241, 8,431 feet; Reject 2292, Censor's decision, 19 January 1960; Appeal Board decision, 26 January 1960; distributor: United Artists.
23. Record 34435, 8,333 feet; Reject 2305, Censor's decision, 7 April 1960; Appeal Board decision, 10 May 1960; certificate issued on 31 May 1960; distributor: Warner-Pathé.
24. Record 34363, 6,227 feet; Reject 2300, Censor's decision, 9 March 1960; Appeal Board decision and certificate issued, 26 April 1960; distributor: Elliman.
25. This seems to be a mistake on O'Hora's part, as his rejection was upheld by the Board, a decision until an appeal after his successor had confirmed the ban. 1960: 9,536 feet; Reject 2326, Censor's decision, 25 August 1960; Appeal Board decision, 27 September 1960. Re-submitted in 1964, 7,950 feet, Reject 2455, Censor's decision, 29 June 1964; ban reversed after appeal, 10 November 1964.
26. As regards this latter film, which centrally concerns the relationship between a teacher and one of her pupils, O'Hora commented that 'no picture of this particular kind has ever come in here before.' (7,648 feet; Reject 2333, Censor's decision, 2 November 1960; Appeal Board decision and Censor's report, 8 November 1960.)
27. Liam O'Hora to Mr Toal, Department of Justice, 6 May 1961, OFC.
28. Record 35278, 7,954 feet; Reject 2362, Censor's decision, 29 May 1961; Appeal Board decision, 20 June 1961; certificate issued on 5 September 1961; distributor: Rank Films.
29. Record 35165, 7,150 feet; Reject 2350, Censor's decision, 13 March 1961; Appeal Board decision and Censor's report, 26 June 1962; *Adam and Eve* was 'the first religious nudist film,' according to *Monthly Film Bulletin* (1958:141). As there was a fifteen month gap between O'Hora's viewing of *Adam and Eve* and the Board's seeing it, and since the Censor's sole problem was nudity, clearly a concern more generally of the Board, it is probable that the version viewed by the Board had such scenes deleted prior to their decision being made.
30. Record 36417, 8,649 feet; Reject 2407, Censor's decision, 4 October 1962, Appeal Board decision and Censor's report, 13 November 1962.
31. Film Censor's report to Minister for Justice, 31 January 1963, OFC.
32. Record 35910, 9,568 feet; Reserve 10502–03, Censor's decision, eleven cuts, 20 February 1962; no certificate issued. Re-submitted in 1964: Record 37405, 9,212 feet; Reserve 10869, Censor's decision, twelve cuts, 20 May 1964; Appeal Board decision, 28 July 1964; Appeal Board Reserve 11154, two cuts, 14 July 1966; distributor: British Lion.
33. Record 37571, 8,190 feet; Reject 2469, Censor's decision, 27 August 1964; Appeal Board decision, 15 September 1964; certificate issued on 8 October 1964; distributor: British Lion.
34. Macken had banned the film because of blasphemy and horror. Record 37542, 7,560 feet; Reject 2464, Censor's decision, 12 August 1964; Appeal Board decision, 8 September 1964; certificate issued on 8 September 1964; distributor: Warner-Pathé.
35. Record 37679, 7,700 feet; Reject 2483, Censor's decision, 4 November 1964; Appeal Board decision and certificate issued, 24 November 1964; distributor: Abbey Films.
36. 2,934 feet; Reject 2487, Censor's decision, 16 November 1964; Appeal Board decision and Censor's report, 8 December 1964; distributor: Warner-Pathé.
37. See Julia Kristeva, *Powers of Horror: An Essay in Abjection*, New York/Oxford: Columbia UP, 1982.
38. Ibid. 3.
39. See Robin Wood, 'An Introduction to the American Horror Film', in *Movies and Methods*, vol. 2, Bill Nichols (ed.), Berkeley/Los Angeles/London: University California Press, 1985:195–220.
40. This has changed in recent decades with work such as Robin Wood and Richard Lippe (eds), *American Nightmares: Essays on the Horror Film*, Toronto: Festival of Festivals, 1979; Gregory Waller (ed.), *American Horrors: Essays on the modern American Horror Film*, Urbana and Chicago: University of Illinois Press, 1987; Mark Jancovich, *Horror*, London: BT Batsford 1992; and Ken Gelder (ed.), *The Horror Reader*, London and New York: 2000.
41. Hardy, *Horror*, 1985:39.
42. Censor's decision, 22 September 1927; ban upheld after appeal (no date).
43. This film was originally due for release in 1925, but Universal withdrew it after adverse publicity in Britain. When the BBFC eventually examined the film, it was passed uncut and with a 'U' certificate on 7 July 1930 (Robertson 1985:36), three weeks before the Irish Censor's decision on 31 July 1930. Record 2795, 8,387 feet; certificate issued on 1 August 1930; distributor: Universal.

44. Record 3486, 6,766 feet; Censor's decision and certificate issued, 21 January 1931; distributor: Universal.
45. Record 16239, 6,569 feet, Censor's decision and certificate issued, 8 September 1931.
46. Robertson 1985: 57.
47. Record 3929, 7,033 feet; Reserve 1388, Censor's decision, 8 May 1931; review and certificate issued, 5 June 1931; distributor: Universal.
48. Robertson, 1985:57.
49. Record 4962 and 13227; Reject 624; Censor's decision, 5 February 1932; Appeal Board decision, 8 March 1932; certificate issued on 9 March 1932; distributor: Universal; length, 6,077 feet.
50. No doubt removing its highly charged eroticism which had led to 731 feet being deleted by the BBFC, Robertson, 1985:58.
51. 7,577 feet; Reject 705, Censor's decision, 27 June 1932. The truncated version was passed by the Appeal Board on 19 August 1932; certificate issued on 23 August 1932.
52. Record 21905, Reject 820, deputy Censor's decision, 6 February 1933; Appeal Board decision, 21 April 1933; certificate issued on 27 April 1932; distributor: Universal.
53. 352 feet were cut by the BBFC.
54. Record 5139 and 21893, 5,669 feet; Reserve 2081, Censor's decision, 16 March 1932; review 19 March 1932; certificate issued on 30 March 1932; distributor: Universal.
55. Record 6157 and 10714, 6,924 feet; Reserve 2219, Censor's decision, 23 January 1933; review, 21 February 1933; certificate issued on 28 February 1933; distributor; Warner Bros.
56. Record 14030, 7,497 feet; Reserve 2476, Censor's decision, 17 August 1933; review, 7 October 1933; certificate issued on 11 October 1933; distributor: Express.
57. Record 7096 and 16963, 6,494 feet; Censor's decision, 4 December 1933; certificate issued on 9 December 1933; distributor: Universal.
58. Record 6740 and 33420, 5,778 feet; Reserve 2726, deputy Censor Joseph Holloway's decision, 10 August 1933; review, 7 October 1933; certificate issued on 11 October 1933; distributor: Express.
59. Record 8124 and 16320, 5,829 feet; Censor's decision, 29 September 1934; certificate issued on 9 October 1934; distributor: Universal.
60. Record 7351, 6,902 feet; Censor's decision, 28 June 1935; certificate issued on 21 June 1935; distributor: Universal.
61. Record 9333 and 20953, 5,521 feet; Censor's decision, 21 July 1935; certificate issued on 25 July 1935; distributor: MGM.
62. Record 9488 and 15141, 5,923 feet; Censor's decision, 22 August 1935; certificate issued on 30 August 1935; distributor: MGM.
63. Record 9273 and 26507, 5,607 feet; Censor's decision, 28 June 1935; certificate issued on 24 July 1935; distributor: Universal.
64. Record 9228 and 34880, 6,518 feet; Censor's decision, 18 June 1935; certificate issued on 21 June 1935; distributor: Universal.
65. Record 10648 and 10772, 6,549 feet; Censor's decision, 10 July 1936; certificate issued on 29 July 1936; distributor: Universal.
66. Record 10795 and 26864, 6,818 feet; Censor's decision, 1 September 1936; certificate issued on 2 September 1936; distributor: Pathé.
67. See entry in *The American Film Institute Catalog: Feature Films, 1931–1940*, Berkeley: University of California Press, 1993:700; Martin F. Norden, *The Cinema of Isolation*, New Brunswick: Rutgers UP, 1994; and Robert Bogdan, *Freak Show*, Chicago: University of Chicago Press, 1998.
68. Robertson, 1989:56.
69. Liam O'Hora had initially decided to order just one cut, the line, 'Mr Parker, do you know what it means to feel like God?', but then changed his mind and banned it. (Record 33380, 6,027 feet, Reject 2237, Reserve 9860, Censor's decision, 12 January 1959; no appeal.)
70. Montgomery told the distributor in this case that 'it may be possible to save this film if the actual murders and scenes of horror [were] cut out' and that if he went through the script 'he may be able to prune the picture for a general certificate.' The Board upheld the Censor's decision. (6,853 feet; Reserve 4255; Reject 1376, Censor's decision, 16 August 1939; ban upheld after appeal.)
71. Hayes initially made ten cuts to the film. Record 18542 and 18512, 6,227 feet; Reject 1712, Reserve 5905, Censor's decision, 18 February 1944; review, 2 March 1944; ban upheld after appeal, 21 March 1944; distributor: Columbia.
72. Hardy, *Horror*, 1985:55.
73. Record 5993 and 34795, 6,275 feet; Reject 795, Censor's decision, 25 November 1932; re-submitted version passed on 6 April 1933; certificate issued on 7 April 1932; distributor: United Artists. What cuts were made by the renter are not known, but it can be assumed that these concerned Montgomery's original criticism. The BBFC had made only minor cuts to the film, Robertson, 1985:58.

74. Record 16043, Reserve 4725, Censor's decision, 19 March 1941; review, 20 March 1941.
75. Record 18100, 6,186 feet; Reserve 5640, Censor's decision, 15 July 1943; review, 9 August 1943; certificate issued on 10 August 1943; distributor: RKO Radio.
76. Lewton's *Cat People* (Jacques Tourneur, 1942) was passed uncut in 1943 (Record 17677, 6,544 feet; Censor's decision, 12 March 143; certificate issued on 20 April 1943; distributor: RKO Radio), and its sequel, *The Curse of the Cat People* (Gunther von Fritsch, Robert Wise, 1944). (Record 18881, 6,279 feet; Censor's decision, 11 July 1944; certificate issued on 18 July 1944; distributor: RKO Radio.) The ban on imports of horror films into Britain during the war does not seem to have affected their availability in Ireland.
77. Jancovich, *Horror*, London: BT Batsford, 1992:61.
78. Record 32283, 8,610 feet; Reserve 9563, Censor's decision, 17 October 1957; review and certificate issued, 29 October 1957; distributor: Columbia.
79. Hardy, 1985:110.
80. Record 18708, 7,234 feet; Reserve 5990, Censor's decision, 14 April 1944; review, 12 May 1944; certificate issued on 16 May 1944; distributor: GFD.
81. Hardy, 1985:84.
82. Record 20625, 6,045 feet; Reserve 6828, Reject 1839 (renter refused cuts), Censor's decision, 24 June 1946; passed uncut after appeal, 8 July 1946; certificate issued on 19 July 1946; distributor: GFD.
83. Record 27183, 6,920 feet; Reject 1960, Censor's decision, 24 April 1952; no appeal; distributor: Elliman/Irish Film Distributors. Robertson, 1985: 134.
84. Record 26846, 5,833 feet; Reserve 8182–3, Censor's decision, 30 January 1952, 'cleaned-up' version viewed at renter's request, Reject 1957 when renter refused to cut further; ban reversed after appeal and certificate issued, 26 February 1952; distributor: Columbia.
85. In act 3, scene 2 of *The Shaughraun*, the play's hero, Conn, rises during his own wake to steal a drink from the mourners unbeknown to them, and later 'resurrects' himself to confront and frighten two of his adversaries who are henchmen of the kidnapper of the film's heroines, one of whom is Conn's sweetheart. Cinema directly borrowed from this scene, an example is the British film *Murphy's Wake* which was made by Walturdaw Co. Ltd in 1906. In these films, sometimes the drink is stolen without the 'corpse' being seen alive, and a fight occurs between the mourners over the missing drink, or else the 'corpse' frightens them, they run away, and he then enjoys the drink left behind. Another version of this trope is the anonymous Irish-American ballad 'Finnegan's Wake' (which was later used with the apostrophe dropped by James Joyce for his last major work) about a bricklayer working in New York who 'fell from a ladder and broke his skull' and is presumed dead. However, at his wake whiskey falls on him, and 'Bedad he revives.'

      Wakes were occasions for a wide variety of ritualized games and other amusements as Seán Ó Súilleabháin demonstrates in *Irish Wake Amusements*, Dublin/Cork: The Mercier Press, 1967; orig. *Caitheamh Aimsire ar Thórraimh*, 1961. Ó Súilleabháin (p. 67) reports that the corpse occasionally became involved in the pranks, citing the story of how an old rheumatic was tied down with ropes to straighten his limbs only to have a trickster loosen them during the wake to frighten the mourners. Another story concerned how a trickster would hide underneath the corpse's bed, and then shake it from side to side to frighten the mourners. Cards might be played either on the bed or even on the corpse itself, with the corpse being dealt a hand of cards, or even given a pipe to smoke. Most shockingly, perhaps, at least because the practice continued into the twentieth century, was when the corpse was taken on to the floor to dance. Ó Súilleabháin cites the clerical pronouncements down the centuries seeking to outlaw the 'pagan' wake amusements, and have them replaced with prayers. By the mid-twentieth century the Catholic church had succeeded in having corpses removed to the church on the evening before the burial, thus neutralizing the drinking and other excesses associated with wakes.
86. Record 24807, 5,708 feet; Reserve 7710, Censor's decision, 5 April 1950; review and certificate issued, 10 May 1950; distributor: Egan Film Service.
87. Record 15821, 5,582 feet; Reserve 4652, Censor's decision, 13 January 1941; certificate issued on 29 January 1941; distributor: Columbia.
88. Record 19275, 5,438 feet; Reserve 6364, Censor's decision, 8 February 1945; review, 27 February 1945; certificate issued on 5 March 1945; distributor: GFD.
89. See Christopher Frayling, *Nightmare: The Birth of Horror*, London: BBC Books, 1996.
90. Record 16679, 10,951 feet; Reserve 4979–80, Censor's decision, 22 December 1941; review, 30 October 1942; certificate issued on 5 November 1942; distributor: MGM.
91. Record 28255, 7,848 feet; Reserve 8497, 26 June 1953; review and certificate issued, 30 June 1953; distributor: Warner Bros.

92. Record 29243, 6,544 feet; Reserve 8693, Censor's decision, 7 July 1954; review and certificate issued, 30 July 1954; distributor: Columbia.
93. Record 29798, 7,719 feet; Reject 2038, Censor's decision, 10 January 1955; Appeal Board decision and Censor's report, 1 February 1955; review and certificate issued, 8 February 1955; distributor: 20th Century-Fox.
94. Record 30370, 7,372 feet; Reject 2082, Censor's decision, 29 August 1955; Appeal Board decision, 7 October 1955; distributor: Irish International Film Agency.
95. Howard Maxford, *Hammer, House of Horror*, London: B.T. Batsford, 1996:28–29.
96. Record 31176, 7,168 feet; Reserve 9278, Censor's decision, 28 June 1956; review and certificate issued, 19 July 1956; distributor: Pathé.
97. Film Censor's report to Minister for Justice, 21 January 1957, OFC.
98. Record 31673, 7,321 feet; Reject 2137, Censor's decision, 6 February 1957; ban reversed after appeal, 19 February 1957; certificate issued on 19 February 1957; distributor: United Artists.
99. Record 33609, 7,331 feet; Reject 2248, Censor's decision, 17 April 1959; Appeal Board decision and Censor's report, 21 April 1959. Re-submitted in 1961: Reserve 10434, Record 35763, Censor's decision, 27 November 1961; review, 18 December 1961; distributor: Abbey Films.
 1. Record 34517, 8,251 feet; Reject 2308, Censor's decision, 16 May 1960; no appeal; distributor: Abbey Films.
 2. Record 34435, 8,333 feet; Reject 2305, Censor's decision, 7 April 1960; Appeal Board decision, 10 May 1960; certificate issued on 31 May 1960; distributor: Warner-Pathé.
 3. Howard Maxford, *Hammer, House of Horror*, 1996:37.
 4. Ibid. 36.
 5. C.A. Lejeune, quoted David Pirie, *A Heritage of Horror: The English Gothic Cinema 1946–1972*, London: Gordon Fraser, 1973:40.
 6. Record 33168, 7,472 feet; Reject 2148, Censor's decision, 26 June 1957; Appeal Board decision and Censor's report, 30 July 1957. Re-submitted in 1958: Record 33168, 7,119 feet; Reserve 9804, Censor's decision, 10 October 1958; review and certificate issued, 20 October 1958; distributor: Warner Bros. *Irish Times*, 24 November 1958:6.
 7. Record 33067, 7,982 feet; Reserve 9774, Censor's decision, 4 September 1958; certificate issued on 16 September 1958; distributor: Columbia.
 8. Record 33067, 200 feet, Reserve 9810, Censor's decision, 21 October 1958.
 9. Hardy, 1985:108.
 10. Ibid. 113.
 11. Record 32861, 7,342 feet; review and certificate issued, 5 June 1958; distributor: Rank.
 12. Record 34630, 7,688 feet; Reserve 10165, Censor's decision, 29 June 1960; certificate issued on 19 July 1960; distributor: J.A. Rank.
 13. He ordered the trailer's 'X' certificate reference to be cut, Record 37203, Reserve 10863, Censor's decision, 13 April 1964.
 14. Record 37203, Reserve 10822, Censor's decision, 15 January 1964.
 15. Hardy, 1985:138.
 16. Record 34724, 7,874 feet; Reject 2328, Censor's decision, 6 September 1960; Appeal Board decision, 11 October 1960; distributor: Columbia.
 17. Record 34724, 5,332 feet; Reject 2408, Censor's decision, 23 November 1962; no appeal; distributor: British Lion.
 18. See 'The Werewolf' in Daniel Cohen, *A Natural History of Unnatural Things*, New York: McCall, 1971: 33–52; See also Emer Rockett and Kevin Rockett, *Neil Jordan: Exploring Boundaries*, Dublin: Liffey Press, 2003, for a discussion of Neil Jordan's *Company of Wolves* (1984).
 19. Hardy, 1985:130.
 20. Record 35278, 7,954 feet; Reject 2362, Censor's decision, 29 May 1961; Appeal Board decision, 20 June 1961; certificate issued on 5 September 1961; distributor: J.A. Rank.
 21. Record 33900, 7,903 feet; Reserve 10002, Censor's decision, 27 August 1959; certificate issued on 1 September 1959; distributor: J.A. Rank.
 22. Record 33930, 7,488 feet; Reserve 10011, Censor's decision, 21 September 1959; certificate issued on 1 January 1960; distributor: Paramount.
 23. Fergus Linehan, *Irish Times*, 1 January 1962:8.
 24. Roger Corman's acolyte, Francis Coppola's first commercial feature, *The Haunted and the Hunted* (aka *Dementia 13*, 1963), which was made in Ireland, also received an 'X' certificate in Britain, but was released in a cut version with a general certificate in Ireland. Set in an Irish castle, it is a murder-mystery-ghost story. In it, the killer of American Louise (Launa Anders) and others is revealed

as her brother-in-law (Bart Patton), who, as a child caused his young sister's death by drowning in the castle pond. Ridden with guilt, he set out on a murderous spree. (Record 37627, 6,570 feet; Reserve 10913, 30 September 1964; certificate issued on 8 October 1964; distributor: Elliman.)

25. Record 34134, 5,600 feet; Reject 2282, Censor's decision, 14 December 1959; no appeal; distributor: Abbey Films.

26. Record 35952, 7,220 feet; Reserve 10499, Censor's decision, 6 March 1962; review, 14 March 1962; certificate issued on 16 March 1962; distributor: Abbey Films. 'Not for children,' declared David Nowlan in the *Irish Times*, 1 October 1962:8.

27. Fergus Linehan commented, 'What it most certainly is not is suitable for children,' *Irish Times*, 25 February 1963:8. See also, *Sunday Independent*, 24 February 1962:17.

28. Record 36786, 7,973 feet; Reserve 10737, Censor's decision, 30 April 1963; review and certificate issued on 29 August 1963; distributor: Warner-Pathé.

29. 7,751 feet; Reject 2549, Censor's decision, 25 March 1966; Appeal Board decision, 3 May 1966; distributor: Warner Bros.

30. Record 37542, 7,560 feet; Reject 2464, Censor's decision, 12 August 1964; Appeal Board decision, 8 September 1964; certificate issued on 8 September 1964; distributor: Warner-Pathé.

31. 7,296 feet; Reject 2495, Censor's decision, 19 January 1965; Appeal Board decision, Over 18s certificate, 1 March 1965.

32. Record 34828, 7,102 feet; Censor's decision and certificate issued, 29 September 1960; distributor: Abbey Films.

33. Record 37109, 7,721 feet; Censor's decision and certificate issued, 8 November 1963; distributor: Warner Bros.

34. Record 37379, 7,311 feet; Censor's decision and certificate issued, 1 May 1964; distributor: National.

35. Record 34519, 9,789 feet; Reject 2309, Censor's decision, 17 May 1960; Appeal Board decision and censor's report, 26 July 1960; distributor: Abbey Films.

36. Record 35216, 9,747 feet; Reject 2325, Censor's decision, 23 August 1960; Reserve 10316, Censor's decision, 12 April 1961; review 10 May 1961; distributor: Paramount. Interestingly, this was the last film on which O'Hora offered a commentary in the Rejects, or Films Banned, book. This policy of silence was continued by his successor, Christopher Macken. Perhaps cinema had gone so far beyond the pale, or had entered the core of that most sensitive of realms, the family, that the censors' vocabulary could not cope with 1960s' cinema.

37. *Sunday Independent*, 2 October 1960:19.

38. *Irish Times*, 3 October 1960:6.

39. For an account of the discussions between Trevelyan and Powell see Aldgate, 1995:53–55, and more generally on the controversy surrounding the film's release see Ian Christie, 'The Scandal of *Peeping Tom*', in Ian Christie (ed.), *Powell, Pressburger and Others*, London: BFI, 1978:53–59.

40. Record 35216, 9,700 feet; Reserve 10316, Censor's decision, 7 April 1961; review and certificate issued, 12 May 1961.

41. Thematic issues such as child labour, neglected or battered children, and, more broadly, children's welfare were features of adult concern from early cinema onwards. The evil or manipulative child accessing forces of darkness can be seen as a post-war cinematic phenomenon.

42. Record 34864, 6,953 feet; Reserve 10225, Censor's decision, 18 October 1960; review, 18 October 1960; certificate issued on 28 October 1960; distributor: MGM.

43. Record 37326, 8,023 feet; Reserve 10850, Censor's decision, 31 March 1964; certificate issued on 8 April 1964; distributor: MGM.

44. Another adaptation was made by Michael Winner as *The Nightcomers* (1971, GB), which was passed with five cuts and an over-18s certificate by Macken's successor, Dermot Breen. (Record 41435, Reserve 11845, Censor's decision, 21 August 1972; review, 28 November 1972, 20 December 1972; distributor: Elliman Films.)

45. Record 35782, 8,920 feet; Reserve 10463, Censor's decision, 19 January 1962; review and certificate issued, 14 February 1962; distributor: 20th Century-Fox.

46. Record 35910, 9,568 feet; Reserve 10502–03, Censor's decision, 11 cuts, 20 February 1962; no certificate issued. Re-submitted in 1964: Record 37405, 9,212 feet; Reserve 10869, Censor's decision, twelve cuts, 20 May 1964; Appeal Board decision, 28 July 1964; Appeal Board Reserve 11154, two cuts, 14 July 1966; distributor: British Lion.

47. See Kevin Rockett, 'From Radicalism to Conservatism: Contradictions within Fianna Fáil Film Policies in the 1930s', *Irish Studies Review*, vol. 9, no. 2, August 2001.

48. Peter Wollen identifies seven differences between mainstream commerical cinema and counter cinema: 1. Narrative transitivity v. Narrative intransitivity. 2. Identification v. Estrangement. 3.

Transparency v. Foregrounding. 4. Single diegesis v. Multiple diegesis. 5. Closure v. Aperture. 6. Pleasure v. Unpleasure. 7. Fiction v. Reality. See Peter Wollen, 'Godard and Counter Cinema: *Vent D'Est*' in Bill Nichols (ed.), *Movies and Method*, vol. 2, Berkeley/Los Angeles: University of California Press, 1985:501; orig. *Afterimage*, no. 4, autumn 1972.

49. Record 35556, 12,965 feet; Reserve 10430, Censor's decision, 31 October 1961; review and certificate issued, 11 December 1961; distributor: National.

50. Record 30974, 10,943 feet; Reserve 10509, Censor's decision, 13 March 1962; review and certificate issued, 19 April 1963; distributor: United Artists.

51. See Aldgate, 1995.

52. Thomas H. Guback, *The International Film Industry: Western Europe and America Since 1945*, Bloomington/London: Indiana UP, 1969:44, includes a table of the nationality of films released in Britain 1946–1966. Fifty-two of the 590 films were over 3,000 feet.

53. Record 25389, 9,905 feet; Reserve 7822–23, Censor's decision, 27 September 1950; certificate issued on 3 October 1950; distributor: Egan Film Service. When the film was re-viewed by the censor in 1965, the only cut retained was of a knife seen during the fight scene near the end of the film (Censor's decision, 12 November 1965). It seems that the other six cuts made in 1950 were restored at that time.

54. Record 24714, 10,460 feet; Reserve 7689, Censor's decision, 7 March 1950; review and certificate issued, 10 April 1952; distributor: Egan Film Service.

55. Record 21571, 9,515 feet; Reserve 7059, Censor's decision, 14 May 1947; review, 28 July 1947; certificate issued on 12 August 1947; distributor: Elliman; London Film Productions.

56. Record 24823, 7,263 feet; Reserve 7727, Censor's decision, 5 May 1950; certificate issued on 9 May 1950; distributor: RKO Radio.

57. Record 28287, 13,255 feet; Reject 1995, Censor's decision, 13 July 1953; cut by renter and re-submitted, Reserve 8517–18, 23 July 1953; renter refused further nine cuts, rejection confirmed; ban upheld after appeal, 8 September 1953; distributor: Eros.

58. Record 32710, 6,606 feet; Reserve 9681, Censor's decision, 17 April 1958; review and certificate issued, 30 June 1958; distributor: Elliman.

59. Record 35345, 7,097 feet; Appeal Board decision, 13 March 1956, 27 March 1956. *Monthly Film Bulletin*, 1956:5.

60. Record 35345, 9,405 feet; Reserve 10359, Censor's decision, 8 June 1961; review, 26 October 1961; certificate issued on 4 November 1961; distributor: Hibernian. *Irish Times* 27 October 1961:8.

61. Record 35238, 15,390 and 15,552 feet; Reject 2356, Censor's decision, 24 April 1961; Appeal Board decision, 9 May 1961; distributor: British Lion. It was screened at the Irish Film Society, but later passed with four cuts by the Appeal Board, 6 July 1965.

62. 12,452 feet, Reject 2465, Censor's decision, 18 August 1964; passed with over-18s certificate and cuts after appeal, 16 June 1965, Appeal Board Reserve 10994, 6 July 1965. This decision was made, of course, by the 'new' Appeal Board appointed in January 1965.

63. 13,050 feet, Reject 2552, Censor's decision, 14 April 1965; the Appeal Board passed the film uncut with an Over 18s certificate over a year later, 10 May 1966.

64. 11,628 feet; Reject 2768, deputy Censor Gabriel Fallon's decision, 29 September 1970; passed with nine cuts, some of them extensive, by the Appeal Board, and with an over-18s certificate. Reserve 11624, 11 January 1971; Appeal Board Reserve, 1 February 1971; distributor: United Artists.

65. Record 41684, 10,612 feet; Reserve 11956, 21 March 1973 (14 March also recorded); Appeal Board decision, 30 July 1973 (21 March 1973 also recorded); distributor: United Artists.

66. Millicent Marcus, *Italian Film in the Light of Neorealism*, New Jersey: Princeton UP, 1996: 96.

67. Record 32143, 7,979 feet; Reserve 9524, Censor's decision, 23 August 1957; no certificate issued; distributor: Hibernian.

68. Record 37128, 14,518 feet; Reserve 10794, Censor's decision, 28 November 1964; review and certificate issued, 16 December 1963; distributor: 20th Century-Fox.

69. Record 27401, 3,320 feet (16mm; approx. 90 mins); Reject 1968, Censor's decision, 5 August 1952; ban reversed after appeal, 12 August 1952; certificate issued on 12 August 1952; distributor: Egan Film Service.

70. Record 31481, 7,837 feet; Reserve 9337, Censor's decision, 29 October 1956; review and certificate issued, 8 November 1956; distributor: Elliman Films.

71. Record 33720, Reserve 9960, Censor's decision, 2 June 1959; certificate issued on 22 October 1959; distributor: Elliman Films.

72. Record 30968, 8,743 feet; Censor's decision, 20 April 1956; ban upheld after appeal, 15 May 1956; distributor: International Film Distributors/Elliman.

73. Record 31691, 8,457 feet; Reject 2138, Censor's decision, 14 February 1957; ban; Appeal Board decision and certificate issued, 12 March 1957; distributor: Elliman Films.
74. Ginette Vincendeau (ed.), *Encyclopaedia of European Cinema*, London: Cassell/BFI, 1995:72.
75. Record 33116, 11,067 feet; Reject 2222, Censor's decision, 19 September 1958; distributor: Elliman Films.
76. Record 33034, 8,091 feet; Reject 2220, Censor's decision, 19 August 1958; Appeal Board decision, 30 September 1958; distributor: Columbia.
77. Record 34745, 8,760 feet; Reserve 10198, Censor's decision, 1 September 1960; review and certificate issued, 26 October 1960; distributor: Hibernian.
78. 8,980 feet; Reject 2584, Censor's decision, 17 November 1966; Appeal Board decision, 5 December 1966; distributor: Elliman Films.
79. Record 36927, 9,200 feet; Reserve 10750, Censor's decision, 9 July 1963; review and certificate issued, 11 December 1964; distributor: Hibernian.
80. Record 35815, 7,860 feet; Reserve 10486, Censor's decision, 5 January or 14 February 1962; review and certificate issued, 21 February 1962; distributor: National.
81. Ania Witkowska, in Vincendeau (ed.), *Encyclopaedia of European Cinema*, 1995:337.
82. Record 34644, Reserve 10173, Censor's decision, 7 July 1960; review, 22 February 1961; distributor: Hibernian.
83. Record 37491, 8,903 feet; Reserve 10884, Censor's decision, 18 July 1964; review and certificate issued on 17 July 1964; distributor: Hibernian.
84. 9,360 feet; Reject 2528, Censor's decision, 16 September 1965; Appeal Board decision deferred, 26 October 1965; Subsequent correspondence with distributor Abbey Films suggested that the appeal be deferred for about six months (10 November 1965); re-submitted, 21 February 1966; appeal rejected; letter to Abbey Films, 3 March 1966.
85. Reject 2562, Censor's decision, 3 May 1966; Appeal Board decision, 31 May 1966; Appeal Board Reserve 11156–57, 14 July 1966; distributor: Abbey Films.
86. 7,470 feet according to *Monthly Film Bulletin*, 1952:61.
87. Record 32137, 7,648 feet; Reject 2161, deputy Censor E.C. Powell's decision, 16 August 1957; Appeal Board decision, 20 September 1957; review and certificate issued on 29 October 1957; distributor: Hibernian.
88. Film Censor's report to Minister for Justice, 1957, OFC.
89. See Vincendeau (ed.), *Encyclopaedia of European Cinema*, 1995:41.
90. Record 34376, 8,661 feet; Reserve 10106, Censor's decision, 10 March 1960; review and certificate issued, 23 March 1960; distributor: Hibernian.
91. 8,730 feet; Reject 2312, Censor's decision, 23 May 1960; Appeal Board decision and Censor's report, 13 September 1960. Re-submitted in 1964, Record 37387, Reserve 10866, passed with cuts, 6 May 1964.
92. Record 36623, 7,787 feet; Reserve 10678, Censor's decision, 15 February 1963; review, 31 May 1963; distributor: Hibernian.
93. Record 37228, 3,240 feet (16mm), Reserve 10829, Censor's decision, 6 February 1964; distributor: Mr Collins.
94. Record 37541, 3,240 feet (16mm); Reserve 10897, Censor's decision, 12 August 1964; review and certificate issued on 21 August 1964; distributor: Independent Film Distributors/Fine Arts.
95. Reject 2607, 7,455 feet; Censor's decision, 13 December 1967; Appeal Board decision, 8 January 1968; Appeal Board Reserve, 5 February 1968; distributor: United Artists. Carty, 1995:51 says about seven minutes were cut from the film. If this is correct, much of it must have been prior to the Board viewing the film, as their three cuts would not have amounted to this.
96. 2,728 feet (16mm); Reject 2730, Censor's decision, 26 March 1970; the Appeal Board viewed the film on 8 June 1970, but no definite decision seems to have been taken; distributor: Independent. The Board viewed the film again on 1 February 1971 and passed it with cuts and an over-18s certificate. The sub-titles cut might have been perceived as 'blasphemous': 'It was God himself. He cut a fillet from God's rump and ate it. Then he felt a pressing need to shit. Having done so he went to the police.' A rape scene was also cut. (Appeal Board Reserve 11622, 1 February 1971.) The Board viewed the film once more in December 1972, and ordered the deletion of 'three scenes portraying phallus (and phalli) in last reel,' and a scene in which a man is seen 'nuzzling [a] girl's body.' (Appeal Board Reserve 11900,10 December 1972.) An explanation for the two Appeal Board decisions may lie in the fact that the first version of the film submitted was a 16mm copy, thus suggesting limited distribution, while the second may have been a 35mm theatrical version of the film.
97. 10,136 feet; Reject 2859, Censor's decision, 12 October 1971; passed with cuts and over-18s certificate after appeal, 17 January 1972; Appeal Board Reserve 11949 (no date); distributor: Abbey

Films. The Board's six cuts mainly concerned David and Karin in bed, the word 'fucking'; and nudity.

98. On the social problem and working-class realist films of this period, see John Hill, *Sex, Class and Realism: British Cinema 1956–63*, London: BFI, 1986.

99. Record 32577, 9,622 feet; Reserve 9647; Censor's decision, 10 February 1958; review and certificate issued, 28 February 1958; distributor: J.A. Rank.

1. 10,555 feet; Reject 2245, Censor's decision, 5 March 1959; also rejected on 30 October 1959 and 16 November 1960.

2. Appeal Board decision and Censor's report, 7 February 1961. The version viewed by the Board was 9,619 feet.

3. 10,555 feet, Reject 2454, Censor's decision, 8 June 1964. Version viewed by Censor was described by him as 'a re-edited version' in his report to Appeal Board, 3 May 1965; Appeal Board Reserve 10984, 4 May 1965; Appeal Board Reserve 11034, three cuts after renter added scenes (no date).

4. Record 34911, 8,011 feet; Reject 2339, Censor's decision, 29 November 1960; Appeal Board decision and Censor's report, 6 December 1960; distributor: British Lion.

5. Record 34133, 9,184 feet; Reject 2283, Censor's decision, 15 December 1959; distributor: Warner-Pathé.

6. Record 36466, Reserve 10634, Censor's decision, 13 November 1962; review, 28 November 1962. See also *Sunday Independent*, 2 June 1963.

7. 7,907 feet, Reject 2506, Censor's decision, 5 March 1965; distributor: National. As Macken put it in his report to the Appeal Board which upheld his ban, the film is 'a pot-pourri of strip-tease, beatniks and violence'. (Appeal Board decision, 2 June 1965.) It had not been submitted to O'Hora upon its British release in 1960.

8. Record 33675, 8,929 feet; Reject 2251, Censor's decision, 14 May 1959; Appeal Board decision, 2 June 1959; distributor: Elliman Films. Re-submitted in 1962: 8,929 feet; Reject 2404, Censor's decision, 31 October 1962; no appeal; distributor: National.

9. Record 34567, 8,691 feet; Reject 2314, Censor's decision, 1 June 1960; ban upheld after appeal, 28 June 1960; distributor: 20th Century-Fox.

10. Record 34586, 12,052 feet; Reject 2316, Censor's decision, 9 June 1960; ban upheld after appeal, 21 June 1960; distributor: Elliman Films/Viceroy Films. Re-submitted with 2,052 feet cut in 1971: 10,000 feet, Reject 2789, Censor's decision, 6 January 1971; Appeal Board issued an over-16s certificate without cuts; distributor: Superama.

11. Reject 2372, Censor's decision, 7 September 1961; distributor: J.A. Rank. Re-submitted in 1970: Reject 2784, Censor's decision, 18 November 1970; no appeal.

12. Record 35674, 9,014 feet; Reject 2376, Censor's decision, 25 October 1961; no appeal; distributor: British Lion. Re-submitted in 1971: over-16s certificate issued after appeal, 2 June 1971.

13. Record 37064, 9,701 feet; Reject 2434, Censor's decision, 17 October 1963; ban was upheld after appeal and Censor's report, 19 November 1963; distributor: British Lion. Re-submitted in 1970, 1,601 feet shorter than in 1963: 8,100 feet, Reject 2774, Censor's decision, 6 November 1970; passed with over-18s certificate and undetermined cuts after appeal, 19 November 1970; distributor: National.

14. Record 35633, 6,628 feet; Reserve 10420, Censor's decision, 12 October 1961; review and certificate issued, 27 November 1961; distributor: British Lion.

15. Record 36622, 11,282 feet; Reject 2414, Censor's decision, 8 February 1963; ban upheld after appeal, 19 February 1963; distributor: British Lion. Re-submitted in 1970: Record 40493; Reserve 11576, Censor's decision, passed with one cut of a nude bed scene between Toby and Jane (reel 8), and an over-18s certificate 20 July 1970; distributor: Abbey Films.

16. Record 33934 and 37138, 8,305 feet; Reject 2267, Censor's decision, 15 September 1959; ban upheld after appeal, 13 October 1959; distributor: 20th Century-Fox. Re-submitted in 1963: Reject 2438, Censor's decision, 5 December 1963; ban upheld after appeal, 9 November 1965; distributor: Hibernian. Re-considered by Appeal Board in 1965: decision deferred, 9 November 1965; appeal rejected 23 November 1965.

17. Record 36461, Reserve 10638, Censor's decision, twelve cuts, 5 November 1962; distributor: British Lion. The sequel, *The New Interns* (John Rich, 1964), which is another hospital drama, was banned: 10,966 feet; Reject 2489, Censor's decision, 8 October 1964; ban upheld after appeal, 27 October 1964. Re-submitted in 1970: 10,966 feet, Reject 2757, 24 August 1970; limited certificate issued after appeal, 1 October 1970. Macken commented on its initial submission that 'the themes around which the picture is built, e.g, the psychiatric test "of a girl's availability," the distasteful scenes of childbirth and the amount of the presentation that concerns rape make this film subversive of public morality.' (Censor's report to Appeal Board, 27 October 1964.)

18. 9,035 feet, Reject 2472, Censor's decision, 6 October 1964; ban upheld after appeal, 13 October 1964. Re-submitted in 1971; passed with over-18 certificate without cuts after appeal. 'The theme in this presentation is criminal abortion and would be subversive of public morality.' (Censor's report to Appeal Board, 13 October 1964.)
19. Record 32439, 7,940 feet; Reject 2178, Censor's decision, 10 December 1957; ban upheld after appeal, 14 January 1958; distributor: Elliman.
20. Record 33504, 8,064 feet; Reject 2244, Censor's decision, 5 March 1959; no appeal; distributor: British Lion.
21. Record 35092, 11,281 feet; Reject 2345, Censor's decision, 2 February 1961; ban upheld after appeal, 9 July 1963; distributor: Paramount. Re-submitted in 1971: issued with an over-18s certificate without cuts by the Appeal Board.
22. Record 37107, 8,387 feet; Reject 2443, Censor's decision, 7 January 1964. Re-submitted in 1971: passed with over-16s certificate, 29 September 1971; certificate issued on 30 September 1971; distributor: Warner-Pathé.
23. Record 37751, 8,590 feet; Reject 2492, Censor's decision, 17 December 1964; ban upheld after appeal, 19 February 1965; distributor: Warner-Pathé. Inevitably, the explicitly titled, *Call Girls* (*Fur zwei Groschen Zärtlichkeit*, Arthur Maria Rabenalt, West Germany/Denmark, 1957), about prostitutes in Denmark, was also banned. (Record 33350, 8,344 feet; Reject 2232, Censor's decision, 30 December 1958; no appeal.) 'A conveniently exploitable subject,' according to *Monthly Film Bulletin* (1958:155). The surprise, perhaps, is that it was ever submitted to the Irish Censor. Also banned was the American *Go Naked in the World* (Ranald MacDougall, 1961), which features a high-class prostitute (Record 35233, 9,286 feet; Reject 2354, Censor's decision, 20 April 1961; ban upheld after appeal, 16 May 1961), and *Irma La Douce* (Billy Wilder, 1963), with Shirley MacLaine as a prostitute and Jack Lemmon trying to 'save' her from life on the Parisian streets. (12,686 feet; Reject 2445, Censor's decision, 30 January 1964. Re-submitted in May 1964: Censor's ban confirmed; ban upheld after appeal, 9 June 1964. Re-submitted in 1970: passed with an over-18s certificate without cuts, in undetermined version.) Also banned because of its prostitution theme was *Never on Sunday* (Jules Dassin, 1959, Greece). (Record 34960, 8,321 feet; Reject 2340, Censor's decision, 30 November 1960; ban upheld after appeal, 13 December 1960; distributor: United Artists.)
24. Among the six cuts to this film were references to prostitution and brothels; and the running down of Jenny, which was deemed to be 'rather shocking'. (Record 35254, 8,722 feet; Reserve 10353, Censor's decision, 1 June 1961; certificate issued on 31 August 1961; distributor: Columbia/British Lion.)
25. Record 36835, 9,607 feet; Reject 2425, Censor's decision, 23 May 1963; ban upheld after appeal, 18 June 1963; distributor: British Lion.
26. 8,069 feet; Reject 2335, Censor's decision, 8 November 1960; ban upheld after appeal, 15 November 1960.
27. Film Censor's report to Minister for Justice, January 1961, OFC.
28. Film Censor's report to Minister for Justice, 31 January 1964, OFC. O'Hora died in office on 22 March 1964, less than three months after writing this report.
29. Noel Moran, *Sunday Independent*, 3 November 1957:15.
30. Noel Moran, *Sunday Independent*, 21 October 1956:15; Noel Moran, ibid. 4 November 1956:15.
31. Noel Moran, *Sunday Independent*, 4 July 1957:13.
32. When first submitted, the film was banned by the Censor (Record 34316, 14,440 feet; Reject 2271, 15 October 1959), a decision upheld by the Appeal Board, 15 December 1959. O'Hora's 'main objection' was to the film's 'utterly clinical dialogue'. (Film Censor's report to Appeal Board, 15 December 1959.) It was re-submitted in the same version two months after the Appeal Board banned it, and on this occasion O'Hora passed it with fifty-three deletions, one of the largest number of cuts made to any film viewed by the censors. (Record 34316, 14,440 feet; Reserve 10089, 24 February 1960; review and certificate issued on 4 April 1960; distributor: Columbia.)
33. *Sunday Independent*, 19 June 1960:23 gives the film's Irish running time as 136 minutes.
34. Cinema correspondent, *Irish Times*, 20 June 1960.
35. M.P.O. Voight, J. Bishton, J.M. Balmforth, *Irish Times*, 23 June 1960:7.
36. Cinema correspondent, *Irish Times*, 27 June 1959:8.
37. Record 36772, 11,608 feet; Reserve 10716, Censor's decision, 23 April 1963; review and certificate issued, 4 June 1963; distributor: J. A. Rank.
38. Record 33919, 9,434 feet; Reserve 10008, Censor's decision, 10 September 1959. O'Hora told the renter that he was primarily concerned with the film's 'nude females'.
39. Roy and John Boulting, *Irish Times*, 31 October 1959:7.

40. John D. Sheridan, ibid. 3 November 1959:7.
41. A.P. McCarty, ibid. 4 November 1959:7.
42. Brian Cleeve, ibid. 5 November 1959:7.
43. John Manning, ibid. 6 November 1959:7. Manning, a brother of writer Mary Manning, had been involved with the Irish Film Society since the 1930s.
44. John D. Sheridan, ibid. 7 November 1959:7.
45. 'Ex-nudist', ibid. 9 November 1959:7.
46. Neil Renton; ibid. 5 November 1959:7.
47. *Irish Times*, 12 November 1959:1.
48. Appeal Board decision, 22 December 1959. See *Irish Times*, 1 January 1960:1.
49. *Irish Times*, 5 December 1960:6.
50. Ibid.
51. Ken Shaw, *Sunday Independent*, 4 December 1960:23. For a discussion of *I'm All Right Jack* see Jeffrey Richards and Anthony Aldgate, *The Best of British: Cinema and Society 1930–1970*, Oxford: Basil Blackwell, 1983:115–130. It is erroneously reported in this book (p. 127), based on a *Daily Telegraph* story, 31 October 1959, that the Boultings did not accept the Irish Censor's cuts.
52. Record 20386, 9,311 feet; Reject 1826, Censor's decision, 6 March 1946.
53. 8,789 feet; Reject 1878, Censor's decision, 8 October 1947.
54. Appeal Board decision, 2 April 1946 and 28 October 1947, respectively.
55. Appeal Board decision, 7 October 1960.
56. *Irish Times*, 23 January 1961:6.
57. Originally censored at Reserve 7056–57, 14 May 1947, but a note saying these 'exceptions' are later said 'to be cancelled' and red marks across both pages perhaps indicate that the film was banned. At Reserve 7214–16, 23 January 1948, there are thirty-three cuts listed, but no record of a certificate being issued.
58. Record 35257, Reserve 10350, Censor's decision, 2 May 1961. The film was released in January 1962. See Fergus Linehan, *Irish Times*, 29 January 1962:8.
59. Record 36117, 9,314 feet; Reserve 10564, 5 June 1962; review and certificate issued, 29 June 1962; distributor: Abbey Films.
60. Fergus Linehan, *Irish Times*, 17 September 1962:8. O'Hora noted in his report that while it had been 'much cut' by the distributor, it was 'no easy picture to pass' because 'in treatment and in theme it is near the bone all the time.' *A Taste of Honey* and another banned British film, *The L-Shaped Room*, were eventually released in 1971, by which time they had been shown on British television. (*Sunday Independent*, 22 August 1971:10.)
61. *Sunday Independent*, 26 May 1963 and *Irish Times*, 27 May 1963:8.
62. *Irish Times*, 27 May 1963:8.
63. Record 36637, cut perhaps from 12,054 to 9,300 feet by renter without formal cuts slip between date of Censor's decision and the review date; Censor's decision, 21 February 1963; review and certificate issued, 22 May 1963; distributor: J. A. Rank.
64. Des Hickey, *Sunday Independent*, 11 November 1962:26.
65. 14,109 feet, Reject 2193, 13 February 1958; ban upheld after appeal, 3 June 1958. O'Hora commented in his report: 'I could not possibly save the picture by cutting as the near-incestuous relationship and the resultant miscarriage and trial for murder would have to be excised and thus the entire broad basis of the picture would be missing.'
66. Des Hickey, *Sunday Independent*. 21 March 1965:6. The film had been banned in 1961 (Record 36009, 11,036 feet; Reject 2364, Censor's decision, 13 June 1961; no appeal; distributor: 20th Century-Fox), and re-submitted in 1962 with 726 feet cut by the distributor and when it was passed with six cuts (10,310 feet; Reserve 10566, 30 May 1962). However, in 1967 it was submitted again in the same shortened version, and was passed with an over-16s certificate by the Appeal Board (Appeal Board decision, 17 April 1967). In this latter instance, the Censor insisted the distributor 'use only description "original version" in advertising,' a clear deception of the public.
67. Des Hickey, *Sunday Independent*, 25 November 1962:24.
68. Record 36404, 11,741 feet; Reserve 10615, Censor's decision, 27 September 1962; certificate issued on 24 October 1962; distributor: Warner-Pathé.
69. Des Hickey, 'Look What Eddie's Father has Done', *Sunday Independent*, 20 December 1964:22. Indeed the Censor's report on the film (Record 36774, Reserve 10714, 22 April 1963), includes four cuts, two of which are references to 'busts' and 'vital statistics'; one to babies; and a line referring to a bedroom door was also excised.
70. *Sunday Independent*, 20 December 1964:22.
71. Ciaran Carty, *Film Directions*, vol. 3, no. 9, 1980:17.

72. Ibid.
73. Haughey 'was a very successful Minister for Justice. He pushed through a radical law reform programme ... He also introduced the Succession Bill ... [which] was one of the most significant contributions to women's rights for decades.' (Vincent Browne (ed.), *The Magill Book of Irish Politics*, Dublin: Magill Publications, 1981.)
74. Interestingly, only a few weeks after the Appeal Board had passed *Adam and Eve* uncut, reversing O'Hora's ban.
75. *Dáil debates*, vol. 196, col. 3463, 26 July 1962. Brendan Corish raised the issue of children attending cinemas on a number of occasions in the Dáil. On the surface his queries may appear to favour limited certificates, but the opposite may in fact have been his intention. It later emerged that despite his prominent position in the Labour Party (a TD since 1945, and its leader for seventeen years, 1960–1977) he was at the same time a secret member of the traditionalist Catholic body, the Knights of St Columbanus, which was highly vocal in its attacks on imported popular culture. Incidentally, Corish's predecessor as leader of the Labour Party, William Norton, was also a member of the Knights.
76. *Dáil debates*, vol. 200, cols. 596–7, 28 February 1963; ibid. vol. 321, 2 June 1964.
77. Des Hickey, *Sunday Independent*, 22 November 1964:24.
78. Record 37670, 9,056 feet; Reject 2482, Censor's decision, 27 October 1964; Appeal Board Reserve 10940–6, 4 February 1965; distributor: MGM.
79. Des Hickey, *Sunday Independent*, 22 November 1964:24.
80. Record 37333, 8489 feet; Reserve 10855, deputy Censor J. Shiel's decision, 2 April 1964. The reason a deputy Censor viewed the film was that Liam O'Hora had died on 22 March and Christopher Macken was not appointed until 13 April.
81. S. Parker, Branch Manager, BLC Films Ltd, 64 Middle Abbey Street, Dublin, to J.T. O'Farrell, 28 August 1964.
82. Appeal Board decision, 1 September 1964. The members present were: J.T. O'Farrell, Canon O'Donnell, Mr A. Russell, Mrs Gibbons, and Sam Stephenson.
83. *Sunday Independent*, 22 November 1964:24.
84. *The Victors* had been passed with six cuts by Macken, Record 37486, 13,992 feet; Reserve 10885, Censor's decision, 8 July 1964. On appeal to the new Board, this was changed to four cuts and an over-16s certificate (Appeal Board decision, 1 February 1965; distributor: British Lion).
85. *Marnie* was passed with five, sometimes long cuts, Record 37629, 11,675 feet; Reserve 10917, Censor's decision, 1 October 1964; the renter appealed cuts, and it was passed uncut with an over-18s certificate by the Board, 1 December 1964.
86. *Becket*, an adaptation of the Jean Anouilh play which focuses on the relationship between the Archbishop of Canterbury, Thomas à Becket and Henry II, was passed with nine cuts by Macken, Record 37651, 13,333 feet; Reserve 10919, Censor's decision, 14 October 1964. The cuts were appealed and the film was passed by the new Board with six cuts and a general certificate, Appeal Board Reserve 10953, 15 February 1965 and 22 February 1965; distributor: Paramount.
87. Macken banned the 'unsavoury' *Girl with Green Eyes*, Record 37372, 8,307 feet; Reject 2452, 28 April 1964; Censor's report to Appeal Board, 12 May 1964. In what was the first of Macken's decisions to be considered by the Appeal Board, it upheld his rejection (12 May 1964). When re-submitted in 1970, it was again rejected by Macken, Record 40526, Reject 2759, 25 August 1970, but passed with an over-16s certificate by the Appeal Board, 19 October 1970.
88. Cut in three places by Macken, Record 37650, 8,717 feet; Reserve 10921, 19 October 1964, but when the renter appealed the cuts, the Board banned the film (3 November 1964).
89. Des Hickey, *Sunday Independent*, 29 November 1964:l. See also readers' letters, ibid. 26.
90. Indeed, in January 1965, just as film censorship was about to be transformed, Hickey published a list of 23 films which had received an 'X' certificate in Britain but which had been approved for general viewing in Ireland, sometimes uncut. (*Sunday Independent*, 10 January 1965:22.) These films included *Blood and Roses* (Roger Vadim, 1960, France); *The Night of the Iguana* (John Huston, 1964) from the play by Tennessee Williams (nineteen cuts); *The Masque of the Red Death*; *Wives and Lovers* (John Rich, 1963) (fifteen cuts); *Night Must Fall* (Karel Reisz, 1964, GB) (two cuts); *Tom Jones* of which the Censor commented that it was 'entirely unfit for children and, because of that very fact, I have to be pretty ruthless with the scissors,' and as such demanded twenty-one cuts, with the Appeal Board adding two more (Record 36942, 11,000 feet, Reserve 10769–70, Censor's decision, 15 July 1963; Appeal Board decision, 4 February 1964; certificate issued on 12 March 1964. Re-submitted in 1971: passed uncut with an over-16s certificate [in undetermined version] by Appeal Board); and a film about an adult who arrives home in New Orleans with a childlike bride, *Toys in the Attic* (George Roy Hill, 1963). As regards this latter film, Macken stated

that it was 'a most adult picture; indeed it is so adult that I am letting children see it,' a very strange comment indeed and one which demonstrates how confused film censorship policy had become. Maybe the explanation for this oddity lies in the fact that he wrote this on New Year's Eve! (Record 37176, Reserve 10818, Censor's decision, 31 December 1963; review, 3 February 1964; distributor: United Artists.)

CHAPTER 6

1. *Dáil debates*, vol. 213, col. 561, 3 December 1964.
2. Ibid., col. 564.
3. For Carroll's views on film censorship see interview in *Film Directions*, vol. 3, no. 9, 1980: 20.
4. Des Hickey, *Sunday Independent*, 7 November 1965: 10.
5. Reject 2500, Censor's decision, 24 February 1965; Appeal Board decision, 10 March 1965: vote 7 to 2 in favour of passing, 18 March 1965; final discussion, 29 March 1965, seven cuts and over-18s certificate. Appeal Board Reserve 10968, 31 March 1965.
6. This film had been banned by O'Hora in 1958: Reject 2231, 7,843 feet, Censor's decision, 11 December 1958; Ban upheld after appeal, 6 January 1959. Re-submitted in 1965 (7,843 feet); Reject 2499, Censor's decision, 18 February 1965, Passed with cuts after appeal, 23 February 1965.
7. Reject 2501, 9,949 feet, Censor's decision, 1 March 1965); passed with cut with over-18s certificate after appeal, 13 April 1965.
8. Censor's report to Appeal Board, 5 April 1965; Reject 2502, 8,000 feet, Censor's decision, 2 March 1965, 'consideration deferred' by Appeal Board, 5 April 1965; ban upheld after appeal, 9 April 1965.
9. Censor's report to Appeal Board, 6 July 1965. Reject 2515, 11,220 feet, Censor's decision, 17 June 1965; passed uncut with over-18s after appeal, 6 July 1965.
10. Reject 2517, 10,298 feet, Censor's decision, 15 July 1965. Appeal Board Reserve 11017, 27 August 1965.
11. Censor's report to Appeal Board, 26 August 1965; Reject 2519, 8,690 feet, Censor's decision, 19 July 1965; ban upheld after appeal, 26 August 1965.
12. Censor's report to Appeal Board, 28 September 1965; Reject 2526, 8,400 feet, Censor's decision, 9 August 1965; Appeal Board Reserve 11038–39, 7,650 feet, over-18s certificate, six cuts, 8 September 1965.
13. Originally banned by Richard Hayes in 1952: Reject 1976, 8,586 feet, Censor's decision, 17 December 1952; no appeal. Re-submitted in 1965; Reject 2521, 10,016 feet, Censor's decision, 23 July 1965; ban upheld after appeal, 9,990 feet, 20 November 1967.
14. Reject 2522, 7,651 feet, 26 July 1965; ban upheld after appeal, 10 September 1965.
15. Reject 2523, 9,043 feet, Censor's decision, 27 July 1965; viewed by Appeal Board, 14 September 1965; Board requested renter to re-edit specified sequences (unrecorded). Reviewed 23 November 1965, over-18s certificate with six cuts, 259 feet, 31 December 1965.
16. Reject 2527, 9,742 feet, Censor's decision, 27 August 1965; Appeal Board Reserve 11041–43, passed with ten cuts and over-18s certificate after appeal, 2 November 1965 and 25 January 1966.
17. Reject 2528, 9,360 feet, deputy Censor Mr J. Shiel's decision, 16 September 1965; ban upheld after appeal. Decision deferred 26 October 1965; Board rejected appeal, but 'indicate to renter that if [he] wishes to re-submit at a later date (say over six months) Board would re-consider film' (10 November 1965). The film was re-submitted on 21 February 1966 and was rejected (Letter to Abbey Films, 3 March 1966. (All at 26 October 1965.)
18. Reject 2529, 8,100 feet (other length recorded, 5,427 feet); Censor's decision, 4 October 1965; Appeal Board Reserve 11027, 8,460 feet, over-18s certificate with two cuts, 12 October 1965.
19. Reject 2531, 11,430 feet, Censor's decision, 23 October 1965; ban upheld after appeal, 7 December 1965.
20. Cited in Douglas Brode, *The Films of the Sixties*, Secaucus, New Jersey: Citadel Press, 1980:150.
21. *Devils of Darkness* (Lance Comfort, 1964, GB), a horror film which concerns how a French count preys on young girls. The other films passed uncut were *The Hill*, a World War Two drama set in North Africa, and *The Night Walker* (William Castle, 1964), a low-budget shocker from the director of *The Tingler*.
22. Appeal Board decision, 2 June 1965.
23. Reject 2508, 11,140 feet, Censor's decision, 12 April 1965; ban upheld after appeal, 19 May 1965.
24. Reject 2516, 6,610 feet, Censor's decision, 18 June 1965; ban upheld after appeal, 27 August 1965.

25. Reject 2496, 8,619 feet, Censor's decision, 20 January 1965, ban upheld after appeal, 4 March 1965.
26. Censor's decision, 8 January 1965.
27. Record 37784, Reserve 10934, 19 January 1965.
28. Censor's decision, 9 April 1965. This is another reflection perhaps of the Censor's attitude to transgressive women.
29. Record 38097, Reserve 110008. Censor's decision, 3 August 1965.
30. Censor's decision, 4 September 1965.
31. Record. 21321, Reserve 6973, 20 January 1946.
32. Reject 2482, 27 October 1964; Censor's report to Appeal Board, 4 February 1965.
33. Reserve 10940–46; 4 February 1965.
34. Reject 2546, 8,159 feet; deputy Censor Gabriel Fallon's decision, 22 February 1965; Appeal Board Reserve 11084, passed with over-18s certificate and three cuts after appeal, 18 March 1966.
35. Reject 2553, 8,100 feet; Censor's decision, 16 February 1966; Appeal Board Reserve 11089, passed with over-18s certificate and two cuts, 18 March 1966.
36. Reject 2566, 10,635 feet; Censor's decision, 30 June 1966; passed with cuts and over-18s certificate after appeal, 22 July 1966; Appeal Board Reserve 11198, 27 September 1966.
37. Reject 2575, deputy Censor Gabriel Fallon's decision, 21 September 1966; passed with over-18s certificate and seven cuts after appeal, 5 October 1966; Appeal Board Reserve 11239–40; 27 February 1967. Fallon commented that it was a 'thoroughly unpleasant slice of French provincial (and immoral) life. [It was] sordid in the extreme without a redeeming feature of any kind.' (Censor's report to Appeal Board, 5 October 1966.)
38. Reject 2576, 8,151 feet, deputy Censor Gabriel Fallon's decision, 22 September 1966. Fallon commented that the film could be rated for over-18s provided its release was confined to 'a recognised "art" cinema'. He went on to comment in his report to the Appeal Board on the 'Photograph' scene which he suggested could be cut, that 'even our "art" cinema audiences are not sufficiently mature to receive this effect, without suspecting an implied mockery or a direct and well-calculated offence,' but the Board deferred a decision for twelve months, by which time the renter had lost the rights to the film (17 October 1966).
39. Reject 2560, 8,283 feet (Reject figure); Censor's decision, 21 June 1966; passed with cuts and over-16s certificate and four cuts after appeal, 8 July 1966; Appeal Board Reserve 11162–3, 29 July 1966. Length also listed as 9,000 feet. Psychiatrist Macken commented that while 'the pictures on the screen give a clear representation of the many and varied auditory and visual hallucinations' of schizophrenia, 'there is very little relieving matter.' (Censor's report to Appeal Board, 8 July 1966.)
40. Reject 2561, 10,530 feet, Censor's decision, 18 April 1966; passed with over-18s certificate and seven cuts after appeal, 26 April 1966; Appeal Board Reserve 11114–15, 2 May 1966 Additional cuts, Appeal Board Reserve 11131 (no date). The cuts ordered included Joe's (Laurence Harvey) 'In Nomine Spiritus Sancti' to 'Fidelio'; and references to sex and being in bed.
41. Reject 2581, 10,240 feet, Censor's decision, 2 November 1966; Appeal Board decision, 18 November 1966.
42. Reject 2570, 10,748 feet, deputy Censor Gabriel Fallon's decision, 5 August 1966; passed with over-16s certificate and eight cuts after appeal, Appeal Board Reserve 11187–8, 13 September 1966; Appeal Board Reserve 11195, further cut, 5 October 1966.
43. Reject 2568, 11,296 feet, Censor's decision, 19 September 1966; on appeal, passed with over-21s certificate and three cuts, Appeal Board Reserve 11861, 28 September 1966.
44. Reject 2578, 13,500 feet, deputy Censor Gabriel Fallon's decision, 11 October 1966; on appeal passed with over-18s certificate and four cuts, Appeal Board Reserve 11212–13, 30 December 1966. 'In Britain it was given a 16 year and over certificate. With this rating I most emphatically disagree. It is in every sense a film for mature adults; and even for exhibition in an "art" cinema in this country, it calls for some selective cutting. It is difficult to believe that some shots were not (even though unintentionally) geared to titillate the viewer.' (Gabriel Fallon's Report to Appeal Board, 24 October 1966.)
45. Reject 2583, 11,133 feet, Censor's decision, 7 November 1966; on appeal, passed over-18s certificate one cut, 5 December 1966; Appeal Board Reserve 11217, 3 January 1967.
46. Reject 2586, 9,907 feet, Censor's decision, 19 December 1966; on appeal, passed with over-18s certificate and one cut, 3 January 1967; Appeal Board Reserve 11224, 9 January 1967.
47. Reject 2569, 9,300 feet, deputy Censor Gabriel Fallon's decision, 25 July 1966; ban upheld after appeal, 2 September 1966.
48. Reject 2564, 7,936 feet, Censor's decision, 22 April 1966; ban upheld after appeal, 17 may 1966; 10 June 1966.

49. Reject 2542, 10,243 feet, deputy Censor Mr Shiel's decision, 27 January 1966; ban upheld after appeal, 1 March 1966. In 1973 it passed with an over-18s certificate and five cuts, Record 41605, Reserve 11933, 29 January 1973.

50. Censor's report to Appeal Board, 19 April 1966. Reject 2554, 8,214 feet, 18 February 1966; passed uncut with over-18s certificate after appeal, 19 April 1966. Those in attendance at the Appeal Board viewing were the Revd Murray, John Carroll and Judge Maguire. However, another 20 films passed with over-18s certificates were cut, including the last in *The Fly* series, *The Curse of the Fly* (Don Sharp, 1965, GB), *The Plague of the Zombies*, *Dracula – Prince of Darkness*, *A Rage to Live* (Walter Grauman, 1965), featuring a nymphomaniac, *Rasputin – The Mad Monk* (Don Sharp, 1966, GB), *Life at the Top* which was one of the last films of the British 'realist' New Wave, *Cul-de-Sac*, *The Silken Skin*, *Diary of a Chambermaid*, *The Group*, *The Chase* and *This Property is Condemned*.

51. Reject 2571, 10,210 feet, 19 July 1966; passed with cuts and over-16s certificate and two cuts of sex scenes after appeal, 16 September 1966; Appeal Board Reserve 11181, 19 September 1966.

52. Reject 2573, 9,540 feet, Censor's decision, 14 September 1966; Appeal Board decision, 10 October 1966.

53. Reject 2580, 8,746 feet, Censor's decision, 6 October 1966; Appeal Board Reserve 11203, 18 November 1966.

54. Quoted, Des Hickey, 'Abuse of Certificates Must be Stopped', *Sunday Independent*, 16 October 1966:22.

55. Record 38368, Reserve 11070, 9,358 feet, Censor's decision, 23 February 1962, review 14 March 1966.

56. Macken issued this film with an over-16s certificate with one cut of a female nude, Record 38528, Reserve 11135, Censor's decision, 8 June 1966. The limited certificate was appealed against over-16s limitation and the Board granted a general certificate provided one further cut was made, Appeal Board Reserve 11150, 12 July 1966; Appeal Board Reserve 11159, 24 July 1966.

57. The Censor's limitation in many instances was not appealed, such as *Bunny Lake is Missing* (Otto Preminger, 1965, GB), John Ford's last film, *Seven Women* (1966), which was also cut twice, and *The Red Desert* (*Il Deserto Rosso*, Michaelangelo Antonioni, 1964, Italy/France).

58. Record 38654, Reserve 11180, Censor's decision, 13 September 1966; Appeal Board Reserve 11214, affirmed cuts (bed scenes between Sarah and Armstrong, and stabbing of Gronek), but it issued general certificate (October 1966).

59. Record 38538, Reserve 11140, Censor's decision, 22 June 1966; Appeal Board Reserve 11147, one cut, over-18s certificate, 7 July 1966; Appeal Board Reserve 11160, restored cut, no date.

60. Record 38306, Reserve 11052, Censor's decision, 7 January 1966. A second cut was of the words 'mistress' and 'kept woman'.

61. Record 38370, Reserve 11069, 24 February 1966.

62. Record 38381, Reserve 11073, 9,230 feet; Censor's decision, 28 February 1966.

63. Record 38394, Reserve 11078, Censor's decision, 9 March 1966.

64. Record 38350, Reserve 11079, Censor's decision, 10 February 1966.

65. Record 38548, Reserve 11144, Censor's decision, 28 June 1966; Appeal Board Reserve 11148, 7 July 1966; Appeal Board Reserve 11155, 14 July 1966.

66. Record 38789, Reserve 11205, Censor's decision, 30 November 1966.

67. Record 38796, Reserve 11207, Censor's decision, 7 December 1966.

68. Reject 2603, 11,880 feet; Censor's decision, 26 October 1967; Appeal Board upheld decision, 11 December 1967. The Board also met on 2 November and 5 December to appraise the film. Re-submitted in 1977: Reject 3121, 9,900 feet; Censor's decision, 8 December 1977 (Dermot Breen). The film was eventually granted a certificate by Sheamus Smith in 2000.

69. Reject 2588, 8,292 feet, Censor's decision, 16 January 1966; passed with six cuts and over-16s certificate after appeal, Appeal Board Reserve 11235, 30 January 1966.

70. Reject 2605, 8,599 feet, deputy Censor Gabriel Fallon's decision, 27 November 1967; appeal on 11 December 1967, 'At request of renter Board will see again film with parts deleted'; Appeal Board Reserve 11352, six cuts (total 577 feet) and over-18s certificate, 4 June 1968.

71. Appeal Board Reserve 11230, 9,866 feet, 23 January 1967.

72. Appeal Board decision, 13 February 1967; 8,280 feet; Appeal Board Reserve 11234, 20 February 1967.

73. Reject 2593, 14 February 1967.

74. Appeal Board Reserve 11263, 1 May 1967. The Rejects book records that the film was 9,000 feet, whereas the Appeal Board gives the length as 9,463 feet.

75. Reject 2600, 10,111 feet, 25 August 1967; appeal, 9 October 1967; 'Re-shown for third and final time,' 19 April 1968; Appeal Board Reserve 11347, 24 May 1968.
76. 8,458 feet, Reject 2610, deputy Censor Gabriel Fallon's decision, 6 February 1968; ban upheld after appeal, 19 February 1968.
77. Reject 2625, 7,383 feet, Censor's decision, 26 June 1968; ban upheld after appeal, 8 July 1968.
78. Reject 2631, 8,100 feet, deputy Censor Gabriel Fallon's decision, 19 September 1968; ban upheld after appeal, 4 October 1968.
79. Reject 2635, 8,600 feet, Censor's decision, 29 October 1968; an upheld after appeal, 2 December 1968.
80. Reject 2638, 8,822 feet, Censor's decision, 5 December 1968). This entry repeated as Reject 2646; ban upheld after appeal, 18 December 1968.
81. Reject 2645, 10,156 feet, Censor's decision, 14 December 1968; ban upheld after appeal, 7 February 1969.
82. Reject 2617, 7,650 feet, deputy Censor Gabriel Fallon's decision, 29 March 1968; re-submitted in 1976: passed with an over-18s certificate, Record 43097, Reserve 12595, Censor's decision, 18 May 1976.
83. Reject 2616, 6,976 feet, deputy Censor Gabriel Fallon's decision, April 1968.
84. Reject 2634, 8,950 feet, Censor's decision, 2 October 1968.
85. Those cut included *Waterhole Three* (William Graham, 1967, GB), which features rape; *Two Weeks in September* (Serge Bourguignon, 1967, France), in which Brigitte Bardot has two lovers; *Mondo Cane No 2* (Italy); *I'll Never Forget Whatshisname* (Michael Winner, 1967, GB); the violent and explicit *Onibaba* (*The Hole*, Kaneto Shindo, 1964, Japan); *The Detective* (Gordon Douglas, 1968), where the ten cuts mainly dealt with homosexuality; *The Bofors Gun* (Jack Gold, 1968, GB), which was cut in eight places; the adaptation of John Fowles' cult novel *The Magus* (Guy Greene, 1968, GB), which the Censor regarded as being thematically 'unsavoury' because it featured abortion and 'perverted sex' (Censor's report to Appeal Board, 27 January 1969); *The Strange Affair* (David Greene, 1968, GB), set among corrupt London police and featuring nymphet Susan George; and *The Anniversary* (Roy Ward Baker, 1968, GB), a black comedy starring Bette Davis.
86. Reject 2640, 8,460 feet, Censor's decision, 30 December 1968; passed with one cut and over-16s certificate after appeal, 21 February 1969; Appeal Board Reserve 11412, 20 March 1969.
87. Reject 2636, 7,645 feet, Censor's decision, 30 October 1968); over-18s certificate after appeal, 18 November 1968.
88. Reject 2621, 9,900 feet, Censor's decision, 29 April 1968; Appeal Board decision, 9,950 feet, 13 May 1968.
89. Reject 2620, 19 April 1968.
90. Appeal Board Reserve 11390–91, December 1968. The appeal was held on 6 May 1968.
91. Reject 2594, 8,810 feet, Censor's decision, 22 February 1967; passed with cuts and over-18s certificate after appeal, 13 March 1967; Appeal Board Reserve 11262, 1 May 1967; Appeal Board Reserve 11288, 24 July 1967.
92. Reject 2619, 10,736 feet, Censor's decision, 18 April 1968; passed with three cuts and over-18s certificate after appeal (10,714 feet), 29 April 1968; Appeal Board Reserve 11353, 4 June 1968.
93. The cuts were outlined in a letter from Judge Maguire to Harry McGuinness, Paramount Branch Manager, 12 December 1966. McGuinness to Maguire, 17 February 1967. The Board approved the final version on 20 March 1967, though it is not recorded if McGuinness' request was acceded to.
94. Record 41259, Reserve 11770, Censor's decision, four cuts and over-18s certificate, 5 April 1972.
95. Record 41490, Reserve 11867, Censor's decision, four cuts and over-18s certificate, five cuts and over-16s certificate, 13 October 1972. Other films in the 1970s with an abortion theme cut or where the film was banned include *Woman Without a Face* (aka *Mister Buddwing*, Delbert Mann, 1966) (Record 39742, Reserve 11376, Censor's decision, two cuts and over-18s certificate, 7 November 1968); *The Engagement* (Paul Joyce, 1970, GB) where even the rejection of abortion: 'I don't want a bloody abortion' was the film's sole cut (Record 404062, Reserve 11562, Censor's decision, 25 June 1970); *Love with the Proper Stranger*, where an abortion scene may have been cut prior to submission, but the fact that abortion is rejected by the woman and marriage serves as the narrative closure, may have encouraged the Board (in 1971) to leave in the word and issue it with an over-18s certificate (Reject 2472, 9,035 feet, Censor's decision, 6 October 1964; ban upheld after appeal, 13 October 1964; re-submitted in 1971; over-18 certificate after appeal, no cuts); *Joanna*; *Next Stop Greenwich Village* (Record 43267, Reserve 12670–71, over-18s certificate with ten cuts, 27 October 1976) and the self-abortion in the adaptation of Sidney Sheldon's bestseller *The Other Side of Midnight* (Charles Jarrott, 1977). (Record 43634, Reserve 12813, Censor's decision, over-18s certificate and two cuts, 24 November 1977.)

96. Record 45271, Reserve 13073, Censor's decision, over-18s certificate with five cuts, 31 August 1983, distributor: Film Services Ltd.
97. Record 45282, Reserve 13078, Censor's decision, twenty-one cuts, no certificate issued, 8 September 1983.
98. Reject 2643, 7,740 feet, Censor's decision, 15 January 1969; ban upheld, 24 February 1969.
99. Reject 2668, 7,290 feet, Censor's decision, 16 April 1969; ban upheld after appeal (7,300 feet), 9 May 1969 and 23 May 1969.
 1. Reject 2665, 8,100 feet, Censor's decision, 10 April 1969; ban upheld after appeal, 13 June 1969.
 2. Reject 2647, 8,308 feet, Censor's decision, 24 January 1969); ban upheld after appeal (7,740 feet), 24 February 1969.
 3. Reject 2648, 8,187 feet, Censor's decision, 24 January 1969; ban upheld after appeal, 10 March 1969.
 4. Reject 2661, 8,820 feet, deputy Censor Gabriel G. Fallon's decision 'rejects regretfully,' 20 March, 1969; ban upheld after appeal, 21 April 1969; re-submitted in 1972: passed over-18s certificate and cut of last bed scene after appeal, Appeal Board Reserve 11859, 28 September 1972.
 5. Reject 2674, 8,370 feet, Censor's decision, 26 May 1969; ban upheld after appeal, 9 June 1969.
 6. Reject 2683, 9,514 feet, Censor's decision, 2 July 1969; ban upheld after appeal, 14 July 1969.
 7. Reject 2687, 9,311 feet, Censor's decision, 12 August 1969; ban upheld after appeal, 29 September 1969.
 8. Reject 2691, 10,428 feet, Censor's decision, 10 September 1969; ban upheld after appeal, 20 October 1969
 9. Reject 2693, 8,155 feet, deputy Censor Gabriel Fallon's decision, 22 September 1969; ban upheld after appeal, 6 October 1969.
10. Reject 2698, 9,591 feet, Censor's decision, 6 October 1969; ban upheld after appeal, 16 February 1970.
11. Reject 2702, 9,173 feet, deputy Censor Gabriel Fallon's decision ('with regret'), 30 October 1969; ban upheld after appeal, 10 November 1969.
12. Reject 2703, 8,762 feet, deputy Censor Gabriel Fallon's decision ('fun and games in a Victorian brothel – no holds barred'), 10 November 1969; ban upheld after appeal, 22 December 1969.
13. Reject 2710, 8,280 feet, Censor's decision, 10 December 1969; ban upheld after appeal, 2 March 1970.
14. These were *That Kind of Girl* (Gerry O'Hara, 1963, GB), *Buona Sera, Mrs Campbell* (Melvin Frank, 1968) *Boom!* (Joseph Losey, 1968), and *The Sergeant* (John Flynn, 1968).
15. Other films of interest in this period given similar treatment are *Rachel, Rachel* (Paul Newman, 1968); *The Night of the Following Day* (Hubert Cornfield, 1969); *Isadora* (aka *The Loves of Isadora*, Karel Reisz, 1968, GB); *The Night They Raided Minsky's* (aka *The Night They Invented Striptease*, William Friedkin, 1968), which was cut in five places; *Three into Two Won't Go* (Peter Hall, 1969, GB), a sex drama about a man (Rod Steiger) who picks up a hitchhiker (Judy Geeson) and has an affair with her and invites her to move into his house, much to his wife's (Claire Bloom) surprise; *Stolen Kisses* (*Baisers Volés*, François Truffaut, 1968, France), the third in Truffaut's Antoine Doinel series, which had bed scenes cut as well as the sub-title, 'For more [money] I'll strip' Reject 2689, 9,000 feet, 20 August 1969; passed with over-18s certificate and cuts after appeal (8,175 feet), Appeal Board Reserve 11466, 27 August 1969; 17 November 1969; *Staircase* (Stanley Donen, 1969, GB), which features gay lovers Richard Burton and Rex Harrison was cut in four places; *The Smashing Bird I Used to Know* (aka *School for Unclaimed Girls*, Robert Hartford-Davies, 1969, GB), a reform school drama; and *Secret Ceremony* (Joseph Losey, 1969, GB), which Fallon objected to because of its 'bizarre sex content'. Reject 2704, 9,787 feet, deputy Censor Gabriel G. Fallon's decision, 12 November 1969, passed with over-18s certificate and eight cuts after appeal, Reserve 11488, 8 December 1969; Appeal Board Reserve 11488, 10 December 1969.
16. Reject 2664, 9,900 feet, Censor's decision, 1 April 1969; Appeal Board Reserve 11455, 30 June 1969. The length of 10,020 feet, recorded by the Appeal Board is 120 feet longer than that on the Censor's reject form. Perhaps, the film was cut by the distributor prior to submitting it and then these unknown cuts were restored before the Board viewed it three months later.
17. Reject 2667, 10,405 feet, Censor's decision, 12 March 1969; passed with three cuts and over-18s certificate after appeal, 21 April 1969; Appeal Board Reserve 11429, 12 May 1969.
18. Reject 2692, 10,169 feet, deputy Censor Gabriel Fallon's decision, 18 September 1969; passed with cuts after appeal (no Reserve slip), over-18s certificate, 8 December 1969.
19. Reject 2706, 11,735 feet, deputy Censor Gabriel Fallon's decision, 28 November 1969; passed with cuts after appeal and over-18s certificate, 2 January 1970; Appeal Board Reserve 11510, 26 January 1970.

20. Seven cuts were made to the western *100 Rifles* (Tom Gries, 1969) and to *If He Hollers, Let Him Go* (Charles Martin, 1969), while the Swedish film, *Who Saw Him Die?* was similarly passed.
21. Reject 2711, 8,198 feet, Censor's decision, 11 December 1969; Reserve 11523, over-12s certificate, 23 February 1970; Appeal Board Reserve 11523, Under 12 with adult certificate, 6 April 1970.
22. Reject 2672, 9,795 feet, Censor's decision, 25 April 1969; passed with three cuts after appeal, 4 June 1969; Appeal Board Reserve 11438, 10 June 1969.
23. Reject 2696, 11,088 feet, Censor's decision, 30 September 1969; passed after appeal, 13 October 1969; Appeal Board Reserve 11480 (no date).
24. Reject 2676, 7,650 feet, Censor's decision, 10 June 1969; on appeal passed uncut and with general certificate subject only to change of title, 20 June 1969
25. Reject 2686, 10,900 feet, Censor's decision, 8 August 1969; passed on appeal (10,700 feet), 20 August 1969. Another two were cut, *But You were Dead* (Italy), and *The Amorous Virgin* (Germany).
26. Bishop Lucey later replied to an attack on the censorship system by the chairman of Player-Wills, the Festival's chief sponsor, by declaring that 'the blind assumption that anything cut by the censor is of artistic value is utter nonsense.' (Carty 1995: 48–49.)
27. Record 41356, Reserve 11810, 12 June 1972.
28. Carty, 1995: 49.
29. Reject 2750, 8,550 feet, Censor's decision, 6 July 1970; passed on appeal, 30 July 1970.
30. Reject 2717, 7,380 feet, deputy Censor Gabriel Fallon's decision, 19 January 1970; passed uncut with over-16s certificate after appeal (7,300 feet), 23 March 1970.
31. Reject 2731, 5,724 feet, Censor's decision, 7 May 1970), on appeal (9,270 feet), passed with cuts, Reserve 11571, and under-12 with adult certificate, 20 July 1970. As can be seen, there is a difference of 3,446 feet in the footage recorded as seen by the Censor and by the Board.
32. Reject 2286, 8,355 feet, Censor's decision, 22 December 1959; ban upheld after appeal, 29 January 1960. Re-submitted in 1970, 8,471 feet, Reject 2785, Censor's decision, 19 November 1970; on appeal passed with one cut (pill being put into coca-cola) and general certificate, 5 April 1971.
33. Ciaran Carty, *Sunday Independent*, 9 January 1972: 10. In this article Carty pointed to the screening that night on BBC TV, which could be received by increasing numbers in Ireland by the 1970s, of *Darling* which had been banned in Ireland. The 'spillover' effect of British television channels to Ireland had become a refrain among censorship campaigners by the 1960s, a condition which was matched by the concern over the 'spillover' effect of Satellite television in the 1980s.

    In 1978 Carty ('Do we really need a censor anymore?', *Sunday Independent*, 14 May 1978: 31) offered another proposal when he suggested that a Registrar of Movies be appointed 'to licence films for public screening.' Films would be classified according to the type of cinema and, thus, presumably, the class of audience, since Carty's proposal was made in the context of the recent opening of Project Cinema Club and the Irish Film Theatre, which were showing uncensored films under club conditions. The Registrar, like the earlier proposal of a Board of Censors, would not have the power to cut films, only to ban or pass them for under-18s, but allow all films for over-18s. Pornography would be confined to special cinemas of less than 200 seats, restricted to over-18s, and 'subject to stiff taxation measures'. Why pornography should be confined to small cinemas and be subject to penal taxation is not explained. However, under the Registrar system, licences carrying a 'porn-rating' would have to 'take their chance with the law and, unlike the other cinemas could be subject to a criminal prosecution.
34. Ciaran Carty, *Sunday Independent*, 11 May 1969: 24.
35. Reject 2715, 8,683 feet, deputy Censor Denis Coakley's decision, 12 January 1970; ban upheld after appeal, 23 February 1970.
36. Reject 2718, 9,480 feet, deputy Censor Gabriel Fallon's decision, 2 February 1970; Appeal Board decision, 6 April 1970.
37. Reject 2745, 10,980 feet, Censor's decision, 22 May 1970); ban upheld after appeal (10,935 feet), 27 July 1970.
38. Reject 2745, 10,980 feet, Censor's decision, 22 May 1970; Appeal Board decision (10,935 feet), 27 July 1970.
39. Reject 2721, 7,815 feet, deputy Censor Gabriel Fallon's decision, 23 February 1970; ; Appeal Board decision, 23 March 1970; 12 May 1970.
40. Passed with cuts but, no doubt, already heavily cut was the sex film, *The Sweet Sins of Sexy Susan* (1967, Austria/Hungary/Italy); *Baby Love* (Alastair Reid, 1968, GB), about a promiscuous nymphet; *The Buttercup Chain* (Robert Ellis Miller, 1970, GB), which features a quartet who swap their sexual partners; and *Cover Me Babe* (Noel Black, 1970), about an unscrupulous student filmmaker;

*Paranoia* (aka *A Quiet Place to Kill*, Umberto Lenzi, 1969, Italy/Spain); the Columbia riots and counter-culture film, *The Strawberry Statement* (Stuart Hagmann, 1970); a melodrama set in 'Swinging London,' *Goodbye Gemini* (Alan Gibson, 1970, GB); the sex education film *Michael and Helga* (1968); *Theorem* (Pier Paolo Pasolini, 1968, Italy); the eighteenth film in the *Carry On* series, *Carry On Loving* (1970). While at least half of the *Carry On* series' twenty-eight films were passed with cuts by the censors, this film was the only one where a banning order was upheld by the Board, though whether *Carry On Camping* (Gerald Thomas, 1972, GB) was passed by the Board after being banned is unclear from the records. *Carry On Screaming* was passed by the Board in 1966 after it was banned by Macken, who complained about 'the constant stream of double entendre' which runs through the film, the very aspect of the series which made it popular and which the censors sought to contain. (Reject 2580, 8,746 feet, Censor's decision, 6 October 1966; Appeal Board Reserve 11203, 18 November 1966.)

41. Reject 2666, 12,227 feet, 14 April 1969; Appeal Board deferred decision, 1 December 1969; no further decision recorded; re-submitted 1977, Reject 3114, Censor's decision, 2 November 1977; distributor: Cinema International, 12,240 feet.
42. Reject 2727, 12,468 feet, deputy Censor Gabriel Fallon's decision, 19 March 1970; Appeal Board decision, 18 May 1970. An exception, though, was the adaptation of Joe Orton's play *Entertaining Mr Sloane* (Douglas Hickox, 1970, GB) in which a man has affairs with a brother and a sister, which was passed with cuts overturning Reject 2751, 8,455 feet, deputy Censor Gabriel Fallon's decision, 7 July 1970; Appeal Board decision, 4 November 1970.
43. Deputy Censor's report to Appeal Board, 6 April 1970. Reject 2719, 11,000 feet, deputy Censor's decision, 5 February 1970.
44. Appeal Board Reserve 11610, 22 December 1970. It seems from the Board's records that the film may have been considered for an over-16s certificate after its initial viewing on 6 April 1970, but the decision was deferred with the Board's minutes recording that it agreed to re-view the film before 7 September 1970 with cuts 'to be suggested to [the] Board by [the] renter to see if they would be acceptable prior to re-show as cuts,' but it was not until more than eight months later, on 22 December 1970, that the Board passed the film with cuts and an over-18s certificate. Indeed, the version seen by Fallon in February 1970, at 11,000 feet, was 2,081 feet less than the one viewed by the Board in April 1970. To add to the complications about versions of the film, there are currently at least three different lengths in circulation: 134 minutes, a re-issued 1981 version at 142 minutes, and a European theatrical version at 144 minutes. (Leonard Maltin, *Movie and Video Guide*, 1993.) It only goes to demonstrate that in the modern era versions of films are being changed depending on the commercial needs of the distributor. The advent of the Avid digital editing system has helped make this task far easier, shifting control over content away from the producer/director towards the distributor/exhibitor, something which has not been in evidence since the early days of cinema.
45. *M.A.S.H.* was cut in ten places by the Board after being banned, Reject 2748, 10,413 feet, 10 June 1970. These cuts varied from four of the film's many operation sequences to areas of continuing concern: sex and religion. While the scene in which 'Hot Lips' and Robert Duvall are making love and which is broadcast throughout the camp seems to have been allowed by the Board, as was the scene where 'Hot Lips' is humiliated as she is taking a shower when the building is torn down while the malicious soldiers look-on, even though she is seen naked, albeit in long shot; the scene where Elliott Gould drunkenly declaims, 'I want sex' and says 'Take her clothes off' was cut. Three scenes relating to Walt's 'suicide' were also cut. These center around the 'Last Supper' sequence, which was completely excised, the priest giving absolution to Walt, and then administrating Holy Communion to him after he takes chewing gum from his mouth, and his subsequent 'revival' with the aid of the female soldier. Appeal Board decision, 29 June 1970; Appeal Board Reserve 11641, 22 March 1971. The time lapse between the Board viewing of the film in June 1970 and the recording of its decision nine months later may suggest that the version cut was not the complete film.
46. Reject 2765, 13,727 feet, Censor's decision, 9 September 1965; Appeal Board, 5 October 1970; Appeal Board Reserve 11609, 22 December 1970; Appeal Board Reserve 11613, 4 January 1971. The Board's minutes record that John O'Connor wanted his rejection of the film to be recorded.
47. Reject 2767, 10,980 feet, Censor's decision, 25 September 1970; Appeal Board, 12 October 1970. Appeal Board Reserve 11595, over-18s certificate, 9 November 1970. Scenes cut by the Board were of female frontal nudity on the raft during one of Yossarian's 'dreams'; the scene in which Yossarian is in bed with Luciana (Olimpia Carlisi) in which her breasts are visible, but where the dialogue between them concerns the effect of not being a virgin will have on marriage; and the scene where Yossarian visits 'Nately's Whore' (Gina Rovere) to tell her that her boyfriend is dead and in which

her underwear is visible. This seems to have been the only cut to the long scene in the brothel with the soldiers lined up waiting for their turn with the prostitutes.

Other films passed with cuts and over-18s certificates by the 1970 Board included *Closely Observed Trains* (Jiri Menzel, 1966, Czechoslovakia), which was banned by deputy Censor Denis Coakley, who had been drafted in to the Censor's office during Macken's holiday periods and during his illness, at least as early as 12 January 1970 because on that day he banned both *Last Summer* and *Me, Natalie* (Fred Coe, 1969), which was later passed by the Board with one cut of Natalie (Patty Duke) in a car scene. In his report to the Board on *Closely Observed Trains*, Coakley wrote that its 'approach to sex [was] completely amoral, promiscuity being less a social evil than inadequacy.' The Board ordered three cuts, including 'fornication in church' near the beginning of the film, a bedroom scene, and towards the end of the film when a young man is seduced. (Reject 2722, 8,530 feet, deputy Censor's decision, 4 March 1970; Appeal Board decision, 13 April 1970; Appeal Board Reserve 11541, 12 May 1970.) Also passed with cuts were *Night Games* (Mai Zetterling, 1966, Sweden), which is about a man in his mid-30s who suffers from memories of his mother's affairs and abberent sexual behaviour; *Castle Keep* (Sydney Pollack, 1969); *The Lawyer* (Sidney J. Furie, 1970), a courtroom drama; *Alice's Restaurant* (Arthur Penn, 1969), the counter-culture film; *The Honeymoon Killers* (Leonard Kastle, 1970), which is based on a real story about a couple who murdered people for their savings; *The Kremlin Letter* (John Huston, 1970), which was cut in two places; *Every Home Should Have One* (aka *Think Dirty*, Jim Clark, 1970, GB) about a salesman who employs sex to sell cereals while his wife becomes an anti-smut campaigner; *Crescendo* (Alan Gibson, 1969, GB) a horror film with sex and heroin; *Explosion* (Jules Bricken, 1969, Canada), about a teenager who is haunted by his brother's death in Vietnam, goes to Canada and becomes involved in crime there; *The Arrangement* (Elia Kazan, 1969), which had two scenes of nudity and the line, 'The screwing I'm getting is not worth the screwing I'm getting' cut; and the sex-change film, *The Christine Jorgensen Story* (Irving Rapper, 1970); while four dialogue cuts of expletives and 'Christ' were made by the Board to *Zabriskie Point* after Macken banned it. Despite its over-18s certificate, extensive cuts were made to the love-making sequence near the end of the film in which the two lovers are intercut with many others strew across the moon-like landscape. (Reject 2742, 10,113 feet, 19 May 1970; Appeal Board decision, 13 July 1970; Appeal Board Reserve 11583, 19 August 1970.). *Leo the Last* (John Boorman, 1970, GB.) also lost scenes which included rape and naked breasts. (Reject 2780, 9,330 feet, 17 December 1970; Appeal Board Reserve 11642, 15 March 1971; Appeal Board Reserve 11642, 22 March 1971.)

Six rejected films were passed by the Board with over-16s certificates with cuts: *The Footbridge* (*Leviathan*, Leonard Keigel, 1961, France), from the novel by Julien Green which features a young man's assault and rape of women; *The Looking Glass War* (Frank R. Pierson, 1970, GB), a Cold War spy story which was cut in five places; *Carry On Up the Jungle* (Gerald Thomas, 1970, GB), a comedy set in Africa in 1900; *Hello-Goodbye* (Jean Negulesco, 1970), a romantic comedy where four cuts of undressing were imposed; *The Rise and Rise of Michael Rimmer* (Kevin Billington, 1970, GB), a political satire with Peter Cook and John Cleese; and *Watermelon Man* (Melvin Van Peebles, 1970), which centers on a white bigot who wakes up a black man and his learning about racial prejudice. Five other rejected films were passed with over-16s certificate but without cuts: *The Virgins*; *Two Mules for Sister Sara* (Don Siegel, 1969), a western in which a nun is raped; *The Tiger and the Pussycat* (Dino Risi, 1967, Italy/USA), a sex comedy featuring Vittorio Gassman and Ann-Margret; *All the Way Up* (James MacTaggart, 1970, GB), which is about a son who follows in his father's corrupt footsteps in business; and *A Man Called Horse* (Elliot Silverstein, 1970) with Richard Harris.

Finally, three rejected films were passed with general certificates, one of them, *The Beat Generation*, as noted was cut, the two uncut films with general certificates were *Until They Sail* (Robert Wise, 1957) and *Oedipus Rex* (Pier Paolo Pasolini, 1967, Italy).

48. These included *Love is a Splendid Illusion*; *The Serpent* (aka *Night Flight from Moscow*, Henri Verneuil, 1971, France/Italy/West Germany), an espionage thriller; *Massacre for an Orgy*; *The Assistant* (John Dooley, 1969, GB); *Chastity* (Allessio de Paola, 1969), in which singer Cher in her acting debut takes to the road to find her own life; *THX-1138* (George Lucas, 1971), a science-fiction tale in which sex is forbidden and all people look alike; *I Love ... My Wife* (Mel Stuart, 1970), a comedy set around Elliott Gould's sexual hang-ups; *The Beguiled* (Don Siegel, 1970), an American Civil War story in which wounded Clint Eastwood is brought to a girls' school, triggering off jealousies and hatred; and *A Very Curious Girl* (*La Fiancée du Pirate*, aka *Dirty Mary*, Nelly Kaplan, 1969, France), a comedy in which a young woman gets a village under her control by selling her body as the women and local priest unsuccessfully try to stop her.

49. Reject 2788, 7,711 feet, Censor's decision, 4 January 1971; ban upheld after appeal, 8 March 1971.

50. Reject 2790, 10,771 feet, Censor's decision, 7 January 1971; ban upheld after appeal, 19 April 1971.
51. Reject 2795, 8,460 feet, Censor's decision, 8 February 1971; ban upheld after appeal, 5 April 1971.
52. Reject 2797, 8,834 feet, Censor's decision, 11 March 1971; ban upheld after appeal, 14 June 1971.
53. Reject 2801, 9,540 feet, Censor's decision, 5 April 1971; ban upheld after appeal, 14 June 1971.
54. Reject 2807, 8,911 feet, 15 April 1971; ban upheld after appeal (8,995 feet), 31 May 1971.
55. Reject 2816, 9,313 feet, Censor's decision, 24 May 1971; ban upheld after appeal, 7 September 1971.
56. Reject 2828, 8,300 feet, Censor's decision, 6 July 1971; ban upheld after appeal, 6 October 1971.
57. Reject 2829, 8,892 feet, Censor's decision, 14 July 1971; ban upheld after appeal, 4 October 1971.
58. Reject 2840, 10,031 feet, deputy Censor Denis Coakley's decision ('Much of the dialogue is vulgar and distasteful'), 10 August 1971; ban upheld after appeal, 8 November 1971, but later released.
59. Reject 2832, 8,370 feet, Censor's decision, 21 July 1971; ban upheld after appeal (9,220 feet), 26 July 1971.
60. Reject 2836, 9,450 feet, Censor's decision, 27 July 1971; ban upheld after appeal (9,617 feet), 16 July 1973.
61. Reject 2799, 8,169 feet, Censor's decision, 24 March 1971; ban upheld after appeal, 10 May 1971.
62. Reject 2827, 8,554 feet, Censor's decision, 6 July 1971; ban upheld after appeal, 30 September 1971.
63. Reject 2841, 9,097 feet, Censor's decision, 1 July 1971; ban upheld after appeal, 29 September 1971 and 21 February 1972.
64. Reject 3039, Censor's decision, 17 December 1974.
65. Reject 2846, 8,121 feet, Censor's decision, 31 August 1971; ban upheld after appeal, 6 December 1971.
66. Reject 2852, 7,501 feet, Censor's decision, 15 September 1971, ban upheld after appeal, 7 February 1972.
67. Reject 2855, 8,549 feet, Censor's decision, 23 September 1971; ban upheld after appeal, 10 January 1972.
68. Reject 2860, 9,858 feet, Censor's decision, 20 October 1971; ban upheld after appeal, 31 January 1972.
69. Reject 2865, 8,457 feet, Censor's decision, 3 November 1971; ban upheld after appeal, 28 February 1972.
70. Reject 2866, 8,100 feet, 4 November 1971; ban upheld after appeal, 14 February 1972.
71. 8,639 feet, Reject 2868, Censor's decision, 9 November 1971; an upheld after appeal, 20 December 1971.
72. These included *The Landlord* (Hal Ashby, 1970), a comedy in which a rich kid buys a Brooklyn tenement; *A Severed Head* (Dick Clement, 1971, GB), a sex comedy-drama from an Iris Murdoch novel in which Lee Remick has an affair with her psychiatrist (Richard Attenborough) while her husband (Ian Holm) looks on; *You Can't Have Everything* (Martin Zweibach, 1970), a teenage sex problem film in which an 18-year-old virgin who is going to Vietnam spends a platonic last twenty-four hours; *One Brief Summer* (John Mackenzie, 1969, GB) in which a wealthy man loses interest in his mistress and courts his daughter's friend, the film also hints of incest; *The Owl and the Pussycat* (Herbert Ross, 1970), a bawdy film with kinky behaviour in which a fellow tenant reports another for prostitution and then moves in with him; *B.S. I Love You* (Steven Hilliard Stern, 1971), where a young advertising man has affairs with a mother and daughter as in *The Graduate*; *A Town Called Bastard* (aka *A Town Like Hell*, *A Town Called Hell*, Robert Parrish, 1971, GB/Spanish), in which Mexican revolutionaries massacre a priest and his parishioners and take over a town, and ten years later a widow seeks revenge; *Husbands* (John Cassavetes, 1970), in which three married men get drunk and fly to London for a weekend of debauchery; *The Statue* (Rod Amateau, 1971, GB) which features a twenty foot statue of David Niven with an enormous penis; *All the Right Noises* (Gerry O'Hara, 1969, GB), in which an electrician with a touring theatre company has an affair with a 15-year-old actress before returning to his wife; *Investigation of a Citizen Above Suspicion* (Elio Petri, 1970, Italy) in which a police chief murders his mistress and then sees if he will be caught; *Doctors' Wives* (George Schaefer, 1971), which had been banned by Miss Twohig during holiday relief work in August 1971, and in which a doctor shoots his unfaithful wife and, as a consequence, others reconsider their sex lives; *Puzzle of a Downfall Child* (Jerry Schatzberg, 1970), in which a fashion model reminisces on a life of sex and high living; *The Hunting Party* (Don Medford, 1970,) in which outlaws kidnap a wife and the husband tracks them down; *Country Dance* (aka *Brotherly Love*, J. Lee-Thompson, 1969, GB), where the 'baptism' of an animal was cut, though the film con-

cerns an eccentric baronet (Peter O'Toole) whose incestuous designs on his sister causes her marriage to break up; *The Seven Minutes*, in which a bookseller is arrested for distributing an obscene novel; *Revenge* (aka *Inn of the Frightened People, Terror from Under the House*, Sidney Hayers, 1971, GB), which is about a girl who is raped and murdered in a northern England town and revenge is taken against a suspect; *Move* (Stuart Rosenberg, 1970), a comedy about a pornography writer (Elliott Gould) as he moves to a new apartment; *Bananas* (Woody Allen, 1971); *Friends* (Lewis Gilbert, 1971, GB), an early teens romance in which a pair run away from home and have a baby; Ken Russell's life of Tchaikovsky, *The Music Lovers* (1971, GB), five scenes of which were cut; *There's a Girl in My Soup* (Roy Boulting, 1970, GB); *Pigsty* (aka *Porcile; Pig Pen*, Pier Paolo Pasolini, 1969); and *The Touch* from which bed scenes were cut. Two films passed with over-18s certificates without cuts were the generation-gap film, *Taking Off* (Milos Forman, 1971), in which suburban parents search for their wayward daughter among hippies, and *Serafino* (aka *Serafino ou l'amour aux champs*, Pietro Germi, 1968, France/Italy).

73. These included the adaptation of the D.H. Lawrence story *The Virgin and the Gypsy* (Christopher Miles, 1970, GB); *The Travelling Executioner* (Jack Smight, 1970), in which an executioner is in love both with the electric chair and a woman prisoner; *Valdez is Coming* (Edwin Sherrin, 1971), a western from which Crucifixion sequences were among the seven cuts; *Violent City* (aka *The Family*, Sergio Sollima, 1970, Italy), an action adventure with Charles Bronson; *Vanishing Point* (Richard C. Sarafian, 1971), an 'existential' road race movie with a blind disk jockey helping driver Barry Newman; *Cat o' Nine Tails* (Dario Argento, 1971, Italy/West Germany/France), a graphic violence and sex film in which blind Karl Malden tracks down a psycho killer with the help of a reporter; *Little Murders* (Alan Arkin, 1971), a New York City black comedy from the play by Jules Ffeifer; and *Satanists (Angeli Bianchi ... Angeli Neri*, Luigi Scattini, 1969, Italy), a documentary about spiritualism, witchcraft and the occult.

74. *Promise at Dawn* (Jules Dassin, 1970, USA/France), a biographical picture about writer Romain Gary; *Red Sky at Morning* (James Goldstone, 1970) about growing up an adolescent in New Mexico during World War Two; *The Hired Hand* (Peter Fonda, 1971), a western; and *Pussycat, Pussycat, I Love You* (Rod Amateau, 1970).

75. The two cut were *Beast of Blood* (aka *Beast of the Dead*, Eddie Romero, 1970), a horror film with a headless monster, and *Kotch* (Jack Lemmon, 1971), in which an old man (Walter Matthau) resists his children's attempts to put him away, and the uncut film was *Tam-Lin* (aka *The Devil's Widow, The Ballad of Tam-Lin*, Roddy McDowell, 1971, GB) in which Ava Gardner plays a sinister widow who influences young people she gathers around her.

76. *One More Train to Rob* (Andrew V. McLaglen, 1971) and *Little Big Man* (Arthur Penn, 1970). *Dirty Dingus Magee* (Burt Kennedy, 1970), a fast-paced comedy in which Frank Sinatra plays an outlaw, was passed uncut.

77. Reject 2821, 8,828 feet, deputy Censor Gabriel Fallon's decision, 8 June 1971; Fallon's Report to Appeal Board, 29 July 1971; Appeal Board Reserve 11679, 9 August 1971.

78. Reject 2833, 10,000 feet, Censor's decision, 21 July 1971; Appeal Board decision, 4 October 1971; Appeal Board Reserve 11698, limited certificate deferred, 5 October 1971; Censor's decision, 10 October 1978.

79. Reject 2878, 8,180 feet, deputy Censor Miss S. Twohig's decision, 3 February 1972; ban upheld after appeal, 17 April 1972.

80. Reject 2880, 8,800 feet, deputy Censor Miss S. Twohig's decision, 28 February 1972; ban upheld after appeal, 9 April 1973; re-submitted in 1979, Record 44224, 10 October 1979.

81. Reject 2881, 8,280 feet, Censor's decision, 6 March 1972; ban upheld after appeal, 5 to 2 vote, 1 May 1972.

82. Reject 2874, 6,480 feet, Censor's decision, 3 January 1972; ban upheld after appeal, 20 March 1972.

83. Reject 2882, 8,290 feet, deputy Censor Miss S. Twohig's decision, 28 February 1972; ban upheld after appeal, 15 May 1972.

84. Reject 2883, 8,490 feet, deputy Censor Miss S. Twohig's decision, 26 May 1972; ban upheld after appeal, 26 June 1972.

85. Reject 2884, 7,660 feet, deputy Censor Denis Coakley's decision, 31 May 1972; ban upheld after appeal, 11 September 1972.

86. Reject 2875, 5,945 feet, Censor's decision, 6 January 1972; Appeal Board decision, 10 April 1972; Appeal Board Reserve 11779.

87. Reject 2876, 7,435 feet, Censor's decision, 5 January 1972; Appeal Board decision, 28 March 1972; Appeal Board, Reserve 11769, 29 March 1972.

88. Reject 2877, 10,584 feet, Censor's decision, 13 January 1972; Appeal Board decision, 3 March 1972; Record 41147, Reserve 13007, 18 June 1981.

89. Reject 2885, 10,080 feet, deputy Censor Miss S. Twohig's decision, 2 June 1972.

90. Reject 2879, 7,000 feet, deputy Censor Miss S. Twohig's decision, 17 February 1972.

91. Reject 2886, 7,380 feet, deputy Censor Miss S. Twohig's decision, 2 June 1972.

92. Carty, 1995: 85–86.

93. Ibid. 49.

94. A new Dublin International Film Festival was established in 2003 with Michael Dwyer (who was the main impetus behind the 'first' Dublin Film Festival when it was set-up in 1986) in charge of programming of the new annual event.

95. Ciaran Carty, 'Censorship Comes Out into the Open', *Sunday Independent*, 30 July 1972: 13.

96. Ciaran Carty, 'The New Look Censor', *Sunday Independent*, 6 August 1972: 11.

97. Carty 1995: 98; *Sunday Independent*, 5 November 1972. In an RTÉ radio discussion he later qualified this comment and claimed his views were misrepresented. However, in a speech at Cork Rotary Club a few years later he rather paranoiacally declared that those opposing censorship were out to destroy civilization as we know it. He said that there were insidious elements in our midst intent on corrupting Irish society by upsetting many of our long established institutions and traditions. He added that some of these groups, perhaps unwittingly or otherwise, were dominating and pressing for the removal of censorship of films, and indeed of all things which were considered decent in accordance with the normal standard of living in a well-orientated society. (Quoted, Ciaran Carty, 'Coming to terms with SINema', *Sunday Independent*, 16 January 1977:2.)

98. Ciaran Carty, *Sunday Independent*, 7 January 1973: 15.

99. *Sunday Independent*, 1 October 1972; Carty 1995: 97. Carty returned to the theme of film censorship in 1978 when the film clubs, Project Cinema Club and the Irish Film Theatre, were opened, and the film society movement was re-organized as the Federation of Irish Film Societies. Both the clubs and societies could show uncensored films, and Carty in such articles as 'It's time to end moral apartheid in cinemas' (*Sunday Independent*, 28 May 1978: 31) and 'Public barred from year's best movies' (ibid., 31 December 1978: 31), highlighted the contradictions in the Film Censor's attitude to the ordinary cinemas and how the 'art' cinemas and film societies could easily avoid censorship through the legal devise of establishing a membership of its patrons, an issue discussed further below.

1. For example, *Nudist Paradise* (Charles Saunders, 1958, GB), *Some Like It Cool* (Michael Winner, 1960, GB), and *Sunswept* (1961, GB).

2. Reserve 6622, Censor's decision, 5 November 1945.

3. Record 41985, Reserve 12075, Censor's decision, 18 October 1973; and *That's Carry On* (Gerald Thomas, 1978), Record 83750, Reserve 12848, Censor's decision, 10 April 1977.

4. Pascall and Jeavons, 1975:176.

5. Reject 2444, Censor's decision, 14 January 1964; Appeal Board decision, 28 January 1964.

6. Reject 2612, Censor's decision, 14 February 1968; Appeal Board Reserve 11325, 1 March 1968.

7. Reject 2459, Censor's decision, 30 June 1964.

8. Record 39698, Reserve 11367, Censor's decision, 1 October 1968.

9. Reject 2567, Censor's decision, 7 July 1966; passed with cuts after appeal with cuts, Appeal Board Reserve 11184–5, 22 September 1966.

10. Pascall and Jeavons, 1975:177.

11. Reject 2799, 8,169 feet, Censor's decision, 24 March 1971; ban upheld after appeal, 10 May 1971.

12. Pascall and Jeavons, 1975:179.

13. Record 39777, Reserve 11386, Censor's decision, 5 December 1968.

14. Reject 2773, Censor's decision, 5 November 1970.

15. Appeal Board Reserve 11589, Censor's decision, 10 September 1970.

16. Record 43085, Reserve 12593, Censor's decision, over-18s certificate with cuts, 18 May 1976. The legislation introduced in 1979 in relation to contraception also ended the banning of books on the grounds they advocated 'unnatural' prevention of conception, while the provision in relation to abortion was lifted following the abortion information referendum in 1995. See, *Irish Times*, 16 June 1998:3.

17. Record 42584, Reserve 12375, Censor's decision, 4 March 1975.

18. Record 42822, Reserve 12482, Censor's decision, 11 September 1975.

19. 9,540 feet; Reject 2801, Censor's decision, 5 April 1971; an upheld after appeal, 14 June 1971.

20. Reject 2861, Censor's decision, 22 October 1971.

21. 8,273 feet; Reject 2887, Censor's decision, 28 June 1972; ban upheld after appeal, 11 September 1972.

22. Record 40813, Reserve 11656, Censor's decision, 16 April 1971; Appeal Board Reserve 11692, 27 September 1971. The Appeal Board's additional cuts were of frontal nudity, two girls in a bath, and a man running his hands over a woman after a game of strip poker.
23. Reject 2889, Censor's decision, 2 August 1972.
24. Reject 2896, Censor's decision, 20 November 1972.
25. 9,990 ft, Reject 2888, 27 July 1972; ban upheld after appeal, 28 September 1972.
26. 8,980 feet, Reject 2891, Censor's decision, 4 September 1972; no appeal
27. Reject 3008, 6,520 feet, deputy Censor Frank Hall's decision, 4 May 1973, distributor: National Films.
28. Reject 3004, 7,650 feet, Censor's decision, 8 February 1973, distributor: National Films.
29. Reject 3006, 2,865 feet, Censor's decision, 23 March 1973, distributor: Paramount, 2,865 feet.
30. Reject 3010, 4,770 feet, Censor's decision, 15 May 1973, distributor: National Films.
31. Reject 3002, 8,640 feet, Censor's decision, 9 February 1973.
32. Reject 3005, 7,844 feet, Censor's decision, 20 March 1973; no appeal. Re-submitted in 1979 in a slightly shorter version (by 104 feet) and passed with two cuts and an over-18s certificate, Reserve 12959, Censor's decision, 22 February 1980.
33. Reject 3017, 9,180 feet, Censor's decision, 19 December 1973.
34. Reject 3018, 12,528 feet, Censor's decision, 1 April 1973.
35. Reject 3021 10,440 feet, Censor's decision, 11 April 1974.
36. Reject 3039, Censor's decision, 17 December 1974.
37. Reject 3053, Censor's decision, 18 March 1975.
38. Reject 3054, 6,390 feet, Censor's decision, 24 March 1975.
39. Reject 3082, 11,520 feet, Censor's decision, 4 March 1976.
40. Reject 3083, 9,520 feet, Censor's decision, 5 March 1976.
41. Reject 3113, 8,370 feet, Censor's decision, 25 October 1977.
42. Record 43588, 13,950 feet, Reserve 12795–69, Censor's decision, over-18s certificate and eight cuts, 12 October 1977; Reject 3119, 6 December 1977; Appeal Board decision, over-18s certificate and two cuts, 29 July 1982.
43. Reject 3120, 10,004 feet, Censor's decision, 8 December 1977.
44. Reject 3123, 11,880 feet, Censor's decision, 8 March 1978; Appeal Board decision, 6 June 1978.
45. Reject 3132, 7,650 feet, Censor's decision, 5 April 1978.
46. Record 42547, Reserve 12357, 4 February 1975.
47. Record 43754, Reserve 12850, Censor's decision, 12 April 1978.
48. Record 44107, Reserve 12911, Censor's decision, 22 June 1979, distributor: National Films. *Love Making – Hot Style* and *Sin, Sun and Sex* (*Le Bal des Voyous*, Jean-Claude Dague, 1967, France/Italy) also had their titles changed.
49. Reject 2830, 9,334 feet, deputy Censor's decision, 14 July 1971; an upheld after appeal, 19 July 1971. Re-submitted in 1978: Record 43904, Reserve 12887, Censor's decision, 22 September 1978.
50. For a discussion of *The Miracle* see Rockett and Rockett, 2003.
51. Reject 3173, 8,640 feet, Censor's decision, 1 January 1982; Appeal Board decision, 19 February 1982.
52. Reject 3180, 8,550 feet, Censor's decision, 23 June 1983; Appeal Board decision, 14 July 1983.
53. Record 45042, Reject 3175, 7,920 feet, Censor's decision, 8 October 1982; Appeal Board Reserve 13048, 29 October 1982.
54. Reject 3177, 8,190 feet, Censor's decision, 17 November 1982; Appeal Board decision, 3 March 1983.
55. Appeal Board decision, 20 May 1993.
56. Reserve 12903, Record 44018, Censor's decision, 14 March 1979.
57. Record 45421, Reserve 13087, Censor's decision, 21 March 1984.
58. Reserve 12960, Censor's decision, 28 February 1980.
59. Record 45381, Reserve 13085, Censor's decision, 3 February 1984, review, 20 March 1984.
60. Record 45348, Reserve 13084, Censor's decision, 9 January 1984.
61. Record 45401, Reserve 13086, Censor's decision, 16 February 1984; review, 7 March 1984.
62. Record 40772, Reserve 11640, Censor's decision, 18 March 1971.
63. Record 40775, Reserve 11644, review 6 April 1971.
64. Record 41010, Reserve 11693, Censor's decision, 21 September 1971.
65. Record 41093, Reserve 11715, Censor's decision, 30 January 1971. See also letter to Miss E. Gleeson, Censor's office, from 20th Century-Fox (20 February 1972) saying eleven cuts to reels 7 and 9 had been effected, OFC.
66. Record 41404, Reserve 11826–27, Censor's decision, 18 July 1972.

67. Record 41534, Reserve 11895, Censor's decision, 5 December 1972; Appeal Board Reserve 11922, reviewed 2 April 1973.
68. Record 41746, Reserve 11979, Censor's decision, 2 May 1973. This film should not be confused with *Imagine: John Lennon* (Andrew Solt, 1988).
69. Record 42620, Reserve 12396–97, Censor's decision, 2 April 1975.
70. Record 43430, Reserve 12799, Censor's decision, 12 October 1977.
71. Record 39226, Reserve 11301, Censor's decision, 25 October 1967.
72. Record 42114, Reserve 12136, Censor's decision, 31 January 1974.
73. Record 42339, Reserve 12245, Censor's decision, 25 July 1974.
74. Record 42579, Reserve 12368, Censor's decision, 26 February 1975.
75. Record 42584, Reserve 12375, Censor's decision, 4 March 1975.
76. Record 42865, Reserve 12503, Censor's decision, 28 October 1975.
77. Record 42915, Reserve 12530, Censor's decision, 17 December 1975.
78. Record 43204, Reserve 12623, Censor's decision, 23 August 1976.
79. Record 43584, Reserve 12794, Censor's decision, 12 October 1977.
80. Record 45282, Reserve 13078, Censor's decision, twenty-one cuts, no certificate issued, 8 September 1983.
81. Record 42643, Reserve 12406, Censor's decision, 24 April 1975.
82. Record 42915, Reserve 12530, Censor's decision, 17 December 1975.
83. Record 43180, Reserve 12609, Censor's decision, 20 July 1976.
84. Reject 3005, 7,844 feet, Censor's decision, 20 March 1973; no appeal. Re-submitted in 1979: Reserve 12959, Censor's decision, 22 February 1980.
85. Reject 3188, 12,690 feet, Censor's decision, 14 December 1984; Reserve 13116, 20 August 1985.
86. See Robert Stam, *Subversive Pleasures: Bakhtin, Cultural Criticism, and Film*, Baltimore and London: John Hopkins UP, 1989; pb: 1992.
87. Reject 2858, Censor's decision, 8 October 1971; Appeal Board Reserve 11773, 6 April 1972.
88. Record 42865, Reserve 12503, Censor's decision, 28 October 1975.
89. Record 42957, Reserve 12540, Censor's decision, 16 January 1976.
90. Record 43386, Reserve 12718, Censor's decision, 15 March 1977.
91. Record 43336, Reserve 12709, Censor's decision, 3 March 1977.
92. Record 43761, Reserve 12852, Censor's decision, 26 April 1978. Five cuts and an over-18s certificate.
93. Record 43761, Reserve 12852, Censor's decision, 26 April 1978.
94. Record 44271, Reserve 12943, Censor's decision, 10 December 1979.
95. Record 44584, Reserve 12997, Censor's decision, 7 January 1981, Review 22 January 1981.
96. Record 44361, Reject 3156, 10,440 feet, Censor's decision, 10 April 1980; Appeal Board decision, 26 June 1980. (This decision was taken on the same day the new Board banned its first film, *Monty Python's Life of Brian*; Appeal Board Reserve 12979, 24 July 1980.)
97. Record 45678, Reserve 13111, Censor's decision, 15 April 1985; Review, 19 April 1985.
98  Reject 3189, 9,360 feet, Censor's decision, 18 November 1985.
99. Record 45876, Reserve 13124, Censor's decision, 29 May 1986, Review, 11 June 1986.
 1. Record 43181, Reserve 12611, Censor's decision, 20 July 1976.
 2. Record 43386, Reserve 12718, Censor's decision, 15 March 1977.
 3. Record 43434, Reserve 12742, Censor's decision, 27 April 1977.
 4. Record 45335, Reserve 13080, Censor's decision, 13 December 1983.
 5. Record 45881, Reserve 13126, Censor's decision, over-18s certificate, 11 June 1985.
 6. Reject 3171, 11,160 feet, Censor's decision, 17 November 1981; Appeal Board decision, 11 December 1981; 22 January 1982.
 7. Record 44532, Reserve 12989, Censor's decision, 6 November 1980, Review, 2 December 1980.
 8. Reject 2877, 10,584 feet, Censor's decision, 13 January 1972; Appeal Board decision, 3 March 1972; Record 41147, Reserve 13007, 18 June 1981.
 9. Record 45180, Reserve 13064, Censor's decision, 13 April 1983; Review, 18 April 1983.
10. Record 45271, Reserve 13073, Censor's decision, over-18s certificate with five cuts, 31 August 1983, distributor: Film Services Ltd.
11. Record 45273, Reserve 13075, Censor's decision, 2 September 1983.
12. Record 44341, Reserve 12961; review, 21 April 1980, 7 March 1980.
13. Reject 3172, 13,230 feet, Censor's decision, 3 November 1981; Appeal Board decision, 29 July 1982.
14. Record 15709, Reserve 4610, Censor's decision, 5 November 1940.
15. Record 15691, Reserve 4609, Censor's decision, 1 November 1940.

16. Record 19689, Reserve 6553, Censor's decision, 10 September 1945.
17. Record 35476, Reserve 10382–83, Censor's decision, 31 July 1961.
18. Record 37392, Reserve 10886, Censor's decision, 12 May 1964.
19. Reject 2568, 11,296 feet, Censor's decision, 19 September 1966; on appeal, passed with over-21s certificate and three cuts, Appeal Board Reserve 11861, 28 September 1966.
20. Appeal Board Reserve 11390–91, December 1968. The appeal was held on 6 May 1968.
21. Record 39800, Reserve 11384–85, Censor's decision, 23 December 1968; Appeal Board Reserve 11442, 13 June 1968.
22. Record 40092, Reserve 11462, Censor's decision, 1 September 1969.
23. Record 40125, Reserve 11469, Censor's decision, 29 September 1969.
24. Record 39938, Reserve 11422, Censor's decision, 2 May 1969.
25. Record 41457, Reserve 11858, Censor's decision, 19 September 1972.
26. Record 42832, Reserve 12483, Censor's decision, 24 September 1975.
27. Record 42833, Reserve 12486, Censor's decision, 23 September 1975.
28. Record 43066, Reserve 12580, Censor's decision, 15 April 1976.
29. Record 43781, Reserve 12858, Censor's decision, 10 May 1978.
30. Record 29021, Reserve 8653, Censor's decision, 21 April 1954.
31. Record 29231, Reserve 8687, Censor's decision, 30 June 1954.
32. Record 36117, Reserve 10564, Censor's decision, 5 June 1962.
33. Record 20487, Reserve 6734, Censor's decision, 28 March 1946.
34. Record 19527, Reserve 6462, Censor's decision, 23 May 1945.
35. Record 19880, Reserve 6542, Censor's decision, 29 April 1945.
36. Censor's decision, 19 January 1956.
37. Record 30164, Censor's decision, 26 May 1956.
38. Record 30655, Censor's decision, 22 December 1955.
39. Appeal Board Reserve 10984, 4 May 1965.
40. Record 35454, Reserve 10378, Censor's decision, 18 July 1961.
41. Record 35716, Reserve 10433, Censor's decision, 14 November 1961.
42. Record 37491, Reserve 10884, Censor's decision, 8 July 1964.
43. Record 38949, 10,842 feet, Reserve 11260, Censor's decision, 22 March 1967; Appeal Board decision, 1 May 1967.
44. Reject 2818, Censor's decision, 25 May 1971; Appeal Board Reserve 11759, 28 February 1972.
45. 'Bugger' was not such a widely used word in Ireland as it was among the English working-class and does not feature, for example, in *Slanguage: A Dictionary of Irish Slang* by Bernard Share, Dublin: Gill and Macmillan, 1997.
46. Record 42657, Reserve 12415, Censor's decision, 6 May 1975.
47. See Anthony Aldgate, 1995:89 ff. for the BBFC's response to the two films.
48. Record 37392, Reserve 10886 Censor's decision, 12 May 1964.
49. Appeal Board Reserve 11156–57, 14 July 1966.
50. Reject 2821, Censor's decision, 8 June 1971; Appeal Board Reserve 11679, 9 August 1971.
51. Record 42015, Reserve 12094, Censor's decision, over-18s certificate with two cuts, 9 November 1973.
52. Record 41483, Reserve 11882–83, Censor's decision, over-18s certificate and fourteen cuts, 15 October 1972; Reserve 11927, 25 January 1973.
53. Record 41614, Reserve 11935, Censor's decision, general certificate and two cuts, 5 February 1973.
54. Record 42232, Reserve 12211–13, Censor's decision, over-18s certificate and seven cuts, 22 May 1974.
55. Record 42320, Reserve 12232, Censor's decision, over-18s certificate and three cuts, 3 July 1974.
56. Record 42521, Reserve 12350, Censor's decision, under-12 with adult certificate and six cuts, 30 January 1975.
57. Censor's decision, 10 October 1978.
58. Record 35782, Reserve 10463, Censor's decision, 19 January 1962.
59. Record 37595, Reserve 10908, Censor's decision, 10 September 1964.
60. Record 37586, Reserve 10912, Censor's decision, 4 September 1964.
61. Reserve 11470, Censor's decision, 3 October 1969.
62. Reject 2742, Censor's decision, 19 May 1970; Appeal Board Reserve 11583, over-18s certificate, 19 August 1970.
63. Record 41129, Reserve 11731, Censor's decision, 21 December 1971.
64. Record 41406, Reserve 11828, Censor's decision, 19 July 1972.

65. Record 41694, Reserve 11958, Censor's decision, 22 March 1973.
66. Record 41703, Reserve 11965, Censor's decision, 3 April 1973.
67. Record 41762, Reserve 11982, Censor's decision, 11 May 1973.
68. Record 41955, Reserve 12064, Censor's decision, 27 September 1973.
69. Reserve 11808, Censor's decision, 30 May 1972.
70. Interestingly, representations of oral sex within mainstream cinema have tended to focus on the female engaging in acts of fellatio which she is forced to do by the sadistic male and where she is clearly coded as submissive. In this regard, *Blue Velvet*'s (David Lynch, 1986) Dorothy both works within and reverses the dominant cinematic stereotype when she forces the young Jeffrey to undress.
71. Record 42135, Reserve 12144–47, Censor's decision, 13 February 1974. Another film from which the word 'cock' was cut was *Lipstick* (Record 43181, Reserve 12611, Censor's decision, 20 July 1976).
72. Record 42139, Reserve 12152–53, Censor's decision, 15 February 1974.
73. Reject 3120, 10,004 feet, Censor's decision, 8 December 1977.
74. Record 43330, Reserve 12688, Censor's decision, 6 January 1977.
75. See Carol J. Clover, *Men, Women and Chainsaws: Gender in the Modern Horror Film*, London: BFI, 1992.
76. Record 42929, Reserve 12536, Censor's decision, 31 December 1975.
77. Record 42481, Reserve 12327, Censor's decision, 10 November 1974.
78. Record 42625, Reserve 12398, Censor's decision, 8 April 1975.
79. Record 43536, Reserve 12779, Censor's decision, 5 August 1977.
80. Record 43767, Reserve 12856, Censor's decision, 4 May 1978.
81. Reserve 12947, Record 44168, Censor's decision, 18 December 1979.
82. Appeal Board decision, 1 February 1955.
83. Record 41512, Reserve 11902, Censor's decision, 16 November 1972.
84. Record 31444, Reserve 9327, Censor's decision, 10 October 1956.
85. Record 31991, Reserve 9488, Censor's decision, 24 June 1957.
86. Record 34353, Reserve 10099, Censor's decision, 6 March 1960.
87. Record 34729, Reserve 10196, Censor's decision, 29 August 1960.
88. Record 34376, Reserve 10106, 10 March 1960.
89. Record 36454, Reserve 10631, Censor's decision, 24 October 1962.
90. Record 36598, Reserve 10669, Censor's decision, 17 January 1963.
91. Record 36926, Reserve 10749, Censor's decision, 9 July 1963.
92. Record 37228, Reserve 10829, Censor's decision, 6 February 1964.
93. Record 37243, Reserve 10834, Censor's decision, 20 February 1964.
94. Record 39419, Reserve 11327, Censor's decision, 5 March 1968.
95. Censor's decision, 28 July 1969.
96. Reject 2712, 8,910 feet, Censor's decision, 15 December 1969; passed with five cuts and over-18s certificate after appeal, 9 February 1970; Appeal Board Reserve 11515, 11 February 1970.
97. Reject 2717, 7,380 feet, deputy Censor Gabriel Fallon's decision, 19 January 1970; passed uncut with over-16s certificate after appeal (7,300 feet), 23 March 1970.
98. Reject 2794, 8,100 feet, Censor's decision, 19 January 1971; passed with two cuts and over-16s certificate after appeal (8,600 feet), 22 February 1971; Appeal Board Reserve 11635, no date.
99. Record 41801, Reserve 11996, Censor's decision, 6 June 1973.
 1. Record 42451, Reserve 12310, Censor's decision, 1 November 1974.
 2. Record 43229, Reserve 12642–43, Censor's decision, 6 October 1976.
 3. Record 43391, Reserve 12721, Censor's decision, 21 March 1977.
 4. Record 43761, Reserve 12852 Censor's decision, 26 April 1978.
 5. Reject 3020, 8,100 feet, Censor's decision, 30 January 1974.
 6. Record 36158, Reserve 10588, Censor's decision, 3 July 1962.
 7. Record 34127, Reserve 10051–52, 15 December 1959; Record 36154, Reserve 10590, 4 July 1962.
 8. Record 31981, Reserve 9485, Censor's decision, 19 June 1957.
 9. Reject 3117, 9,990 feet, Censor's decision, 3 November 1977; Appeal Board decision and Censor's report, 12 December 1977.
10. Censor's report to Appeal Board, 28 September 1972.
11. Reject 2897, 10,000 feet, Censor's decision, 29 November 1972; Appeal Board decision, 18 December 1972; Appeal Board Reserve 11931, 29 January 1973.
12. Record 45430, Reserve 13090, Censor's decision, 3 April 1984.
13. Record 41684, 10,612 feet, Reserve 11956, Censor's decision, 21 March 1973.
14. Record 43545, Reserve 12781, Censor's decision, 16 August 1977.

15. Record 43792, Reserve 12901, 8 June 1978, Review, 9 February 1979.
16. Record 41392, Reserve 11840, Censor's decision, 8 August 1972. A detailed synopsis of the film may be found in Rockett, 1996:429.
17. Record 41423, Reserve 11839, Censor's decision, 9 August 1972.
18. Record 43588, 13,950 feet, Reserve 12795–69, Censor's decision, over-18s certificate and eight cuts, 12 October 1977; Reject 3119, 6 December 1977; Appeal Board decision, over-18s certificate and two cuts, 29 July 1982.
19. Record 43113, Reserve 12589, Censor's decision, 11 May 1976.
20. Record 42958, Reserve 12568, Censor's decision, 19 January 1976.
21. Record 42232, Reserve 12211–13, Censor's decision, over-18s certificate and seven cuts, 22 May 1974. *The Exorcist* was re-released in 1998; see *Irish Times*, 31 October 1998:Weekend 5; *Irish Independent*, 29 October 1998:12; *Sunday Tribune*, 1 November 1998:6.
22. Record 43136, Reserve 12596, Censor's decision, 25 May 1976.
23. Record 43503, Reserve 12768, Censor's decision, 13 July 1977.
24. Record 43022, Reserve 12559, Censor's decision, 5 March 1976.
25. Record 43747, Reserve 12847, Censor's decision, 10 April 1978.
26. Record 43324, Reserve 12704, Censor's decision, 7 February 1977.
27. Reject 3074, 9,400 feet, Censor's decision, 19 November 1975; Appeal Board decision and Censor's report, 4 December 1975.
28. Record 42294, Reserve 12224, Censor's decision, 21 June 1974.
29. Record 42568, Reserve 12331, Censor's decision, 19 December 1974. A scene referred to in Breen's report, and most likely cut prior to submission, is of a living Mahler brought in a coffin by Nazis and includes a black-clad woman mourner performing a striptease as well as dancing topless with the Nazis, and sitting on a giant phallus-like gramophone horn.
30. Appeal against Reserve 12331, 14 April 1975. Nevertheless, a question mark hangs over this appeal as the Appeal Board report, written four months after Breen's decision, does not record the film's length as viewed and mysteriously declares that the 'Appeal is allowed subject to no notion of the Censor's original cut being ever in advertising material or trailer,' a suggestion, perhaps, that the approved version was cut prior to submission.
31. Reserve 12660, Censor's decision, 27 September 1976; Appeal Board decision and Censor's report, 27 September 1976.
32. Record 43190, Reserve 12616, Censor's decision, 6 August 1976.
33. Reject 2313, 8,700 feet, Censor's decision, 24 May 1960; ban upheld after appeal, 6 September 1960. Re-submitted in 1974: Record 42156, Reserve 12159, Censor's decision, 28 February 1974.
34. Record 43181, Reserve 12611, Censor's decision, 20 July 1976.
35. Record 43169, Reserve 12612, Censor's decision, 1 July 1976.
36. Reject 3002, 8,640 feet, 9 February 1973.
37. Reject 3001, Censor's decision, 9,829 feet, 3 January 1973, 14 May 1973; Appeal Board decision and Censor's report, 14 May 1973.
38. Reject 2898, 9,376 feet, Censor's decision, 6 December 1972; Appeal Board decision and Censor's report, 15 January 1973; passed with cuts and over-18s certificate after appeal.
39. Record 44163, Reserve 12922, Censor's decision, 26 July 1979.
40. Record 44834, Reserve 13019, Censor's decision, 1 December 1981.
41. Record 44302, Reserve 12952, Censor's decision, 17 January 1980.
42. Record 44165, Reserve 12923, Censor's decision, 27 July 1979.
43. Record 45164, Reserve 13062, Censor's decision, 31 March 1983.
44. Record 45437, Reserve 13091, Censor's decision, 6 April 1984.
45. Record 44059, Reserve 12907, Censor's decision, 24 April 1979.
46. Reject 3155, 12,780 feet, Censor's decision, 24 March 1980.
47. Record 45979, Reserve 13129, Censor's decision, over-16s certificate with cuts, 8 January 1987.
48. In 1981 the European Court of Human Rights overturned a Northern Ireland anti-homosexual law identical to the one in the Republic of Ireland. Following that decision, gay campaigner David Norris took a case to the Court which was heard in 1988, but the Irish government in its submission declared it reserved the right to legislate on private morality. See Colm Boland, 'State defends right to legislate on moral issues', *Irish Times*, 26 April 1988:8. Following its defeat there, the Irish government was forced to change the Irish law. See David Norris, 'Homosexuality legislation', in Brian Lalor (ed.), *The Encyclopaedia of Ireland*, 2003:498–99.
49. Reject 2661, 8,820 feet, 20 March 1969; Appeal Board Reserve 11859, 28 September 1972.
50. Reject 2833, 10,000 feet, Censor's decision, 21 July 1971; Appeal Board decision, 4 October 1971;

Appeal Board Reserve 11698, limited certificate deferred, 5 October 1971; Censor's decision, 10 October 1978.

51. Record 41910, Reserve 12042, Censor's decision, 24 August 1973.
52. Record 42785, Reserve 12458, Censor's decision, 31 July 1975.
53. Record 42995, Reserve 12554, Censor's decision, 13 February 1976.
54. Record 43073, Reserve 12577, Censor's decision, 12 April 1976.
55. Record 43210, Reserve 12627, Censor's decision, 8 September 1976.
56. Reject 3011, 10,067 feet, deputy Censor Frank Hall's decision, 13 June 1973, Appeal Board decision and Hall's report, 30 July 1973.
57. Record 43921, Reserve 12900, Censor's decision, 27 October 1978.
58. Record 43930, 7,560 feet, Reject 3138, Censor's decision, 10 November 1978.
59. Reject 3069, 9,910 feet, deputy Censor Frank Hall's decision, 22 July 1975; Hall's report to Appeal Board, 15 September 1975.
60. Those for the film were Isobelle Byrne, Padraic Gearty, Robert V. Kiely, and the Protestant clergyman, Canon John D. Murray. Those voting to uphold Hall's decision were John Carroll, John A. O'Connor, Justice Rochford, and Fr O'Donoghue (15 September 1975). On the second vote, the member absent from the first viewing, Margaret Skehan, had no objection to the certificate except for a bedroom scene, while Rochford, Murray and Gearty were absent (29 September 1975).
61. Reject 3101, 8,460 feet, Censor's decision, 9 September 1976; Appeal Board decision and Censor's report, 27 May 1977.
62. Reject 3169, 9,540 feet, Censor's report, 5 May 1981.
63. Reject 3141, Censor's decision, 10 January 1979; Appeal Board decision, 18 May 1981.
64. Reject 3176, 10,710 feet, Censor's decision, 29 November 1982; Appeal Board decision, 17 December 1982.
65. Record 44374, Reject 3158, 8,370 feet, Censor's decision, 29 April 1980; Appeal Board decision, 26 June 1980; Censor's decision, 7 August 1987.
66. Reject 3181, 9,450 feet, Censor's decision, 27 June 1983; Appeal Board decision, 14 July 1983.
67. Record 44178, Reserve 12925, Censor's decision, 30 August 1979.
68. Record 44207, Reserve 12927, Censor's decision, 24 September 1979.
69. Record 44268, Reserve 12941, Censor's decision, 6 December 1979.
70. Record 43976, Reject 3142, 10,088 feet, Censor's decision, 23 January 1979.
71. Record 44979, Reject 3174, 23 July 1982; Appeal Board decision, 6 September 1982. Those against were Carroll, O'Donoghue and Liddy; those for: Sheehan and Ryan.
72. Record 44366, Reserve 12969, Censor's decision, 25 April 1980.
73. Record 44402, Reserve 12974, Censor's decision, 9 June 1980.
74. Record 45026, Reserve 13047, Censor's decision, 9 September 1982.
75. Record 45163, Reserve 13061, Censor's decision, 30 March 1983.
76. Record 43430, Reserve 12799, Censor's decision, 12 October 1977.
77. Record 45681, Reserve 13112, Censor's decision, 16 April 1985.
78. For a related discussion of Neil Jordan's *The Butcher Boy* (1997) see Rockett and Rockett, 2003.
79. Laffoy Commission's third interim report, Dublin: Stationary Office, 2004.
80. *Irish Times*, 29 December 1994:13.
81. *Film West*, no. 15, Spring 1993:15.
82. *Irish Times*, 29 December 1994:13.
83. *Sunday Business Post*, 13 October 1995:26.
84. Interview with author, 15 August 2000.
85. *Film West*, no. 15, spring 1993:15.
86. Record 47748, Reserve 13148, Censor's decision, 27 June 1997.
87. Record 45934, Reserve 13127, Censor's decision, 19 September 1986.
88. Record 45935, Reserve 13128, Censor's decision, 22 September 1986.
89. Record 45979, Reserve 13129, Censor's decision, 8 January 1987.
90. Record 46023, Reserve 13131, Censor's decision, 10 April 1987.
91. Record 46162, Reserve 13132–33, Censor's decision, 15 January 1988.
92. Record 46233, Reserve 13134, Censor's decision, 28 June 1988.
93. Record 46251, Reserve 13135, Censor's decision, 10 August 1988.
94. *Sunday Tribune*, 13 October 1995:26.
95. Record 46418, Reserve 13136, Censor's decision, 12 July 1989.
96. Record 46548, Reserve 13138, Censor's decision, 10 April 1990.
97. Record 46593, Reserve 13139, Censor's decision, 8 August 1990.
98. Record 46761, Reserve 13141, Censor's decision, 23 July 1991.

99. Appeal Board decision, 23 March 1992.
1. Appeal Board decision, 13 July 1992.
2. Record 47312, Reserve 13144, Censor's decision, 20 January 1995.
3. Record 47497, Reserve 13145, Censor's decision, 23 February 1996.
4. Reject 3226, Reserve 13149, Censor's decision, 18 January 1999; Appeal Board decision, 24 March 1999.
5. Interview with author, 15 August 2000.
6. Reject 3190, 9,540 feet, Censor's decision, 13 March 1987, Appeal Board decision, 12 May 1987.
7. Reject 3191, 8,190 feet (91 mins), deputy Censor Jerome Hegarty's decision, 12 August 1987; Appeal Board decision upheld in vote of 7 to 1.
8. Reject 3202, 7,380 feet (82 mins), deputy Censor Jerome Hegarty's decision, 9 August 1991, Appeal Board 'couldn't come to an agreement' but on review , 20 September 1991, unanimously rejected the film.
9. Reject 3206, 8,820 feet (98 mins), Censor's decision, 29 January 1993; ban upheld by Appeal Board, 18 February 1993.
10. Reject 3208, 7,200 feet, Censor's decision, 7 February 1994.
11. Reject 3211, 8,100 feet (90 mins), Censor's decision, 13 May 1994.
12. Reject 3214, 10,710 feet (119 mins), Censor's decision, 11 October 1994; ban upheld by Appeal Board after appeal, 20 January 1995.
13. Reject 3215, 11,790 feet (131 mins), Censor's decision, 8 October 1995; ban upheld by Appeal Board after appeal, 25 January 1996.
14. 9,270 feet (108 mins), Censor's decision, 1 May 1996.
15. Reject 3,223, 99 mins, 34 secs, Censor's decision, 28 October 1997.
16. Michael Dwyer, *Irish Times*, 31 October 1997:9.
17. Reject 3198, 7,290 feet, Censor's decision, 19 December 1990; Appeal Board Reserve 13140, 11 February 1991.
18. *Seanad debates*, vol. 117, col. 1277, 4 November 1987.
19. *Irish Times*, 25 November 1995:4.
20. Ibid., 11 March 1994:13.
21. Record 44374, Reject 3158, 8,370 feet, Censor's decision, 29 April 1980; Appeal Board decision, 26 June 1980; Censor's decision, 7 August 1987.
22. See Fiachra O'Marcaigh, 'Only nine years late', *Irish Times*, 1 July 1988:12.
23. Anon., 'Archbishop attacks film on Christ', *Irish Times*, 15 September 1988:1, 9.
24. Michael Finlan, 'The first temptation is to go see it', *Irish Times*, 2 September 1988:10; and Nuala O'Faoláin, *Irish Times*, 5 September 1988:10. Smith passed the film uncut for over-18s certificate with two unusual conditions. No member of the public is to be admitted after the film has begun to ensure that audiences see a statement from Martin Scorsese that the film is based on the book by the Greek writer Nikos Kazantakis, and not the Gospels. The other condition is that this statement is to appear on signs outside the cinema in a display equal to the size of the posters advertising the film. (*Irish Times*, 21 October 1988:1,6.)
25. For an interesting re-interpretation of the notions of tradition and modernization, see Luke Gibbons, 'Coming out of Hibernation? The Myth of Modernity in Irish Culture', in Richard Kearney (ed.), *Across the Frontiers: Ireland in the 1990s*, Dublin: Wolfhound Press, 1988.158.
26. Interview with author, 15 August 2000.
27. Appeal Board decision, 18 February 1993.
28. *Sunday Independent*, 21 March 1993:12.
29. *Video Home Entertainment Ireland*, vol. 3, no. 3, March 1994:9.
30. *Film Ireland*, no. 53, June/July 1996: 5.
31. David Kerekes and David Slater (eds), 2000:337.
32. Ian O'Doherty, *Irish Independent*, 12 May 1998:9.
33. Ibid.
34. Bernadette Murphy, *Irish Independent*, 23 April 1996:8.
35. *Irish Independent*, 27 July 2000:36.
36. Ibid. 5 July 2000:13.
37. *Reservoir Dogs* had also been cited in other cases. One of these concerned a deranged man who, according to his girlfriend, had become obsessed with the film, identifying with the same character and scene. He was jailed for life after he inflicted severe facial burns on her after she was doused with petrol and he lit a cigarette he had given her, causing the injuries. (*Irish Independent*, 27 July 2000:36. See also, and Jackie Bourke, 'Tales of guns and gore', *Irish Times*, 17 November 1999:10.)
38. *Irish Independent*, 23 April 1996:8.

39. Ibid. 27 July 2000:36.
40. *Irish Times*, 13 September 1993.
41. Ibid. letters, 17 September 1993.
42. Bernie O'Toole, 'Porn films blamed for rise in sadistic sex crime', *Irish Independent*, 29 March 1999:5. See also, Mary Banotti, 'Biting the bullet to oppose pornography', *Irish Times*, 30 August 1993:10.
43. In the USA four boys claimed after raping a nun that had been inspired by the film, but it later emerged that they had not seen the film. Blake Morrison, *Independent on Sunday*, 21 April 1995:31.
44. Quoted, Lyons 1997:15; the speech was delivered on 31 May 1995.
45. *Irish Times*, 29 October 1994:8.
46. Interview with author, 15 August 2000.
47. *Irish Times*, 29 October 1994:8.
48. Unpublished section of taped interview with Colum Kenny, 22 October 1986.
49. I was the film programmer at Project Cinema Club at the time.
50. Interview with author, 15 August 2000.
51. Ibid.
52. These events generated a considerable amount of criticism of both the Film Censor and of the Film Institute board. See, for example, *Evening Press*, 31 March 1995:1, 11; Des Crowley, 'Vicious satire, not violence, marked out banned film', *Sunday Press*, 2 April 1993:33; Emmanuel Kehoe, 'Sense and censorship', *Sunday Press*, 2 April 1995:17; Laoise MacReamoinn, 'Natural Born Controversy', *Sunday Business Post*, 2 April 1995:27; Susan McKay, 'Film censor denies he was behind the IFC's decision', *Sunday Tribune*, 2 April 1995:3; Kevin Myers, 'An Irishman's Diary', *Irish Times*, 4 April 1995:13.
53. See Ben Walters' review of the film in *Sight and Sound*, vol.14, no. 1, 2004:60. He sums it up as a 'relentless' film which is 'indulgent of, or entertained by, its characters' excesses and pains' and is the 'equivalent of a well-dressed Cheech and Chong film'.
54. Reject 3244, 101 mins, Censor's decision, 30 June 2003; distributor: Pathé Distribution. Letter from John Kelleher to Paul O'Higgins, Appeal Board register, 21 July 2003, OFC.
55. Interview with the author, 20 April 2004.
56. Appeal Board decision, 27 January 2003.
57. The BBFC also awarded the film an over-18s certificate. See review by Leslie Felperin in *Sight and Sound*, vol. 13, no. 3, 2003: 47–8.
58. Philip Molloy, 'See no evil', *Irish Independent*, 12 March 2004, Day & Night: 4–5. In addition, the Department of Justice agreed to allow for a two-tier fee system to aid the distribution of minority or foreign language films with less than six prints available in Ireland as part of its review of the cost of submitting a film for a certificate. However, the cost of certifying a film is quite high. While educational films cost nothing to certify, for those films with six prints or less in distribution at any one time in Ireland, from 1 April 2004, the cost was set at €3 per minute, or €300 for a 100 minute feature film. For other films, that is mainly feature films with more than six prints in circulation, the cost was set at €12 per minute, or €1,200 for a 100 minute feature film. The cost of an appeal was set at €1,000. (Censorship of Films (fees) Order 2004 (Statutory Instrument 114 of 2004).) Considering that in 2003 distributors paid €167,917 in fees for film classification with a further €693,196 for video certification, or a total of €1,081,153 when video licence fees are included, this cost (a 'tax') is no doubt being passed on to consumers. (Official Film Censor's Annual Report for 2003.) Nevertheless, censorship fees had remained static since 1987 (Statutory Instrument 341 of 1987). Video fees were also revised upwards at the same time. The cost of certifying a video is €10 per minute for the first hour; €8 per minute for the second hour; and €6 per minute thereafter. Thus, a 100 minute video would cost €920, while an appeal would cost a further €1,000. (Statutory Instrument 113 of 2004.)
59. Interview with the author, 20 April 2004.
60. Hugh Linehan, 'The parable of the censor and the cert', *Irish Times*, 13 March 2004: Weekend 40. Ironically, the most complaints received during Kelleher's first year in office concerned a decision made by his predecessor who awarded a 12PG to Jim Sheridan's *In America* (2003) as some argued that the film's explicit love-making scene warranted a higher rating. Indeed, the BBFC certified the film for over-15s only.
61. Pat Stacey, 'God's guts', *Irish Independent*, 12 March 2004, Day & Night:4–5.
62. Hugh Linehan, *Irish Times*, 13 March 2004: Weekend 4.
63. Ibid. 20 March 2004:Weekend 5.
64. Michael Dwyer, 'Give me that old time religion', ibid. 11 March 2004, The Ticket: 8–9. See also, Michael Dwyer, 'A haunting film of excruciating violence and horror', ibid. 26 February 2004:16.

65. Ibid., 26 February 2004:1, 16.
66. See Patsy McGarry, 'Papal silence on film generating tensions', ibid, 2 March 2004: 14.
67. Ibid., 10 March 2004:3; ibid., 12 March 2004:7.
68. Ibid., 17 March 2004:6. The film also developed a diverse correspondence in the *Irish Times*. See, for example, 2 March 2004:15; 4 March 2004:17; 6 March 2004:15.
69. Breda O'Brien, '"Passion" challenges believers on nature of faith,' ibid., 13 March 2004:14.

CHAPTER 7

1. *Seanad debates*, vol. 117, col. 1270, 4 November 1987.
2. 'Censorship of Television Films', TV6049, Office of the Minister for Posts and Telegraphs, January 1960, OFC.
3. *First Supplemental Report*, Television Committee, p. 11, State Paper Office, Dept. of the Taoiseach, S 14996A, NAI; quoted Robert J. Savage Jnr, *Irish Television: The Political and Social Origins*, Cork: Cork UP, 1996:46.
4. 'Censorship of Television Films', 1960.
5. *Seanad debates*. vol. 52, col. 20, 20 January 1960,
6. *Dáil debates*, vol. 179, col. 759, 24 February 1960.
7. Ibid., vol. 180, col. 1575, 31 March 1960.
8. Liam O'Hora to Minister for Justice, Oscar Traynor, 1 February 1960, OFC.
9. Liam O'Hora to Minister for Justice, Oscar Traynor, January 1961, OFC.
10. Liam O'Hora to Minister for Justice, Charles Haughey, 8 February 1962, OFC.
11. Adapted from a memorandum by Telefís Éireann's Head of Management, J.A. Irvine, 30 May 1962, OFC.
12. J.A. Irvine to A. Ingoldsby, 28 May 1962, OFC.
13. S. Ó Seaghdha, Dept. of Posts and Telegraphs to J.A. Irvine, 29 May 1962, OFC.
14. J.A. Irvine to S. Ó Seaghdha, 29 May 1962, OFC.
15. T.A. Irvine, 30 May 1962, OFC.
16. *Dáil debates*, vol. 195, col. 1870, 30 May 1962.
17. 'TV Authority Acts as its own censor', *Irish Times*, 31 May 1962:16. See also 'Television Film is Criticised by Labour Party Chief', *Irish Independent*, 31 May 1962:14.
18. *Leinster Leader*, 9 June 1962:3.
19. Liam O'Hora to Minister for Justice, Charles Haughey, 31 January 1963, OFC.
20. Charles Haughey to Liam O'Hora, 5 February 1963, OFC.
21. 'TÉ Acts as Own Censor', *Irish Press*, 31 May 1962:4.
22. Liam O'Hora to Minister for Justice, Charles Haughey, 11 February 1963, OFC.
23. Peter Berry, Department of Justice, to Leon Ó Broin, Secretary, Department of Posts and Telegraphs, 29 April 1963.
24. See Robert J. Savage Jnr, *Irish Television*, 1996, for the broader policy contexts to what is discussed in the opening section of this chapter.
25. Mention is made of this in a reply from Telefís Éireann's Director-General, Kevin C. McCourt, to Leon Ó Broin, 7 August 1963; Ref. TW. 41447/62.
26. Ibid.
27. Kevin C. McCourt, to Leon Ó Broin, 7 February 1964.
28. RTÉ memo dated 28 June 1971, OFC.
29. *Dáil debates*, vol. 230, col. 1530–32, 24 October 1967.
30. Ibid. vol. 245, col. 1018, 8 April 1970.
31. Ibid. col. 1019.
32. *Seanad debates*, vol. 68, col. 194, 27 May 1970.
33. Ibid. col. 202.
34. *Irish Times*, 26 January 1987:9. See reviews of *Lamb* in ibid., 3 October 1986, and *Sunday Independent*, 5 October 1986:15.
35. It is rarely a week passes without one such film being screened, and many of the films discussed in this book were recorded off-air for research purposes.
36. '*Ulysses* ban: RTÉ Wasn't Swayed', *Sunday Independent*, 17 June 1979:1.
37. *Irish Independent*, 29 January 2000:8; *Irish Times*, 29 January 2000:4; *Sunday Business Post*, 30 January 2000:6; *Sunday Business Post*, 6 February 2000:6. This short-lived controversy also raised the spectre that 'public exhibition' as defined in the Censorship of Films Act included television, jurisdiction which had never been even implied by censors prior to this.

38. Section 31 is discussed in the next chapter.
39. Jack Dowling, Lelia Doolan and Bob Quinn, *Sit Down and Be Counted: the cultural evolution of a television station*, Dublin: Wellington, 1969: 65.
40. Ten episodes of the series had been filmed, but it was withdrawn after the fifth episode was shown. The offending scene featured an art teacher played by David Kelly and the model was played by Madeleine Erskine. The founder of the League of Decency, J.B. Murray, reportedly had a heart-attack from the shock of watching the scene. For an account of the series and the controversy, see Helena Sheehan, *Irish Television Drama: A Society and its Stories*, Dublin: RTÉ, 1987:162–177.
41. *Sunday Press*, 6 January 1980:4.
42. Record 44168, Reserve 12947, Censor's decision, 18 December 1979.
43. Jim Farrelly, *Irish Independent*, 16 January 1980:1. Other films mentioned in the report were *The Happy Hooker*, *The Lustful Vicar*, *Bedroom Mazurka*, and *Deep Throat*.
44. *Dáil debates*, vol. 370, col. 805, 27 November 1986.
45. Deaglán de Bréadún, 'Show your own blue movies', *Irish Times*, 6 July 1981:10 and 'Public-house picture shows', ibid., 6 July 1981:10.
46. *Controls on Video Nasties*, Tenth Report of the Select Committee on Crime, Lawlessness and Vandalism, Dublin: Stationary Office, 1986:5; hereafter *Controls ... 1986*.
47. *Irish Times*, 6 July 1981; ibid., 6 July 1981:10.
48. *Irish Times*, 21 July 1981.
49. *Dáil debates*, vol. 335, col. 1277–78, 9 June 1982; The issue was raised by Workers' Party TD Paddy Gallagher, Waterford.
50. *Dáil debates*, vol. 337, col. 2847, 15 July 1982.
51. *Controls ... 1986:8.*
52. *Irish Times*, 18 September 1987:8. See *Irish Times*, 27 February 1988:4, which details the pressure applied by the American Ambassador to Ireland on Industry and Commerce Minister Albert Reynolds to take action against the piracy of American companies' intellectual property rights, and *Irish Times*, 30 July 1981 for a report of the prosecution of a video club owner distributing pirated tapes.
53. *Video Home Entertainment Ireland*, vol. 3, no. 3, March 1994:1.
54. Ibid., vol. 3, no. 8, August 1994:8. By 1995, consumer spending on video was £65.8 millions, while in 1996, 72 per cent of Ireland's approximately one million households had a VCR. (Roddy Flynn, *Film Ireland*, no. 58, p. 18.)
55. *Irish Times*, 9 April 1998:7; *Irish Times*, 10 April 1998:4.
56. See for example, Derek Malcolm, 'Stand Up to the New Censorship', the *Guardian*, 15 March 1984; and Nigel Andrews in Martin Barker (ed.), *The Video Nasties: Freedom and Censorship in the Media*, London/Sydney: Pluto Press, 1984.
57. *Dáil debates*, vol. 346, col. 752, 30 November 1983.
58. *Dáil debates*, vol. 364, col. 1442, 11 March 1986.
59. *Controls ..., 1986: 1.*
60. Ibid. 20.
61. Ibid. 21.
62. *Video Home Entertainment Ireland*, vol. 3, no. 6, June 1994:7. The occasion was the opening by the minister of an extension to the film censors' premises to allow for the accommodation of six video censors.
63. Clodagh Corcoran, *Pornography: The New Terrorism*, Dublin: Attic Press, 1989:5.
64. Ibid. 4.
65. For a detailed account of the film's history, content, its production, and, most importantly, its marketing, see David Kerekes and David Slater, *Killing for Culture: An Illustrated History of Death Film From Mondo to Snuff*, London: Creation Books, 1994. See also Phil Hardy (ed.), *Horror*, 1985:297. The FBI, whose report on the film's first screening in Indianapolis in 1976 is reproduced in David Kerekes and David Slater, *See No Evil: Banned Films and Video Controversy* (Manchester: Critical Press, 2000), concluded that the film was fiction, and the Federal authorities decided against prosecuting it 'in view of the absence of any hard core pornography.' (Ibid. 376.) Though there were many imitations, this is most likely to be the unnamed film referred to by Corcoran. Ireland, as elsewhere, it should be noted, had its own popular interest in 'real' killings with the *Mondo Cane* films of the 1960s, the first of these was banned, but the second *Mondo Cane 2* (aka, *Mondo Pazzo*, Gualtiero Jacopetti and Franco Posperi, 1963) was released in 1968 in a cut version with an over-18s certificate. In an otherwise thoughtful speech during the Second Stage of the debate on the Video Recordings Bill, 1987, Senator David Norris, along with many other senators, accepted with-

out question the existence of 'snuff' movies. (*Seanad debates*, vol. 117, cols. 1281–82, 4 November 1987.)

66. See Pamela Church Gibson and Roma Gibson (eds), *Dirty Looks: Women, Pornography, Power*, 1993 for a wide selection of essays on the topic.

67. Ibid. 1993:3.

68. *Controls ...* 1986:17.

69. Robin Wood, *Hitchcock's Films Revisted*, London: Faber and Faber, 1991: 306; orig. 1989.

70. See Hitchcock's appreciation of this in relation to Grace Kelly in François Truffaut, *Hitchcock*, New York: Simon & Schuster, 1983: 73.

71. Carol J. Clover, *Men, Women and Chainsaws: Gender in the Modern Horror Film*, London: British Film Institute, 1992:160.

72. In Martin Barker (ed.), *The Video Nasties: Freedom and Censorship in the Media*, London/Sydney: Pluto Press, 1984:52.

73. Carol J. Clover, *Men, Women and Chainsaws*, 1992:51.

74. Ibid. 115.

75. Ibid. 120.

76. Ibid. 151.

77. Ibid. 228. When I finally got to see *I Spit on Your Grave* at Dublin's Irish Film Centre as part of a 1999 Halloween event organized by the IFC and Dublin's Horrorthon Club, the film was the only one singled out for special notice. At the box office, attention was drawn to a sign warning that the film contained graphic images, while, prior to the screening, the chairman of the Club gave personal testimony as to why he wouldn't be watching the film again (having seen it once) and repeated the warnings about the film's graphic nature. This squeamishness illustrated better than anything the much-hyped fear surrounding the film. The displacement on to the film's violence, when in fact there are far more offensive images within mainstream cinema, suggests two things. One, there was an implicit understanding on the part of the male spectators, who remained silent throughout the screening, that this is a feminist text in which a woman, on her own, gets even (*Thelma & Louise* though without a heroic suicide. The original title of the film – *Day of the Woman* – supports this). Secondly, there is an attendant recognition of male mutilation which, post the fact, allows for identification with the rapists even though they do not function to attract such empathy or identification. However, that the rape is represented as within a male context of competition and sport (to establish the male pecking order) – the group dynamic so familiar to males – there is an awareness of their own guilt and function within this community. Consequently, the film acts to make complex their viewing position. Of course, the level of violence against the male is clearly problematic given the general misogyny within (classical) mainstream cinema, often, even more pronounced in Irish literary and film work. Recent Irish film examples might include *Saltwater* (Conor McPherson, 2000) and *Intermission* (John Crowley, 2003). Other forbidden or controversial films in the Horrorothon series were: *Alice, Sweet Alice* (aka *Communion, Holy Terror*, Alfred Sole, 1976), *Zombie Flesh Eaters* (aka *Zombie 2*, Lucio Fulci, 1979, Italy), *Maniac* (William Lustig, 1980), *Suspiria* (Dario Argento, 1976, Italy), *The Rage: Carrie 2* (Kath Shea, 1999), *Tenebrae* (*Sotto gli Occhi dell' Assassino*, Dario Argento, 1982, Italy), *Phantasm* (aka *Phantasmes; Phantasmes Pornographiques*, Jean Rollin, 1975, France), *The Beyond* (*... E Tu Vivrai nel Terrore!*; aka *L'Aldila*, Lucio Fulci, 1981, Italy), *The Evil Dead* (Samuel M. Raimi, 1982), and *The Driller Killer*.

78. Video Prohibition 701/1994 and 1/2000.

79. Quoted Senator Maurice Manning, *Seanad debates*, vol. 117, col. 1260, 4 November 1987.

80. *Controls ...* 1986:24.

81. Ibid. 9.

82. Ibid. 5.

83. Ibid. 6.

84. Taylor also entered the public arena when he condemned the screening on RTÉ in 1987 of the film *This is Katie Bennett* which has a violent opening sequence. He claimed that if RTÉ did not 'show some form of restriction,' Ireland would have a Hungerford-type massacre. (This reference was to Michael Ryan who, on 20 August 1987, went on a killing spree in this English town, and for which the tabloid newspapaers wrongly claimed that he had been influenced by the Sylvester Stallone screen character Rambo. He killed 6 people.) Taylor declared that he was 'satisfied excessively [that] violent programmes could lead to violent crime.' (*Sunday Independent*, 30 August 1987:3.)

85. *Seanad debates*, vol. 117, col. 1277, 4 November 1987.

86. Ibid., vol. 118, col. 1475 ff., 17 February 1988.

87. Ciaran Carty, *Sunday Tribune*, 20 April 1992: B3.

88. *Seanad debates*, vol. 118, col. 1465, 17 February 1988.

89. Ibid., col. 1459, 17 February 1988.
90. Ibid., vol. 117, col. 1287, 4 November 1987.
91. Ibid., col. 1220. This particular piece of panic was fuelled by an evening newspaper report, a version of which is featured in David Cronenberg's media theory savvy film, *Videodrome* (1983).
92. *Seanad debates*, vol. 117, col. 1215.
93. Ibid., col. 1221–22. For an account of the operation of the British act four years after its passing, see Julian Petley, 'Video with red tape', *Independent*, 18 August 1988:11.
94. *Seanad debates*, vol. 117, col. 1224, 4 November 1987.
95. Ibid., vol. 117, col. 1675, 19 November 1987.
96. *Irish Press*, 5 November 1987:8.
97. Ibid.
98. *Irish Times*, 30 September 1987:11.
99. Ibid., 8 October 1987:11. See also, Patsy McGarry, 'Women in Revolt on the Video Bill', *Irish Press*, 8 June 1988:4.
 1. *Irish Times* 22 April 1988:4; *Sunday Tribune* 24 April 1988:6.
 2. *Irish Times*, 6 May 1988:13. The dispute within the ICCL over the Video Recordings Bill had come in the wake of another bitter conflict within the organization when proposals concerning the Rape Crisis Centre's submission in 1986 to the Law Reform Commission on reform of the rape laws were considered. See *Irish Press*, 8 June 1988:4.
 3. *Irish Press*, 8 June 1988:4.
 4. For press accounts on the event see *Evening Herald*, 24 November 1987:8; *Evening Press*, 5 December 1987:1; *Sunday Press*, 6 December 1987:3; *Irish Times*, 7 December 1987:10.
 5. Kevin Rockett, convenor of conference, to Minister for Justice, 7 December 1987.
 6. John Kirwan, Private Secretary, Minister for Justice, to Kevin Rockett, 7 January 1988.
 7. *Irish Times*, 29 December 1994:13.
 8. *Film Ireland*, no. 58, April–May 1997:5.
 9. Author's interview with Sheamus Smith, 15 August 2000.
10. *Film Ireland*, No. 58, April–May 1997:5.
11. *Irish Times*, 15 August 2002:3; *Irish Times*, 22 August 2002, The Ticket:28.
12. For an account of the reception of *Crash* internationally, see Martin Barker, Jane Arthurs and Ramaswami Harindranath, *The Crash Controversy: Censorship Campaigns and Film Reception*, London/New York: Wallflower Press, 2001. For the Paul McCarthy exhibition, see *Paul McCarthy*, Butler Gallery catalogue August 2002 (Kilkenny; Butler Gallery, 2002). A forum on the controversy held in Kilkenny after the police and censors' interventions was addressed by artist and academic Alastair MacLennan, artist Valerie Connor, art critic Slavka Sverakova, and myself.
13. Ciaran Carty, 'New Censors to Vet Videos We Watch', *Sunday Tribune*, 26 April 1992: B3.
14. Ibid. In 1988 in the Dáil the Minister for Justice had given the figure of 1,000 per annum as the number of new videos coming on the market each year. (*Dáil debates*, vol. 384(a), col. 8, 10 November 1988.)
15. Film Censor's annual reports.
16. Of course, it is these which are being squeezed out of the system with inspections by Gardaí for the Censor's authorized labels on video/DVD cases. In relation to sex shops trading in porn videos and claiming they were released prior to the act, see Ian Kilroy, 'Sex shops beat censorship laws', *Sunday Tribune*, 7 March 1999:6. See also, 'Porn ring smashed', *Evening Herald*, 11 April 1997:1; *Irish Independent*, 12 April 1997:7, which reported that in the previous two years, £2 million worth of pornographic material had been seized by customs officers; *Irish Independent*, 24 March 1999:6; Paul Melia, 'Porno shop still selling its sleaze', *Irish Times*, 20 January 2000:4; *Irish Times*, 19 February 2000:4; *Evening Herald*, 9 March 2000:2; *Irish Independent*, 15 November 2001:10.
17. Martha Kearns, 'Video chief hits out at "failure" to enforce laws', *Irish Independent*, 20 August 1996:7.
18. Prohibition Order 539/1994. According to Michael Dwyer, Smith banned the film because of a 'violent scene of anal rape'. (*Irish Times*, 23 November 1994:1.)
19. Prohibition order 17/1997.
20. Prohibition order 679/1997.
21. Prohibition order 25/1997.
22. *Irish Independent*, 5 August 1997:3.
23. Prohibition order 13/2002. See *Irish Times*, 27 March 2003:9.
24. *Irish Times*, 16 May 2002, The Ticket:28.
25. See Michael Dwyer, 'X marks the rot', *Irish Times*, The Ticket:6 for a hostile review of *Baise-Moi*; a more generous review which points out two key elements – the central female duo take power, if

not in a politically correct way, and they enjoy having sex – that make the non-conventionally enjoyable or 'stimulatingly' pornographic film worth seeing is one by Ginette Vincendeau in *Sight and Sound*, vol. 12, no. 5, May 2002: 38.

26. These include *The Secret Agent Club* (John Murlowski, 1996) starring Hulk Hogan, which had an over-15s limitation changed to over-12s (12 November 1996), bringing it closer in line with the British rating of PG; the blockbuster special effects science-fiction alien invasion comic film with Will Smith, *Independence Day* (Roland Emmerich, 1996) had its over-15s certificate replaced by a General one (12 November 1996); a comedy with Jennifer Aniston (of *Friends*) and Cameron Diaz, *She's the One* (Edward Burns, 1996) was changed from an over-18s certificate to over-15s certificate uncut (4 July 1997); and *Jurassic Park*'s sequel, *The Lost World: Jurassic Park* (Steven Spielberg, 1997) had its over-12s certificate confirmed (22 January 1998).

27. Prohibition order 13/2002; Appeal Board decision, 27 January 2003, distributor: Universal Picture. Those in attendance were Kevin Myers, Anne Walsh, Anne Mooney, Cathy Herbert, Paul O'Higgins (chair), David Pierpoint.

28. Prohibition order 221/1995; ban upheld after appeal, 18 August 1995. This was the first video banning to be appealed. A film with a slightly different title, *Secret Games III* was banned two years later, 26/1997; there was no appeal on that occasion.

29. Prohibition order 1/1998; Appeal Board decision, 22 April 1998.

30. Prohibition order 35/1999; Appeal Board decision, 28 April 1999.

31. Prohibition order 40/2000; Appeal Board decision, 31 August 2000. In this case, the majority decision (of four present) was to grant an over-18s certificate upheld after appeal.

32. Prohibition order 3/1991; Prohibition revoked, 2 September 1999.

33. Prohibition order 335/1995; Prohibition revoked, 1 May 2001.

34. Prohibition order 97/1997; Prohibition revoked, 20 November 1997.

35. *Evening Herald*, 7 October 1987:1.

36. Smith gave this interview to *Video Home Entertainment Ireland*, which was published in vol. 3, no. 3, March 1994:1. The above comments were not included in the published interview, but I am grateful to the interviewer, Colum Kenny, for supplying me with the full text of the article.

37. For a discussion of Muybridge, see Linda Williams, *Hardcore: Power, Pleasure, and the 'Frenzy of the Visible'*, London: Pandora, 1991; orig. 1990.

38. Audrey Conlon interview with author, 15 August 2000. In a 2000 newspaper article, Smith drew attention to the 'more liberal', ratings he gave to a number of films compared with his UK counterpart: *The End of the Affair*: Ireland, over-15; UK over-18; *The World is Not Enough*: Ireland, PG; UK, over-12; and *Stigmata*: Ireland, over-15; UK, over-18. He regarded the 'matter-of-fact way' in which abortion was treated in *The Cider House Rules* as inappropriate for 15-year-olds 'given the context of that subject in this country at the moment.' Sheamus Smith, 'A Day in the Life', *Irish Independent*, 28 March 2000:10.

39. Author's interviews with Smith and Conlon, 15 August 2000.

40. One extreme example of this displacement, was the multi-billion dollar lawsuit lodged in 2001 by parents of fifteen school-children killed at Columbine High School, near Denver, Colorado in 1999, against makers of violent computer games, blaming them for inspiring the massacre. (Niall McKay, 'Internet not to blame for Littleton massacre', *Irish Times*, 7 May 1999:Business 10.) A case related to *The Basketball Diaries*, as mentioned in the previous chapter, was dismissed by a judge the following year. See *Irish Independent*, 7 June 2001:36. See also, Ian O'Doherty, *Irish Independent*, 12 May 1998:9; 'Horrific game [Carmageddon II] to go on sale here', *Evening Herald*, 15 October 1998:1; Jackie Bourke, 'Games for a laugh?', *Irish Times*, 10 November 1999:8; and Eddie Gibb, 'Programmed for violence?', *Sunday Tribune*, 13 February 2000:2. For an excellent general introduction to video games and their cultural impact and meaning, see Eugene F. Provenzo Jnr, *Video Kids: Making Sense of Nintendo*, Cambridge: Harvard UP, 1991.

41. By 2004, 'search engine' Google had indexed six *billion* pages of internet text. However, Google itself came under scrutiny with some regarding such claims of text-indexing as exaggerated. See Karlin Lillington, 'Facts are hard to find when you google Google', *Irish Times*, 14 May 2004:Business 7.

42. MUD (Multiple User Dimension/Dungeon) interchangeable with MUSH (Multiple User Shared Hallucination) essentially describes a (virtual) role playing game in which characters assume certain identities and act out fantasies with other players. See Sheery Turkle, 'MUD Rape: Only Words?' in her *Life on the Screen*, London: Phoenix, 1995:250–3.

43. See Mark Slouka, *War of the Worlds*, Basic Books/HarperCollins, 1995.

44. Marjorie Heins, *Not in front of the Children*, 2002, New York: Hill and Wang, 2002:8; orig., 2001.

45. *Evening Herald*, 29 April 1997:15. Due to diet and other factors, puberty is happening earlier than in the past.

46. See 'Birth of tween spirit', *Irish Independent*, 16 April 2001:13 and *Evening Herald* 4 June 2001:12 for accounts of the tweenager in Ireland. It should be noted that while the 1990s saw rapid change, the child/teenager as a consumer was already a reality, especially with regard to music even if it was not sold as explicitly on sex and image appeal, while specialist brands and clothes outlets were available from the 1980s. See also Marie Murray, 'Reclaiming childhood', *Sunday Tribune*, 2 April 2000:5, for parental strategies to desexualize children's clothes.

47. Michel Foucault, *The History of Sexuality*, London: Allen Lane, 1979; orig.,1976; English translation, 1978.

48. See Marjorie Heins, *Not in front of the Children*, 2002; Laurence O'Toole, *Pornocopia: Porn, Sex, Technology and Desire*, London: Serpent's Tail, 1998.

49. See Tom Inglis, *Truth, Power and Lies: Irish Society and the Case of the Kerry Babies*, Dublin: UCD Press, 2003.

50. Fintan O'Toole, *A Mass for Jesse James: A Journey Through 1980s Ireland*, Dublin: Raven Arts Press, 1990: 10.

51. Despite the level of media hysteria about the internet, a number of insightful articles appeared in the press, among them, Kathryn Holmquist's 'On the dark side of the Net', *Irish Times*, 28 October 2000:Weekend 1. Notwithstanding its misleading eye-catching headline about how researcher Rachel O'Connell feared for her life as a result of her work entrapping internet paedophiles online, the report was otherwise balanced and informative, and concluded with the suggestion: 'We must keep the risks of online victimisation in perspective: according to research, one in eight Irish boys and one in four Irish girls will be sexually abused in "real life", as opposed to virtual reality. For most abused children, this happens in their own homes or in the homes of trusted friends or relatives. Many others will be physically attacked by other youths. Internet victimisation is new, but as challenging and harmful as it may seem, it is not the most significant nor the most likely peril for our children.' Since this article, there has been a decided increase in the number of unprovoked street attacks by and on young people.

52. There is considerable material devoted to this, even if much of it is written from a populist and techno-fetishistic stance. Possible starting points for further exploration are Howard Rheingold, *Virtual Reality*, London: Quality Paperbacks Direct, 1991; Claudia Springer, 'The Pleasure of the Interface' *Screen* vol. 32, no. 3, 1991 and reprinted in her book-length study of bodies, desire and the internet, *Electronic Eros*, London: Athlone, 1996; Michael Heim, *The Metaphysics of Virtual Reality*, New York: Oxford UP 1993; Mark Dery (ed.), *Flame Wars* (special issue) *The South Atlantic Quarterly*, 92: 4, Duke UP, fall/autumn 1993; James Brook and Iain A. Boal (eds), *Resisting the Virtual Life*, San Francisco: City Lights, 1995.

53. The nearest to this, at present, at least with regard to democratic access, is largely limited to works of (science) fiction, computer games or in terms of Ireland's obsession with real estate, virtual online tours through prestigious properties.

54. Though sex always sells (see Frank Rose, 'Sex Sells', *Wired*, vol. 5 no. 12, December 1997: 218–224; 276–284, a discussion of the internet's Seth Warshavsky and the sex business,) in Ireland, at least, according to the first survey of general Irish internet usage, 'Irish surfers prefer cars to sex,' as a *Sunday Tribune* headline put it. (23 January 2000:5; 13.)

55. 'Library staff fear Internet porn browsers', *Evening Herald*, 2 March 2000:18. Although third level colleges have also restricted access by some, usually student, users because of porn surfing, it was a senior administrator of such an institution who was suspended because of his surfing and downloading of illegal material. See, John Walshe, 'Top college official in web porn probe', *Irish Independent*, 2 June 2001:6. Three years later, a report by PixAlert on private sector employees accessing internet pornography sites stated that while one in ten companies said that the downloading of pornography was responsible for their most serious breaches of security, half of all companies surveyed reported incidents of staff downloading and distributing pornography. Additionally, the distribution of explicit material on company servers had led to a series of financial settlements with female employees who claimed sexual harassment after receiving pornography from other employees. (See 'Internet porn epidemic hits half of all firms', *Sunday Tribune*, 23 May 2004:1, 9.) Almost simultaneous with the publication of this report, Bank of Ireland managing-director Michael Soden resigned after he was found to have breached company guidelines on internet usage by accessing a Las Vegas escort agency, itself a completely legal activity. The response to Soden's resignation was tempered by the simultaneous discovery of widespread over-charging of customers by the bank's main rival, AIB, with many commentators declaring that bankers should be forced to resign, not for accessing internet sites which is legal, but for what many regard as a serious breach of the law

at AIB. (See, for example, Kieran Fagan, 'We have become bigger hypocrites than Victorians', *Irish Times*, 1 June 2004:16, and Fintan O'Toole, 'A culture of total impunity', ibid.)

56. Nonetheless, while it may exaggerate conventional gender difference which serves the male fantasy, 'it does not always conform to traditional sexual representations.' (Claudia Springer, *Electronic Eros*, 1996:68.)

57. SPAM refers to unsolicited emails from individuals or organizations the content of which is largely advertising.

58. Dennis Howitt, *Paedophiles and Sexual Offences Against Children*, Chichester: J. Wiley, 1995.

59. Laurence O'Toole, *Pornocopia*, 1998:231.

60. *Irish Times*, 3 November 1997:20.

61. *Irish Independent*, 9 September 1996:5. See also, Aideen Sheehan, 'Porn slips through the 'Net: Paedophiles are using websites to contact young children', *Evening Herald*, 16 July 1997:14–15.

62. *Irish Independent*, 24 June 1996:8. See also, Jim Cusack, 'Global net users who trade on child misery', *Irish Times*, 7 September 1996:9. This was one of three articles mainly concerning the need to introduce controls on the internet published in the context of the capture of the notorious child murderer and paedophile, Belgian Mark Dutroux. Nowhere in the articles was it reported that Dutroux or his associates used the internet for his activities. Indeed, during his 2004 trial, psychiatric evidence suggested that far from being a networker, he was a pathological loner. See also Carissa Casey, 'Who's policing the Net paedophiles?', *Sunday Business Post*, 1 September 1996:16. One of the first Irish articles about the internet was Aine O'Connor's 'Love and lust on-line', *Sunday Independent*, 3 September 1995.

63. This age can vary considerably in different jurisdictions: in Italy the age is 13. Additionally the media-driven interest in westerners engaging in Asian sex tourism is complicated by the fact that in many Asian societies such as Cambodia, adult males having sex with children has been ritualized in religious practice for centuries; indeed, 90 per cent of those having sex with children are locals. See Ann McElhinney, 'Foreign tourists only part of the child sex problem', *Irish Times*, 27 May 2003:13.

64. *Irish Times* letters, 17 March 1998:15.

65. See Mark Jolly, 'Growing up fast', *Sunday Times*, 30 July 1995.

66. Prohibition order 163/1999. Original running time, 105 mins; re-submitted at 96 mins later in 1999 and passed with an over-18s certificate.

67. Garrett Reynolds, 'Who will censor cyberspace?', *Irish Independent*, 14 July 1997: 16. The organization was formally established in January 1998.

68. Eoin Licken, 'Child porn law flawed?', *Irish Times*, 13 October 1997:10.

69. Ibid., 13 October 1997:10.

70. See Catherine Cleary, 'Report claims evidence of paedophiles on Internet', ibid., 23 March 1998:1.

71. Ibid., 13 May 1998:13.

72. Ibid., 15 May 1998:B12.

73. Laurence O'Toole, *Pornocopia*, 1998:259.

74. *Evening Herald*, 24 October 2000:2. An investigation two years earlier concerned a single man in his 50s whom police detained when they found him video-taping young children as they undressed on Laytown beach, Co. Meath. A follow-up search of the man's home revealed further amateur videos of children, but police admitted at that time that current legislation might not cover such activities. See 'Naked children filmed', *Irish Independent*, 8 June 1998:6.

75. See, for example, Gemma O'Doherty and Jerome Reilly, 'Exposed: Ireland's vile child-sex rings', *Irish Independent*, 11 July 1998: Focus 1, 4. Buried in the bowels of this 'sensationalist' report is the comment by one policeman: 'To be honest, there has been precious little evidence so far to support the view of a large-scale organised network.'

76. See, for example, a commentary on a tragic Irish case, Mebh Ruane, 'Most risky place for child is within own family', *Irish Times*, 7 September 2001:14.

77. Laurence O'Toole, *Pornocopia*, 1998:222.

78. *Irish Independent*, 13 January 1999:6; 'Child porn convict may help Gardaí', *Sunday Tribune*, 5 December 1999.

79. 'Paedophile caught peddling child porn from website here,' *Irish Independent*, 7 February 2000:1; *Irish Times*, 31 July 2002:4.

80. *Manga* relies on a host of codes and symbolic substitutes whereby the reader is able to insert what would be otherwise censored or deemed forbidden. These include the standard schoolgirl in uniform as object of paedophilic desire, candle as torture device, conch shell as cunnilingus, train or plane in motion as penetration, Japanese white radish as phallus substitution or erection. The list of pornography codes, reminiscent of mainstream cinema, is, Sandra Buckley points out, endless

and constantly changing but clearly understood by 'informed' and 'regular' readers. (Sandra Buckley 'Penguin in Bondage', *Technoculture*, Constance Penley and Andrew Ross (eds), Minneapolis, Oxford: University of Minnesota Press, 1991:187–188.) Examples of codes within classical cinema include Alfred Hitchcock's train in the tunnel representing sexual relations at the end of *North By Northwest*, or, more explicitly, waves breaking on a seashore to represent sexual climax, as in the famous beach scene in *From Here to Eternity*. Ironically, as noted in chapter 3, such classical cinema codes were developed in response to film censorship restrictions in the 1930s, and, as some have argued, led to a more subtle and sophisticated cinema. See, for example, Stephen Prince, *Classical Film Violence: Designing and Regulating Brutality in Hollywood Cinema, 1930–1968*, New Brunswick, New Jersey: Rutgers UP, 2003, on violence becoming codified in the censorship era. See also the British Film Institute compilation film *A Personal Journey with Martin Scorsese through American Movies* (Martin Scorsese and Michael Henry Wilson, 1995, UK/USA) in which Scorsese discusses the 'smuggler' and inventive film director.

81. Laurence O'Toole, *Pornocopia*, 1998, chapter 6.
82. The middle-class profile of internet child pornography users was confirmed in the Britain's Operation Magenta when 75 raids yielded up teachers, doctors, and other care workers, as well as a 15-year-old boy, among the 30 arrested; *Irish Times*, 25 April 2002:13.
83. *Irish Independent*, 14 January 2000:4.
84. Ibid. 17 May 2001:7; see also, ibid. 11 August 2000:1.
85. Ibid. 14 January 2000:4.
86. *Sunday Independent*, 5 August 2001:4.
87. See Andrea Dworkin, *Pornography: Men Possessing Women*, New York: Perigee, 1981; and Catharine MacKinnon *Feminism Unmodified: Discourses on Life and Law*, Cambridge, Mass.: Harvard UP, 1987.
88. *Irish Times*, 28 May 2002:5; ibid. 30 May 2002:8; ibid. 1 June 2002:8.
89. Ibid. 18 January 2003:1, 3, 15; Weekend:1.
90. Ibid. 22 November 2002:6. The prosecution of offences relating to child pornography was the theme of the fifth National Prosecutors' Conference held in May 2004 under the auspices of the Director of Public Prosecutions.
91. Ibid. 13 May 2003:5; ibid. 18 January 2003:3.
92. Ibid. 2 July 2003:4.
93. Ibid. 23 July 2003:4; ibid. 3 December 2003:1, 5.
94. Ibid. 19 September 2003:4.
95. Ibid. 21 November 2003:4.
96. Ibid. 12 June 2003: 4; ibid. 19 December 2003:4; ibid. 17 February 2004:4; ibid. 2 April 2004:2; ibid. 21 April 2004:3; ibid. 24 April 2004:1,4,5,17.
97. Ibid. 20 March 2004:4.
98. Ibid. 3 April 2003:2.
99. Ibid. 24 July 2003:4.
 1. *Irish Independent*, 18 July 2002:11.
 2. *Irish Times*, 9 July 2003:4; ibid. 4 February 2004:4.
 3. *Irish Independent*, 5 July 2003:3.
 4. *Irish Times*, 20 May 2003: 9; ibid. 22 July 2003:4. After pleading guilty to possessing 23 offensive images, ex-Garda Conor Brough had his sentence adjourned until he received treatment at the Granada Institute for Sex Offenders, Dublin. (Ibid. 15 April 2004:4.)
 5. Ibid., 20 May 2003:4; ibid., 10 July 2003:4.
 6. Sandra Buckley, 'Penguin in Bondage,' in Penley and Ross (eds), *Technoculture*, 1991:183. This material offers an easy transition to the new pornographic software games that are often advertised within these 'comics' and are available in bookstores and by mail order. As Buckley points out, more explicit and violent games are available on the black market including 'do-it-yourself sexual violence games [which] come in a variety of "flavours" including sadomasochism, bestiality, rape and pedophilia.' (p. 163.)
 7. *Irish Times*, 2 April 1999:4. Max Taylor is co-author with Ethel Quayle of *Child Pornography: An Internet Crime*, London: Routledge, 2002.
 8. Kathryn Holmquist, 'On the dark side of the Net', *Irish Times*, 28 October 2000: Weekend 1. However, the focus of O'Connell's own work (with a €0.75 million grant) was for the development of educational programmes for the protection of children on the net. By 2003, according to another Holmquist article, *Irish Times*, 18 January 2003: Weekend 1, COPINE research suggested that 'in excess of 50,000 abusive images of children' were being posted monthly to internet newsgroups.

9. This comment was made in 1996 by Manchester police sergeant Oliver Clarke, chairman of CommUnity, a UK based on-line campaigning organization quoted in Laurence O'Toole, *Pornocopia*, 1998:259.

10. *Irish Independent*, 6 December 2003:5.

11. *Illegal and Harmful Use of the Internet*, 1998:33–34.

12. The dangers, though, of chat rooms were graphically illustrated by the case of a 12-year-old English girl who was befriended on the internet by a 31-year-old American, with whom she eloped. Following an international search the pair were found, the man later being charged with abduction. (See *Sunday Independent*, 20 July 2002:3.) Perhaps realizing the potential dangers posed by chat rooms Microsoft closed down thousands of the internet chat rooms on its system. Ireland's Eircom.net is one of the few ISPs not to offer a chat room service. (See, Jamie Smyth, *Irish Times*, 25 September 2003:14.)

13. Catherine Lumby, 'Porn Again', *21·C*, no 4, 1996:33.

14. The report received wide publicity on its release. See *Irish Times*, 23 March 1998:1; *Irish Independent*, 10 July 1998:7, 12; ibid., 14 July 1998:16.

15. Catherine Lumby, 'Porn Again', *21·C*, no. 4, 1996:34.

16. 'Internet hotline for users' pornography complaints', *Irish Times*, 12 February 2000:3.

17. '100 arrested as Internet paedophile ring uncovered', *Irish Times*, 3 September 1998:1, 15; *Sunday Independent*, 5 August 2001: 1, 4; Lynda Lee-Potter, 'Vile depravity on the internet', *Irish Independent*, 5 September 1998:3.

18. In this instance, it was reported, after 46 men were arrested in 12 countries that hundreds of thousands of still images and video clips were found, including some depicting torture of children and sexual abuse of babies, *Irish Independent*, 3 July 2002:34.

19. 'German police smash child porn network', *Irish Times*, 27 September 2003:10.

20. An Italian organization put the number of websites featuring child pornography in 2003 at 17,016, up 70 per cent up on the previous year, with more than half of them originating in the USA. (*Irish Times*, 17 January 2004:10.)

21. Laurence O'Toole (*Pornocopia*, 1998:264) cites the case of a Catholic priest in Scotland who was convicted in autumn 1996 for possession of computer child pornography. Contributing to a self-declaring paedophile exchange system on-line, he was caught as a direct result of boasting about his 'conquests' of his young parishioners, rather than as a consequence of trading pornographic images.

22. Ibid. 268.

23. *Irish Times*, 10 December 1999: Business 12.

24. *Illegal and Harmful Use of the Internet*, 1998:12.

25. 'Irish groups may plead pornography case at UN', *Sunday Tribune*, 28 November 1999:17. In order to stop 'unsuitable programmes' the National Parents Council Secretary, Nick Killian, called for European Union controls on terrestrial and satellite television content. (*Evening Herald*, 29 April 1997:15.) In 1993, Senators had engaged in an excited discussion on the Danish pornography channel, Red Hot Television, because it could be viewed in Ireland. (See, 'Porn creates a heated debate', *Irish Times*, 8 April 1993:7.) The issue of gaining some measure of regulatory control over satellite television beamed from another country, such as Sky's UK base, was one which the Irish government pursued until finally admitting defeat in 2004 when the European Commission ruled that such a service was trans-European in the same way as other products were sold without national regulation across Europe.

26. 'Hotline move to halt child porn on Internet', *Irish Independent*, 30 November 1999. For the international context of ISPs and government regulation, see 'Net films caught in censorship crossfire', *Irish Times*, 3 December 1999: Business 11. This is a reprint of a *Financial Times* article.

27. *Irish Independent*, 31 August 2001:12; 'Parliament no to use of personal communications', *Irish Times*, 7 September 2001:4.

28. Jamie Smyth, 'Government to sign crime treaty despite concerns', *Irish Times*, 18 January 2002:Business Supplement 8.

29. See Karlin Lilington, 'War on liberties escalates', *Irish Times*, 22 November 2002:7.

30. See, *Irish Times*, 26 May 2003: 18.

31. *Irish Times*, 20 March 2004:1.

32. *Sunday Tribune*, 5 December 1999:7.

33. *Illegal and Harmful Use of the Internet* 1998:36.

34. See *Irish Times*, 4 March 2004:4.

35. See Karlin Lillington's stinging reply, 'Positive aspects of Internet for Children', *Irish Times*, 13 February 2002: 16.

36. *Illegal and Harmful Use of the Internet* 1998:15–16.
37. 'Raids a first step to protect children', *Irish Times*, 28 May 2002: 12.
38. 'This evil menace needs more laws', *Irish Independent*, 19 December 1997:9. Though the relationship or kinship of the abuser to the child was not explained, as the conference title suggests they were not strangers. Perhaps the most disturbing aspect of the American police investigation of the Texas website already discussed, was not the sale/purchase of child pornographic images, but the content of the classified internet advertisements listed. Frequently, the police uncovered instances where parents or guardians posted notices offering a child for sex with an adult in return for money.
39. 'Internet child abuse increases', *Irish Times*, 11 February 2004:14.
40. *Irish Independent*, 23 January 2004:5; Paul Gilligan, Chief Executive, ISPCC, 'Camera phones and the threat to children', ibid.; *Irish Times*, 23 January 2004:6, 8; 'Focus on identifying schoolgirl criticised', *Irish Times*, 28 January 2004:10; ibid., 17 February 2004:7.
41. 'Call for schools to ban photo phones', *Irish Times*, 11 February 2004:10.
42. 'Pool bans phones after woman pictured', *Irish Times*, 10 February 2004:2.
43. See Martin Jay, *Downcast Eyes: The Denigration of Vision in Twentieth Century French Thought*, Berkeley/Los Angeles/London: University of California Press, 1994.
44. Quoted Marjorie Heins, *Not in Front of the Children*, 2002:3.
45. Ibid. 14.
46. Internet Advisory Board Report, 2002:vii. The report does not detail how many of these children *deliberately* accessed material forbidden by their parents.
47. 'Pre-teens "seeing porn on internet in their homes"', *Irish Independent*, 18 July 2002:11.
48. Matthew Magee, 'Censor regulates computer games', *Sunday Tribune*, 10 January 1999:4. See also Pio Stack, 'Dying To Play', *Irish Independent*, 9 February 1998:14.

     While games in Ireland are monitored by the Film Censor, a joint agreement exists between the Censor and games' manufacturers whereby a classification system used throughout European applies to Ireland. Thus, the ratings produced by the European Leisure Software Publishers Association are voluntarily accepted in Ireland, 'and only in exceptional circumstances is the Film Censor asked to classify a game.' ('Violent child computer games to be X-rated', *Irish Independent*, 6 November 2000:4.)
49. For discussions of 'X-rated' music videos, see 'Courting controversy?', *Irish Times*, 18 November 1998:3 and Peter Murphy, 'Massacre of good taste?', *Sunday Independent*, 23 May 1999:9L, who concludes that if you switch on MTV after midnight 'there's no shortage of prohibited images from which to choose.' He also notes that German techno and heavy metal bands such as Rammstein and RMFDM, as well as American 'gothic' singer Marilyn Manson, were cited as contributing to the psychopathology of the Columbine school killers, yet another example of how gun lobbyists in the USA seek to displace responsibility for gun-killings from themselves on to popular culture.
50. *Sunday Tribune*, 22 October 1995:1.
51. 'The Internet and Your Child', *Irish Times* Education and Living supplement, 7 March 2000:2.
52. It was this commercialization of childhood and the extent to which children are targets of television advertisements which led to Irish independent filmmaker Bob Quinn resigning from the RTÉ Authority – the station's governing body – in 1999. See Bob Quinn, *Maverick: A Dissident's View of Broadcasting Today*, Dingle, Co. Kerry: Brandon, 2001, which details his failed attempts to ban or restrict child-centered advertising, which is worth between six and eight million euro annually to the station. Belatedly, in 2004 the Broadcasting Commission of Ireland introduced some limits on advertisements aimed at children ('Child ad code will not cover British stations', *Irish Times*, 20 April 2004:5), while Quinn was one of the promoters of a new lobby group, Stop Television Advertising to Children (STOP), set up in 2004, which is seeking a complete ban on advertisements aimed at children between 2 p.m. and 7 p.m. (Breda O'Brien, 'Kidnapping our children's imaginations', *Irish Times*, 1 May 2004:16). See also, Breda O'Brien, 'Shaping our children to the consumerist ethos', *Irish Times*, 20 July 2002:14. Ironically, it is not toys, but fashion clothes and make-up, which now interests many pre-teens, and advertisers target them with these products, resulting in the decline of the traditional toy market. See Kim Bielenberg, 'Old head on young shoulders', *Irish Independent*, 19 November 1999:13.
53. 'Pokemon craze really hits home', *Sunday Tribune*, 9 April 2000:6;. See also 'Poke-craze is now a monster out of control', *Evening Herald*, 3 April 2000:11; 'The toy that got 'em all', *Irish Times*, 5 April 2000:5.
54. It was distributed to 10,000 children.
55. One report of the findings after they were presented to a 'Children and the Media' conference organized by the Family and Media Association is Fergal Maddock, 'Alarm over children's access to

"X" videos', *Irish Independent*, 9 September 1996:5. See also the first newspaper reports of the findings: Yvonne Healy, 'What are videos doing to our kids?', *Irish Times*, 28 February 1995:EL4; John Roper, '"Adult" films seen by 96% of children – survey', *Sunday Tribune*, 22 October 1995:1, 2; and Jackie Bourke, 'Peaceful kids in a violent world', *Irish Times*, 13 May 1997:Education 5.

56. *Irish Independent*, 30 September 1997:14. For another instance of moral outrage generated by the press see 'Fury at Video Sickener; Explicit Scenes Show Kids Mutilating Genitalia With Nails,' *Evening Herald*, 7 May 1998:1, in which the passing by the British Board of Film Classification of the video *Physical Graffiti* was used by two journalists, Bairbre Power and Katie Hannon, to elicit the outraged response from the Minister for Children, Frank Fahey, that 'obviously that kind of material shouldn't be available here.' He undertook to take up the matter with the Film Censor, Sheamus Smith, even though the video had not even been submitted for a certificate. The fact that the *Herald* led with it as a page one story, though it was displaced by other stories in later editions, is evidence enough of the manufactured nature of the news. Needless to say, neither the journalists nor the minister indicated that they had seen the video. As of June 2004, it has not been submitted to the Irish Censor.

57. *Irish Independent*, 17 April 2000:12.

58. Prior to the submission of *Lolita* (Adrian Lyne, 1997, GB/France) to the Irish Film Censor, Cian Ó Tighearnaigh was interviewed on RTÉ's current affairs radio programme *Morning Ireland* in early 1998. His acknowledgment that he had not seen the film did not stop him from calling for it to be banned on the basis that a film dealing with the relationship between an adult male and a teenage girl was not a fit subject for a film. As it happened, *Lolita* was passed uncut with an over-18s certificate by Sheamus Smith. Irish critics were generally favourable in their comments on the film. Prior to its release, Aine O'Connor ('Lolita getting old waiting for a date', *Sunday Independent*, 13 July 1997:3L and *Sunday Independent*, 5 April 1998:11L), and Fintan O'Toole ('The problem of paedophilia in art', *Irish Times*, 3 September 1996:10) argued the liberal case for the film's release, while Philip Molloy (*Irish Independent*, 18 April 1998:3), gave the film a positive review. See also the article by John Mortimer (*Evening Herald*, 9 May 1998:6), which supported its release.

59. *Sunday Tribune*, 22 October 1995:2. Indeed, the discourse around mobile phones led by the 2000s to such anguished articles as 'Should we give mobile phones to children?', *Irish Independent*, 4 January 2000:11.

60. Clodagh Sheehy, 'Can we police kids' TV?', *Evening Herald*, 29 April 1997:14.

61. One piece of research examining the influence of television advertisements on under-7s showed that children who watched a lot of advertisements during November and December sought five or six presents from Santa compared to those who watched little or no television who requested only one. The research was based on a study of 1,300 advertisements screened during children's programmes in the five weeks prior to Christmas 1999. In Sweden, where advertising to under-12s is banned, a study of children found that they wanted significantly less toys than their British counterparts. See *Irish Independent*, 31 March 2001:R7.

62. *Sunday Tribune*, 22 October 1995:2.

63. *See Irish Times*, 13 July 2001:9.

64. *Illegal and Harmful Use of the Internet* 1998:32.

CHAPTER 8

1. Thomas Coyne, 'Memo on censorship', September 1945, Dept. of the Taoiseach, S11445/8, NAI.

2. See Luke Gibbons in *Cinema and Ireland*, 1988:203.

3. See Kevin Rockett, ibid. 24.

4. Tim Pat Coogan, *The IRA*, London: Fontana/Collins, 1987:69; orig. 1970.

5. Quoted Ciaran Carty, *Film Directions*, vol. 3, no. 9, 1980:17.

6. For the history of Irish film production during the 1910s to the 1930s see Rockett in *Cinema and Ireland*, Rockett et al., 1988, chapters 1–3.

7. Cosgrave approved the released version on 30 April 1931.

8. Rachael Low, *Films of Comment and Persuasion of the 1930s*, London: George Allen & Unwin, 1979:21–22.

9. John Horgan, *Seán Lemass: The Enigmatic Patriot*, Dublin: Gill & Macmillan, 1997:39.

10. Ibid. Coogan, *The IRA*, 1987:69 reports that the Masterpiece 'was blown up' by the IRA.

11. Rachael Low, *The History of the British Film 1918–1929*, London: George Allen & Unwin, 1971:293.

12. Coogan, *The IRA*, 1987:69.
13. Horgan, *Seán Lemass*, 1997:39.
14. Coogan *The IRA*, 1987:69.
15. See Rockett, chapter 4, in Rockett et al., *Cinema and Ireland*, 1988.
16. '500 People Rioted in Cinema', *An Phoblacht*, 8 December 1934:1.
17. '400 Men Dash Into Cinema – Screen Torn at Protest Against Film', *Irish Press*, 4 December 1934:1.
18. 'Dublin Cinema Outrage', *Irish Times*, 4 December 1934:7.
19. Ibid.
20. 'Why Cinemas are Wrecked', *Republican Congress*, 8 December 1934:1.
21. 'Tyranny', *Irish Times*, 5 December 1934:5.
22. 'Two Different Casements', *Republican Congress*, 22 December 1934:4. Others were aware of the decision by the BBFC to discourage the production of a feature film about Roger Casement (see next section).
23. These events prompted a letter writer to recall the events when in 1913 Na Fianna, the youth wing of the nationalist movement, raided a recruitment film. See 'When the Fianna Raided a British Propaganda Film', *An Phoblacht*, vol. 9, no. 47, 22 December 1934:1. See also, Rockett, *Cinema and Ireland*, 1988:32–33.
24. '*Irish Times* Hysteria', *An Phoblacht*, 8 December 1934:4.
25. *Irish Times*, 5 December 1934:7.
26. *Irish Times*, 10 October 1934:4.
27. Rachael Low, *Film Making in 1930s Britain*, London: George Allen & Unwin, 1985:168.
28. 'A Fine English Film', *Irish Times*, 2 January 1934:9.
29. For an account of this controversy see Rockett, 'From Radicalism to Conservatism', *Irish Studies Review*, 2001: 155–165.
30. 'The Cinema Evil; *Irish Press* Hypocrisy', *An Phoblacht*, vol. 10, no. 8, 23 March 1935:1.
31. Quoted Jeffrey Richards, *The Age of the Dream Palace: Cinema and Society in Britain 1930–1939*, London: Routledge & Kegan Paul, 1984:139.
32. *Irish Times*, 30 April 1935:4. Predictably, the *Irish Times* described it as 'an outstanding film'. (Ibid.)
33. Record 8738 and 19676, 10,027 feet; Reserve 3243, Censor's decision, 25 February 1935; review and certificate issued, 14 March 1935.
34. Richards, 1984:270.
35. He attended the official opening by President Cosgrave of the Savoy in 1929.
36. Quoted Richards, 1984:269.
37. *Irish Times*, 7 May 1935:6.
38. Ibid. A week later, the *Irish Times'* film reviewer complained about the 'intolerance' of those who were opposed to the royal newsreels being shown. (12 May 1935:4.)
39. Low, *Film Making in 1930s Britain*, 1985:124. The film was not subsequently submitted to the Irish Censor.
40. 'A New Censorship: No Special Coronation Films', *Irish Times*, 11 May 1937:4. In an editorial, 'Government by – Whom?', the same day, the *Irish Times*, p. 6, identified the 'Committee of Republican and Labour Organisations' who visited the renters as consisting of Cumann Phoblachta na hÉireann; Dublin Constituents Committee; the Labour Party; Republican Congress; National Association of the Old IRA; the Irish Citizens' Army; and Cumann na mBan.
41. 'Films of Coronation: not to be Shown Here in any Detail', *Irish Press*, 8 May 1937:6. Lewis, who was a pioneer newsreel cameraman and feature film producer in Ireland during the late 1910s, and was himself subject to censorship by the British military authorities during the War of Independence, may even have known some of those engaged in the 'boycott' of British royal films. See Rockett, in Rockett et al., 1988: 33–37.
42. Sinn Féin asked ITGWU members to ban screenings of Coronation films. It said that labour should be withdrawn since English cinema interests would not heed their request. (The *Cinema*, 29 April 1953.)
43. 'Southern Irish See Coronation Film', *Manchester Guardian*, 9 June 1953. During the 1937 controversy, the *Irish Times* (21 May 1937:5) also reported that 'hundreds' were travelling to Belfast to see film of the Coronation and that a special train was arranged for 22 May.
44. Richards, 1984: 264.
45. Low, *Film Making in 1930s Britain*, 1985:250.
46. Record 12317 and 33783, 10,485 feet; Censor's decision, 29 October 1937; certificate issued on 14 December 1937.

47. Record 13602, 8575 feet; Censor's decision, 8 November 1938; certificate issued on 7 December 1938.
48. *Irish Times*, 30 January 1939:5.
49. *Irish Press*, 31 January 1939:5.
50. This renewed militancy was treated in many British feature films including *I See a Dark Stranger* (Frank Launder, 1946), *Odd Man Out* (Carol Reed, 1947), *The Gentle Gunman* (Basil Dearden, 1952) and *A Terrible Beauty* (Tay Garnett, 1960). In most of these, and other such films, as John Hill argues, they operate to show the behaviour of the IRA activist (leader) as primarily pathological. Hill, *Cinema and Ireland*, 1988:147 ff. Most of these, mainly British-produced, films dealing with IRA activities in contemporary Northern Ireland were passed uncut by Irish censors, perhaps further indication that distorted representations of the IRA, or even pathological anti-Treaty characters such as that played by James Cagney in *Shake Hands with the Devil* (Michael Anderson, 1959), fitted within the South's demonization of any view which challenged the status quo.
51. Martin Quigley, 1999:181.
52. For a discussion of such films during 1910–1920, see Rockett, chapter 1, *Cinema and Ireland*, 1988.
53. James C. Robertson, *The British Board of Film Censors Film Censorship in Britain, 1896–1950*, London: Croom Helm, 1985:86.
54. Ibid. 50.
55. British Board of Film Censors Scenario notes (hereafter BBFC scenarios), 1933, 128, 8 February 1933, held at British Film Institute Library.
56. Ibid., 1934, 349, 29 October 1934. Shortly after his execution, Casement was the barely disguised subject of an American fiction film, *Whom the Gods Destroy* (William P.S. Earle, 1916). For an account of this film, see Rockett, 1996:291–292.
57. Robertson, 1985:88. The version released in Britain was 7,919 feet while the one submitted to the Irish Censor, perhaps the complete film, was 8,481 feet, or over 6 minutes longer. American versions have been variously given as 91, 95 and 97 minutes.
58. James Montgomery's report to the Appeal Board, 28 June 1935. Record 9270 and 16988, Reject 1218, 28 June 1935. The Appeal Board viewed the film on 9 July 1935 and the certificate was issued on 22 July 1935.
59. BBFC scenarios, 1935, 415, 7 May 1935.
60. Ibid. 8 May 1935.
61. Robertson, 1985:88.
62. BBFC scenarios, 1936, 46, 3 April 1936.
63. Robertson, 1985:89.
64. Ibid.
65. For a detailed note on the film see Rockett, 1996:349–350.
66. BBFC scenarios, 1938, 65a, 27 July 1938.
67. Ibid. 1938, 65, 29 July 1938.
68. Ibid. 1939, 28, 8 May 1939.
69. Ibid. 28b, 4 May 1939.
70. Coogan, *The IRA*, 1987:166–67.
71. BBFC scenarios, 1942, 30a, 4 March 1942.
72. Ibid. 1944, 75, 21 January 1944.
73. Ibid. 1944, 83, 31 May 1944.
74. See Rockett, 1996:147.
75. BBFC scenarios, 1945, 120, 17 May 1945.
76. See John Hill, 'Images of Violence', *Cinema and Ireland*, 1988.
77. Rachel Low, *The History of the British Film 1918–1929*, 1971:172.
78. Record F2028 (Reject book 2), 8,375 feet; Reject 51, 18 October 1926; distributor: Gaumont.
79. Record F2229 (Reject book 2), 10,895 feet; Reject 66, Censor's decision, 6 December 1926; passed with cuts after appeal; distributor: Famous Players-Lasky.
80. *American Film Institute Catalog of Motion Pictures Produced in the United States, Feature Films, 1921–1930*, Berkeley/Los Angeles/London: University of California Press, 1997:186–7; orig. 1971.
81. Record G2405 (Reject book 2), 6,657 feet; Reject 66, Censor's decision, 27 January 1927; distributor: Gaumont.
82. Record G3047 (Reject Book 2), 7,482 feet; Reject 110, Censor's decision, 15 July 1927; distributor: First National.
83. Record C674 (Reject Book 1), 6,000 feet; Reject 27; Censor's decision, 20 August 1924; distributor: E. Grattan Milloy.

84. Record F1112 (Reject book 2), 6,433 feet; Reject 16, Censor's decision, 4 February 1926; Phoenix Film Co.
85. Record F1169 (Reject book 2), 2,110 feet; Reject 23, Censor's decision, 18 February 1926; distributor: Levy & Co.
86. Record H3919 (Reject book 2), Reject 161, 9,272 feet; Censor's decision, 23 April 1928; passed with cuts after appeal; distributor: Fox Film Co.
87. Record C929 (Reject book 2), 8,471 feet; Reject 5, Censor's decision, 2 December 1925; passed with cuts after appeal; Stoll Films.
88. Record F2262, 9,586 feet; Reject 62, Censor's decision, 13 December 1926; distributor: Jury-Metro-Goldwyn.
89. Record 15,375, 9,045 feet; Reserve 1433; Reject 489, Censor's decision, 8 June 1931; distributor: United Artists. Certificate revoked under Emergency Powers Order (no. 196) on 18 September 1942.
90. 12,837 feet; Reserve 903; Censor's decision, 2 July 1930; certificate issued on 7 July 1930.
91. Robert Fisk, *In Time of War; Ireland, Ulster and the Price of Neutrality, 1939–45*, London: Palladin Books, 1985:165; orig. 1983.
92. Quoted, ibid. 279.
93. Quoted, ibid. 561.
94. Ibid. 162.
95. 'Memoranda on Film Censorship' by Connolly; and Connolly letter to Aiken, 15 September 1939, Dept. of Justice, NAI.
96. Ibid.
97. Coyne to Aiken memo, 16 September 1939, OCC 5/5, MA.
98. Dept of Justice, 16 September 1939, NAI.
99. Connolly, 'Memoranda on Film Censorship', 20 September 1939, Dept. of Justice, NAI.
1. Dept. of Justice memo, 21 September 1939, Dept. of the Taoiseach, S11450, NAI.
2. Michael Powell in Ian Christie (ed.), *Powell, Pressburger and Others*, London: British Film Institute, 1978:25.
3. *Irish Press*, 2 September 1939:5.
4. Department of Justice memo, 21 September 1939; NAI, Dept. of the Taoiseach, S11450. See also Fisk, *In Time of War*, 1983:162. Two months earlier the *Irish Times* reported ('Banned in Eire', 7 July 1939:7) that the American film, *Confessions of a Nazi Spy* (Anatole Litvak, 1939) had been refused a certificate by both the Censor and the Appeal Board. (Record 14369, 9,398 feet; Censor's decision, 28 June 1939; Appeal Board decision, 4 July 1939; distributor: First National.) The newspaper added that 'it is believed that the reasons for the banning of the film are that it is calculated to engender racial hatred, and to be "subversive of public morals".' The film was being widely screened in the USA and Britain.
5. Record 14568, 5,559 feet; Censor's decision, 8 September 1939; certificate issued on 19 September 1939; distributor: Columbia.
6. Record 14474 and 14838, 8,815 feet; Reserve 4244 and 4310, Censor's decision, 28 July 1939; review, 6 September 1939; certificate issued on 13 September 1939; Re-submitted under EPO, 8 November 1939; Certificate revoked, 2 December 1939; distributor: GFD. Another EPO title change was *Military Academy* (D. Ross Lederman, 1940) to *The Great Tradition*, Censor's decision, 30 October 1940.
7. Record 8542 and 11368, 10,442 feet; Reserve 5400, Censor's decision, 8 January 1937; certificate issued on 15 January 1937; reviewed by Censor under EPO, 22 January 1943; five cuts were demanded, one of which was of the first part of the introduction, while four were of Union Jacks; review, 29 January 1943; distributor: Warner Bros. Though it seems that the Union Jack was routinely cut by distributors prior to submission, or by Montgomery, in the 1930s, no cuts are recorded as having been made to this film when first submitted in 1937 which suggests that it was cut prior to submission, and that the 1943 version viewed under EPO was the complete film.
8. Record 9062; Reserve 5697; Censor's decision, 27 August 1943. At the time of its American release, the *New York Times* described it as 'a handsome tribute to the glory of British rule in India' (quoted, Jeffrey Richards, 1984:139), a view also shared, though from an anti-imperialist perspective, by those who visited a Dundalk cinema and took away the film. ('Film Taken in Dundalk: Two Men Detained', *Irish Times*, 8 April 1937:8.)
9. Record 10174, Reserve 5885, 2 February 1944; 17 February 1944; 18 February 1944; 31 March 1944. Two shots of the English sailors with native girls were also cut, but not under EPO.

10. 'Memoranda on Film Censorship', Joseph Connolly to Frank Aiken, 19 September 1939, Dept. of Justice, NAI.
11. Connolly memo, 20 September 1939, Dept. of Justice, NAI.
12. See *Irish Press*, 1 December 1936:5; ibid. 2 December 1936:2.
13. Record 24255, Reject 1420, Censor's decision, 1 June 1940; original decision, 5 May 1936. There was no appeal; distributor: ABPC.
14. James Montgomery to film distributors, September 1939, MA.
15. *British Movietone News*, 535A, Record 10243; Reserve 4265, Censor's decision, 9 September 1939. See also *Pathé Gazette*, 97411.
16. *Pathé Gazette*, 'The Crime of the Athenia', 39/75; Reserve 4276, Censor's decision, 20 September 1939. *Movietone*, 537; Reserve 4278, Censor's decision, 20 September 1939. *Gaumont News*, 596; Reserve 4279, 20 September 1939.
17. *Movietone*, Reserve 4312, 544, Censor's decision, 9 November 1939. Two other entries, *Pathé Gazette*, 34/90; Reserve 4313, and *Irish News*, 410, are identical to Reserve 4314.
18. *Pathé Gazette*, 549; Reserve 4334, 11 December 1930.
19. *Pathé Pictorial*, 194; Reserve 4340, 18 December 1939.
20. *Pathé Gazette*, 'Eire Bombed', 41/6. Record 98507; Reserve 4662; Censor's decision, 20 January 1941. Fisk 1985:391 refers to a 35-second item on the bombing, *Pathé* 41/4, 'Eire Bombed', but the item submitted to the Irish Censor seems to have been a more extended version of this item. The one Fisk refers to may have been the British release version of the event.
21. *Irish News*, 776; Reserve 4792; 13 June 1941. Again, the 45-second item referred to by Fisk, 1985:392, 'Germans Bomb Dublin', *Pathé Gazette*, 41/46, may be a British release version of this event as it ends with the line, 'Maybe this is the price that Éire has to pay for – sitting on the fence!' Fisk, ibid. pp. 392–96, details a 10-minute news film made by *British Paramount News* in 1942, 'Ireland – The Plain Issue' (1140, 2, 2), which does not seem to have been submitted to the Irish Film Censor because of its openly anti-Irish bias, and is described by Fisk as a 'grotesque carica-ture of the Irish' (p. 395). The item includes interviews with de Valera, Northern Ireland Prime Minister Andrews, and an expert on naval strategy since the focus of the item was on the use by the British Navy of Irish naval bases. It was the subject of a formal complaint from the Irish Government. See M.J. Reid, *British State Propaganda on Irish Neutrality in the Second World War*, MA dissertation, Thames Valley University; and BUFVC website. See also, *British Movietone News*, 11723, 'Dublin Bombed'. See also Ó Drisceoil, 1996:42–43.
22. *Pathé Gazette*, 41/104; Reserve 6481; 12 June 1945.
23. Reserve 4408, 21 Censor's decision, March 1940.
24. Irish News; Reserve 4929; 13 November 1941. Two newsreels included this item in its British edi-tions: *Gaumont British News*, 62239, 'Irish Cattle Arrive at British Port', 819,7; and *Pathé Gazette*, 99131, 'Good News for Farmers', 4191, 6.
25. Reserve 5290; Censor's decision, 19 October 1942.
26. *Seanad debates*, vol. 25, cols 222–23, 29 January 1941.
27. Ibid. col. 305 (Alton); col. 360–61 (Aiken on basis of censorship); 368–69 (Aiken on newsreels). See also *Kine Weekly*, 2 February 1941:2; ibid. 27 February 1941.
28. *Kine Weekly*, 12 February 1942:4.
29. *Seanad Debates*, vol. 25, col. 362, 30 January 1941.
30. Ó Drisceoil 1996:34.
31. Hayes was responsible for breaking the codes of several German spies in Ireland.
32. Quigley 1999:70.
33. Ibid. 145.
34. Ibid. 125.
35. Ibid. 159.
36. Ibid. 163.
37. Ibid. 164. However, the relative absurdity of the Censor's actions can be measured by his decision to cut a reference to Kaiser, the American shipbuilder, because it was asserted that some in the cinema audience might think it meant Kaiser Wilhelm of World War One. (Ibid. 104.)
38. Ibid. 165.
39. Ibid. 167.
40. Ibid. 173.
41. Even the previously friendly Hayes kept his distance – his 'greatest problem' during the time Quigley was in Ireland was in relation to *A Yank in the RAF*, Quigley 1999:169 ff. – believing, perhaps, that Quigley was somehow responsible for Aiken's intervention.
42. Quigley 1999:183.

43. Ibid. 70. In the Dáil, Fine Gael's James Dillon questioned Aiken about, among other film censor-
    ship matters, the withdrawal of a film featuring army chaplins, in a probable reference to *Army
    Chaplin*. Aiken replied that the film was withdrawn because it was 'repugnant to Catholic teach-
    ing' and that it was 'at the instance [*sic*] of Catholic authorities.' (*Kine Weekly*, 4 May 1944:5.) If
    this is true, it makes Quigley's attempt to secure the papal nuncio's support to have the film re-
    released all the more ironic, as well as providing further proof of how Dublin's Archbishop McQuaid
    interfered in film censorship issues.
        Indeed, during an interview with de Valera, Quigley enquired about the banning of *The Eternal
    Gift*, in which the Catholic High Mass is celebrated by the Servite Fathers of Chicago. It was
    endorsed by the archbishop of Chicago and is narrated by the Catholic University's Fr Fulton J.
    Sheen, an Irish-American author and preacher who was very popular with Irish Catholics during
    his frequent trips to the country. De Valera declared that 'so far as public exhibition was concerned
    as this country is so Catholic that representation of a Catholic religious service, no matter how
    treated, would be objectionable.' (Quigley, 1999:121.) This confirms that it was not just senior
    Catholic clergy who introduced and maintained the prohibition on the representation of religious
    services from the 1920s onwards.
44. Ibid. 202.
45. As the spy reports in his final communiqué from Ireland in mid-November 1943, ibid. 204.
46. Reserve 6218–19, Censor's decision, 9 October 1944.
47. Fr Richard S. Devane SJ, wrote widely on the cinema from the 1920s to the 1940s, usually advo-
    cating a broad-based government-sponsored institution and influenced by the then fashionable
    Catholic ideology of Vocationalism. See, for example, the articles by him: 'National Film Control',
    *The Standard*, 27 September 1940:3 and 'The Problem in Éire!', ibid., 25 October 1940:7. See also
    Devane's widely-circulated *Challenge from Youth: A Documented Study of Youth in Modern Youth
    Movements*, Dublin: Browne and Nolan/The Richview Press, 1942.
48. *Dáil debates*, vol. 93, col. 2108, 3 May 1944.
49. Ibid. vol. 123, col. 1232, 23 November 1950.
50. Ibid. vol. 122, col. 259, 28 June 1950.
51. Ibid. vol. 124, cols. 770–71, 28 February 1951.
52. Ibid. vol. 124, cols. 1865–86, 14 March 1951.
53. John Gerrard, 'Irish Censorship – or Fighting for Cleaner Cinema', *Sight and Sound*, summer
    1949:82.
54. Established by the Minister for External Affairs Seán MacBride in 1949, it published *Éire-Ireland*,
    edited by Conor Cruise-O'Brien, but it was abolished by Frank Aiken in 1957. The 1948–1951
    inter-party government of which MacBride was a member also promoted the production of indige-
    nous documentaries.
55. The *Irish Times* ('Try Again, Mr Nolan' [David Nolan, the producer], 1 April 1946:5) was not
    impressed. 'Much as one dislikes to write uncharitably of a new native enterprise,' the newspaper
    began its review of the film, 'the news that it is hoped to expand this feature in exchange for other
    news reel items from foreign parts surely justifies a little immediate and straightforward criticism.'
    Complaining about how badly an Abbey Theatre Gaelic pantomime was photographed and describ-
    ing the poor synchronization of Seamus Locke's lip movements as 'comically inaccurate,' the film
    also featured an introductory message from Dublin's Lord Mayor, Alderman Doyle, and the
    England–Ireland and France–Ireland rugby internationals at Lansdowne Road. During the war, an
    Army film unit had operated, while modest independent companies were set up, such as the Irish
    National Film Unit, formed by Richard Hayward, Michael Scott and Roger Greene, which had
    made *Our Daily Bread* (1943) on the wheat-growing campaign. Another war-time film was *Ireland's
    Call to Arms*, made by Gordon Lewis, though this was a *Gaumont British News* production, 60555.
56. Switzerland was cited as an example where during the war the country had laid the basis of its film
    industry by compelling Swiss exhibitors to book the native newsreel.
57. Public information drama and documentary films which began to be produced during the 1948–1951
    inter-party government are discussed in Rockett at al, *Cinema and Ireland*, 1988, and are to be
    seen in Kieran Hickey's 1986 documentary *Short Story: Irish Cinema 1945–1958*.
58. John Leydon, Secretary to the Ministry of Industry and Commerce, to M.W. O'Reilly, 30 April
    1947.
59. There were a number of proposals to government in the immediate post-war period, the most
    grandiose of which featured producer Gabriel Pascal and playwright Bernard Shaw. For a detailed
    account of these activities, see Kevin Rockett, *Cinema in Ireland*, vol. 1, D.Phil. thesis, University
    of Ulster, 1989:196–211.

60. Gael-Linn, an Irish language body, was established in 1953 with Dónal Ó Móráin as director. Through a football pool, it financed the fostering the Irish language, including helping the economic development of the Gaeltacht. Besides its cinema newsreel, Gael Linn also produced a series of documentaries from the late 1950s to the early 1970s, while it has also played a prominent role in the development of traditional Irish music.

61. Record 14843, 8,635 feet; Reserve 4348, Censor's decision, 22 December 1939; review, 29 December 1939; certificate issued on 5 January 1940; distributor: MGM.

62. Record 14862, 6,670 feet; Reserve 4356, 10 January 1940; review, 11 January 1940; Reserve 4464, 15 May 1940; certificate issued on 8 May 1940; distributor: D. Egan.

63. Record 14968, 11,712 feet; Reserve 4374; Censor's decision, 15 February 1940; review, 16 February 1940; certificate issued on 26 February 1940; distributor: Columbia.

64. Record 14871, 7,820 feet; Reserve 4358, Censor's decision, 16 January 1940; distributor: Paramount.

65. Record 15739, Censor's decision, 22 November 1940.

66. Record 16201, 7,890 feet; Reserve 4797, Censor's decision, 19 June 1941; passed after appeal, 6 September 1941; certificate issued 25 September 1941; distributor: GFD.

67. Record 16975, 10,654 feet; Reserve 5094; Censor's decision, 30 April 1942; review, 5 May 1942; certificate issued on 14 May 1942; distributor: 20th Century-Fox.

68. Record 16332, 11,591 feet; Reserve 4843, Censor's decision, 29 July 1941; Reserve 7273, Censor's decision, revised cuts, 10 June 1948; distributor: United Artists.

69. Record 17332, Reserve 5237; Censor's decision, 22 September 1942.

70. Record 11807 and 12060, 8,246 feet; Reserve 5271, Censor's decision, 26 May 1937; certificate issued on 16 June 1937; reviewed under EPO, 10 August 1942; review, 20 October 1942; distributor: United Artists.

71. Thomas Schatz, *Boom and Bust*, 1997:119.

72. On review in 1940, 'Rule Britannia' was cut from this film at three points. Record 15739, Censor's decision, 22 November 1940.

73. On review in 1943, the cuts were of a 'certain foreign power' and 'They're spies. Foreigners.' Record 9223 and 31018, 7,800 feet; Censor's decision, 17 June 1935; certificate issued on 21 June 1935; review under EPO, Reserve 5756, 7 October 1943' distributor: Gaumont.

74. Record 18576, 8,390 feet; Reject 1707 under EPO, Censor's decision, 17 February 1944; Record 19577, Reserve 6467; 12 June 1945; review, 15 June 1945; certificate issued on 19 June 1945; distributor: 20th Century-Fox.

75. Record 18577, 6,097 feet; Reject 1711 under EPO, 29 February 1944; on re-submission, 6,635 feet; Reserve 6478; deputy Censor Michael Dolan's decision, 21 June 1945; certificate issued on 25 June 1945; distributor: Paramount.

76. Record 19136, 5,485 feet; Reserve 6277; Censor's decision, 27 November 1944; Reject 1779 after renter refused to cut the film; Appeal Board decision, 23 January 1945; review, 26 January 1945; certificate issued on 2 February 1945; distributor: Columbia.

77. For an account of the controversy see Richards and Aldgate, 1993: 61–74.

78. Record 19275, 13,933 feet; Reserve 5736–41; Censor's decision, 29 September 1943; 2 October 1943; certificate issued on 27 June 1945; distributor: GFD.

79. 9,583 feet; Reserve 4420–21; Censor's decision, 4 April 1940. Re-submitted, when Hayes commented that it 'a very unsavoury gangster film and rather drastic cutting is required.'(18 January 1951.)

80. Record 16490, 8,044 feet; Reserve 4891; Censor's decision, 1 October 1941; review, 2 October 1941; certificate issued on 19 March 1942; distributor: Anglo-American.

81. Record 15041, 8,072 feet; Reserve 4398, Censor's decision, 13 March 1940; review and certificate issued, 14 March 1940; distributor: Warner Bros.

82. Record 15608, 9,136 feet; Reserve 4591, 3 October 1940; Reserve 4608, 24 October 1940, when Montgomery re-viewed the film with recently-appointed Censor, Richard Hayes, and when Reject 1440 was issued after the renter appealed the cuts; passed after appeal, 12 November 1940, but there is no record of any cuts demanded by the Appeal Board; distributor: MGM.

83. Record 18215, 6,970 feet; Reserve 5702, Censor's decision, 3 September 1943; review, 12 and October 1943; certificate issued on 18 October 1943; distributor: 20th Century-Fox.

84. As Montgomery put it, 'the most difficult thing in the film … There is no indication of repentance for her life as a prostitute – it is a gesture of a materialist. There is not a trace of a Christian outlook.' (24 October 1940.)

85. Record 14796, 6,775 feet, Reject 1395, Censor's decision, 5 December 1939; decision upheld after appeal, 15 December 1939; distributor: United Artists.

86. Ian Christie (ed.), *Powell, Pressburger and Others*, 1978:26.
87. 'Censorship of Films' memo, July 1942, OCC 5/39, MA.
88. Emergency Powers Order (No.196), *Statutory Rules and Orders*, No.296 of 1942, 24 July 1942.
89. *March of Time* 6th Year, no. 8; Reserve 4656, Censor's decision, 14 January 1941; following complaint, amended Reserve 4656, 18 March 1941.
90. Swiss minister Benzinger to Dept. of External Affairs, 22 February 1941, Dept. of External Affairs, 216/303, NAI; Record 15748, 7,629 feet; Reserve 4689, Censor's decision, 7 February 1941; certificate issued on 22 February 1941; distributor: RKO Radio.
91. Dept. of External Affairs note, 5 June 1942, 216/303, NAI. Hayes passed the film with thirteen cuts on first viewing, but following the representations made by the Italian minister, a further six cuts were made of references to Italians in the film. Record 16848, 8,178 feet; Reserve 5034 (EPO), Censor's decision, 16 February 1942 and 27 June 1942; certificate issued on 2 April 1942; distributor: United Artists. The film was issued with a 16mm certificate on 3 April 1950, apparently without cuts.
92. Record 18619, 14,080 feet; Reserve 5956–57, Censor's decision, 29 March 1944, Reserve 6149, extra cut, 19 August 1944; review, 2 May 1944, 15 May 1944, 6 July 1944, 17 July 1944; distributor: Paramount. Minister for Justice memo, 7 June 1944, Dept. of External Affairs, 216/303, NAI.
93. KRS to John Dulanty, 30 March 1942, Dept. of External Affairs, 323/203, NAI.
94. *Kine Weekly*, 19 March 1942:5, See also *Daily Mail* 7 April 1942.
95. *Kine Weekly*, 26 March 1942:1.
96. Dept. of External Affairs note, June 1942, NAI; *Daily Film Renter* 24 June 1942.
97. Dept. of the Taoiseach to Controller of Censorship, 24 July 1942.
98. Minutes of meeting, 18 September 1942, OCC 5/39, MA.
99. *Today's Cinema*, 10 December 1943.
 1. Record 18463, 9,451 feet; Reject 1691, Censor's decision, 5 January 1944; distributor: Egan Film Service.
 2. The *Cinema*, 23 February 1944.
 3. Frank Aiken's cuts, perhaps in conjunction with the Film Censor, are at Record 18463, Reserve 5907–08, decision, 22 February 1944. However, Aiken's second viewing, at review stage, on 20 March was two days *after* that recorded at Reserve 5943, 18 March 1944, when a further three cuts under the EPO were demanded; review, 22 March 1944; certificate issued on 3 July 1944. See also *Today's Cinema*, 12 April 1944.
 4. Record 18175 and 18989, 8,779 feet; Reserve 5665–67, Censor's decision, 10 August 1943; review and certificate issued on 10 September 1943; certificate suspended by direction of the Minister for Co-ordination of Defensive Measures with effect from 24 September 1943. Re-submitted in 1945: Record 19793, Reserve 6510, passed with five cuts, Censor's decision, 27 July 1945; review, 21 August 1945; distributor: 20th Century-Fox. These cuts were of Carol 'underdressed' singing a song; the suggestive line, 'You've been turning it in all evening'; the toning down of the two last kissing scenes; the comment in Carol's flat, 'Nobody could get under her bed'; and what Hayes described as a 'rough-tumbling' scene in reel 9.
 5. Minutes of meeting, 30 October 1943, OCC 5/39, MA.
 6. Record 18259, 1,336 feet; Reject 1661 (EPO), Censor's decision, 20 September 1943. Aiken viewed the film on 8 November 1943 and confirmed the rejection. Record 19771, 1,335 feet; Censor's decision, 6 September 1945; certificate issued on 13 September 1945.
 7. Minutes of meeting between Frank Aiken and Theatre and Cinema Association delegation, 1 October 1943, OCC 5/39, MA. It was not just the shortage of film product which was causing concern to the exhibitors. Due to fuel shortages in 1944 electricity supply was cut to as little as 20 per cent of normal. This reduced the light intensity from projectors and lead to restrictions on cinema opening hours. As a result, many cinemas did not open until 6.30 p.m. instead of the normal 2 p.m., while provincial cinemas had to eliminate shows on several days of the week. It was not until July 1944 that exhibitors were restored to 40 per cent of normal electricity supply, a percentage which increased to 90 per cent in September. Additionally, train transport which had been restricted to two trains weekly saw an increase to four trains weekly in July 1944. This allowed for an improvement in services to provincial areas which were dependent on trains to deliver films. City bus and train services finished at 9.30 p.m., thus also limiting city centre cinema attendances. (*Kine Weekly*, 6 April 1944:37; ibid. 20 July 1944:5; ibid. 21 September 1944:7.)
 8. Martin Quigley Jnr, 'Exhibition in Éire', *Motion Picture Herald*, 4 September 1943:6.
 9. Minutes of meeting, 30 October 1943, OCC 5/39, MA.
10. The Irish Film Society's Liam O'Laoghaire sought permission from Coyne to publish an article by Quigley, 'Hollywood at War', in the Society's magazine *Scannán*, in which he lamented the limited

view of American cinema seen in Ireland during the war. O'Laoghaire to Coyne, 1 February 1944. Coyne refused the request in a letter to O'Laoghaire, 5 February 1944; 7/55, MA.

11. Gray to de Valera, 5 October 1943 and 29 November 1943; de Valera to Gray, 25 October 1943; Coyne to Gray, 13 December 1943. Dept. of Justice, 1/41, NAI.

12. The film was the surprise top-grossing hit of 1941 following a sell-out run for six weeks at a 1,000 seat New York first-run theatre, and then moving to a larger venue. (Thomas Schatz, *Boom and Bust*, 1997:67; *MPH*, 10 August 1941.)

13. Record 16617, 12,055 feet; Reject 1503, Censor's decision, 20 November 1941; ban upheld after appeal, 27 November 1941; distributor: Warner Bros.

14. Coyne to J. O'Connor, Dept of Justice, 30 December 1941, OCC 7/48, MA.

15. Schatz, *Boom and Bust*, 1997:117.

16. See 'Walsh and Warner Bros' in Phil Hardy (ed.), *Raoul Walsh*, Edinburgh Film Festival, 1974.

17. These early films include *Confessions of a Nazi Spy*, *Espionage Agent* (both 1939) and *The Fighting 69th* (1940).

18. Record 18457, 951 feet; Reserve 5864, Censor's decision, 8 January 1944; review, 28 January 1944; distributor: Columbia.

19. Minister's decision 17 January 1944.

20. Columbia Pictures Corporation to Irish High Commissioner's Office, London, undated and 10 March 1944, Dept. of External Affairs, 323/203, NAI.

21. Schatz, *Boom and Bust*, 1997:117.

22. *Kine Weekly*, 13 June 1940.

23. Coyne to F.H. Boland, 31 December 1943.

24. Liam O'Laoghaire, 3 February 1944.

25. Record 17090, 5,204 feet; Reserve 5126, 2 June 1942; certificate issued on 17 July 1942; distributor: Irish Photoplays. This certificate was suspended by order of government on 18 July 1942, noted in ibid.

26. Record 19796, 2,820 feet; Reject 1588, Censor's decision, 2 June 1942; distributor: Irish Photoplays. This certificate was suspended by order of the Minister for the Co-ordination of Defensive Measures on 29 July 1942; Reject 1587; also noted in ibid.

27. 'Suspension of cert. granted by Official Censor', OCC 5/40, MA.

28. See *Irish Press* 18 July 1942 on the film's planned release.

29. Cited by Ó Drisceoil, 1995:38.

30. Jay Leyda, *Kino: A History of the Russian and Soviet Film*, London: George Allen & Unwin, 1960.

31. 'Irish Film Society', OCC 7/55, MA.

32. Quigley, 1999:186. Government interest in the Soviet Union is exemplified by the treatment of *Mission to Moscow* (Michael Curtiz, 1943), about real-life American Ambassador Joseph Davies, who introduces the film, played by Walter Huston, in peace-time USSR. According to Quigley, 'the whole cabinet' attended a screening of the film (Quigley 1999:154), but the film was rejected because, as Richard Hayes recorded, it 'tries to place the responsibility for the war on Nazi Germany and Japan. It must be regarded as propaganda in favour of the Soviet regime.' (Record 18176, 10,884 feet; Reject 1653, Reject 1653, Censor's decision, 13 August 1943; distributor: Warner Bros.)

33. Record 17218, 1,058 feet; Reject 1565, Censor's decision, 29 July 1942; review, by Aiken and Walsh from External Affairs, 10 August 1942; distributor: Irish Photoplays.

34. This screening took place under the auspices of the Dublin Little Theatre Guild on 21 February 1936. The *Irish Independent* described it as 'one of the finest examples of Eisenstein's work,' and the article went on to focus on 'the main interest ... the technique, the application of what is known as montage, the rhythmical relation of the shots to one another and to the plot as a whole,' a commentary which suggests that it was written by one of those involved in its presentation, and which de-politicizes the film. (*Irish Independent*, 22 February 1936:6.) The *Irish Times* (25 February 1936:4; see also 21 February 1936:4) congratulated the Little Theatre Guild on showing the 'film classic *Potemkin*'. Later, a strong attack on the film appeared in the *Irish Catholic*.

35. Mary Davoran, 14 December 1943, 7/55, MA.

36. This may be wrong as there is no mention of this title in the film censorship register before 1945. Record 19686, 10,965 feet; Reserve 6520, Censor's decision, 9 August 1945, one cut of man being clubbed with rifle butt, which Censor regarded as 'rather brutal'; review, 14 August 1945; distributor: GFD.

37. *Irish Times*, 14 May 1945.

38. Peter Stead, 'The People as Stars', in Philip M. Taylor (ed.), *Britain and the Cinema in the Second World War*, London: Macmillan, 1988:72.

39. Record 18749, 2,400 feet (16mm); Reject 1720, 24 April 1944; distributor: Irish Film Society.

40. The other three were René Clair, Jean Renoir and Marcel Carné, whose films also regularly appeared in IFS programmes.
41. Richard Abel, *French Film Theory and Criticism, 1907–1939*, vol. 2, Princeton, 1988:177.
42. O'Laoghaire to Coyne, 3 February 1944, OCC 7/55, MA.
43. Comments attributed to Greene on the Hendring Ltd 'Russian Classics' video release.
44. O'Laoghaire to Coyne, 3 February 1944, OCC 7/55, MA.
45. Coyne to Aiken, 9 February 1944, OCC, 7/55, MA.
46. 'Instructions to Press Censorship Staff', 12 February 1944, Dept, of Justice, NAI. While a review of the film in the *Irish Times* was stopped by the censors, see issue of 14 May 1945, a hostile review of the film was published in the *Catholic Standard*.

    In 1952 another Soviet film, *Friendship Delegation to U.S.S.R.*, was submitted for a certificate, it seems, by a private individual. Ms H. Allberry, 37 Fitzwilliam Square, Dublin 2. It focused on a delegation from Finland visiting the Soviet Union and they being given a tour of factories and farms by Soviet officials. Hayes viewed the film, which he regarded as 'staged for propaganda use,' with Maurice Linnane, representing the Revenue Commissioners, probably because the film was seized at customs. The two men agreed 'that, while there are small parts of it here and there which could be regarded as educational, the film as a whole does not come within the educational category. The film as a whole is not suitable for public presentation in this country' because 'it symbolises an ideology that is destructive of western civilisation and if shown in a cinema or public hall it would undoubtedly lead to disturbances.' (Record 27442, Censor's decision, 15 August 1952.)
47. Coyne to Aiken, 26 September 1944, OCC, 7/55, MA.
48. Coyne met O'Kelly on 3 October 1944; letter from Coyne to Kelly, 4 October 1944; Liam O'Laoghaire to Coyne, 11 October 1944, enclosing reviews; O'Laoghaire to Coyne, 14 October 1944, OCC 7/55, MA.
49. Record 15077, 8,242 feet; Reserve 4422, Censor's decision and review, 5 April 1940; certificate issued on 12 April 1940; distributor: Columbia.
50. Purcell to Aiken, 13 October 1944, OCC 7/55, MA.
51. *Monthly Film Bulletin*, August 1939.
52. Peter G. Sherry to Aiken, 17 October 1944, OCC 7/55, MA.
53. Aiken to Sherry, 19 October 1944, OCC 7/55, MA.
54. Coyne to Aiken, 30 October 1944, OCC 7/55, MA. *Storm in a Teacup* had been passed uncut in 1937: Record 12087 and 29783, 7,894; Censor's decision, 26 August 1937; certificate issued on 21 September 1937; distributor: United Artists.
55. It was eventually released in 1946. Record 20321, 8,996 feet; Censor's decision, 6 February 1946; certificate issued on 8 February 1946; distributor: GFD.
56. Roy Armes, *A Critical History of British Cinema*, New York: Oxford UP, 1978:173.
57. *Monthly Film Bulletin* December 1943.
58. Coyne to Aiken, 18 October 1944, OCC, 7/55, MA.
59. Coyne to Sherry, 20 October 1944; Sherry to Coyne acknowledging restriction, OCC, 7/55, MA.
60. Coyne to Sherry, 20 November 1944, OCC, 7/55, MA.
61. 'Refusal to Grant Licence for Importation of *Target for Tonight*', December 1941, OCC 7/49, MA.
62. Dan Bryan (G2) to Joseph Walshe (Secretary, Dept. of External Affairs), 11 April 1945, F/A (Sec.) A 8 (1), NAI.
63. *Dáil debates*, vol. 95, cols. 1497–98, 24 January 1945.
64. Coyne memo, 24 January 1945, OCC 8/51, MA. Coyne noted the ongoing question of 'propaganda' films being distributed by the American legation in Dublin.
65. Record 19346, 11,776 feet; Reserve 6385 (under EPO), Censor's decision, 23 February 1945; review, 16 April 1945; certificate issued on 12 April 1945; distributor: 20th Century-Fox. See *Irish Times*, 14 May 1945:3; *Irish Press* 14 May 1945.
66. *Unknown Battle* had been banned because of its depiction of the Allied bombing of Germany only four days before the EPO was lifted, *March of Time*, tenth year, no. 9, Record 19496, 1,779 feet; Reject 1798, 7 May 1945; distributor: 20th Century-Fox. See *Irish Times*, 17 May 1945, 18 May 1945; Irish Press 21 May 1945.
67. The one cut to the film was of a 'Java Dance' with a dancer's words, 'like they do in the movies,' which, had it remained, would have been somewhat bewildering for an Irish audience as they had not been allowed to see such dances. Record 19520, 12,267 feet; Reserve 6359, 18 May 1945; certificate issued, 19 May 1945; distributor: Paramount.
68. *Irish Times*, 25 May 1945 See *Irish Times*, 24 May 1945:1 on war films being released.
69. The Bellman, 'Meet Dr. Hayes: or The Genial Censor', *The Bell*, vol. 3, no. 2, November 1941:109.

During the war censorship was also applied to any exposed negative film sent out of the country, usually to Britain, for processing. This regulation was administered by the Irish military censors and there was a 'Dad's Army' approach to its application. This is well illustrated by the manner in which 16mm amateur as well as official film was dealt with. While the film was in Britain it was examined by British military and civilian censors before being sent back to Ireland. A contemporary account reported that 'after its return from the Allied authorities who could, if they wished, have made innumerable copies, the Irish Military Censor [Coyne] solemnly viewed it and deleted any scenes which might be of military or strategic importance and which might have imperiled our national security when shown to family audiences in quiet homes. Even in the humblest aspect of the cinema, chaotic stupidity is the keynote of the official position.' (T.J.M. Sheehy, 'The Cinema and Irish Culture', *Irish Catholic*, 28 June 1946:1.) See also Ó Drisceoil, 1996.

70. Record 15976 (1941) and 19704 (1945), 11,244 feet (1941) and 11,692 feet (1945); Reject 1459, Censor's decision, 22 February 1941; ban upheld after appeal, 8 March 1941; re-submitted in 1945: Reserve 6498, Censor's decision, 11 July 1945; review, 2 October 1945; certificate issued on 9 October 1945; distributor: United Artists.
71. Record 18564, 8,666 feet; Reject 1708, Censor's decision, 18 February 1944; distributor: Paramount.
72. Benedict Kiely, the *Standard*, 22 June 1945:3. Kiely, like his colleague at the *Standard*, Patrick Kavanagh, also a film reviewer there, later became an established writer. Kiely has commented that Kavanagh was 'a reluctant film reviewer,' having walked out of *Gone with the Wind*, and took to writing his reviews 'straight off the press releases'. It might be added that Kavanagh was not (and perhaps still not) unique in this regard. (See profile of Kiely, *Irish Times*, 15 August 1989:10.) For an assessment of how Irish film reviewers discussed the release of Irish films see Kevin Rockett, 'Re-Viewing the Green', *The Green on the Screen*, 1984. Kiely wrote perhaps the most interesting and pertinent review of *Rock around the Clock* upon its release in 1956, as discussed in chapter 5. He said that 'at least the young people who dance like that are alive. They're not just slithering around the floor, jaded, dreary-looking, half-asleep.' Bill Haley and the Comets 'have perfected their back-leaping art in healthy rural places, so the rocking, rolling dancing can be regarded as a healthy gust of fresh air blowing from wide open spaces.' (*Irish Press*, 25 June 1956:6.) Such a view was far removed from the official view of the body in 1950s Ireland, but, of course, it also suggests that (even) in that, and earlier decades, repressive ideology was resisted, by a few, publicly, but by many others, silently.
73. T.J.M. Sheehy, *Irish Catholic*, 21 June 1945:1. In its report on the critical comments on the war films the British film trade newspaper, the *Cinema* ('War Films do not Amuse Éire Critics', 27 June 1945) changed, rather mischievously, Sheehy's sarcastic 'enthusiastic anti-West Britons' to 'enthusiastic anti-Britons'.
74. The Censor only demanded that the words 'persistent bastards' be cut. Record 19527, 10,295 feet; Reserve 6462, Censor's decision, 23 May 1945; review, 24 May 1945; certificate issued on 25 May 1945; distributor: British Lion.
75. No cuts were demanded. Record 19530, 6,882 feet; Censor's decision, 23 May 1945; certificate issued on 24 May 1945; distributor: C & G.
76. Liam MacGabhann, 'De Mortuis Nil Nisi Boloney', *Irish Press*, 18 June 1945:2.
77. Record 15041, 8,072 feet; Reserve 4398, Censor's decision, 13 March 1940; review and certificate issued, 14 March 1940; distributor: Warner Bros.
78. Record 18273, 5,485 feet; Reserve 5752, Censor's decision, 5 October 1943; certificate issued on 21 December 1943; distributor: GFD.
79. *Pathé Gazette*, 41/104; Reserve 6481; 12 June 1945.
80. Record 19806, 8,936 feet; Reserve 6582, 14 September 1945; review, 29 September 1945 and 10 October 1945; certificate issued on 17 October 1945; distributor: Paramount.
81. Record 19686, 10,965 feet; Reserve 6520, Censor's decision, 9 August 1945, 14 August 1945; distributor: GFD.
82. Record 19527, 10,295 feet; Reserve 6462, Censor's decision, 23 May 1945; review, 24 May 1945; certificate issued on 25 May 1945; distributor: British Lion.
83. Record 17253, 12,010 feet; Reject 1555, Censor's decision, 13 August 1942; reviewed by the Minister for the Co-ordination of Defensive Measures, rejection upheld, 5 October 1942; distributor: MGM.
84. Coyne memo, Dept. of the Taoiseach, September 1945, S 11445/8, NAI.
85. Maurice Gorham, *Forty Years of Irish Broadcasting*, Dublin: Talbot Press, 1967:59–60.
86. Ibid. 154–56.
87. Ibid. 203.

88. Ibid. 245.
89. Ibid. 275–76.
90. Desmond Fisher, *Broadcasting in Ireland*, London: Routledge and Kegan Paul, 1978:27.
91. Dermot Keogh, 'Ireland and "emergency culture": between Civil War and normalcy 1922–1961', *Ireland: A Journal of History and Society*, vol. 1, no. 1, p. 32.
92. John Horgan, *Seán Lemass: The Enigmatic Patriot*, Dublin: Gill & Macmillan, 1997:316.
93. *Dáil debates*, vol. 254, cols. 1045–46, 12 October 1966.
94. There are a number of excellent accounts of censorship of the British broadcast media. See especially, Liz Curtis, *Ireland: The Propaganda War*, London: Pluto Press, 1984; and Bill Rolston and David Miller (eds), *War and Words: The Northern Ireland Media Reader*, Belfast: Beyond the Pale Publications, 1996.
95. *Dáil debates*, vol. 254, cols. 2494–99, 24 June 1971. During this debate, both Conor Cruise O'Brien and Garret Fitzgerald, a future Taoiseach, favoured allowing members of illegal organizations to present their arguments on radio and television and to be answered by their critics.
96. John Horgan, *Irish Media: A Critical History Since 1922*, London: Routledge, 2001:91.
97. Ibid.
98. Curtis, *Ireland: The Propaganda War*, 1984:191.
99. These events were not unique to the Republic of Ireland. In 1971 a BBC reporter, Bernard Falk, spent four days in prison when he refused to identify a defendant charged with IRA membership as the same he had interviewed for television. (Horgan 2001: 99.)
1. See his lengthy Dáil contributions just as the RTÉ Authority was about to be axed by the Government, *Dáil debates*, vol. 263, cols. 2470–2500, 23 November 1972.
2. Horgan, 2001: 116.
3. Curtis, 1984:193. Another Cruise O'Brien proposal was that rather than develop a second RTÉ television channel, as happened in 1978, he advocated the re-broadcasting by RTÉ of the BBC service, presumably as part of a process of further anglicizing the Irish in the wake of violent republicanism.
4. Horgan, 2001: 122. The guidelines were further revised in 1978 (21 January) by Director-General Oliver Moloney.
5. Horgan, 2001: 123.
6. Quoted Horgan, 2001: 122.
7. See Horgan, 2001: 130–132; Curtis, 1984.
8. See Betty Purcell, 'The Silence of Irish Broadcasting' in Bill Rolston and David Miller (eds), *War and Words: The Northern Ireland Media Reader*, 1996:253–264; orig. in Bill Rolston (ed.), *The Media and Northern Ireland: Covering the Troubles*, London: Macmillan, 1991: 51–68.
9. However, RTÉ did invest in the television feature *Dear Sarah* (Frank Cvitanovich, 1990) about the relationship of imprisoned Guiseppe Conlon, his wife Sarah, and their son Gerry, as well as others wrongfully imprisoned after the 1974 Guildford pub bombing. Jim Sheridan's feature film *In the name of the Father* (1993) is based on the same events.
10. See, for example, 'Decoding Higgins on Section 31', *Irish Times*, 14 October 1993:14.
11. See Betty Purcell, 1996: 261.
12. *Irish Times*, 5 August 1992:3. Boyd is also reported as calling for the repeal of Section 31 following the court decision.
13. Quoted Niall Meehan, *Sunday Business Post*, 20 April 2003.
14. Michael Foley, 'Section 31 issue still left up in the air', *Irish Times*, 2 October 1993:4.
15. Niall Meehan, *Sunday Business Post*, 9 August 1992.
16. *Irish Times* letters, 18 October 1990:11.
17. Niall Meehan, *Sunday Business Post*, 9 August 1992.
18. The interview took place on 23 March 1988. See *Irish Times*, 25 March 1988:8. The *Irish Times* reported on 26 March 1988 ('Ignorance of the law at RTÉ') that Brian MacAonghusa, Controller of Programmes, Radio One, did not regard the item as breaching Section 31 since Ms Comiskey did not represent Sinn Féin, but this viewpoint was quickly suppressed as it did not conform to the policy of RTÉ's senior management.
19. Quoted, Niall Meehan, '(Self)Censoring the Talks: How Section 31 of the Broadcasting Act affected RTÉ's coverage of the John Hume–Gerry Adams talks', 1993, downloaded from CAIN website, 2004.
20. See survey of period by Niall Meehan and colleagues, '(Self)Censoring ...CAIN website, 2004.
21. Farrell Corcoran, *RTÉ and the Globalisation of Irish Television*, London: Intellect, 2003:36–41.

# Select bibliography

Adams, Michael, *Censorship: The Irish Experience*, Alabama: University of Alabama Press, 1968.

Aldgate, Anthony, *Censorship and the Permissive Society: British Cinema and Theatre, 1955–1965*, Oxford: Clarendon Press, 1995.

Barker, Martin (ed.), *The Video Nasties: Freedom and Censorship in the Media*, London/Sydney: Pluto Press, 1984.

The Bellman, 'Meet Dr Hayes: or The Genial Censor', *The Bell*, vol. 3, no. 2, November 1941.

Black, Gregory D., *Hollywood Censored: Morality Codes, Catholics, and the Movies*, Cambridge: Cambridge UP, 1994.

——, *The Catholic Crusade against the Movies, 1940–1975*, Cambridge: Cambridge UP, 1998.

Bordwell, David, Janet Staiger and Kristin Thimpson, *The Classical Hollywood Cinema: Film Style & Mode of Production to 1960*, London: Routledge & Kegan Paul, 1985.

Bowser, Eileen, *The Transformation of Cinema 1907–1915*, vol. 2, History of the American Cinema, Berkeley/Los Angeles/London: University of California Press, 1994.

Breakwell, Ian and Paul Hammond, *Seeing in the Dark: A Compendium of Cinemagoing*, London: Serpent's Tail, 1990.

Burns-Bisogno, Louisa, *Censorsing Irish Nationalism: The British, Irish and American Suppression of Repubican Images in Film and Television, 1909–1995*, Jefferson, North Carolina/London: McFarland & Co., 1997.

Byrne, Helen, 'Going to the Pictures: The Female Audience and the Pleasures of Cinema', in Mary J. Kelly and Barbara O'Connor (eds), *Media Audiences in Ireland*, Dublin: UCD Press, 1997.

Carlson, Julia (ed.), *Banned in Ireland: Censorship & the Irish Writer*, London: Routledge, 1990.

Carty, Ciaran, *Confessions of a Sewer Rat: A Personal History of Censorship and the Irish Cinema*, Dublin: New Island Books, 1995.

Chester, Gail and Julienne Dickey (eds), *Feminism and Censorship: The Current Debate*, Bridport, Dorset: Prism Press, 1988.

Church Gibson, Pamela and Roma Gibson (eds), *Dirty Looks: Women, Pornography, Power*, London: BFI, 1993.

Clover, Carol J., *Men, Women and Chainsaws: Gender in the Modern Horror Film*, London: BFI, 1992.

Collins, David (ed.), *Film Directions*, special censorship issue, vol. 3, no. 9, 1980.

Couvares, Francis G. (ed.), *Movie Censorship and American Culture*, Washington/London: Smithsonian Institution Press, 1996.

Daly, Mary, *Dublin: The Deposed Capital: A Social and Economic History, 1860–1914*, Cork: Cork UP, 1984.

Doherty, Thomas, *Teenagers and Teenpics: The Juvenilization of American Movies in the 1950s*, Boston: Unwin Hyman/London, 1988.

——, *Pre-Code Hollywood: Sex, Immorality, and Insurrection in American Cinema, 1930–1934*, New York; Columbia UP, 1999.

Drennan, Professor Max, 'The Cinema and its Dangers', *Irish Monthly*, vol. 45, February 1917:74–82.

Gerrard, John, 'Irish Censorship – or Fighting for Cleaner Cinema', *Sight and Sound*, vol. 18, no. 70, Summer 1949.

Gibbons, Luke, *Transformations in Irish Culture*, Cork: Cork UP, 1996.

Gunning, Tom, *D.W. Griffith and the Origins of American Narrative Film: The Early Years at Biograph*, Urbana and Chicago: University of Illinois Press, 1994.

Hardy, Phil (ed.), *The Aurum Film Encyclopaedia-Horror*, London: Aurum Press, 1985.

Heins, Marjorie, *Not in front of the Children*, New York: Hill and Wang, 2002; orig. 2001.

Herr, Cheryl, *Joyce's Anatomy of Culture*, Urbana and Chicago: University of Illinois Press, 1986.

Horgan, John, *Irish Media: A Critical History since 1922*, London: Routledge, 2001.

Hunnings, Neville March, *Film Censors and the Law*, London: George Allen & Unwin, 1967.

Jacobs, Lea, *The Wages of Sin: Censorship and the Fallen Woman Film*, Madison: University of Wisconsin Press, 1991.

Kerekes, David and David Slater, *Killing for Culture: An Illustrated History of Death Film from Mondo to Snuff*, London: Creation Books, 1994.

—, *See No Evil: Banned Films and Video Controversy*, Manchester: Critical Press, 2000.

Kinnard, Roy and Tim Davis, *Divine Images: A History of Jesus on the Screen*, New York: Citadel Press, 1992.

Kuhn, Annette, *Cinema, Censorship and Sexuality, 1909–1925*, London/New York: Routledge, 1988.

Leff, Leonard J., and Jerold L. Simmons, *The Dame in the Kimono: Hollywood, Censorship, and the Production Code from the 1920s to the 1960s*, New York: Anchor Books, Doubleday, 1990.

Magennis, William, 'The Cinema as a Social Evil', *Studies*, vol. 33, March 1944.

May, Lary, *Screening out The Past: The Birth of Mass Culture and the Motion Picture Industry*, Chicago and London: University of Chicago Press, 1983; orig. 1980.

Montgomery, James, 'The Menace of Hollywood', *Studies*, vol. 31, no. 124, December 1942.

Musser, Charles, *The Emergence of Cinema: The American Screen to 1907*, vol. 1, History of the American Cinema, Berkeley/Los Angeles/London: University of California Press, 1994; orig. 1990.

O'Connor, James A. (Seamus), 'Censorship of Films, 1894–1970: Hollywood, London & Dublin', PhD thesis, University College Dublin, 1996 (unpublished; copies of film censors' annual reports to 1970, assorted correspondence, and censors' reports on the films discussed in this thesis are held at University College Dublin Archives).

Ó Drisceoil, Donal, *Censorship in Ireland 1939–1945: Neutrality, Politics and Society*, Cork: Cork UP, 1996.

O'Toole, Laurence, *Pornocopia: Porn, Sex, Technology and Desire*, London: Serpent's Tail, 1998.

Phelps, Guy, *Film Censorship*, London: Victor Gollancz, 1975.

Pascall, Jeremy and Clyde Jeavons, *A Pictorial History of Sex in the Movies*, London/New York: The Hamyln Publishing Group, 1975.

Quigley, Martin S., *A U.S. Spy in Ireland*, Dublin: Marino Books, 1999.

Richards, Jeffrey, *The Age of the Dream Palace: Cinema and Society in Britain, 1930–1939*, London: Routledge & Kegan Paul, 1984.

— and Anthony Aldgate, *The Best of British: Cinema and Society, 1930–1970*, Oxford: Basil Blackwell, 1983.

Robertson, James C., *The British Board of Film Censors: Film Censorship in Britain, 1896–1950*, London: Croom Helm, 1985.

—, *The Hidden Cinema: British Film Censorship in Action, 1913–1972*, London/New York: Routledge, 1989.

Rockett, Emer, and Kevin Rockett, *Neil Jordan: Exploring Boundaries*, Dublin: The Liffey Press, 2003.

Rockett, Kevin, Luke Gibbons, and John Hill, *Cinema and Ireland*, London: Croom Helm, 1987; London: Routledge, 1988.

—, 'The Irish Migrant and Film', in Patrick O'Sullivan (ed.), *The Creative Migrant*, vol. 3, *The Irish World Wide* series, Leicester: Leicester UP, 1994

—, *The Irish Filmography: Fiction Films, 1896–1996*, Dublin: Red Mountain Media, 1996.

—, 'From Radicalism to Conservatism: Contradictions Within Fianna Fáil Film Policies in the 1930s,' *Irish Studies Review*, vol. 9, no. 2, August 2001.

—, '(Mis) Representing the Irish Urban Landscape', in Mark Shiel and Tony Fitzmaurice (eds), *Cinema and the City: Film and Urban Societies in a Global Context*, Oxford: Blackwell Publishers 2001.

—, 'Something Rich and Strange: James Joyce, Beatrice Cenci and the Volta', *Film and Film Culture*, 2004.

Rothery, Sean, *Ireland and the New Architecture*, Dublin: The Lilliput Press, 1991.

Schatz, Thomas, *Boom and Bust: American Cinema in the 1940s*, vol. 6, History of American Cinema, Berkeley/Los Angeles/London: University of California Press, 1997; pbk,1999.

Schumach, Murray, *The Face on the Cutting Room Floor: The Story of Movie and Television Censorship*, New York: Da Capo Press, 1975; orig. 1964.

Vincendeau, Ginette (ed.), *Encyclopaedia of European Cinema*, London: BFI, 1995.

Vizzard, Jack, *See No Evil: Life Inside a Hollywood Censor*, New York: Simon & Schuster, 1970.

Watters, Eugene and Matthew Murtagh, *Infinite Varieties: Dan Lowry's Music Hall 1979–97*, Dublin: Gill and Macmillan, 1975.

Williams, Linda, *Hard Core: Power, Pleasure, and the 'Frenzy of the Visible'*, London: Pandora/HarperCollins, 1990.

Woodman, Kieran, *Media Control in Ireland, 1923–1983*, Galway: Officina Typographica, Galway University Press, 1985.

# Index of film titles

# General index

Italicized numbers refer to plates.